An Introduction to Chinese Poetry

Harvard East Asian Monograph Series 408

An Introduction to Chinese Poetry

From the *Canon of Poetry* to the Lyrics of the Song Dynasty

Michael A. Fuller

Published by the Harvard University Asia Center
Distributed by Harvard University Press
Cambridge, Massachusetts 2017

Printed in the United States of America

The Harvard University Asia Center publishes a monograph series and, in coordination with the Fairbank Center for Chinese Studies, the Korea Institute, the Reischauer Institute of Japanese Studies, and other faculties and institutes, administers research projects designed to further scholarly understanding of China, Japan, Vietnam, Korea, and other Asian countries. The Center also sponsors projects addressing multidisciplinary and regional issues in Asia.

Library of Congress Cataloging-in-Publication Data

Names: Fuller, Michael Anthony, author.
Title: An introduction to Chinese poetry : from the canon of poetry to the lyrics of the Song dynasty / Michael A. Fuller.
Other titles: Harvard East Asian monographs ; 408.
Description: Cambridge, Massachusetts : Published by Harvard University Asia Center, 2017. | Series: Harvard East Asian monographs ; 408 | English and Chinese. | Includes bibliographical references and index.
Identifiers: LCCN 2016053059 |
ISBN 9780674977013 (hardcover : alk. paper)
ISBN 9780674983885 (paperback : alk. paper)
Subjects: LCSH: Chinese poetry--History and criticism. | Chinese poetry--Translations into English.
Classification: LCC PL2307 .F856 | DDC 895.11009--dc23 LC record available at https://lccn.loc.gov/2016053059

Contents

Author's Note

This textbook grew out of many years of teaching undergraduate courses in Chinese poetry at the University of California, Irvine. From the beginning I was unhappy with assigning students extensive readings from English-language anthologies and with attempting to do close readings of poems in translation. To help students without knowledge of Chinese get closer to the poems, I developed the four-part format I use in chapters 3–10 of this textbook: the Chinese text of the poem, a word-by-word rendering, my "technical" translations and, where available, a polished professional translation. In my technical translation I try—as much as possible—to capture the specificity of wording and syntax of the original poem without making it unreadably awkward or opaque. Comparing my minimally aesthetic rendering to more finished versions allows students to be aware of the compromises that are part of the art of translation.

The other elements of the presentation of the poems in this book—the brief framing accounts to introduce periods and authors, and the study guides with notes and questions that follow most poems—conform to the standard practice for textbooks on English poetry. Through the background information I give and the questions I ask about the poems, I encourage students to pay attention to formal issues and, at the same time, to see the relevance of linguistic, literary, social, and historical contexts. I hope that, through this process, students will learn how to actively read poems. The textbook surely will work best in a classroom context where the teacher can guide students, but I believe that it may also be of value for individual self-study.

I have included a chapter on the distinctive features of classical Chinese language (chapter 1) because poets exploited these linguistic elements to create effects that translate poorly and are not readily apparent in English. Introducing students to the formal features of the classical language provides them with the analytic tools needed to clarify these aspects of poetic construction that are otherwise difficult to approach. A presentation of the syntax of Classical Chinese also helps students get from the usually rather bare Chinese text to the English renderings that must supply information (like number and tense and logical connectives) not explicitly present in the original. Moreover, because I have found that at UCI many students come into the classroom with little experience reading poetry and with little sense of the power of poetic form, I have added a brief overview of formal features like couplets, rhyme, metaphor, voice, etc., that the Chinese and English poetic traditions share (chapter 2).

In modeling my textbook on the rather open format used to teach poetry in English, I differ significantly from the approach of Cai Zong-qi's *How to Read Chinese Poetry: A Guided Anthology* (New York: Columbia University Press, 2007). In that textbook Cai assembles a panel of expert readers to lead students through poems. In contrast, I require significant student participation in discovering how the poems work. In a classroom at the beginning of the term, the first tentative steps in this process can be painful since most students lack experience with poetry. I therefore have organized the textbook chronologically—rather than by themes or formal features—to ease students into the art of reading Chinese poems. The lessons begin, in chapter 3, with poems from the *Canon of Poetry* that have minimal formal structure and plain, direct language. After setting the stage with a few additional poems from the *Lyrics of Chu* in chapter 3, I continue in chapter 4 with songs from the Han dynasty, out of which the *shi* 詩 poetic tradition grew. Though simple in language, form, and meaning, these poems already reveal features that become important in the later tradition. The textbook then helps students trace the growth of this tradition: if students start with poems like the "Nineteen Old Poems" (chapter 4) and progress through Tao Qian, Xie Lingyun, and the later Southern Dynasties poets (chapter 5), they gain experience with both language and form that helps them to approach Wang Wei's and Du Fu's more demanding regulated verse (chapters 6 and 7) and the wide range of innovations of the Mid- and Late Tang (chapter 8). As the textbook follows the development of the five-character and seven-character *shi* verse traditions, I hope students will learn to see the power of poetic form and how the innovations in form helped to broaden and deepen poetry's representational possibilities. I include the final two chapters, chapters 9 and 10, on the song lyrics (*ci* 詞) of the Tang and Song dynasties because of the intrinsic merit of the verse form, because it provides an important comparison with the *shi* tradition, and because the development of its formal features follows an arc different from that found in *shi* poetry.

Finally, I stress that although these are the concerns around which I have selected the poems and organized the chapters, I have tried to give teachers substantial freedom to use the textbook for other goals in the classroom. I hope *An Introduction to Chinese Poetry* proves useful, and I look forward to suggestions about how I might improve the textbook to serve a wider range of teachers and students.

How to Use This Book

In this textbook, I try to present the most immediately relevant information for each poet and poem in the body of the text when I discuss them. However, I also provide additional material both for convenient referral and to allow students to explore the writers and poems more deeply.

1. Students should first read the introductory chapters, chapters 1 and 2, for an overview of the classical Chinese language and the unique features, as well as important poetic forms, of Classical Chinese poetry.
2. The textbook provides romanizations in modern Mandarin for various technical poetic terms as well as romanizations for rhyme words that rely on reconstructions of Old Chinese or Middle Chinese. By convention, romanizations in italics represent modern Mandarin; those in roman type preceded by an asterisk are Old Chinese reconstructions, while those in roman type without an asterisk are reconstructions of Middle Chinese readings. I take the reconstructions of Early Middle Chinese (around AD 600), Late Middle Chinese (around 800), and Early Mandarin (around 1300) from Edwin G. Pulleyblank, *Lexicon of Reconstructed Pronunciation in Early Middle Chinese, Late Middle Chinese, and Early Mandarin* (Vancouver: University of British Columbia Press, 1991). For Old Chinese, I rely on William H. Baxter and Laurent Sagart, *Old Chinese: A New Reconstruction* (Oxford: Oxford University Press, 2014).
3. The textbook uses *pinyin* romanization for modern Mandarin but preserves the earlier Wade-Giles romanization in translations when it is used by the translator.
4. Chapters 3–10 present poems in the Classical Chinese tradition chronologically. They should ideally be covered in chronological order.
5. The textbook provides Chinese characters for poets' names, as well as information on their birth and death years, when poets are first introduced in the text. Chinese characters and life dates for major poets also appear in appendix 1, the "List of Poems, Sources, and Translators."
6. Although the textbook provides dates for dynasties where relevant, it also includes a chronological list of the dynasties for easy reference.

7. Appendix 1, the "List of Poems, Sources, and Translators," is organized in the order of presentation in each chapter and provides a citation of a standard Chinese edition for each poem. The entry for the poem also includes source information on translations, if there are any. Poems that are briefly mentioned in the introductory chapters 1–2 but fully translated and discussed in later chapters (chapters 3–10) appear under the chapter where they are translated and discussed in detail.
8. The poems presented in this textbook date from 600 BC to AD 1300, and the editions that have preserved these poems through the centuries do not have completely consistent texts for the poems. The modern Chinese scholarly editions of these poems record the variant characters introduced either because the transmitted texts relied on different sources for the poems or because the compilers of the texts amended the poems according to their best judgment, or simply because of mistakes in copying. The textbook notes these variant texts when they raise serious issues for the understanding of a poem. In most cases, however, I, like the modern Chinese editors, select what I consider the most compelling choice among the variant characters and simply list the alternatives in appendix 2, a "List of Variant Characters," for those students who are interested in problems of the stability of texts and readings.
9. The textbook also provides a list of Suggested Readings organized by chapter for students wishing to explore the poets and their writings in greater detail.

Chronology

Dynastic History

The Legendary Emperors

- Fu Xi 伏羲
- Shen Nong 神農
- Huang Di 黃帝 (the Yellow Emperor)
- Yao 唐帝堯
- Shun 虞帝舜

The Three Dynasties

- Xia 夏(before 2070 BC)[1]
  - Yu 禹, "the sage founder"
  - Jie 桀, "the bad last emperor"
- Shang 商 (before 1700–1046 BC), also known as Yin 殷
  - Tang 成湯 (before 1700 BC), "the sage founder"
  - Zhòu 紂 (1087–1045 BC), "the bad last emperor"
- Zhou 周 (1046–255 BC)
  - Western Zhou 西周 (1046–771 BC)
    - Wu Wang 武王 (1045–1043 BC)
    - Cheng Wang 成王 (1042–1006 BC)
      - (Regency of Duke of Zhou 周公)
  - Eastern Zhou 東周 (770–255 BC)
    - Spring and Autumn Period 春秋 (770–476 BC)
    - Warring States Period 戰國 (476–221 BC)

Early Imperial China

- Qin 秦 (255–207 BC)
- Han 漢 (206 BC–AD 220)
  - Western Han 西漢 (206 BC–AD 8)
  - Wang Mang 王莽, the usurper (AD 8–23)
  - Eastern Han 東漢 (25–220)
- Wei 魏 (220–65)
- The Three Kingdoms Period 三國
  - (Wei 魏, Shu Han 蜀漢, Wu 吳)
- Jin 晉 (265–420)

Poetic History

- Earliest poems in the *Canon of Poetry* (*Shi jing* 詩經) [Western Zhou]
- Latest poems in *Canon of Poetry* [Spring and Autumn Period]
- *Lyrics of Chu* (*Chu ci* 楚辭) [Warring States Period]
- *Yuefu* 樂府 (folk poetry) [Western Han]
- Han *fu* 賦 (rhyme-prose)
- "Nineteen Old Poems" (古詩十九首) [Eastern Han]
- Seven Masters of the Jian'an 建安七子 (Cao Cao 曹操, Cao Zhi 曹植, Wang Can 王粲)
- Ruan Ji 阮籍 [Wei]

1. The estimated dates for the founding of the Xia and Shang dynasties come from the work of the Xia-Shang-Zhou Chronology Project. The nature of the Xia and early Shang "states" is still much debated.

Dynasty	Poets
Western Jin 西晉 (265–316)	Pan Yue 潘岳, Zuo Si 左思, Lu Ji 陸機, Guo Pu 郭璞
Eastern Jin 東晉 (317–420)[2]	Tao Qian 陶潛, Xie Lingyun 謝靈運
The Northern and Southern Dynasties	
Song 宋 (420–79), also called the Liu Song 劉宋	Bao Zhao 鮑照
Qi 齊 (479–502), also called the Southern Qi 南齊	Xie Tiao 謝朓
Liang 梁 (502–57)	Hu Xun 何遜, Xiao Gang 蕭綱, Yu Jianwu 庾肩吾
Chen 陳 (557–89)	Yu Xin 庾信
Imperial China	
Sui 隋 (581–618)	
Tang 唐 (618–907)	Early Tang (618–712): Wang Bo 王勃, Song Zhiwen 宋之問, Shangguan Wan'er 上官婉兒, Chen Zi'ang 陳子昂 High Tang (712–56): Wang Wei 王維, Meng Haoran 孟浩然, Cui Hao 崔顥, Wang Zhihuan 王之渙, Li Bai 李白, Du Fu 杜甫 Mid-Tang (780–824): Bai Juyi 白居易 , Meng Jiao 孟郊, Han Yu 韓愈, Li He 李賀, Jia Dao 賈島, Liu Yuxi 劉禹錫 Late Tang (824–60): Li Shangyin 李商隱, Du Mu 杜牧, Wen Tingyun 溫庭筠, Yu Xuanji 魚玄機
The Five Dynasties 五代 (907–79)	Wei Zhuang 韋莊, Feng Yansi 馮延巳, Li Yu 李煜
Song 宋 (960–1279), also called the Zhao Song 趙宋	
Northern Song 北宋 (960–1127)	Yan Shu 晏殊, Zhang Xian 張先, Liu Yong 柳永, Su Shi 蘇軾, Zhou Bangyan 周邦彥, Li Qingzhao 李清照
In the South	
Southern Song 南宋 (1127–1279)	Xin Qiji 辛棄疾, Jiang Kui 姜夔,Wu Wenying 吳文英, Zhang Yan 張炎
In the North	
Jin 金 (1115–1234)	
Yuan 元 (1271–1368)	
Yuan 元 (1271–1368)	
Ming 明 (1368–1644)	
Qing 清 (1636–1912)	

2. Although called the Eastern Jin, in fact the Jìn was reestablished south of the Yangzi.

List of Terms

Formal Terminology

Length of the Line

Four-character verse: in four-character verse, there are four Chinese characters in each line. This is the main format for poems in the *Canon of Poetry* (*Shijing* 詩經), the venerated collection of early Zhou dynasty poetry. Most poetry in the Han, Wei, and Western Jin continued to be written in four-character verse forms, but with the increasing popularity of five-character verse, later writers primarily used four-character verse for many types of very formal and ritual poetry.

Pentasyllabic verse, also called **five-character verse**: in pentasyllabic verse, there are five Chinese characters in each line. Although pentasyllabic lines do appear in the *Canon of Poetry*, as a verse form, it came to prominence in the late Eastern Han dynasty. It became the most common line length in Southern Dynasties poetry.

Heptasyllabic verse, also called **seven-character verse**: in heptasyllabic verse, there are seven Chinese characters in each line. Poets began to write heptasyllabic verse based on popular song forms in the Southern Dynasties, but this line length came to particular prominence during the Tang dynasty.

Length of the Poem

Quatrain: a quatrain is a poem with four lines. Early quatrains perhaps were modeled on popular songs, but poets learned to use the quatrain for other purposes as well.

Octave: an octave is a poem with eight lines. This is the standard length for regulated verse (see below).

Genre

Shi **詩 (poetry)**: the earliest form of poetry is preserved in the *Canon of Poetry*. Very little poetry survives from the Warring States period. The major collection of verse from the Warring States is the *Lyrics of Chu* (*Chu ci* 楚辭), written in distinctive song meters very different from the poetry of the *Canon of Poetry*. When authors in the Han dynasty began to write poems modeled on the *Canon of Poetry*, they referred to these compositions as *shi*, "poems." Ever since the Han dynasty, writers have used the term *shi* to refer to the basic types of four-character, pentasyllabic, and heptasyllabic verse compositions.

Fu **賦 (rhyme-prose)**: the *fu* is a verse genre that developed in the Han dynasty, modeled on the verse forms of the *Lyrics of Chu*. Early *fu* were long, spectacular court presentation forms that mixed passages in verse that used Chu meters (see below) with sections of prose. Although writers continued to compose long *fu*, they also developed a smaller, more intimate and personal type of *fu* (see chapter 4 for an example of this type of personal *fu*). The *fu* was the most prestigious genre of verse composition well into the Tang dynasty.

Ci **詞 (song lyric)**: the song lyric is a genre in which writers fill in the words of the poem based on the requirements of the tune. Initially, this genre was strongly tied to musical performance—as the role of the tune title in shaping the verse suggests—but as more writers adopted the genre, it became increasingly independent of the music, although the metrical requirements remained. However, the most important writers of song lyrics in the Southern Song dynasty reacted against this separation of lyrics and music and restored their close connection in their compositions.

Terms from the Early Poetic Tradition

***Xing* 興 (affective image)**: this is an image from the natural world that poets used to evoke emotional associations. This style of imagery was modeled on images in the *Canon of Poetry*, where poems often begin with a natural image and then shift into the topic of the poem. For example, the first line of a poem celebrating a marriage (an epithalamium), "The Peach Is Fresh-Blooming," starts with the image of a peach before turning to the theme of marriage (see chapter 3). Later poets explored this evocative usage of natural images, and it became an important rhetorical device in the poetic tradition.

Chu meters (Chu song style): these are styles of line-construction based on the model of the *Lyrics of Chu*. They usually have the pause character *xi* 兮 either in the middle of the line or at the end of the first line of a couplet. If the *xi* is at the end of the first line, there often is a grammatical function word in a middle position, for example, X X X *xi* X X X / X X X *xi* X X X (rhyme) or X X X *fw* X X X *xi* / X X X *fw* X X X (rhyme). Poets used Chu meters to evoke the ambience of the *Lyrics of Chu*, with its sorrowful laments for loss and its lush Southern landscapes (see chapter 3 for the poetry of the *Lyrics of Chu*.)

***Yuefu* 樂府 (folk song)**: *yuefu*, which literally means "music bureau," is the standard term for folk poetry in the Chinese tradition. The Han dynasty emperors emulated what they believed to be the practice of the Zhou dynasty court by sending officials from the Music Bureau into the countryside to collect popular songs, which they believed reflected the mood of the populace and thus served as a measure of the success of dynastic policies. Although this effort to collect folk songs soon was abandoned, the early Han folk poems that survived were called *yuefu*, and the later tradition continued to use this name for folk poetry.

Southern folk songs: the aristocratic culture of the Southern Dynasties discovered a tradition of folk songs usually in quatrain form and sung by women. These songs often relied on paranomasia, a form of punning that relies on the sounds of words. Thus "lotus" (*lian* 蓮) sounds like "to be fond of" (*lian* 憐), and "silk thread" (*si* 絲) sounds like "to long for" (*si* 思). Later poets used these puns to evoke the ambience of the Southern folk songs, with their simplicity, forthrightness, and Southern folk ambiance. The two major groups of folk songs from the Southern Dynasties are the **"Western Songs"** (*xi quge* 西曲歌) and the **"Wu Songs"** (*Wu sheng gequ* 吳聲歌曲).

Terms from the Tang Dynasty

"Modern"-style poetry (*jinti shi* 今體詩): "modern"-style poetry evolved in the Tang dynasty as a regularization of the prosodic constraints on lines and couplets that Southern Dynasties court writers developed as they increasingly explored the role of the tonal system of the Middle Chinese language in creating euphonic effects. In "modern"-style poetry, words in the "level" tone were to be properly balanced with words in the "oblique" tones (the "rising," the "departing," and the "entering" tones; see chapter 1 for a discussion of the phonology). In general, the second line of a "modern"-style couplet also mirrored the tonal pattern of the first line. (That is, where the first line had a "level" tone, the second line had an "oblique," and vice versa.) Although tonal rules became strict later in the poetic tradition, during the Tang, approaches to achieving proper balance within a line and within a couplet had some flexibility. There were three main types of "modern"-style verse: the **regulated quatrain**; the **regulated octave**, usually simply called regulated verse; and an extended form of regulated poetry with more than eight lines, called *pailü* 排律.

Regulated verse (*lü shi* 律詩): as explained above, "regulated verse" is an eight-line verse form, usually in either the pentasyllabic or heptasyllabic line. In addition to the prosodic conventions for balancing tones within the line and the couplet, the two middle couplets usually were parallel. That is, the words in each position in the second line were supposed to be in the same category as the word in the corresponding position in the first line of the couplet. Verbs matched verbs; adjectives matched adjectives; and nouns were to be either similar or opposite within a category. For example, "river" in the first sentence often was paired with "ocean" in the second as being of the same type within the category of "topography," but "river" also could be paired with "mountain" as an opposite and complementary type within the category.

Old-style verse (*guti shi* 古體詩): during the Tang dynasty, "old-style" verse developed as the opposite of "modern"-style poetry, violating the prosodic rules and parallelism of regulated verse. It often took the form of "**songs**," not associated with music, but as a form of freely flowing verse in which line lengths varied significantly and in which authors used grammatical function words to give a prose-like quality to the verse line that was avoided in the "modern" forms.

Terms from the Song Lyric Tradition

Tune title: every song lyric was associated with a tune title that determined the prosodic rules for the composition. In many cases, the lyric provides just the tune title (indicated in this textbook with bold brackets **【. . . 】**) without any additional information.

"Short lyric" (*xiao ling* 小令): this is the simplest form of a lyric in just a single stanza (*dan diao* 單調).

"Dual stanza" (*shuang diao* 雙調): the "dual stanza" is the next more complicated form of a lyric: it has two stanzas that repeat the prosodic structure of the tune in each stanza, with slight variations allowed. Some scholars suggest that this is a less-than-useful term since there are also song lyrics in several stanzas where the prosody differs significantly in the second stanza. In any case, Zhang Xian's "To the Tune 'Heavenly Immortal' " in chapter 9 is an example of a "dual stanza" lyric.

"Extended form" (*man ci* 慢詞): the "extended form," as the name suggests, is a lyric written to a version of a tune that extends the prosodic structure to create a longer, more varied composition.

"Governing word" (*ling zi* 領字): "governing words" are a technical feature of the song lyric that provides additional semantic structure. These can be time words (like "gradually" *jian* 漸) that are to be applied to a succession of lines, or they can define the speaker's attitude toward a series of lines to follow (like "how can I bear to . . . " *nakan* 那堪).

CHAPTER ONE

The Classical Chinese Language

"Poetry is what is lost in translation."
—Robert Frost

Poetry, like all art, draws on the material resources of its medium. Poetry is an art of language. Since languages differ from one another, the properties authors exploit in writing poetry also differ from language to language. For this reason, poetry usually does not translate well. The linguistic effects of a poem—ranging from the sound, to the cadence, to the ordering of words and structuring of sentences—find no easy correspondences when moving from one language to another. To understand Chinese poetry, then, we need to begin with a basic understanding of the classical Chinese language in which the works were composed.

Classical Chinese in Historical Perspective

The poetic traditions discussed in this book span a period from roughly 1000 BC through AD 1300. The languages spoken in what we think of as the Chinese heartland—the areas around the Yellow River in the north and the Yangzi River in the south—changed significantly during these two thousand years. They changed in every way, from their morphology, phonology, and syntax, to their vocabulary and written forms. Scholars usually divide the language spoken in the courts of the Zhou (1046 BC–255 BC) and later dynasties into three historical periods. Old Chinese (subdivided into early and late) was spoken until the early part of the Han dynasty (206 BC–AD 220), which saw the emergence of Middle Chinese. The courts spoke versions of Middle Chinese through the Tang dynasty (618–907), but some of the features of modern Mandarin Chinese began to appear in the late Tang. The situation is further complicated because the Chinese empire covered a large domain, and many regions surely developed distinct dialects for which we have little information.

Old, Middle, and early Mandarin Chinese were *spoken* languages, but all we have are the written texts based on those languages. Scholars persistently have debated the relationship of the written to the spoken forms: that is, did the Chinese actually speak as they wrote? Some skeptics have suggested that given the apparent fluidity of word classes in Old Chinese texts, it is not possible that the written record accurately reflects a living language. The situation for Middle Chinese is simpler because, on the whole, the texts no longer reflected a spoken language. That is, by the middle of the Han dynasty, Classical Chinese had become *a written language* with a fairly stable form based on the conventions of late Old Chinese. Some texts that perhaps record the spoken language survive, but most types of elite documents—including poetry—are in the conventionalized written dialect. Still, when writers composed in Classical Chinese, the characters they wrote did have sound values based on the words in the spoken language of the time. And although Classical Chinese is a conventionalized written language, it still *is* a language, with a regular grammar that plays an important role in shaping the poetic tradition.

Classical Chinese as a language has three components—phonology, morphology, and syntax—that linguists see as the most important parts of any language's *grammar*. That is, languages are made up of words and ways of putting the words together. Words, of course, have sounds, but in any given language, only some of the sounds humans can produce are used as parts of words. *Phonology* is the study of the sound system and its rules. The words in a language also have structure, like the "s" in "words" that makes it a plural noun or the "s" in "draws" in the first sentence of this chapter that makes it a third-person singular present-tense verb. *Morphology* is the study of how words in a language are assembled out of parts. Finally, the grammatical rules for combining words in phrases, clauses, and sentences are called the *syntax* of a language.

The Basis for the Written Record: Chinese Characters

In Western cultures, writing is alphabetic: little bits of representations of sound are strung together to make complete sounds (syllables) that in turn combine to make longer intelligible sound-structures called words. Because Chinese characters are based on a different strategy of representation, a mystique has grown around them: they are thought of as somehow more holistic and able to convey their meaning with an immediacy not available in Western alphabetic scripts. The task of introducing characters would be simpler if these notions could be completely dismissed, but they have some small grain of truth to them.

The basic strategy for Chinese characters as they evolved to represent the Old Chinese language was very simple: one character for one word. Two distinctive features of Old Chinese, however, shaped this development. First, the language was essentially monosyllabic, that is, one *syllable* for each word. Second, words did not have a complex morphology. While sounds may have been added at the beginning or end of a syllable (like an initial s- or a final glottal stop -ʔ), one character represented the entire sound cluster. In contrast, inflectional languages like Japanese, for example, have a large array of syllables added to the ends of verb root forms that convey important information. When the Japanese borrowed Chinese characters to write their own language, they needed a way to represent these extra syllables and thus developed an additional phonetic (strictly sound-based) script. For instance:

食	*tabe-*	"eat"
食て	*tabe- te*	"eating"
食ない	*tabe- nai*	"[he, she, it, I, you, we, they] does/do not eat"
食る	*tabe- ru*	"[he, she, it, I, you, we, they] eat/eats"
食た	*tabe- ta*	"[he, she, it, I, you, we, they] ate"
	and so on . . .	

Because in Old Chinese almost all words were single syllables, there was no need to develop a phonetic system like those in Japanese and Korean to represent such additional sounds.

The common belief encouraged by simplistic accounts of Chinese writing is that characters are *ideographs*, the graphic representation of *ideas*. However, characters represent *words*. The distinction is easy to miss because the earliest forms of characters—pictograms and graphic representations of simple concepts—do use a strategy of drawing the idea expressed by the word to represent the word itself. These are the easiest characters to learn, and they are the examples usually introduced to explain the visual nature of Chinese writing. Nonetheless, they represent a small percentage of the total and only the earliest stratum of writing. There are many standard examples:

SEAL SCRIPT	MODERN WRITING	MODERN READING	MEANING
上	上	*shàng*	on top
下	下	*xià*	below
木	木	*mù*	tree
日	日	*rì*	sun
月	月	*yuè*	moon
口	口	*kǒu*	mouth

This sort of approach goes only so far, however. Some simple concepts and some of the most common objects can perhaps be represented in this manner, but one quickly confronts the limitations of simple drawing.

A slightly more complex approach to depicting words is to combine graphs to present a corresponding composite idea represented by the word. Some examples of this strategy are:

伐 "to attack" = 人 [person] + 戈 [halberd (a type of weapon)]

牧 "to herd [cattle]" = 牛 [ox] + 攴 [a hand holding a stick]

Still, these three approaches (drawing objects, representing concepts, and compounding concepts) present serious constraints. Differentiating words referring to similar objects and finding ways to depict words for complex concepts both prove difficult. To represent these, Chinese scribes turned to two related strategies. In the first approach, *phonetic borrowing*, scribes simply used one pre-existing character to represent another word that sounded the same.[1] Common examples of this type of direct borrowing are:

來 (來) a type of wheat (麥)➔ "to come"

其 (其) a winnowing basket (later written 箕 [箕])➔ "his, hers, its, their"

Phonetic compounding is the second, slightly more complex approach to reusing graphs based on their sound. Here, the new graph combines two components, a *radical*—in most cases indicating the general category of object or action—that has been added to a *phonetic*, a character that sounds approximately like the word to be represented (here I use Baxter and Sagart's reconstruction of Old Chinese):[2]

1. For the different types of characters, I use the terms in Jerry Norman's *Chinese* (Cambridge: Cambridge University Press, 1988), pp. 58–82, which offers a good account of the development of the Chinese script.

2. William H. Baxter and Laurent Sagart, *Old Chinese: A New Reconstruction* (Oxford: Oxford University Press, 2014).

CHARACTER	MEANING		RADICAL	+ PHONETIC
髻 (*kˤits)	hair knot	=	髟 (hair)	+ 吉 (*qit)
排 (*bˤrəj)	to push	=	手 (hand)	+ 非 (*pəj)

There are far more characters built on phonetic compounding than on any other approach.

Among the five ways of creating a character, in only one (phonetic borrowing) is the meaning of the character completely divorced from the form of its representation. In all the others, at least some semantic information—however attenuated—remains in the writing.

The Sound Systems of Classical Chinese

The Phonology of Middle Chinese

The authors who wrote most of the poetry in this book spoke dialects that were close to Middle Chinese. This Middle Chinese, however, is something of a scholarly construct: it is based on rhyme books that survive from the Tang dynasty, but we do not know for sure whether the rhyming information reflects the speech of a single "official" dialect or whether it is a compromise between practices from several regions. In any case, the most important point to be stressed in this brief overview of the sound system is that the language in which the authors wrote—what they heard in their heads as they wrote and chanted aloud when they read—is different from any modern dialect or modern Mandarin, although some modern dialects do have features that were important in Middle Chinese but have been lost in modern Mandarin.

The rhyme books on which reconstructions of Middle Chinese are based were essentially rhyming dictionaries to help authors use proper rhyme schemes when writing poems for formal occasions. The books were divided into four large sections—one for each tone in Middle Chinese—and then divided into chapters for every possible rhyme in a given tone.

A Brief Aside on Tones

A "tone" is a pitch contour that is part of the pronunciation of a word in Chinese. In English we change the relative pitch we use in asking a question (going from lower to higher) as opposed, for example, to giving an exasperated command (higher to lower). Consider the difference between "Now?" and "Now!" In both Middle Chinese and the modern dialects, each word has a pitch contour that is not part of sentence-level inflection but is simply part of the pronunciation of the word itself. Changing the pitch of a syllable does not change a word's meaning from a question to a command, for instance: instead, it becomes another word altogether. Words in modern Mandarin, for example, have one of four tones represented by diacritic marks over the vowels: a high level tone, as in *mā* (媽 "mother"), a high rising tone *má* (麻 "hemp"), a falling-then-rising tone *mǎ* (馬 "horse"), and a falling tone *mà* (罵 "to scold"). Modern Cantonese has a yet more complex set of tones, including two sets of so-called "entering" tones that end in *-p*, *-t*, or *-k* inherited from Middle Chinese that Mandarin lost in the Yuan dynasty (1280–1368).

For the purposes of this book, the four-tone system of Middle Chinese is most important, but the tones differ from those in modern Mandarin:

1. level　平 *píng*　example: 安 ʔan[3]
2. rising　上 *shǎng*　匽 ʔián
3. departing　去 *qù*　晏 ʔjàːn
4. entering　入 *rù*　揠 ʔjaːt

Note that all the characters in the examples use 安 as the basic phonetic element and that a *-t* final entering tone corresponds to words that end in *-n* in the other three tones because both *n* and *t* are sounds made at the tip of the tongue. Similarly, a *-p* entering tone corresponds to an *-m*, and a *-k* corresponds to an *-ng* in the other tones.

The actual number and nature of the rhyme groups within each of the four tonal categories are details that are perhaps not so crucial in our understanding of the language. More directly relevant to poetic practice is the existence of *tongyong* ("used together") groups of rhyme words: words whose final sounds were close enough in Tang dynasty China to be considered acceptable "near rhymes" when formal requirements were less strict.

The Sounds of Old Chinese

The earliest Chinese poetry is written in Old Chinese. Unfortunately, there are no extant rhyme books to help scholars reconstruct what the language sounded like. However, based on information from the rhyming patterns in the early poetry and from the pattern of phonetic borrowings in the creation of characters, historical phonologists have developed an approximate model for the sound system. The idea of *system* here is important: what scholars have constructed are relative rather than absolute sound systems.[4] Phonologists can identify characters that speakers of Old Chinese considered to refer to words with mutually differentiating sounds, but they cannot be sure exactly what those sounds were.[5] Thus the account that follows is a good guess but cannot be entirely certain.

---

3. By convention, romanizations in italics represent modern Mandarin; those in roman type preceded by an asterisk are Old Chinese reconstructions, while those in roman type without an asterisk are reconstructions of Middle Chinese readings. I take the reconstructions of Early Middle Chinese (around AD 600), Late Middle Chinese (around 800), and Early Mandarin (around 1300) from Edwin G. Pulleyblank, *Lexicon of Reconstructed Pronunciation in Early Middle Chinese, Late Middle Chinese, and Early Mandarin* (Vancouver: University of British Columbia Press, 1991).

4. That is, the human lips, tongue, mouth, nose, and throat are capable of making a wide range of sounds that potentially can be used in forming words in a language. Only a fraction of these sounds, however, are used in any given language. Moreover, the sounds that *are* used need to be distinguished from one another and form a system of mutual differentiation. Sanskrit, for example, distinguishes between *b-* and *bh-* (a "b" with breath coming out), while English does not. English distinguishes between *l-* and *r-* while Japanese does not.

5. The consonant values are somewhat easier to reconstruct because the points of articulation (where the sound is made) are fairly distinct. Vowels, in contrast, depend on the position of the tongue and the shape of the lips and mouth, all of which allow shading from one sound into another. So phonologists may know that there were four nuclear vowels, but they cannot say exactly what they sounded like.

Old Chinese did not sound like modern Mandarin or like any modern dialect, or even like Middle Chinese. This is perhaps the most important point to be made: the Chinese language changed significantly over the two thousand years of the poetic tradition covered in this book. The specific details are merely a means to stress how different the sound systems of the languages were at different points in their historical development.

The first major difference from later Chinese dialects is in the initial sounds of words. Early in the study of Old Chinese, researchers exploring words made as phonetic compounds noticed that scribes used the same character to represent words that have significantly different initials in the modern language. This usage compelled the scholars to conclude that the borrowed words had more complex clusters of initial consonants than exist in the modern dialects.[6] For example,

	Modern Mandarin	Old Chinese
京	*jīng*	*krang
涼	*liáng*	*C.rang
數	*shǔ*	*s-roʔ
屢	*lǚ*	*roʔ-s

A second difference appears in the third and fourth examples above: the *final* sound also was more complex. This seemingly small addition of a final -ʔ or -s is part of a much more significant difference: Old Chinese probably did not have the sort of pitch-contour tones that are part of Middle Chinese and modern Chinese dialects. Careful sifting of evidence increasingly has led scholars to believe that these types of tones were not part of the early language, and that instead, Old Chinese words ending in -ʔ, -s, -p, -t, or -k evolved into Middle Chinese words in 2nd, 3rd, or 4th tones.

A third difference in Old Chinese derives from the patterns of meaning when comparing sets of words with and without particular initial or final consonants that seem to be pairs. For example:

藏	*m-tsʰˤaŋ	to store
倉	*tsʰˤaŋ	granary
屰	*ŋrak	to go against, reverse
朔	*s-ŋrak	first day of month (moon waning > waxing)
見	*kˤen-s	to see
現	*N-kˤen-s	to appear
磨	*mˤaj	to grind
磨	*mˤaj-s	inkstone
受	*duʔ	to receive
授	*duʔ -s	to give, hand over[7]

6. In this account of Old Chinese, I follow Baxter and Sagart, *Old Chinese.*

7. These examples come from Baxter's and Sagart's discussion of affixes in *Old Chinese*, pp. 54–59. They propose a set of specific functions for the prefixes, infixes, and suffixes that are beyond the scope of this initial survey of the language.

The roles of these prefixes and suffixes are difficult to determine, but they appear to serve a variety of grammatical functions. Changing between nouns and verbs seems to be one well-established pattern, but various proposals have been made to account for the variations in the evidence. Despite the uncertainties in the evidence, it remains important to keep in mind that the sound system of Old Chinese probably reflects morphological components whose meanings likely were lost by the Han dynasty. We, like later readers in the Chinese tradition itself, no longer have access to important shades of meaning in those early texts.

The Morphology of Classical Chinese

It's easy to regard words as not particularly worthy of attention. They are rather simple in English and even simpler in Chinese. Yet words do have properties that affect how they are used in poetry. Words in English have little bits and pieces that we stick on them to help identify what sort of words they are. The famous example is Lewis Carroll's "Jabberwocky," which begins:

> Twas brillig, and the slithy toves
>   Did gyre and gimble in the wabe:
> All mimsy were the borogoves,
>   And the mome raths outgrabe.

The rules for making words in English tell us that "slithy" and "mimsy" must be adjectives, while "toves," "borogoves," and "raths" must be specifically *plural* nouns. "Wabe," as the object of a prepositional phrase, must be a noun, and "gyre," "gimble," and "outgrabe" all must be verbs. What, however, is "mome"? Since it precedes the plural noun "raths," it must be either a noun (like "river rats") or an adjective (like "large spiders"): we cannot be sure, but the ambiguity is not too disconcerting, since we don't know what's going on anyhow.

English, compared to German and Latin, has few ways of explicitly marking the *case* of nouns in order to indicate the function of the noun in the sentence (as, for example, subject, object, possessive modifier, or instrument), and we rely on word order, as in "in the wabe," to indicate function. Even simpler than English, Classical Chinese does not have verb endings and pluralizing suffixes to help distinguish nouns from verbs. With no affixes at all, Classical Chinese relies almost entirely on word order to indicate the function of a word in a sentence.[8]

Words in Classical Chinese poetry usually are a single syllable. Although prose writers beginning particularly in the Han dynasty started using phrases made of two words to express ideas with greater precision, the sub-units of those phrases remain distinct words. This contrasts with a few two-syllable words that cannot be split apart:

芙蓉 "lotus"
葡萄 "grape"

8. It is important to stress that Classical Chinese is the conventionalized written language, distinct from the spoken languages of Old Chinese and Middle Chinese.

Words in Classical Chinese are either nouns or verbs. And both nouns and verbs, depending on word order, can easily become modifiers:

人	person/people
生	(n) life, (v) to be born, to bring to life
人生	human life
月明	The moon (月) is bright (明).
明月	bright moon

Only a few special-purpose words serve strictly as modifiers:

不	"not"	a modifier of verbs
其	"his, her, their, our, its"	a modifier of nouns
于 or 於	marker of locatives (see below)	a modifier of nouns

Verbs in Classical Chinese often serve as the topics of sentences or the objects of other verbs and thus can become nouns, but nouns forced to serve as verbs are rare:

Verb as Topic

問	to ask
答	to answer
問答乃未已	**Asking and answering** were not yet finished.

Verb as Object

笑	to laugh/smile
但見新人**笑**	[He] only sees the new person **smile**.

Noun Forced to Act as Verb

父	father
兄	older brother
父不**父**，兄不**兄**	Fathers do not **act as fathers**, nor brothers **as brothers**.

Because the morphology of Classical Chinese specifies neither the number (singular or plural) of nouns nor the tense (past, present, future) and aspect (completed action, on-going, etc.) of verbs, Chinese poetry leaves much unspoken. Translators must make explicit decisions as they render these lines into other languages. Nonetheless, the indeterminate nature of words in Classical Chinese rarely creates unintended difficulties for the reader. As we shall see, however, poets do call upon ambiguities—especially of tense—in writing poetry.

The Syntax of Classical Chinese

The syntax of Classical Chinese is a complex topic about which there remain many questions. For the purposes of this introduction, I will stress those features not present in English that play an important role in Chinese poetry (and are therefore difficult to capture in translation) rather than give a complete picture of our understanding of Classical Chinese.

Sentences in Classical Chinese are built upon a set of four syntactic relationships to be explained below:

1. Topic—Comment
2. Verb—Object
3. Modifier—Modified
4. Coordination (of nouns, verbs, phrases, or sentences)

The elements that can participate in these relationships are single words, longer phrases, or entire sentences. In the sentence above, "He only sees the new person smile," for example, a complete verbal sentence (新人笑 "The new person smiles") is the object of the verb 見 "to see."

Topic—Comment

Although the "subject" as a syntactic category remains important in the technical analysis of the formal syntax of Classical Chinese, Classical Chinese is what is called a "topic-prominent" language. That is, at the level of surface syntactic structure, the language stresses—and has explicit mechanisms to mark—topics rather than subjects. The topic, as the name suggests, is what a sentence is about. The comment is what the sentence has to say about the topic. Consider a sentence from a poem by Li Bai 李白 (701–62):[9]

長	安	不	見	使	人	愁	Chang'an cannot be seen,
Chang	An	not	see	cause	person	grieve	causing one to grieve.

The first four characters are a complete sentence in which Chang'an (the Tang dynasty capital) is the topic, about which the comment is "[I] do not see [it]." In English we render such a sentence as a passive construction, so that the topic becomes the subject. In the Chinese text itself, however, the subject remains "I" or "we" or a more general "one" (to allow Li Bai, the poet, to identify himself with all those who have climbed Phoenix Terrace before him and all those to follow). Moving "Chang'an" to the topic position creates a form of rhetorical focus on the phrase. The entire four-character sentence in turn is the topic about which the comment is "[it] causes one to grieve."

Comments can be either verb phrases—like an English sentence—or noun phrases, which is unlike English usage. The basic function of a nominal sentence (when the comment is a noun) is to make identity statements, as in this poem by Du Fu 杜甫 (712–70):

---

9. Li Bai, "Climbing Phoenix Terrace in Jinling"《登金陵鳳凰臺》.

夫	婿	輕	薄	兒	My husband [was] a man of shallow feelings.[10]
husband		light	slight	lad	

The line identifies a topic—"husband"—with a noun comment: "(light-and-slight) lad." The two verbs in the sentence ("light" and "slight," which taken together meant "fickle") simply modify the noun comment, "lad," rather than turning the sentence into a verbal statement about an action or about the current state of some object. Although this sort of assertion of identity is the basic role of nominal sentences, we shall encounter many variations on this theme in the poems in the following chapters. Verbal sentences are largely like those in English and therefore are rather straightforward.

Verb—Object

When working in one's own language, verbs seem simple enough. It turns out, however, that what can serve as the object of a verb and why are by no means simple questions. Consider the following variations:

1. George asked a question.
2. George asked Sally.
3. George asked Sally a question.
4. George asked Sally out.
5. *George asked out. (Linguists use an asterisk [*] to indicate an ungrammatical sentence)

The fourth sentence is acceptable because it's a contraction of "George asked Sally [to go] out." The final sentence, however, is nonsensical. While "out" serves as the object of the elided "to go" in sentence 4, we don't view sentence 5 as a contraction, and we expect "ask" to take as an object only questions (either as words like "how" or "why" or as complete phrases like "why she shot him") or prepositional phrases like "for more" or "about it."

TYPES OF OBJECTS

In the English sentence "George asked Sally a question," the person being asked the question (Sally) is the *indirect object* (coming between the verb and the direct object), while what was asked (a question) is the *direct object*. Classical Chinese, in contrast, treats the person asked as a *locative object*, that is, as a place (in time, place, or some other system of relationship):

吾	問	之	王	I asked the king about it.
I	ask	it	king	

That is, in any language the roles of the participants in an action are defined by the sorts of noun slots a verb requires to be filled. The noun slots are the "thematic roles" that verbs define as items in the

10. Du Fu, "The Fair One"《佳人》. The first two characters more literally mean "husband and son-in-law."

language's vocabulary list, or lexicon. These thematic roles appear in sentences in the form of subjects, objects, and, in English, prepositional phrases.

The two most important and common thematic roles are *agent* (the doer of the action) and *patient* (the done-to). In an **active** sentence with a transitive verb, the **agent** corresponds to the **subject**, and the **patient** serves as the **object** of the verb:

A ping-pong ball hit George.

In a *passive* sentence, the agent disappears as a required element, but it can be reintroduced (in English) through a prepositional phrase:

George was hit.
George was hit by a ping-pong ball.

In English, some verbs require a *location* provided by a prepositional phrase. One commonly cited example is

Sally leaned against the wall.

One can simply say "Sally leaned," but that would mean something quite different, that Sally tilted to one side.

In English, an object is optional for some verbs:

The boat sank.
Hitting an iceberg sank the boat.

The second sentence is essentially the *causative* form of the first: "Hitting an iceberg caused the boat to sink."

Classical Chinese has categories for thematic roles and objects that are similar to the English examples above, but the manner in which it represents them syntactically is different. For instance, verbs in Classical Chinese have three possible types of objects: direct, indirect, and (as mentioned above) locative.

Locative Objects

A locative object names a place (in time, space, or a relational system) that somehow participates in the action of the verb. In many cases, the manner of participation is clear and easily corresponds to English usage:

行	到	水	窮	處	Walking, I arrive where the water ends.[11]
walk	arrive	water	end	place	

11. Wang Wei 王維, "The Villa in the Zhongnan Mountains"《終南別業》.

Verbs of motion (come, go, enter, leave, etc.) take locations as their objects:

> He went home.
> Fools rush in where angels fear to tread.

and so on.

In English, we often use prepositional phrases with these verbs:

> I went to school.
> He traveled to the ends of the earth.

In many cases, English translations of Classical Chinese sentences with locative objects must supply an appropriate preposition. Although the role of the locative object in the action may diminish through the addition, the shift is not great:

涼	風	起	天	末	A cool wind rises at the sky's edge.[12]
cool	wind	rise	sky	tip	

Another important function of locative objects in Classical Chinese is in comparative constructions:

霜	葉	紅	於	二	月	花	The frosted leaves are redder than the flowers of the Second Month.[13]
frost	leaves	red	than	second	month	flower	

The function word 於 is frequently used in prose but rarely in poetry to explicitly mark locative objects. Here Du Mu 杜牧 (803–53) relies on it to make the syntax—and the comparative construction—clear.

A final important function of locative objects is to mark the agent in passive constructions:

有	備	則	制	人,		If one is prepared, one controls people.
have	prepare	then	control	people		
無	備	則	制	**於**	人	If one is not prepared, then one *is controlled by people.*[14]
not have	prepare	then	control	(loc.)	people	

It becomes clear that the function word 於 marking the locative object can be indispensable in clarifying who did what to whom. However, 於 is a "prosy" character usually avoided in poetry so that on occasion uncertainty can creep into a line. This syntactic ambiguity becomes a resource that authors can exploit:

---

12. Du Fu, "Thinking of Li Bai at the Sky's Edge"《天末懷李白》.

13. Du Mu, "Traveling in the Mountains"《山行》. This poem is fully discussed in chap. 8; see appendix 1 for source information.

14. Huan Kuan 桓寬 (fl. 80 BC), "The Strategic and Secure"《險固》in *Discourses on Salt and Iron* 鹽鐵論.

瓦	溝	鳴	急	雪	The rooftile channels sing out with driven snow;
tile	channel	sing	urgent	snow	
睡	鴨	照	華	鐙	The sleeping duck illumines the florid lantern.[15]
sleep	duck	shine	florid	lamp	

This couplet, by the Song dynasty poet Huang Tingjian 黃庭堅 (1045–1105), is difficult to read with certainty. It is possible that the roof tiles themselves cause the wind-driven snow to sing out, or the tiles are made to sing by the snow. Similarly, the "sleeping duck" is a metal incense burner, but are we to see it in the light of the lamp, or are we to see the lamp reflected in the metal of the incense burner?[16]

Indirect Objects

Indirect objects are perhaps the simplest type of object to describe. The combination of **verb + indirect object + direct object** is very similar to English and to modern Mandarin syntax, where the indirect object precedes the direct:

與	之	一	杯	酒	[I] gave him (i.o.) one glass of ale (d.o.).[17]
give	him	one	glass	wine	

There of course are some differences between the Classical Chinese and English versions of indirect objects, but they have no significant impact on poetic usage.

Direct Objects and Causative Constructions

Nouns used as direct objects also are very similar to English usage:

美	人	捲	珠	簾	The beautiful one rolls up (v.) the bead curtain (d.o.).[18]
lovely	one	roll	bead	curtain	

And just as in English, verbs that tend to not take an object, when forced to do so, become causative. English verbal forms of adjectives provide common examples:

> The sky **darkened** as the storm approached.
> He **darkened the new paint** to match the old.[19]

---

15. I thank Stuart Sargent for pointing this couplet out. My translation is a version of his modified to stress the problem of ambiguity. See Sargent's discussion of the couplet in Stuart Sargent, "Huang T'ing-chien's 'Incense of Awareness': Poems of Exchange, Poems of Enlightenment," *Journal of the American Oriental Society* 121, no. 1 (Jan. 2001): 65.

16. Sargent notes that the duck refers to an incense censer. He also stresses that the interest in the couplet is precisely in working out the relationships set out through the syntax.

17. From Yuan Jie 元結 (719–72), "Instructing a Former Campaigner"《喻舊部曲》.

18. Li Bai, "Resentment"《怨情》.

The situation in Classical Chinese poetic usage is similar. The following line is by Wang Wei 王維 (701?–761), one of the great Tang dynasty masters of landscape description:

日	色	冷	青	松	The sun's appearance chills the green pines.[20]
sun	color	cold	green	pine	

One can interpret the "green pines" as the *locative* rather than direct object of "cold": "The sun's appearance is cold on the green pines." Weakening the 冷 from the active verb "chills" to the stative verb "cold," however, destroys the animated quality of the landscape Wang Wei describes here. This type of causative construction is important in poetry because it syntactically enforces a connection between aspects of a scene that often are weakened in English translation:

墟	里	上	孤	煙	The hamlet sends forth a lone [column of] smoke.[21]
hamlet		go up	lone	smoke	

Although one can argue that this word order is a form of "poetic" inversion—"goes up, the lone [column] of smoke" (i.e., a lone column of smoke rises)—little in the poetic tradition justifies or particularly requires this reading.

Verbs can also serve as the objects of other verbs, but in many ways, the similarities to English make these constructions rather simple.

(1) Verbs as the Simple Objects of Verbs of Perception and Cognition

In English we say things like "I know that . . . " or "He saw that . . . " and so on. Classical Chinese has similar constructions without a character analogous to the "that":

空	悲	清	夜	徂	In vain I sorrow that the pure night passes.[22]
in vain	sorrow	pure	night	depart	

These are the simplest cases. The two other types of constructions with verbs as objects—auxiliaries and pivot constructions—are a bit more complex but have useful English analogies.

(2) Auxiliary Constructions

Auxiliary verbs in Classical Chinese express what is called *modality*, the desirability or probability of the action they take as their object. For example:

---

19. That is, he caused the new paint to become darker.

20. More literally, "The sun's appearance makes cold the green pines." Wang Wei, "Visiting Incense Accumulation Temple" 《過香積寺》.

21. More literally, "The hamlet makes go up the lone [column of] smoke." Wang Wei, "At Wang River Living at Ease, Presented to Pei Di" 《輞川閑居贈裴秀才迪》.

22. Du Fu, "Weary Night" 《倦夜》. This poem is fully discussed in chap. 7; see appendix 1 for source information.

他 人 **應** 已 睡 — Other people *surely* have already gone to sleep.[23]
other people ought already sleep

不 **必** 取 長 途 — [I] *need* not set out on a long road.[24]
not must select long road

吏 不 **敢** 聽 — The official does not *dare* listen.[25]
official not dare listen

A distinctive feature of auxiliary constructions is that—usually—nouns cannot come between the auxiliary verb and its object. Du Fu's poetry shows, however, that even this rule can be broken:

鬢 髮 還 **應** 雪 滿 頭 — My temples and hair, when I return, *surely* will be snow covering my head.[26]
temple hair return ought snow fill head

(3) Pivot Constructions

In Classical Chinese, *pivot constructions* describe situations where one person asks, orders, urges, compels, or allows someone else to do an action:

勸 君 更 盡 一 杯 酒 — [I] urge you to finish another glass of wine.[27]
urge you again finish one glass wine

In the above sentence, "urge" is the pivot verb which takes "finish" as its direct object. "You," the indirect object, is called the *pivot* because it is both the recipient of the action of asking and the agent who will carry out the request. The sentence is analogous to sentences in English like

I let him wait.

in contrast to

I ordered that he wait.

where the "him" in the first sentence serves as an indirect object while "wait" is the direct object of "let." (The "ordered" in the second sentence acts like a verb of cognition, except that the verb in the following clause is in the subjunctive mood.)

---

23. Jia Dao 賈島, "Enjoying the Moon"《玩月》.

24. Du Fu, "The Yangzi and Han Rivers"《江漢》. This poem is fully discussed in chap. 7; see appendix 1 for source information.

25. Li He 李賀, "Ballad of the Fierce Tiger"《猛虎行》.

26. Du Fu, "Sent to Du Wei"《寄杜位》.

27. Wang Wei, "Seeing Off Yuan Two to Serve as Envoy to Anxi"《送元二使安西》.

Modifier—Modified

In English we speak of adjectives modifying nouns and adverbs modifying verbs and adjectives. In Classical Chinese, verbs can modify nouns, and nouns can modify verbs (which usually become nominalized in the process) as well as other nouns. There is just one major constraint: the modifier *precedes* the modified word:

1.	靜	to be quiet or still	verb
2.	山	mountain	noun
3.	靜山	a quiet mountain	verb modifying noun
4.	山(之)靜	the stillness of a mountain	noun modifying verb

There are many types of mountains: tall, densely forested, denuded, mountains with roaring waterfalls or trickling springs, and so on. Phrase (3) refers specifically to mountains that are quiet. Similarly, there are many types of stillness: the quiet of ancient ruins, or that of a house where all are asleep, or of a temple when the monks are deep in meditation. Phrase (4) points to the stillness of an empty mountain. In English we have suffixes like "-ness" that change adjectives into nouns and make the syntax clear, but Classical Chinese lacks such morphological aids, and uncertainty can arise. In particular, since 靜 is a verb, the two words, "mountains" + "still," can be read as a short but complete sentence, "The mountains are still." The optional character 之, however, serves to remove the ambiguity and explicitly inform us that "mountain" here *modifies* "still[ness]."

Despite the general ease with which words shift categories in Classical Chinese, there are a few important words that are specifically restricted to serving as modifiers of either nouns or verbs:

MODIFIERS OF NOUNS:
其 "his, her, its, their"
諸 "all the . . . "

MODIFIERS OF VERBS:
不 "not"
未 "not yet"
所 [function word pointing to verb's object]

Beyond a few such syntactically restricted cases, words in Classical Chinese are allowed to bind together as modifier and modified with few restraints.

This lack of morphological and syntactic constraints in allowing one character to modify another in Classical Chinese played a role in the development of poetic technique. As the tradition matured, Chinese poets used the looseness of the rules for modification to explore how we carve up our perception of the world and how we allow perceptions to inform one another. For example, Du Fu writes:

竹 bamboo	涼 cool	侵 invade	臥 bedroom	內 within	Bamboo coolness invades the bedroom.
野 outland	月 moon	滿 fill	庭 court	隅 corner	The outland moon fills a corner of the courtyard.[28]

28. Du Fu, "Weary Night" 《倦夜》. This poem is fully discussed in chap. 7; see appendix 1 for source information.

What is a "bamboo coolness," and how can it invade Du Fu's bedroom? Du Fu most certainly is pointing to a slight breeze coming from a window screened by bamboo. The breeze carries the scent of bamboo and perhaps a rustling sound as well. Similarly, one may ask what an "outland moon" is. Du Fu sees the walled courtyard itself and not the vast expanse of open land beyond the walls. Yet the moon retains and conveys the qualities of the broad outlands he seems to be trying to shut out. The effect of the modification relationships in the first two words of each line is not a condensed, difficult "poetic" pair of images. They are in fact fairly easy and "natural" precisely because the language facilitates these sorts of juxtapositions. We shall encounter many such examples in the following chapters.

Coordination

Coordination is the pairing of two nouns, verbs, or sentences: Jack and Jill, eat and run, for better or worse, and so on.

Pairs of nouns present no problem at all. The only slight difference from English usage is that Classical Chinese does not require an explicit conjunction like "and" or "or":

李	**杜**	文	章	在	The compositions of *Li [Bai] and Du [Fu]* remain.[29]
Li	Du	composition		remain	

In most cases, there is no uncertainty about whether an "and" or an "or" is implied.

Pairs of verbs prove to be more complicated than nouns because verb phrases in a coordinate relationship in Classical Chinese tend to imply more than simple juxtaposition. There usually is some relationship between the two actions. The two most common types of connections are:

1. Action One happens *with the result that* Action Two happens
2. Action One is performed *in order to make* Action Two possible

For example,

抽	刀	斷	水	水	更	流	[I] *pull* a knife to *cut* the water, [with the result that] the water *flows* all the more.
pull	knife	break	water	water	more	flow	
舉	杯	銷	愁	愁	更	愁	[I] *lift* a glass to *dispel* sadness, [with the result that] sadness *becomes yet more sad.*[30]
lift	glass	dispel	sad	sad	more	sad	

and

煖	湯	濯	我	足	[He] *heated* water [in order to] *wash* our feet,
heat	water	wash	my	feet	
剪	紙	招	我	魂	And *cut* paper [in order to] *summon* our souls.[31]
cut	paper	summon	my	soul	

29. Han Yu, "Teasing Zhang Ji"《調張籍》. This poem is fully discussed in chap. 8; see appendix 1 for source information.

30. Li Bai, "At the Tower of Xie Tiao in Xuanzhou, a Farewell Feast with Editor Shu Yun"《送元二使安西》.

31. Du Fu, "Ballad of Pengya"《彭衙行》. This poem is fully discussed in chap. 7; see appendix 1 for source information.

In addition, the two actions can be in a logical sequence ("and") or the second can happen despite the first ("but"). The couplet by Li Bai above is a good example of coordination that implies "but": "I pull a knife to cut the water, but the water flows more swiftly. / I lift a glass to dispel sorrow, but the sorrow grows more intense." Sometimes, however, the relationship between the two actions is enigmatic. For example, Du Fu's famous first couplet of "Spring Vista" 春望 is:

國	破	山	河	在	The capital is broken: mountains and rivers remain.
country	break	mountain	rivers	remain	
城	春	草	木	深	The city wall in spring: the grasses and trees grow thickly.[32]
wall	spring	grass	tree	deep	

What is the relationship between the catastrophic An Lushan Rebellion and the constancy of the landscape that Du Fu observes?[33] Is there solace to be found, or is the landscape entirely indifferent to the fate of empires? Is such indifference a model to emulate, or should Du Fu strive for constancy on a human scale? The nature of Classical Chinese syntax suggests that surely the coordinate actions in the first line are related, but the relationship here remains uncertain. Indeed, this uncertainty in the relationship between the human and the natural realm becomes the central problem the poem explores.

One final aspect of verb coordination is worth mentioning to complete this overview of Classical Chinese syntax. In pairs of coordinate verbs, as discussed above, the first action very often sets the condition for the second. Some actions, however, set out abstract causal conditions and became part of the structural components of the language. They are transitive verbs (i.e., verbs with objects) that became *grammaticalized* into what are called coverbs, function words that are still verbal in character but more closely resemble English prepositional phrases. They help explain how the action of the *main verb* (m.v.) came about. The most frequently used coverbs are:

COVERB	USUAL TRANSLATION	MEANING AS A VERB
以	with	to use . . . in order to [m.v.]
從	from	to follow . . . in doing [m.v.]
自	from	to start from . . . in doing [m.v.]
與	with	to accompany . . . in doing [m.v.]
為	for	to do [m.v.] for the sake of . . .
因	relying on	to rely on . . . to accomplish [m.v.]
由	following	to follow the route of . . . in doing [m.v.]
緣	following	to follow along . . . in doing [m.v.]

Coverbs in most cases come before the main verb. However, because coverbs remain verbs in a coordinate relationship with the main verb, syntax allows the two to be reversed. When the main verb comes first, one needs to look for a rhetorical reason for the change in word order. Since *focus*—the stressed part of the sentence—usually is at the *end* of the sentence (though there are rhetorical devices to move the focus

32. Du Fu, "Spring Vista"《春望》. This poem is fully discussed in chap. 7; see appendix 1 for source information.

33. For an extended discussion of Du Fu and the An Lushan Rebellion, see chapter 7.

to the beginning), shifting the coverb to the end of the sentence usually is done in order to stress the object of the coverb.

Conclusion

This overview of Classical Chinese as a language is by no means complete. Its primary function is to serve as a resource in discussing the poems in the chapters ahead. In order to explain the particular qualities of a line or a poem, one must at times point out technical features of the phrasing, and this can only be done on the basis of some knowledge of the classical language.

Perhaps the key features to keep in mind—because they differ so much from English usage—are the topic-comment structure of sentences, the importance of word order in a language without grammatical affixes, and the corresponding ease with which words shift from one word class to another.

Chapter Two

The Formal and Rhetorical Features of Chinese Poetry

In 1950 the Black Mountain poet Charles Olson advocated a break from the closed forms of traditional poetry and proposed a careful, minutely precise, yet free-flowing linkage of structure and intent in his seminal essay "Projective Verse":[1]

> If a contemporary poet leaves a space as long as the phrase before it, he means that space to be held, by the breath, an equal length of time. If he suspends a word or syllable at the end of a line (this was most [*sic*]l Cummings' addition) he means that time to pass that it takes the eye—that hair of time suspended—to pick up the next line. If he wishes a pause so light it hardly separates the words, yet does not want a comma—which is an interruption of the meaning rather than the sounding of the line—follow him when he uses a symbol the typewriter has ready to hand:
>
> What does not change / is the will to change[2]
>
> Observe him, when he takes advantage of the machine's multiple margins, to juxtapose:
>
> Sd he:
>   to dream takes no effort
>   to think is easy
>   to act is more difficult
> but for a man to act after he has taken thought, this!
> is the most difficult of all[3]
>
> Each of these lines is a progressing of both the meaning and the breathing forward, and then a backing up, without a progress or any kind of movement outside the unit of time local to the idea.

Olson's goal that the line be an organic structure which captures the precise flow of meaning leads to his maxim:

---

1. Charles Olson, "Projective Verse," *Poetry New York*, no. 3 (1950): 13–22.

2. This is the first line of Olson's poem "The Kingfishers." *The Collected Poems of Charles Olson* (Berkeley: University of California Press, 1987), p. 86.

3. From Olson's "The Praises," *The Collected Poems of Charles Olson*, p. 98.

the HEAD, by way of the EAR, to the SYLLABLE
the HEART, by way of the BREATH, to the LINE[4]

and to the principle, written in capital letters, that he borrows from fellow Black Mountain poet, Robert Creeley: FORM IS NEVER MORE THAN AN EXTENSION OF CONTENT.[5] This principle is part of a manifesto proclaiming a new poetry of the "open field." Taken at face value as a historical fact about the nature and function of poetic form, it is wrong except at the deepest level: throughout most of human history, poets have used the conventions of their poetic traditions to extend the possibilities for language, have conceived of their poetry *through* form, and used form to provide an additional dimension for the shaping of meaning.

The difficulty for the student of poetry is that Olson and Creeley, in their efforts to naturalize form, to make it follow from the movement of head and heart, are clearly right: traditional form is not natural. It is a set of *conventions* about sound and language and about how to build poems out of lines, couplets, and ever-larger units of organization. To fully understand poems written through the manipulation of these conventions, the reader must be almost viscerally aware of them. Most people, however, do not have this sort of sure familiarity with the formal and rhetorical features of earlier poetic traditions. Poems from other places and other ages seem accordingly stilted, academic, and hollow: they cannot speak effectively to an untrained ear. Yet to learn poetic conventions well enough to begin to hear poets through the language of form in which they wrote is not simple. It requires an imaginative leap to begin to recognize what form adds to language in poetry and to recover the human experience within the conventional practice, and to understand that, in its deepest nature, form is, as Olson demands, "an extension of content."

The goal of this chapter is to begin this process of familiarization with the formal and rhetorical features that Chinese poets drew upon in their writings. Some of these features—like line length, prosody, rhyme, voice, and tone—are shared by many different poetic traditions since they deal with the basics of composition. Some, like tonal regulation and parallelism, are more specific features of the language and the intellectual universe of early and medieval China. The chapter begins with formal aspects of poetry—lines, couplets, and stanzas, as well as prosody and rhyme—and then turns to rhetorical features like metaphor, allegory, and allusion. The survey ends with large-scale features like the shaping of poetic voice.

4. Olson, "Projective Verse," p. 16.

5. Olson, "Projective Verse," p. 14. Olsen attributes the principle to Creeley in the essay.

The Formal Structures of Chinese Poetry

The Line

THE LINE AS PROSODIC UNIT

In many traditions, the line is a *prosodic* unit, a number of stressed syllables—with or without rhyme—that interacts with syntax in complex ways. Consider the beginning of a sonnet by Shakespeare:

Let me not to the marriage of true minds
Admit impediments. Love is not love
Which alters when it alteration finds,
Or bends with the remover to remove:
(William Shakespeare, Sonnet 116, ll. 1–4)

We are taught (or at least I was) to read the sentence ending with "impediments" without a pause for the end of the first line. Yet there is a rhyme word, "minds," at the end of the line. Similarly, the opening lines of William Wordsworth's "Ode: Intimations of Immortality from Recollections of Early Childhood" are shaped by rhyme, while the rhythm of the lines is governed by the punctuation rather than the line breaks:

There was a time when meadow, grove and stream,
The earth and every common sight
To me did seem
Apparelled in celestial light,
The glory and the freshness of a dream. (ll. 1–5)

In the Chinese tradition as well, the line was a prosodic unit, but unlike in Western poetic genres, it also largely served as a complete grammatical unit. The earliest poetic texts, from the *Canon of Poetry* (*Shijing* 詩經), were part of the musical repertoire of the Zhou court: they were sung and accompanied by music and dance. They typically had a four-beat meter:

桃之夭夭	The peach so fresh in its bloom:
灼灼其華 (*hwra)	Radiant are its flowers.
之子于歸	This [girl] goes to her new home:
宜其室家 (*kra)	All aright is her chamber and house.[6]

6. "The Peach Is Fresh-Blooming"《桃夭》, Mao 6, ll. 1–4. This poem is fully discussed in chap. 3; see appendix 1 for source information.

This stanza has an *abcb* rhyme scheme and is typical of Chinese rhyme in general, where just the last stressed ("full") word in each couplet rhymes. In this poem, as in most Chinese poems, the line, while shaped by prosodic constraints, also is a syntactically complete unit, a sentence.

While the *Canon of Poetry* reveals a significant range of line lengths and rhyming schemes, by the Han dynasty (206 BC–AD 220) when the elite poetic tradition of the imperial period was beginning to form, ritual poetry of archaic correctness and grandeur modeled on the *Canon of Poetry* used a four-character line. This sense of the ritual propriety of the four-character line in fact persisted throughout the premodern tradition in that funerary poems and other highly formal genres continued to use this meter. However, by the Han, a second musical and poetic tradition from the state of Chu introduced a variety of new prosodic patterns. The Warring States (ca. 450 BC–221 BC) verse in the Chu meters and the Han dynasty imitations of the earlier poems were gathered together into a collection called the *Lyrics of Chu* (*Chu ci* 楚辭). The longest and most famous poem in that collection is *Encountering Sorrow* (*Li sao* 離騷), traditionally attributed to Qu Yuan, an upright, ill-fated minister of Chu, who is said to have written the poem to express his sorrow, vexation, and regret before he threw himself into the Miluo River. Its meter, in a longer line than the poems of the *Canon*, is basically:

X X X O X X 兮 [ɣɛj]
X X X O X R (rhyme)

That is, the lines of the couplet have five stressed syllables (X), an unstressed word (O), and a breathing mark (ɣɛj) between lines. Two couplets from *Encountering Sorrow* suffice as an example; note that the two characters in the fourth position (其 and 之) are both grammatical function words.

日月忽其不淹兮，	The days and months hurried on, never lingering;
春與秋其代序。[ziǝ̆]	Springs and autumns replaced one another:
惟草木之零落兮，	I thought of the verdure's fading,
恐美人之遲暮。[mɔʰ]	And feared that the Fair One would grow old[7]

The *Lyrics of Chu* also had poems with a shorter line:

X X X 兮 X X
X X X 兮 X R (rhyme)

The following example is from the *Nine Songs* (*Jiu ge* 九歌), another set of verses in the *Lyrics of Chu*:

浴蘭湯兮沐芳	I bathe in orchid water—and wash my hair with fragrances:
華采衣兮若英	Florid, bright clothes—are like flowers.[8]

Like the poems of the *Canon of Poetry*, all six lines in the above examples are end-stopped: each line is a complete sentence.

7. Qu Yuan, *Encountering Sorrow*. This poem is fully discussed in chap. 3; see appendix 1 for source information.

8. *Lyrics of Chu*, "Lord amidst the Clouds" 《雲中君》, ll. 1–2. This poem is fully discussed in chap. 3; see appendix 1 for source information.

These prosodic patterns from the *Lyrics of Chu* became part of the Chinese poetic tradition and were strongly associated with a southern ambience and an antique emotional intensity and moral high-mindedness. The important Tang dynasty writer Wang Wei, for example, invokes the Chu meter in an old-style song:

天路來兮雙黃鵠	From the Heavens' road comes—a pair of yellow swans.
雲上飛兮水上宿	They fly above the clouds—and spend the night on the water.[9]

The Han dynasty contributed one more set of prosodic patterns to the poetic tradition as it looked back to its past for models. The Han emperors emulated the Zhou kings, who reportedly sent out envoys to collect the folk songs of the realm as a way of assessing the moral, social, and economic effectiveness of their rule. The Han dynasty Music Bureau (Yuefu 樂府) was charged with this task of gathering folk songs, and poems said to be from the Music Bureau collection survived into later times. Some poems are in a mixture of three-, five-, and seven-character lines, but others are more irregular. Consider, for example, the anonymous poem "Oh, Above" 上邪:

我欲與君相知。[tri]	I want to get to know you,
長命無絕衰。[ʂwi]	Eternally decreed without end or decline.
山無陵，	When the mountains are without peaks,
江水為竭，[giat]	The river waters run dry,
冬雷震震夏雨雪，[swiat]	Winter thunder rumbles, and snow falls in summer,
天地合，	When Heaven and Earth collapse together,
乃敢與君絕。[dzwiat]	Only then would I dare to break with you.[10]

As the Chinese tradition evolved, writers looked back to these Han dynasty songs and saw an emotional directness and a spontaneity of composition free of premeditated crafting. When writers used this sort of variation in line length and rhyme scheme, especially in poems labeled as songs or ballads, they invoked this ancient simplicity and unadorned honesty. One famous example is "Song of Climbing Youzhou Terrace" 登幽州臺歌 by Chen Zi'ang 陳子昂 (661–701), a strong advocate of returning to older styles of verse in the Tang dynasty:[11]

前不見古人	Ahead, one cannot see men of old.
後不見來者	Behind, one cannot see those to come.
念天地之悠悠	Thinking on the vastness of Heaven and Earth,
獨愴然而涕下	Alone, I am stricken with sorrow, and tears fall.[12]

9. Wang Wei, "Song of a Pair of Yellow Swans: A Farewell" 《雙黃鵠歌送別》.

10. Anonymous, "Oh, Above" 《上邪》. This poem is fully discussed in chap. 4; see appendix 1 for source information.

11. The Youzhou Terrace is close to the Tang northeastern frontier, near modern Beijing. Chen Zi'ang traveled there as part of the army of the Prince of Jian'an in a campaign against the Khitan.

12. Chen Zi'ang, "Song of Climbing Youzhou Terrace" 《登幽州臺歌》. This poem is fully discussed in chap. 6; see appendix 1 for source information.

The two overwhelmingly predominant prosodic patterns from the later Southern Dynasties throughout the remainder of the premodern tradition were poems with five-character or seven-character lines. Although there are examples of the five-character line in early verse, it attained a new importance in the final years of the Han dynasty and developed rapidly in the Wei, Jin, and early Southern Dynasties (i.e., from AD 200 to AD 450). In contrast, although writers employed the seven-character line in the Southern Dynasties, it really came into its own during the Tang.

Once these two meters developed as the norm for polite composition, the earlier meters came to signal conscious, intentional deviation from formal elegance. The High Tang poet Li Bai, for example, invokes the roughness of the "old" through extended line lengths and prosaic syntax in a poem written to a Han dynasty Music Bureau title:

匈奴以殺戮為耕作。	The Xiongnu treat slaughter as plowing:
古來唯見白骨黃沙田。	From of old, one only sees white bones on the fields of yellow sand.[13]

In contrast, the Mid-Tang poet Li He 李賀 (790–816) used a very short line to create striking effects in a poem about the grave of a Southern Dynasties courtesan. The poem is titled "The Grave of Little Su" 蘇小小墓:

幽 蘭 露	The dew on secluded orchids
如 啼眼 [ŋja:n´]	Resembles weeping eyes.
無物結同心	There is nothing "to bind our hearts as one."
煙 花不堪剪 [tsian´]	The misty flowers: I cannot bear to cut them.
草如茵	The grass resembles a mat.
松如蓋 [kaj`]	The pine resembles an awning.
風 為裳	The wind becomes a skirt.
水為 珮 [pɦuaj`]	The water becomes pendants.
油壁車	An oil-cloth carriage
夕相待 [tɦaj`]	At dusk awaits him.
冷翠燭	A cold blue-glinting candle
勞光彩	Labors to become bright.
西陵下	At the foot of West Mound
風吹雨	The wind blows rain.[14]

The choice of line length in Chinese poetry, and especially the choice to write in a form that differed from five- or seven-character verse, clearly signaled the mode of the poem through the prosodic pattern's association with ancient exemplars.

While formal innovation in verse forms did not come to an end with the contrast between the early styles and the dominant five- and seven-character meter, *shi* 詩 poetry as a genre largely became

13. Li Bai, "Fighting South of the Wall" 《戰城南》, ll. 9–10. This poem is fully discussed in chap. 6; see appendix 1 for source information.

14. Li He 李賀, "The Grave of Little Su" 《蘇小小墓》. This poem is fully discussed in chap. 8; see appendix 1 for source information.

fixed.[15] The five- and seven-character verse forms, like the earlier prosodic models, initially developed when elite writers appropriated contemporary song forms. Once these forms grew popular among the literati, however, this initial linkage between poetry and musical performance faded. Still, this pattern of elite borrowing of popular musical forms remained a continuous undercurrent in the evolution of prosody. In the last major development during the period covered in this book, writers during the Tang dynasty began to compose lyrics to new song forms that had far greater variety both in the length of lines and in syntactic organization. Unlike earlier innovations, however, this manner of writing remained distinct from *shi* poetry and developed into a separate tradition, that of *ci* 詞, "song lyric." The Late Tang poet Wen Tingyun 溫庭筠 (ca. 812–66), for example, wrote to the tune "Geng lou zi" 【更漏子】:

柳絲長，	The willow catkins are long.
春雨細，[siajˋ]	The spring rain is fine.
花外漏聲迢遞。[tɦiajˋ]	Beyond the flowers, the sound of the water-clock is distant.
驚塞雁，	Startling the frontier geese,
起城烏，[ʔuǎ]	Arousing the crows on the city wall:
畫屏金鷓鴣。[kuǎ]	The golden partridge on the painted screen.[16]

Later ages continued to develop new verse forms, but, like the *ci*, they evolved into distinct genres, while the *shi* poetic form—still dominant—remained unchanged.

TONAL PROSODY

Prosody refers to the rhythm and pattern of sounds in a poem. In many poetic traditions, not only does the *number* of syllables matter, but so do differences in *weight* between the syllables of the line. Ancient Greek and Latin poetry, for example, gave greater weight to long vowels and diphthongs (as well as short vowels followed by two consonants), and their prosody was based on patterns of feet (combinations of syllables) with differing *vowel lengths*. French and English traditions, in contrast, are based on stress rather than vowel length. Shakespearean blank verse, for example, uses an iambic (da-DA) pentameter as its basic line:

> But sòft, what lìght through yònder wìndow breàks?
> It ìs the eàst, and Jùliet ìs the sùn.
> (Shakespeare, *Romeo and Juliet*, act 2, scene 2)

In all these traditions, different genres of poetry used different meters, and authors used the violation of the expected metrical patterns as a tool in composition.

In the Chinese tradition, the fundamental metrical unit is the character and not the foot (the disyllabic [iamb, trochee, spondee, etc.] or trisyllabic grouping [dactyl, anapest, etc.]). Still, distinctions in stress matter in some poetic forms: the *Lyrics of Chu* and poems based on it rely on a small set of

---

15. While there were other forms of rhymed verse in China from the Han dynasty onward, the term *shi* 詩 encompasses most of what we typically think of as "poetry."

16. Wen Tingyun, "To the tune 'Geng lou zi'" 【更漏子】.

words—largely grammatical function words that were lightly stressed—to fill out the metrical pattern. We have seen the pattern:

X X X O X X 兮
X X X O X R

The "O" word is an unstressed function word. However, this use of unstressed words to define meter did not continue into the five- and seven-character verse genres.

What did develop was a prosody based on the four tones of Middle Chinese. This evolution remains a topic of active research, complicated by the problem of the history of the four tones themselves. The first extant discussion of tones dates to Shen Yue 沈約 (441–513) in the Qi dynasty (483–93). Linguists largely believe that tones evolved during the transition from Old Chinese to Middle Chinese as the final -ʔ and -s changed to rising (上 *shang*) and departing (去 *qu*) tones. However, when and where the transition started and finished is unclear.[17] In any case, Shen Yue and his colleagues began to stress the organization of tonal patterns in lines and couplets. The preferences they proposed in a rather sketchy form gradually evolved into conventional practices during the next 150 years as the tonal system of Middle Chinese fully emerged. These conventions of euphony in tonal prosody became the "regulated verse" (*lü shi* 律詩) of the Tang dynasty.

The conventions for tonal prosody in Tang regulated verse provided a set of norms within which, and at times against which, poets composed their verse. There remain debates about how strict these conventions were and whether social occasion determined the strictness of prosodic rules. However, as the most basic and general rule, the prosody requires either of two patterns for a five-character couplet, where 平 (*ping*) is a level tone and 仄 (*ze*) is a "deflected" tone (i.e., rising, departing, or entering):

仄仄平平仄 / 平平仄仄平 (R) or 平平平仄仄 / 仄仄仄平平 (R)

In both patterns, the second and fourth and the third and fifth characters are in opposite tonal categories, and the last character of the second line of the couplet is a rhyme word that must be in the level tone. Moreover, the tonal pattern in the second line of the couplet is the mirror-image of the first line. In an eight-line regulated verse poem, the two patterns alternate. The situation for seven-character verse is almost identical:

平平仄仄平平仄 / 仄仄平平仄仄平 (R) or
仄仄平平平仄仄 / 平平仄仄仄平平 (R)

Some scholars have argued that the prosody was looser, that the tones of the first and third characters in five-character verse and the tones of the first, third, and fifth characters in seven-character verse do not matter. This simple model, in any case, is an after-the-fact generalization, and the corpus of Tang dynasty

17. Edwin Pulleyblank, for example, argues that characters used for Buddhist terms show that the final -s began to disappear in northern China in the early fourth century but persisted much longer in the south. Indeed, Pulleyblank argues that for Shen Yue some words in the "departing tone" retained the -s, while others had an intermediate -h, and still others may have acquired a tonal pitch contour. See Edwin G. Pulleyblank, "Some Further Evidence Regarding Old Chinese -s and Its Time of Disappearance," *Bulletin of the School of Oriental and African Studies* 36, no. 2 (1973): 368–73.

regulated verse shows that actual practice was more complicated. First, in seven-character verse in particular there was a strong tendency for the first line to rhyme: this required—at its simplest—switching the pairings of tonal patterns.[18] Second, poets systematically violated expectations in the first line of a couplet and then "rebalanced" the couplet by a matching violation in the second half. Huang Tingjian in the Song dynasty is especially famous for this technique, but scholars cite the Tang poet Du Fu as Huang's inspiration. In the chapters on Tang poetry, I shall provide the arrangement of level and oblique tones for regulated verse and note particularly salient violations.

THE CAESURA

Poetry orchestrates sound and meaning as an interplay of phonology and syntax. Poets use the grammar of a language to control the flow of a poem in a counter-rhythm to the prosodic features. The caesura, a strong pause in a line required by syntax and/or semantics (i.e., the sense of the line), most clearly reveals the role of counter-metrical rhythms in reading. Standard examples in English (with the caesura marked by ||) are

> To be or not to be: || that is the question.[19]
> To err is human; || to forgive, divine.[20]

In English poetry, caesurae are commonly marked by punctuation that clarifies syntax.

In Chinese poetry, the five-character line usually has a caesura after the second character, and in seven-character verse, there are possible breaks after the second and fourth characters. The pause built into the syntax of the line can range from almost non-existent to a full stop. This 2–3 pattern appeared at the very beginning of the five-character verse tradition, as in the second of the "Nineteen Old Poems" 古詩十九首:

> 蕩子 || 行不歸， The rover || travels and does not return,
> 空床 || 難獨守。 An empty bed || is hard to maintain alone.[21]

Here the first two characters are the topic; the last three are the comment. When writers during the Jian'an reign period (196–220) began to adopt the five-character format, they also used the 2–3 pattern, but the syntactic features and the strength of the caesura varied to create a flexible line. Wang Can 王粲 (177–217) in his poem "Seven Laments" 七哀詩 writes:

---

18. That is, the second (rhyme word) line of the first pattern matched with the second line of the second pattern:
(beginning with 仄) 仄仄平平仄仄平 (R) / 平平仄仄仄平平 (R) or
(beginning with 平) 平平仄仄仄平平 (R) / 仄仄平平仄仄平 (R)

19. William Shakespeare, *Hamlet*, Act III, Scene 1.

20. Alexander Pope, "An Essay on Criticism" (l. 525).

21. Anonymous, "Nineteen Old Poems," no. 2《古詩十九首》第二, ll. 9–10. This poem is fully discussed in chap. 4; see appendix 1 for source information.

出門 ‖ 無所見	Going out the gate, ‖ there is nothing [else] to see:
白骨 ‖ 蔽平原	White bones ‖ cover the broad plain.
路有 ‖ 饑婦人	On the road is ‖ a starving woman:
抱子 ‖ 棄草間	Hugging her child, ‖ she abandons it in the grass.[22]

In the first and fourth lines above, the caesura falls between two coordinate verb phrases. In the second line, the break is between topic and comment. In the third line, the caesura, between a verb and its object, is very weak.

By the Tang dynasty, poets learned to violate the normal 2–3 pattern as one more technique in writing. Chen Zi'ang in "Song of Climbing Youzhou Terrace," for example, not only employed irregular line lengths to create an "old" effect; in the five-character lines of the poem, he also used a 1–4 rhythm with the caesura coming after the first character:

前 ‖ 不見古人	Ahead, ‖ one cannot see men of old.
後 ‖ 不見來者	Behind, ‖ one cannot see those to come.

The seven-character line gives writers greater room to vary the rhythms that come from syntax, but the general pattern was similar to the five-character line. The first couplet of Wang Wei's regulated-verse poem "After Long Rain, Written at Wang River Villa" 積雨輞川莊作 shows the flexibility within a 2–2–3 rhythm:

積雨 **‖** 空林 ‖ 煙火遲	After long rains, **‖** in the empty forest ‖ the fires are slow:
蒸藜 ‖ 炊黍 **‖** 餉東菑	With steamed pulse ‖ and cooked millet **‖** [workers] eat in the east fields.[23]

In both lines, the first four characters are pairs of nouns modified by verbs, but in the first line, the first pair is a topic to which the next five characters are the comment, while in the second line, the two pairs are coordinate noun phrases that serve as the topic for the last three characters of the line. As a result, in the first line, the break between the second and third characters is stronger than that between the fourth and fifth, while in the second line, the caesura after the fourth character is strongest. The shifting cadences are subtle but effective.

The Couplet

Rhyme helped shape the couplet as the fundamental unit in Chinese *shi* poetry. From as early as the songs of the "Airs of the States" (*Guo feng* 國風) in the *Canon of Poetry*, stanzas were built upon couplets where the last character of the couplet rhymed with the last character of the couplet before and after it (i.e., A**B**C**B**D**B**E**B** . . .). Yet the couplet, even in the beginning, took on a role greater than simply that of a rhyming unit. This couplet-wise rhyming linked the individual lines—which tended to be a

---

22. Wang Can, "Seven Laments"《七哀詩》. This poem is fully discussed in chap. 4; see appendix 1 for source information.

23. Wang Wei, "After Long Rain, Written at Wang River Villa"《積雨輞川莊作》. This poem is fully discussed in chap. 6; see appendix 1 for source information.

syntactically complete sentence—into a larger unit of meaning. Consider once again the first stanza of "The Peach Is Fresh-Blooming":

桃之夭夭	The peach so fresh in its bloom:
灼灼其華 [*hwra]	Radiant are its flowers.
之子于歸	This [girl] goes to her new home:
宜其室家 [*kra]	All aright is her chamber and house.

Although each line is a sentence, the second line in each couplet serves as a comment that fills out the statement of the first line. This pattern continued in the early development of the five-character verse form, as in the opening lines of the first of the "Nineteen Old Poems":

行行重行行	Traveling on and on, on and on:
與君生別離 [li]	Living parted from you.
相去萬餘里	Having gone more than ten thousand *li* from one another,
各在天一涯 [ngɛ:j]	Each is at one edge of the sky.[24]

The role of the second line of the couplet in complementing the first led to early examples of parallel couplet construction. The first of the "Nineteen Old Poems," for example, continues:

胡馬依北風	The Hu horse leans to the north wind.[25]
越鳥巢南枝	The Yue bird nests in the southern branches.[26] (ll. 7–8)

In the couplet, the northern name "Hu" matches the southern place-name "Yue"; "horse" matches "bird," and "leans to" as a verb corresponds to "nests." "North" is opposite "south," while the noun "wind" as an element of the natural scene matches "branches." Three of the five characters in the first line have straightforward complements in the second. The power of parallel construction is in bringing the other two sets of characters into alignment, so that one asks "How is 'lean' like 'nest' and 'wind' like 'branch'?" This creation of contextual correspondence through the couplet proved very powerful and extended the representational reach of poetry as the art of parallel couplet-crafting grew in sophistication.

The development of parallelism intensified the focus on the couplet as the basic unit of composition. In the regulated octave (eight-line) poetry that reached maturity in the Tang, the second and third couplets had to be parallel, and finding new and interesting ways to handle this requirement became central to the art of poetry. Wang Wei, for example, could achieve an austere grandeur and simplicity:

大漠孤煙直，	Across the great plain, a lone column of smoke [rises] straight.
長河落日圓。	On the long river, the setting sun is round.[27]

24. Anonymous, "Nineteen Old Poems, no. 1" 《古詩十九首》第一. This poem is fully discussed in chap. 4; see appendix 1 for source information.

25. The Hu are specifically *northern* barbarians.

26. Yue is a southern region.

27. Wang Wei, "Arriving at the Border as an Envoy" 《使至塞上》. This poem is fully discussed in chap. 6.

Du Fu had a large range of styles in couplet-crafting. He could be loose-jointed and prosy:

花徑不曾緣客掃	The flower-strewn path has never been swept for a guest.
蓬門今始為君開	[My] bramble gate now for the first time [I] open for you.[28]

He could be elegant and ornate:

香霧雲鬟濕	The fragrant mist of your cloud-ringlets has become damp.
清輝玉臂寒	In the pure gleam your jade arms are cold.[29]

More significantly, he could be difficult. He was a complicated poet and wrote couplets that at times defied explication. Perhaps the most famous is:

香稻啄殘鸚鵡粒	The fragrant rice: the pecking-remains of parrot kernels.
碧梧棲老鳳凰枝	Jade-green pawlonia: roosting-aged phoenix branches.[30]

Late Tang writers learned much from Du Fu's range of technique in couplet-crafting, and they achieved complex effects through parallelism, but they sought to avoid Du Fu's density and difficulty. Jia Dao 賈島 (779–854), who came to represent the Late Tang style, wrote the highly crafted yet simple couplet:

流星透疏木	The flowing stars penetrate the sparse trees;
走月逆行雲	The running moon goes against the moving clouds.[31]

The "flowing" stars shift slowly in the night sky, so slowly as to be imagined but not seen. In contrast, the "running" moon is an optical illusion created by the clouds moving across its face.

Much can be written on the art of couplet-crafting in the Chinese poetic tradition, but the goal in this chapter is simply to introduce it as one of the formal tools writers had at their disposal as they composed poetry. Later chapters will consider many examples in greater detail.

The Quatrain Stanza and the Octave Poem

Couplets combine to form larger units. In the Chinese tradition, long poems occasionally grew to a hundred couplets or more, but they had little formal scaffolding comparable to Western stanza structures upon which to build, and their organization drew largely upon their author's inspiration. To construct long poems, writers at times used quatrain units with an *aaba* rhyme scheme where the rhyme shifted

28. Du Fu, "A Guest Arrives" 《客至》. This poem is fully discussed in chap. 7; see appendix 1 for source information.

29. Du Fu, "Moonlit Night" 《月夜》. This poem is fully discussed in chap. 7; see appendix 1 for source information.

30. Du Fu, "Autumn Meditations, no. 8" 《秋興八首》第八. This poem is fully discussed in chap. 7; see appendix 1 for source information.

31. Jia Dao, "Staying the Night at a Mountain Temple" 《宿山寺》. This poem is fully discussed in chap. 8; see appendix 1 for source information.

with each quatrain.[32] At other times, authors wrote long series of quatrains or octave poems to produce a sequence of discrete if interconnected poems rather than a single, integrated poem. Nothing like the *ottava rima* or the canto of Italian poetry developed. In the Chinese tradition shorter forms prevailed; the quatrain and the eight-line poem were the central forms and had their own conventional practices.

The quatrain, made up of twenty to twenty-eight characters, necessarily was an art form of quick strokes that relied on the reader to fill in unspoken implications and contexts. One source for the development of the quatrain was Southern folk songs (usually about love) from which elite writers borrowed language, attitudes, themes, and ambience:

年少當及時 When young, one should act in season.
蹉跎日就老 [law'] While hesitating, one daily grows older.
若不信儂語 If you don't believe my words,
但看霜下草 [tshaw'] Just look at the grass covered by frost.[33]

The sentiments are simple, and the poem is a form of direct address. The poem, however, already reveals a common feature of later quatrain structure: the third line raises an issue (here, the question of proof for the *carpe diem*) that the writer resolves in the fourth.

During the Southern Dynasties writers appropriated the quatrain form for serious and personal matters, as in Yu Xin's 庾信 (513–81) "Again Parting from Secretarial Minister Zhou" 重別周尚書. Yu Xin wrote this poem while living in north China, where the Western Wei and its successor, the Northern Zhou court, refused to allow him to return to the south:

陽關萬里道 On the ten-thousand *li* road from Yang Pass,[34]
不見一人歸 [kuj] One does not see a single person return.
惟有河邊雁 There are only the geese by the Yellow River,
秋來南向飛 [puj] That, when autumn comes, fly toward the south.[35]

The last line of a quatrain must be highly resonant to bring a short poem to a compelling finish, and poets learned to use "objective closure," a final image like the geese flying southward that embodies—but does not articulate—the matrix of thoughts and emotions evoked by the occasion of the poem. Another Southern Dynasties poet, He Xun 何遜 (d. 518), used objective closure to particularly beautiful effect in "At Parting" 相送:

客心已百念 In the traveler's heart, already a hundred concerns.
孤游重千里 [li] Wandering alone for again a thousand *li*.

32. Wen Tingyun 溫庭筠, "Song: Naval Battle on Kunming Lake" 《昆明治水戰詞》. This poem, which uses the *aaba* form, is fully discussed in chap. 8; see appendix 1 for source information.

33. Anonymous, "Midnight's Song" 《子夜歌》 ("When young, one should act in season" 年少當及時). This poem is fully discussed in chap. 5; see appendix 1 for source information.

34. Yang Pass in fact is on the border of China's frontier with the Inner Asian Steppe, far to the northwest.

35. Yu Xin, "Again Parting from Secretarial Minister Zhou" 《重別周尚書》. This poem is fully discussed in chap. 5; see appendix 1 for source information.

江暗雨欲來	The river darkens; rain is about to come:
浪白風初起 [khi]	The billows whiten when the wind first rises.[36]

The octave form also acquired conventions for its structuring. Later writers described the organization of the four couplets of a regulated verse octave as "begin, continue, turn, and close" (*qi cheng zhuan he* 起承轉合). Stephen Owen has simplified this account into a three-part structure of "begin, develop, and close" that better accords with Tang dynasty practice, in which the two middle couplets of regulated verse develop the themes and images of the first couplet, and the final couplet provides an appropriate conclusion drawing on the transitions of the middle couplets. Du Shenyan's 杜審言 (ca. 646–ca. 708) "Matching the Rhymes of Assistant Lu of Jinling's 'Early Spring Excursion'" 和晉陵路丞早春遊望 [37] offers a good example of the tripartite form:

獨有宦遊人	It is especially officials who are traveling
偏驚物候新	Who are startled by the renewal of the season.
雲霞出海曙	Clouds and mist in the dawn light rising from the sea;
梅柳渡江春	The plum and willow [reveal] spring on crossing the River.
淑氣催黃鳥	The purified air urges the yellow oriole;
晴光轉綠蘋	The clear-sky radiance stirs the green duckweed.
忽聞歌古調	Suddenly I hear [you] singing an ancient melody:
歸思欲霑巾	In my longing to return, I am about to soak my kerchief.[38]

The first couplet sets up the event named in the poem's title: the two men, on official assignment, encounter a spring vista. The middle couplets then describe the new elements of the spring scene that most moved Du Shenyan. The last couplet turns to the recipient, Mr. Lu, his poem, and Du's response to it. The ending neatly draws together the themes of being away from home, the passage of time, and the stirring to which spring gives rise in the scene—in the plants and animals—and in his companion, who has now written a poem that corresponds with the scene and moves Du to the verge of tears. The organization of the poem—establishing the situation, developing elements of it, and then synthesizing the situation and its particular features into a personal response at the conclusion—exemplifies the conventional structure of eight-line regulated verse. Poets then exploited the expectations that were part of the form: at times they fulfilled the generic expectation in subtle ways that required thoughtful reading; at others they deviated from the norm for rhetorical effects. We shall see many variations in how writers drew upon the formal structure of regulated verse to inflect the meaning of the poem.

---

36. He Xun, "At Parting"《相送》. This poem is fully discussed in chap. 5; see appendix 1 for source information.

37. See the discussion of the tripartite form in Stephen Owen, *The Poetry of the Early T'ang*, rev. ed. (Basel: Quirin Press, 2012), pp. 328–29. Jinling (modern Changzhou) is just south of the Yangzi River, east of Nanjing.

38. Du Shenyan, "Matching the Rhymes of Assistant Lu of Jinling's 'Early Spring Excursion'"《和晉陵路丞早春遊望》,

Rhetorical Features of Chinese Poetic Language

Within the formal framework constructed by generic expectations, Chinese poets drew on a wide range of rhetorical devices that broadened and deepened the representational and expressive possibilities of the language. Among these rhetorical resources are the tropes that should be familiar from the study of the Western poetic tradition. The most important of these are perhaps metaphor, metonymy, and synecdoche. Others that play a central role in the Chinese are related to—as particular instances of—the basic techniques of metaphor and metonymy. These include various forms of ornamental language and allusion that developed in sophistication as the tradition evolved.

Because poems are constructed, they inevitably are a type of performance, and, as performance, they present to the poem's audience a performer *within* the poem who can never be fully identical to the author. This distinction between the author of the poem and the speaking voice within the poem produces a second group of rhetorical features, namely voice, persona, and implied author. Chinese poets, like those in other traditions, learned to modulate qualities of voice to create a range of personae within their verse. Becoming aware of these qualities of voice will be important in learning to read Chinese poetry.

Rhetorical Tropes

METAPHOR AND SIMILE

Metaphor is a use of language that "improperly" equates two terms.[39] John Donne in "The Canonization," for example, offers a string of metaphors to describe his love:

> Call us what you will, we are made such by love,
> Call her one, me another fly,
> We're tapers too, and at our own cost die,[40]
> And we in us find the eagle and the dove.
> (ll. 19–22)

The persona in the poem equates himself and his love in succession to flies (which live very short lives), candles (that burn themselves out all the more quickly for burning brightly), and eagles (strength) and doves (purity). The effect of creating these equivalences through metaphorical figuration is to set off a search that finds the commonalities between the two juxtaposed images. As I. A. Richards explains,

> In the simplest formulation, when we use a metaphor we have two thoughts of different things active together and supported by a single word, or phrase, whose meaning is a resultant of their interaction.[41]

39. "Improper" is a somewhat technical term. Some comparisons are "proper" in that they derive from the meaning that we consider as belonging to ("proper to") a term. An improper comparison is one that cannot be considered part of the usual meaning of either term.

40. "Die" had the added meaning of sexual intercourse in the Elizabethan period.

41. *The Philosophy of Rhetoric* (New York and London: Oxford University Press, 1936), p. 93.

Metaphorical usage of language is so common even in daily life that we usually do not even notice it. Since metaphor is an "improper" equation of terms, when the metaphor has become completely normal (like "the time has flown quickly"), it is a "dead metaphor."

A simile is a metaphor that has hedged its bet with the addition of an "as" or "like." Perhaps two of the most famous examples are:

> O my Luve's like a red, red rose
> That's newly sprung in June;
> O my Luve's like the melodie
> That's sweetly played in tune.
> (Robert Burns, "A Red, Red Rose," ll. 1–4)

and

> I wandered lonely as a cloud
> that floats on high o'er vales and hills.
> (William Wordsworth, "I Wandered Lonely as a Cloud," ll. 1–2)

A simile does not assert the equivalence of terms but just resemblance. Still, effective similes require an effort of the imagination: the loneliness of a cloud is a very particular sort that is profoundly different from the loneliness of the customers in Edward Hopper's painting *Nighthawks*.

In the Chinese poetic tradition, metaphor of the sort seen in Donne's poem is relatively rare, while similes abound. A decade ago, the question of "metaphor in Chinese poetry" sparked an intense debate in the scholarly community, but the perspective of this textbook is that writers in the Chinese tradition developed different techniques to require readers to think about difficult equivalences of terms. In part, this difference is based on a broader sense of the categories of correspondence within which people live their lives, so that the sort of "improper" equivalence of the Western metaphor is not the center of imaginative effort in Chinese poems. For example, consider the central, parallel couplets from Du Fu's "Weary Night" 倦夜:

重露成涓滴	The heavy dew forms water drops that fall.
稀星乍有無	The sparse stars flicker, now there, now gone.
暗飛螢自照	Fireflies gleam in their own light as they fly in the dark.
水宿鳥相呼	The birds stopping for the night on the water call out to one another.[42]

The parallelism asserts the equivalence of the dew and the stars, and the fireflies and the geese. In addition, the poem suggests that Du Fu, staying up late and restless, also is like the fireflies and the geese, but this final step of finding equivalence comes in part from readers' bringing to their engagement with a poem an expectation that "things of the same category move one another" (*tonglei xiangan* 同類相感).

Although direct assertions of equivalence of terms are relatively rare in the Chinese tradition, such equivalence still exists as an option. Consider, for example, the opening couplet of Wang Can's

42. Du Fu, "Weary Night"《倦夜》. This poem is fully discussed in chap. 7; see appendix 1 for source information.

"Seven Laments," in which he explains his decision to leave Chang'an, the Han dynasty capital, as it was falling into chaos:

西京亂無象 The Western Capital is chaotic, without manifest [order].
豺虎方遘患 Jackals and tigers just now await the disaster.[43]

Here Wang Can refers to the various armies about to descend on Chang'an simply and directly as "jackals and tigers."

In contrast to the relative scarcity of metaphor as a trope (rather than more implicit forms of asserting equivalence of terms), simile is an important figure in Chinese poetry. Pan Yue 潘岳 (247–300), describing his lingering sorrow after the loss of his wife, for example, writes:

如彼翰林鳥。 [We] **were like** those birds in the thicket:
雙棲一朝隻。 A pair roosting, then one morning just one.
如彼游川魚。 [We] **were like** those fish swimming in the river:
比目中路析。 Paired eyes split apart mid-journey.[44]

METONYMY AND SYNECDOCHE

Metonymy and synecdoche are tropes of contiguity. That is, they refer to objects through other terms associated with the object. Metonymy is more general, while synecdoche is a specific type of metonymy that refers to a whole by a part or to a part by the whole, and it is perhaps the most common type of metonymy. In *Doctor Faustus*, for example, Christopher Marlowe uses synecdoche to describe Helen of Troy, whose abduction led to the Trojan War, and the Greek response: "Was this the face that launched a thousand ships, / And burnt the topless towers of Ilium?" Helen's beauty of form, more than just her face, enraptured Paris and led to his rash action, while the Greek cities launched more than ships: the ships carried an army to lay siege to Troy. However, using a narrower, more concrete term to refer to a larger one allows the poet to focus intently on a compelling image that carries with it broader resonances.

Metonymy uses not just part/whole relations but also connections like cause/effect or instrument/action. For example, when in Genesis Adam is expelled from Eden, he is told: "By the sweat of your brow, you will eat your food," the sweat is the *effect* of the hard labor of farming. He cannot directly turn sweat into food. In the familiar phrase "the pen is mightier than the sword," the "pen" refers to writing, while the sword points to forcible coercion. The force of these specific images that stand in for more abstract concepts contributes to the success of the phrasing.

Metonymy is a common feature of Chinese poetry. As in Western practice, synecdoche is the most common form. Tao Qian, for instance, writes

43. Wang Can, "Seven Laments"《七哀詩》. This poem is fully discussed in chap. 4; see appendix 1 for source information.

44. Pan Yue, "Mourning the Departed," 3 poems, no. 1《悼亡詩》三首 第一. The image here is of a fish like the flounder that has eyes only on one side: the belief was that a pair of fish was needed in order for the two to be able to see where they were going. This poem is fully discussed in chap. 4; see appendix 1 for source information.

窮巷隔深轍 The dead-end alley is apart from the deep wheel ruts [of the great][45]

The wheel ruts refer to wheels that in turn refer to the elite society that rides in carriages. However, Chinese poets also used a broader range of metonymic figures. In Du Fu's "Weary Night," he concludes

萬事干戈裏 Ten thousand affairs all hemmed in with halberds and spears:
空悲清夜徂 In vain I sorrow that the pure night passes.

The "halberds and spears" stand in for the armies and warfare of the An Lushan Rebellion.

Ornamentation

In China, the early writers of pentasyllabic verse during the Jian'an reign period at the end of the Han dynasty became famous in the later tradition for their simplicity of style. Cao Cao 曹操 (155–220), the famous general who sought to reunite the empire as it was disintegrating into the turmoil of the Three Kingdoms period, wrote of the devastation using verse in a five-character meter based on folk poetry:

白骨露於野， White bones were exposed on the plains.
千里無雞鳴。 For a thousand *li*, there was not a cock crowing.[46]

The "white bones" are the picked-over remains of dead soldiers, while "cock crowing" refers to a settled rural society, but these are not complex figures.

When the Western Jin briefly reunited the territories of the former Han, writers at the Jin court continued to explore pentasyllabic *shi*, but they applied their training in the more important *fu* 賦 (rhyme-prose) to make the new genre more elegant. One of the most talented writers was Lu Ji 陸機 (261–303), who tried his hand at writing in the style of the anonymous "Nineteen Old Poems" of the late Han but added further polish. In his "Imitation of 'In the Northwest There Is a Tall Tower'" 擬西北有高樓, for example, his word choice is refined:

佇立望日昃 Standing long, I watch the sun decline.[47]

"Decline" (昃, *tʂik*) here is an elegant, educated verb. In this poem striving for an "old" style Lu Ji is restrained, but he switches to a more ornamented diction when writing other types of poems, as in the second and third couplets of "Going to Luoyang, Written on the Road, Second of Two" 赴洛道中作詩二首第二:

45. Tao Qian, "Reading the *Canon of Mountains and Seas*," 13 poems, no. 1《讀山海經詩》十三首之一. This poem is fully discussed in chap. 5; see appendix 1 for source information.

46. Cao Cao, "Ballad of Bramble Village"《蒿里行》. This poem is fully discussed in chap. 4; see appendix 1 for source information.

47. Lu Ji, "Imitation of 'In the Northwest There Is a Tall Tower'"《擬西北有高樓》.

振策**陟崇丘**	Plying my whip, I **ascend** the **looming hillock**;
安轡遵平莽	With easy reins I follow the level scrubland.
夕息**抱影**寐	At dusk I rest, sleeping **embracing my shadow**;
朝徂**銜思**往	At dawn I depart, traveling **bridling my longing**.[48]

Lu Ji brings courtly crafting to this poem: in the first line above, he replaces the simple diction of "go up a tall hill" 上高山 with "ascend the looming hillock" 陟崇丘. The second couplet is parallel and uses elegant figuration: "embracing my shadow"—that is, with no loved one in his arms—parallels "bridling my longing"—more literally "holding longing in my mouth as a bit"—and these are forms of periphrasis, decorously "talking around" a topic. These types of ornamental substitutions, borrowed from the *fu*, quickly became part of the *shi* poetic tradition.

Allusion

Allusion is another rhetorical technique authors employed from the very beginning of the Chinese poetic tradition. Allusions are words or phrases that call to mind texts or other pieces of cultural lore shared by the author and the reader. Bob Dylan's line "There are no truths outside the gates of Eden," for example, concisely draws upon the biblical banishment from Eden and the implicit hope of final return to represent the moral failures of the human condition and a critique that it could have been different.

In both English and Chinese poetry, there is a considerable range in the function of allusive reference. Sometimes it can be fairly casual, as in the last sentence of D. C. Berry's short poem "On Reading Poems to a Senior Class at South High":

They went to another class
I suppose and I went home

where Queen Elizabeth
my cat met me
and licked my fins
till they were hands again.
(Berry, ll. 24–29)

Here it does not even matter whether Berry is referring to Queen Elizabeth the first or second: the reader simply assumes that his cat has the hauteur of royalty. (The grand naming also reinforces the whimsical character of the voice in the poem.) In contrast, on other occasions, the details of the allusive reference matter in making sense of the poem. Thomas Hardy, for instance, in "Channel Firing," uses his readers' knowledge of the Christian lore of the Judgment Day announced by the apocalypse at which time all graves are to be flung open and the dead brought to final judgment:

48. Lu Ji, "Going to Luoyang, Written on the Road," 2 poems, no. 1《赴洛道中作詩》二首第二. This poem is fully discussed in chap. 4; see appendix 1 for source information.

That night your great guns, unawares,
Shook all our coffins as we lay,
And broke the chancel window-squares,
We thought it was the Judgment-day

And sat upright....
(Hardy, ll. 1–5)

The usage here is neither deep nor complex, but it is effective. (The poem continues the theme with God and the dead lamenting the unchanging folly of war.)

The Chinese poetic tradition used allusion from the very beginning. In the poem "Barred Gate" 衡門 from the *Canon of Poetry* (Mao 138), the singer alludes to royalty much as D. C. Berry does, with little specificity needed:

豈其食魚，	When eating fish, who needs
必河之魴。	bream of the river?
豈其取妻，	When taking wife, who needs
必齊之姜。	a Jiang princess of Qi?[49]

However, as the *shi* tradition evolved, poets learned to use allusion with increasing subtlety, and it became a central rhetorical technique, which correspondingly put great demands upon the reader to acquire the mastery of cultural lore upon which the poets drew. The Mid-Tang poet Li He offers a more complex allusion in the first line of his "Song of the Bronze Immortal Bidding Farewell to the Han" 金銅仙人辭漢歌, in which he imagines the thoughts of a bronze dew-catcher being carted off to the Wei capital at the end of the Han dynasty:

茂陵劉郎秋風客	Young Master Liu of Maoling, a traveler in the autumn wind:
夜聞馬嘶曉無跡	At night one heard a horse neigh; at dawn, there are no tracks.[50]

Maoling was the great burial mound under which Emperor Wu of the Han was buried, while "young Master Liu" refers to Emperor Wu himself. The bronze statue thinks of the emperor as still young, compared with its own mix of long survival and agelessness. Being an immortal statue rather than human, it also refers to the emperor by his surname rather than by his title, which is meaningful only in the human realm. The statue then describes Emperor Wu as a traveler in the autumn wind. At one level, this presents Emperor Wu as a restless, ghostly figure inhabiting the sere autumn landscape of the old capital of the now-ended dynasty. Yet "autumn wind" also alludes to Emperor Wu's famous "Song of the Autumn Wind," which ends with his lament for the brevity of youth and strength. Li He's dense series of

---

49. The translation is by Stephen Owen, *An Anthology of Chinese Literature: Beginnings to 1911* (New York: W. W. Norton & Co., 1996), p. 53.

50. Li He, "Song of the Bronze Immortal Bidding Farewell to the Han"《金銅仙人辭漢歌》. This poem is fully discussed in chap. 8; see appendix 1 for source information.

allusive references in this first line allows him to present a powerful, complex interplay of mortality, loss, and the strange persistence of presence through memory that are the themes of the poem.

Qualities of Voice: The Person in the Poem

Poetic genres in China originated in song performance, first in the poems of the *Canon of Poetry*, then in the *Lyrics of Chu*, next in the late Han dynasty pentasyllabic verse preserved in the "Nineteen Old Poems," and finally in the Tang dynasty song lyrics that survive in Dunhuang manuscripts. This idea of performance for an audience continued to inform the writing of poetry in the Chinese tradition.

In writing for an audience, poets shaped their self-presentation. They crafted the voice in which they spoke in the poem and, through that voice, they created a persona, a version of themselves speaking in a specific key. Behind this persona and voice, we infer an author, not the real author to whom we have no direct access, but an implied author, the person with values and sensibility that is hinted at by the ways in which the poem was shaped.

In this section, we explore some of the ways in which poets used qualities of voice to create the personae through which they spoke.

Voice

Consider, for example, the final stanza of Percy Bysshe Shelley's "Ode to the West Wind":

Make me thy lyre, even as the forest is:
What if my leaves are falling like its own!
The tumult of thy mighty harmonies

Will take from both a deep, autumnal tone,
Sweet though in sadness. Be thou, Spirit fierce,
My spirit! Be thou me, impetuous one!

Drive my dead thoughts over the universe
Like withered leaves to quicken a new birth!
And, by the incantation of this verse,

Scatter, as from an unextinguished hearth
Ashes and sparks, my words among mankind!
Be through my lips to unawakened Earth

The trumpet of a prophecy! O Wind,
If Winter comes, can Spring be far behind?

The poem's strong, even rapturous invocation to the West Wind, spoken in direct address, presents us with an urgent, intense voice and an utterly sincere persona filled with desire and, unhappy in its narrow selfhood, searching for grandeur and self-transcendence.

Contrast this with the playful voice in Emily Dickinson's "I'm Nobody":

I'm Nobody! Who are you?
Are you – Nobody – too?
Then there's a pair of us!
Don't tell! they'd advertise – you know!

How dreary – to be – Somebody!
How public – like a Frog –
To tell one's name – the livelong June –
To an admiring Bog!

Note how this poem also uses direct address, but here Dickinson is not apostrophizing the wind but speaking to the reader in an amused, conspiratorial voice. The sharply different qualities of the voices in these poems do not arise just from their different themes and messages. Shelley's formal language, long words, flowing lines, and sentences that span as many as four lines complement the imperative mood in forming a drivingly urgent voice. In contrast, Dickinson relies on short words and a staccato rhythm to define her whimsical voice.

Chinese poetry from its earliest texts presented a wide range of voices from sarcasm to plaintive longing to bluff camaraderie. For example, in the *Canon of Poetry*, a collection of Western Zhou ritual songs that are the oldest extant Chinese poems, we encounter this voice of protest, assumed to be aimed at extortionate officials:

碩鼠碩鼠，　Big rat, big rat,
無食我黍。　Don't eat our millet!
三歲貫女，　For three years we have served you,
莫我肯顧。　[Yet] you never are willing to heed us.
逝將去女，　[We] vow to leave you soon,
適彼樂土。　And go to that happy land.
樂土樂土，　Happy land, happy land:
爰得我所。　There we will find our place.[51]

Later writers greatly valued the directness of such voices in the *Canon of Poetry*. They also valued the women's voices in the *Canon of Poetry* that provided later poets with models for how a male author might assume a female persona. The following simple song of longing from the *Canon of Poetry* is a good example:

彼采葛兮，　There [I] pick kudzu, hey!
一日不見，　One day not seeing [him]
如三月兮。　Is like three months, hey!

51. Anonymous, "Big Rat"《碩鼠》, Mao 113 in the *Canon of Poetry*.

彼采蕭兮， There [I] pick southernwood, hey!
一日不見， One day not seeing [him]
如三秋兮。 Is like three autumns, hey!

彼采艾兮， There [I] pick mugwort, hey!
一日不見， One day not seeing [him]
如三歲兮。 Is like three years, hey![52]

Compare this poem with the voices in two Southern Dynasties quatrains written in the style of a "Midnight's Song":

自從別郎來 Ever since I parted from him,
何日不咨嗟 What day have I not sighed?
黃蘗鬱成林 Wormwood, dense, becomes a grove:
當奈苦心多 What can be done about so much bitterness of heart?[53]

and

攬裙未結帶 I throw on my skirt, not yet tying its belt.
約眉出前窗 Arranging my brows, I go out to the front window.
羅裳易飄颺 My gauzy skirt is easily blown:
小開罵春風 If it opens a little, I'll scold the spring wind.[54]

The first quatrain quite literally introduces a note of bitterness into the young woman's longing.[55] The voice in the second quatrain, in contrast, is playful and flirtatious. Both of these poems probably were written by men, courtiers at one of the Southern Dynasties courts, who had adopted a female persona, that is, created a woman's voice through which to present the poem.

PERSONA

A persona is a crafted identity. It can be simply the part of a poet's identity that finds expression in a particular poem at a particular moment. Indeed, since poems inevitably are partial things, limited speech acts that cannot convey the fullness of the author's character, writing through a delimited, created self—a persona—is inescapable. Thus writers must choose what part of themselves to foreground in a given poem. However, personae also can be a way for poets to explore identities radically different from their

52. Anonymous, "Picking Kudzu"《采葛》, Mao 72 in the *Canon of Poetry*.

53. Anonymous, "Midnight's Song"《子夜歌》("Ever since I parted from him" 自從別郎來). This poem is fully discussed in chap. 5; see appendix 1 for source information.

54. Anonymous, "Midnight's Song"《子夜歌》("I throw on my skirt, not yet tying its belt" 攬裙未結帶). This poem is fully discussed in chap. 5; see appendix 1 for source information.

55. The "bitterness" is in fact a well-established play on words in that "heart" refers both to the young woman's heart and to the core of the wormwood tree, which produces a very bitter sap.

own. The medieval Chinese courtier writing in the voice of a young woman in a "Song of Midnight" poem, for example, has adopted a persona.[56] The Mid-Tang poet Meng Jiao 孟郊 (751–814) takes on the "folk" persona of a wife separated from her husband when he writes a self-consciously "old" quatrain, "Ancient Grievance" 古怨:

試妾與君淚	You and I, let us try with our tears—[57]
兩處滴池水	In two places, drop them into pond's water.
看取芙蓉花	Watch, in picking lotus flowers,
今年為誰死	This year, for whose [tears] will they die?[58]

Meng Jiao here quickly sketches an extremely pained, disturbed sensibility. We cannot know for sure why he created this voice. It may give indirect expression to his own turmoil, but surely in part the poem is an exploration of persona as a poetic resource that stands behind, shapes, and distorts the engagement with the world structured in the poem. In English poetry, perhaps the most famous explorations in explicitly distorted personae that parallel Meng Jiao's poems are those of Robert Browning's dramatic monologues, as in the first stanza of his "Childe Roland to the Dark Tower Came":

My first thought was, he lied in every word,
  That hoary cripple, with malicious eye
  Askance to watch the workings of his lie
On mine, and mouth scarce able to afford
Suppression of the glee, that pursed and scored
  Its edge, at one more victim gained thereby.
      (Browning, ll. 1–6)

Browning writes through a persona whose judgments the readers discover they cannot trust, but the reader cannot see beyond this obsessive narrator, so that the poem is unsettling and disorienting.

However, the creation of personae also can be liberating and just plain fun, as in Don Marquis's poems about Archy, a cockroach, and his (eventual) friend Mehitabel, an alley cat:

expression is the need of my soul
i was once a vers libre bard
but i died and my soul went into the body of a cockroach
it has given me a new outlook upon life
i see things from the under side now
thank you for the apple peelings in the wastepaper basket
but your paste is getting so stale i cant eat it

56. For a study of the male use of the female voice in medieval literature, see Paul Rouzer, *Articulated Ladies: Gender and the Male Community in Early Chinese Texts* (Cambridge: Harvard University Asia Center, 2001).

57. The speaker is a wife, as indicated by *qie* 妾, the humble first-person status pronoun, "secondary wife."

58. Meng Jiao, "Ancient Grievance" 《古怨》. This poem is fully discussed in chap. 8; see appendix 1 for source information.

there is a cat here called mehitabel i wish you would have
removed she nearly ate me the other night why dont she
catch rats that is what she is supposed to be for
there is a rat here she should get without delay[59]

Meng Jiao, Browning, and Marquis provide clear examples of explicitly created personae. However, the Chinese poetic tradition began with the assumption that a writer was driven to compose to express keenly felt reactions to encountered events, so that there is a strong presumption that the speaker in the poem is the author and that the poem faithfully records the author's own intentions and feelings. While we shall see poems that reflect these commitments—especially at the beginning of the five-character verse tradition in chapter 4—this simple story soon gave way to a far more complex array of strategies as poets explored the representational possibilities of poetry. This textbook, especially in the chapters on the later tradition, will return to the question of how poets craft and use personae as part of the shaping of their poems.

Implied Author

The implied author is the writer whom the poem suggests stands behind the text. In many cases, when the persona in the poem is sincere, there is no significant difference between the persona informing the poem and the implied author. This identity between the two is the case in Li Shangyin's 李商隱 (ca. 812–58) lovely quatrain "Night Rain, Sent North" 夜雨寄北:

君問歸期未有期	You ask the date set for my return: no date has yet been set.
巴山夜雨漲秋池	In the Ba Mountains the night rain swells the autumn pools.
何當共剪西窗燭	When shall we together trim the candle at the west window,
卻話巴山夜雨時	And talk about the time of night rain in the Ba Mountains?[60]

In some cases, like the two "Midnight's Songs" above, the poem gives us no sense of an author standing behind the persona. Other poems, however, create an ironic view of the narrator who serves as the poem's focus—ironic in that the reader sees more deeply into the narrator's actions than does the narrator himself—and thereby create an implied author who winks to the reader. Li Bai offers such a deluded persona and indulgent implied author in "Decanting Alone, under the Moon" 月下獨酌, which begins

花間一壺酒	Amid the flowers, one pot of ale:
獨酌無相親	Pouring alone, without a friend.
舉杯邀明月	I raise my cup to invite the bright moon.
對影成三人	Facing my shadow, we become three people.

59. From "The Coming of Archy" in *archy and mehitabel.*

60. Li Shangyin, "Night Rain, Sent North" 《夜雨寄北》. This poem is fully discussed in chap. 8; see appendix 1 for source information.

月既不解飲	Not only does the moon not understand drinking,
影徒隨我身	My shadow pointlessly follows me.
暫伴月將影	For the moment, I'll accompany the moon and my shadow:
行樂須及春	Our finding pleasure should last through spring.
我歌月徘徊	I sing, and the moon wavers.
我舞影零亂	I dance, and my shadow grows wild.[61]

The whimsical persona here creates friends out of his shadow and the moon and persists in misunderstanding why his shadow "grows wild" and the moon wavers in order to maintain the willful fiction of separate identities. The reader, of course, sees the direct connection to the narrator's actions: singing includes moving one's head to follow the rhythm. As readers, we imagine Li Bai the poet standing behind the poem to create this amused self-presentation. In reading Chinese poetry, seeing the distinction between persona and implied author becomes crucial when authors are exploring ways of shaping the personae they create, as Li Bai is in "Decanting Alone, under the Moon."

Summary

Despite the differences in language and in the specific genres of Chinese and English poetry, the *types* of formal features that Chinese poets used in their writing are in many ways very similar to those in the English poetic tradition. Lines, couplets, stanzas, and end rhymes are key organizing components in both traditions. Poets worked within—and exploited—fixed prosodic constraints and tight organization in such poetic forms as the sonnet in English and regulated verse (*lü shi* 律詩) in Chinese. The types of rhetorical tropes are similar as well, although Chinese poetry relies far less on metaphor in its strict sense. In both traditions, some poets are famous for their mastery of rhetorical crafting while others stand out for their search for simplicity and directness and the rejection of crafting.

Developing a feel for form and for the range of rhetorical crafting writers used in shaping their poems will be an important part of learning to hear the distinctive voices of the poets in this textbook. Understanding the development of the Chinese poetic tradition crucially also depends on tracing the evolution of poetic forms and rhetorical resources as well as some poets' reaction against the growing sophistication of the tradition. I hope this brief overview of these basic components of poetic crafting will help as we read the poems in the chapters that follow.

61. Li Bai, "Decanting Alone, Under the Moon" 《月下獨酌》. This poem is fully discussed in chap. 6; see appendix 1 for source information.

Interlude: On the Translation of Poetry

The modern Russian poet and novelist Vladimir Nabokov begins his poem "On Translating *Eugene Onegin*":

> What is translation? On a platter
> A poet's pale and glaring head,
> A parrot's screech, a monkey's chatter,
> And profanation of the dead.[1]

As the poem suggests, Nabokov was skeptical about the possibility of doing justice to a poem through translation. Many translators agree and consider the task impossible: they hope merely for a few hard-won moments when they manage to convey into English some of the qualities and effects of poems they love that are written in foreign languages.[2] Translators of Chinese poetry have shared this broader sense of impossibility matched by a determination to keep trying anyway.

Translating a Chinese poet who exploits the verse forms of the tradition and the distinctive features of the Classical Chinese language seems a particularly hopeless project: Chinese and English are too different, and the forms of Chinese verse lack effective English equivalents. We have discussed, for example, the implications of Classical Chinese being a topic-prominent isolating language: that is, in Classical Chinese one need not include an explicit subject in a sentence—so pronouns are mostly dropped in poetry—and nouns have no suffixes to indicate number and gender while verbs have no inflections for tense. English, in contrast, requires explicit subjects in sentences, numbers for nouns, and tenses for verbs. The translator has to add these, even when it is not entirely clear who is doing the action in the poem and when exactly it is being done.

Consider, for example, the first four lines of Du Fu's "Spring Vista" 春望, discussed in chapter 7:

國 country	破 broken	山 mountain	河 rivers	在 remain	The capital is broken: mountains and rivers remain.
城 wall	春 spring	草 grass	木 tree	深 [ɕim] deep	The city wall in spring: the grasses and trees grow thickly.
感 moved	時 time	花 flower	濺 drench	淚 tear	Moved by the times, flowers drenched with tears.
恨 resent	別 parting	鳥 bird	驚 startle	心 [sim] heart	Resenting the parting, birds startle the heart.[3]

1. Vladimir Nabokov, "On Translating *Eugene Onegin*."

2. For a good discussion of the problems of translating poetry, see David Connolly, "Poetry Translation," in Mona Baker and Kirsten Malmkjær, eds., *Routledge Encyclopedia of Translation Studies* (London: Routledge, 1998), pp. 170–76.

3. Du Fu, "Spring Vista"《春望》. This poem is fully discussed in chap. 7; see appendix 1 for source information.

The translation above is a "technical" translation like those that I provide next to each poem in this textbook; it is a minimal translation without aesthetic embellishment in which I try to preserve as much of the literal reading of the lines as possible. Even so, English usage requires that I provide a subject in lines 3 and 4, where there is none in the original text. It is not clear whether Du Fu is moved by the time and drenches the flowers with tears or whether Du Fu attributes this sadness to the flowers and thus describes the dew as tears. Similarly, we do not know if Du Fu resents parting from his family and thus is startled by the birds, or whether even the birds have been cut off by the larger turmoil. These two possibilities precisely echo the divide in the first line: is nature indifferent to human turmoil, or is the persistence of the mountains and rivers a sign that the basis for human civilization remains and simply awaits renewal? Yet renewal itself can be ambivalent, since an "overgrown city" (蕪城) is a ruined, abandoned city overgrown with vegetation, as nature slowly reclaims its land from the human realm. The very title of the poem, "Spring Vista," raises the question of what the seasonal cycle of return means for Du Fu and the Tang state, which the poem explores through its juxtapositions of the human and the natural. Whatever translation one offers compels one to take a position about the relationship that Du Fu can leave in suspension because of the nature of the Classical Chinese language. David Hawkes, for example, gives a prose translation of the poem that does not attempt to capture any formal qualities of the original. Still he has to commit to an interpretation:

> The state may fall, but the hills and streams remain. It is spring in the city: grass and leaves grow thick. The flowers shed tears of grief for the troubled times, and the birds seem startled, as if with the anguish of separation.[4]

Hawkes hedges on the fate of the nation: it "may fall," but it has not yet failed utterly. And while he takes a clear stance on the flowers—they do indeed shed tears—he is much less certain about the birds: they *seem* startled, and it is *as if* they feel the anguish of separation. David Hinton, a professional translator, brings Du Fu's poem more into the realm of modern American poetry in that he does not end-stop his lines but lets sentences run over the boundaries:

> The country in ruins, rivers and mountains
> Continue. The city's grown lush with spring.
>
> Blossoms scatter tears for us and all these
> Separations in a bird's cry startle the heart.[5]

Hinton drops "moved by the times" in the third sentence and pads it with "for us." Similarly, "resentment" disappears entirely in the fourth line. Gary Snyder, an important American poet who became interested in Chinese verse, takes a bit of license in the fourth line:

> The nation is ruined,   but mountains and rivers remain.
> This spring the city   is deep in weeds and brush.

4. David Hawkes, "Spring Scene," *Little Primer of Tu Fu* (Hong Kong: Renditions, 1987), p. 48.

5. David Hinton, "Spring Landscape," *Classical Chinese Poetry: An Anthology* (New York: Farrar, Straus, and Giroux, 2008), 1988), p. 198.

Touched by the times even flowers weep tears.
Fearing leaving the birds tangled hearts.[6]

Note that Snyder reproduces the caesura between the second and third characters in Du Fu's five-character line. Snyder is much truer to the original than Hinton, even if it is not entirely clear what "birds tangled hearts" means. Comparison shows that all three translators provide elements of paraphrase to make the original intelligible to an English-speaking readership, but only Snyder preserves, even if he does not stress, the parallelism in the third and fourth lines.

As the various strategies for handling Du Fu's couplets suggest, form presents a challenge as great as or even greater than that of syntax. Some modern poets in English continue to write using the sonnet, villanelle, and other traditional forms, but many contemporary readers are more familiar with free verse or—at most—with Shakespeare's blank verse in iambic pentameter. Using rhyming couplets in English would be "poetic" and distort the qualities of the poem in Chinese. Thus neither Hinton nor Snyder attempts any sort of rhyme in translating "Spring Vista." Similarly, the sort of parallelism in "Spring Vista," which is typical of Chinese poetry, appears as mechanical rather than resonant in English and lingers only in the background for the observant reader. Finally, the prosodic rules for balancing tones in regulated verse are impossible to reproduce in English.

Given these challenges, translators have kept experimenting with methods to render Chinese verse into English. What works—it turns out—has depended in part on the dominant styles of English poetry at the time.[7] André Lefevere argues that it is not fair to blame W. J. B. Fletcher (b. 1879), a British Consul in China, for translating Wang Wei's poems into elegantly phrased rhyming couplets in 1919: anything less would have been considered crude, and Fletcher did not want to present the great Tang poet as crude.[8] With the rise of Modernism, however, poets and translators began to appropriate Chinese verse for the Modernist cause. Ezra Pound (1885–1972) famously used its characteristic succinctness and focus on simple naturalistic images as an inspiration for his Imagist revolt against the traditional rhetoric and forms of English poetry. Knowing no Chinese but working from notes written by the scholar Ernest Fenollosa given to him by Fenollosa's widow, Pound produced his epochal volume of translations, *Cathay*, in 1915. Pound assisted in publishing the initial translations of Arthur Waley (1889–1966), an immensely talented scholar and translator with affiliations to the Bloomsbury group of writers, who had taught himself both Classical Chinese and Classical Japanese. Waley, a far more faithful—if less brilliant—translator of Chinese poetry, committed himself to using a form of Gerard Manley Hopkins's sprung rhythm with syllabic stresses that approximated the number of characters in the original Chinese text. (Among later translators, Kenneth Rexroth (1905–82) also used stresses that matched the character count in the original poem.) Waley's many translations became a major source of English readers' encounters with Chinese poetry in the first half of the twentieth century.

Since Waley—who was both a poet and a scholar—published his translations, a split has developed between poets (working largely in free verse forms) who have translated Chinese poems—

6. Gary Snyder, *The Gary Snyder Reader* (Berkeley: Counterpoint, 1999), p. 542.

7. John Cayley presents a good overview of this historical dimension to translation in "Classical Chinese Poetry," in Chan Sin-wai and David E. Pollard, eds., *An Encyclopaedia of Translation: Chinese-English, English-Chinese* (Hong Kong: Chinese University Press, 1995), pp. 758–72.

8. André Lefevere, "Factors of Poetic Translation," in Chan Sin-wai and David E. Pollard, eds., *An Encyclopaedia of Translation*, p. 749.

usually with the aid of a scholarly informant—and professional scholars whose translations rarely reach the broader public. The translations of some scholars nonetheless have found a larger audience: David Hawkes's *Songs of the South* is a translation of the *Lyrics of Chu* (see chapter 3) that was published by the mass-market Penguin Press. Angus C. Graham also published a slim volume of Middle and Late Tang poems (see chapter 8) through Penguin. Moreover, Burton Watson's *Columbia Book of Chinese Poetry: From Early Times to the Thirteenth Century* (1984) and Stephen Owen's *An Anthology of Chinese Literature: Beginnings to 1911* (Norton, 1996) are large single-translator compilations by scholars directed toward students and a general readership.

This textbook includes translations by poet-translators like Pound, Witter Bynner, Robert Payne, Kenneth Rexroth, and Gary Snyder, as well as by important scholar-translators like Hawkes, Graham, Watson, and Owen. It also includes translations by the current generation of scholars of Chinese poetry. Since no translation can capture all the qualities of the original Chinese text, I provide several perspectives on each poem to help readers overcome the limitations of any single translation. The first version presents the original Chinese text with my word-by-word translation below each character and my unadorned "technical" translation next to the Chinese text. In this, I follow Robert Browning's advice that a translation "ought to be absolutely literal, with exact rendering of words, and words placed in the order of the original. Only a rendering of this sort gives any real insight into the original."[9] However, this approach by itself is too austere, and thus for most of the poems, I also include a more polished translation, and sometimes two when comparing the differences in approach, to illuminate important aspects of the Chinese poem.

9. This is from John Addington Symonds's account of Browning's comments recorded in his diary, quoted in Paul Selver, *The Art of Translating Poetry* (London: John Baker, 1966), p. 26.

Chapter Three

Origins of the Poetic Tradition

The *Canon of Poetry* (*Shijing*)

The Origin of the Canon of Poetry

The *Canon of Poetry* is a collection of 305 poems from the Zhou dynasty's repertoire of songs used in court ceremonies. These ceremonies ranged from religious rituals performed before the altar of the Zhou ancestral hall to songs for feasting with feudal lords. However, the ceremonial context for many of the poems, particularly those in the first section—the Airs of the States—is unclear. Indeed, from the very establishment of the imperial Confucian canon by the Emperor Wu of the Han in 136 BC, explaining why many of these poems are in the collection at all has been a challenge to the exegetes charged with teaching the canon.

Much about the collection is a mystery. We do not know who compiled it or when. The poems themselves span much of the Zhou dynasty, from the eleventh century BC to the seventh century BC. One tradition states that the kings of Zhou sent officials from the Music Bureau into the countryside to collect songs as a way to gauge the mood of the populace and learn about the successes and failures of their rule. A further elaboration of the story states that Confucius went to the Music Bureau and selected the current 305 poems from among the 3,000 some poems that had accumulated in the archives and arranged them in the present order. The collection thus is worthy of canonical status—the argument goes—because Confucius selected the particular poems as perfect aesthetic responses to the ethically and politically charged situations that inspired their composition.

Whatever his actual role, we do know that the *Canon of Poetry* existed as a collection of poems (known as the *Shi*, "Poems") by the time of Confucius because he refers to it on numerous occasions in anecdotes recorded in the *Analects*. Both the *Analects* and another early text, *Mo Zi* 墨子, specifically refer to the "three hundred poems" of the *Shi*, although we cannot be sure that the Han version of the collection was the same as the ritual repertoire known when Confucius was alive during the Spring and Autumn period of the late Eastern Zhou. The *Analects* and the *Tradition of Zuo* (*Zuo zhuan* 左傳), a chronicle recounting events from the Spring and Autumn period, record a variety of functions that the *Shi* served. First, songs from the *Shi* continued to be part of ritual performances, although Confucius complains that feudal lords were improperly appropriating Zhou dynasty ritual songs for use in their own clan ceremonies. Proper mastery of the ritual use of the *Shi* repertoire remained part of a young man's education. Recitation of songs from the *Shi* came to be part of diplomacy during the period: the choice of the poem was seen as obliquely reflecting the goals of the chanter. More generally, as the *Analects* shows, lines from the poems proved to be useful catch-phrases to express ideas, particularly ideas about moral self-cultivation.

The Canon of Poetry *and the Development of the Poetic Tradition*

In 136 BC, the ambitious young Emperor Wu of the Han (r. 140 BC–87 BC) decided he needed to shift the ideological underpinnings of the Han dynasty, which had been in existence for seventy years. He proclaimed that all officially appointed scholars in his employ were to focus on collating, annotating, interpreting, and teaching the various extant versions of five collections of Confucian texts. These five texts were: the *Canon of Documents*, the *Canon of Poetry*, the *Canon of Changes*, the *Records of the Rites* (*Liji* 禮記), and the *Spring and Autumn Annals*. In 124 BC, he created the Imperial Academy as a center for scholarship and teaching of the newly designated canon. Specialists in other, competing traditions were dismissed. At the time, there were three major imperially sponsored oral traditions that defined the texts and interpretation of the *Canon of Poetry*: the Lu, Qi, and Han traditions. A fourth version of the text appears to have been largely based not on oral transmission but on written texts that had survived the fall of the Qin. This tradition, the Mao recension, was supported by Emperor Wu's half-brother, Prince Xian of Hejian, and seems to have been established around 150 BC, that is, not long before the designation of the Confucian canon. However, there was no imperial scholarly post (*boshi* 博士, "erudite") assigned for the Mao text until the reign of Emperor Ping (r. AD 1–6). During the two hundred years of the Eastern Han dynasty, the Mao version of the *Poetry* gradually became more widely used, while the other three traditions waned. At present, we have only fragments of the Lu and Qi commentaries, and what survives of the Han tradition appears to be more of a manual on rhetoric based on the interpretive uses of the poems rather than a focused commentary. Modern editions of the *Canon of Poetry* largely depend on the Mao version of the text and on the commentaries written on the Mao text. Citations of poems from the *Canon of Poetry* in this textbook refer to the poems by their entry number in the Mao text.

For writers after the Han dynasty, the *Canon of Poetry* had a dual identity. It was part of the Confucian canon: that is, they knew that the poems were worthy of veneration and could serve as exemplars of morally correct thought and writing. At the same time, the poetry in the poems still shone through. The many folk songs in the collection presented ideals of simplicity and spontaneity of expression. The more weighty poems provided both models for unadorned stateliness and excuses for satire in which "the speaker does not offend and the hearer takes warning." For these later readers, the "Great Preface" to the Mao version of the *Canon of Poetry*—an essay of uncertain date but traditionally attributed to Zixia, a disciple of Confucius—served as a framework through which to think of the poetry.

毛詩大序

The "Great Preface" to Mao's *Canon of Poetry*

詩者，志之所之也。在心為志，發言為詩。情動於中而形於言。言之不足，故嗟嘆之，嗟嘆之不足，故永歌之，永歌之不足，不知手之舞之，足之蹈之也。情發於聲，聲成文謂

Poetry is where the resolve goes. In the heart, it is resolve; manifested in words, it is a poem. Emotion moves within and takes shape in words. Words are not enough, and so one sighs it. Sighing it is not enough, and so one draws it out in song. Drawing it out in song is not enough, and so unknowingly one's hands dance it and one's feet tread it. Emotion is manifested in the voice. When voice is patterned, we call it tone. The tone of a well-governed state is peaceful and happy; its government is

之音。治世之音安以樂，其政和。亂世之音怨以怒，其政乖。亡國之音哀以思，其民困。故正得失，動天地，感鬼神，莫近於詩。先王以是經夫婦，成孝敬，厚人倫，美教化，移風俗。故詩有六義焉。一曰風，二曰賦，三曰比，四曰興，五曰雅，六曰頌。

harmonious. The tone of a chaotic age is resentful and angry; its government is perverse. The tone of a lost state is full of sorrow and longing; its people are in straits. Thus for correcting gain and loss, moving Heaven and Earth, and affecting the spirits, nothing comes close to poetry. The early kings used [poetry] to regulate [relations between] husbands and wives, to perfect filiality and respect, to enrich human relations, to adorn the moral transformation [of the people] and to change customs. Thus poetry has Six Principles: the first is called "Air." The second is called recitation; the third is called "analogy"; the fourth is called "stimulus"; the fifth is called "*Ya*," and the sixth is called "Hymn."

上以風化下，下以風刺上。主文而譎諫，言之者無罪，聞之者足以戒，故曰風。至於王道衰，禮義廢，政教失，國異政，家殊俗，而變風變雅作矣。國史明乎得失之跡，傷人倫之廢，哀刑政之苛，吟詠情性，以風其上，達於事變，而懷其舊俗者也。故變風發乎情，止乎禮義。發乎情，民之性也。止乎禮義，先王之澤也。是以一國之事，繫一人之本，謂之風。言天下之事，形四方之風，謂之雅。雅者，正也，言王政之所由廢興也。政有小大，故有小雅焉，有大雅焉。頌者，美盛德之形容，以其成功告於神明者也。是謂四始，詩之至也。

Superiors use the Airs to transform those below. Those below use the Airs to criticize their superiors. They stress elegance [of expression] and remonstrate obliquely: the speaker does not offend, and it allows the hearer to take warning. Thus they are called "Airs." When the kingly way declined and rites and right action were discarded, when the teaching of governance was lost, so that states had different governance and clans different customs, then the Changed Airs and Changed *Ya* were made. The state historians clearly knew the traces of success and failure. They grieved at the discarding of [correct] human relations and lamented the cruelty of governance using punishment. They sang of their nature and feelings in order to influence their superiors. They penetrated the changes in affairs and cherished the old customs. Thus the Changed Airs come from feelings and yet stop with [the bounds of] ritual and duty. Their coming from feelings reflects the nature of the populace. Their stopping within rites and duty reflects the beneficent legacy of the early kings. Thus when the affairs of an entire state are tied to the person of a single individual, we deem this an "Air." When [a poem] speaks of the affairs of the realm, giving form to the manners of the four directions, we deem it *Ya*. "*Ya*" is "correctness": it speaks of the process by which kingly governance rises and falls. In governance there are lesser and greater [matters]; thus there are the Lesser *Ya* and the Greater *Ya*. The hymns praise the form and appearance of flourishing virtue in order to tell the [ancestral] spirits of their successes. These are called the four beginnings: they are the perfection of poetry.[1]

1. Cf. Steven Van Zoeren, *Poetry and Personality: Reading, Exegesis, and Hermeneutics in Traditional China* (Stanford: Stanford University Press, 1991), pp. 95–97.

Study Notes and Questions

As we study Classical Chinese poetry, we discover that the writers and their audiences understood themselves, their world, and the meaning of their experiences in ways that differed profoundly from approaches in contemporary America. The "Mao Preface" provides a first encounter in which we can begin to see these differences.

1. The Preface appears to present an "expressive" model for poetry, in which writers pour forth their inner feelings; "emotions move within and take shape in words." How do you understand poetry? Why do people write poetry? Why do you read it?

2. Note the progression at the beginning of the Preface. "Poetry is where the resolve goes. In the heart, it is resolve; manifested in words, it is a poem." What is *resolve* (*zhi* 志)?

3. In the Chinese tradition, the heart (*xin* 心) is the physical organ of thought, and many authors translate it as "mind" rather than "heart." What difference does it make if one thinks of the *xin* as the heart or the mind? Is the mind more abstract?

4. Next the Preface asserts that "emotion (*qing* 情) moves within and takes shape in words." What is the relation of resolve to the emotions here? Does emotion come from resolve? How? What, for you, is emotion?

5. The Chinese tradition treats the emotions captured in the poems of the *Canon of Poetry* as exemplary. In the *Canon of Poetry*, resolve is morally sound, and the emotions are appropriate to the occasions to which they respond. The poems, moreover, all succeed in conveying this mix of circumstances and morally informed response. Is this how morally—and perhaps politically—exemplary poetry works in the United States? The Psalms in the Bible are a good example. Think of some other examples.

6. The Preface explains that the deeply moved authors write their poems because "words are not enough, and so one sighs it. Sighing it is not enough, and so one draws it out in song. Drawing it out in song is not enough, and so unknowingly one's hands dance it and one's feet tread it." Why are they dancing? What does dancing have to do with the poems?

The Structure of the Canon of Poetry

The *Canon of Poetry* has four sections:

1. The Airs of the States (160 poems from 15 states)
2. The Lesser *Ya* (74 poems)
3. The Greater *Ya* (31 poems)
4. The Hymns (40 poems divided between Zhou, Lu, and Shang)

1. The "Airs of the States"

The story that the officials of the Zhou Music Bureau collected poems from the populace provides at least a plausible explanation for the "Airs of the States." The poems largely are folk songs that deal with the sort of daily joys and tribulations of life that typically inspire song: love, friendship, partings, longing, celebrations, and so on. If the poems came from the regions of China indicated in the sections of the "Airs," they appear to have gone through a process of standardization so that they reflect the language of the central Zhou court rather than whatever must have been the dialect of the specific region.

The poems mostly are short. They also are built around a tight stanza structure, where each stanza is essentially the same except for variations in the rhyme words at the end of each couplet. (See "The Peach Is Fresh-Blooming" discussed later in this chapter.)

2. The "Lesser *Ya*"

Ya means "correct" and also refers to the people of the central Chinese cultural sphere in contra-distinction to the tribal cultures of the four directions. Thus *yayan* 雅言 ("*ya* speech") referred to the normative speech of the Zhou court. Why the middle sections of the *Canon of Poetry* are called *Ya* is unclear, but the "Great Preface" to the Mao version of the collection states:

> When [a poem] speaks of the affairs of the realm, giving form to the manners of the four directions, we deem it *Ya*. "*Ya*" is "correctness": it speaks of the process by which kingly governments rise and fall. In government there are greater and lesser [matters]; thus there are the Greater *Ya* and the Lesser *Ya*.

Michael Nylan suggests that *ya* simply refers to the court and thus translates the section as "Minor Court Songs." In any case, the "Lesser *Ya*" does indeed seem to deal with lesser matters of state: the feasting of retainers, descriptions of the hardships of serving the state either as an envoy or in the army, and many other aspects of the life of a low-ranking member of the feudal hierarchy of Zhou society. However, many of the poems—like the epithalamium (marriage song) "Luxuriant Is the Tarragon" 菁菁者莪 (Mao 176)—are indistinguishable from poems in the "Airs of the States" in both style and topic.

3. The "Greater *Ya*"

The poems of the "Greater *Ya*" in fact are, in general, poems of the Zhou court. Some recount founding myths and celebrate the great ancestors. Some describe ancestral rituals. However, there also are poems of complaint like "The Populace Is Weary" 民勞 (Mao 253) and "Grand" 板 (Mao 254) that caution the ruler not to give in to bad advice, become arrogant, or overwork the people. Indeed, much of the poetry in this section seems intent on warning the current occupant of the throne that the mandate—gloriously attained by his ancestors—is easily lost and that he needs to listen to advice and remain humble or risk the fate of the earlier Shang dynasty (before 1700–1046 BC).

4. The "Hymns"

The poems in the final section of the *Canon of Poetry* are mixed. Those in the "Hymns of Zhou" are songs for the Zhou royal ancestral rites. Those from the "Hymns of Lu" and "Hymns of Shang," however, more closely resemble the poems recounting ancestral glory in the "Greater *Ya*." The poems from Lu explain why the Lu ancestors are worthy. The "Hymns of Shang" are from the state of Song, which the Zhou conquerors created in order to continue the ancestral rites for the fallen Shang dynasty. The poems in this section recall the Shang's great dynastic founders. The songs in the "Hymns of Zhou" and to a lesser extent those in "Hymns of Shang" are metrically distinct from all the others in the collection in that many of them are not rhymed and are very irregular in meter. Modern scholars believe that the songs from Lu and Shang were written quite late in the development of the collection (i.e., mid–Spring and Autumn period) in imitation of the authentically early Zhou hymns.

Selections from the *Canon of Poetry*

From the "Airs of the States"

"The Peach Is Fresh-Blooming" (Mao 6)

桃夭				The Peach Is Fresh-Blooming[2]
桃	之	夭	夭	The peach so fresh in its bloom:
peach	's	young and vigorous		
灼	灼	其	華 [*qʷʰˤra]	Radiant are its flowers.
brilliant		its	flowers	
之	子	于	歸	This [girl] goes to her new home:
this	child	is on	going to husband	
宜	其	室	家 [*kˤra]	All aright is her chamber and house.
proper	her	room	house	
桃	之	夭	夭	The peach so fresh in its bloom:
peach	's	young and vigorous		
有	蕡	其	實 [*mə.lit]	Plentiful [will be] its fruit.
there is	plentiful	its	fruit	
之	子	于	歸	This [girl] goes to her new home:
this	child	is on	going to husband	
宜	其	家	室 [*s.tit]	All aright is her house and chamber.
proper	her	house	room	
桃	之	夭	夭	The peach so fresh in its bloom:
peach	's	young and vigorous		
其	葉	蓁	蓁 [*tsrin]	Its leaves are so luxuriant.
its	leaves	luxuriant		

2. The "technical" translations of the poems from the *Canon of Poetry* derive from Bernard Karlgren's *The Book of Odes* (Stockholm: Museum of Far Eastern Antiquities, 1950), and the reconstructions of Old Chinese rhymes are from Baxter and Sagart, *Old Chinese*.

之 that	子 child	于 is on	歸 going to husband	This [girl] goes to her new home:
宜 proper	其 her	家 house	人 [*niŋ] people	All aright are the people of her house.

JOSEPH R. ALLEN'S TRANSLATION

Young Peach

The peach is young and strong
Blossoming into buds
This girl goes to her new home
All is right with house and chamber

The peach is young and strong
Coming into color is its fruit
This girl goes to her new home
All is right with chamber and house

The peach is young and strong
Its leaves lush and luxuriant
This girl travels to her new home
All is right with the family

Mao Preface: "'Young Peach' is created by the royal consort. She is not jealous, thus men and women are thereby proper, weddings are thereby timely, and the states have none without wives."[3]

Zheng Xuan: "This [the peach] is an evocative image, describing how all women are able, with the flourishing of the year, to carry this [the marriage ceremony] out at the correct time."

Zhu Xi: "This is written in reference to women being married. A woman marrying is called 'going home.' According to the *Rites of Zhou*, mid-spring is when men and women meet. That being so, then the proper time for weddings is just when the peach is blossoming. . . . Under the influence of King Wen, from family to the state, men and women acted with propriety, married in a timely way. Thus this is what the poet saw and he used the emotive image to exclaim the worthiness of the woman, knowing it must be that all is right with chamber and house."

3. Joseph R. Allen includes the three major commentaries in his translations of the *Canon of Poetry*. The "Mao (lesser) preface" (*xiao xu* 小序) for each poem was an integral part of the Mao edition of the *Canon of Poetry*. Zheng Xuan 鄭玄 (127–200) was a late Han dynasty scholar whose annotation of the *Poetry* became authoritative until it was largely replaced by the commentary of Zhu Xi 朱熹 (1130–1200), the great synthesizer of Neo-Confucianism (Daoxue 道學) whose annotations were accepted as canonical until the fall of the Qing dynasty (1644–1912).

Study Notes and Questions

1. Note how Zheng Xuan's commentary quietly replaces the specificity of the Mao reading of the poem.

2. Scholars since Zhu Xi have considered this poem to be an epithalamium. Why?

3. How important is the sequence of stanzas in this poem? The first two stanzas seem to offer a progression, but does the third follow the pattern?

"In the Field There Is a Dead Deer" (Mao 23)

野有死麕					In the Field There Is a Dead Deer
野 field	有 there is	死 dead	麕 [krun] deer		In the field there is a dead roe-deer.
白 white	茅 straw	包 wrap	之 it		With white straw we wrap it.
有 there is	女 woman	懷 embrace	春 [tʰun] spring		There is a girl cherishing spring [thoughts].
吉 luck	士 knight	誘 entice	之 it		A fine gentleman entices her.
林 grove	有 there is	樸 thicket	樕 [sok]		In the grove there is a thicket.
野 field	有 there is	死 dead	鹿 [mə.rˤok] deer		In the wilds there is a dead deer.
白 white	茅 straw	純 wrap	束 [s-tʰok] bind		With white straw [we] wrap and bind [it].
有 there is	女 woman	如 resemble	玉 [ŋrok] jade		There is a girl like jade.
舒 slow	而 and	脫 easy	脫 easy	兮 [mə.l̥ˤot] ho!	Slowly! Gently!
無 don't	感 shake	我 my	帨 kerchief	兮 [l̥ˤot-s] ho!	Don't pull my kerchief!
無 don't	使 cause	尨 shaggy dog	也 bark	吠 [Cə.bots]	Don't cause the dog to bark.

Ezra Pound's Translation

Lies a dead deer on younder plain
whom white grass covers,
A melancholy maid in spring
                    is luck

for
lovers.

Where the scrub elm skirts the wood,
be it not in white mat bound,
as a jewel flawless found,
dead as doe is maidenhood.

Hark!
Unhand my girdle-knot,
stay, stay, stay
or the dog
may
bark.

Joseph R. Allen's Translation

In the wilds is a dead doe,
With white rushes he wraps her.
There is a girl with spring desires,
A fine young man lures her.

In the woods are scrub and brush.
In the wilds is a dead deer,
With white rushes bound tight.
There is a girl like a jewel.

Slowly now, not so fast,
Don't remove my sash,
Don't start the hound to bark.

Mao Preface: "'In the Wilds Is a Dead Doe' condemns the lack of propriety. When the empire is in chaos, then brute force is used to violate others, and thereupon follows licentious practices. Having received the influence of King Wen, although in times of chaos, they still condemn the lack of propriety."

Zheng Xuan: "When the people are hard-pressed in chaotic times, brutish men act even more without propriety. Therefore it is pure girl's feeling, wishing to have one use white rushes to wrap up the pieces of venison and come with this as a proper gift."

Zhu Xi: "When the southern states received the influence of King Wen, women had chastity and guarded themselves; they were not sullied by those acting brutishly. This is what the poet observed to use to make an evocative image with this to praise them. Some say this is a description that speaks of praising the fine young man who wraps the dead doe in white rushes to lure the girl with spring desires."

Study Notes and Questions

1. What might have been an appropriate context for the performance of this song?

2. What is the relation between the roe-deer and the young woman in the poem? What is the effect of starting the poem with the image? Ezra Pound pads his translation to suggest one link.

3. Describe the very short scenario at the end of the poem: what is happening?

4. Guided by the three major commentaries, traditional readers of the *Canon of Poetry* read it as a collection of morally illuminating poems approved by Confucius. Zhu Xi struggles to compellingly rework the Mao and Zheng readings, yet he adds an additional perspective suggesting doubt. How might you read the conclusion of the poem as a reflection of moral virtue?

"My Lord Is on Campaign" (Mao 66)

君子于役					My Lord Is on Campaign
君 lord	子 son	于 at	役 service		My lord is on campaign:
不 not	知 know	其 his	期 [g(r)ə] time-period		[I] don't know his expected time [to return].
曷 "?"	至 arrive	哉 "!"			When will [he] arrive?
雞 chicken	棲 roost	于 at	塒 [də] wall-hole		The chickens roost in the wall-holes.
日 sun	之 's	夕 eve	矣 [perfective aspect]		Already the dusk of the day:
羊 sheep	牛 ox	下 below	來 [rə] come		The sheep and oxen come back.
君 lord	子 son	于 at	役 service		My lord is on campaign:
如 resemble	之 it	何 what	勿 not-it	思 [sə] long	How can I not long for him?
君 lord	子 son	于 at	役 service		My lord is on campaign:
不 not	日 day	不 not	月 [ŋ^{w}at] month		Nor days nor months [do I know].
曷 "?"	其 his	有 exist	佸 [g$^{w\text{ʕ}}$at] join		When will we meet?

雞	棲	于	桀 [N-k<r>at]	The chickens roost on perches.
chicken	roost	at	wall-hole	
日	之	夕	矣	Already the dusk of the day:
sun	's	eve	[perfective aspect]	
羊	牛	下	括 [$k^{wʕ}$rat]	The sheep and oxen gather on return.
sheep	ox	below	bind	
君	子	于	役	My lord is on campaign:
lord	son	at	service	
苟	無	饑	渴 [Nə.$k^{hʕ}$at]	May he be without hunger or thirst.
[modal]	not-exist	hunger	thirst	

Ezra Pound's Translation

He's to the war
for the duration;
Hens to wall-hole,
beasts to stall,
shall I not remember
him at night-fall?

He's to the war
for the duration,
fowl to their perches,
cattle to byre;
is there food enough;
drink enough
by their camp fire?

Joseph R. Allen's Translation

My Man is on Corvee Duty

My man is away on corvée duty,
No knowing for how long,
Or where he goes.
Chickens are resting in their roosts,
It is the evening of the day,
The sheep and cattle have come in.
My man is away on corvée duty,
Being so, how can I not miss him?

My man is away on corvée duty,
Not just for days, not for months.
When will we ever meet again?

Chickens are resting in their stands,
It is the evening of the day,
Cattle and sheep have been herded in.
My man is away on corvée duty,
Let him be without hunger or thirst.

Study Notes and Questions

1. Ezra Pound's translation of this poem is not nearly as accurate as Joseph Allen's, but it is a far more brilliant rendering of the poem.

2. What is the effect of the short lines in Pound's version? What is the effect of the rhyming and repetitions in Pound's translation?

"The Cock Crows" (Mao 96)

雞鳴					The Cock Crows
雞	既	鳴 [m.reng]	矣		"The cock already crows.
cock	already	crows	[completed]		
朝	既	盈 [leng]	矣		Dawn already is fully here."
dawn	already	full	[completed]		
匪	雞	則	鳴 [m.reng]		"It's not the cock that crows.
not	cock	[topic]	crows		
蒼	蠅	之	聲 [l̥eng]		It's the sound of flies."
dark	fly	's	sound		
東	方	明 [mrang]	矣		"The east is bright.
east	region	bright	[completed]		
朝	既	昌 [t^{h}ang]	矣		Dawn already glows."
dawn	already	gleams	[completed]		
匪	東	方	則	明 [mrang]	"It's not the east that's bright.
not	east	region	[topic]	bright	
月	出	之	光 [$k^{wʕ}$ang]		It's the gleam of the moon rising."
moon	come out	's	radiance		
蟲	飛	薨	薨 [m̥^{ʕ}əng]		"Insects buzz as they fly.
insects	fly	buzz	buzz		
甘	與	子	同	夢 [C.məng-s]	Gladly would I still dream with you,
gladly	with	you	share	dream	
會	且	歸	矣		And return home with you.
Surely	will	return	[completed]		
無	庶	予	子	憎 [ts^{ʕ}əng]	I would not want to hate you."
Without	hope	my	you	hate	

Joseph R. Allen's Translation

The Cock Crows

The cock has crowed,
And the court has filled.
Tis not the cock that crowed,
But the sound of houseflies.

The eastern sky brightens,
And the court is already teeming,
Tis not the eastern sky that brightens,
But rather the glow of the moon.

Bugs fly about buzzing;
Sweet it'd be to lie with you and dream.
They will be returning soon;
Let's not give them reason to scorn you.

Mao Preface: "'The Cock Crows' contemplates the virtuous consort. Duke Ai had fallen into licentiousness and neglect, therefore this describes the virtuous consort and pure women so as to warn him to perfect his Way in this matter."

Zheng Xuan (first stanza): "The cock crows and the court fills, the lady and the lord can arise and perform the standard etiquette. . . . The lady thinks the sound of flies is the cock's crow, thus she gets up early to perform the standard etiquette and pay her respects."

Zhu Xi: "A description. It speaks of the virtuous consort going to where the lord is, arriving at the time just before dawn, she has to tell the lord, 'The cock has crowed, the gathering officials have filled the court. I want to ask the lord to arise early and attend to court.' Yet, in fact it is not the crow of the cock; it is rather the sound of houseflies. Probably when the virtuous consort awakes in the early morning, in her mind she often is afraid of being late. Therefore when she hears something like this, she thinks that it is real. It is not that her mind is focused on warnings to be afraid, nor does she dwell on her lingering desire. How could she be so? Therefore the poet narrates this affair, and praises her."

Study Notes and Questions

1. Some scholars have argued that early Chinese culture had no sense of the inner self. However, consider the role of judgments of perception in the poem as a way of portraying subjectivity.

2. What is the situation set out in the poem?

3. This poem presented a challenge to readers from the Han dynasty onward who very much wanted to consider the poems of the *Canon of Poetry* to be morally exemplary. Note the three quite different accounts offered by Mao, Zheng Xuan, and Zhu Xi.

"Yellow Bird" (Mao 131)

黃鳥				Yellow Bird
交 twitter	交 twitter	黃 yellow	鳥 bird	Twitters the Yellow Bird:
止 stop	于 at	棘 [*krək*] buckthorn		[It] stops on the buckthorn.
誰 who	從 follow	穆 Mu	公 Duke	Who follows Duke Mu?[4]
子 Ziju (a surname)	車	奄 Yan-	息 [sək] -xi (name)	Ziju Yanxi.
維 [is]	此 this	奄 Yan-	息 [sək] -xi	This Yanxi
百 100	夫 men	之 's	特 [dˤək] special	Was special among the throng of men.
臨 approach	其 his	穴 [Gʷˤit] cave		Approaching the pit,
惴 shudder	惴 shudder	其 his	慄 [C-rit] tremble	[He (?)] was shivering with fear.
彼 that	蒼 blue	者 [thing]	天 [l̥ˤin] Heaven	That blue Heaven
殲 exterminate	我 our	良 fine	人 [niŋ] person	Exterminates our finest men.
如 if	可 can be	贖 redeem	兮 !	If he could be redeemed,
人 person	百 100	其 his	身 [n̥iŋ] body	[The lives of] a hundred men [would be worth] his.
交 twitter	交 twitter	黃 yellow	鳥 bird	Twitters the Yellow Bird:
止 stop	于 at	桑 [sˤang] mulberry		[It] stops on the mulberry.
誰 who	從 follow	穆 Mu	公 Duke	Who follows Duke Mu?
子 Ziju	車	仲 Zhong-	行 [gˤang] -hang	Ziju Zhonghang.
維 [is]	此 this	仲 Zhong-	行 [gˤang] -hang	This Zhonghang
百 100	夫 man	之 's	防 [m-pang] match	Is a match for the throng of men.

4. Duke Mu of Qin died in 621 BC and had more than 100 people buried alive in his tomb.

臨 approach	其 his	穴 [Gʷˤit] cave		Approaching the pit,
惴 shudder	惴 shudder	其 his	慄 [C-rit] tremble	[He (?)] was shivering with fear.
彼 that	蒼 blue	者 [thing]	天 [l̥ˤin] Heaven	That blue Heaven
殲 exterminate	我 our	良 fine	人 [niŋ] person	Exterminates our finest men.
如 if	可 can be	贖 redeem	兮 !	If he could be redeemed,
人 person	百 100	其 his	身 [n̥iŋ] body	[The lives of] a hundred men [would be worth] his.

交 twitter	交 twitter	黃 yellow	鳥 bird	Twitters the Yellow Bird:
止 stop	于 at	楚 [s.r̥aʔ] thornbush		[It] stops on the thornbush.
誰 who	從 follow	穆 Mu	公 Duke	Who follows Duke Mu?
子 Ziju	車	鍼 Qian-	虎 [qʰˤraʔ] -hu	Ziju Qianhu.
維 [is]	此 this	鍼 Qian-	虎 [qʰˤraʔ] -hu	This Qianhu
百 100	夫 man	之 's	禦 [m-qʰ(r)aʔ] guard against	Is the equal of the throng of men.
臨 approach	其 his	穴 [Gʷˤit] cave		Approaching the pit,
惴 shudder	惴 shudder	其 his	慄 [C-rit] tremble	[He (?)] was shivering with fear.
彼 that	蒼 blue	者 [thing]	天 [l̥ˤin] Heaven	That blue Heaven,
殲 exterminate	我 our	良 fine	人 [niŋ] person	Exterminates our finest men.
如 if	可 can be	贖 redeem	兮 !	If he could be redeemed,
人 person	百 100	其 his	身 [n̥iŋ] body	[The lives of] a hundred men [would be worth] his.

Study Notes and Questions

1. The topic of this poem, the sacrificial burial of Duke Mu of Qin's worthy advisors with him to accompany him in death, certainly is stunning. Who would sing such a song? On what sort of occasion?

2. Consider the images of the poem: what role does the "Yellow Bird" play in the poem? Does its action, its landing on various plants, select the victims, or is the poet working backwards from the names of the victims to the plants? How can one tell?

From the "Greater Ya*"*

"The Birth of the People [of Zhou]" (Mao 245)

生民					The Birth of the People [of Zhou]
厥 its	初 beginning	生 give birth	民 populace		The first birth of [our] people:
時 this	維 is	姜 Jiang	嫄 Yuan		This was Jiang Yuan.
生 give birth	民 populace	如 resemble	何 what		How did [she] give birth to [our] people?
克 can	禋 give offering	克 can	祀 [s-ɢəʔ] give sacrifice		[She] could present offerings and could sacrifice,
以 by [this]	弗 clear away	無 without	子 [tsəʔ] child		So that she would not be childless.
履 tread on	帝 Lord	武 footprint	敏 big toe	歆 accept gladly	She stepped on a toe-print of the Lord on High,
攸 what-is	介 aided	攸 what-is	止 blessed		She was enriched; she was blessed.
載 then	震 pregnant	載 then	夙 [suk] early		She then became pregnant; it then came quickly;
載 then	生 give birth	載 then	育 [m-quk] nourish		She gave birth; she nourished [a son].
時 this	維 is	后 Hou-	稷 [tsək] ji		This was Houji.
誕 reach	彌 fill	厥 her	月 [ŋʷat] month		When she had fulfilled her months,
先 first	生 born	如 and	達 [lˤat] arrive		Her first-born came forth.

不	坼	不	副		Not bursting, not rending,
not	rend	not	split		
無	菑	無	害 [N-kˁat-s]		There was no injury, no hurt;
without	calamity	without	harm		
以	赫	厥	靈 [rˁeng]		To make brilliant his spiritual power.
by [this]	blazon	his	spiritual power		
上	帝	不	寧 [nˁeng]		The Lord on High greatly comforted [her].[5]
above	Lord	greatly	comfort		
不	康	禋	祀 [s-ɢəʔ]		[He] was greatly pleased with the sacrifice,
greatly	approve	giving sacrifice			
居	然	生	子 [tsəʔ]		So that easily she bore her son.
peaceful-	ly	give birth	son		
誕	寘	之	隘	巷	When they placed him in a narrow lane,
then	place	him	narrow	lane	
牛	羊	腓	字	之 [mə-dzəʔ-s]	The oxen and goats protected him.
ox	goat	shelter	nurture	him	
誕	寘	之	平	林 [rəm]	When they placed him in a forest on the plain,
then	place	him	level	forest	
會	伐	平	林 [rəm]		He met wood-cutters in the forest on the plain.
meet	cut	level	forest		
誕	寘	之	寒	冰 [p.rəng]	When they placed him on the cold ice:
then	place	him	cold	ice	
鳥	覆	翼	之		Birds screened him with their wings.
bird	cover	wing	him		
鳥	乃	去	矣 [kʰ(r)ap-s]		The birds then went away.
bird	then	depart	[perfective]		
后	稷	呱	矣 [kʷˁa]		Houji wailed.
Hou-	ji	wail	[perfective]		
實	覃	實	訏 [qʷʰ(r)a]		[His cry] was long and loud:
thus	long	thus	big		
厥	聲	載	路 [Cə-rˁak-s]		His voice was great.
his	sound	then	great		
誕	實	匍	匐 [bˁək]		When thus he crawled:
then	thus	crawl			
克	岐	克	嶷 [ŋ(r)ək]		He could step and he could stand,
can	[stand] tall	can	[stand] firmly		

5. The traditional commentary took "not comforted" (*buning* 不寧) as "comforted" (*ning* 寧), seemingly unaware that "not" (*bu* 不) here should have been "greatly" (*pi* 丕).

以 就 口 食 [mə-lək]	by [this[go to mouth eat	To reach food for his mouth.
蓺 之 荏 菽	plant it large beans	He planted [the land] with large beans.
荏 菽 旆 旆 [bˤat-s]	large beans banner-like	The large beans waved in rows;
禾 役 穟 穟 [s-ɢʷit-s]	grain work sprout sprout	The grain, tended, grew abundantly;
麻 麥 幪 幪 [mˤongʔ]	hemp wheat luxuriant	The hemp and wheat grew thick;
瓜 瓞 唪 唪 [pʰrongʔ]	melon small melon plentious	The melons were plentious.
誕 后 稷 之 穡	then Hou- -ji 's farming	Thus the farmwork of Houji,
有 相 之 道 [lˤuʔ]	there is help 's way	Had the way of helping [the growth].
茀 厥 豐 草 [tsʰˤuʔ]	clear away its abundant grass	Clearing away the abundant grass,
種 之 黃 茂 [m(r)uʔ]	sow it yellow grain	He sowed [the ground] with the yellow grains.
實 方 實 苞 [pˤ<r>u]	thus sprout thus flourish	Thus it sprouted; thus it flourished;
實 種 實 褎 [sə.lu-s]	thus sow thus grow tall	Thus it was sown; thus it grew tall;
實 發 實 秀 [s-luʔ-s]	thus flower thus produce ears	Thus it flowered; thus it set ears [of grain];
實 堅 實 好 [qʰˤuʔ]	thus firm thus fine	Thu it grew firm; thus it grew fine;
實 穎 實 栗 [rit]	thus ears thus complete	Thus it[s ears] ripened; thus it matured;
即 有 邰 家 室 [s.tit]	then there is Tai clan dwelling	Then he had his household in Tai.[6]

誕 降 嘉 種	then send down fine seed	Then he sent down [to the people] the fine grains:
維 秬 維 秠 [pʰrəʔ]	it is black millet it is double-kernelled millet	The black millet, and the double-kernelled;
維 穈 維 芑 [C.qʰrəʔ]	it is red-sprout it is white-sprout	The red-sprouting, and the white.

6. According to legend, Emperor Yao enfeoffed Houji in Tai, in modern Shaanxi Province.

恆	之	秬	秠 [p^{h}rəʔ]		He broadly planted the ground with the black and the double-kernelled,
broadly	it	black millet	double-kernelled		
是	穫	是	畝 [məʔ]		This he reaped and this he piled.
this	reap	this	pile in field		
恆	之	穈	芑 [C.q^{h}rəʔ]		He broadly planted the red-sprouting and the white,
broadly	it	red-sprout	white-sprout		
是	任	是	負 [bəʔ]		This he carried on his shoulders and this on his back:
this	shoulder	this	bear on back		
以	歸	肇	祀 [s-ɢəʔ]		Returning home, he used it to found the sacrifices.
by [this]	return	begin	sacrifice		

誕	我	祀	如	何	Then our sacrifices: what are they like?
then	we	sacrifice	resemble	what	
或	舂	或	揄 [lu]		Some hull [the grain]; some take it from the mortar;
some	mortar	some	take from mortar		
或	簸	或	蹂 [nu]		Some winnow it; some tread it.
some	winnow	some	tread		
釋	之	叟	叟 [sru]		[We] rinse it swishing;
rinse	it	swish	swish		
烝	之	浮	浮 [m.b(r)u]		[We] steam it billowing.
steam	it	billow	billow		
載	謀	載	惟 [ɢwij]		Then [we] plan; then we reflect;
then	plan	then	consider		
取	蕭	祭	脂 [kij]		[We] take artemisia and offer it with the fat;
take	artemisia	offer	fat		
取	羝	以	軷 [b^{ʕ}at]		[We] take a ram and skin it;
take	ram	by [this]	skin		
載	燔	載	烈 [rat]		Then [we] roast and then [we] broil,
then	roast	then	broil		
以	興	嗣	歲 [s-q^{wh}at-s]		And by this start the coming year.
by [this]	start	successor	year		

卬	盛	于	豆	We fill the footed platters [with offerings],
we	fill	on	footed platter	
于	豆	于	登 [k-t^{ʕ}əng]	Onto the footed platters and onto the covered.
on	footed	on	covered platter	
其	香	始	升 [s-təng]	When the fragrance starts to ascend,
its	fragrance	start	rise	
上	帝	居	歆 [q^{h}rəm]	The Lord on High tranquilly accepts [the sacrifice].
high	Lord	peacefully	accepts gladly	

胡 distant	臭 breath	亶 truly	時 [də] good	The pervading fragrance is truly good.
后 Hou-	稷 -ji	肇 begin	祀 [s-ɢəʔ] sacrifice	Houji began the sacrifice,
庶 crowd	無 is without	罪 blame	悔 [m̥ˤəʔ] regret	The multitude is without blame or regret,[7]
以 by [this]	迄 reach	于 to	今 [krəm] now	By this we reach the present day.

Study Notes and Questions

1. What sort of hero is Houji? The poem sets out the signs pointing to divine protection: What virtues does he reveal? Why do you think he was abandoned three times?

2. What is the ritual occasion of the poem?

3. Although scholars argue that the Zhou people replaced the corporate "ancestors on high" of Shang state ritual and religion with Heaven, the sacrifices in this poem are to these ancestors (translated as "Lord on High"). The king has the right and duty to offer sacrifices to his ancestors: how does this ritual bind those present together?

7. There is some debate whether "multitude" 庶 here should be taken as "fortunately," as it is used in a similar phrase elsewhere in the *Canon of Poetry*.

From the "Hymns of Zhou"

"Fruitful Year" (Mao 279)

豐年				Fruitful Year
豐 bounty	年 year	多 much	黍 [s-tʰaʔ] millet	In the fruitful year, much millet,
多 much	稌 [lˤaʔ] rice			Much rice.
亦 also	有 are	高 high	廩 granary	And there are high-piled granaries.
萬 10^4	億 10^5	及 reach	秭 [tsijʔ] 10^6	Thousands and millions:
為 make	酒 wine	為 make	醴 [rˤijʔ] sweet wine	We [use to] make clear wines and sweet wines
烝 present	畀 give	祖 ancestor	妣 [pijʔ] ancestress	To offer to our ancestors.
以 by [this]	洽 complete	百 100	禮 [rˤijʔ] rites	By this we complete the hundred rites,
降 send	福 blessing	孔 very	皆 [kˤrij] complete	And they send down blessings throughout [our land].

STUDY NOTES AND QUESTIONS

This is a song to accompany a harvest sacrifice in the Zhou ancestral temple. Who is the speaker? What is his role? What is his relationship to the populace? What is his relationship to the ancestors? How do these two relationships shape one another and the wording of the poem?

The *Lyrics of Chu* (*Chu ci*)

On one level, it is easy to describe the *Lyrics of Chu* (*Chu ci* 楚辭): it is an extremely important anthology of late Warring States (476–221 BC) poetry from the large southern state of Chu, along with early Han poetry written in imitation of that southern tradition, that Wang Yi 王逸 (fl. 140) compiled during the later Eastern Han dynasty. Beyond this, however, much about the collection is wrapped in mystery. Although Sima Qian 司馬遷 included a biography of Qu Yuan 屈原 (ca. 340–278 BC) as the author of *Encountering Sorrow* (*Li sao* 離騷)—the main poem in the collection—in the *Records of the Grand Historian* (*Shi ji* 史記), that biography has many internal problems and is not a trustworthy guide. The language, meaning, authorship, and roles of the poems are largely opaque, since we have little more than the biography of Qu Yuan, the bare texts of the poems, and Wang Yi's often less-than-helpful commentary to go on. Despite much archeological work on Chu culture in the past fifty years, modern scholars tracing the poems' origins have had little success.

The current *Chu ci* is a collection of seventeen groups of poems:

Chu Texts

1. *Encountering Sorrow*	attributed to Qu Yuan
2. *Nine Songs*	attributed to Qu Yuan
3. *Heaven's Questions*	attributed to Qu Yuan
4. *Nine Pieces*	attributed to Qu Yuan
5. *Far Wandering*	attributed to Qu Yuan
6. *Divining a Dwelling*	attributed to Qu Yuan
7. *The Fisherman*	attributed to Qu Yuan
8. *Nine Transformations*	attributed to Song Yu
9. *Summoning the Soul*	attributed to Song Yu
10. *Great Summoning*	attributed to Qu Yuan

Han Dynasty Texts

11. *Lamenting a Vow [Betrayed]*	Jia Yi
12. *Summoning the Recluse*	Liu An
13. *Seven Remonstrances*	Dongfang Shuo
14. *Lamenting My Fate*	Yan Ji
15. *Nine Regrets*	Wang Bao
16. *Nine Laments*	Liu Xiang
17. *Nine Longings*	Wang Yi

As David Hawkes reconstructs the origins of the *Lyrics of Chu*, it began as a collection of poems from Chu compiled at the court of Liu An 劉安 (179 BC–122 BC), the Prince of Huainan, who had an extensive library and had attracted a very talented group of writers and scholars to his service. Liu An's connection with Chu culture was strong. The Han imperial clan initially was from the south, and Liu An's realm was in what formerly had been Chu. His capital, Shouchun, had once served briefly as the capital of the Chu state after the fall of Ying (the earlier Chu capital) and before Chu's defeat by Qin.

Emperor Wu of the Han, upon coming to the throne, began a policy of curbing the princely courts and centralizing power. Eventually Liu An plotted rebellion, was discovered, and committed suicide. Emperor Wu had Liu An's books brought to Chang'an and incorporated them into the imperial archives, where the next part of the story of the *Chu ci* occurred. Hawkes suggests that Liu Xiang 劉向 (79 BC–8 BC), a great bibliographer, put the anthology together from materials he found in the imperial archive. This collection found its way into Wang Yi's hands; he in turn added his own poems to the end of the compilation and wrote a commentary.[8]

Selected Poems from the *Lyrics of Chu*

Encountering Sorrow

Encountering Sorrow is the central poem of the *Lyrics of Chu*. It is a long narrative poem (of 372 lines) in which the writer laments that his "fair one" has been misled by jealous rivals, plans to go off to seek a more enlightened love, and, at the last moment, hesitates. Its language, meter, and imagery are entirely different from the poetry in the *Canon of Poetry*. Since, however, at least three hundred years of social, political, and intellectual turmoil separate the last poems of the *Poetry* and the writing of *Encountering Sorrow*, this difference is not unexpected.

According to a tradition that already was fully developed by the time Sima Qian wrote the *Records of the Grand Historian*, *Encountering Sorrow* was composed by Qu Yuan, a loyal minister to King Huai (r. 328 BC–299 BC) and King Xiang (r. 299 BC–278 BC) of Chu. In this tradition, Qu Yuan, an ardent Chu loyalist, sought to prevent the northern state of Qin's slow rise to power by seeking alliances with other states like Qi while blocking any cooperation with Qin. At various times during his long career, however, Qu Yuan was slandered by fellow officials and banished. In the traditional account, he wrote the various poems of the *Lyrics of Chu* attributed to him during these periods of exile. Qu Yuan wrote *Encountering Sorrow* in particular after King Xiang banished him in 292 BC. Eventually he despaired of ever returning to King Xiang's favor and, losing all hope for his homeland, threw himself into the Miluo River.

Scholars have described *Encountering Sorrow* as marking the "birth of the author" in China. That is, the poem reflects a strong personality, and its twists and turns directly reflect the shifting moods of the informing authorial voice. There is an intense and explicit self-consciousness in the author's effort to get the "fair one" to understand him by creating an external form that adequately expresses his inner self. In many ways, however, this reflecting, inward self already exists inchoately in many poems of the *Canon of Poetry*. In the *Poetry*, writers frequently lament that "those who know me" say one thing, while those who do not know me misunderstand: the sense of the distance between the inner self and external appearances and the role of poetry in trying to overcome that distance serves as a leitmotif throughout the collection. *Encountering Sorrow* makes this project central, and, importantly, it fails in the short term: the commentary tradition interprets the conclusion of the poem as expressing Qu Yuan's resolve to kill himself (although the poem itself provides an alternative ending where he becomes a proto-Daoist

8. David Hawkes gives an excellent overview of what is known about the origins of the collection in *The Songs of the South: An Ancient Chinese Anthology of Poems by Qu Yuan and Other Poets* (Harmondsworth: Penguin, 1985), pp. 28–38.

recluse). Despite the concluding uncertainty, *Encountering Sorrow* became the canonical statement of the problem of self-representation.

From *Encountering Sorrow* by Qu Yuan (first seventy-six lines)

	離騷								Encountering Sorrow
	帝	高	陽	之	苗	裔	兮		Descendant of the high lord Gao Yang,
	Lord	Gao	Yang	’s	sprout	descendant	xi!		
	朕	皇	考	曰	伯	庸 [juawng]			Bo Yong was my father’s name.
	my	august	elder	say	Bo	Yong			
	攝	提	貞	于	孟	陬	兮		When She Ti pointed to the First Month of the year,[9]
	She	ti	just now	at	beginning	1st Month	xi!		
	惟	庚	寅	吾	以	降 [kaɨwng^{h}]			On the day *gengyin* I was delivered.
	is	*geng*	*yin*	I	by [this]	descend			
	皇	覽	揆	余	于	初	度	兮	My august [father], examining my [time of] birth,
	august	examine	reckon	my	on	first	cross	xi!	
6	肇	錫	余	以	嘉	名 [mjiajng]			Divined to give me a fine name.
	divine	present	me	by [this]	fine	name			
	名	余	曰	正	則	兮			[He] named me Correct Norm:
	name	me	say	correct	norm	xi!			
	字	余	曰	靈	均				The capping name was Divine Balance.[10]
	capping	me	say	numinous	balance				
	紛	吾	既	有	此	內	美	兮	Profusely having this inward beauty,
	profuse	I	since	have	this	inside	beauty	xi!	
	又	重	之	以	修	能 [nəng]			I also added refined ability.
	also	double	it	by	refined	ability			
	扈	江	離	與	辟	芷	兮		I dressed in river selinea and secluded angelica,
	wear	river	selinea	and	secluded	angelica	xi!		
12	紉	秋	蘭	以	為	佩			and twined autumn orchids to make a sash.[11]
	twist	autumn	orchid	by [thi]	make	sash			

9. David Hawkes gives a lengthy account of this line, which describes the position of a constellation, She Ti, that indicated the beginning of the new year.

10. Men in premodern China had two personal names, a private name that was used by the family, and a “capping name” given at the capping ceremony when a boy became an adult. The problem in these lines is that the author is supposed to be Qu Ping, whose capping name was “Yuan,” but these are not the names the speaker of the poem announces here.

11. Throughout this textbook I use the much later meaning of “orchid” for *lan* 蘭, which in early China referred to an aromatic plant with the inelegant rendering of “thoroughwort.”

汩	余	若	將	不	及	兮	Swiftly I went, as if I could not catch up,
swift	I	resemble	about to	not	reach	xi!	
恐	年	歲	之	不	吾	與 [jiă']	Afraid the years would not be given me.
fear	year	year	's	not	me	give	
朝	搴	阰	之	木	蘭	兮	In the mornings I gathered the magnolia on the mountains;
morning	gather	mound	's	magnolia		xi	
夕	攬	洲	之	宿	莽		In the evenings I plucked the evergreen sedges of the islets.
evening	pluck	islet	's	persist	sedge		
日	月	忽	其	不	淹	兮	The days and months hurried on, never lingering;
day	month	hurry	their	not	linger	xi!	
春	與	秋	其	代	序 [ziǒ']		Springs and autumns replaced one another:
spring	and	autumn	their	replace	in order		
惟	草	木	之	零	落	兮	I thought of the verdure's fading,
think	grass	tree	's	fade	fall	xi!	
恐	美	人	之	遲	暮	[mɔ^h]	And feared that Fair One would grow old.
fear	fair	person	's	tardy	sunset		
不	撫	壯	而	棄	穢	兮	"You do not grasp your prime years to cast aside the impure!
not	stroke	prime	and	cast aside	impure	xi!	
何	不	改	乎	此	度 [dɔ^h]		Why do you not change this conduct?
why	not	change	at	this	conduct		
乘	騏	驥	以	馳	騁	兮	Mount fine steeds to gallop:
mount	fine steed		by [this]	gallop	gallop	xi!	
來	吾	導	夫	先	路 [lɔ^h]		Come, I will lead you on the road ahead!"
come	I	lead	that	ahead	road		
昔	三	后	之	純	粹	兮	"The purity and refinement of the three kings of old[12]
former	three	lord	's	pure	refined	xi!	
固	眾	芳	之	所	在		Was indeed where fragrant flowers thronged.
indeed	throng	fragrant	's	where	exist		
雜	申	椒	與	菌	桂	兮	They mixed doubled pepper and sweet-olive:
mix	extend	pepper	and	sweet-olive		xi!	
豈	維	紉	夫	蕙	茝		How did they only braid melilot and angelica?
how	only	braid	that	melilot	angelica		
彼	堯	舜	之	耿	介	兮	The glorious greatness of those Yao and Shun,
those	Yao	Shun	's	glorious greatness		xi!	

12. The long commentary tradition has suggested various possibilities for who these three excellent rulers were. One compelling proposal is that these are three sage rulers who preceded the sage emperors Yao and Shun, who are mentioned next in the poem.

30	既	遵	道	而	得	路 [lɔ^h]				Since they followed the way and attained the road.
	since	follow	way	and	attain	road				
	何	桀	紂	之	猖	披	兮			How reckless were Jie and Zhou,[13]
	how	Jie	Zhou	’s	reckless		xi!			
	夫	唯	捷	徑	以	窘	步 [bɔ^h]			Who took narrow paths and could move no further.
	now	only	take	shortcut	by [this]	block	step			
	惟	夫	黨	人	之	偷	樂	兮		For those who cabal and seize pleasure,
	it is	those	cabal	person	’s	steal	pleasure	xi!		
	路	幽	昧	以	險	隘				The road is dark, steep, and narrow
	road	secluded	dark	by [this]	steep	narrow				
	豈	余	身	之	憚	殃	兮			How do I fear for my own peril:
	how	my	body	’s	fear	peril	xi!			
36	恐	皇	輿	之	敗	績				I fear the crash of the August Carriage.
	fear	august	carriage	’s	crash and destroy					
	忽	奔	走	以	先	後	兮			I hurriedly rushed ahead and behind,
	hurry	rush	run	by [this]	ahead	behind	xi!			
	及	前	王	之	踵	武				To reach the tracks of the former kings.”
	reach	former	king	’s	heal	step				
	荃	不	察	余	之	中	情	兮		The Fragrant One did not examine my inner feelings:
	calamus	not	examine	I	’s	inner	feeling	xi!		
	反	信	讒	而	齌	怒 [nɔ^h]				Instead he trusted slander and grew enraged.
	contrary	trust	slander	and	burst	anger				
	余	固	知	謇	謇	之	為	患	兮	I surely know that forthrightness creates calamity;
	I	surely	know	forthrightness		’s	make	calamity	xi!	
42	忍	而	不	能	舍	也				Yet I will endure: I cannot give it up.
	endure	and	not	able	set aside	it is				
	指	九	天	以	為	正	兮			I point to the ninefold heaven to be my witness:
	point	nine	heaven	by [this]	become	witness	xi			
	夫	唯	靈	修	之	故	也 [kɔ^h]			This is for the sake of the Divine One.[14]
	now	is	numinous refined		’s	reason	it is			
	曰	黃	昏	以	為	期	兮			[He] said that dusk would be [our] time to meet,
	say	yellow	dusk	take	make	appointment				
	羌	中	道	而	改	路 [lɔ^h]				But in mid-route he changed his path.
	also	middle	way	and	change	road				

13. These were the “bad last” emperors whose violence and depravity were said to have destroyed the Xia and Shang dynasties.

14. The commentaries agree that the Divine One (literally, “numinous and refined”) refers to the Chu king.

初 既 與 余 成 言 兮	beginning since with me complete say xi!	In the beginning he completed arranging with me,
後 悔 遁 而 有 他	later regret equivocate and there is other	But later he regretted and had other [thoughts].
余 既 不 難 夫 離 別 兮	I since not complain that separate part xi!	While I do not object to separation,
傷 靈 修 之 數 化	hurt numinous refined 's often transform	I grieve that the Divine One changes so often.
余 既 滋 蘭 之 九 畹 兮	I since plant orchid 's nine *wan* xi!	I have planted many acres of orchids,[15]
又 樹 蕙 之 百 畝	and plant melilotus 's hundred *mu*	And planted a hundred *mu* of melilotus.
畦 留 夷 與 揭 車 兮	border peony and *jieju* xi!	I bordered the fields with peony and *jieju*,[16]
雜 杜 衡 與 芳 芷	mix asarum and fragrant angelica	And mixed asarums with fragrant angelica.
冀 枝 葉 之 峻 茂 兮	hope branch leaf 's soar abundant xi!	I hoped that branch and leaf would flourish;
願 俟 時 乎 吾 將 刈 [ŋiaj^h]	vow await season at I about to mow	I vowed to await the season when I would harvest.
雖 萎 絕 其 亦 何 傷 兮	although wither its also what harm xi!	Although they withered, what was the harm?
哀 眾 芳 之 蕪 穢 [ʔwiaj^h]	lament crowd fragrant 's overgrown weeds	I lamented that the thronging fragrance was overwhelmed by weeds.
眾 皆 競 進 以 貪 婪 兮	crowd all compete advance by [this] greed gluttony xi!	The crowd competes to advance in greed and gluttony,
憑 不 厭 乎 求 索 [sak]	full not sate in seek search	Filled but never sated in their seeking.
羌 內 恕 己 以 量 人 兮	also within take model self by [this] measure people xi!	And within they use their own self to assess others,
各 興 心 而 嫉 妒 [tɔ^h]	each arise mind and envy spite	Each filling their minds with envy and spite.

15. It appears that "nine" was used in Chu to mean "many." One *wan* was twelve *mu*, and one *mu* was a strip of land of 240 paces by one pace. The "one hundred *mu*" in the next line is about eleven acres, the amount of land needed to support one family.

16. *Liuyi*, tentatively translated as peony, and *jieju* clearly are fragrant plants, but no one has very specific information.

	忽 馳 騖 以 追 逐 兮	hurried gallop dash by [this] chase pursue xi!	Hurriedly they wildly gallop in pursuit:
	非 余 心 之 所 急 [kip]	is not my heart 's what urgent	This is not what my heart keenly seeks.
	老 冉 冉 其 將 至 兮	old age gradual its about to arrive xi!	For old age comes gradually and soon will arrive;
66	恐 修 名 之 不 立 [lip]	fear fine name 's not establish	I fear I shall not establish a fine reputation.
	朝 飲 木 蘭 之 墜 露 兮	dawn drink magnolia 's fall dew xi!	At dawn I drank dew falling from the magnolia;
	夕 餐 秋 菊 之 落 英 [ʔiajng]	dusk eat autumn chrys… 's fall petals	At dusk I ate the falling petals of the autumn chrysanthemum.
	苟 余 情 其 信 姱 以 練 要 兮	if my feelings be truly fine by [this] refine essential xi!	If my feelings are truly fine, refined and essentially focused,
	長 顑 頷 亦 何 傷 [ɕiang]	always yellow from starving also what harm	What harm is there if I am gaunt with hunger?
	擥 木 根 以 結 茝 兮	clasp tree stalk by [this] tie angelica xi!	I clasped the stalks to bind angelica,
72	貫 薜 荔 之 落 蕊 [ɲwi']	thread creeping fig 's fall stamen	And thread the creeping fig's fallen stamens.
	矯 菌 桂 以 紉 蕙 兮	straighten sweet-olive by [this] twist melilotus xi!	I straightened sweet-olive for twining with melilotus,
	索 胡 繩 之 纚 纚 [şi']	string vine 's strong rope	And strung strong ropes of vines.
	謇 吾 法 夫 前 修 兮	direct I model that former refined xi!	I take as my model former worthies:
	非 世 俗 之 所 服 [buwk]	is not generation custom 's what wear	It is not what [those in the] current mode wear.
	雖 不 周 于 今 之 人 兮	although not accord at present 's people xi!	Although it does not accord with people today,
78	願 依 彭 咸 之 遺 則 [dzək]	vow rely Peng Xian 's left-over norm	I vow to rely on the pattern that Peng Xian has left.[17]

17. Later commentaries, probably basing their readings on the legend of Qu Yuan, state that Peng Xian was a worthy official of the Shang dynasty who drowned himself when the emperor ignored his forthright advice. See the discussion in Hawkes, *Songs of the South*, pp. 84–86.

STUDY NOTES AND QUESTIONS

1. The self-presentation at the beginning has the quality of a ritual introduction to proclaim Qu Yuan's worthiness to participate in a sacrificial offering, yet no ritual follows. What is the effect of framing the poem in this manner?

2. The first-person narrator (pronouns for "I" or "me" appear eight times in the first fourteen lines) quickly turns to the theme of time passing too quickly. "Time" (lit. "years and harvests") here has interlocking linear and cyclical components. How do they interact and inform the images of adornment with flowers? Explain the narrator's injunction to "gather the flowers of youth and cast out the impure." Who is the audience for the narrator's monologue?

3. In the second section, the narrator gives the allegorical elements of flowers and "the road" an explicitly political dimension. Who were Yao, Shun, Jie, and Zhou?

4. In the second section, the narrator also introduces the theme of the disjunction between inner worth and external appearance (inner commitments and outer actions) from several angles. How does he present this theme?

5. The final section of this first part of *Encountering Sorrow* develops the connected themes of isolation and independence. How might this section have resonated with the post-conquest Chu elite?

6. *Encountering Sorrow* was popular at the Han imperial court. Liu Bang, the founder of the Han, was a southerner: what role could a song of Chu nostalgia that portrays highly individuated, if ritualized, political protest play in the project of creating a unified realm on the collapse of Qin's first version of a universal empire?

The Nine Songs

In Wang Yi's account, while Qu Yuan was in exile, he witnessed the religious rites of the local populace in a region south of the capital. Although Qu Yuan considered the wording of the songs performed during the rites to be crude, he nonetheless was moved by the sentiments expressed, since they matched his own unhappy state. He therefore provided new lyrics for the ritual hymns and created what we now know as the *Nine Songs*.

Scholars since the early twentieth century have considered this story unlikely. David Hawkes suggests that instead, the eleven poems of the *Nine Songs* formed a set of hymns to be performed for the dead during spring and autumn sacrifices. Hawkes further suggests that two of the eleven poems are specific to the spring ritual, and two are specific to autumn, so that in each cycle, nine poems in fact would be performed. That is, although there is good evidence that "nine" was an early Chinese stand-in for "many," by the late Warring States period when these poems were composed, the devisers of the ritual cycle took the number quite literally.

Most modern scholars have pointed to the strong religious element in these poems. Earlier scholars attempted to connect the ritual practices described in the poems to forms of shamanism that survive in both Siberia and Taiwan. More recent research has argued, however, that comparisons with contemporary examples are less useful than simply reconstructing the practices from the poems. In the *Nine Songs*, the religious adepts who perform the song first purify themselves for an encounter with a daemonic spirit, then entice the spirit, experience the encounter (which can involve a journey in the company of the spirit), and finally suffer pangs of abandonment as the spirit withdraws.

The final two poems of the cycle are different. "Those Who Died for the State" was perhaps the culmination of the ritual performance in which the spirits of those who died in battle were appeased through ritual acknowledgment of their suffering and sacrifice. The very short "Ritual for the Souls" is a coda announcing the completion of the cycle and committing to continue the ritual in perpetuity.

The meter of a couplet in the *Li sao* is basically:

X X X O X X 兮 (xi)
X X X O X R (rhyme)

where the O is a light, grammatical particle. In contrast, the meter for the *Nine Songs* is:

X X X 兮 X X
X X X 兮 X R (rhyme)

The two clearly are related variations on a five-stress line, but the actual historical connection is not certain. These meters came to represent the "Chu song style" that later poets used to invoke the ambience of Chu and its mix of lushness and sorrow.

"Lord amidst the Clouds" (second of the *Nine Songs*)

雲中君						Lord amidst the Clouds
浴	蘭	湯	兮	沐	芳 [p^{h}uang]	I bathe in orchid water and wash my hair with fragrances:
bathe	orchid	hot water		shampoo	fragrant grass	
華	采	衣	兮	若	英 [ʔiajng]	Florid, bright clothes, like flowers.
florid	colored	clothes		resemble	flower petals	
靈	連	蜷	兮	既	留	The spirit descends and tarries,
spirit	drawn in	curve		already	remain	
爛	昭	昭	兮	未	央 [ʔiang]	He blazes brightly, without stopping.
blaze	bright	bright		not yet	stop	
謇	將	憺	兮	壽	宮	Halting, he is about to rest in the Palace of Long Life.[18]
stop	about to	settled		Longevity	Palace	
與	日	月	兮	齊	光 [kwang]	He is equal in radiance to the sun and moon.
with	sun	moon		equal	radiance	
龍	駕	兮	帝	服		A dragon chariot and blazon of the Ancestor on High:
dragon	carriage		divine	clothes		
聊	翱	遊	兮	周	章 [tɕiang]	He will soar aloft, wander throughout [the sky].
would	soar	wander		all over	travel	

靈	皇	皇	兮	既	降	Having descended, the spirit is of dazzling majesty,
spirit	dazzling	majesty		already	descend	
猋	遠	舉	兮	雲	中 [truwng]	In a whirl he rises afar, amidst the clouds.
whirlwind	far	raises		clouds	midst	
覽	冀	州	兮	有	餘	He inspects Jizhou and all beyond.[19]
inspect	Ji	zhou		there is	extra	
橫	四	海	兮	焉	窮 [guwng]	Crossing the four seas, how could he cease?
traverse	four	seas		how	exhaust	

思	夫	君	兮	太	息 [ɕik]	Longing for that lord, I sigh deeply,
long	that	lord		great	sigh	
極	勞	心	兮	忡	忡 [sik]	Greatly troubled at heart with grief.
extreme	toil	heart		grieved	grieved	

18. This seems to be the temple dedicated to providing sacrifices for the spirits.

19. Commentary states that this refers to the land "between the two rivers," that is, between the Yellow and the Yangzi Rivers.

David Hawkes's Translation

The Lord within the Clouds

We have bathed in orchid water and washed our hair with perfumes,
And dressed ourselves like flowers in embroidered clothing.
The god has halted, swaying, above us,
Shining with persistent radiance.

He is going to rest in the House of Life.
His brightness is like that of the sun and moon.
In his dragon chariot, dressed in imperial splendour,
Now he flies off to wander round the sky.

The god has just descended in bright majesty,
When off in a whirl he soared again, far into the clouds.
He looks down on Ji-zhou and the lands beyond it;
There is no place in the world that he does not pass over.
Thinking of that lord makes me sigh
And afflicts my heart with a grievous longing.

Study Notes and Questions

1. The poem is a story of encounter. What happens? Does anything change because of the encounter?

2. If this is a ritual poem, what might the ritual be?

3. The poem defines a ritual space in the first few lines. The narrator then describes the travels of the Lord amidst the Clouds in what some scholars have described as a form of ritual theater. What theatrical elements do we see in the text?

4. The translation provides all the pronouns ("we," "he," and "my"): there are none in the text. Yet we know the poem ends as a first-person narrative. How? What is the effect of presenting the conclusion in the first person?

"Those Who Died for the State" (tenth of the *Nine Songs*)

國殤							Those Who Died for the State
操 grasp	吳 Wu	戈 halberd	兮	被 wear	犀 rhino	甲 [kaːp] armor	Wielding Wu halberds, Wearing rhino armor,
車 chariot	錯 cross	轂 hub	兮	短 short	兵 weapon	接 [tsiap] meet	Their chariots hub to hub, Their short [swords] crossed.
旌 banner	蔽 block	日 sun	兮	敵 enemy	若 resemble	雲 [wun] clouds	Banners blocked the sun; The foe [numerous] as clouds.

矢	交	墜	兮	士	爭	先 [sɛn]	Arrows were exchanged in fire,
arrow	cross	fall		knight	compete	first	The knights vied to be first.
凌	余	陣	兮	躐	余	行 [ɣang]	They breached our ranks,
breach	my	ranks		tread	my	line	They overran our lines.
左	驂	殪	兮	右	刃	傷 [ɕiang]	The left horse killed by an arrow,
left	outer horse	shoot& kill		right	blade	wound	The right wounded by sword.
霾	兩	輪	兮	縶	四	馬 [maɨ']	Our chariot wheels sank,
bury	pair	wheels		tether	four	horse	Our horse teams tethered.
援	玉	枹	兮	擊	鳴	鼓 [nɔ^h]	Holding the jade-gilt drum-stick,
hold	jade	drum-stick		strike	sing	drum	He strikes the sounding drum.
天	時	墜	兮	威	靈	怒 [kɔ']	Heaven now casts [us] away,
Heaven	time	fall		awesome	spirits	angry	The awesome spirits are angry.
嚴	殺	盡	兮	棄	原	壄 [jia']	All killed, we
stern	kill	complete		abandon	plain	wilds	Were left on the battlefield.
出	不	入	兮	往	不	反 [puan']	We left [camp] to enter no more,
go out	not	enter		leave	not	return	We set out, not to return.
平	原	忽	兮	路	超	遠 [wuan']	The level plain is vast,
level	plain	distant		road	distant	far	The road so distant.
帶	長	劍	兮	挾	秦	弓	Wearing long swords,
belt	long	sword		clasp	Qin	bow	And clasping Qin bows,
首	身	離	兮	心	不	懲 [dring]	[Even] with heads and body apart,
head	body	separate		heart	not	subdue	[Their] hearts are not subdued.
誠	既	勇	兮	又	以	武	Truly, being brave,
indeed	already	brave		again	by [this]	martial	And martial
終	剛	強	兮	不	可	凌 [ling]	To the end tough and strong,
end	tough	strong		not	can be	breach	They could not be breached.
身	既	死	兮	神	以	靈 [lɛjng]	Their bodies having died,
body	already	dead		spirit	by [this]	numinous	Their spirits are thus divine.
魂	魄	毅	兮	為	鬼	雄 [wuwng]	Their souls are strong,
soul	spirit	strong		become	ghost	hero	Becoming heroes among ghosts.

David Hawkes's Translation

Hymn to the Fallen

Grasping our great shields and wearing our hide armour,
Wheel-hub to wheel-hub locked, we battle hand to hand.

Our banners darken the sky; the enemy teem like clouds:
Through the hail of arrows, the warriors press forward.

They dash on our lines; they trample our ranks down.
The left horse has fallen, the right one is wounded.

The wheels are embedded, the foursome entangled:
Seize the jade drumstick and beat the sounding drum!
The time is against us: the gods are angry.
Now all lie dead, left on the field of battle.

They went out never more to return:
Far, far away they lie, on the level plain,
Their long swords at their belts, clasping their Qin bows,
Head from body sundered: but their hearts could not be vanquished.

Both truly brave, and also truly noble;
Strong to the last, they could not be dishonoured.
Their bodies may have died, but their souls are living:
Heroes among the shades their valiant souls will be.

Study Notes and Questions

1. What makes this poem seem like a hymn to the dead? How did they die? According to the poem, at their time of death, were they given proper burial? The spirits of the dead that have not received proper burial remain restless and dangerous in many cultures. How might this ritual satisfy such spirits?

2. In contrast to "Lord amidst the Clouds," this poem provides explicit first-person pronouns. In what line do they appear? What is the effect of introducing first-person speech?

3. Does the poem switch perspective from first person to third person? At what point and to what effect?

4. Is the "level plain" in the poem real or symbolic?

The Nine Pieces

The *Nine Pieces* is a collection of nine late Warring States poems from Chu written in the tradition already defined by *Encountering Sorrow* and the *Nine Songs*. Some, like "Lament for Ying," are topical, while others adopt the style of a generalized lament for the times. Many follow the *sao* meter, derived from *Encountering Sorrow* (*Li sao*), of

XXXOXX (xi)
XXXOXR (rhyme)

The tradition attributes the nine poems to Qu Yuan, and Wang Yi explains that they were all written during Qu Yuan's long exile in King Xiang's reign. Later scholars proposed different scenarios to account for the content of the particular compositions, but all were committed to Qu Yuan's authorship.

Seeing the nine poems as being self-consciously in the tradition of the *Li sao* puts stress on the ways in which the basic conventions of language, imagery, and persona came to be used to handle a variety of topics that were not part of the *Li sao* itself.

"Lament for Ying" from the *Nine Pieces*

	哀郢							Lament for Ying[20]
	皇 august	天 heaven	之 's	不 not	純 pure	命 mandate	兮 xi!	August Heaven is not perfect in its mandate:
	何 why	百 hundred	姓 surname	之 's	震 agitate	愆 [*kʰrjan] offend		Why are the people unsettled and meet punishment?
	民 populace	離 separate	散 scatter	而 and	相 mutual	失 lose	兮 xi!	The people are scattered and lose one another:
	方 just	仲 middle	春 spring	而 and	東 east	遷 [*tsʰan] move		Just in the middle of spring I moved eastward.
	去 leave	故 old	鄉 village	而 and	就 go to	遠 distant	兮 xi!	I left my old village to set off for a distant [place]:
	遵 follow	江 Jiang	夏 Xia	以 by [this]	流 flow	亡 [*maŋ] depart		Following the waters of the Jiang and Xia, I drifted into exile.
4	出 go out	國 capital	門 gate	而 and	軫 grieve	懷 breast	兮 xi!	I went out through the capital's gate and grieved in my heart:

20. Ying was the capital of Chu. The sack of the city and the eastward migration mentioned in the poem refer to the Qin general Bo Qi's capturing of the city in 278 BC. However, the route in the poem differs from the actual move of the capital, so some scholars take this as the author's personal journey. Also see Hawkes's translation in *The Songs of the South*, pp. 161–66.

甲	之	鼂	吾	以	行 [*graŋ]		On the *jia* day in the morning, I started my travels.[21]
jia	's	morning	I	by [this]	travel		
發	郢	都	而	去	閭	兮	I set out from Ying and left my ward [in the city]:
set out	Ying	city	and	leave	ward	xi!	
荒	忽	其	焉	極 [*g(r)jɨk]			This dazed confusion, when will it end?[22]
dazed	confused	its	where	reach limit			
楫	齊	揚	以	容	與	兮	The oars lifted in unison, and we moved haltingly:
oar	evenly	lift	by [this]	haltingly		xi!	
哀	見	君	而	不	再	得 [*tɨk]	I lamented that I shall not again get to see my lord.
lament	see	lord	and	not	again	attain	
望	長	楸	而	太	息	兮	I gazed on the tall catalpa trees and sighed deeply:
gaze	long	catalpa	and	great	sigh	xi!	
涕	淫	淫	其	若	霰 [*s(k)ens]		Tears flowed unrestrainedly, like sleet.
tears	flow without stop		its	resemble	sleet		
過	夏	首	而	西	浮	兮	We passed the head of the Xia River and drifted westward:
pass	Xia	head	and	west	drift	xi!	
顧	龍	門	而	不	見 [*kens]		I looked back for the Dragon Gate but could not see it.[23]
look back	Dragon	Gate	and	not	see		
心	嬋	媛	而	傷	懷	兮	My heart was filled with longing, and I grieved:
heart	longing		and	harm	breast	xi!	
眇	不	知	其	所	蹠 [*tjak]		In the distance, I do not know where I shall tread.
distant	not	know	its	where	tread		
順	風	波	以	從	流	兮	Following the wind and waves, I went with their flow:
follow	wind	wave	by [this]	follow	flow	xi!	
焉	洋	洋	而	為	客 [*khrak]		Where would I drift as a traveler?
where	drift		and	become	traveler		
淩	陽	侯	之	氾	濫	兮	We traversed the great billows of the God of Waves,
traverse	Yang	Marquis	's	billowing-waves		xi!	
忽	翱	翔	之	焉	薄 [*phak]		In an instant soaring, where will we moor?
sudden	soaring		's	where	moor		
心	絓	結	而	不	解	兮	My heart was tethered without release;
heart	snag	tie	and	not	release	xi!	
思	蹇	產	而	不	釋 [*hljAk]		My longings were tangled with no relief.
longing	twisted about		and	not	release		

21. *Jia* is the first stem in the counting system for the calendar: journeys *should* begin on a *jia* day.

22. Some texts have *chao* 怊 (aggrieved and dispirited) at the beginning of the line.

23. Dragon Gate was the east gate of the capital, Ying.

	將	運	舟	而	下	浮	兮		I moved my boat, floating downstream,
	about to	move	boat	and	down	float	xi!		
	上	洞	庭	而	下	江 [*kroŋ]			Up to Dongting Lake and down to the [Yangzi] River.
	up	Dong-	ting	and	down	River			
	去	終	古	之	所	居	兮		I had left where I dwelt for all time:
	leave	end of	old	's	where	reside	xi!		
	今	逍	遙	而	來	東 [*toŋ]			And now I roamed and came to the East.
	now	roam		and	come	east			
	羌	靈	魂	之	欲	歸	兮		My soul desired to return:
	also	numinous	soul	's	desire	return	xi!		
	何	須	臾	而	忘	反 [*pjanʔ]			For what instant have I forgotten about returning?
	what	brief time		and	forget	return			
16	背	夏	浦	而	西	思	兮		I turned my back on the banks of the Xia and longed to go westward,
	turn back	Xia	shore	and	west	long for	xi!		
	哀	故	都	之	日	遠 [wjanʔ]			I lamented that my old city grew daily more distant.
	lament	old	city	's	daily	distant			
	登	大	墳	以	遠	望	兮		I climbed a high hill and gazed into the distance,
	climb	big	mound	by [this]	distant	gaze	xi!		
	聊	以	舒	吾	憂	心 [*səm]			That I might ease my sorrowing heart.
	for now	by [this]	ease	my	sorrow	heart			
	哀	州	土	之	平	樂	兮，		I lamented my land's constant joys
	lament	state	land	's	level	joy	xi!		
	悲	江	介	之	遺	風 [*prəm]			And sorrowed for the remnant winds of the river's edge.[24]
	sorrow	river	border	's	remnant	wind			
	當	陵	陽	之	焉	至	兮		Facing the challenge of getting to Lingyang,[25]
	just at	Ling-	yang	's	where	arrive	xi!		
	淼	南	渡	之	焉	如 [*na]			In the vast distance, crossing south, where does one go?
	vastness	south	cross	's	where	go			
20	曾	不	知	夏	之	為	丘	兮	Did I not know that the palaces would become mounds?
	once	not	know	palace	's	become	mound	xi!	
	孰	兩	東	門	之	可	蕪 [*ma]		How could the two east gates [of Ying] become overgrown with weeds?
	which	two	east	gate	's	can be	overgrown		
	心	不	怡	之	長	久	兮		Long has my heart not felt joy;
	heart	not	joyful	's	long	long time	xi!		

24. The commentaries explicitly reject taking 遺風 in its usual sense of "remnant customs."

25. Lingyang is indeed a place name (in modern Anhui Province), but some scholars relate the phrase to the earlier Marquis of Yang 陽侯, the god of the waves.

憂	與	愁	其	相	接 [*tsap]		Grief and sorrow succeed one another.
grief	and	sorrow	its	mutual	connect		
惟	郢	路	之	遼	遠	兮	I think of the great distance of the road to Ying,
think	Ying	road	's	distant	far	xi!	
江	與	夏	之	不	可	涉 [*djap]	And the [Yangzi] River and the Xia cannot be crossed.
River	and	Xia	's	not	can be	cross	
忽	若	去	不	信	兮		Suddenly it seems as if leaving was not true,[26]
suddenly	resemble	leave	not	trust	xi!		
至	今	九	年	而	不	復 [*b(r)juk]	Yet now it has been nine years, and I have not returned.
arrive	now	nine	year	and	not	return	
慘	鬱	鬱	而	不	通	兮	Sadness swells within and cannot find release;
sad	stifled swelling		and	not	penetrate		
蹇	侘	傺	而	含	慼 [*Sthiwk]		Dispirited and vacillating, I hold my grief within.
blocked	vacillating		and	hold in	grief		
外	承	歡	之	汋	約	兮	When externally they expressed delight in tender pleasing,[27]
outside	receive	delight	's	tending pleasing		xi!	
諶	荏	弱	而	難	持 [*drji]		Truly they were weak and could not hold firm.
certain	weak	weak	and	hard to	uphold		
忠	湛	湛	而	願	進	兮	My loyalty was deep, and I vowed to approach you,
loyal	deep and firm		and	vow	approach	xi!	
妒	被	離	而	鄣	之 [*tji]		But jealousy swarmed and blocked it.
jealous	disordered swarm		and	block	it		
堯	舜	之	抗	行	兮		Yao and Shun's lofty actions
Yao	Shun	's	lofty	action	xi!		
瞭	杳	杳	而	薄	天 [*hlin]		Reached the vast heights and approached Heaven.
reach	vast heights		and	near	Heaven		
眾	讒	人	之	嫉	妒	兮	[Yet] the crowd of slanderers was envious and jealous
crowd	slander	people	's	envious	jealous	xi!	
被	以	不	慈	之	偽	名 [*mjeŋ]	And gave them the false reputation of being unkind.
apply	by	not	kind	's	false	name	
憎	慍	惀	之	脩	美	兮	They hate the sincerely loyal, refined and fair,
hate	sincerely loyal		's	refined	fair	xi!	

26. Hawkes takes *xin* 信 to mean "stay a second night." See Hawkes, *Songs of the South*, p. 165.

27. This final section seems to be a later addition to the poem and is made of couplets that appear in the later *Nine Transformations*.

	好	夫	人	之	忼	慨 [*k^{h}ɨts]			But are fond of those people's agitated ardor.
	fond of	that	person	's	agitated ardor				
	眾	踥	蹀	而	日	進	兮		The crowd rushes and daily advances [in the ruler's favor].
	crowd	rush about		and	daily	advance	xi!		
	美	超	遠	而	逾	邁 [*mrats]			The fair grow distant and ever more far off.
	fair	exceed	distant	and	increase	go far			

亂曰：

The Envoy says:

	曼	余	目	以	流	觀	兮		Long have my eyes gazed about,
	extend	my	eye	by [this]	flow	observe	xi!		
	冀	壹	反	之	何	時			I hoped to finally return, but when?
	hope	one	return	's	what	time			
32	鳥	飛	反	故	鄉	兮			Birds fly to return to their old place,
	bird	fly	return	old	village	xi!			
	狐	死	必	首	丘				And when the fox dies, it invariably turns its head toward its lair.
	fox	die	must	head	mound				
	信	非	吾	罪	而	棄	逐	兮	Truly it was not for my crime that I was rejected and banished.
	truly	is not	my	crime	and	reject	banish	xi!	
	何	日	夜	而	忘	之			What day or night can I forget [Ying]?
	what	day	night	and	forget	it			

STUDY NOTES AND QUESTIONS

1. What is the story set out in this poem? Do the concluding lines before the envoy seem consistent with the earlier part of the poem? Why do you think these concluding lines, modeled on *Encountering Sorrow*, were added to the poem?

2. Compare this poem to *Encountering Sorrow*. What has changed in the author's self-presentation? Comment on the overall narrative coherence and the development of the poem.

3. Compare the use of imagery in *Encountering Sorrow* with this poem.

4. This poem has left the world of ritual performance; however, might someone have performed this song? Would it have been a private or a public occasion?

The Nine Transformations

This text, traditionally divided into nine sections, is attributed to Song Yu 宋玉, who was believed to have been a student of Qu Yuan. Sima Qian briefly mentions Song Yu in his biography of Qu Yuan, and several important early compositions in the *fu* 賦 ("rhyme-prose" or "exposition") genre were ascribed to him, but he is a shadowy, half-mythological figure at best.

The *Nine Transformations* provides important insight into a "domesticated" Chu style. Its meter is irregular within a general "Chu" format. It is not about the spirit-ridden world of *Encountering Sorrow* and the *Nine Songs*; instead it presents the author confronting a sorrowful but natural landscape. The imagery in *Encountering Sorrow* is allegorical. In the poems of the *Nine Pieces* like "Lament for Ying," the landscape is part of a political and personal geography of loss. In the *Nine Transformations*, in contrast, the images begin to take on a weight of experiential meanings derived from the patterns of seasonal shifts and the weariness of unending travel.

Nine Transformations (first section)[28]

九辯							Nine Transformations
悲 sad	哉 !						Sad indeed,
秋 autumn	之 's	為 become	氣 *qi*	也 it is			the autumn in the air.[29]
蕭 desolate and dreary	瑟	兮 xi!					Desolate and drear,
草 grass	木 tree	搖 quaver	落 fall	而 and	變 transform	衰 [ʂwi] decline	grasses and leaves quaver, fall, and turn to decline.
憭 chill and forlorn	慄	兮 xi!					Chill and forlorn,
若 resemble	在 is at	遠 distant	行 travel				as if on a long journey,[30]
登 climb	山 mountain	臨 overlook	水 water	兮 xi!			Climbing a mountain overlooking a river,
送 see off	將 about to	歸 [kuj] return					One sees off [a friend] about to return.

28. Compare this translation with the one by David Hawkes in *Songs of the South*, pp. 209–10.

29. "Air" is literally *qi*.

30. The commentaries assume that Song Yi *is* on a long journey and thus gloss 若 ("resemble") as 乃 ("thus"). Being on a far journey significantly changes the setting of the poem.

泬	寥	兮						Vast and void,
vast and void		xi!						
天	高	而	氣	清 [tsʰiajng]				The sky is high, and the air is limpid.
sky	high	and	air	pure				
宗	廫	兮						Still and vast,
void and vast		xi!						
收	潦	而	水	清 [tsʰiajng]				the river has received the torrential rains, and the water is clear.
receive	torrent	and	water	pure				
憯	悽	增	欷	兮				Heart-sick and dejected, I sigh yet more:
heartsick	dejected	increase	sigh	xi!				
薄	寒	之	中	人 [ɲin]				the approaching cold strikes into one.
approach	cold	’s	strike	person				
愴	怳	懭	悢	兮				Disappointed, distraught, and discontented:
disappointed		discontented		xi!				
去	故	而	就	新 [sin]				I leave the old and go to the new.
leave	old	and	go to	new				
坎	廩	兮						Afflicted,
frequently	afflicted	xi!						
貧	士	失	職	而	志	不	平 [biajng]	the poor officer has lost his post and his resolve is unsettled.
poor	officer	lost	post	and	resolve	not	level	
廓	落	兮						Desolate,
desolate		xi!						
羇	旅	而	無	友	生 [ʂiajng]			bound to journey long, I am without friends.
harness	travel	and	is without	friend				
惆	悵	兮						With grieving disappointment
grieving	disappointment	xi!						
而	私	自	憐 [lɛn]					I inwardly pity my plight.
and	privately	myself	pity					
燕	翩	翩	其	辭	歸	兮		Swallows flutter as they depart homeward;
swallow	flutter	flutter	its	take leave	return home	xi!		
蟬	宗	漠	而	無	聲 [ɕiajng]			The cicadas are still and silent, without sound.
cicada	still and silent		and	is without	sound			
鴈	廱	廱	而	南	遊	兮		The wild geese call out as they travel southward;
goose	call out		and	south	travel	xi!		
鶤	雞	啁	哳	而	悲	鳴 [miajng]		The partridges twitter and sadly sing.
partridge		twittering		and	sad	sing		
獨	申	旦	而	不	寐	兮		Alone until dawn and not sleeping;
alone	extend to	dawn	and	not	sleep	xi!		

哀	蟋	蟀	之	宵	征 [tɕiajng]		I mourn the crickets' night-time travel.[31]
lament	cricket		's	night	journey		
時	亹	亹	而	過	中	兮	The season passes quickly, already half gone:
season	pass quickly		and	exceed	middle	xi!	
蹇	淹	留	而	無	成 [dʑiajng]		He halts, waiting, with nothing completed.
halt	tarry		and	is without	complete		

Study Notes and Questions

1. This poem is an evocative meditation on autumn. List all the seasonal elements.

2. What is the occasion of the poem, and how does the landscape described by the author intensify the emotions of the occasion?

3. Does this poem follow the principles set forth in the "Mao Preface": is there a resolve that is stirred by external events to produce an emotional response?

31. This image reflects a belief that crickets sang out as they wandered at night.

"The Fisherman"

One of the fascinating aspects of the *Lyrics of Chu* anthology is the way in which its compiler included material directly attacking Qu Yuan's obsessive moral self-understanding. Qu Yuan needed to define himself vis-à-vis his slanderers and his benighted ruler: he could not stand outside these futile commitments. This question of whether one needs to serve the state or if one can just go it alone (especially when one judges the ruler to be unworthy) became a constant theme in later elite culture. "The Fisherman," at the very beginning of the tradition, provides a powerful, enduring counter-statement to Qu Yuan's resolve.

"The Fisherman" 漁父

屈原既放，遊于江潭，行吟澤畔，顏色憔悴，形容枯槁。漁父見而問之曰："子非三閭大夫與？何故至于斯？"屈原曰："舉世皆濁我獨清，眾人皆醉我獨醒，是以見放。"漁父曰："聖人不凝滯于物，而能與世推移。世人皆濁，何不淈其泥而揚其波？眾人皆醉，何不哺其糟而歠其釃？何故深思高舉，自令放為？"屈原曰："吾聞之，新沐者必彈冠，新浴者必振衣。安能以身之察察，受物之汶汶者乎？寧赴湘流，葬于江魚之腹中。安能以皓皓之白，而蒙世俗之塵埃乎？"漁父莞爾而笑，鼓枻而去，

Qu Yuan, having been banished, wandered along the riverbank. He chanted as he walked; his appearance was haggard, his form withered. A fisherman saw him and asked, "Are you not the Minister of the Three Gates? What brings you here?" Qu Yuan replied, "All the world is sullied; I alone am pure. The masses of men are all drunk; I alone am sober, and for this I was banished." The fisherman said, "A sage is not mired in things and can shift with the world. If all the world is sullied, why not stir up the mud and splash the waves? If the masses of men are drunk, why not feed on their lees and drink their dregs? Why must you think deeply, take a lofty stance, and cause yourself to be banished?" Qu Yuan replied, "I have heard that one who has just washed his hair must rap his hat; one who is newly washed must shake his clothes. How can I in my purity accept filthy things? I would rather go to the currents of the Xiang and bury myself in the belly of a river fish. How can I in my brilliant whiteness receive the dirt of vulgar custom?" The fisherman smiled slightly, beat on the side of his boat and left, singing:

歌曰						The song was:
滄 Cang-	浪 lang	之 's	水 water	清 pure	兮 xi! [*N-s-ɾeŋ]	When the waters of the Canglang are pure,
可 can be	以 use	濯 wash	吾 my	纓 hatstring [*ʔeŋ]		they can be used to wash my hatstring.
滄 Cang-	浪 lang	之 's	水 water	濁 dirty	兮 xi! [*N-tˤrok]	When the waters of the Canglang are dirty,
可 can be	以 use	濯 wash	吾 my	足 foot [*[ts]ok]		they can be used to wash my feet.

遂去，不復與言。

He then left and did not speak to Qu Yuan again.

Chapter Four

Poetry in the Han, Wei, and Jin Dynasties

During the late Eastern Han, literati began to use five-character song forms to write poetry. Much of this verse expressed very general themes of longing and the hardships of travel that were part of the popular poetry of the day. However, a very talented group of writers primarily associated with the great warlord Cao Cao and his son Cao Pi 曹丕 (187–226) took an extraordinary step beyond these generic compositions. Relying on the venerable model of the *Canon of Poetry*, they began to use the five-character form to write very personal poems in response to the painful events of their times. They discovered that these poems gave them a powerful tool for self-presentation that, as it proved, endured for centuries. While continuing to use four-character and Chu song forms, literati in the next century adopted five-character verse and began to experiment with formal and rhetorical techniques to extend the range of its representational possibilities.

The origins of this pentasyllabic (five-character) song in the popular culture of the mid-Han dynasty have proven difficult to trace. A few alleged early examples are clearly forgeries: they are quite wonderful forgeries, but fakes nonetheless. Contemporary scholars point to the folk songs that survive from the Han and to the manner in which pentasyllabic segments appear within more elaborate suites of songs that comprised performance sets. The earliest Han dynasty folk poetry is called *yuefu*, or "Music Bureau," poetry. Han dynasty court scholars believed that during the Zhou dynasty, the officials of the Music Bureau were sent into the countryside to record the songs of the day to assess the success of imperial policies. Emperor Wu, emulating this model, commissioned his Music Bureau to do the same. However, because courtiers began planting songs supporting themselves and attacking enemies, the effort was soon abandoned. Still, scholars in successor dynasties believed that the Han folk poems that had survived in written form were preserved through the efforts of the officials in the Music Bureau. Many of the early texts are short and in irregular meters.

There are also many poems in pentasyllabic verse, like "Watering My Horse by the Great Wall," which are of uncertain authenticity and may date from the Han but probably are of later origin (at least in the forms we have them). We do not know whether the surviving pentasyllabic songs—if they are related to Han compositions—had an original performance context consisting of a suite of songs in various meters that was lost long ago. Despite the textual problems, it seems in any case that by the late Han, five-character verse had become independent of any framing suite and that elite writers had begun to take an interest in the form; the so-called "Nineteen Old Poems" surely are literati versions of the pentasyllabic song forms that were popular at the very end of the dynasty. Their themes make them suitable for performance in convivial settings, and the poems seem to be closely linked with their origins in song. The writers in Cao Cao's group during the Jian'an reign period at the end of the Han crafted poems essentially identical to the "Nineteen Old Poems" and also wrote poems using *yuefu* titles. These compositions presumably were set to tunes and performed. However, whether these writers also composed their more serious and personal poems as songs to be sung is unclear and seems unlikely to me. I cannot imagine an occasion when Wang Can might think the first of his "Seven Laments" appropriate for performance.

The step from social performance to semi-private composition seems strange until we see these poems as the extension of a tradition in which the poems of the *Canon of Poetry* were read as morally informed personal responses to intense encounters. Why write in "Seven Laments" about a peasant mother abandoning her child? It is not a "poetic" topic, for it has a quality of specificity very different from such generic lines as "White bones covered the wild plains." Is the wrenching event a symbol created out of Wang Can's imagination, or are we to assume that in fact the author actually witnessed it? The model of the *Canon of Poetry* suggests that we should take the incident as more-or-less real: Wang Can was deeply moved and found himself compelled to write about it. In writing in the *Shijing* mode, moreover, he found he could articulate his own moral convictions as they intertwined with his emotional responses. Why did he do this? There is, of course, the possibility of an ulterior motive: writing as articulating the inner meaning of events always presents the possibility of manipulating one's self-presentation for the sake of an audience. Surely Cao Zhi 曹植 (192–232), for example, crafted his verse-letter to his brother Cao Biao 曹彪 (195–251) knowing full well that it would be read by Cao Pi, their brother and the newly enthroned, very suspicion-ridden emperor of the Wei dynasty. Yet Cao Zhi's poem series is not a polite fiction constructed for Cao Pi's sake. It deals with hard issues and risks self-exposure at a very dangerous moment. Cao Pi himself explained what was at stake in his "Discourse on Literature." He proclaimed:

> Glory and pleasure go no further than this mortal body. To extend both of these to all time, nothing can compare with the unending permanence of a work of literature. It was for this reason that writers of ancient times gave their lives to the ink and brush and revealed what they thought in their writings. Without recourse to a good historian or dependence on a powerful patron, their reputations have been passed on to posterity on their own force.[1]

In a world of turmoil and decay, literature—and poetry in particular—can preserve the self.

1. The translation is from Owen, *An Anthology of Chinese Literature*, p. 361. See the full translation in the appendix at the end of this chapter.

Anonymous Poetry from the Music Bureau

"There Is One I Long For"

有所思					There Is One I Long For
有	所	思			There is one I long for,
there-is	what	long-for			
乃	在	大	海	南 [nam]	Who is to the south of the Great Sea.
and	is-at	great	sea	south	
何	用	問	遺	君	With what should I inquire of you?
what	use	ask	leave-to	you	
雙	珠	瑇	瑁	簪 [tsam]	A pair of pearl and tortoise-shell hair pins,
pair	pearl	tortoise-shell		hair-pin	
用	玉	紹	繚	之 [lɛw]	With jade to wrap around it.
use	jade	wrap around		it	
聞	君	有	他	心	I hear that your mind has thoughts of another.
hear	you	there-is	other	heart	
拉	雜	摧	燒	之 [ɕiaw]	I will pull it apart, shatter and burn it.
pull	admix	shatter	burn	it	
摧	燒	之			Shatter and burn it,
shatter	burn	it			
當	風	揚	其	灰 [xwəj]	And let the wind carry away the ashes.
be-at	wind	lift	its	ash	
從	今	以	往		From now on,
from	now	use	go forward		
勿	復	相	思 [si]		I will not again long for you.
don't	again	[d.o.]	long-for		
相	思	與	君	絕	My longings will be cut off from you,
[d.o.]	long-for	with	you	cut-off	
雞	鳴	狗	吠 [buaj^h]		As the cock crows and dogs bark,
chicken	call	dog	bark		
兄	嫂	當	知	之 [tri]	My elder brother's wife surely will know of this.
brother	wife	ought	know	it	
妃	呼	狶			Ah, oh, alas,
ah	oh	alas			

秋	風	肅	肅	晨	風	颸 [tʂʰi]	The autumn wind gusts, the pheasant [calls out] in longing.[2]
autumn	wind	rustle-rustle		morning-wind		long-for	
東	方	須	臾	高	知	之 [tri]	The east will soon be bright, and I will know it.
east	region	soon		high	know	it	

STEPHEN OWEN'S TRANSLATION

The One I Love

The one I love
is south of the sea.
What gift can I send him?—
a hair-clasp of tortoise shell,
  set with paired pearls,
and wound all about with jade.

Then I heard that his heart had changed,
I broke it and burned it in a pile,
broke and burned it,
threw the ash to the wind.
From this day on,
no more longing, no more love,
my love for him is done.

When roosters crow and the dogs all bark,
my brother, his wife will know,
tra-la-la,
the autumn winds howl, the pheasants shrill,
soon the east will grow bright
  and all will be known.

STUDY NOTES AND QUESTIONS

1. Comparing early Chinese "folk poetry," even if it is an elite imitation of folk models, to the lyrics of American popular songs seems to me hard to resist. Many early Chinese laments mine the same materials—jealousy, longing, regret, the desire to forget for just this night—that are the staples of country and Western and blues. Do the modern Western counterparts share the sort of discontinuity between the second and third stanzas of "There Is One I Long For"? How do you explain the final stanza?

2. The phrase "morning-wind" appears to represent "pheasant." The character 颸 is "wind" 風 + "long for" 思, and is taken simply to mean "long for."

2. The pearls and the tortoise-shell hair pin signify wealth: do they imply a high-born audience or perhaps one with merely enough contact with elite culture to dream of being so extravagant as to destroy such objects of value in a fit of pique?

"Oh, Above"

上邪							Oh, Above!
上 above	邪 "!?"						Oh, Above!
我 I	欲 want	與 with	君 you	相 mutual	知 [tri] know		I want to get to know you,
長 long	命 fate	無 not-exist	絕 cut-off	衰 [ʂwi] decline			Eternally decreed without end or decline.
山 mountain	無 not-exist	陵 peak					When the mountains are without peaks,
江 river	水 water	為 make	竭 [giat] use-up				The river waters run dry,
冬 winter	雷 thunder	震 rumble-rumble	震	夏 summer	雨 rain	雪 [swiat] snow	Winter thunder rumbles, and snow falls in summer,
天 heaven	地 earth	合 combine					When Heaven and Earth collapse together,
乃 then	敢 dare	與 with	君 you	絕 [dzwiat] cut-off			Only then would I dare to break with you.

Stephen Owen's Translation

Heaven Above

By Heaven above,
I will be your true love,
let it be forever and never wane.
When hills no longer rise,
when the river's water dries,
when winter thunder rolls,
and snow in summer falls,
when sky and earth fuse,
I'll stop loving you.

Study Notes and Questions

1. Note that in the first full line, the speaker *wishes* to become acquainted with the object of her undying affection. How does that opening line frame the poem?

2. Does it make a difference if lines 4 and 5 are in reality a single line with a 3 + 4 caesura break to match the sixth line ("Winter thunder rumbles, and snow falls in summer") and create a rhyming couplet? I take line 6 as one long line, but it could also could be a pair of shorter lines (4 + 3), so that there would be an ABCB rhyme scheme. Note the parallelism in these lines: "mountain" matches "water" in lines 4 and 5, while "winter" matches "summer" in the two halves of line 6. Should this latter pairing be an argument for taking line 6 as being in fact two lines?

3. Note the prosiness of the language. The first line (我**欲與**君**相**知, "I want to get to know you") and the last (**乃**敢**與**君絕, "Only then would I dare to break with you") in particular use essentially prose syntax and are filled with grammatical function words, marked in a bold font. What is the relation between this prosiness and the qualities of simplicity and directness that later readers admired in the poem?

"A Ballad: Watering My Horse by the Great Wall"

飲馬長城窟行					A Ballad: Watering My Horse by the Great Wall
青 luxuriantly	青 green	河 river	畔 bank	草 [ts^{h}aw’] grass	Flourishing green is the riverbank grass.
綿 long and tangled	綿	思 longing	遠 distant	道 [daw’] road	Ceaselessly I long for [the one on] the distant road.
遠 distant	道 road	不 not	可 can be	思 [si] long for	[The one on] the distant road cannot be longed for.
宿 overnight	昔 formerly	夢 dream	見 see	之 [tɕi] her/him	Last night I dreamed of him.[3]
夢 dream	見 see	在 be at	我 my	傍 [baŋ] side	I dreamed I saw him by my side.
忽 suddenly	覺 awake	在 be at	他 other	鄉 [xɨaŋ] region	Suddenly I awoke: [he was] in another region.
他 other	鄉 region	各 each	異 differ	縣 [ɣwɛn^{h}] county	Another region: each in a different district.
展 toss-and-turn	轉	不 not	相 mutually	見 kɛn^{h}] see	Tossing and turning, I cannot see him.
枯 withered	桑 mulberry	知 know	天 sky	風 wind	From the withered mulberries, I know the sky is windy;
海 sea	水 water	知 know	天 sky	寒 [ɣan] cold	From the sea's water, I know the sky is cold.
入 enter	門 gate	各 each	自 self	媚 adore	On entering one's gate, each cherishes his own:
誰 who	肯 willing	相 [d.o.]	為 for sake	言 [ŋɨan] speak	Who is willing to convey word to him for me?
客 traveler	從 from	遠 distant	方 place	來 come	A traveler come from a distant land,
遺 leave	我 me	雙 pair	鯉 carp	魚 [ŋɨă] fish	Leaves me a pair of carp.[4]
呼 call	兒 boy	烹 boil	鯉 carp	魚 [ŋɨă] fish	I call the boy to boil the carp.
中 middle	有 there is	尺 chi	素 white silk	書 [ɕɨə̆] letter	In its middle there is a letter on a foot-long piece of white silk.
長 long	跪 kneel	讀 read	素 white silk	書 [ɕɨə̆] letter	Kneeling erect, I read the silk letter.

3. Commentaries treat 昔 ("formerly") as 夕 ("night").

4. The commentaries want this "pair of carp" to be a carp-shaped case for carrying letters.

書 letter	中 middle	竟 in the end	何 what	如 [ɲɨɔ̆] resemble	What is in the letter?
上 top	言 say	加 add	餐 meal	食 [ʑik] eat	At the beginning, it tells me to eat well.
下 bottom	言 say	長 long	相 mutual	憶 [ʔik] recall	At the end he says he will always keep thinking of me.

STEPHEN OWEN'S TRANSLATION

Watering My Horse by the Great Wall

Green, green the grass by the river,
thoughts on far travels go on and on.
I can't bear to think on his travels,
I saw him last night in my dreams,
in dream I saw him right by my side,
when I woke, he was off in another land,
in another land and a different place,
I tossed and turned and saw him no more.
The mulberry, bare, knows Heaven's wind,
the ocean's waters know Heaven's cold.
Whoever comes shows love for his own,
and no one wants to comfort me.

A stranger came from a far-off land,
and gave me a paired-carp letter case;
I called for the boy to cook the carp
and in it I found the letter.
I read the letter on my knees,
and what did the letter say?—

It began, "Take care of yourself,"
and ended, "I love you forever."

STUDY NOTES AND QUESTIONS

1. The beginning of the poem, after the first line, is a tightly integrated progression. How does the first line fit in? Is it a *xing* 興, an affective image, in the manner of the poems of the *Canon of Poetry*?

2. Later commentaries want to explain the "carp" as a carp-shaped letter case (note also the assumption of the wife's literacy), but the wife orders the carp cooked and takes the letter from within the carp. This puzzle points to a world not fully understood, but does it add to or detract from the poem?

3. What is the effect of the repetition in the poem that connects the last phrase of one rhyming couplet with the first phrase of the next?

Early Pentasyllabic Poetry

From the Series "Nineteen Old Poems"

古詩十九首第一 / Nineteen Old Poems, no. 1

行 travel	行 travel	重 again	行 travel	行 travel	Traveling on and on, on and on, on and on:
與 with	君 you	生 alive	別 part	離 [li] separate	Living parted from you.
相 mutually	去 leave	萬 10,000	餘 plus	里 [li'] *li*	Having gone more than ten thousand *li* from one another,
各 each	在 is at	天 sky	一 one	涯 [ngɛːj] shore	Each is at one edge of the sky.
道 path	路 road	阻 blocked	且 and	長 long	The road is hard and long.
會 meet	面 face	安 how	可 can be	知 [tri] know	How can we know when we shall meet again?
胡 Hu	馬 horse	依 leans	北 north	風 wind	The Hu horse leans to the north wind.[5]
越 Yue	鳥 bird	巢 nests	南 south	枝 [tɕi] branch	The Yue bird nests in the southern branches.[6]
相 mutually	去 leave	日 day	已 already	遠 [wuan'] far	Each day we are further apart.
衣 clothes	帶 belt	日 day	已 already	緩 [ɣwan'] loose	Each day my clothes and belt grow looser.
浮 float	雲 cloud	蔽 block	白 white	日 sun	Floating clouds block the white sun.
遊 wander	子 son	不 not	顧 look	返 [puan'] return	The wandering one does not look to return.
思 long for	君 you	令 makes	人 person	老 [law'] old	Thinking of you makes one old.
歲 year	月 month	忽 suddenly	已 already	晚 [muan'] late	The year suddenly has grown old.
棄 reject	損 harm	勿 do not	復 again	道 [daw'] say	"Rejected," don't say again:
努 exert	力 strength	加 add	餐 meal	飯 [buan'] eat	Exert yourself to eat well.[7]

5. The Hu are specifically *northern* barbarians.

6. Yue (Yüeh in Wade-Giles romanization) is a southern region.

BURTON WATSON'S TRANSLATION

On and on, going on and on,
away from you to live apart,
ten thousand *li* and more between us,
each at opposite ends of the sky.
The road I travel is steep and long;
who knows when we meet again?
The Hu horse leans into the north wind;
the Yüeh bird nests in southern branches:
day by day our parting grows more distant;
day by day robe and belt dangle looser.
Shifting clouds block the white sun;
the traveler does not look to return.
Thinking of you makes one old;
years and months suddenly go by.
Abandoned, I will say no more
but pluck up strength and eat my fill.

STUDY NOTES AND QUESTIONS

1. This poem proved very influential in the later tradition as a model of aesthetically compelling simplicity. The language, imagery, and sentiments are indeed all very simple, yet consider the structure of the poem. Consider the transition from one couplet to the next, how the poem presents and develops its themes in a pattern of repetition that is by no means simple.

2. Later poets especially tried to capture the effect of the first line. What is the effect of the repetition?

3. Going word by word, explain the parallelism of the couplet about the Hu horse and the Yue bird.

---

7. Watson interprets these last two lines quite differently. He removes the quotation marks from "Rejected," to get the lines "Abandoned, I will say no more / but pluck up strength and eat my fill."

From the Series "Nineteen Old Poems"

古詩十九首第二					Nineteen Old Poems, no. 2
青	青	河	畔	草	Green, green is the riverbank grass,
green	green	river	shore	grass	
鬱	鬱	園	中	柳 [luw']	Densely flourishing is the garden willow.
dense	dense	garden	middle	willow	
盈	盈	樓	上	女	Elegant is the woman in the tower,[8]
elegant		tower	on	woman	
皎	皎	當	窗	牖 [juw']	Brightly gleaming next to the window.
moon-bright		just-at	window	frame	
娥	娥	紅	粉	妝	Alluring is her make-up of rouge and powder.
alluring	alluring	red	powder	make-up	
纖	纖	出	素	手 [ɕuw']	Slender: she extends her white hand.
slender	slender	come-out	white-silk	hand	
昔	為	倡	家	女	Before she was a girl in a singing house;
formerly	enact	singer	household	woman	
今	為	蕩	子	婦 [buw']	Now she is the wife of a rover.
now	enact	wander	person	wife	
蕩	子	行	不	歸	The rover travels and does not return,
wander	person	travel	not	return	
空	床	難	獨	守 [ɕuw']	An empty bed is hard to maintain alone.
empty	bed	hard-to	alone	guard	

Arthur Waley's Translation

Green, green,
The grass by the river-bank.
Thick, thick,
The willow trees in the garden.
Sad, sad,
The lady in the tower.
White, white,
Sitting at the casement window.
Fair, fair,
Her red-powdered face.
Small, small,
She puts out her pale hand.
Once she was a dancing-house girl,

---

8. The commentaries take *ying ying* 盈盈 to be the same as *ying ying* 嬴嬴 ("elegant").

Now she is a wandering man's wife.
The wandering man went, but did not return.
It is hard alone to keep an empty bed.

Study Notes and Questions

1. This poem seems strongly tied to musical performance. What is the effect of the series of six "reduplicatives," or pairs of repeated characters? Such pairs usually function as adjectives or stative verbs, but here, at the beginning of each line, they serve as focal topics.

2. Think of this poem as a performance by a female singer. The translations present the poem in the third person, but there are no pronouns in the Chinese. Could it be in the first person? How would first-person presentation change the first part of the poem? How would it change the end?

From the Series "Nineteen Old Poems"

古詩十九首第五					Nineteen Old Poems, no. 5
西	北	有	高	樓	To the northwest there is a tall tower;
west	north	exists	tall	tower	
上	與	浮	雲	齊 [dzεj]	Its top is even with the drifting clouds.
upper	with	float	cloud	even	
交	疏	結	綺	窗	Silk screens the patterned carving of the window;
crossed	carved	tie	silk	window	
阿	閣	三	重	階 [kε:j]	The deep-eaved tower is of three stories.
corner-eave	tower	three	again	story	
上	有	絃	歌	聲	At its top: the sound of voice and string:
upper	exist	string	song	sound	
音	響	一	何	悲 [pi]	The resonant sound is oh so sorrowful.
tone	echo	one	"?"	sad	
誰	能	為	此	曲	Who could have made this tune?
who	can	make	this	tune	
無	乃	杞	梁	妻 [ts^{h}εj]	Is it not Qi Zhi's wife.[9]
won't be	then	Qi	Liang	wife	
清	商	隨	風	發	The clear *shang*-mode comes on the wind.[10]
clear	shang	follow	wind	emit	

9. Qi Zhi, with a capping name of Liang, was a person of the Spring and Autumn period. When he died in battle, his wife wrote a number of songs for the zither to lament his death. After writing the songs, she threw herself into the river and drowned.

10. *Shang* is one of the five modes for music in early China: it corresponds to autumn.

中	曲	正	徘	徊 [ɣwɛj]	At the middle of the tune, it tarries.
middle	tune	just-now	pace-pace		
一	彈	再	三	歎	One pluck and three sighs:
one	pluck	again	three	sigh	
慷	慨	有	餘	哀 [ʔɛj]	Deeply moving, it has an excess of lament.
deeply moved		exist	excess	sorrow	
不	惜	歌	者	苦	I do not grieve at the bitter sadness of the singer;
not	regret	song	-er	suffer	
但	傷	知	音	稀 [xɨj]	I am just wounded that those who can "recognize the sound" are few.
only	harm	know	tone	few	
願	為	雙	鴻	鵠	I pray we may become a pair of swans,
make vow	make	pair	swan	goose	
奮	翅	起	高	飛 [puj]	With a stir of pinions, rising to fly on high.
bestir	pinion	rise	high	fly	

Burton Watson's Translation

Northwest the tall tower stands,
its top level with floating clouds,
patterned windows webbed in lattice,
roofs piled three stories high.
From above, the sound of strings and song;
what sadness in that melody!
Who could play a tune like this,
who but the wife of Ch'i Liang?
The clear *shang* mode drifts down the wind;
halfway through, it falters and breaks,
one plucking, two or three sighs,
longing, a grief that lingers on—
It is not the singer's pain I pity,
but few are those who understand the song!
If only we could be a pair of calling cranes,
beating wings, soaring to the sky!

Study Notes and Questions

1. What is the gender of the speaker of the poem? Given an assumed elite male audience, what difference does it make if the speaker is female or male?

2. Transitions often are abrupt in early poems. The first twelve lines present a coherent account, but then the perspective shifts. What is the effect of this turn in the next couplet?

3. What is the quality of the speaker's lamenting the woman's lack of an understanding friend? Is it agitated? rueful? resigned? How does the wish of the final couplet offer a response to the speaker's regret? How does this ending work as the conclusion of a performance?

From the Series "Nineteen Old Poems"

古詩十九首第十五					Nineteen Old Poems, no.15
生 live	年 year	不 not	滿 fill	百 100	The years of our lives do not fill out 100,
常 always	懷 cherish	千 1000	歲 year	憂 [ʔuw] sorrow	Yet we always harbor sorrows of a thousand years.
晝 daytime	短 short	苦 suffer	夜 night	長 long	The days are short, and we grieve that nights are long.
何 "?"	不 not	秉 hold	燭 candle	遊 [juw] wander	Why not go roaming with candle in hand?
為 enact	樂 joy	當 ought	及 arrive-at	時 season	Making merry, we should seize the moment.
何 "?"	能 can	待 wait	來 come	茲 [tsi] this	How can we wait for the coming year?
愚 dolt	者 -thing	愛 love	惜 concern	費 spend	The foolish regret the expense,
但 only	為 enact	後 after	世 generation	嗤 [tɕʰi] jeer	But are just jeered at by later generations.
仙 immortal	人 person	王 Wang	子 Zi-	喬 -qiao	The immortal Wang Ziqiao:[11]
難 hard	可 can	與 with	等 equal	期 [gi] expect	We cannot expect to attain an equal [fate].

Burton Watson's Translation

Man's years fall short of a hundred;
a thousand years of worry crowd his heart.
If the day is short and you hate the long night,
why not take the torch and go wandering?

11. According to the *Biographies of Immortals* (*Liexian zhuan* 列仙傳), a Western Han work attributed to Liu Xiang, Wang Ziqiao was the heir apparent to King Ling of Zhou. He excelled in music and practiced proto-Daoist longevity techniques on Mt. Song before eventually ascending as an immortal. "Immortals" in early Chinese culture were adepts who, by mastering certain arts of refining the physical form and *qi*, transcended death.

Seek out happiness in season;
who can wait the year to come?
Fools who cling too fondly to gold
earn no more than posterity's jeers.
Prince Ch'iao, that immortal man—
small hope we have of matching him!

Study Notes and Questions

1. The theme of the poem is *carpe diem*, "seize the day." What action does it urge? Is the song appropriate for a gathering of friends?

2. Once again, does it make any difference if the speaker of the poem is male or female?

From the Series "Nineteen Old Poems"

古詩十九首第十九					Nineteen Old Poems, no. 19
明 bright	月 moon	何 how	皎 gleam	皎 gleam	How radiant is the bright moon:
照 shine	我 my	羅 net	床 bed	幃 [wuj] curtain	It brightens my gauze bed curtain.
憂 sorrow	愁 sad	不 not	能 able	寐 sleep	Worried and sad, I cannot sleep.
攬 pull	衣 clothes	起 rise	徘 pace	徊 [ɣwəj] pace	Gathering up my clothes, I rise to pace.[12]
客 traveler	行 travel	雖 though	云 said	樂 happy	Although it is said a traveler's journey is joyful,
不 not	如 resemble	早 early	旋 turn	歸 [kuj] return	It cannot compare with an early return home.
出 go out	戶 door	獨 alone	彷 pace	徨 [ɣwang] pace	Going out the door, alone, I walk back and forth:
愁 sad	思 longing	當 ought	告 inform	誰 [dʑwi] who	My sad longings, to whom should I speak them?
引 pull	領 neck	還 return	入 enter	房 [buang] chamber	Straining to look, I return to my chamber:
淚 tears	下 go down	沾 wet	裳 clothes	衣 [ʔɨj] clothes	Tears fall, wetting my garments.[13]

12. In early China, clothing was long enough to impede movement. So the narrator of the poem has to gather up his or her clothes before walking.

13. Some texts switch 衣 ("upper clothing") and 裳 ("lower clothing") so that 裳 [dʑɨang] rhymes with 房 [buang].

Arthur Waley's Translation

The bright moon, oh, how white it shines,
Shines down on the gauze curtains of my bed.
Racked by sorrow I toss and cannot sleep.
Picking up my clothes, I wander up and down.
My absent love says that he is happy,
But I would rather he said he was coming back.
Out in the courtyard I stand hesitating, alone.
To whom can I tell the sad thoughts I think?
Staring before me I enter my room again;
Falling tears wet my mantle and robe.

Study Notes and Questions

1. How do you know the speaker of the poem is a woman?

2. This poem is a very influential "boudoir lament," a woman's expression of sadness and longing for a husband compelled to travel. Why would the performance of such a poem be popular?

Poets of the Jian'an Reign Period

Cao Cao 曹操 *(155–220)*

Cao Cao established his reputation as a shrewd leader through his role in suppressing the Yellow Turban uprising in the late Han dynasty. In 189, generals in the Eastern Han capital, Luoyang, summoned the border general Dong Zhuo 董卓 in an effort to wrest control from court eunuchs. The eunuchs struck first, but Dong Zhuo's battle-hardened troops arrived, eliminated the eunuchs, put a new emperor on the throne, and moved the capital to Chang'an in the west. In the meantime, Cao Cao, having left Luoyang, raised his own troops and created a regional power base. In 192 Dong Zhuo was assassinated, and in 196 Cao Cao persuaded the emperor to move the capital yet again, to the city of Xuchang, where Cao Cao could keep an eye on his ruler, who was not much more than a puppet monarch under his control. Cao Cao gradually solidified his control over north China. In 208 he became prime minister to the emperor and led a large army south to attack the forces of Sun Quan 孫權 (182–252) and Liu Bei 劉備 (161–223), the warlords who controlled south China. Cao Cao famously was defeated at the Battle of Red Cliff and had to abandon his hope of reestablishing a unified empire. He died before his son Cao Pi deposed the last Han emperor and established the Wei dynasty in north China, but Cao Pi gave him the posthumous title of "Martial Emperor of the Wei" (Wei Wudi 魏武帝).

Cao Cao strongly advocated the policy of advancing those with ability regardless of hereditary status and worked to remove the entrenched aristocratic lineages that clung to power as the Han dynasty collapsed. He was an excellent judge of talent and gathered an impressive coterie of writers to his side. These writers, including his sons Cao Zhi and Cao Pi, as well as Wang Can, Chen Lin, and Xu Gan, established pentasyllabic verse as an important elite poetic form. The later tradition looked back to the "Jian'an style"—named for the Jian'an 建安 reign period (196–219), the last reign period of the Han dynasty—as capturing strong responses to stirring events with simple yet elegant and powerful language.[14] Although Cao Cao as a writer primarily excelled at the older styles of *yuefu* ballads, he was also able to use the new five-character verse form effectively.

14. Cao Pi's "A Discourse on Literature" (translated as an appendix at the end of this chapter) commemorated the group of writers in his father's entourage and helped to define the Jian'an regin period as a distinctive moment in literary history.

"Ballad of Bramble Village" by Cao Cao

蒿里行					Ballad of Bramble Village[15]
關	東	有	義	士	East of the pass, there are righteous officers:[16]
pass	east	exist	righteous	officer	
興	兵	討	群	凶 [xuawŋ]	[They] raise troops to attack the gathered evil ones.
raise	weapon	attack	flock	evil-ones	
初	期	會	盟	津	At first, they expected a meeting like Meng Ford,[17]
at-first	expect	meet	Meng	ford	
乃	心	在	咸	陽 [jiaŋ]	Yet their thoughts were on Xianyang.[18]
and then	heart	is at	Xian-	yang	
軍	合	力	不	齊	[Although] the armies united, [their] strength was not coordinated.
army	unite	strength	not	even	
躊	躇	而	雁	行 [ɣaŋ]	Pacing uncertain and traveling undirected.
pace back and forth		and	goose	travel	
勢	利	使	人	爭	The disposition of advantage caused men to compete:
disposition	advantage	cause	people	compete	
嗣	還	自	相	戕 [dziaŋ]	Soon after, [they] were killing one another.
soon thereafter		self-	mutual	kill	
淮	南	弟	稱	號	South of the Huai, the younger brother proclaimed his reign:[19]
Huai	south	brother	proclaim	reign-title	
刻	璽	於	北	方 [puaŋ]	[They] carved an imperial seal in the northern region.[20]
carve	imperial seal	at	north	region	
鎧	甲	生	蟣	虱	Our armor grew lice,
armor	plate	born	larva	louse	
萬	姓	以	死	亡 [muaŋ]	The populace thus died or fled.
10,000	surname	use	die	flee	
白	骨	露	於	野	White bones were exposed on the plains.
white	bone	expose	at	wild field	

15. In 190, generals from eastern China gathered to fight Dong Zhuo, who reportedly intended to depose the reigning emperor. They picked Yuan Shao as their leader. However, internal dissension never ceased. The title of the poem, "Ballad of Bramble Village" is a *yuefu* title for a coffin-pulling song. According to one explanation, "Bramble Village" was a village of the dead. Cao Cao here does not appear to be drawing upon the origin of the song but uses it simply as a *yuefu* tune.

16. This is the Han'gu Pass between Chang'an, which Dong Zhuo had made the capital, and eastern China.

17. This is where King Wu of Zhou, the founder of the Zhou, met with other leaders to foment rebellion against the Shang dynasty.

18. Xianyang, near Chang'an, was the Qin capital. Here, however, it stands in for Chang'an itself.

19. Yuan Shu, Yuan Shao's half-brother, declared himself emperor in Shouchun (once a capital of Chu) in 197.

20. Yuan Shao planned to have Li Yu, the Protector of Youzhou in the north, declared emperor in 191.

千 1000	里 *li*	無 not exist	雞 chicken	鳴 [miajŋ] call out	For a thousand *li*, there was not a cock crowing.
生 born	民 populace	百 100	遺 leave	一 one	Of our populace, one in a hundred remained.
念 recall	之 it	斷 break	人 people	腸 [driaŋ] innards	Thinking of this rends one's vitals.

Meow Hui Goh's Translation

Wormwood Village Song

East of the pass were righteous men;
They raised troops to assail the bands of outlaws.
At the beginning they gathered at the Ford of Alliance,
Their hearts set firmly on Xianyang.
Their armies united but their strength uneven;
Unsteadily, they advanced in geese formation.
Power and profit brought rivalry among men;
One's descendants turned against each another.
In Huainan, a younger brother claimed a title;
While in the north an imperial signet was engraved.
Armors were left to breed nits and lice;
Ten thousand people had perished.
White bones lay exposed in the wild;
Across a thousand *li*, no sound of cock's crow.
Among the living, one out of a hundred remains—
Brooding on it severs one's bowels!

Study Notes and Questions

1. Perhaps the most fascinating aspect of this poem is its very existence. Cao Cao here uses a *yuefu* title to write about very serious matters. Who would have been his audience? What would have been the advantage of setting his criticism of the behavior of the generals to music?

2. Note how the poem reworks a well-established opening: "East of the Pass there are righteous officials." What other parts of the poem use language or tropes seen elsewhere in Han five-character verse?

"Short Ballad" by Cao Cao

短歌行				Short Ballad
對 face	酒 ale	當 just at	歌 [ka] sing	Facing ale, as I sing:
人 people	生 life	幾 how many	何 [ɣa] "?"	How long is human life?
譬 compare	如 resemble	朝 dawn	露 dew	It is like the morning dew;
去 leave	日 day	苦 suffer	多 [ta] many	My departed days are painfully many.
慨 move	當 ought	以 use	慷 [kʰaŋ] feel deeply	One should feel what moves one deeply;
憂 sad	思 longing	難 difficult	忘 [muaŋ] forget	Sad thoughts are impossible to forget.
何 "?"	以 use	解 cut	憂 sad	How can one dispel sadness?
唯 only	有 exist	杜 Du	康 [kʰaŋ] Kang	There is only Du Kang's [brew].[21]
青 green	青 green	子 master	衿 [kim] collar	"Blue, blue is his collar:
悠 distant-longing	悠	我 I	心 [sim] mind	Longing, longing is my heart."[22]
但 only	為 for	君 you	故 reason	Only for your sake,
沈 sink	吟 chant	至 arrive	今 [kim] now	Do I chant quietly to this moment.
呦 "Yo"	呦 "Yo"	鹿 deer	鳴 [miajŋ] call out	"Yo, yo cries the deer,
食 eat	野 wild field	之 's	苹 [biajŋ] vegetation	As it eats the greens of the wilds.
我 I	有 exist	嘉 fine	賓 guest	I have a fine guest:
鼓 beat	瑟 zither	吹 blow	笙 [ʂiajŋ] "reed-organ"	Play the zither and blow the reed-organ."[23]

21. Du Kang supposedly was the first brewer of ale.

22. This couplet is a direct quote from "Your Collar"《子衿》, Mao 91 in the *Canon of Poetry*.

23. These four lines are taken directly from "The Deer Calls Out"《鹿鳴》, Mao 161 in the *Canon of Poetry*.

明 bright	明 bright	如 resemble	月 [ŋuat] moon	Bright, bright like the moon:
何 "?"	時 season	可 can be	輟 [trwiat] stop	When can it be stopped?
憂 sad	從 from	中 middle	來 come	Sorrow comes from within:
不 not	可 can be	斷 break	絕 [dzwiat] cut-off	It cannot be brought to cease.
越 surpass	陌 path	度 cross	阡 [ts^{h}ɛn] field-path	Crossing the paths, passing over the trails,
枉 err	用 use	相 [d.o.]	存 [dzwən] inquire	[You] have errantly come to ask of me.
契 meet after separation	闊	談 chat	讌 banquet	Meeting after long parting, we talk and banquet:
心 mind	念 recall	舊 old	恩 [ʔən] kindness	My mind recalls [your] former kindness.
月 moon	明 bright	星 star	稀 [xij] few	The moon is bright; the stars few.
烏 rook	鵲 magpie	南 south	飛 [puj] fly	The magpie flies south:
繞 circle	樹 tree	三 three	匝 circuit	It circles the tree three times
何 "?"	枝 branch	可 can be	依 [ʔij] rest-on	On what branch can it rest?
山 mountain	不 not	厭 sate	高 high	The mountain is not sated in its height;
海 sea	不 not	厭 sate	深 [ɕim] deep	The sea is not sated in its depth.[24]
周 Zhou	公 Duke	吐 spit	哺 chew	The Duke of Zhou spat out his food:[25]
天 sky	下 below	歸 return	心 [sim] mind	The realm's mind turned [to him].

24. This couplet seems to derive from the book of political philosophy *Guan Zi*《管子・形勢解》, in which the enlightened leader never tires of searching for men of talent, just as the sea never turns water back and mountains never cast away stones: 「海不辭水，故能成其大。山不辭土石，故能成其高。明主不厭人，故能成其眾。士不厭學，故能成其聖。」

25. In both the *Records of the Grand Historian* and the *Unofficial Commentary to the Han Poetry* (*Han shi waizhuan* 韓詩外傳), the Duke of Zhou, sage brother to King Wu of Zhou, states, "Having just started washing my hair, or having just started chewing my food, I would rise to attend upon officers because I still was afraid to lose one of the worthies of the realm." 「一沐三握髮，一飯三吐哺，起以待士，猶恐失天下之賢人。」

Stephen Owen's Translation

Short Song

The wine before me as I sing:
how long can a man's life last?
I liken it to morning's dew,
and the days now past are too many.
The feeling is strong in me,
brooding thoughts I can't ignore.
How can I banish melancholy?—
by Du Kang's gift of wine.

"Blue, blue are your gown's folds,
ever you are in my heart,"
and only because of you,
my concerns keep on till now.
"*Yoo, yoo* cry the deer,
eating the shoots in the meadow:
Worthy guests are here with me
so play the harp and blow the pipes."

Bright and full is the moon—
when will its passage cease?
cares come from deep within,
nor can they be halted.
You crossed the paths and lanes,
taking the trouble to visit me,
now feasting and chatting after hard times,
your hearts consider old kindness done.

The moon is bright, the stars are few,
and magpies come flying south,
three times around they circle the tree,
where is the branch on which to roost?
The mountain does not mind its height,
the ocean does not mind its depth.
The Duke of Zhou broke off his meals,
and all the world turned to him in their hearts.

Study Notes and Questions

1. Cao Cao makes the occasion a theme in the poem. What is that occasion?

2. Cao Cao uses the four-character form very effectively here. Looking at the Chinese and the word-for-word gloss, consider how Cao Cao varies the syntax of the lines. What sort of syntactic constructions does he use? How does this variety help animate the poem?

3. Given the tone of the poem, what is the function of the couplets drawn directly from the *Canon of Poetry*? Are they obtrusive?

4. Is the magpie in the poem allegorical? How does it compare to the Hu horse and the Yue bird from the first of the "Nineteen Old Poems"?

Cao Zhi 曹植 *(192–232)*

Cao Zhi was Cao Cao's third son and younger brother of Cao Pi. As the younger brother of the future emperor, Cao Zhi's position was always precarious, and he seems to have led a life designed to demonstrate to Cao Pi that he had no intention of competing with him for the throne. He acquired the reputation of an arrogant wastrel. However, Cao Cao and Cao Pi were not fools, and they took measures to make sure that neither Cao Zhi nor his many half-brothers could contest the succession. On Cao Cao's death, Cao Pi had Cao Zhi's main advisors executed and ordered Cao Zhi and his brothers to return to their feudal domains rather than remain in the capital. After Cao Pi's death in 226, the new emperor—Cao Pi's son—continued to keep Cao Zhi away from the capital and denied him any opportunities to serve in office. Cao Zhi died of illness on his estate at the age of 40.

Despite his fraught political position, Cao Zhi was the greatest poet of the Jian'an period. He mastered his father's *yuefu* style and the generalized pentasyllabic verse style represented by the "Nineteen Old Poems." He also encouraged the development of the pentasyllabic verse form as a medium for deeply personal poems: he juxtaposed stock images and sentiments with specific places and moments to create a new particularity of poetic voice, the voice of the individuated author.

"Miscellaneous Poem" by Cao Zhi

雜詩					Miscellaneous Poem
高 high	臺 terrace	多 much	悲 sad	風 wind	On the high terrace, much sad wind:
朝 dawn	日 sun	照 shines	北 north	林 [lim] grove	The dawn sun shines on the northern grove.
之 this	子 man	在 is at	萬 10,000	里 *li*	That man is ten thousand *li* away,
江 river	湖 lake	迥 distant	且 and	深 [ɕim] deep	And the rivers and lakes are distant and deep.
方 paired	舟 boat	安 how	可 can be	極 go to limit	How can [my] double-hulled boat reach its limit?
離 separate	思 longing	故 of old	難 hard	任 [ɲim] bear	The longing of separation, from of old, is hard to bear.
孤 lone	雁 goose	飛 fly	南 south	遊 wander	A lone goose flies off southward;

過 cross	庭 court	長 long	哀 lament	吟 [ŋim] call out	Crossing over [my] courtyard, it gives a long mournful cry.
翹 pinion	思 longing	慕 envy	遠 far	人 person	With soaring longing, I think on the distant one:
願 request	欲 want	託 entrust	遺 left-over	音 [ʔim] sound	I wish to entrust [word] to [the bird's] fading voice.[26]
形 shape	景 shadow	忽 suddenly	不 not	見 see	Its shape and shadow suddenly vanish:
翩 flutter	翩 flutter	傷 wound	我 my	心 [sim] heart	Fluttering, it wounds my heart.

MEOW HUI GOH'S TRANSLATION

Miscellaneous Poem

The lofty terrace invites much grievous wind;
The morning sun shines upon the northern groves.
The one I miss is ten thousand *li* away;
The rivers and lakes are wide and deep.
How can two boats be lashed together?
Thoughts of separation have always been hard to bear.
A lone goose flies, heading to the south;
Passing above my courtyard, it lets out a long cry.
My thoughts soar as I pine for the one faraway—
I wish to entrust them to the bird's echoes.
Its form and shadow suddenly leave my sight:
Flapping swiftly, it pains my heart.

STUDY NOTES AND QUESTIONS

1. The poem begins in a way strongly reminiscent of the "Nineteen Old Poems." At what point does the poem begin to introduce an individuated sensibility?

2. Is the goose in the poem allegorical, or are we to assume that it was part of an actual experience that Cao Zhi brought to the poem? What is the difference in the reading of the poem?

3. "Soaring longing" in the poem (line 9) is more literally "pinion longing," which is an odd phrase even in Classical Chinese.

4. Although the poem ends with a conventional "wounds my heart," the final couplet gives this assertion a distinctive complexity. What is the sorrow of losing sight of the goose, and what does "fluttering" add to the sense of sorrow?

---

26. That is, here Cao Zhi refers to the conventional idea of tying a letter to the leg of the migrating goose.

"Seeing Off Mr. Ying"

送應氏二首第一					Seeing Off Mr. Ying (the first of two poems)
步	登	北	邙	坂	On foot I ascend the slope at North Mang:[27]
step	climb	north	Mang	slope	
遙	望	洛	陽	山 [ʂɛːn]	Afar I gazed for the hills of Luoyang.
far	gaze	Luo-	-yang	mountain	
洛	陽	何	寂	寞	Luoyang—how desolate!
Luo-	-yang	"?"	desolate		
宮	室	盡	燒	焚 [bun]	The buildings all utterly burnt.
buildings		entirely	burn	burn	
垣	牆	皆	頓	擗	The walls entirely cast down;
wall	wall	all	cast down		
荊	棘	上	參	天 [tʰɛn]	Brambles rise to touch the sky.
bramble	thorn	ascend	participate	sky	
不	見	舊	耆	老	I do not see the old ones of former times.
not	see =	former	old	old	
但	睹	新	少	年 [nɛn]	I look at the newly [arrived] youths.
only	see	new	young	year	
側	足	無	行	徑	Turning my feet sideways, there are no paths to travel.
turn aside	foot	not exist	travel	path	
荒	疇	不	復	田 [dɛn]	Overgrown fields are not cultivated again.
wild	field	not	again	field	
遊	子	久	不	歸	A wandering one long has not returned:
wander	person	long time	not	return	
不	識	陌	與	阡 [tsʰɛn]	[You] do not recognize the paths and lanes.
not	recognize	field-path	and	field-path	
中	野	何	蕭	條	The midst of the wilds, how forlorn:
middle	wilds	"?"	forlorn		
千	里	無	人	煙 [ʔɛn]	For a thousand *li*, no smoke of human habitation.
thousand	*li*	not exist	people	smoke	
念	我	平	生	親	Recalling one with whom I have been close all my life,
recall	I	normal	life	close	
氣	結	不	能	言 [ŋian]	My breath constricts, and I cannot speak.
breath	tie up	not	can	speak	

27. North Mang was a hill to the northeast of Luoyang where many of the nobility had their grave sites.

ARTHUR WALEY'S TRANSLATION

The Ruins of Lo-yang

I climb to the ridge of Pei Mang Mountain
And look down on the city of Lo-yang
In Lo-yang how still it is!
Palaces and houses all burnt to ashes.
Walls and fences all broken and gaping,
Thorns and brambles shooting up to the sky.
I do not see the old old-men:
I only see the new young men.
I turn aside, for the straight road is lost:
The fields are overgrown and will never be ploughed again.
I have been away such a long time
That I do not know which street is which.
How sad and ugly the empty moors are!
A thousand miles without the smoke of a chimney.
I think of the house I lived in all those years:
    I am heart-tied and cannot speak.

STUDY NOTES AND QUESTIONS

1. Consider the relation of this poem to the "Nineteen Old Poems": what makes this text a poem of a specific time and place, written by one individual to another, rather than a generic performance?

2. Is the landscape a real landscape, a symbolic landscape, or both? Or does it depend on the particular image?

3. This is a farewell poem. According to the poem, what are the important aspects of the farewell?

Wang Can 王粲 *(177–217)*

Wang Can came from an illustrious clan with a long tradition of service to the Han court. His own career, however, reflected the turmoil of the final decades of Han rule. When Dong Zhuo brought the emperor west to Chang'an, Wang Can, a youth at the time, traveled there to establish himself and search for patrons. In 194, after Dong Zhuo's death, Wang Can went south to the court of the southern warlord Liu Biao 劉表 (142–208) but did not find employment. When Liu Biao died, however, Wang Can reportedly had a role in persuading his successor Liu Cong to surrender to Cao Cao. Cao Cao recognized Wang Can's abilities and employed him in various capacities. Wang Can died in 217 while accompanying Cao Cao on a campaign against the southern warlord Sun Quan.

Wang Can was one of the "Seven Masters of Jian'an" whom Cao Pi discussed in his "Discourse on Literature."[28] His surviving works are few but important. His "*Fu* on Climbing the Tower" reveals a new approach to handling the venerable Han *fu* (rhyme-prose) genre. His two-poem series "Seven Laments" shows how Jian'an writers used the forms and conventions of late Han pentasyllabic verse to create intense poetry with an autobiographical authorial voice.

From the Series "Seven Laments" by Wang Can

七哀詩					Seven Laments, 2 poems, no. 1
西 west	京 capital	亂 chaos	無 without	象 image	The Western Capital is chaotic without manifest [order].[29]
豺 jackal	虎 tiger	方 now	遘 meet	患 [ɣwain^h] calamity	Jackals and tigers just now await the disaster.
復 again	棄 reject	中 central	國 state	去 leave	I'll abandon the central realm, leave,
遠 distant	身 self	適 go to	荊 Jing	蠻 [main] barbarians	Distance myself, go to the Jing barbarians.[30]
親 family	戚 kin	對 face	我 me	悲 sorrow	My relatives face me in sorrow.
朋 friends	友 friends	相 mutually	追 chase	攀 [p^{h}ain] climb	My friends chase after me, holding on.

28. Cao Pi's full list: Kong Rong 孔融, Chen Lin 陳琳, Wang Can 王粲, Xu Gan 徐幹, Ruan Yu 阮瑀, Ying Chang 應瑒, and Liu Zhen 劉楨. See the appendix at the end of this chapter for a translation of Cao Pi's essay.

29. The Western Capital was Chang'an, modern Xi'an, to which Dong Zhuo had moved. Wang Can was leaving Chang'an after the death of Dong Zhuo as contending strongmen vied for control. The phrase "chaotic without manifest [order]" comes from the *Zuo zhuan*, 9th year of Duke Xiang《左傳・襄公九年》: "When a state is chaotic, there is no portent; it cannot be known."「國亂無象，不可知也。」

30. Jing is another name for Chu and, here, for south China in general. Wang Can went to seek employment in the court of the southern warlord Liu Biao.

出 go out	門 gate	無 is not	所 [object]	見 see	Going out the gate, there is nothing [else] to see:
白 white	骨 bones	蔽 cover	平 level	原 [ŋuan] plains	White bones cover the broad plain.
路 road	有 there is	饑 starve	婦 wife	人 person	On the road is a starving woman:
抱 hug	子 child	棄 reject	草 grass	間 [kəɨn] midst	Hugging her child, she abandons it in the grass.
顧 look back	聞 hear	號 wail	泣 weep	聲 sound	Looking back, she hears the sound of wailing.
揮 wipe	涕 tears	獨 alone	不 not	還 [ɣwaɨn] return	Wiping tears, alone, she does not return.
未 not yet	知 know	身 self	死 die	處 place	"I don't know where I shall die:
何 how	能 can	兩 two	相 mutually	完 [ɣwan] complete	How can I keep both of us intact?"
驅 gallop	馬 horse	棄 reject	之 it	去 leave	I gallop my horse, leaving her behind.
不 not	忍 endure	聽 listen	此 this	言 [ŋɨan] speech	I cannot endure to listen to these words.
南 south	登 climb	霸 Ba	陵 Mound	岸 bank	South, I climb the bank of Ba Mound,[31]
回 return	首 head	望 look for	長 Chang	安 [ʔan] an	Turning my head, I gaze on Chang'an.
悟 realize	彼 that	下 Falling	泉 Spring	人 person	I understand that "Falling Spring" person.[32]
喟 deep sigh	然 -ly	傷 wound	心 hear	肝 [kan] liver	With a deep sigh, I feel wounded within.

WENDY SWARTZ'S TRANSLATION

At the western capital, such chaos denied portents,
Wolves and tigers hatched up this calamity.
So I abandoned the Central Plains and left,
To consign myself to the land of Jingman.
My kinfolks stood before me in sadness,
Friends ran along my carriage, clinging on.
Out the gate, I saw nothing,

---

31. Ba Mound, to the southeast of the capital, was the tomb of the great Emperor Wen of the Han.

32. "Falling Spring" is the title of *Shijing* poem Mao 153, a poem lamenting benighted times and longing for the rule of the early Zhou sage kings. It has the line "I recall that Zhou capital."

But white bones covering the plains.
On the road there was a famished woman,
Who carried a baby which she abandoned in the grass.
She turned around when she heard his cries and wails,
But wiped away her tears and did not go back.
"I do not even know where I will die,
How can I keep both of us alive?"
I spurred on my horse and left them there,
Unable to bear listening to such talk.
Toward the south, I ascended the slopes of the Ba Tumulus,
And turned my head to gaze at Chang'an.
I now understand he who wrote the "Falling Spring,"
Sighing, I feel that pain inside.

STUDY NOTES AND QUESTIONS

1. Wang Can has left the entertainment hall far behind in composing this poem. Who is his audience? Specific friends? Family? A generalized elite readership?

2. Like Cao Zhi's "Seeing Off Mr. Ying," this poem begins by placing itself in a vista of destruction, but Wang Can is even more direct. Still, Wang constructs the poems through conventional images. The "jackals and tigers" clearly are metaphorical. What about the bones?

3. Does the vignette with the woman and infant, in contrast, seem to reflect actual rather than conventionalized suffering? How does Wang Can create the sense of actuality?

4. What is the effect of the citation from the *Canon of Poetry* in the second-to-last line? What are the implications of the comparison Wang Can draws here? What happens to the present moment in the allusion? Is he distancing himself from the present, intensifying it, or framing it, or doing all three at once?

5. The poem is clearly about Wang Can's decision to leave Chang'an for the court of Liu Biao in 194, but what if Wang Can *wrote* it after 208, when he was said to have persuaded Liu Biao's son to surrender to Cao Cao and when Wang Can himself joined the circle of writers gathered around the Cao clan?[33] Would a lapse of years between the events and their recollection change your reading of the poem?

33. See Robert Ashmore's arguments in *Transports of Reading: Text and Understanding in the World of Tao Qian (365–427)*, Harvard East Asian Monographs 327 (Cambridge: Harvard University Asia Center, 2010), pp. 257–58, n21.

The Wei Dynasty

When Cao Pi deposed the last Han dynasty emperor to establish the Wei dynasty in 220, he could not claim to hold authority over all the territory of the former Han. In 221 Liu Bei proclaimed himself Emperor of Shuhan in Sichuan, and in 222 Sun Quan in the south renounced his loyalty to the Wei and took up hostilities. Sun declared himself Emperor of Wu in 229. The Wei dynasty was a time of constant warfare between the three "empires," each vying to establish itself as the legitimate inheritor of the Han dynasty mandate. Cao Pi ruled for six years, and on his death, his son Cao Rui 曹叡 (204?–39), although young when he came to the throne, proved sufficiently adroit to maintain the military stalemate and keep control of his court. Cao Rui, however, died young and left his son in the protection of two regents: Cao Shuang, a distant relative from his own clan, and Sima Yi, an important general. This did not end well: Cao Shuang proved no match for Sima Yi, who consolidated his power, ousted Cao Shuang, and had him executed in 249. For the last sixteen years of the dynasty, the Sima clan effectively ruled the state, and in 265 Sima Yan 司馬炎 (236–90)—Sima Yi's grandson—accepted the abdication of the fifth emperor and founded the Jin dynasty (265–420).

Most of the Seven Masters of Jian'an who made Cao Cao's retinue so brilliant died before Cao Pi became emperor. Thus the Wei court, pressed by constant warfare and deadly political maneuvering, had little of the allure of the Jian'an, and its most famous poet, Ruan Ji, spent his life trying to avoid the dangers of court life.

Ruan Ji 阮籍 (210–63)

Ruan Ji was the son of Ruan Yu 阮瑀, one of the "Seven Masters of Jian'an." He was also one of the "Seven Worthies of the Bamboo Grove," a retrospectively designated group of talented eccentrics who sought to distance themselves from the intrigues at the Wei court as it was coming under the domination of the Sima clan. The Seven Worthies developed philosophical positions based on Zhuang Zhou 莊周 (ca. 369–ca. 286 BC) that stressed spontaneity and freedom in a world in flux and rejected the claims of a Confucian ritual and ethical system that—from their perspective—contemporary events had shown to be completely hollow formalisms.[34]

Ruan Ji probably did not write the series of eighty poems entitled "Chanting My Thoughts" as a coherent set. The texts explore a variety of themes and moods but in general have an abstracted, philosophical quality that some scholars attribute to a prudent refusal to reveal specific views about events of the day in the manner of the Seven Masters of Jian'an.

34. Zhuang Zhou was a brilliant proto-Daoist philosopher of the late Warring States period. He was intensely skeptical about human knowledge of the world, language, and the categories imposed on the world through language. *Zhuang Zi* 莊子, the work that preserves his writings as well as those of his followers, is intensely imagined, with many exuberant flights of fancy, and had a powerful influence on the classical Chinese literary tradition.

From the Series "Chanting My Thoughts" by Ruan Ji

詠懷 第一					Chanting My Thoughts, no. 1
夜 night	中 middle	不 not	能 able	寐 sleep	In the middle of the night, I cannot sleep.
起 rise	坐 sit	彈 pluck	鳴 sing	琴 [gim] zither	Rising, I sit and play my resounding zither.
薄 thin	帷 curtain	鑒 mirror	明 bright	月 moon	[Through] thin curtains, the mirror of the bright moon.
清 pure	風 wind	吹 blow	我 my	襟 [kim] collar	A fresh wind blows my collar.
孤 lone	鴻 swan	號 call	外 outer	野 wilds	A lone swan calls in the outer wilds;
翔 soar	鳥 bird	鳴 sing	北 north	林 [lim] grove	Soaring birds sing in the north grove.
徘 pace back & forth	徊	將 about	何 what	見 see	Pacing restless, what will be seen?
憂 sorrow	思 longing	獨 alone	傷 hurt	心 [sim] heart	Sorrowful longings especially wound the heart.[35]

Stephen Owen's Translation

Songs of My Cares, 1

In the night I could not sleep,
restless I rose and plucked the harp.
Thin curtains mirrored the bright moon,
cool breeze blew into gown-folds.
A lone swan screeched out on the moors,
in the north woods birds flew singing.
I wavered then, what would I see?—
troubled thoughts injure a heart all alone.

Study Notes and Questions

1. In this short poem, Ruan Ji sets up a conventional scene and draws on many images seen before, yet he also offers something new. The third line, for example, literally says "The thin curtain *mirrors* the bright moon": it strikingly takes the noun "mirror" and forces it to become a verb. Yet if it is a verb, what does it mean? Think of a full moon seen through a thin gauze curtain.

35. The Chinese commentary points out that the last four lines describe both the narrator and the birds.

2. The third couplet puts together the lone swan of line 5 with the soaring (small) bird of line 6. Are these visual or aural images? What elements are stressed for each animal? What is the effect of this comparison?

3. This poem seems to be a series of fragments. How do the events and images of the poem articulate the "sorrowful longing" of the final line? How do the shifts from image to image convey a sensibility?

The Western Jin Dynasty

When Sima Yan forced the last Wei emperor to abdicate in 265, he was determined not to repeat the mistakes of the Cao clan. Cao Pi had distrusted Cao Zhi and his other kinsmen and, as a result, had left his son isolated without broad support. In contrast, when Sima Yan took the throne as Emperor Wu of the Jin, he established his many relatives as princes with domains to provide them with independent sources of income and armies. This redistribution of power, although it weakened the dynasty decades later, initially brought Sima Yan and the new Jin dynasty sufficient stability to allow him to defeat the state of Wu in the south and reunify much of the territory of the former Han dynasty.

Political tensions, however, began to grow around Sima Yan's determination to have his mentally deficient son succeed him. When Sima Yan died in 290 the political intrigue over control of that son, the newly enthroned Emperor Hui, grew bloody as Emperor Hui's wife—Jia Nanfeng—and her clan consolidated power. Empress Jia was sufficiently adroit as to retain power until 300, when she ordered the assassination of the crown prince, Emperor Hui's son by a concubine, and provoked a coup within the imperial clan. Her suicide marked the beginning of a decade in which Jin imperial princes, supported by their independent resources, relentlessly struggled to control the throne. Eventually, in 307 Sima Yue, the regent at the time, (probably) had Emperor Hui poisoned and installed a new emperor. This unceasing internecine bloodletting, called the War of the Eight Princes, so weakened the dynasty that in 311 the resurgent Xiongnu, a Central Asian tribal group, along with their allies, inflicted devastating defeats on the Jin army and attacked, captured, and sacked the capital of Luoyang. The new emperor and the heir apparent both were captured, but enough of the court fled to south China, along with a significant part of the population, to regroup as the Eastern Jin.

The first two decades of the Western Jin, although filled with warfare, were stable enough for the reestablishment of a grand court culture in which poets explored how to give more nuance to poetry.[36] Although poets inherited from the Jian'an writers a model of poetry based on one's response to events, they very early discovered a conundrum: if one is too honest, one might invite disaster. The intense, anguished, yet direct poets of the Jian'an period gave way to the more prudently abstract musings of Ruan Ji in the next generation. For the Western Jin poets, the goal of setting out revealing responses to events remained unchanged, but there was an increasing sense of the complexities of meaning both for events and for the responding person. Poets brought greater historical and literary self-awareness to the act of composition. They experimented with rhetorical techniques borrowed from other genres and explored the formal possibilities created by the couplet structure of pentasyllabic verse.

36. Most of the important Western Jin writers died in Sima Yan's reign, during the regency of Empress Jia or soon after. Zhang Hua was executed along with Empress Jia in 300. Pan Yue and his entire clan were executed in 301. Zuo Si, who successfully retired in 300, died of illness in 302. Lu Ji and his brother were executed in 303.

The Dominant Western Jin Literary Form: The Fu

The court culture of the Western Jin held two traditional verse forms in higher esteem than they did the more recent five-character *shi* form. The lesser of the two traditional forms was the four-character *shi* form inherited from formal Han dynasty courtly composition. The most prestigious inherited form, however, was the *fu* 賦, sometimes translated as rhyme-prose. Writers at the imperial court during the height of the Han dynasty had produced spectacular *fu* that celebrated the dynasty, mixing together prose narration with long rhymed passages that used exuberant, highly elaborate language and a meter inherited from the Chu song tradition. As the *fu* form evolved during the Eastern Han, however, it became less associated with court performance and was increasingly used for more personal purposes within elite society. It became shorter and simpler. The Western Jin court saw some revival of the longer, more elaborate *fu* genre, but most of what has survived is in the short, more personal mode. Many of the complete *fu* from the period are elegant, courtly allegories composed on objects, but it is also clear from the many fragments and extant titles that writers wrote on a wide range of topics.

The *fu*, as the central verse form of the period, provided Western Jin authors with basic literary tools like a courtly vocabulary, the art of crafting parallel couplets, and approaches to rhetorical elaboration. As they continued to assimilate the five-character verse form, they experimented with ways in which they could apply the techniques of *fu* composition to transform *shi*, with its roots in popular song genres, into a more elegant elite form.

Xiang Xiu 向秀 (ca. 227–300), whose life spanned the Wei and the early Western Jin, provides us with an example of the short, personal *fu*. As the preface makes clear, he wrote the *fu* to commemorate a visit to the former residence of Xi Kang 嵇康 (223–62), who ran afoul of Sima Yan's father and had been executed.

"Thinking of Former Times," a *Fu*, with a Preface, by Xiang Xiu

余與嵇康呂安居止接近，其人並有不羈之才。然嵇志遠而疏，呂心曠而放，其後各以事見法。嵇博綜技藝，於絲竹特妙。臨當就命，顧視日影，索琴而彈之。余逝將西邁，經其舊廬。于時日薄虞淵，寒冰淒然。鄰人有吹笛者，發聲寥亮。追思曩昔遊宴之好，感音而歎，故作賦云。

In former times, I lived near Xi Kang and Lü An. They both were men of unbridled talent, but Xi's resolve was distant, and he paid little heed [to worldly matters] while Lü's mind was expansive but unconstrained. After [our time together] each was sentenced [to execution] over a dispute.[37] Xi broadly mastered the arts and was particularly wonderful with strings and pipes [i.e., the *qin* and flute]. When he was about to face execution, he turned to look at the [lengthening] shadows, asked for his *qin*, and played it. I was departing to travel west and went past his former house. At the time, the sun was nearing the Abyss of Yu, and the chill was forlorn.[38] Among the neighbors was a flute player, whose sound was

37. Lü An accused his brother of adultery with his wife, but his brother then accused Lü An of beating their mother. Xi Kang sought to defend Lü An, but they both were arrested and executed in 262 under orders from Sima Zhao, Sima Yan's father.

38. When the sun set, it sank into the Abyss of Yu in the west and then rose again from the eastern ocean.

clear and resonant. Thinking back to the joys of our excursions in times past, I was moved by the sound and sighed. I therefore composed a *fu*:

思舊賦							Thinking of Former Times[39]
將	命	適	於	遠	京	兮	By imperial command, I was going to the distant capital,[40]
take	command	go to	at	distant	capital	xi!	
遂	旋	反	而	北	徂 [dzɔ]		Then soon returned and went north.
then	soon	go back	and	north	go		
濟	黃	河	以	汎	舟	兮	Crossing the Yellow River, I was aboard a boat,
go across	yellow	river	by [this]	float	boat	xi!	
經	山	陽	之	舊	居 [kɨə̆]		And then passed [his] former residence at Shanyang.
pass	Shan-	yang	's	former	reside		
瞻	曠	野	之	蕭	條	兮	I gazed at the forlornness of the vast wilds,
gaze	broad	wilds	's	forlorn		xi!	
息	余	駕	乎	城	隅 [ŋuă]		And rested my carriage by the corner of the city wall.
rest	my	ride carriage	at	city	corner		
踐	二	子	之	遺	跡	兮	Treading the traces of footsteps of the two masters,
tread	two	master	's	remain	footstep	x!	
歷	窮	巷	之	空	廬 [lɔ]		I went by [their] empty houses in a destitute lane.
pass by	destitute	alley	's	empty	hut		
歎	黍	離	之	愍	周	兮	I sigh over "Shuli's" lamenting over Zhou;[41]
sigh	Shu-	li	's	lament	Zhou	xi!	
悲	麥	秀	於	殷	墟 [kʰɨə̆]		And grieve that the grain was ripe on the ruins of Yin.[42]
sorrow	grain	ripen	at	Yin	mound		
惟	古	昔	以	懷	今	兮，	I think of former times to cherish the present;
think	old	former	by [this]	cherish	now	xi!	
心	徘	徊	以	躊	躇 [drɨə̆]		My mind is irresolute as I pace back and forth.
mind	go back and forth		by [this]	pace back and forth			

39. David Knechtges translates this *fu* in *Wen xuan or Selections of Refined Literature, Volume 3* (Princeton: Princeton University Press, 1996), pp. 167–69.

40. Xiang Xiu was from Henei in modern Henan Province and was summoned to Luoyang, the capital, to offer his services to Sima Zhao.

41. The Mao preface to the poem "Shuli" (Mao 65) in the *Canon of Poetry* describes the poem as the lament of a Zhou dynasty official as he passed by the ruins of the old Zhou capital.

42. The *Canon of Documents* records that Song Weizi, an older brother of the last Shang dynasty ruler who tried but failed to prevent the downfall of the dynasty, composed a "Song of the Ripening Grain" when he later passed by the ruins of the old Shang [Yin] dynasty capital and saw only fields of ripening grain.

	棟	宇	存	而	弗	毀	兮	The beams and roof remain and are not destroyed;
	beam	roof	remain	and	not-it	destroy	xi!	
	形	神	逝	其	焉	如 [ɲɨə̆]		[Yet] their form and spirit have departed, gone where?
	form	spirit	depart	its	where	go		
	昔	李	斯	之	受	罪	兮	Formerly when Li Si received his punishment,
	former	Li	Si	's	receive	punish	xi!	
16	歎	黃	犬	而	長	吟 [ŋim]		He sighed over his brown dog and sighed long.[43]
	sigh	brown	dog	and	long	chant		
	悼	嵇	生	之	永	辭	兮	I lament Master Xi's eternal farewell,
	mourn	Xi	Master	's	long	take leave	xi!	
	顧	日	影	而	彈	琴 [gim]		Looking back at the shadows and playing the *qin*.[44]
	look back	sun	shadow	and	play	*qin*		
	託	運	遇	於	領	會	兮	He entrusted his chances to his understanding,
	entrust	fate	encounter	at	understand	encounter	xi!	
20	寄	餘	命	於	寸	陰 [ʔim]		And lodged his remaining fate within an inch of shadow.[45]
	lodge	remaining	fate	at	*cun*	shadow		
	聽	鳴	笛	之	慷	慨	兮	I listen to the deep sorrow of the singing flute;
	listen	sing	flute	's	deep sorrow		xi!	
	妙	聲	絕	而	復	尋 [zim]		Its wondrous sound breaks off and then continues again.
	wondrous	sound	break off	and	again	follow		
	停	駕	言	其	將	邁	兮	I stop my carriage as I am about to pass beyond,
	stop	carriage		its	about to	cross over	xi!	
24	遂	援	翰	而	寫	心 [sim]		And then grasp the brush to set out my mind.
	then	grasp	feather	and	depict	mind		

STUDY NOTES AND QUESTIONS

1. What is the role of the preface? Would the effect of the rhymed portion of the *fu* be the same without the prose introduction? What does the preface contribute?

---

43. Li Si, minister to the First Emperor of the Qin (Qin Shihuang), lamented to his son as he was being led to the execution ground, "I wish I could again lead out the brown dog and, together with you, chase nimble rabbits outside the east gate of [our home,] Shangcai, but how can I get that!"

44. Xi Kang was famous as a master of the *qin*. As the time for his execution was approaching, he asked for his *qin*, played it, and explained that because he had previously refused to teach the tune "Guangling san" to a student, now it would be lost forever.

45. The image here is time as measured on a sundial.

2. In form, the rhymed section uses couplets of six-character lines where the fourth character in each line is a grammatical word (於 *yu* = [locative marker], 而 *er* = [verb coordination marker], 之 *zhi* = [noun modification marker], 其 *qi* = "his/her/their/its," or the coverb 以 *yi* "use it to"). The end of the first line of each couplet is marked by the character 兮, a "breathing" word like "hey." Compare this form to that of the songs in the *Lyrics of Chu* in chapter 3.

3. Note the parallelism in the *fu*. For example, explain the fairly simple parallelism in lines 9 and 10. "The beams and roof remain" in line 13 and "their form and spirit have departed" in line 14 use a more complicated pairing. Moreover, Xiang Xiu writes entire couplets in roughly parallel patterns: consider lines 15–16 and lines 17–18.

4. The language throughout the rhymed section relies on ornamental substitutions of both nouns and verbs. For example, Xiang uses the more formal 駕 (harness) for 車 (carriage) and verbs like 徂 (advance toward) for "go" and 息 (breathe) for "rest." These two verbs reappear in Lu Ji's courtly *shi* poem below.

5. Note that Xiang Xiu is explicit about the purpose of the *fu*, "to set out [his] mind." This goal is very similar to that being assigned to *shi* poetry at the time. Compare this *fu* to Cao Zhi's "Seeing Off Mr. Ying." Discuss the differences in content, structure, and feel between the two compositions.

Pan Yue 潘岳 *(247–300)*

Pan Yue went to the Jin court with a reputation as a "child prodigy." According to his biography, he was ambitious but easily provoked and always unhappy with positions that did not match his abilities. An active participant in court politics, he eventually was caught up in its web and was executed.

Pan Yue understood the dangers of service, and one of his most famous compositions is the "*Fu* on Living at Leisure," about the joys of retirement, but he could not quit. Pan Yue was known for the elegant, elaborate rhetorical crafting of his writing and was especially good at commemorative funerary compositions. His most famous series of poems, "Mourning the Departed," however, is powerful for the simplicity and directness of language with which he describes his grief over his wife's death.

From the Series "Mourning the Departed" by Pan Yue

悼亡詩 三首第一					Mourning the Departed, 3 poems, no. 1
荏	苒	冬	春	謝	Gradually winter and spring take leave.
gradually		winter	spring	take leave	
寒	暑	忽	流	易 [jiajk]	Cold and hot suddenly shift and change.
cold	hot	sudden	flow	change	
之	子	歸	窮	泉	The traveling one has returned to the remote spring.[46]
go	person	return	end	spring	
重	壤	永	幽	隔 [kəijk]	The layered earth forever separates [us].
layer	earth	always	secluded	separate	
私	懷	誰	克	從	Private longing: who can follow it?
private	cherish	who	can	follow	
淹	留	亦	何	益 [ʔjiajk]	[Yet] what is the benefit of tarrying?
tarry	remain	also	"?"	increase	
僶	俛	恭	朝	命	[I] am diligent in following the court's command:
diligent		respect	court	command	
迴	心	反	初	役 [jwiajk]	I turn my heart to return to what I first [did in] service:
return	mind	go back	at first	serve	
望	廬	思	其	人	Gazing for [my] house, [I] long for its person.
gaze for	hut	long for	its	person	
入	室	想	所	歷 [lɛjk]	Entering the room, [I] imagine what [we] had been through.
enter	room	imagine	what	experience	
幃	屏	無	髣	髴	The bed-curtain and screen convey no semblance[of her]:
curtain	screen	not exist	faint semblance		

46. "Traveling one" is an old phrase used frequently in the *Canon of Poetry* and here refers to his wife. The dead were believed to go to the "Yellow Springs" under the ground.

翰 quill	墨 ink	有 exist	餘 left over	跡 [tsiajk] trace	Brush and ink preserve remnant traces.
流 flow	芳 fragrant	未 not yet	及 reach	歇 exhaust	The floating fragrance has not yet vanished:
遺 leave	掛 hang	猶 still	在 is at	壁 [pɛjk] wall	Remaining, hanging, still on the wall.[47]
悵 distracted	怳	如 resemble	或 some	存 remain	[I] am distracted as though [she] still were there,
回 return	惶 apprehensive	忡 worried	驚 startle	惕 [t^{h}ɛjk] apprehensive	And turn apprehensive, worried, and affrighted.
如 resemble	彼 that	翰 quill	林 grove	鳥 bird	[We] were like those birds in the thicket:
雙 pair	棲 roost	一 one	朝 dawn	隻 [tɕiajk] [bird counter]	A pair roosting, one morning just one.
如 resemble	彼 that	游 swim	川 river	魚 fish	[We] were like those fish swimming in the river:
比 align	目 eye	中 middle	路 road	析 [sɛjk] split	Paired eyes split apart mid-journey.[48]
春 spring	風 wind	緣 follow	隟 crack	來 come	The spring wind comes from a crack;
晨 dawn	霤 dripping	承 receive	檐 eaves	滴 [tɛjk] drop	The dripping of water at dawn collects from the eaves.
寢 sleep	息 rest	何 "?"	時 time	忘 forget	When [I] rest, when will I forget?
沉 sink	憂 sad	日 day	盈 increase	積 [tsiajk] accumulate	Brooding sorrow accumulates by the day.
庶 let it be that	幾	有 exist	時 time	衰 decline	I hope it will decline in time:
莊 Zhuang	缶 pot	猶 still	可 can be	擊 [kɛjk] strike	Master Zhuang's pot still can be banged.[49]

47. The modern scholar Yu Guanying 余冠英 suggests that both lines refer to her calligraphy. The ink, made of pine soot, carried a fragrance. See Yu Guanying, *Han Wei Liuchao shi xuan* 漢魏六朝詩選 (Hong Kong: Joint Publishing, 1993), p. 183.

48. As previously noted, the image here is of a fish like the flounder that has eyes only on one side: the belief was that a pair of fish was needed in order for the two to be able to see where they were going.

49. A passage in "Utmost Happiness"《至樂》in *Zhuang Zi* describes how Zhuang Zi was disconsolate when his wife died. Then he reflected that he could not be sure whether death was in fact a stage of transformation in which his wife passed to greater happiness such that she would look back on life as but a sad interlude. Realizing that he was just being self-centered in mourning his loss rather than celebrating her transformation, he then passed his days making merry—if rustic—music by banging on a pot.

BURTON WATSON'S TRANSLATION

Lamenting the Dead

Before I know it, winter and spring depart,
cold and heat suddenly trading places,
and she has gone to the deepest springs;
heaped earth forever seals her apart.
My secret longings I cannot fulfill;
what good would it do to linger there?
Swearing allegiance to the sovereign's command,
I turn my heart back to former tasks.
But seeing the house, I think of her;
entering its rooms, I recall the past.
Curtains and screens hold no shadow of her,
her writings the only trace that remains,
the drifting scent that never quite fades,
her things left forgotten, hung on the wall.
Dazed by longing, I think she is here,
then come to myself with a twinge of pain—
We were a pair of birds winging to the wood,
mated, then suddenly one morning alone;
a pair of fish swimming the stream,
eye to eye, then parted midway—
Spring wind filters in through the cracks,
morning rain drips down from the eaves;
lying at rest, when will I forget?
Each day I sink into deeper sorrow.
Perhaps a time will come when it will fade
and I, like Chuang Tzu, can pound the tub.

STUDY NOTES AND QUESTIONS

1. Five-character verse as an expressive medium evolved with great speed. Poets learned techniques to begin and end poems with ever greater subtlety and organized poems with ever greater sophistication in the service of deeply personal ends. Consider the first couplet of this poem: how is it effective in beginning a meditation on loss? How does the seasonal theme return in the poem? How does the final couplet offer one last version of the reflection on time and loss?

2. Part of the tone of this poem comes from features of language all but impossible to capture in English. Consider the 或 "some" in line 15. By the time the poem was written, it also (almost) meant "or": here it conveys a tentativeness in the poet's distracted state that leads to the sense at moments that his wife is still alive. Can you think of a way to convey this quality in an English rendering?

3. Pan Yue turns away from the conventional ending, "it wounds the heart," and finds a new approach. Does Pan Yue's reference to Zhuang Zi's coming to realize the foolishness of his mourning (because his wife had rejoined the great cycle of creation) stand in for Pan Yue's resolution, or does it present a consolation he cannot find?

Zuo Si 左思 *(ca. 250–ca. 305)*

Zuo Si was from a minor clan at a time when lineage mattered. He went to the capital in search of patronage but was not adept at making the sort of contacts needed to advance in the world of politics. Instead, he turned his ambitions toward writing, for this provided an alternative route to renown. He resolved to write a monumental *fu* on the capitals of Shu, Wu, and Wei as a self-conscious continuation of the earlier tradition of *fu* on capitals. He reportedly spent ten years meticulously researching and writing his monumental *fu*, but when he initially presented it, it was poorly received. He persevered and brought it to the attention of an important cultural figure of the time, who recognized its value and introduced it to other leading writers who took it up with enthusiasm. The story goes that it became so popular that the price of paper rose in Luoyang because so many people were copying it and because it was so long. He attained the fame he sought and then prudently refused office, moved away from the capital, and eventually died at home of illness.

Not much of Zuo Si's poetry survives. What survives, however, shows a movement away from the rhetorical ornamentation that had become part of the Jin court style. His poem series "Chanting of History," composed of eight poems reflecting on accounts of incidents from early history with an eye to contemporary events, is his best-known work.

From the Series "Chanting of History" by Zuo Si

詠史詩八首第六					Chanting of History, 8 poems, no. 6
荊 Jing	軻 Ke	飲 drink	燕 Yan	市 market	Jing Ke drank in the marketplace of Yan,[50]
酒 ale	酣 tipsy	氣 *qi*	益 increase	震 [tɕinʰ] earthquake	Growing tipsy with ale, his *qi* increasingly stirred.
哀 mourn	歌 song	和 accompany	漸 Jian	離 Li	In a mournful song he accompanied [Gao] Jianli.

50. Jing Ke was a noble-minded ruffian who tried but failed to assassinate the Qin ruler on behalf of the heir apparent of the state of Yan. Zuo Si here recounts part of Jing Ke's biography as it appears in the *Records of the Grand Historian* 《史記・刺客列傳》: "When Jing Ke reached Yan, he was fond of the dog-butcher of Yan, Gao Jianli, who also excelled at playing the zither. Jing Ke had a taste for ale; each day he drank with Gao Jianli in the market square in Yan. After they had become tipsy, Gao would play the zither, and Jing Ke would accompany him with song to their mutual delight. When it ended they would both weep as if there were no one around them."「荊軻既至燕，愛燕之狗屠及善擊筑者高漸離。荊軻嗜酒，日與狗屠及高漸離飲於燕市。酒酣以往，高漸離擊筑，荊軻和而歌於市中，相樂也。已而相泣，旁若無人者。」

謂 say	若 resemble	傍 side	無 not exist	人 [ɲin] people	They said he [acted] as if there was no one nearby.
雖 although	無 not exist	壯 robust	士 officer	節 regulate	Although he lacked the deportment of a stalwart man,
與 with	世 generation	亦 also	殊 different	倫 [lwin] type	In his generation, he still was exceptional.
高 high	眄 look down	邈 slight	四 four	海 sea	With lofty pride, he disdained [all within] the four seas.
豪 grand	右 superior	何 "?"	足 suffice	陳 [drin] set out	The aristocrats were beneath mention.
貴 noble	者 -thing	雖 although	自 of itself	貴 noble	Although the nobility take themselves as noble,
視 see	之 it	若 resemble	埃 dust	塵 [drin] dirt	I look at them like dust.
賤 lowly	者 -thing	雖 although	自 of itself	賤 lowly	Although the lowly take themselves as lowly,
重 heavy	之 it	若 resemble	千 1000	鈞 [kwjin] [weight]	I value them as worth a thousand pounds [of gold].

STUDY NOTES AND QUESTIONS

1. This is a poem opposing courtly values both in content and style, yet its audience was the aristocratic elite. What are some of Zuo Si's anti-court arguments? Why might the court have enjoyed them?

2. Why is it titled "chanting of history"? What is the role of Jing Ke's example in the poem? What is the relation of the poem to the account of Jing Ke in the *Records of the Grand Historian*?

3. Note the prose function words in the poem like "as if" 若, "although" 雖, "with" 與, "it" 之, and "-thing" 者. They contribute significantly to the plain syntax. Look at the last four lines in particular. What is the effect of this studied plainness?

Lu Ji 陸機 *(261–303)*

Lu Ji's father and grandfather both were important generals in the southern state of Wu. After the Jin conquest of Wu in 280, Lu Ji remained at his family estate, but at the end of the Taikang reign period (280–89), he and his younger brother Lu Yun went to Luoyang, where they quickly established their reputations as writers. However, Lu Ji had both a scholarly and a military background, and he was appointed general in a campaign that went disastrously wrong. He was blamed for the failure and executed.

As a writer Lu Ji had an intense sense of literary tradition. He drew on earlier writers to expand the rhetorical repertoire for poetry and also studied the origins of the pentasyllabic tradition in an attempt to recapture the power of the poems from the late Han dynasty and the Wei while bringing to it the sophistication of later developments. His most famous and important work is the "*Fu* on Writing," which reflects on all the various aspects of writing, from its resources and its genres to the difficulties of the actual process of composition. Much of his poetry is in the ornately ornamented and structured Jin court style, but he also tried his hand at explicitly imitating exemplary works from the beginning of the pentasyllabic verse tradition.

"Imitating 'How Radiant Is the Bright Moon'" by Lu Ji

擬明月何皎皎					Imitating "How Radiant Is the Bright Moon"
安	寢	北	堂	上	When I was resting at ease in the north hall,
at ease	lie down	north	hall	on	
明	月	入	我	牖 [juw']	The bright moon entered my window.
bright	moon	enter	I	window	
照	之	有	餘	輝	The gleam cast radiance that spread,
shine	it	exist	surplus	gleam	
攬	之	不	盈	手 [ɕuw']	[Yet], holding it, it did not fill the hands.
hold	it	not	fill	hand	
涼	風	繞	曲	房	A cool wind wound around the curving room;[51]
cool	wind	circle	curve	room	
寒	蟬	鳴	高	柳 [luw']	A cold cicada sang out in the tall willow.
cold	cicada	call out	high	willow	
踟	躕	感	節	物	Pacing, I was moved by the seasonal scene.
pace back and forth		move	season	thing	
我	行	永	已	久 [kuw']	I have been traveling long now.[52]
I	travel	long	already	long time	

51. A "curving room" is a room with a winding porch railing.

52. Commentaries are not sure how to interpret this line: has he really traveled, or does this refer to someone else?

遊 wander	宦 official	會 meet	無 not exist	成 complete	My official journeys have not accomplished anything,
離 separate	思 longing	難 difficult	常 always	守 [ɕuw'] guard	The longings of separation are hard to constantly endure.

Meow Hui Goh's Translation

Imitating "How the Bright Moon Is Gleaming"

As I sleep soundly above the northern hall,
The bright moon enters my window.
Facing it, I see its abundant brilliance;
Grasping it, nothing fills my hand.
A cool wind circles the secluded chamber;
Chilly cicadas call from tall willows.
I pace back and forth, moved by seasonal things;
My endless travels have gone on for too long.
I wander in officialdom, accomplishing little,
Yet it's hard to always keep my thoughts on separation.

Study Notes and Questions

1. The title of the poem informs us that it is an imitation of "How Radiant Is the Bright Moon," ("Nineteen Old Poems, no. 19"). Compare the two poems. Are the situations of the two personae in the poems similar? Are the scenes the same?

2. What about the language? Does Lu Ji capture the simplicity and directness of the earlier poem?

3. How well structured is this poem? Does it introduce a time, a place, and a theme and then develop the theme through further exploration of the scene? What is the function of abstract statement in the poem? Can it help to portray the mood Lu Ji sets out? Explain.

4. How does the final couplet of this poem compare to the final couplet of "How Radiant Is the Bright Moon"? Does the implied author Lu Ji maintain an individuated voice or does he slip into a persona?

From the Series "On the Road to Luoyang" by Lu Ji

又赴洛道中作詩二首第二					Again on the Road to Luoyang, 2 poems, no. 2
遠 distant	遊 excursion	越 cross	山 mountain	川 river	Wandering afar, I cross mountains and rivers.
山 mountain	川 river	修 long	且 and	廣 [kwaŋ'] broad	Mountains and rivers are long and broad.
振 shake	策 whip	陟 ascend	崇 exalted	丘 hill	Wielding my whip, I ascend lofty hills;
安 ease	轡 reins	遵 follow	平 level	莽 [maŋ'] thicket	With loose reins, I follow the level grasslands.[53]
夕 dusk	息 breathe	抱 embrace	影 shadow	寐 repose	At dusk I rest and sleep embracing shadows.
朝 dawn	徂 advance	銜 hold in	思 longing	往 [wuaŋ'] go toward	At dawn I depart, go out, holding in longings.
頓 pause	轡 reins	倚 lean	嵩 high	巖 cliff	Pausing my reins, I lean against a high cliff;
側 turn aside	聽 listen	悲 sad	風 wind	響 [xiaŋ'] echo	Aside, I listen to the echoes of the sad wind.
清 pure	露 dew	墜 fall	素 white silk	輝 gleam	Pure dew falls with a sheer white gleam:
明 bright	月 moon	一 one	何 how	朗 [laŋ'] luminous	How luminous is the bright moon!
撫 stoke	枕 pillow	不 not	能 able	寐 repose	Stroking the pillow-block, I cannot sleep:[54]
振 shake	衣 clothes	獨 alone	長 long	想 [siaŋ'] imagine	Throwing on my clothes, alone, I ponder long.

Study Notes and Questions

1. Lu Ji wrote this poem when he was leaving the south to go to Luoyang: what mood does he convey? He continues the Jian'an practice of using five-character verse to convey a particular, personal event, but the reading of the event through the structuring of specific elements has become complex. Lu Ji describes a conventionally "sad" wind. In contrast, what is the significance of the dew and moonlight?

2. Consider the use of time in the poem: what is the effect of describing at least two days and nights?

3. Lu Ji uses courtly language and more elegant and arresting words to replace more common ones. In line 2, for example, he uses 修 "long" (elongated) to apply to mountains. In line 3, he uses 陟 ("ascend")

53. There is a textual variant here: some texts have 案, taken as 按 ("to control [reins]"), for 安.

54. There is another textual variant in this line: some texts have 几 ("low desk") for 枕 ("pillow-block").

for "climb" and 崇 "exalted" for "high." Lu Ji also uses the pairing of 息 and 徂 for "rest" and "go" respectively already seen in Xiang Xiu's *fu*.

4. The poem also introduces arresting images with complex resonances. In particular, what does it mean to sleep "embracing a shadow"? The parallel image in the second half of the couplet is "holding in longing." The word *xián* 銜 is a horse's bit and turns into the verb "clench in the teeth": what would it mean to hold in longing like a bit?

5. Despite the impulse toward crafted language, the poem still builds on the conventions of the "Nineteen Old Poems," which Lu Ji clearly had studied and admired. What elements of the narrator's emotions and situation are shared with the nineteenth of the "Nineteen Old Poems"?

6. What difference do the two variants make in the meanings of the lines?

Guo Pu 郭璞 *(276–324)*

Guo Pu lived through the chaotic events that ended the Western Jin and served the Eastern Jin. His father had served in the Secretariat of the Jin court, so that Guo Pu presumably had the resources of the imperial library to help develop his extraordinarily broad talents as a scholar. He annotated the early dictionary *Erya* and wrote commentaries on the *Canon of Mountains and Seas*, the *Lyrics of Chu*, and other works.[55] He also was adept at divination, but this talent led to his violent death. When the military commander Wang Dun was planning a rebellion, Guo Pu at the time was serving as his adjutant. Wang sought a divination about whether he would succeed, and Guo's answer was "Surely not." Wang had him killed.

Guo Pu was the preeminent writer of the early Eastern Jin. His "River *Fu*" was a showcase for his lexicographical erudition. Only twenty-two poems survive, and of those, fourteen are in a group known as "Poems on Wandering Immortals." In these Guo Pu develops a persona that scorns the trappings of success and instead yearns for the simple life of reclusion. The language of the poems, in contrast to their themes, shows strong traces of Jin courtly rhetorical embellishment and erudition.

From the Series "Poems on Wandering Immortals" by Guo Pu

遊仙詩十四首第一					Poems on Wandering Immortals, 14 poems, no. 1
京 capital	華 florid	遊 wander	俠 knight	窟 pit	The capital is a lair of wandering knights.
山 mountain	林 grove	隱 hide	遯 withdraw	棲 [sɛj] roost	Mountain forests provide a roost for the recluse.
朱 vermillion	門 gate	何 "?"	足 suffice	榮 glory	How is a vermillion gate worth glorifying?
未 not yet	若 resemble	托 entrust	蓬 Peng-	萊 [lɛj] -lai	It is not so good as lodging in Penglai.[56]
臨 stand by	源 spring	挹 decant	清 pure	波 wave	Standing by the springhead, I decant [its] pure waves.
陵 ridge	岡 knoll	掇 gather	丹 cinnabar	荑 [dɛj] sprout	On ridges and knolls I gather cinnabar sprouts.[57]
靈 numinous	溪 ravine	可 can be	潛 submerge	盤 coil	At Mystic Ravine one can dwell in hiding.
安 why?	事 work at	登 climb	雲 cloud	梯 [tʰɛj] ladder	Why strive to ascend the cloud ladder?

55. The *Erya* 爾雅, translated tentatively as *Approaching Correctness*, perhaps dates to the end of the Warring States period.

56. Penglai was one of the fabled Isles of the Immortals in the eastern ocean.

57. According to traditional lore, this is an herb that confers long life.

漆 lacquer	園 garden	有 exist	傲 haughty	吏 clerk	In the Lacquer Garden there was a haughty clerk.[58]
萊 Lai	氏 clan	有 exist	逸 lofty	妻 [ts^{h}ɛj] wife	In the Lai clan, there was an untrammeled wife.[59]
進 advance	則 then	保 preserve	龍 dragon	見 see	If one advances [as a recluse], one preserves the "seeing of the dragon."[60]
退 withdraw	為 make	觸 hit against	藩 hedge	羝 [tɛj] ram	If one withdraws [from reclusion], one becomes a "ram entangled in a hedge."[61]
高 high	蹈 step	風 wind	塵 dust	外 outside	Treading on high, beyond the wind and dust:
長 long	揖 bow	謝 take leave	夷 Yi	齊 [dzɛj] Qi	Bowing long, [I] take leave of Bo Yi and Shu Qi.[62]

STUDY NOTES AND QUESTIONS

1. What do you make of the persona in the poem? Think of the language of the *Lyrics of Chu*—the wild shifts of topic and action and the elaborate symbolism—all representing the discontent, sorrow, and anger of the speaker. Is the persona in this poem wild or self-controlled?

2. Jin authors experimented with forms of ornamented language. One approach was the search for elegant substitute phrasing. "Cloud ladder," for example, is a metaphorical expression for entering into high government service. Another aspect was the use of striking phrasing: what does Guo Pu gain by using the term "lair," more literally a "pit," at the end of the first sentence?

---

58. According to Zhuang Zi's biography in the *Records of the Grand Historian*, he served as the clerk of the Lacquer Garden in Meng. The King of Chu, hearing of him, sent an envoy requesting that Zhuang Zi serve as a high minister in Chu. Zhuang Zi laughed and spurned the offer. 「莊子者，蒙人也，名周，嘗為蒙漆園吏。楚威王聞莊周賢，使使厚幣迎，許以為相。莊周笑謂楚使者曰：亟去，無污我。」

59. The *Biographies of Virtuous Women* (*Lienü zhuan* 烈女傳) records the story of a Master Lai, a recluse who farmed in the mountains. The King of Chu, hearing of him, invited him to serve as a minister, and Lai assented. Lai's wife, however, stated that given the chaos of the times, if she had to obey, it would lead to calamity. She affirmed she would not be compelled to go with her husband, put down her work, and fled into seclusion. Her husband decided to accompany her.

60. The phrase comes from the line commentary to the first hexagram in the *Canon of Changes*. In context, the hexagram line, "The dragon is seen in the field," points to a dragon still in the wilds that preserves its great virtue. Some commentaries, however, take this in the opposite way: the line refers to coming out of reclusion to serve the emperor [the dragon]. They explain the image in the second half of the couplet by saying that once one has served, it is difficult to retreat.

61. This image comes from the line commentary to hexagram 34 of the *Canon of Changes* and presents a ram whose horns have become entangled in a hedge and can neither advance nor withdraw. In this case, to withdraw is taken as returning to worldly pursuits, which inevitably lead to inextricable entanglements.

62. Bo Yi and Shu Qi were noble recluses who protested the Zhou conquest of the Shang as a violation of proper ritual decorum. They "refused to eat the grains of Zhou" and so starved to death on Mt. Shouyang.

3. What is the effect of the allusions in the poem? Is it part of Guo Pu's effort to gather around him a lineage and culture of reclusion? When he announces at the end that he is bidding farewell to Bo Yi and Shu Qi, what does he mean? To what is he bidding adieu?

Appendix to Chapter 4

Cao Pi 曹丕

典論·論文

文人相輕，自古而然。傅毅之於班固，伯仲之間耳，而固小之，與弟超書曰，「武仲以能屬文為蘭臺令史，下筆不能自休。」夫人善于自見，而文非一體，鮮能備善，是以各以所長，相輕所短。里語曰，「家有弊帚，享之千金。」斯不自見之患也。今之文人，魯國孔融文舉、廣陵陳琳孔璋、山陽王粲仲宣、北海徐幹偉長、陳留阮瑀元瑜、汝南應瑒德璉、東平劉楨公幹，斯七子者，於學無所遺，於辭無所假，咸以自騁驥騄於千里，仰齊足而并馳。以此相服，亦良難矣。蓋君子審己以度人，故能免於斯累，而作論文。

A Discourse on Literature[63]

Literary men have always insulted one another. Fu Yi and Ban Gu were virtually brothers, but Ban Gu made fun of Fu Yi in a letter to his elder brother Ban Zhao: "Fu Yi got to be Imperial Librarian because he had a 'facility' in writing—that is, whenever he put his writing brush to paper, he couldn't stop himself." Everyone is good at putting himself forward, but since literature is not restricted to one particular norm, few people can be good at everything. Therefore each person makes light of those things in which he is weakest by the criteria of his strengths. As the saying in the villages has it, "A worn-out broom is worth a thousand pieces of gold, so long as it belongs to me." This is a failure due to lack of self-awareness. The great literary men of the day are Kong Rong, Chen Lin, Wang Can, Xu Gan, Ruan Yu, Ying Chang, and Liu Zhen. These seven masters have a full store of learning, and their language does not simply borrow the colors of their predecessors. Yet they have found it hard to gallop head to head on their mighty steeds a thousand leagues, thus to pay one another the respect due. A superior person looks to himself when taking the measure of others and in this way avoids such entanglements of envy. Thus I have written the discourse on literature.

王粲長於辭賦，徐幹時有齊氣，然粲之匹也。如粲之初征、登樓、槐賦、征思，幹之玄猿、漏卮、圓扇、橘賦，雖張、蔡不過也，然於他文未能稱是。琳、瑀之章表書記，今之雋也。應瑒和而不壯，劉楨壯而不密。孔融體氣高妙，有過人者，然不能

Wang Can excels in poetic expositions. Even though Xu Gan sometimes shows a certain languor of energy, he remains Wang Can's match. Even the great Han writers such as Zhang Heng and Cai Yong have not done better than works like Wang Can's "Beginning of the Journey," "Climbing High in a Building," "The Locust Trees," or "Thoughts on Travel," or works like Xu Gan's "The Black Gibbon," "The Syphon," "The Circular Fan," or "The Orange Tree." Their other writings are not on a par with these. In memorials, letters, and records, Chen Lin and Ruan Yu are preeminent. Ying Chang's style is agreeable but lacks vigor. Liu Zhen's style is vigorous, but entirely on the surface with nothing held in reserve. Kong Rong's mastery of form and the

63. This translation is by Stephen Owen, in *An Anthology of Chinese Literature*, pp. 360–61.

持論，理不勝辭；以至乎雜以嘲戲，及其所善，揚、班儔也。

quality of energy in his work is lofty and subtle, with something about it that surpasses everyone else. But he cannot sustain an argument, and the presentation of natural principle in his work is weaker than his command of diction—to the point that he sometimes includes playful spoofing. But at his best he rivals the Han writers Yang Xiong and Ban Gu.

常人貴遠賤近，向聲背實，又患闇於自見，謂己為賢。夫文本同而末異，蓋奏議宜雅，書論宜理，銘誄尚實，詩賦欲麗。此四科不同，故能之者偏也，唯通才能備其體。

Most people value what is far from them and treat what is close at hand with contempt. They respect reputation but disregard real substance. They also suffer all the hazards of a failure of self-awareness in claiming to be men of great worth. On a basic level all literature is the same, but it acquires differences as it unfolds in its various branches. Generally speaking, memorials to the throne and disquisitions should have dignity; letters and discourses should be based on natural principles; inscriptions and eulogies should respect the facts, poems and poetic expositions should be beautiful. Each of these four categories is different, and a writer's abilities will lead him to favor some over others. Only a comprehensive talent can master all these forms.

文以氣為主，氣之清濁有體，不可力強而致。譬諸音樂，曲度雖均，節奏同檢，至於引氣不齊，巧拙有素，雖在父兄，不能以移子弟。

Qi, "vital force" or "breath," is the most important factor in literature. *Qi* has its own norms, either clear or murky. And it is not something that can be brought about by force. As "breath" we may compare it to flute music. Two performers may be equal in knowing the melody and following the rules of the rhythm; but when there is an inequality in drawing on a reserve of *qi* or breath, we can tell a skillful player from a clumsy one. A father cannot pass this on to his son, and an elder brother cannot pass it on to his younger brother.

蓋文章，經國之大業，不朽之盛事。年壽有時而盡，榮樂止乎其身，二者必至之常期，未若文章之無窮。是以古之作者，寄身于翰墨，見意於篇籍，不假良史之辭，不托飛馳之勢，而聲名自傳於後。故西伯幽而演易，周旦顯而制禮，不以隱約而弗務，不以康樂而加思。夫然，則古人賤尺璧而重寸陰，懼乎時之過已。而人多不強力，貧賤則懾於飢寒，富貴則流于逸樂，遂營目前之務，而遺千載之功。日月逝于上，體貌衰於下，忽

Literary works are the greatest accomplishment in the workings of a state, a splendor that never decays. Glory and pleasure go no further than this mortal body. To extend both of these to all time, nothing can compare with the unending permanence of a work of literature. It was for this reason that writers of ancient times gave their lives to the ink and brush and revealed what they thought in their writings. Without recourse to a good historian or dependence on a powerful patron, their reputations have been passed on to posterity on their own force. When King Wen of Zhou was in prison, he wrote additions to the *Classic of Changes*; even in his glory the Duke of Zhou made the prescriptions that are the *Rites*. The former did not forsake writing even in hardship; the latter was not distracted by health and pleasure. We can see from this that the ancients cared nothing for those great jade disks that were marks of wealth, but instead treasured the moment, fearful lest time pass them by. Yet people tend not to exert themselves in this way. In poverty and low position, they fear hunger and cold; when they are rich and honored, they let themselves drift in the distractions of pleasure. They occupy themselves with immediate demands and neglect an accomplishment that will last a thousand years. The days and months pass overhead; here below the face and

然與萬物遷化，斯志士之大痛也。融等已逝，唯幹著論，成一家言。

body waste away. We will pass suddenly into change with all the things of this world—and this causes great pain to a man with high aspirations. Kong Rong and the others have all passed away, and only the discourses composed by Xu Gan represent a truly individual accomplishment.

Chapter Five

The Maturing of Convention: The Poetry of the Northern and Southern Dynasties

Although the Jin emperors had reunited the old Han domain by AD 280, they could not maintain control as internecine strife eroded the dynasty. The generals who founded the Jin had given their kin large domains to provide both tax revenue and soldiers. However, the successors to the throne could not prevent their kinsmen from drawing on their great resources and regional powerbases and rebelling to seize power. After a short period of constant warfare, one of the rebellious princes invited a local Xiongnu chieftain to join his side, but instead Xiongnu troops under a succession of generals captured and sacked the two capitals of Chang'an and Luoyang and drove the Jin court south in 316. Thus began the two hundred years of division between non-Chinese rule in the North and successive military regimes in the South known as the Northern and Southern Dynasties.

North and South

Throughout the late Eastern Han, Wei, and Jin dynasties, as imperial authority weakened in the countryside, the great landholding clans had established their own armies and forts. Many farmers displaced by warfare voluntarily or involuntarily became part of these large estates as slaves or bondsmen. In order to rein in the power of these families at the imperial court and recruit officials as impartially as possible from these clan-controlled localities, Cao Cao had set up a process of recommendation and evaluation known as the Nine-Rank system. However, during the Jin, this system of evaluation designed to break the pattern of inherited rank began to evolve into yet another form of hereditary entitlement to office, since those who held the higher ranks controlled both the processes of recommendation and subsequent assessment.

When the Jin court fled south in 316, it was joined by at least a million refugees who resettled in the still sparsely settled lands of the middle and lower Yangzi basin. The elite families among the refugees brought with them a political, social, and economic order that shaped the aristocratic culture that emerged in the South. These aristocratic émigrés reestablished a Jin court and recreated great estates from lands either newly opened or seized and worked by slaves or bondsmen drawn from the large pool of landless farmers who joined the exodus south. Although the reconstituted Eastern Jin dynasty (317–420) continued for another hundred years, the court was in constant competition with its generals and with the aristocratic clans who had claims on bureaucratic office and exemption from taxation on the vast estates. In the end, Huan Wen 桓溫 (312–73), the greatest of the Eastern Jin generals, extended the dynasty's control into Sichuan but later came to dominate the court. His son usurped the throne in 403. Although the Jin was restored, Liu Yu 劉裕 (363–422), one of the generals responsible for the restoration, seized the throne in 420 to found the Song dynasty. Liu Yu was of humble background outside of the great clans, and he drew his major officials from outside the aristocracy as well, leaving the great lineages to hold hereditary offices that increasingly were becoming mere sinecures. Liu Yu died soon after founding the dynasty, but his trusted chief ministers decided that the heir whom Liu Yu had chosen was incompetent, and he deposed him for a younger brother, Liu Yilong 劉義隆 (407–53). Liu Yilong proved an exceptionally talented, hard-working administrator whose long rule brought peace and growing prosperity to the South as Emperor Wen of the Song. Still, Emperor Wen had to rely on regional commanders—rather than a strong palace army—to support his rule, and this inevitably led to palace intrigues in which his sons formed alliances to plot their ways into succession. In the end, the crown prince assassinated Emperor Wen, claimed the crown, and was then deposed by another brother who ruled with a firm grip at court but still was unable to control the provinces. The Liu Song dynasty continued to spiral downward in palace intrigue, and the last emperor was deposed in 479 by Xiao Daocheng 蕭道成 (427–82), the general in command of the palace guard, who founded the Qi dynasty (479–502).

Repeating the pattern seen in the Liu Song, the founding emperor died soon after taking the throne but was fortunate in having an effective successor, Emperor Wu 齊武帝 (440–93), whose Yongming reign period (483–93) defined a distinctive moment in the development of court poetry. Because Emperor Wu's successors were in continual fear of palace coups, however, they took violent measures to eliminate their rivals and reigned only briefly. Eventually a regional commander who was a distant member of the Xiao clan, Xiao Yan 蕭衍 (464–549), deposed the Qi ruler during a period of internecine turmoil and proclaimed the Liang dynasty in 502.

Xiao Yan, unlike earlier rulers, reigned for forty-seven years as Emperor Wu of Liang. Although his rule brought relative stability, warfare with the northern states and rebellions by provincial generals resisting Xiao Yan's efforts to assert greater authority continued to plague the state. His rule took a fateful turn in the spring of 548 when he accepted the surrender of Hou Jing 侯景 (d. 552), a northern commander who had controlled provinces on the border with the Liang but was forced to flee south with only a few troops. Xiao Yan then allowed Hou Jing to retain control of a province he had captured. However, in the summer of 548, fearing he was being outmaneuvered by Xiao Yan's negotiations with his former nominal rulers in the North, Hou Jing attacked the capital, Jiankang 建康. Although he had an army of only several thousand soldiers, the imperial clansmen who held positions as regional governors decided not to send aid in hopes of exploiting Hou Jing's rebellion to ascend to the throne. Thus Hou Jing was able to capture the capital, the emperor Xiao Yan, and the crown prince Xiao Gang 蕭綱 (503–51). When Xiao Yan died shortly after his capture, Hou Jing placed Emperor Wu's nephew (Xiao Zhengde 蕭正德) on the throne but quickly deposed and executed him, and in 549 replaced him with Xiao Gang. The provinces surrounding the capital were devastated in the ensuing warfare between Hou Jing, the provincial governors, and a succession of increasingly aggressive northern dynasties, and many peasants fled yet further south to the areas of Fujian and Guangdong. Hou Jing was killed by a subordinate in 552, and Chen Baxian 陳霸先 (503–59), who had gained a reputation fighting in Vietnam and had created a powerbase in Guangdong, eventually came to control the capital region. In 557 he deposed the last nominal Liang emperor and founded the Chen dynasty. He died two years later.

The odds against Chen Baxian's successor, his nephew Chen Qian 陳蒨 (522–66), were wretched: the heartland of the Liang dynasty had been devastated, the provincial governors had become independent warlords, and the Northern Zhou and Northern Qi pressed him on the border. Still, in the seven years of his rule, Chen Qian managed to suppress the regional warlords within his empire, and after his death, his oldest son was deposed by an energetic and competent younger son, Chen Xu 陳頊 (530–

82), who managed to hold the Chen state together against increased northern aggression. In 577, the Northern Zhou in the west defeated the Northern Qi in the east to unify all of north China. Two years later, the new Northern Zhou ruler turned his attention southward but—luckily for the Chen—died in 580. The next year, a northern general, Yang Jian 楊堅 (541–604), who was the father-in-law of the new ruler of the Northern Zhou, deposed his son-in-law to found the Sui dynasty (581–619). In 582 Chen Xu died, and the crown prince Shubao 陳叔寶 (553?–604), also known as Chen Houzhu 陳後主 the "final ruler of the Chen," came to the throne. After Yang Jian consolidated his rule, he initially refrained from attacking Chen in acknowledgement of the death of its emperor, but he later ordered a campaign against the Chen, and Chen Shubao surrendered when the capital Jiankang was captured in 589. Jiankang was razed to the ground.

This is the complex historical context within which the milieu of sophisticated princely salons nurtured the significant poetic developments of the Southern Dynasties period. Most of the famous poets of the age were descendants of northern émigré families who held their position in society through their lineage, through the offices to which their pedigree gave them access, and through their mastery of the cultural forms linked to the traditions of the lost Chinese heartland in the North. The salons in which they participated, given the historical context, were fraught with tensions in the constant battle for power between the provincial courts and the imperial throne. Many writers were caught up in the intrigues of their day and died because of it, while others sought to retreat from the court and its aristocratic values.[1]

1. Wang Xizhi's 王羲之 (321–79) "Preface to the *Orchid Pavilion Collection*" (translated as an appendix to this chapter) captures both the elegance and the anxieties of the courtly salons in the South.

Tao Qian 陶潛 (365–427)

Tao Qian's biography in the *History of the Song* appears in the chapter on recluses: his contemporaries viewed what later readers most valued in his poetry as merely interesting eccentricity. Tao Qian certainly was well known in his own day: Yan Yanzhi 顏延之 (384–456), one of the most important poets of the next generation, wrote his funerary ode. Moreover, his work continued to intrigue readers throughout the Southern Dynasties: Xiao Tong 蕭統 (501–31), heir apparent to the Liang throne, for example, wrote a biography and a preface for Tao Qian's collection. The aristocratic salons, however, stressed wit, understatement, and crafted elegance in their poetry: all values quite different from the style Tao Qian developed at his estate far away from court. The real impact of his work came during the Tang dynasty, when writers sought poetic values beyond the artifice of court style.

Tao Qian was from a minor aristocratic lineage. Both his grandfather and father had held regional posts as prefects, and Tao, in his turn, held a variety of minor positions away from the capital. In the end, however, he famously quit to return to his small estate, where he lived out the remainder of his days. Tao Qian's collection shows that he could write with the ornate craft of the imperial court; but once he returned to his farm, he sought out a different style to serve different ends. He wrote about his life on the farm: about his family, his neighbors, his experiences working the land, and his idle moments. He developed a very simplified style with easy couplet structure and little ornamental language that matched what he saw to be the values of simplicity he discovered in his agrarian life. His poetry preserved—even restored—the basic commitment to "speak of resolve," to record his responses to objects and events in a way that articulated his grasp of their meaning. In focusing this poetic commitment on a humble yet meaningful life away from the grand events of the day and finding a poetic voice to match that life, he created new possibilities for later poets and has been acclaimed as "the father of agrarian poetry."

From the Series "Reading the *Canon of Mountains and Seas*" by Tao Qian

讀山海經詩 十三首第一

Reading the *Canon of Mountains and Seas*, 13 poems, no. 1[2]

孟	夏	草	木	長	In the beginning of summer, grasses and trees grow tall.
first	summer	grass	trees	grow long	
遶	屋	樹	扶	疏 [ʂuə̆]	Around the roof, trees become dense.
encircle	roof	tree	[densely grown]		
眾	鳥	欣	有	託	The flocks of birds delight in having lodging.
group	birds	happy	have	entrust	
吾	亦	愛	吾	廬 [lyə̆]	I also love my hut.
I	also	love	my	hut	
既	耕	亦	已	種	Having plowed and also having planted,
since	plow	also	already	plant	
時	還	讀	我	書 [ʂyə̆]	At this time, I read my books.
time	return	read	my	writings	
窮	巷	隔	深	轍	The dead-end alley is apart from the deep wheel ruts [of the great]:
end	alley	separate	deep	wheel track	
頗	迴	故	人	車 [kyə̆]	It usually turns back the carriages of my acquaintances.
rather	turn back	old	people	cart	
歡	然	酌	春	酒	With pleasure I pour out spring ale;[3]
happy	-ly	pour	spring	wine	
摘	我	園	中	蔬 [ʂuə̆]	I pluck vegetables from my garden.
pick	my	garden	middle	vegetables	
微	雨	從	東	來	A light drizzle comes from the east;
slight	rain	from	east	come	
好	風	與	之	俱 [kyə̆]	A pleasant breeze accompanies it.
fine	wind	with	it	together	
汎	覽	周	王	傳	I browse through the biography of Zhou [Mu] Wang,[4]
float	look	Zhou	king	biography	
流	觀	山	海	圖 [tɦiuə̆]	And look over the maps of the mountains and seas:
flow	observe	mountain	sea	chart	
俯	仰	終	宇	宙	Thus in a moment's gaze I go to the ends of the universe:
look down	look up	end	universe		
不	樂	復	何	如 [ryə̆]	If this is not joy, then what is?
not	joy	again	what	resemble	

---

2. The *Canon of Mountains and Seas* was a Han dynasty text filled with exotic lore. Much Daoist imagery is preserved in it. For an English translation, see Anne Birrell, trans., *Classic of Mountains and Seas* (Harmondsworth: Penguin, 1999).

3. Ale was brewed from the fall harvest and was fully fermented by late spring.

4. The "Biography of Emperor Mu" has many extravagant tales of the king's wanderings to the four corners of the earth.

STEPHEN OWEN'S TRANSLATION

Reading the Classic of Mountains and Seas

Summer's first month, all plants grow tall;
around my cottage, trees dense and full.

There flocks of birds rejoice to find lodging,
and I too cling with love to my cottage.

With the plowing done and the sowing,
now and then I can read my books.

These narrow lanes keep out deep ruts,
and tend to turn away old friends' carts.

In pleasure I pour out the wine of spring
and pick from the garden's vegetables.

A light rain is moving in from the east,
a nice breeze comes along with it.

I browse in the tales of the King of Zhou
and look through the charts of the *Mountains and Seas.*

In an instant I have covered the universe—
if this is not joy, what is?

STUDY NOTES AND QUESTIONS

1. How is this poem about reading the *Canon of Mountains and Seas*? Consider the poem couplet-by-couplet and trace how it leads up to Tao Qian's looking over the text and the charts of the *Canon of Mountains and Seas.*

2. What is the theme that Tao Qian presents in the first two couplets of the poem? How does he develop it? How do the imaginative wanderings at the end relate to the earlier parts of the poem? (It is too easy to conclude that Tao Qian here simply contradicts himself. Think of your own habits of reading.)

From the Series "Returning to the Fields to Live" by Tao Qian

歸園田居 五首第一					Returning to the Fields to Live, 5 poems, no. 1
少 young	無 is no	適 accord	俗 vulgar	韻 rhyme	When young, I was not inclined to the common mode.
性 nature	本 origin	愛 loves	邱 hills	山 [ʂɛːn] mountains	By nature I loved the hills and mountains.
誤 mistake	落 fall	塵 dust	網 net	中 midst	Erring, I fell into the dusty net.[5]
一 one	去 leave	三 thirty	十	年 [nɛn] years	Having left [home], I was away for thirty years.[6]
羈 tethered	鳥 bird	戀 fond of	舊 old	林 grove	A tethered bird pines for its old grove.
池 pond	魚 fish	思 longs	故 old	淵 [ʔwɛn] pool	A fish in a pond longs for its old deep waters.
開 open	荒 wasteland	南 south	野 wilds	際 border	Opening up wasteland on the border of the south wilds,
守 maintain	拙 clumsy	歸 return	園 garden	田 [dɛn] field	Maintaining my clumsiness, I return to the fields.
方 square	宅 estate	十 ten	餘 extra	畝 *mu*	A square farmstead of ten or so *mu*,
草 grass	屋 roof	八 eight	九 nine	間 [kɛːn] bays	A grass-thatched house of eight or nine bays.
榆 elm	柳 poplar	蔭 shade	後 rear	簷 eaves	Elms and poplars shade the rear porch.
桃 peach	李 pear	羅 spread	堂 court	前 [dzɛn] before	Peaches and pears are arrayed before the courtyard.
曖 shady-darkened	曖	遠 distant	人 people	村 village	In the distance, the shade marks a village;
依 vague-indistinct	依	墟 small-	里 village	煙 [ʔɛn] smoke	Vaguely the smoke from the village [rises].
狗 dog	吠 bark	深 deep	巷 lane	中 in	Dogs bark in the deep lanes;
雞 cock	鳴 crow	桑 mulberry	樹 tree	顛 [tɛn] top	Cocks crow from the tops of the mulberry trees.[7]

5. The image here is of a bird straying too close to the ground and getting snared in a net.

6. A variant text for this line, which Hightower uses in his translation below, has "thirteen years" 十三年 rather than "thirty years" 三十年. Some scholars suggest that thirteen years is a more precise reckoning of the years Tao Qian spent in office.

戶 door	庭 courtyard	無 is no	塵 dust	雜 mix	The courtyard has no admixture of dust.
虛 empty	室 room	有 there is	餘 extra	閒 [ɣɛːn] leisure	My empty rooms have a surplus of leisure.
久 long	在 is in	樊 cage	籠 basket	裏 inside	Long in a cage,
復 again	得 obtain	返 return	自 of itself	然 [ɲian] is thus	I again get to return to the Thus-of-itself.

JAMES ROBERT HIGHTOWER'S TRANSLATION

Returning to the Farm to Dwell

From early days I have been at odds with the world;
My instinctive love is hills and mountains.
By mischance I fell into the dusty net
And was thirteen years away from home.
The migrant bird longs for its native grove.
The fish in the pond recalls the former depths.
Now I have cleared some land to the south of town,
Simplicity intact, I have returned to farm.
The land I own amounts to a couple of acres
The thatched-roof house has four or five rooms.
Elms and willows shade the eaves in back,
Peach and plum stretch out before the hall.
Distant villages are lost in haze,
Above the houses smoke hangs in the air.
A dog is barking somewhere in a hidden lane,
A cock crows from the top of a mulberry tree.
My home remains unsoiled by worldly dust
Within bare rooms I have my peace of mind.
For long I was a prisoner in a cage
And now I have my freedom back again.

---

7. This couplet alludes to the *Lao Zi* 老子 (section 80): "Though adjoining states are within sight of one another, and the sound of dogs barking and cocks crowing in one state can be heard in another, yet the people of one state will grow old and die without having had any dealings with those of another."「鄰邦相望，雞犬之聲相聞，民至老死，不相往來。」The translation is by D. C. Lau, from Lao Tzu, *Tao Te Ching*, translated by D. C. Lau (Harmondsworth: Penguin, 1963), p. 142.

The *Lao Zi* ("Old Master"), also known as the *Canon of the Way and Its Power* (*Daodejing* 道德經), is the seminal text of Daoism. Its provenance is uncertain. According to Lao Zi's biography in the *Records of the Grand Historian*, he lived during the time of Confucius (i.e., late 6th–early 5th century BC), but the text of the *Lao Zi* is probably a Warring States compilation of sayings associated with the emerging religious, philosophical, and political tradition of Huang-Lao thought. The *Lao Zi* stresses non-action (*wuwei* 無為), spontaneity (*ziran* 自然), and simplicity.

STUDY NOTES AND QUESTIONS

1. Tao Qian is considered the "father" of agrarian poetry. This poem shows how he invests his life on the farm—in its particularity—with significance. One way to see this process at work is to compare the third couplet ("A tethered bird . . .") with the sixth ("Elms and poplars . . ."). The bird and fish of the third couplet are metaphoric: what about the trees of the sixth? What do they signify? How do the previous four lines set up that significance?

2. The eighth couplet mentions the sounds of dogs barking and cocks crowing. It alludes to the *Lao Zi*, but as you read the poem, do you hear these sounds as part of the actual landscape? Think of your own experience: how can images be symbolic and real at the same time?

3. How is the agrarian world (as opposed to the forests of the hermit) an abode of the spontaneous ("Thus-of-itself")?

From the Series "Twenty Poems on Drinking Ale" by Tao Qian

飲酒 二十首第五					Twenty Poems on Drinking Ale, no. 5
結 weave	廬 hut	在 is at	人 people	境 region	I thatched a hut in a populated area,
而 and/but	無 is no	車 cart	馬 horse	喧 [xuan] clamor	Yet there is no clamor of horses and carts.
問 ask	君 you	何 how	能 can	爾 like this	"I ask you how it can be like this."
心 heart	遠 far	地 land	自 of itself	偏 [pʰjian] peripheral	If the heart is distant, the place will be outland.
採 pick	菊 chrysan-themum	東 east	籬 hedge	下 below	I pick chrysanthemums by the east hedge
悠 distant	然 -ly	望 gaze	南 south	山 [ʂɛːn] mountain	And distantly gaze on South Mountain.
山 mountain	氣 vapors	日 day	夕 evening	佳 fine	The vapors on the mountain are lovely at dusk.
飛 fly	鳥 birds	相 mutually	與 with	還 [ɣwɛːn] return	Flying birds return following one another.
此 this	中 midst	有 there is	真 true	意 intent	Midst all this there is a truth of purpose,
欲 about to	辨 discern	已 already	忘 forget	言 [ŋɨan] words	About to explain, I've forgotten the words.

WENDY SWARTZ'S TRANSLATION

I built my hut in the realm of men,
Yet hear no clamor of horse and carriage.
You ask me how can it be done?
With a distant mind, one's place becomes remote.
Plucking chrysanthemums beneath the eastern hedge,
At a distance I see the southern mountain.
The mountain air turns finer at dusk,
As flying birds return together in flocks.
In these things there is true meaning,
I wish to explain, but have forgotten the words.

STUDY NOTES AND QUESTIONS

1. This is a remarkably easy-going yet well-structured poem. What is the problem the first couplet sets up? In case the inattentive reader missed the issue, Tao Qian has an interlocutor intervene in the third line to seek an explanation for the seeming contradiction of the opening lines. The answer in the fourth line is a bit cryptic: how does the rest of the poem fill out the explanation?

2. Follow the line of sight in the poem. Explain how Tao Qian structures it.

3. The sixth line occasioned a very famous textual debate. Some versions of the text have "gaze on South Mountain" 望南山 while others have "see South Mountain" 見南山. "Gaze" is a volitional word: Tao Qian makes an active effort to look to the mountains in the distance. "See" suggests happy coincidence: Tao Qian looks up, and there they are: the distant mountains. Su Shi 蘇軾 (1037–1101), a central cultural figure in the Northern Song, argued that surely "see" better conveyed Tao Qian's intent. (Swartz follows Su Shi's emendation in her translation.) Explain what is at stake in the debate.

4. Is Tao Qian being truthful in the final couplet? This is a very elegant form of poetic closure. Can you explain why?

Xie Lingyun 謝靈運 (385–433)

Xie Lingyun, Duke of Kangle 康樂公, was the grandson of the great Jin dynasty general Xie Xuan 謝玄. His membership in one of the most important clans in the realm afforded him great advantages but also came with corresponding risks. Proud and rash, he spent much of his life entangled in the maneuverings for power that marked the final years of the Eastern Jin (317–420) and the usurpation that created the Song court (420–79). As a child, Xie Lingyun grew up not in Jiankang, the capital, but in Kuaiji 會稽 (also pronounced Guiji), near modern Hangzhou. However, at fifteen he moved to the capital and at age twenty-one was assigned to office.

Liu Yu took the throne and founded the Song in 420. When Liu Yu died, in 422, Xie Lingyun was demoted to the post of prefect of Yongjia 永嘉 in the southeast near Kuaiji. He neglected his duties and soon retired to the clan estate in Kuaiji. The retirement, however, was brief: the emperor summoned him back to the capital where Xie established himself as a preeminent man of letters. Xie, not satisfied with being a mere literary ornament, grew dissatisfied and increasingly reckless. The emperor allowed him to return to Kuaiji, where he threw himself into improving his considerable estate. Xie Lingyun could not keep out of trouble, however: he created suspicions that he was plotting rebellion and, after numerous twists and turns, was exiled to Guangzhou in the far south, and then finally executed.

Xie Lingyun was not an adroit politician, but he was a fine poet. He mastered the court style and, in a pattern that recurs throughout the history of the poetic tradition, then extended the range of the rhetorical and formal skills he had honed at court to reflect on a world of new experiences. Xie Lingyun wrote extensively about his life in Yongjia and Kuaiji. Deeply moved by the mountain scenery there, he explored the nature of the meaning he found in his experiences. Scholars often point to the role of Buddhism in Xie's creation of a form of landscape poetry, but he also read the landscape through the formal structuring made available by an increasingly sophisticated use of parallelism and through the vast lore of the earlier literary tradition. The later tradition acknowledged his compelling synthesis of these many components by calling him the "father of landscape poetry."

"Returning from the Purification Hall at Stonewall" by Xie Lingyun

石壁精舍還湖中作

Returning from the Purification Hall at Stonewall, Written on the Lake

昏	旦	變	氣	候	Dusk to dawn changes the weather.
dusk	dawn	change	weather		
山	水	含	清	暉 [xuj]	The mountains and water hold in a pure gleam.
mountain	water	hold in	pure	gleam	
清	暉	能	娛	人	The pure gleam can delight one:
pure	gleam	can	allure	person	

遊 wander	子 person	憺 calm	忘 forget	歸 [kuj] return	The wanderer, at ease, forgets he must return.[8]
出 go out	谷 valley	日 sun	尚 still	早 early	When I left the valley, the day was still young.
入 enter	舟 boat	陽 sunny	已 already	微 [muj] faint	As I entered the boat, the sunlight already was waning.
林 grove	壑 glen	斂 gather	暝 darken	色 aspect	The wooded glens gathered in the darkening colors.
雲 clouds	霞 mist	收 receive	夕 twilight	霏 [p^{h}uj] wisps	The high clouds took in the twilight mists.
芰 caltrop	荷 lotus	迭 successive	映 shine	蔚 glisten	The water chestnuts and lilies glistened in succession.
蒲 rushes	稗 reed	相 mutually	因 rely	依 [ʔij] lean	Reeds and rushes lean on one another.
披 open	拂 brush	趨 hasten	南 south	徑 path	Pushing them aside, I hasten through the south path.
愉 pleased	悅 happy	偃 rest	東 east	扉 [puj] gate	Happy, I rest at the east gate.
慮 reckon	澹 placid	物 things	自 of itself	輕 light	Reckonings calmed, things then weigh lightly;
意 intention	愜 pleased	理 pattern	無 is no	違 [wuj] astray	Intentions well pleased, the pattern [unfolds] without straying.[9]
寄 send	言 word	攝 nourish	生 life	客 traveler	I send word to seekers of long life:[10]
試 try	用 use	此 this	道 way	推 [t^{h}wəj] push	Try using this way in your practice.

BURTON WATSON'S TRANSLATION

The weather changeable at dusk and dawn,
mountain waters shot through with clear light,
a clear light that makes men joyful:
the wanderer, lulled, forgets to go home.
Out of the valley, the sun still high;

8. This line echoes "Lord of the East," from the *Nine Songs* in the *Lyrics of Chu*: "Ah, the sound and sight delights one: / The observer, calmed, forgets he [must] return" (羌聲色兮娛人 / 觀者憺兮忘歸).

9. The terms "thing" (物, better translated as "phenomenon") and "pattern" (理) are paired categories in Buddhism. The first refers to the objects of perception as they arise, and the second refers to the logic of the arising of phenomena.

10. These seekers of long life are specifically Daoist adepts who developed alchemy, herbal lore, and yogic breath exercises in order to extend their lifespans.

boarding the boat, the light fading now,
forest and ravine clothed in sombering color,
clouds of sunset wrapped in evening mist;
lotus and caltrop, their leaves one by one shining;
reeds and cattails propped against each other—
push through, hurry down the trail to the south,
returning contented to bed behind the eastern door.
Thoughts at ease, outside things weigh lightly;
mind relaxed, nothing going wrong.
A word to you gentlemen "nourishers of life"—
try using this method for a while!

Stephen Owen's Translation

Written on the Lake, Returning from the Chapel at Stone Cliff

Dawnlight to dusk transmuted the atmosphere,
streams and hills infused with a luminous glow:

Such luminous glow can so beguile a man
that the traveler, rapt, neglects to go.

The sun was still low when I left the valley,
its light now grows faint as I board my boat.

These wooded canyons gather hues of the dark,
as the white clouds and red draw back twilight haze.

Caltrop and lotus alternate shining verdure,
cattails and reeds rest each on the other.

Pushing back brush, I rush down the southbound trail,
and cheerfully lie by my eastern portal.

When man's cares calm, the world's things grow light,
With the will content, the patterns don't go amiss,

These words I send to those nurturing life:
just try using this Way to search for it.

Study Notes and Questions

1. This is a poem about returning to the affairs of the lay world after visiting a Buddhist retreat. How does the first couplet present the issues surrounding return? Are there images of change and constancy? Do these issues transform the landscape into a symbolic order or do they inhere in the world as Xie Lingyun sees it here?

2. After the first couplet, Xie recounts the events of the day through his description of the landscape. What is that narrative?

3. While Xie creates a narrative, he also offers arresting images. Look carefully at the parallelism of the fourth couplet. How do the glens "gather in" the darkening colors as sunset approaches? If you have ever been in the mountains at dusk, draw on your own experience to explain the image. (If not, a vivid and precise imagination helps.)

4. Explain the last four lines in the context of the poem's occasion. What is "this way" to which Xie Lingyun refers? How does this conclusion echo and explain the opening couplet?

"Climbing the Tower by the Pond" by Xie Lingyun

登池上樓詩					Climbing the Tower by the Pond
潛 submerge	虯 dragon	媚 allure	幽 secluded	姿 manner	A submerged dragon adds allure to [the pond's] secluded manner.[11]
飛 fly	鴻 swan	響 echo	遠 distant	音 [ʔim] sound	A flying swan echoes its distant sound.
薄 near	霄 high cloud	愧 ashamed	雲 cloud	浮 float	Nearing the high mists, I am ashamed before the clouds' drifting.[12]
棲 roost	川 river	怍 ashamed	淵 pool	沉 [drim] sink	Roosting by the river, I feel shame before sinking into the abyss.[13]
進 advance	德 virtue	智 wisdom	所 what	拙 clumsy	"Advancing in virtue": wherein my wisdom is clumsy.[14]
退 withdraw	耕 plow	力 strength	不 not	任 [ɲim] bear	Retiring to plow: my strength cannot endure it.
徇 seek	祿 salary	反 return	窮 dead-end	海 sea	Seeking a salary, I have returned to the brink of the sea.
臥 lie down	痾 sick	對 face	空 empty	林 [lim] grove	Lying sick, I face the empty forest.
衾 coverlet	枕 pillow	昧 dark	節 season	候 period	With coverlet and pillow, I was unaware of the season.
褰 lift	開 open	暫 briefly	窺 peek	臨 [lim] look over	Opening [the curtain], I briefly peek out.

11. This image reflects an old belief that a dragon living in a pool adds luster to it.

12. That is, the swan sets the example of drifting off into the clouds, an example he cannot follow.

13. Similarly, the dragon shows the way to plunge into the depths, but he cannot.

14. The *Wenyan* commentary to the Qian hexagram in the *Canon of Changes* 《易・乾・文言》has the line, "The noble man advances his virtue and cultivates his task because he wants to be timely."「君子進德修業，欲及時也。」

傾	耳	聆	波	瀾	Inclining my ears, I listen for the billows.
tilt	ear	listen	wave	billow	
舉	目	眺	嶇	嶔 [k^{h}im]	Lifting my eyes, I gaze for the soaring peaks.
lift	eye	stare	soaring	steep	
初	景	革	緒	風	The incipient scene changes the remnant winds.[15]
at first	scene	change	remnant	wind	
新	陽	改	故	陰 [ʔim]	The new radiance transforms the old gloom.
new	radiance	change	old	shade	
池	塘	生	春	草	The pool bank grows spring grasses.
pool	dike	grow	spring	grass	
園	柳	變	鳴	禽 [gim]	The garden willow changes its singing birds.
garden	willow	change	call	small bird	
祁	祁	傷	豳	歌	"So much": I am stricken by the song of Bin.[16]
many-many		hurt	Bin	song	
萋	萋	感	楚	吟 [ŋim]	"So luxuriant": I am moved by the chanting of Chu.[17]
luxuriant-luxuriant		move	Chu	chant	
索	居	易	永	久	"Living apart" is easy to extend forever.[18]
apart	reside	easy	long	long time	
離	羣	難	處	心 [sim]	Separated from the crowd, it is hard to control one's heart.
separate	flock	hard	manage	heart	
持	操	豈	獨	古	Holding fast, how is [this] only in ancient times?
hold	grasp	how	alone	ancient	
無	悶	徵	在	今 [kim]	"Being without vexation" I confirm here now.[19]
not exist	vexation	confirm	exist	now	

15. "Scene" 景 does *not* seem to be an alternative form for "radiance" 影. The term "remnant wind" comes from "Crossing the River"《涉江》from the *Lyrics of Chu*: "I sigh at the lingering wind of autumn and winter."「欸秋冬之緒風」.

16. The phrase comes from "The Seventh Month"《七月》 from the "Airs of Bin"《豳風》,Mao 154 in the *Canon of Poetry*:

春日遲遲	The spring days come slowly, slowly.
采蘩祁祁	Picking white artemisia so many.
女心傷悲	The girl's heart is stricken with sadness,
殆及公子同歸	Likely she will return married to his lord's son.

17. The phrase is from "Summoning the Recluse" in the *Lyrics of Chu*《楚辭・招隱士》: "The princeling roams and does not return. The spring grasses grow so luxuriant."「王孫遊兮不歸，春草生兮萋萋。」

18. The phrase is from "Tangong" (Part 1)《檀弓, 上》in the *Record of Rites* 禮記: "Zixia said, 'I have lived long now apart from the crowd in seclusion.'"「吾離群索居，亦已久矣。」

19. The phrase comes from the Qian hexagram in the *Canon of Changes*: "One with the dragon's virtue who hides in reclusion does not change to follow the times, does not seek out reputation, and is without vexation in avoiding the world."「龍德而隱者也，不易乎世，不成乎名，遯世無悶。」

Stephen Owen's Translation

Climbing an Upper Story by the Pool

A dragon, submerged, enhances sequestered charms,
the swan in flight sends its voice echoing far.

Chagrined by one reaching the drifting cloud-wisps,
shamed by the other, settled in stream's deepest chasm.

My wisdom too awkward to rise by virtue;
my strength that cannot bear retiring to plow.

Now to sea's very edge in pursuit of income,
I lie here ailing, facing barren woods.

Quilt and pillow have blinded me to seasons,
now lifting the curtain, I briefly peer out.

I turn my ear to hearken to waves,
lift eyes to catch sight of towering cliffs.

In this new scene are altered the lingering winds,
fresh sunlight transfigures the shadows that were.

Pond and pool grow with grasses of spring,
garden willows vary the birds that there sing.

Such bounty brings pain at the songs of Bin.
lush growth touches the thoughts of Chu's lays.

Dwelling solitary easily comes to last long,
apart from others, hard to steady the heart.

Holding fast to standards is not only of old—
"Being free from distress" is confirmed right now.

Study Notes and Questions

1. This poem is more typical of Xie Lingyun's approach to reading the landscape through reference to textual traditions. How many different texts does he cite in these twenty-two lines?

2. Xie Lingyun asserts that the dragon and swan of the first two lines give depth to the landscape he confronts as he climbs the tower. The two animals are emblematic, yet the power of their examples sets the poem in motion. From the first four lines, what will the poem be about? How does the next couplet rephrase the theme?

3. By line 7, Xie has turned to the time of composition and begins to explain the particular significance of his making his way to climb the tower. The next six lines (7–12) provide the context for what he sees in lines 13–16. Try to paraphrase that context.

4. Lines 15–16 became very famous in the tradition, in part because of the use of the verbs in the third position in each line. The language is simple, but the effect of the causative syntax (see chapter 1) strongly animates the couplet. Explain how the pool bank gives renewed life to the grasses and how the garden willow "changes" its singing birds. A second reason the couplet became famous is that Xie Lingyun claimed he was inspired to compose it in a dream (and hence the couplet appears natural rather than labored and crafted). What does this account say about the time of the poem's writing and about poetry as an art of reflection rather than spontaneity? Is there anything in the poem to suggest that it was *not* written at the time of climbing the tower?

5. The poem ends with a series of reflections on the experience. What role do the allusions play in shaping the conclusion? How does the conclusion respond to the themes introduced in the opening couplets?

Bao Zhao 鮑照 (ca. 415–70)

In contrast to Tao Qian and Xie Lingyun, Bao Zhao was a complete outsider. He attained office and rose in rank through a mixture of pluck, diligence, and ability. The various princes, vying in the splendor and cultural attainments of their courts, were always interested in discovering new talent; Bao Zhao tried his luck with the Prince of Lin'an, Liu Yiqing, whose brilliant coterie of writers had assembled the famous collection of anecdotes titled *New Tales of the World* (*Shishuo xinyu* 世說新語). Bao Zhao impressed Liu Yiqing, who gave him a post. Bao Zhao proved able in office and attracted the notice of the emperor. His last post was as military adjutant to yet another prince. When the prince's troops rebelled, Bao Zhao died in the uprising.

Bao Zhao was the talented outsider who brilliantly defined the role of "talented outsider." His best-known works were not in the urbane, crafted forms of the court but in rugged, energetic imitations of earlier *yuefu* models. Later critics in the tradition praised him for writing out of his own experience of the hardship of commoners in a way that aristocrats like Xie Lingyun could not.

From the Series "Imitating 'Traveling the Road Is Hard'" by Bao Zhao

擬行路難第六							Imitating "Traveling the Road Is Hard," no. 6
對	案	不	能	食 [ʑik]			Facing the table, I cannot eat.
face	table	not	able	eat			
拔	劍	擊	柱	長	歎	息 [sik]	Drawing my sword, I strike the pillar and sigh long.
pull	sword	strike	column	long	sigh	sigh	
丈	夫	生	世	能	幾	時	A man born in this world: how much time does he have?
a manly man		born	age	able	how much time		
安	能	疊	燮	垂	羽	翼 [jik]	How can I tread carefully and sit with folded wings?
how	can	small steps		hang	feathers	wings	
棄	檄	罷	官	去			I'll throw away my documents, quit office, and leave.
discard	order	quit	office	leave			
還	家	自	休	息 [sik]			Returning home, I'll take my rest:
return	home	myself	rest	breathe			
朝	出	與	親	辭			In the morning, bid my parents farewell as I leave,
dawn	go out	with	parents	take leave			
暮	還	在	親	側 [tʂik]			At dusk, return to be at my parents' side,
dusk	return	be at	parents	side			
弄	兒	床	前	戲			Dandling children, playing before the bed,
play with	child	bed	in front	play			

看	婦	機	中	織 [tɕik]			Watching my wife as she weaves at the loom.
watch	wife	loom	middle	weave			
自	古	聖	賢	盡	貧	賤	From of old, the sage and worthy all have been poor and lowly.
from	old	sage	worthy	all	poor	lowly	
何	況	我	輩	孤	且	直 [drik]	How much more so my generation, isolated and straight?
how much more		my	ilk	alone	and	straight	

Paul Rouzer's Translation

Hard Traveling VI

I faced the table but could not eat;
I drew my sword and struck the pillar
    and uttered a lengthy sigh.
Just how long a time is it
    a man lasts in this world?
And how can he go limping along,
    dragging his wings behind?
I'll leave behind my post and go,
Come home again and take my rest —
Where I part with loved ones in the morn
And still come back to them at dusk.
I hang with my son as he plays by the bed;
Watch my wife as she weaves at her loom.
Since times gone by, the sages and worthies
    are always humble and poor —
True all the more for men like us
    who are upright in our solitude.

Study Notes and Questions

1. How different is the life that Bao Zhao portrays in the poem from that of Tao Qian? The tone and the dilemma that Bao Zhao presents to himself in the second couplet are very different from what one finds in Tao Qian's poems. Explain the tone and the issue with which Bao Zhao wrestles.

2. How does the *yuefu* folk song form contribute to the poem and to Bao Zhao's presentation of vexation and conflicted restlessness?

Xie Tiao 謝朓 (464–99)

Xie Tiao was from the same illustrious clan as Xie Lingyun. His route to office therefore was easy, but he also acquitted himself well in his posts, unlike Xie Lingyun. Although on occasion he tried to decline appointments, the emperor was free to accept or reject such refusals, and he refused to allow Xie Tiao to withdraw. In the end, Xie Tiao was implicated in a palace succession plot and executed.

Xie Tiao is known in the poetic tradition as the "Lesser Xie," in contrast to his kinsman Xie Lingyun. Xie Tiao, along with Shen Yue, came to define the so-called Yongming 永明 style (after the Yongming reign period [483–93] of the Qi dynasty). Xie and Shen developed the conventions for couplet construction—both in terms of tonal balance and of sophistication of parallelism—to a new level that opened the way for the regulated poetry of the Tang dynasty.

"Jade Staircase's Grievance" by Xie Tiao

玉階怨					Jade Staircase's Grievance
夕 evening	殿 palace	下 lower	珠 pearl	簾 curtain	In the night palace, she lowers the bead curtain.
流 flow	螢 firefly	飛 fly	復 again	息 [sik] rest	The flowing fireflies flit and stop.
長 long	夜 night	縫 mend	羅 gauze	衣 clothes	During the long night, she mends her sheer clothing.
思 long	君 you	此 this	何 when	極 [gik] end	This longing for you, when will it end?

XIAOFEI TIAN'S TRANSLATION

Grievance on the Jade Stairs

The twilight palace lowers pearl blinds,
Floating fireflies flit and come to rest.
Through long nights she sews his silken robe,
Longing for you, when will it ever end?

STUDY NOTES AND QUESTIONS

1. Explain the title. What is the ambience?

2. In the last line, the word *jun* 君, literally "lord," is a polite status pronoun that can mean either "you" or "him" ("her gentleman"). What difference do the two readings make in interpreting the poem?

3. As you read the poem, do you picture Xie Tiao as seeing this woman or just imagining her? What is the vantage point of the scene? Inside the room, outside, or indeterminate? Some critics write of the "male gaze" that turns women into objects of aesthetic contemplation. What role might the vantage point play in such an objectification?

4. We saw the Han dynasty version of a boudoir lament in chapter 2. Xie Tiao uses the much more compressed form of the quatrain and, because the themes and moods of the boudoir lament were well established, can afford to use just a handful of elements to sketch the scene. What elements does Xie Tiao evoke, and what does each contribute to the scene? (For example, what elements refer to the season, and why does the season matter?)

Southern Folk Songs

When the northern aristocratic lineages fled south with the fall of the Western Jin, they discovered a landscape and culture very different from that of the north China plain. The south was a land of rivers, lakes, and mists. Its winters were less harsh, its summers long and languorous. They also discovered folk traditions very different from those of north China. The aristocratic courts developed a taste for the "Wu song" 吳聲歌曲 styles popular among the young women of the southeast and for the "Western songs" 西曲歌 from regions further inland. Among the "Wu songs," the quatrain style of popular tunes entitled "Midnight's Songs" and "Midnight's Songs of the Four Seasons" proved particularly influential. Later writers used the style, language, and imagery of the songs to invoke the soft folk ways of the South.

From the Series "Midnight's Songs"

1. 子夜歌 Midnight's Song

自	從	別	郎	來	Ever since I parted from him,
from	since	part	master	come	
何	日	不	咨	嗟 [tsia]	What day have I not sighed?
what	day	not	sigh	sigh	
黃	蘗	鬱	成	林	Wormwood, dense, becomes a grove:
wormwood		dense	become	grove	
當	奈	苦	心	多 [ta]	What can be done about so much bitterness of heart?[20]
ought	what	bitter	heart	many	

2. 子夜歌 Midnight's Song

年	少	當	及	時	When young, one should act in season.
years	few	ought	reach	time	
蹉	跎	日	就	老 [law']	While hesitating, one daily grows older.
waiver		day	arrive	old	
若	不	信	儂	語	If you don't believe my words,[21]
if	not	believe	my	words	
但	看	霜	下	草 [ts^{h}aw']	Just look at the grass covered by frost.
only	look	frost	below	grass	

20. "Heart" refers both to the center of the wormwood bush, which produces a very bitter sap, and to the persona's own heart. "Bitter" means both "suffering" and bitterness of taste.

21. The poem uses a formulaic, "Southern" pronoun 儂 for "my."

3. 子夜歌 — Midnight's Song

攬	裙	未	結	帶	I throw on my skirt, not yet tying its belt.
grab	skirt	not yet	tie	belt	
約	眉	出	前	窗 [tʂ^{h}aiwng]	Arranging my brows, I go out to the front window.
arrange	eyebrow	go out	front	window	
羅	裳	易	飄	颺	My gauzy skirt is easily blown:
gauze	skirt	easy	breeze	blow	
小	開	罵	春	風 [puwng]	If it opens a little, I'll scold the spring wind.
little	open	scold	spring	wind	

4. 子夜歌 — Midnight's Song

我	念	歡	的	的	I recall our pleasure so clearly:
I	recall	delight	bright and clear		
子	行	由	豫	情 [dziajng]	Your conduct is with unsteady feelings.
you	travel	uncertain		feelings	
霧	露	隱	芙	蓉	Mists and dew hide the lotus blossoms:
mist	dew	hides	lotus		
見	蓮	不	分	明 [miajng]	Seeing the lotus is not distinct.[22]
see	lotus	not	distinct	clear	

STUDY NOTES AND QUESTIONS

1. Compare the "folk songs" with the quatrain by Xie Tiao above. Is the language similar? Is the voice in the poems similar? Do they use the four-line form in a similar way?

2. The "Wu Songs" are famous for their use of plays on words. Explain the double meanings in poems 2 and 4.

3. Explain who you imagine is the audience for the "Wu Songs."

22. The word 蓮 "lotus" sounds like 戀, "to be fond of," while 見 can mean "to see" or can mark a passive construction, i.e., "to be loved."

He Xun 何遜 (d. 518)

He Xun was recommended to the Liang court as a talented youth. He held a variety of positions but failed to impress Emperor Wu of Liang. He died while serving in the court of the Prince of Luling. His writing was much admired during his lifetime, and he had a reputation for writing few but excellent poems that were "limpid and new" 清新.

"At Parting" by He Xun

相送					At Parting
客	心	已	百	念	In the traveler's heart, already a hundred concerns.
traveler	heart	already	hundred	thoughts	
孤	遊	重	千	里 [li]	Wandering alone for again a thousand *li*.
lone	wander	twice	thousand	*li*	
江	暗	雨	欲	來	The river darkens; rain is about to come:
river	darken	rain	about to	come	
浪	白	風	初	起 [k^hi]	The billows whiten when the wind first rises.
billows	white	wind	at first	rise	

BURTON WATSON'S TRANSLATION

The traveler's heart has a hundred thoughts already,
his lonely journey piling mile on endless mile.
The river darkens, rain about to fall;
waves turn white as the wind comes up.

STUDY NOTES AND QUESTIONS

1. Was this poem written at the parting or after it? Is the writer the "traveler" or is the recipient of the poem? Why is the traveler's heart "already" filled with myriad concerns?

2. Who is seeing the scene described in the final couplet? Where is he standing?

3. The final line is a great example of the art of "objective closure," the use of a compelling image to stand in for the author's final response. Is the scene, by itself, beautiful? Is it troubling? What does it convey about the writer's thoughts and feelings at this parting?

Xiao Gang 蕭綱 (503–51)

Xiao Gang was the third son of Xiao Yan 蕭衍 (Emperor Wu of Liang 梁武帝, r. 502–49). After the death of Xiao Tong, Xiao Gang became the heir apparent. Xiao Yan, however, lived a long time, and when Xiao Gang came to the throne as Emperor Jianwen 梁簡文帝, it was under dire circumstances. In 547 the general Hou Jing of the northern Eastern Wei dynasty surrendered his army to the Liang. The next year, however, he rebelled and captured the Liang capital of Jiankang. He deposed Emperor Wu and put a new emperor, Xiao Zhengde, on the throne. Xiao Zhengde proved inadequate for Hou Jing's purposes, so in 549 Hou deposed and executed him and proclaimed Xiao Gang emperor. In 551 Hou Jing then deposed Xiao Gang and had him killed.

Even before he became heir apparent, Xiao Gang had attracted a group of talented writers to his salon. When he became next in line to the throne, he returned to the capital with an even more impressive coterie of writers at his side. They as a group developed the "Palace style" 宮體 (the name derives from the fact that the heir apparent lived in the "Eastern Palace" 東宮). This style, built upon the formal, tonal, and rhetorical proprieties of the earlier Yongming style of the Qi, sought yet greater poetic refinement. The scope of topics it treated was narrow, and the plight of palace women—as imagined by the male courtier—was a common theme. Xiao Gang and his salon, which included Xu Ling 徐陵 and Yu Xin 庾信, compiled the famous anthology of love poetry *New Songs of the Jade Terrace* (*Yutai xinyong* 玉臺新詠).

"Chanting about Late Evening in the Bedroom" by Xiao Gang

詠晚閨					Chanting about Late Evening in the Bedroom
珠 pearl	簾 curtain	向 face	暮 dusk	下 lower	The pearl curtain lowers in the setting sun:
妖 alluring	姿 manner	不 not	可 can be	追 [trwi] pursue	Her alluring manner cannot be divined.
花 flower	風 wind	暗 dark	裏 in	覺 aware	In the dark, she becomes aware of the flower-strewing wind;
蘭 orchid	燭 candle	帳 hanging	中 middle	飛 [puj] fly	The scent of the orchid candle flies within the bed curtain.
何 what	時 time	玉 jade	窗 window	裏 in	When, by the jade window frame,
夜 night	夜 night	更 again	縫 mend	衣 [ʔij] clothes	Will she night after night again mend clothes?

XIAOFEI TIAN'S TRANSLATION

Another Three Couplets on "Spring Boudoir Feelings"

The bead curtain is drawn shut towards evening,
her alluring demeanor cannot be pursued.
A breeze among the flowers is felt in the dark,
the perfumed candle glides behind the draperies.
When will she sit by the jade window,
night after night, sewing clothes?

STUDY NOTES AND QUESTIONS

1. Compare this poem to Xie Tiao's "Jade Staircase Grievance." What elements does Xiao Gang repeat? What does he add?

2. From whose perspective is "Jade Staircase Grievance" written? What signals this in the poem? What about the perspective in "Late Evening in the Bedroom"—which line refers to the viewer? How does the viewer's perspective change the imagery, tone, and significance of the poem?

3. Notice that Tian translates 覺 (*jue*) in the passive as "is felt . . . ," while I propose "[she] becomes aware . . . ." What difference does the translation make in shaping the perspective of the poem?

4. This poem conveys a small vignette of disappointment. What is the writer of the poem asking and hoping in the last two lines?

"At Night, Gazing at a Lone Flying Goose" by Xiao Gang

夜望單飛雁							At Night, Gazing at a Lone Flying Goose
天 sky	霜 frost	河 river	白 white	夜 night	星 star	稀 [xij] sparse	The sky brings frost, the Milky Way is white, the night stars are few.
一 one	雁 goose	聲 sound	嘶 call out	何 what	處 place	歸 [kuj] return	One goose calls out: to what place does it return?
早 early	知 know	半 half	路 road	應 surely	相 mutual	失 lose	If it had known early that, halfway, it surely would lose [its flock],
不 not	如 resemble	從 from	來 come	本 original	獨 alone	飛 [puj] fly	[This] is not so good as from the start flying alone.

Xiaofei Tian's Translation

Gazing at a Lone Wild Goose Flying at Night

The sky is frosty, the Milky Way pale, the evening stars few,
one wild goose cries a mournful note: where can he go?
Had he known he would lose his companions halfway,
it would have been better for him to always fly alone.

Study Guide and Questions

1. We have encountered the sense of volition in the term "gaze" (*wang* 望) in Tao Qian's poem. What would have changed in Xiao Gang's framing of the vignette in the poem if the title had been "At Night, Hearing a Lone Flying Goose?" Does he in fact see the goose?

2. In this poem Xiao Gang casts off the courtly style and returns to the simplicity and directness of Jian'an. However, for a sophisticated court writer like Xiao Gang, style is a choice, and the challenge is to decide whether the author or just his persona is speaking the poem's anguished final line. Critics take this as a moment of authentic self-expression because the line breaks through the clichéd sentiments one would expect from a well-crafted persona.

3. Xiao Gang uses the quatrain form very effectively in the poem. In the quatrain form, the third line typically presents a turn in the poem to which the final line is a response. Here, the third line by itself appears to be simply "It knew early on . . . " rather than the concessive "*If* it had known early on . . . ," but the final line recasts the third line as a condition about which it draws a conclusion.

4. One final aspect of the poem that is very hard to capture in English is the "empty" (*xu* 虛) quality of the language of the second couplet, that contributes an affective, subjective, interior quality in contrast to the "substantive" (*shi* 實) first line. The adjective "half," the adverbs "early" and "mutually," along with the auxiliary verb "surely [is]," in the third line all are "empty" while in the fourth line, only "fly" is substantive. Consider the use of nouns, verbs, adjectives (and nouns serving as adjectives), and adverbs in the poem. Why might the first line be considered "full" and the last line "empty"?

Yu Jianwu 庾肩吾 (487–551)

The life of Yu Jianwu followed the fortunes of his patron and pupil, Xiao Gang. He joined Xiao Gang's staff while Xiao was still the Prince of Jin'an. When Xiao Gang transferred to Yongzhou, Yu Jianwu and nine other writers received appointments as his resident scholars. When Xiao Gang became heir apparent, Yu Jianwu followed him to the capital and was given a position in a palace literary and scholarly office, the Wendesheng 文德省. During Xiao Gang's captive reign as emperor under the control of Hou Jing, Yu Jianwu managed to escape. He was captured once more but managed to get free and made his way to the camp of another son of Emperor Wu who had declared himself emperor in opposition to Hou Jing. Yu Jianwu died soon thereafter.

Yu Jianwu, like his son Yu Xin (see below), is associated with the "Palace style" of Xiao Gang's salon. His poetry is highly crafted, elegant, and narrow in scope.

From the Series "Matching the Poems of the Prince of Xiangdong" by Yu Jianwu[23]

奉和湘東王應令春宵 / Responding to Command: Spring Night

征 journey	人 person	別 parting	未 not yet	久 [kuw'] long	Parting from the traveler is not yet long.
年 year	芳 fragrant	復 again	臨 look over	牖 [juw'] window	As the year flourishes, I again look out the window.
燭 candle	下 beneath	夜 night	縫 mend	衣 clothes	By candlelight I mend clothes at night.
春 spring	寒 cold	偏 one-side	著 attach	手 [ɕuw'] hand	The spring chill lodges especially in the hands.
願 request	及 reach	歸 return	飛 flying	雁 goose	I want to reach a returning goose
因 rely	書 letter	寄 send	高 High	柳 [luw'] Willow	And use it to send a letter to High Willow.[24]

23. The Prince of Xiangdong was Xiao Yi 蕭繹 (508–55), who became Emperor Yuan of the Liang 梁元帝 (r. 552–55).

24. High Willow had been a fortress and military district in the distant northeast since Han dynasty times.

XIAOFEI TIAN'S TRANSLATION

Spring Night Respectfully Presented as a Companion Piece Written at the Prince of Xiangdong's Command

The soldier on a campaign has long been gone,[25]
spring's fragrance once again comes into the window.
In the candlelight she sews clothes all night,
she feels spring's chill particularly in her hands.
"I wish I could catch the wild geese returning north,
to send a letter to the Fortress of Tall Willow."

STUDY NOTES AND QUESTIONS

1. Note the conventionality of the items in the poem. Is the simplicity of the language at odds with the poem's occasion, an imperial command to write on the topic of "Spring Night"?

2. One standard argument concerning elite poetry about lonely women is that it is a metaphor for the plight of the official longing to serve his ruler. How well does that approach work for this poem? What elements might support the argument for allegory? What aspects work against it?

25. Tian accepts the variant *lai* 來 ("come") for *wei* 未 ("not yet") in the early Tang encyclopedia *Yiwenleiju* 藝文類聚.

Yu Xin 庾信 (513–81)

As the talented son of a well-established aristocratic lineage, Yu Xin, the son of Yu Jianwu, moved easily in court circles. However, when Xiao Gang's sad reign was nearing its end, Yu Xin joined other members of Xiao Gang's entourage in fleeing Jiankang. Yu Xin, on leaving the city in 551, made his way to Jiangling 江陵, where he joined his father at the court of Xiao Yi 蕭繹 (508–55; the future Emperor Yuan 元帝), who was organizing resistance to Hou Jing. In 554 Yu Xin was sent on an important mission as envoy to the northern state of the Western Wei 西魏, which was using the turmoil to gain territory. In 557, while Yu Xin was still serving as an envoy, the Liang was overthrown by the Chen dynasty. Because the Western Wei court admired Yu Xin's talents, he was kept captive in Chang'an. When the Northern Zhou replaced the Western Wei, its emperor greatly respected Yu Xin, who was persuaded to serve in office. When diplomatic relations were established between the Northern Zhou and the Chen, the Chen emperor asked for the return of the captive envoys. Zhou Wudi allowed all except Yu Xin and another well-known poet, Wang Bao 王褒 (fl. 570), to return south. Yu Xin died in the first year of the Sui dynasty.

Yu Xin and Xu Ling were the preeminent masters of the "Palace style" associated with the salon of Xiao Gang. During his northern captivity, Yu Xin drew upon this mastery of form to reflect upon his newly straitened and difficult situation. Critics argue that he brought new depth and substance to the arid formalism of the "Palace style."

"Dusty Mirror" by Yu Xin

塵鏡					Dusty Mirror
明 bright	鏡 mirror	如 resemble	明 bright	月 moon	The bright mirror resembles a bright moon.
恆 always	常 constant	置 place in	匣 case	中 [truwŋ] middle	Always I place it in its case.
何 what	須 need	照 shine on	兩 pair	鬢 temple-hair	What need is there to shine on my paired temple hairs?
終 end	是 this is	一 one	秋 autumn	蓬 [bəwŋ] tumbleweed	To the end, they are one autumn tumbleweed.

XIAOFEI TIAN'S TRANSLATION

Dusty Mirror

The bright mirror is like the bright moon,
I always keep it in the mirror-case.
For what's the point of looking at my temple hair?
It is but one mess of autumn tumbleweed.

STUDY NOTES AND QUESTIONS

1. "Dusty Mirror" is in the courtly genre of "poems chanting about objects" (*yongwu* 詠物). Since Yu Xin writes about a bright mirror kept in its case, why is the poem entitled "Dusty Mirror"?

2. Comparing a round hand mirror to the full moon was a cliché by Yu Xin's time, but he greatly complicates the simile. In the second line, Yu Xin shifts to questions of time: the mirror may be like a full moon, but how long is a moon full? How long is the mirror bright? Can the mirror be bright when locked in the case that preserves its eternal brightness?

3. The poem is in the borrowed voice of an aging court woman but takes on new resonances because the author is a courtier who has been compelled to travel far away from his native land. For him, the tumbleweed, detached from its roots and constantly blown about by the wind, has an emblematic quality. What thoughts and emotions about his circumstances does Yu Xin convey through this brief account of a mirror he never uses?

"Again Parting from Secretarial Minister Zhou" by Yu Xin

重別周尚書					Again Parting from Secretarial Minister Zhou[26]
陽 Yang	關 Pass	萬 10^4	里 *li*	道 road	On the ten thousand *li* road from Yang Pass,[27]
不 not	見 see	一 one	人 person	歸 [kuj] return	One does not see a single person return.
惟 only	有 there is	河 river	邊 beside	雁 goose	There are only the geese by the Yellow River:
秋 autumn	來 come	南 south	向 toward	飛 [puj] fly	When autumn comes, they fly toward the south.

STUDY NOTES AND QUESTIONS

1. The language of the poem—and especially the reference to Yang Pass—invokes the many southern "border poems" in which writers imagine husbands serving on the frontier missing their wives. Does the specificity of the occasion transform our reading of the generic language?

2. This is another poem that relies on "objective closure." Yet what do the geese flying south signify for the author on this occasion? For example, why do the geese fly south? Are we supposed to think of the particular reasons or simply consider it their nature? What difference does it make? Why is Zhou heading south? Since Yu Xin served a dynasty that no longer existed, is he like the geese or like Zhou? Or is the contrast relevant?

---

26. Zhou Hongzheng 周弘正 once served as Secretariat Minister of the Left for the Liang dynasty in the South. As an ambassador for the new Chen dynasty, he visited Yu Xin in captivity in the Northern Zhou capital of Chang'an.

27. Yang Pass in fact is on the border of China's frontier with the Inner Asian Steppe, far to the northwest.

3. Consider the scales of time in the poem: what period of time is invoked in the first couplet? Is it linear or cyclical time? What about the second couplet? Where does Zhou Hongzheng fit into these patterns? Where does Yu Xin? What happens to that sliver of time, the present moment of farewell, in this context?

Appendix to Chapter 5

Wang Xizhi 王羲之 *(321–79)*

蘭亭集序

Preface to the Orchid Pavilion Collection[28]

永和九年，歲在癸丑，暮春之初，會於會稽山陰之蘭亭修褉事也。群賢畢至，少長咸集。此地有崇山峻嶺，茂林修竹。又有清流激湍映帶左右，引以為流觴曲水。列坐其次，雖無絲竹管弦之盛，一觴一詠，亦足以暢敘幽情。

In the ninth year of the Eternal Harmony era in the beginning of the last month of spring when the calendar was in *kuei-ch'ou*,[29] we met at the Orchid Pavilion in Shan-yin, Kuei-chi to celebrate the Bathing Festival.[30] All the worthy men assembled; the young and senior gathered together. Here were lofty mountains and towering hills, thick groves and tall bamboo. And, there was a clear, rapid stream reflecting everything around that had been diverted to play the game of floating wine-cups along a winding course. We sat down in order of precedence. Though we had none of the magnificent sounds of strings and flutes, a cup of wine and then a poem was enough to stir our innermost feelings.

是日也，天朗氣清，惠風和暢。仰觀宇宙之大，俯察品類之盛。所以遊目騁懷，足以極視聽之娛，信可樂也。

This was a day when the sky was bright and the air was pure. A gentle breeze warmed us. Upwards we gazed to contemplate the immensity of the universe; downward we peered to scrutinize the abundance of living things. In this way, we let our eyes roam and our emotions become aroused so that we enjoyed to the fullest these sights and sounds. This was happiness, indeed!

夫人之相與，俯仰一世，或取諸懷抱，晤言一室之內。或因寄所託，放浪形

Men associate with each other but for the brief span of their lives. Some are content to control their innermost feelings as they converse inside a room. Some are prompted to give rein to their ambitions and lead wild, unfettered lives. There is all the difference between

28. Orchid "pavilion" is perhaps more accurately but less poetically rendered as "Orchid District," since a *ting* 亭 is an administrative unit. The translation is by Richard Strassberg in Victor Mair, ed., *Columbia Anthology of Traditional Chinese Literature.*

29. April 22, 353: *gui-chou* is a set of symbols from a repeating sixty-year cycle.

30. This initially was a festival of ritual purification, but by Wang Xizhi's time it had become a good excuse for a spring outing.

骸之外。雖取舍萬殊，靜躁不同，當其欣於所遇，暫得於己，快然自足，曾不知老之將至。及其所之既倦，情遂事遷，感慨係之矣。向之所欣，俯仰之間，已為陳跡，猶不能不以之興懷。況修短隨化，終期於盡。古人云，死生亦大矣，豈不痛哉。

controlled and abandoned natures, just as the quiescent and the frenzied are unalike. Yet, both take pleasure from whatever they encounter, possessing it but for a while. Happy and content, they seem unaware that old age is fast approaching. And, when they tire of something, they let their feelings change along with events as they experience a deep melancholy. What they had taken pleasure in has now passed away in an instant, so how could their hearts not give rise to longing? Furthermore, a long or short life depends upon the transformation of all things: everything must come to an end. An ancient said, "Life and death are the greatest of matters, indeed!" Isn't this reason enough to be sad?

每覽昔人興感之由，若合一契，未嘗不臨文嗟悼，不能喻之於懷。固知一死生為虛誕，齊彭殤為妄作。後之視今，亦猶今之視昔，悲夫。故列敘時人，錄其所述，雖世殊事異，所以興懷，其致一也。後之覽者，亦將有感於斯文。

Whenever I read the causes of melancholy felt by men of the past, it is like joining together two halves of a tally.[31] I always feel sad when I read them, yet I cannot quite understand why. But I know that it is meaningless to say life and death are the same; and to equate the longevity of P'eng-tsu with that of a Shang-tzu is simply wrong.[32] Future readers will look back upon today just as we look back at the past. How sad it all is! Therefore I have recorded my contemporaries and transcribed what they have written. Over distant generations and changing events, what gives rise to melancholy will be the same. Future readers will also feel moved by these writings.

31. Both here and below, what Strassberg translates as "melancholy" is better understood as "strong emotion."

32. "Shang-tzu" (*pinyin*: Shangzi) is a child who dies young. Strassberg treats the term as a proper noun.

Chapter Six

Early and High Tang Poetry before Du Fu

When Li Shimin 李世民 (600–649, r. 626–49) urged his father to seize the throne from the Sui emperor and proclaim the founding of the Tang, they did not know that they were at the beginning of a three-hundred-year-long dynasty. Later, before the ignominious collapse of Emperor Tang Xuanzong's 唐玄宗 (685–762, r. 712–56) reign into catastrophic rebellion, the officials of his court did not know that they would become part of the legend of the glorious height of Tang rule. And when Du Fu 杜甫 and Li Bai 李白 died, they had every reason to believe that they were failures: they did not know that within a generation they would be hailed as the greatest poets of their age and that history would view them as the greatest poets in the Chinese tradition. We later readers, in contrast, know all of this, and we tend to allow our knowledge to shape our reading of the poetry. Our backward glance imparts a sense of necessity to Tang poetry that is not part of the poetry itself. The Tang dynasty *was* the great age of Chinese poetry, but this claim is a cliché and of little value. The challenge is to allow the poetry—with its astonishing variety of voices, moods, styles, and topics—to speak for itself.

The Tang rulers, like those of the brief Sui dynasty, were northerners. They were suspicious of the allure of the Southern courts and at the same time intrigued by it. Moreover, as the new masters of a reunited China, the early Tang emperors felt the need to bring together the divergent cultures of the North and South that had grown apart during the years of disunion. Southern scholars, for example, were central to the grand textual compilation projects for the Confucian canon at the beginning of the dynasty that were to demonstrate that the Tang was the worthy inheritor of the Han universal empire. In literature, the Tang court sought to demonstrate that it could master the full legacy of the South yet improve upon it with the strength and seriousness of Northern values. The Tang emperor and princes invited the best of the remaining Southern poets to serve as advisors and to join them in versifying at imperial banquets and all the many occasions that called for poetry. The Tang court largely continued the elegant styles of the Southern salons, stripped perhaps of their most frivolous topics and hyper-refined mannerisms. Fortunately for poetry—though not for the poets—the Tang court was as dangerous a place as were the princely courts of the Southern dynasties. As before, courtiers were banished or prudently withdrew from the centers of power, and they took their mastery of poetic technique with them. They wrote of serious personal concerns through the courtly style and, in demanding more from it, changed it.

Another set of historical circumstances also intervened to shape poetry during the first century of the Tang. Empress Wu Zetian 武則天 (623–705, r. 690–705), the wife of Emperor Gaozong 唐高宗 (628–83, r. 649–83), was a formidable power even during her husband's lifetime. After his death, she dominated her sons. Two were declared emperors in succession—while she still remained regent—and she removed both. In the end she declared her own dynasty. Eventually Tang loyalists within the court organized resistance and restored the deposed emperors to the throne. During the period of Wu Zetian's ascendancy, however, she sought to marshal support among "new men"—talented commoners and the lesser branches of the great clans—who were less committed to the Tang imperial clan and who would owe their rising status to her support. One mechanism by which she sought to recruit the new elite was through greater use of the "presented scholar" (*jinshi* 進士) examination system, which underwent major reform in 681. The *jinshi* examination after 681 demanded policy essays but also required candidates to compose poems in the "regulated verse" form that had evolved out of palace poetry. Thus one important result of Empress Wu's political maneuverings was that ambitious young men from good families throughout the empire sought to master the regulated verse form. The center of poetic composition began to shift from the court itself to the elite society of the capital, Chang'an 長安.

The short reigns of the two Tang emperors, the sons of Wu Zetian who were restored to the throne in succession after the empress's death, were extremely unstable, filled with brutal palace intrigue and marked by institutional drift. When Xuanzong came to the throne, however, he restored morale and efficiency to the civil bureaucracy, and his military campaigns expanded the empire to its greatest reach. Chang'an became the glittering, cosmopolitan capital of a vast realm that stretched from northern Vietnam in the south to outposts in Central Asia in the west. Later critics deemed the bold, expansive poetry of his reign, with its grand vision, to be "High Tang" 盛唐 poetry. Some of the major poets of the period like Wang Wei came from long established lineages, while others like Zhang Jiuling 張九齡 (678–740)—who came from Guangzhou—were "new men" recruited through the examination system. Du Fu, the greatest Tang poet, to be discussed in the next chapter, was from a minor branch of a declining aristocratic lineage, while Li Bai was of very uncertain ancestry and was an outsider who briefly attracted interest in the capital for his outlandish ways. Indeed, the capital's brilliance, wealth, and hunger for the new during the height of Xuanzong's power attracted talented writers and encouraged poetic innovation.

This chapter looks at writers from the beginning of the Tang through Xuanzong's reign and tries to suggest the richness and variety of the poetry of the period.

Wang Bo 王勃 (650–76)

Wang Bo was from a well-established aristocratic lineage. His grandfather was the important scholar Wang Tong 王通 (584–617). Wang Bo was a precocious child and passed an imperial examination at age sixteen. He was appointed to a nominal office in the imperial court, found and quickly lost employment at one of the princes' courts, and then traveled to Sichuan both to sightsee and to seek patronage. However, because he murdered a slave who had committed a crime and whom he was concealing, he was stripped of his status. His father, however, suffered a yet worse fate for Wang Bo's crime: he was exiled to serve in Jiaozhi 交趾 in what is now northern Vietnam. Wang Bo traveled to see him but drowned in the ocean en route.

Wang Bo, one of the "Four Talents of the Early Tang," is famous primarily as a prose stylist. In poetry he excelled at pentasyllabic regulated verse and quatrains.

"The Pavilion of the Prince of Teng" by Wang Bo

			滕王閣				The Pavilion of the Prince of Teng
滕	王	高	閣	臨	江	渚 [tɕia’]	The tall pavilion of the Prince of Teng
Teng	prince	high	pavilion	overlook	river	sandbar	overlooks river sandbars.[1]
佩	玉	鳴	鸞	罷	歌	舞 [muə’]	Pendant jades and chiming phoenix-bells
pendant	jade	call	phoenix	stop	sing	dance	stopped their singing and dancing.[2]
畫	棟	朝	飛	南	浦	雲	Among the painted beams, South Bank
painted	beams	morning	fly	south	bank	clouds	clouds that fly in the morning,[3]
珠	簾	暮	捲	西	山	雨 [wuǎ’]	Bead curtains rolled up at dusk:
bead	curtains	dusk	roll	west	mountain	rain	rain on the western mountains.[4]
閒	雲	潭	影	日	悠	悠 [juw]	Day after day, idle clouds and deep pool
idle	clouds	pool	shadow	sun	far	far	reflections are in the far distance.

1. The Prince of Teng was Li Yuanying, twenty-second son of the first Tang emperor. He was rather wild and frequently in trouble. Nonetheless, he seems to have died a natural death. The Pavilion is in Jiangxi Province, near modern Nanchang, facing the Gan River. Wang Bo wrote this poem while traveling to Vietnam to visit his father. The preface to the collection of poems to which this poem belongs became an important text in establishing Wang Bo's fame as a prose writer. The preface explains that the occasion for the gathering was to celebrate the Double Nine festival. It was soon after writing this that Wang Bo drowned.

2. The bells were attached to carriages. The jades were ornaments tied to the belt: for men, they usually indicated the person's official rank.

3. South Bank, an allusion to the *Lyrics of Chu*, was a conventional reference to a place of farewell.

4. Most commentaries take "western mountains" to be simply mountains to the west of the tower. I suspect, however, that they also suggest the mountains where the Queen Mother of the West had her tryst with Emperor Wu of the Han. The phrase "clouds and rain" is conventional for sexual dalliance.

物	換	星	移	幾	度	秋 [ts^{h}uw]	Things replace one another, the stars shift through how many autumns?
things	exchange	stars	shift	how many times		autumn	
閣	中	帝	子	今	何	在	The emperor's son in the pavilion, where is he now?
pavilion	in	emperor	son	now	where	is at	
檻	外	長	江	空	自	流 [luw]	Beyond the railing, the great river flows to no end.
railing	beyond	long	river	empty	of itself	flow	

Study Notes and Questions

1. This poem presents Wang Bo's "reading" of the Pavilion of the Prince of Teng, a place with strong contemporary resonances. Wang Bo evokes how the pavilion still reveals the abiding presence of its past. Consider the movement between past and present, presence and absence, in the poem. For example, was Wang Bo referring to the present gathering at which he wrote the poem when he wrote line 2? Or was he referring to the parties of the Prince of Teng?

2. Picture the scene described by the second couplet. How high are the painted beams? Is the rain in the present? What does the image invoke? What role does it play in Wang Bo's account?

3. What is the perspective of the two halves of the third couplet? "Abstraction" is a pulling away that at the same time forms links at a different, less immediate, level. What types of simultaneous pulling away and shifting of levels do you see in this couplet? What do they contribute to representing Wang Bo's encounter with the pavilion?

4. The last line, as an answer to the seventh line and as a final turn in the theme of past and its continuing presence in the poem, is a great example of objective closure. What emotions and thoughts does Wang Bo capture in the final image?

Song Zhiwen 宋之問 (ca. 651–712)

Song Zhiwen was from a notable clan. After passing the *jinshi* examination in 675 (i.e., before its reform), he came to the attention of Empress Wu and held various literary posts during her reign. However, he ran into difficulties and was banished when Emperor Zhongzong was restored in 705. He returned without permission to Luoyang and, having proven a useful toady in court power struggles, was restored to the good graces of the court. He eventually received a succession of capital appointments but was caught taking bribes while administering an imperial examination and banished to the far south (Guangdong and then Guangxi). In the end, he was given the privilege of killing himself (rather than being executed) probably during the first years of Xuanzong's reign.

Along with Shen Quanqi 沈佺期 (650–729), Song Zhiwen was one of the most important poets in the court of Wu Zetian. The two men are credited with bringing regulated verse to its full maturity of form. Song produced elegant parallelism that still maintained some sense of ease in its crafting, and he was especially adept at pentasyllabic regulated verse. His poems as he headed into final exile brought great refinement and precision to his reflections on his increasingly difficult situation.

"Written on the Wall of the North Post Station of the Dayu Range" by Song Zhiwen

題大庾嶺北驛					Written on the Wall of the North Post Station of the Dayu Range[5]
陽 Yang	月 month	南 south	飛 fly	雁 geese	In the Month of Yang the south-flying geese,
傳 transmit	聞 hear	至 arrive	此 here	回 [ɣwəj] return	It is said, reach here and turn back.[6]
我 I	行 travel	殊 particular	未 not yet	已 end	My traveling, however, is not over:
何 what	日 day	復 again	歸 return	來 [ləj] come	What day shall I return here?
江 river	靜 quiet	潮 tide	初 begin	落 fall	The river is quiet when the tide first falls.
林 grove	昏 dark	瘴 miasma	不 not	開 [khəj] open	The trees remain dark: the miasma does not disperse.[7]

5. The Dayu Mountains are on the border of Guangdong and Jiangxi Provinces. Song Zhiwen crossed the range when going into exile in Guangdong, which during Tang times was the *far* south.

6. The Month of Yang was the tenth month of the Chinese lunar calendar, i.e., the first month of winter; it corresponds to December. Since *yin* reaches its peak in the tenth month, therefore *yang* begins to reassert itself at that moment.

7. The far south was known for its malarial swamps. The mists were considered unhealthy.

明 bright	朝 dawn	望 gaze	鄉 home	處 place	Tomorrow morning, where one gazes towards home,
應 ought	見 see	隴 ridge	頭 top	梅 [məj] plum	I'll surely see the plum flowering on the ridgetop.

Study Notes and Questions

1. "Written on the wall of . . ." is a sub-genre of poetry that commemorates passing through a particular place. Thus in the poem, the poet gives an account of what brought him or her there and records an impression of the place. Here, Song Zhiwen focuses on how far south the Dayu Mountains are. What is the point of the opening contrast between himself and the geese? What does the phrase "it is said" add? That is, how does cultural lore help shape Song's encounter with the scene? Does it help assuage his feelings as he goes further into exile, or does it make matters worse?

2. What function do the contrasts of the third couplet serve? Line 5 depicts a pleasant scene, but line 6 is more ominous. Do they simply balance one another, or is there a progression from good to foreboding?

3. The fourth line surely must be an allusion to a poem written by Lu Kai 陸凱 (d. ca. 500) to Fan Ye 范曄 (398–445) while Lu Kai, a northern aristocrat from the Northern Wei, was serving in south China:

折梅逢驛使	I break a [branch] of plum flowers when I meet a post messenger.
寄與隴頭人	And send it to the person at the head of the field dividers.
江南無所有	There is nothing here in the southland,[8]
聊附一枝春	So I'll just attach one branch of spring.

4. The conclusion is a form of projected recognition that provides Song Zhiwen's sense of place at the courier station. What is a "gaze home place": why gaze homeward, and why there? What would seeing a plum, the first flowering tree to bloom in the spring, signify? How does the allusion shape the interpretation?

8. The phrase *jiangnan* 江南 literally means "south of the [Yangzi] River" but refers in general to the South, with its distinctive physical and cultural ambience.

Shangguan Wan'er 上官婉兒 (664–710)

Empress Wu's court played an important role in developing the shared conventions for elite poetry—the proprieties of vocabulary, prosody, and the handling of poetic themes—that evolved into the rules for regulated verse. Shangguan Wan'er (also known as Shangguan Zhaorong 上官昭容) was an influential arbiter of court tastes. She was the granddaughter of Shangguan Yi 上官儀 (608–65), an important minister during Emperor Gaozong's reign who unsuccessfully opposed Empress Wu's efforts to control the court and was subsequently executed by her. As an infant, Shangguan Wan'er followed her mother in becoming an inner palace slave. However, Empress Wu discovered that Shangguan Wan'er was a precociously talented writer and brought her into her entourage. After the coup that restored Emperor Zhongzong 中宗 (r. 684, 705–10) to power, Shangguan became one of his concubines and was a trusted associate of his wife, Empress Wei. On Zhongzong's death, however, Empress Wei sought to emulate Empress Wu and gain control of the court. The future Emperor Xuanzong discovered the plan and had Empress Wei—and Shangguan Wan'er—executed.

Shangguan Wan'er presided over many imperial poetry competitions and helped define the court style. She was also a prolific writer. However, only thirty-four poems from her twenty-*juan* collection survive.

From the Series "An Excursion to Princess Changning's Pond of Floating Cups" by Shangguan Wan'er

遊長寧公主流杯池二十五首第九 An Excursion to Princess Changning's Pond of Floating Cups, 25 poems, no. 9[9]

登	山	一	長	望	Climbing a mountain to take a long look,
climb	mountain	one	long	gaze	
正	遇	九	春	初 [tʂʰuǎ]	We just now encounter the beginning of spring.
just now	encounter	nine	spring	begin	
結	駟	填	街	術	Thronging carriages with harnessed horses fill the streets.[10]
tie	horse-team	fill up	street	urban street	
閭	閻	滿	邑	居 [kyǒ]	The populace fills the city residences.
alley-gate	lane-gate	fill	town	residence	
鬪	雪	梅	先	吐	Vying with snow, the plum trees first sprout blossoms.
contend	snow	plum	first	spit out	
驚	風	柳	未	舒 [ʂyǒ]	In gusting wind, the willows have not yet stretched forth.
startle	wind	willow	not yet	stretch	

9. Princess Changning was Empress Wei's daughter. The pond was part of her palace in Chang'an.

10. *Jiesi* 結駟 refers to *jiesilianqi* 結駟連騎, a phrase from the *Records of the Grand Historian* describing a thoroughfare thronging with carriages.

直 only	愁 sorrow	斜 slant	日 sun	落 fall	I only lament that the slanting sun sets
不 not	畏 fear	酒 ale	尊 beaker	虛 [xyǒ] empty	But do not fear that the ale flagon will be empty.

Study Notes and Questions

1. Shangguan Wan'er's poem is a good example of a court composition. It is not brilliant and does not reflect much individuality, as these traits would not be proper for an imperial banquet. The poem follows what Stephen Owen has described as the three-part structure of courtly regulated verse. The first couplet sets the time, place, and occasion of the poem. The middle two parallel couplets expand on the first couplet and provide additional details. The final couplet brings the event and the poem to a proper end with an appropriate sentiment. Compare it with Song Zhiwen's final couplet that Shangguan Wan'er praises in the poetry competition described below.

In 709, Shangguan Wan'er presided over a poetry competition. An account of this event was preserved in the *Record of Events Concerning Tang Poetry* (*Tang shi jishi* 唐詩記事) and translated by Stephen Owen:

> On the last day of the First Month [709], Zhongzong visited Kunming Pool and composed a poem on the occasion. The courtiers then composed more than a hundred pieces to imperial command. In front of the royal tent a brightly colored frame tower was set up, and His Majesty commanded Shangguan Wan'er to select one poem as the new imperial composition. He then had his courtiers gather beneath the tower, and in an instant papers started flying down. As each competitor recognized his own poem, he clasped it to him. This went on until only the poems of Shen Quanqi and Song Zhiwen had not been tossed down. Everyone rushed to look at it, and it was Shen's. Then they heard Shangguan Wan'er's evaluation: "Both poems were equally matched in craftsmanship, but Shen's last couplet went:
>
> 微臣彫朽質 This humble courtier would carve rotting stuff,
> 羞覩豫章材 And is ashamed to perceive the material of Camphor Terrace.
>
> In my opinion the energy of his line stops here. Song's poem closed:
>
> 不愁明月盡 I do not grieve that the bright moon is gone,
> 自有夜珠來 For the pearl that shines by night comes in its stead.
>
> This ends the poem on the upbeat." Shen Quanqi submitted and did not dare contest the matter.[11]

2. How do the couplets fit together? Where are the people, and where are the plum and willow trees? What is the relation of the second to the first couplet and of the third to the second couplet?

11. Stephen Owen, *The Poetry of the Early Tang*, revised ed. (Melbourne: Quirin Press, 2012), p. 237.

Chen Zi'ang 陳子昂 (661–702)

Chen Zi'ang was from Shu 蜀 (modern Sichuan Province) and claimed to have been from a family with a long tradition of extravagant gallantry.[12] His father had passed the examination in classical scholarship (*mingjing* 明經) but did not serve. Chen asserted that until he was seventeen or eighteen, he was a proud, dashing young bravo who had no book learning. Then he set his mind on learning, soon mastered the textual tradition, and developed a literary style much like that of the great Han dynasty writers Sima Xiangru 司馬相如 and Yang Xiong 揚雄, both of whom were also from Shu. That is, Chen Zi'ang, as an outsider, crafted a history for himself in which he played the familiar role of the young swashbuckler from Shu ready to take the capital by storm.

Chen Zi'ang went to Chang'an in search of knowledge, patronage, and an official post. He passed the newly reformed *jinshi* examination in 682 just before Emperor Gaozong's death. Although he did not receive a post and returned to Shu, in 684 he impressed Empress Wu, who gave the young man a literary post in the eastern capital, Luoyang. In 690, the term of the post ended, and Chen was reassigned to another minor position. However, when his stepmother died in late 691, he needed to go home to Shu for mourning. When Chen returned to Luoyang in late 693, he received another relatively minor post in the capital with which he was unhappy, so in 696 he sought out the opportunity to participate in a military campaign against the Khitan in the far northeast. He soon discovered, however, that his role on the staff of the general leading the expedition was merely to copy documents rather than to offer his advice. The campaign initially proved a disaster, but the empress committed significant resources to suppressing the Khitan, who eventually were subdued. Finding no advancement through his participation in the successfully concluded campaign, in 698 Chen Zi'ang again returned home to Shu to tend to his father, who died in 699. While Chen was still in mourning, a local official, believing that Chen had hidden a considerable fortune in his house, threw him into prison to pressure him to pay, in essence, a ransom. Chen died while imprisoned.

Chen Zi'ang, consistent with his outsider persona, presented himself as a poet who rejected the crafted blandness of court versifying. His most famous poems are a series of thirty-eight poems entitled "Moved by What I Encounter" 感遇 that have a mix of abstraction, intensity, and discontent similar to Ruan Ji's "Chanting My Thoughts" and that use a language stripped of courtly ornament.

12. Because there is no syllable *ziang* (in contrast to *xiang* or *jiang*), Chen Zi'ang's name does not need the apostrophe, but I add it here to make clear that it is two separate syllables.

"Song of Climbing Youzhou Terrace" by Chen Zi'ang

登幽州臺歌						Song of Climbing Youzhou Terrace [13]
前	不	見	古	人		Ahead, one cannot see men of old.
before	not	see	old	men		
後	不	見	來	者		Behind, one cannot see those to come.
behind	not	see	come	one		
念	天	地	之	悠	悠	Thinking on the vastness of Heaven and Earth,
recall	Heaven	Earth	's	vast	vast	
獨	愴	然	而	涕	下	Alone, I am stricken with sorrow, and tears fall.
alone	stricken	-ly	and	tears	fall	

Robert Payne's Translation

The Ancients

I look before, and do not see the ancients.
Looking after I do not see the coming ages.
Only Heaven and Earth will last forever:
Alone I lament, and my tears fall down.

Study Notes and Questions

1. This poem, about an ancient place in the far northeast of the realm, is self-consciously "ancient poetry." As a "song" written in one five-character couplet and one six-character couplet, it harkens back to *yuefu* traditions. What is the rhyme scheme?

2. Chen here uses a variety of techniques to make the poem "ancient." From the word-by-word gloss, where is the caesura in the first two lines? What is the effect of the repetitions of wording in those lines?

3. Where is the caesura in the two lines of the second couplet? Each line could have been written with five characters, but Chen pads them with grammatical particles in the fourth position. What is the effect of this determinedly prosy construction?

13. The Youzhou Terrace is close to the Tang northeastern frontier, near modern Beijing. Chen Zi'ang traveled there as part of the army of the Prince of Jian'an in a campaign against the Khitan.

Wang Zhihuan 王之渙 (688–742)

Wang Zhihuan is a good example of the sort of talented young man from a good family who attained some success—if not great fortune—in the bureaucratic milieu during the reign of Xuanzong. He was not from a prominent clan but had sufficient patronage to serve in the minor post of assistant magistrate in Jizhou 冀州 in north China. Encountering slander, he returned home to live for fifteen years. Late in life he served again in a minor local post and earned the reputation of a good administrator.

Wang Zhihuan was admired as a poet in his own time and was a master of the quatrain form in particular. Unfortunately only six of his poems survive, but among them, "Climbing Stork Tower" is a small masterpiece.

"Climbing Stork Tower" by Wang Zhihuan

登鸛雀樓					Climbing Stork Tower[14]
白 white	日 sun	依 leans	山 mountain	盡 end	The white sun goes out against the mountains.
黄 Yellow	河 River	入 enter	海 sea	流 [luw] flow	The Yellow River flows to enter the sea.
欲 desire	窮 exhaust	千 thousand	里 *li*	目 eye	Wishing to exhaust a thousand-*li* gaze,
更 again	上 ascend	一 one	層 level	樓 [ləw] tower	Go up one more flight.

RICHARD BODMAN'S TRANSLATION

Climbing the Stork Pavilion

The white sun leaning on the mountain disappears,
The Yellow River flows on into the sea;
To stretch your gaze a thousand leagues,
Climb up still another story.

14. Stork Tower was in what is now the town of Yongji in Shanxi Province. It overlooked the Yellow River. It is important to the poem that the tower is on the *west* side of the mountains, that is, that looking west one cannot see the mountains far off in the distance.

Stephen Owen's translation

Climbing Stork Tower

The bright sun rests on the hill and is gone,
the Yellow River flows into the sea.
If you want to see a full thousand miles,
climb one more story of this tower.

Study Notes and Questions

1. In a "climbing high" poem, one gives an account of the significance of ascending the heights. A standard clichéd explanation offered in such poems was that, being closer to Heaven, one gained a vantage point far above mundane, worldly concerns. Wang Zhihuan here writes a very elegant quatrain that subtly explores the "climbing high" theme. However, standing and looking out from the top of Stork Tower, one cannot in fact see the sun setting among the mountains, nor can one see the river entering the ocean: how can these two images seen only in the mind's eye then serve to introduce a "climbing high" poem?

2. Discuss the parallelism of the first couplet character by character. "Mountain" and "sea" make a conventional abstract pairing, yet there is more to it: what about their roles in setting out directions, movements, and modes of completion in the couplet?

3. What is a "thousand-*li* gaze"? Did the first couplet describe one? Since the scenes in the first couplet are imagined, what does the concluding gesture of climbing one more story signify? Why climb?

4. The quatrain is a form that, by the quick sketch and the evocative gesture, tries to distill the significance of a moment. Consider the poem as a realization of the quatrain form. From that perspective, how does the final gesture capture the significance of "climbing Stork Tower"?

5. Contemporary students in China learn this poem as a call for them to study yet harder. Investigate this interpretation.

Meng Haoran 孟浩然 (689–ca. 740)

Meng Haoran was from Xiangyang (in modern Hubei Province) and remains strongly associated with the city. He does not have a biography in either of the official Tang histories, and the details of his life are poorly understood. He was an enthusiastic traveler and was a friend of most of the important poets of the day. He repeatedly took the *jinshi* examination in the capital but always failed. In the end, he gave up hope of an official career and spent his remaining years comfortably in Xiangyang entertaining friends as they passed through the region.

Meng Haoran, with little training in the poetic decorum of the styles developed in the aristocratic capital milieu, went his own way in writing. He was strongest in informal pentasyllabic compositions, which included both old-style verse and regulated forms. The later tradition linked him to Wang Wei, and the pair became known as the two great masters of landscape poetry during Xuanzong's reign. Yet Meng Haoran, with great skill, delineates the temporal shifts of moving through the landscape to produce effects quite different from Wang Wei's more austere style.

"On Pengli Lake, Gazing at Mount Lu" by Meng Haoran

彭蠡湖中望廬山					On Pengli Lake, Gazing at Mount Lu
太 great	虛 void	生 is born	月 moon	暈 halo	When the Great Void brings forth a halo around the moon,[15]
舟 boat	子 man	知 know	天 sky	風 [piung] wind	The boatmen know the sky's wind.
挂 hang	席 mat	候 await	明 bright	發 set-out	Raising the sail, [we] await first light
渺 vast & vague	漫	平 level	湖 lake	中 [tiung] middle	In the vastness of the calm lake.
中 middle	流 flow	見 see	匡 Kuang	阜 mountain	From the middle of the current, we see Kuang's Mountain:[16]
勢 stance	壓 suppress	九 Nine	江 Rivers	雄 [jiung] bold	Its stance overawes the mighty [scenery] of Jiujiang.[17]
黤 pitch-black	黮	容 contain	霽 clearing	色 appearance	Pitch black, it encompasses the scene of clearing clouds:

15. The commentaries cite a saying, "Moon halo and wind, damp foundation stones and rain."

16. Kuang's Mountain 匡阜 is another name for Mt. Lu; there are many stories about who Mr. Kuang was. None are especially reliable.

17. This is the city of Jiujiang 九江 (lit. "nine rivers"), also called Xunyang 潯陽 in history. There are various accounts of what the "nine" rivers are. This line echoes a letter written by Bao Zhao to his younger sister.

崢 soaring-steep	嶸	當 be at	曉 dawn	空 [k'ung] void	Soaring massively, it stands in the dawn void.[18]
香 incense	爐 burner	初 at first	上 ascend	日 sun	Incense Burner Peak when the sun first rises:[19]
瀑 waterfall	布	噴 spurt	成 become	虹 [ɣung] rainbow	A waterfall, shooting out, becomes a rainbow.
久 long	欲 desire	追 pursue	向 Xiang	子 Master	I long have desired to pursue Master Xiang;[20]
況 yet more	茲 this	懷 cherish	遠 Yuan	公 [kung] Duke	Even more do I now cherish Lord [Hui]yuan.[21]
我 I	來 come	限 restrain	于 [within]	役 duty	My coming is constrained by duty:
未 not yet	暇 leisure	息 rest	微 slight	躬 [kiung] body	I do not have leisure to rest my insignificant self.
淮 Huai	海 Ocean	途 road	將 almost	半 half	My journey to the Huai River and the sea is about half done;
星 stars	霜 frost	歲 year	欲 about	窮 [giung] run-out	Stars and frost [tell us] the year is almost at an end.
寄 send	言 word	巖 cliff	棲 roost	者 -ers	I send word to the cliff dwellers:
畢 finish	趣 interest	當 ought	來 come	同 [dung] share	When I've exhausted my interest [in roaming], I surely will come join you.

Study Notes and Questions

This is an old-style narrative poem that describes sunrise on Pengli Lake. It has wonderful descriptive couplets, but it requires some imagination to visualize the succession of scenes.

1. The first two couplets set the stage. What is the time of the first line? What does the lore of the second line tell us? Think about issues of persona and voice as well as the immediate narrative function.

2. The six lines of description (lines 5–10) seem utterly devoid of symbolic or metaphorical meaning. This landscape simply *is*. Does this sheer presence of the visual have its own meaning? How does the rest of the poem explore, contextualize, and respond to this moment in the poem?

---

18. Since Mt. Lu is famous for its Buddhist temples, the pairing of "scene" (色, Sanskrit: *rupa*) and "void" (空, Sanskrit: *sunyata*), two important Buddhist terms about perception, is probably not accidental.

19. Incense Burner Peak is one of the main peaks of Mt. Lu.

20. Master Xiang was a late Han dynasty recluse. After taking care of the marriages of his sons and daughters, he set off to tour the great mountains of China and, with a few friends, led the life of a recluse.

21. Huiyuan 慧遠 (334–417) was an eminent monk of the Jin dynasty. While the South was still sparsely populated, he established a monastic retreat on Mt. Lu and, with several other monks, founded the White Lotus Society.

"Staying the Night on the Jiande River" by Meng Haoran

宿建德江					Staying the Night on the Jiande River[22]
移 move	舟 boat	泊 moor	煙 mist	渚 sandbank	Moving the boat, we moor on a misty bank.
日 sun	暮 dusk	客 traveler	愁 sorrow	新 [sin] new	As the sun sets, a traveler's sorrow renews.
野 wilds	曠 broad	天 sky	低 low	樹 trees	The wilds are broad: the sky lowers the trees.
江 river	清 clear	月 moon	近 close	人 [ɲin] people	The river is clear: the moon comes close.

STEPHEN OWEN'S TRANSLATION

Spending the Night on the Chien-te River

I move the boat on to moor by a misty isle,
At sunset a traveler's sorrow strikes anew:
The wilderness vast, heaven low upon the trees,
The river clear, the moon, near the person.

STUDY NOTES AND QUESTIONS

1. Note the simplicity and efficiency of the set-up in the first couplet. The first line introduces the fact of "staying the night" in the title. Line two gives us the time and part of the visual image. What is the effect of the third-party statement, "a traveler's sorrow renews"? What might be meant by "a traveler's sorrow," and why is it renewed here?

2. The syntax of the second couplet gives us four objects in the landscape that are the topics for four coordinate verbal sentences in which the first sentence of each line serves as the antecedent condition for the second. Explain the interaction. The sky and the moon in the second sentences also become active. How does the sky come low on the trees? How can the moon come close? What is the relation of these images to the first couplet?

22. The Jiande River is a part of the upper region of the Qiantang River as it flows through modern Zhejiang Province.

Wang Wei 王維 (701?–61)

Wang Wei was from a branch of the great Taiyuan Wang clan. As the talented son of a noble lineage, he went to Chang'an to learn its ways and establish connections. He passed the *jinshi* examination in 721 at age twenty-one and received an appointment as a music specialist. For some unknown reason, however, he soon was demoted to a prefectural position in Jizhou (in modern Shandong Province). What happened over the next thirteen years is not known. In 733 Zhang Jiuling returned to power at court, and through his influence Wang Wei returned to Chang'an. After that, he served in a variety of positions including a brief tour as an emissary on the northwestern frontier. Presumably during this period he also frequently returned to his estate on the Wang River at the foot of the Zhongnan mountain range south of the capital.

In the mid-750s, when Xuanzong had been on the throne for over forty years, tension began to grow between his chief ministers and the largely non-Chinese military governors who guarded the empire's northern borders. In 755 this tension turned into open warfare as An Lushan, military governor of the northeast border, rebelled.[23] After the rebellion broke out and Xuanzong and his immediate entourage fled to Shu in 756, Wang Wei was captured by An Lushan's army and pressed into service as an official. The next year An Lushan was assassinated, and imperial troops reclaimed the capital. While Wang Wei, who as an official who had cooperated with the rebels, could have encountered serious problems, in fact the new Emperor Suzong 肅宗 (r. 756–62) restored him to the position he held before the rebellion. In 759, as part of a conservative retrenchment, Suzong promoted Wang Wei to ministerial rank, but Wang died soon thereafter.

Wang Wei was perhaps the greatest of the capital poets.[24] That is, he was a master of all the styles popular in the Chang'an aristocratic milieu, from the most decorous of regulated verse and witty quatrains to energetic heptasyllabic songs. However, Wang Wei expanded beyond these styles. On many occasions, he took the self-effacing tendency in court poetry to an extreme in largely disappearing behind the text of the poem. Perhaps the most famous example of this enigmatic style is the series of quatrains he wrote with his friend Pei Di at his Wang River estate. He also adopted the simplified poetry of Tao Qian to depict his life on the estate as a rural idyll. He is known as both a landscape poet and a Buddhist poet. Moreover, his conservative regulated verse style became extremely influential in the next generation, before the shifting cultural values of the early ninth century came to focus on Li Bai and Du Fu as the central poetic figures of Xuanzong's reign.

---

23. See chapter 7 for a more detailed account of the rebellion.

24. See Stephen Owen's extensive discussion of the capital poets of the High Tang in *The Great Age of Chinese Poetry: The High Tang* (New Haven: Yale University Press, 1981), pp. 52–70.

From the Series “Twenty Poems on Wang River”

輞川集 二十首
鹿柴

Twenty Poems on Wang River
Deer Stockade

空 empty	山 mountain	不 not	見 see	人 people	In the empty mountains, one sees no people.
但 only	聞 hear	人 people	語 speak	響 [xiang’] echo	One only hears the echoes of people’s speech.
返 return	景 gleam	入 enter	深 deep	林 grove	The returning sunbeams enter the deep grove,[25]
復 again	照 shine	青 green	苔 moss	上 [dʑiang’] on	And shine upon the green moss.

WITTER BYNNER’S TRANSLATION

Deer-Park Hermitage

There seems to be no one on the empty mountain . . .
And yet I think I hear a voice,
Where sunlight, entering a grove,
Shines back to me from the green moss.

RICHARD W. BODMAN AND VICTOR H. MAIR’S TRANSLATION

Deer Enclosure

On the empty mountain, seeing no one,
Only hearing the echoes of someone’s voice;
Returning light enters the deep forest,
Again shining upon the green moss.

25. “Returning sunbeams” are the rays of the late afternoon sun.

竹里館					Bamboo Village Hostel
獨	坐	幽	篁	裏	Sitting alone in a deep bamboo thicket
alone	sit	hidden	brake	in	
彈	琴	復	長	嘯 [siàw]	I play a zither and chant low and long.
pluck	zither	again	long	whistle	
深	林	人	不	知	In the deep grove: no one knows;
deep	grove	people	not	know	
明	月	來	相	照 [tṣiàw]	The bright moon comes to shine on me.
bright	moon	come	[d.o]	shine	

Burton Watson's translation

Bamboo Mile Lodge

Alone I sit in dark bamboo,
strumming the lute, whistling away;
deep woods that no one knows,
where a bright moon comes to shine on me.

Witter Bynner's translation

In a Retreat among Bamboos

Leaning alone in the close bamboos,
I am playing my lute and humming a song
Too softly for anyone to hear—
Except my comrade, the bright moon.

Study Notes and Questions

1. This series of quatrains describes various sites that were part of Wang Wei's estate. People often take them as embodiments of Buddhist principles concerning the perception of emptiness within the phenomenal realm. What elements in these two poems might carry double meanings? In particular, pay attention to light and illumination. Can the poems be both about specific sites and Buddhist perception?

"Arriving at the Border as an Envoy" by Wang Wei

使至塞上					Arriving at the Border as an Envoy
單 single	車 cart	欲 about to	問 inquire	邊 [pjian] border	In my single cart, I am going to inquire at the border.[26]
屬 vassal	國 state	過 pass	居 Ju-	延 [jian] -yan	Among the vassal states, I pass Juyan.[27]
征 campaign	蓬 tumbleweed	出 go out	漢 Han	塞 outpost	A traveling tumbleweed leaves the Han outpost.
歸 return	雁 goose	入 enter	胡 Hu	天 [t^{h}ian] sky	A returning goose enters the Hu sky.
大 great	漠 desert	孤 lone	煙 smoke	直 straight	Across the great plain, a lone [column of] smoke rises straight.
長 long	河 river	落 fall	日 sun	圓 [yan] round	In the long river, the setting sun is round.
蕭 Xiao	關 Pass	逢 meet	候 await	騎 rider	At the Xiao Pass, I meet a mounted scout.[28]
都 Protector-General	護 	在 is at	燕 Yan-	然 [rian] -ran	The Protector General is at Yanran.[29]

STEPHEN OWEN'S TRANSLATION

Arriving at the Frontier on a Mission

With a single coach I'll visit the frontiers,
And of client kingdoms, pass by Chü-yen.
Voyaging tumbleweed leaves the passes of Han,
A homebound goose enters Tartar skies.
Great desert: one column of smoke stands straight;
Long river: the setting sun hangs round.

---

26. Li Ling, "Answering Su Wu's Letter"《答蘇武書》: "In the past you, as a lone envoy (lit. "envoy of a single cart"), approached an enemy with ten thousand chariots."「足下昔以單車之使，適萬乘之虜。」Li Ling was a Han dynasty general.

27. The Juyan Marsh is in the northwest, on the Chinese border with Mongolia.

28. He Xun 何遜, "Watching a Soldier's Parting"《見征人分別》: "Mounted scouts go out from Xiao Pass. / Pursuing soldiers approach Ma city"「候騎出蕭關 /追兵赴馬邑。」Xiao Pass is in modern Gansu Province; like most passes, it was a fortified check-point and military stronghold.

29. The "Protector General" was the title of a Tang military governor assigned to control important northern border regions. Yanran was a mountain where the Han dynasty general Dou Xian 竇憲 built a monument to commemorate his great victory over the Xiongnu, a powerful northern barbarian confederation.

At Hsiao ramparts I met a mounted messenger—
"The Grand Marshall is now at Mount Yen-jan."

Study Notes and Questions

1. This is a courtly treatment of "border poetry." What do the allusions contribute to Wang Wei's encounter with the frontier?

2. Later readers greatly admired the geometric patterns of the third couplet. Explain how the images work.

"At Farewell" by Wang Wei

送別					At Farewell
下 descend	馬 horse	飲 drink	君 you	酒 wine	Dismounting, I urge you to drink.
問 ask	君 you	何 where	所 [place]	之 [tʂi] go	I ask you, where are you going?
君 you	言 say	不 not	得 obtain	意 intent	You say you are not content:
歸 return	臥 lie down	南 south	山 mountain	陲 [ʂɦyj] foot	And return to rest at the foot of South Mountain.
但 only	去 leave	莫 don't	復 again	問 ask	Leave then; I'll ask no more:
白 white	雲 clouds	無 with no	盡 end	時 [ʂɦi] time	White clouds are without end.

Robert Payne's Translation

On Going Away

Dismounting from my horse to drink with you,
"Where are you going?" I asked.
You said, "Because I cannot go where I want to go,
I shall return to the south mountain border,
There I shall not care what happens outside.
The white clouds flow on for ever."

STUDY NOTES AND QUESTIONS

1. The language here is simple and repetitive. What is the tone of the poem? (This is not an easy question.) How do the repetitions of "you" 君 contribute to it?

2. Wang Wei uses the white clouds in the final line as a form of objective closure. How do they relate to the person's departure and return to the mountains? Do they offer a model? (Clouds "return [to the mountains] without intent" 無意而歸.) Are they a form of solace? Some commentaries connect the clouds with Buddhist emptiness. Can they be real clouds and Buddhist emblems at the same time?

"Written on Returning to Mount Song" by Wang Wei

		歸嵩山作			Written on Returning to Mount Song
清	川	帶	長	薄	The pure stream is edged with long thickets;
pure	river	belt	long	thicket	
車	馬	去	閒	閒 [ɣɛ:n]	Carts and horses set out at a leisurely pace.
cart	horse	leave	idle	idle	
流	水	如	有	意	The flowing water seems to have an intent.
flow	water	seems	have	intent	
暮	禽	相	與	還 [ɣwɛ:n]	The sunset birds return with one another.
sunset	birds	mutual	give	return	
荒	城	臨	古	渡	The overgrown outer walls overlook an old ford.
overgrown	city wall	overlook	old	ford	
落	日	滿	秋	山 [ʂɛ:n]	The setting sun fills the autumn mountains.
falling	sun	fill	autumn	mountain	
迢	遞	嵩	高	下	In the distance, beneath the height of Mount Song,
distant	distant	Song	height	below	
歸	來	且	閉	關 [kwɛ:n]	I return and for now close my gate.
return	come	for now	close	gate	

STEPHEN OWEN'S TRANSLATION

Returning to Mount Sung

A clear stream lined by long tracts of brush,
There horse and coach go rumbling away.
The flowing waters seem to have purpose,
And birds of evening join to turn home.
Grass-grown walls look down on an ancient ford,
As setting sunlight fills the autumn mountains,
And far, far beneath the heights of Mount Sung,
I return and close my gate.

Study Notes and Questions

1. If this poem is Wang Wei's account of returning to his estate, how does he structure the meaning of that return in the poem? This first couplet does not explicitly mention "return" and instead simply states that he "leaves" 去. What is the manner of his leaving?

2. The stream and the birds are active elements in the landscape in the second couplet. However, it is easy to over-read the parallels between these images and Wang Wei's own actions because his touch here is very light. He states merely that the stream "seems" to have an intention and that the birds return with one another, quite indifferent to whatever Wang Wei is doing.

3. Returning always is an interplay of presence and absence, past and present, what passes away, what remains. How does Wang Wei's much-admired third couplet (line 6 is considered especially grand) present these elements in the context of his homeward journey?

4. The conclusion draws on distinctions of near and far, open and closed: how do the last two lines work together as a final version of the gesture of return?

"After Long Rains, Written at Wang River Villa" by Wang Wei

積雨輞川莊作							After Long Rains, Written at Wang River Villa
積	雨	空	林	煙	火	遲 [dri]	After long rains, in the empty
piled	rain	empty	grove	smoke	fire	late	forest the fires are laggard:
蒸	藜	炊	黍	餉	東	菑 [tʂi]	With steamed pulse and cooked millet
steamed	pulse	cooked	millet	eat	east	field	[workers] eat in the east fields.
漠	漠	水	田	飛	白	鷺	In the vastness of the flooded
vast	vast	water	paddy	fly	white	egret	paddies flies a white egret;
陰	陰	夏	木	囀	黃	鸝 [li]	In their shade, the summer trees
shade	shade	summer	tree	warble	yellow	oriole	warble with orioles.[30]
山	中	習	靜	觀	朝	槿	In the mountains, practicing calm,
mountain	midst	practice	calm	observe	dawn	hibiscus	I observe the dawn hibiscus;[31]
松	下	清	齋	折	露	葵 [gjwi]	Beneath fir trees, keeping a pure
fir	below	purify	fast	break	dew	mallow	fast, I break off a dewy mallow.

30. An old commentary argues that this couplet derives from a five-character couplet by Li Jiayou 李嘉祐—and that Wang added two characters (漠漠 and 陰陰) to the beginning of each line—but this story largely has been rejected.

31. The hibiscus is well known as a flower that blooms in the morning and loses its petals by nightfall.

野	老	與	人	爭	席	罷	An old rustic, I have stopped vying with people over a mat:[32]
wilds	old-man	with	people	struggle	mat	stop	
海	鷗	何	事	更	相	疑 [ŋi]	Why should the seagulls again doubt me?[33]
ocean	gull	what	affair	again	[object]	suspect	

PAUL ROUZER'S TRANSLATION

Written at My Estate at Wang Stream, after Long Rains

After long rains in the empty wood
  smoky fires are slow to light:
The men on the new-plowed fields to the east
  are eating steamed goosefoot and millet.
In a vast expanse of flooded paddy
  up starts a snowy egret;
In the gloomy shade of summer trees
  the yellow orioles sing.
I practice stillness within these hills,
  observe the dawn hibiscus;
I fast in purity below the pines,
  break off a dewy mallow.
This old rustic has surrendered the fight
  for a place to sit on the mat—
So why should sea gulls come to doubt
  my motives once again?

STUDY NOTES AND QUESTIONS

Wang Wei was a skilled poet well trained in regulated verse composition. Yet this poem has an odd structure. In regulated verse, the poet usually sets out an initial image that embodies themes to be explored in the poem. The middle couplets explore the theme by expanded or shifting images, often with a significant reworking of the theme in the third couplet. The final two lines then provide a response to

32. The allusion here is to a story in the "Lodged Words" chapter of *Zhuang Zi*《莊子・寓言》in which Yang Zhu returned to an inn where he had once been treated with great respect. Since receiving instruction from Lao Zi, however, Yang Zhu now practiced humility and emptiness, so the people at the inn made no room for him and even fought over the mat on which he was sitting. 「其往也，舍者迎將，其家公執席，妻執巾櫛，舍者避席，煬者避灶。其反也，舍者與之爭席矣。」

33. This allusion comes from the "Yellow Emperor" chapter in the Han dynasty Daoist miscellany *Lie Zi* 列子: There was a boy who liked to play with the seagulls on the beach. Each morning when he would arrive, some hundred gulls would swirl about him. One day the boy's father suggested that he catch a gull so that the father could have one to play with as well. The next morning the gulls would not come near him. 「海上之人有好漚鳥者，每旦之海上，從漚鳥游，漚鳥之至者百住而不止。其父曰，吾聞漚鳥皆從汝游，汝取來，吾玩之。明日之海上，漚鳥舞而不下也。」

the developments presented in the first six lines. In this poem, however, there is a significant split between the two halves, and the concerns of the final couplet are in tension with the opening images.

1. What do the rains—the occasion of the poem—signify in the first couplet? What is the relation of human activity to the rural scene?

2. The second couplet is a very famous "landscape" couplet: what is the vision of order it presents? Where is the human within that order?

3. What is the relation of the third couplet to the first four lines?

4. Many famous poems continue to be powerful precisely because they "don't work": they structure forces that cannot come to rest; and readers, feeling the poem does cohere despite the internal tensions, are compelled to work to create an aesthetic whole behind those tensions. Consider the relation of the squabbling and the doubt in the fourth couplet to the rest of the poem. Do they raise questions of unease that contradict the earlier lines, or do they recast those lines as an implicit argument about his relation to the landscape? How is this poem a coherent whole? What holds it together?

Cui Hao 崔顥 (704?–54)

If Chen Zi'ang, a generation earlier, played the outsider from Shu, Cui Hao played the dissolute young man of noble birth. His family was from Bianzhou (Kaifeng) and may have been related to the great Cui clan of Boling. What we know of him largely are bits and pieces of legend. He seems to have started out in the same princely court as Wang Wei. He passed the *jinshi* examination in 723 but did not have much interest in an official career. He gained notoriety for marrying women for their looks (rather than for useful connections) and for readily divorcing them. He also reportedly used a poem of introduction to offend an important official who had considered helping him in his career. Later in the Tianbao reign period (742–56), he appears to have changed his ways and held several posts.

Only forty-three poems by Cui Hao survive. They reflect the popular aesthetic values of the capital. Befitting the persona of the dissolute young aristocrat, he wrote many "unbridled" *yuefu* poems ranging from long seven-character song forms to quatrains. His most famous poem is "Yellow Crane Tower," which Li Bai reportedly admitted he could not outdo.

"Yellow Crane Tower" by Cui Hao

黃鶴樓							Yellow Crane Tower[34]
昔 former	人 person	已 already	乘 ride	白 white	雲 cloud	去 leave	The man of old already has ridden away on white clouds:
此 this	地 land	空 empty	餘 remain	黃 yellow	鶴 crane	樓 [ləw] tower	At this place there vainly remains the Yellow Crane Tower.
黃 yellow	鶴 crane	一 one	去 leave	不 not	復 again	返 return	The yellow crane, having once left, will not return again.
白 white	雲 cloud	千 thousand	載 year	空 empty	悠 distant	悠 [juw] distant	White clouds for a thousand years drift aimlessly.
晴 clear sky	川 river	歷 distinct	歷 distinct	漢 Han-	陽 -yang	樹 tree	Across the sunlit river the trees of Hanyang stand distinct.
春 spring	草 grass	萋 flourish	萋 flourish	鸚 parrot	鵡	洲 [tɕuw] isle	Spring grasses flourish on Parrot Isle.
日 sun	暮 dusk	鄉 village	關 pass	何 what	處 place	是 this	The sun sets: where is the pass to my home?
煙 mist	波 waves	江 river	上 on	使 cause	人 person	愁 [dʑuw] grieve	Misty waves on the river make one grieve.

34. The poem is based on a story of a Daoist immortal who painted a picture of a yellow crane on the wall of the tavern, which later took its name from the painting. When customers sang, the crane would dance. The tavern soon became famous and the proprietor wealthy. One day, the Daoist reappeared, played his flute to call the crane, and rode off on it.

Stephen Owen's Translation

Yellow Crane Tower

That man of old has already ridden
  white clouds away.
And here in this land there remains only
  Yellow Crane Tower.
The yellow crane, once it has gone,
  will never come again,
But white clouds of a thousand years
  go aimlessly on and on.
Clear and bright in the sunlit stream
  the trees of Han-yang,
Springtime's grasses, lush and green,
  all over Parrot Isle.
Sun's setting, the passes to home—
  where can they be?
Beside this river of misty waves
  it makes a man sad.

Study Notes and Questions

1. Compare this poem with Wang Bo's "Pavilion of the Prince of Teng" (pp. 179–80). Both authors write about a location with a history that is somehow inscribed in the landscape, yet Cui Hao is far more focused on reading the scene before his eyes than on reflecting on the past. In particular, compare the middle couplets of the two poems. (Note, of course, that Wang Bo's poem is not regulated verse, and only one of its couplets is parallel.)

2. This poem is considered regulated verse even though the phrase "yellow crane" appears two (or three) times in the first three lines, a violation of the norms for regulated verse as understood in later periods. Although some later readers worried about such a violation, this way of beginning a poem also drew praise. Describe the progression here and its effect in both connecting the past to the present and liberating the present from that past.

3. The third couplet presents a moment of warm, sunlit clarity. What does the moment signify?

4. Explain the relation of the final couplet to the third couplet.

Li Bai 李白 (701–62)

Li Bai was an outsider in the Tang lineage-based society and played the part to an audience that was fickle but enamored of the exotic. He was born in 701 either in Shu (Sichuan) or on the frontier to the northwest (in Gansu 甘肅), which was largely inhabited by Turkic-speaking tribes. In any case, by the time he was five, his father, a merchant, had brought him to Shu. His two main biographies state that when he was ten, he had mastered the *Canon of Documents* and *Canon of Poetry* and had read the Warring States philosophers. By fifteen, the accounts continue, he had taken up swordsmanship and Daoist texts. After this, the biographies give different years for when various events in his early years occurred, but the general outlines are similar. Li Bai played the role of the heedlessly gallant noble youth in the manner of Chen Zi'ang but with further embellishments. He was said to have killed someone and to have given away large sums of money. By twenty-five or twenty-six, he had left Shu to try his fortune in the Jiangnan region. He found a patron in the town of Anlu 安陸 (in modern Hubei Province), married, and remained there until 734 when he was thirty-four. He appears to have taken excursions to various parts of China during this period and met various important poets of the day. Both biographies agree that in 742 when he was forty-two, he met the Daoist master Wu Yun 吳筠. It was Wu Yun who recommended Li Bai to the emperor. Li Bai proved amusing, and Xuanzong gave him a post in his private bureau of writers, the Hanlin Academy. During this period in the capital, Li Bai presented himself as a man of extraordinary genius and gained the epithet of "banished immortal" 謫仙. However, by 744 Li Bai had worn out his welcome, was dismissed, and traveled once more in east and south China. Years passed peripatetically until the An Lushan Rebellion broke out. In 757, the second year of the rebellion, the Prince of Yong was sent by the new Emperor Suzong to pacify the south but instead attempted to carve out his own state. Li Bai joined his campaign, perhaps in ignorance of the prince's plans but more probably fully aware of them. In any case, the Prince of Yong's rebellion failed and Li Bai was briefly imprisoned. He was banished to Yelang 夜郎 in south China, but a pardon arrived in 759. He spent the remaining three years of his life traveling between Jinling 金陵, Yangzhou 揚州, and the other major cities of the Jiangnan region.

Li Bai indeed was the brilliant outsider. When he arrived for his brief stay in Chang'an at age forty-two, he brought with him a mature poetic sensibility trained not through writing verse in the capital milieu but through reading the great poetry of the past. His best poetry is a deeply innovative reimagining of earlier traditions. His *yuefu* in particular derive from the Han models but are wholly his own: his voice rings loudly—often very loudly—in them. He loved the world of Jiangnan and wrote poems that captured the delicate lushness of the South. He brought a new fictive imagination to these poems: he did not so much "cherish the old" 懷古 as recreate how a scene must have appeared through the eyes of the participants at the time.

"Song of the Roosting Crows" by Li Bai

烏棲曲							Song of the Roosting Crows
姑	蘇	臺	上	烏	棲	時 [dʑi]	When the crows roosted on
Gu-	-su	Terrace	on	crow	roost	time	Gusu Terrace,[35]
吳	王	宮	裏	醉	西	施 [ɕi]	In the palace of the king of Wu,
Wu	king	palace	in	drunk	Xi	Shi	drunk Xi Shi.
吳	歌	楚	舞	歡	未	畢 [pjit]	Songs of Wu, Chu dances: before
Wu	song	Chu	dance	pleasure	not yet	end	the joy had ended,
青	山	欲	銜	半	邊	日 [ɲiː]	Green mountains would soon hold
green	mountain	about to	hold in	half	border	sun	a sun filling half the border.
銀	箭	金	壺	漏	水	多 [ta]	From the silver arrow, in the gold pot
silver	arrow	gold	pot	drip	water	much	the dripped water was deep.[36]
起	看	秋	月	墜	江	波 [pa]	She rose to look at the autumn moon
rise	look	autumn	moon	fall	river	waves	fallen into the river waves:
東	方	漸	高	奈	樂	何 [ɣa]	In the east, [the sun] grows gradually
east	section	gradual	high	avail	joy	what	higher: what avails our joy?

Stephen Owen's Translation

Song of the Roosting Crows

The time when the crows are roosting
 on the terrace of Ku-su
Is when, in the Wu king's palace,
 Hsi Shih is growing drunk.
The songs of Wu and dances of Ch'u—
 their pleasure had not reached its height,
As the green hills were about to swallow
 a half side of the sun.
From the waterclock more and more drips away,
 from the basin of gold with its silver arrow,

35. Gusu Terrace was a spectacular palace complex built by Fuchai 夫差, the King of Wu (r. 495–473 BC). In 494 BC Fuchai defeated Goujian 勾踐, the King of Yue, who then planned his revenge by finding a young peasant girl, Xi Shi 西施, whom he trained as a courtesan. He then had Xi Shi presented to Fuchai so that she would distract him from his duties as ruler. The plan worked, and in 473 BC Wu was conquered by Yue.

36. This refers to a water-clock, which dripped at a steady rate, by which palace officials told the hours of the night.

And they rise and they watch the autumn moon
sink down in the river's waves,
As in the east the sun grows higher,
what shall their joy be then?

STUDY NOTES AND QUESTIONS

1. This poem, a vivid re-imagining of a famous story, presents images presaging danger both as a form of dramatic irony and as a suggestion of some awareness on Xi Shi's part of the end soon to come. What elements in the poem point to the fall of Fuchai? How do they contribute to the tone of the poem?

2. Note the unusual form and rhyme scheme: *aabbccc*. What impact does this have on the ending of the poem?

3. To suggest the distinctiveness of Li Bai's poem and his creativity in his use of past poetry, it is helpful to recall that the title of this poem refers to a Southern Dynasties *yuefu* tune. Liang dynasty writers adopted this title to compose highly stylized, slightly erotic quatrains. Xiao Gang, for example, wrote:

烏棲曲	*Song of the Roosting Crows*, no. 4
織成屏風金屈膝	The folding screen of brocade, with gold hinges—
朱脣玉面鐙前出	her red lips and jade face emerge in lamplight.
相看氣息望君憐	They gaze at each other, breathing hard, expecting love—
誰能含羞不自前	who can be so shy, as to not come forward?[37]

What elements of the scene in Xiao Gang's poem does Li Bai retain in his poem, and what new elements does he add?

37. Translation by Tian Xiaofei, *Beacon Fire and Shooting Star: The Literary Culture of the Liang* (Cambridge: Harvard University Asia Center, 2007), p. 244.

"Fighting South of the Wall" by Li Bai

戰城南									Fighting South of the Wall[38]
去	年	戰		桑	乾	源			Last year we fought at the Sanggan Spring.[39]
depart	year	fight		Sang	gan	spring			
今	年	戰		蔥	河	道 [daw']			This year we fight on the road to Zong River.[40]
now	year	fight		Zong	river	road			
洗	兵	條	支	海	上	波			We wash our blades in the waves of the Tiaozhi Sea,[41]
wash	weapon	Tiao	zhi	sea	on	waves			
放	馬	天	山	雪	中	草 [tshaw']			Loose our horses in the grass midst the snows of the Tian Mountains.[42]
loose	horse	Tian	mountain	snow	midst	grass			
萬	里	長	征	戰					Fighting on a campaign of ten thousand *li*,
104	*li*	long	campaign	fight					
三	軍	盡	衰	老 [law']					The Three Armies are all worn and old.[43]
three	army	complete	worn	old					
匈	奴	以	殺	戮	為	耕	作		The Xiongnu take slaughter as plowing[44]
Xiong	nu	take	kill	slaughter	to be	plow	make		
古	來	惟	見	白	骨	黃	沙	田 [dɛn]	From of old, all one sees are white bones on fields of yellow sand.
ancient	come	only	see	white	bone	yellow	sand	field	
秦	家	築	城	備	胡	處			Where the Qin clan built the Wall to prepare for the Hu,[45]
Qin	clan	build	wall	prepare	Hu	place			
漢	家	還	有	烽	火	燃 [ɲian]			The Han clan then had beacon fires burn.
Han	clan	still	have	beacon	fire	burn			

38. This is an old *yuefu* (folk song) title. See the Study Notes and Questions for this poem for the original Han dynasty version.

39. The Sanggan River is in the far northern part of Shanxi Province, just south of the Great Wall. Xuanzong had fought the Tujue 突厥 (Eastern Turks) there.

40. The Zongling River flows into Xinjiang Province from the Pamir Plateau in central Asia. Xuanzong had fought the Tibetans there.

41. Tiaozhi is a Chinese rendering of Antiochia and refers to Syria. The "sea" is the Mediterranean.

42. This is a mountain range in Xinjiang Province, in Central Asia.

43. The "three armies" are the imperial armies.

44. The Xiongnu were a powerful, militarily effective nomadic people during the Han dynasty.

45. Hu is a general name for "northern barbarian."

烽	火	燃	不	息				The beacon fires burn without rest.
beacon	fire	burn	not	cease				
征	戰	無	已	時 [dʑi]				The war campaigns are without end.
campaign	fight	is no	end	time				
野	戰	格	鬬	死				Fighting in the wilds, one dies in struggle.
wilds	fight	fight afar	fight	die				
敗	馬	號	鳴	向	天	悲 [pi]		Tired horses, sad, call out to the Heavens.
defeat	horse	call out	cry	face	heaven	sad		
烏	鳶	啄	人	腸				Crows and kites peck at men's guts,
crow	kite	peck	person	guts				
銜	飛	上	挂	枯	樹	枝 [tɕi]		Holding them, they fly to hang them on the branches of withered trees.
hold	fly	ascend	hang	dried	tree	branch		
士	卒	塗	草	莽				Officers and troops smear the grass.
knight	troops	smear	grass	grass				
將	軍	空	爾	為 [wi]				The General has acted in vain.
leader	army	empty	this way	do				
乃	知	兵	者	是	凶	器		Thus we know that weapons are indeed evil instruments:
thus	know	weapon	thing	this	evil	instrument		
聖	人	不	得	已	而	用	之 [tɕi]	The Sage only when he has no choice will use them.
sage	person	not	obtain	stop	and	use	it	

STUDY NOTES AND QUESTIONS

1. This is one of Li Bai's justly famous reworkings of old *yuefu* topics. The original anonymous *yuefu* poem from the Han Dynasty is:

戰城南	Fighting south of the wall,
死郭北	Dying north of the outer rampart,
野死不葬烏可食	Dying in the wilds, unburied, [we] can be eaten by crows.
為我謂烏	For me address the crows:
且為客豪	"For the moment, weep for the travelers.
野死諒不葬	Having died in the wilds, truly not buried,
腐肉安能去子逃	How can [our] rotting flesh flee from you?"
水深激激	The water is deep and clear;
蒲葦冥冥	The reeds and cattails grow dark.
梟騎戰鬬死	The valiant horsemen died in strife of war;
駑馬徘徊鳴	Weary horses pace back and forth and neigh.

〔梁〕築室	We build a dwelling:[46]
何以南	How can we go south?
何以北	How can we go north?
禾黍不穫君何食	The rice and millet unharvested, how will our lord eat?
願為忠臣安可得	We wished to be loyal servants, but how can we?
思子良臣	Think on your fine servants.
良臣誠可思	Fine servants truly can be thought of:
朝行出攻	At dawn they went out to battle,
暮不夜歸	At dusk they did not return for the night.[47]

2. Consider the voice in the poem. The persona here is an old campaigner, and on one level Li Bai entirely disappears. However, he speaks strongly through the energy of the style. Look at all the traditional elements of a song lamenting a frontier campaign and consider the elements of specificity that Li Bai adds to them to make them fresh.

3. The language of the poem is extremely prosy. That is, it uses prose syntax and includes many explicit function words. Consider, for example, the second-to-last line (乃知兵者是凶器) in which three of the seven characters (乃, "thus;" 者, "thing;" 是 "this [is]") are function words. Lines also vary greatly in length: they follow the syntax of the sentence rather than metrical rules. How is this prosy style appropriate to the themes and persona of the poem?

4. By the Tang dynasty, poets had developed many subtle ways to bring poems to a conclusion that avoided baldly direct statements (in the Chinese commentary tradition, such direct phrasing was called a "straightforward brush," *zhibi* 直筆). For later writers, using *zhibi* rhetoric in concluding a poem echoed the unembellished simplicity and honesty of the early poetic tradition. Explain the final couplet as this sort of "old" approach to closure.

46. Yu Guanying argues that *liang* 梁 is just a sound-word with no meaning. See Yu Guanying, *Han Wei Liuchao shi xuan*, p. 29. The version of the poem in the *Yuefu shiji* 樂府詩集, a major source for *yuefu* poetry compiled in the Northern Song dynasty by Guo Maoqian 郭茂倩, does not have the 梁.

47. Compare this translation with that of Stephen Owen in *An Anthology of Chinese Literature*, pp. 228–29.

"Bring in the Ale" by Li Bai

將進酒							Bring in the Ale
君 you	不 not	見 see					Don't you see:
黃 Yellow	河 River	之 's	水 water	天 Heaven	上 on	來 [ləj] come	The Yellow River's waters that come from Heaven,
奔 rush	流 flow	到 reach	海 ocean	不 not	復 again	回 [ɣwəj] return	Rush to the sea and never return.
君 you	不 not	見 see					Don't you see:
高 high	堂 hall	明 bright	鏡 mirror	悲 sorrow	白 white	髮 [fjyat] hair	Before the bright mirror in the tall hall, grieving at white hair:
朝 morning	如 like	青 blue	絲 silk	暮 dusk	成 become	雪 [syat] snow	In the morning like dark silk, by dusk, changed to snow.
人 human	生 life	得 obtain	意 intent	須 must	盡 exhaust	歡 pleasure	In life, when it meets your inclination, you must exhaust the pleasure.
莫 don't	使 cause	金 gold	樽 beaker	空 empty	對 face	月 [ŋyat] moon	Don't let the gold beaker stand empty facing the moon.
天 Heaven	生 grow	我 my	材 talent	必 must	有 have	用 use	Heaven gave birth to my talent: it must have a use:
千 1,000	金 gold	散 scatter	盡 exhaust	還 return	復 again	來 [ləj] come	A thousand pieces of gold tossed away, it shall return again.
烹 boil	羊 lamb	宰 slaughter	牛 ox	且 for now	為 make	樂 joy	Boil a lamb, slaughter an ox, let's make merry!
會 surely	須 must	一 one	飲 drink	三 three	百 hundred	杯 [pəj] cup	Given the chance, at one sitting, you must drink three hundred cups.
岑 Cen	夫 noble	子 master					Master Cen,
丹 Cinnabar	丘 Hill	生 mister					Master Cinnabar Hill,[48]
進 bring in	酒 wine	君 you	莫 don't	停 [tɦiajŋ] stop			Bring in ale, don't you stop.
與 with	君 you	歌 sing	一 one	曲 song			I'll sing a song for you.

48. These two men seem to be good friends of Li Bai.

請 ask	君 you	為 for	我 me	傾 incline	耳 ear	聽 [thiajŋ] listen	I ask you to incline your ear and listen to me.
鐘 bell	鼓 drum	饌 eat	玉 jade	不 not	足 worth	貴 esteem	Bells, drums, fine delicacies are not worthy of esteem.[49]
但 only	願 request	長 long	醉 drunk	不 not	用 use	醒 [siajŋ] sober	I only wish to be always drunk, no use to be sober.
古 old	來 forward	聖 sage	賢 worthy	皆 all	寂 silent	寞 [mak] quiet	The sages and worthies from ancient times all are silent.
惟 only	有 there is	飲 drink-	者 -ers	留 leave	其 their	名 [mjiajŋ] name	Only the drinkers have left their names.
陳 Chen	王 prince	昔 former	時 time	宴 party	平 Level	樂 [lak] Joy	The Prince of Chen in former times feasted at the Level Joy Temple:
斗 quart	酒 wine	十 ten	千 thousand	恣 unbridled	歡 pleasure	謔 [xɨak] jest	“A quart of ale for ten thousand in gold,” with unbridled joy and jesting.[50]
主 preside	人 person	何 why	為 sake	言 say	少 little	錢 cash	Host, why do you say you have little money?
徑 immediate	須 must	沽 buy wine	取 take	對 face	君 you	酌 [tɕɨak] decant	I’ll right away buy ale to pour out for you.
五 five	花 flower	馬 horse					The dappled horse,
千 thousand	金 gold	裘 [guw] fur					The furs worth a thousand cash,
呼 call	兒 boy	將 take	出 out	換 exchange	美 fine	酒 wine	Call the boy: take them out to exchange for fine ale.
與 with	爾 you	同 share	銷 melt	萬 10,000	古 ancient	愁 [dʑuw] sorrow	With you I’ll dissolve the sorrows of all antiquity.

Burton Watson’s Translation

Bring the Wine

Have you not seen
    the Yellow River waters descending from the sky,
    racing restless toward the ocean, never to return?
Have you not seen
    bright mirrors in high halls, the white-haired ones lamenting,

49. These are the accouterments of a feast, namely, the music and food.

50. Cao Zhi 曹植 was enfeoffed as the Prince of Chen. In a poem titled “A Famous City” 《名都篇》, he writes, “I return to feast at Level Joy Temple, A quart of fine wine for ten thousand cash.” 「歸來宴平樂，美酒斗十千。」

their black silk of morning by evening turned to snow?
If life is to have meaning, seize every joy you can;
do not let the golden cask sit idle in the moonlight!
Heaven gave me talents and meant them to be used;
gold scattered by the thousand comes home to me again.
Boil the mutton, roast the ox—we will be merry,
at one bout no less than three hundred cups.
Master Ts'en!
Scholar Tan-ch'iu!
bring wine and no delay!
For you I'll sing a song—
be pleased to bend your ears and hear:
Bells and drums, food rare as jade—these aren't worth prizing;
all I ask is to be drunk forever, never to sober up!
Sages and worthies from antiquity—all gone into silence;
only the great drinkers have left a name behind.
The Prince of Ch'en once feasted in the Hall of Calm Delight;
wine, ten thousand coins a cask, flowed for his revelers' joy.
Why does my host tell me the money has run out?
Buy more at once—my friends have cups to be refilled!
My dappled mount,
my furs worth a thousand—
call the boy, have him take them away and barter for fine wine!
Together we will wash away ten thousand years of care.

Study Notes and Questions

1. Like "Fighting South of the Wall," "Bring in the Ale" is an old *yuefu* title. Unfortunately, we have only fragmentary texts for earlier versions of the song.

2. Li Bai brings the same extravagance and energy to both the form and the language of this poem that he shows in "Fighting South of the Wall." The persona here is yet more intense: a carouser who seems to almost literally "seize the day" in his acute awareness of the fleetingness of life's pleasures and the inevitability of sorrow. Consider the elements in the poem that contribute to the intensity of the voice.

3. Whose horse and furs does Li Bai want sold to buy wine?

From the Series “Ancient Airs” by Li Bai

古風五十九首第一					Ancient Airs, 59 poems, no. 1
大	雅	久	不	作	The Greater *Ya* have long since stopped:[51]
Greater	*Ya*	long	not	made	
吾	衰	竟	誰	陳 [trɦin]	I have grown weak; who, then, will set it out [anew]?[52]
I	frail	finally	who	set forth	
王	風	委	蔓	草	The King’s Airs have become neglected and overgrown.[53]
King	Air	decline	creeper	grass	
戰	國	多	荊	榛 [tsɦin]	During the Warring States weeds flourished.[54]
warring	states	many	brambles		
龍	虎	相	啖	食	Dragons and tigers devoured one another.
dragon	tiger	mutually	greedily	eat	
兵	戈	逮	狂	秦 [tsɦin]	The rule of weapons continued until crazed Qin.[55]
weapons	spears	reach	crazed	Qin	
正	聲	何	微	茫	How diffuse had grown the rectifying sound.[56]
correct	sound	how	slight	vague	
哀	怨	起	騷	人 [rin]	Sorrow and resentment gave rise to the *Sao* poets.[57]
lament	resent	arise	Sao	people	
揚	馬	激	頹	波	Yang Xiong and Sima Xiangru stirred up crashing waves.[58]
Yang	Ma	agitate	crumble	waves	

---

51. The “Greater *Ya*” is one of the sections of the *Canon of Poetry*.

52. “The King’s Regulations” 王制 in the *Record of Rites* 禮記 explains, “He orders the Grand Archivist to set out poems in order to observe the folkways of the populace” 「命太史陳詩以觀民風。」

53. The “King’s Airs” is a section of the “Airs of the States” in the *Canon of Poetry*. The phrase, however, is more general, as in the “Great Preface” to the *Canon of Poetry*: “The transformations of ‘Osprey Cries’ and the ‘Unicorn’s Footsteps’ are the influence (風) of the true king” 「關雎麟趾之化，王者之風。」.

54. The Warring States period (5th–3rd centuries BC) was a time of many small warring kingdoms following the final collapse of the Zhou dynasty.

55. The Qin united all of China at the very end of the Warring States period. However, the severity of its measures was said to have led to its collapse soon after the death of the founding emperor. The line alludes to the twentieth of Tao Qian’s “Twenty Poems on Drinking Wine”: “[Confucius, who taught between] the Zhu and Si Rivers, stopped his fading echo: they drifted until they reached crazed Qin” 「洙泗輟微響，漂流逮狂秦。」.

56. The phrase “correct sound” is both the sound that is produced by a time that is correctly governed and a sound that, when heard, can lead to a transformation in behavior. Both meanings apply here.

57. The “*Sao* poets” refers foremost to Qu Yuan, author of *Encountering Sorrow*, the most important poem in the *Lyrics of Chu*. The phrase also refers to all the other poets of the collection. The poems were considered political allegory about the ruler’s foolish neglect of his worthy ministers.

58. Yang Xiong and Sima Xiangru are two of the most famous Han dynasty writers of *fu* 賦 (rhyme-prose), an elaborate, energetic form of verbal display.

	開 open	流 flow	蕩 stir	無 without	垠 [ŋin] border	They opened a flow that flooded without border.
	廢 discard	興 flourish	雖 although	萬 10,000	變 changes	Although rise and decline has ten thousand transformations,
12	憲 regulate	章 order	亦 also	已 already	淪 [lyn] sunk	Proper ordering had disappeared entirely.[59]
	自 since	從 from	建 Jian	安 -an	來 forward	Ever since the Jian'an reign period,[60]
	綺 patterned	麗 pretty	不 not	足 worth	珍 [trin] rare	The artful prettiness has not been worth valuing.
	聖 sage	代 age	復 return	元 primal	古 old	Our sage dynasty has returned to the original ways of ancient days.
16	垂 hang	衣 clothes	貴 value	清 pure	真 [tʂin] genuine	In "straightening one's clothes" one values the pure and genuine.[61]
	群 crowd	才 talents	屬 belong	休 fine	明 bright	The assembled talents belong among the brilliant.
	乘 ride	運 move	共 together	躍 jump	鱗 [lin] fish scales	Riding the changing times, they together are like [thronging] fish scales.
	文 adorn	質 substance	相 mutually	炳 shine	煥 blaze	Adornment and substance set one another ablaze:[62]
20	眾 gathered	星 stars	羅 spread	秋 autumn	旻 [min] sky	The gathered stars arrayed across the autumn sky.
	我 my	志 resolve	在 is at	刪 edit	述 transmit	My resolve is to edit and transmit,[63]
	垂 hang	輝 gleam	映 shine	千 1,000	春 [tʂhyn] springs	Leaving a radiance to shine for a thousand springs.

59. The phrase "proper ordering" appears in Ban Gu's 班固 "*Fu* on the Eastern Capital"《東都賦》as well as in the "Doctrine of the Mean." That is, it has old, proper, canonical associations.

60. The Jian'an reign period was part of the Han dynasty and lasted from AD 196–220. This was the great age of direct, simple, committed poetry that marks the beginning of the five-character verse tradition.

61. The line alludes to the sentence from the "Great Commentary"《繫辭傳》to the *Canon of Changes*: "The Yellow Emperor, Yao, and Shun set their clothes aright and the realm was ruled."「黃帝、堯、舜垂衣裳而天下治。」. Li Bai praises Emperor Xuanzong as the embodiment of the Daoist sage ruler, who rules by non-action.

62. The line points to Confucius's *Analects* 6.18: "When adornment and substance are matched, only then is one a noble man."「文質彬彬，然後君子。」.

63. These are the activities associated with Confucius's organizing of the Zhou dynasty canonical texts. In *Analects* 7.1 Confucius asserts, "I transmit but do not create."「述而不作。」.

希 aspire	聖 sage	如 if	有 have	立 accomplish	Aspiring to sagehood, if I establish a legacy,
絕 stop	筆 brush	於 at	獲 capture	麟 [lin] unicorn	I shall stop my brush at the capture of the unicorn.[64]

Victor Mair's Translation

Poems in an Old Style, No. 1

Ages have passed since the stately Odes flourished,
I am growing old and there is no one else to present them;
The folk songs became tangled with creeping grasses,
In the Warring Kingdoms, thorny bushes grew thickly.

Dragons and tigers devoured each other,
Armed hostilities lasted until rabid Ch'in;
How feeble had the orthodox tradition grown!
In its place arose the sad and complaining bard.

Yang and Ssu-ma revived Ch'ü Yüan's declining ripples,
And opened a new current which reached a boundless swell;
Although there has been a myriad of changes in its fortune,
Ars poetica finally sank into oblivion.

Ever since the Chien'an period at the end of the Han,
Prettiness itself has not been considered fine enough;
In our own hallowed age, we have returned to antiquity,
Our majestic monarch values purity and truth.

The assembled talents are handsome and smart,
"They have mounted fate's carriage and joined the leaping dragons";
Style and substance glitter together—
A host of stars spread over the Autumn Sea.

My determination is but "to edit and transmit,"
So that this brilliance may shine through a thousand springs;
If my task is accomplished, I would hope, like the sage,
To lay down my brush with the capture of the unicorn.

Study Notes and Questions

1. This poem, the first in Li Bai's series "Ancient Airs," provides a summary of the history of poetry from its beginning until the present. His account repeats the truisms of the oppositional aesthetics associated

64. When Confucius heard that a unicorn—an auspicious beast—had been captured during his turbulent times, he knew that the Way of the Former Kings would not be reestablished. This news was the last entry in the *Spring and Autumn Annals* (Ai Gong 14) that Confucius was writing in order to preserve the Way for future ages.

with the ideal of "restoring the ancient" (*fugu* 復古) that is an appropriate introduction to poems written as "Ancient Airs."

2. Li Bai takes on yet another persona in this poem. Who is he this time? Consider the many resources he uses to define that persona. For example, what types of allusions does he use, and do they shift during the poem?

3. Into what role is Li Bai casting himself in the last four lines? Does it mirror the opening couplet? How seriously should we accept this persona as speaking for Li Bai? Does the difficulty of answering this question contribute to the character of the poem?

"Jade Staircase's Grievance" by Li Bai

玉階怨					Jade Staircase's Grievance
玉 jade	階 stair	生 grow	白 white	露 dew	White dew grows on the jade stairs.
夜 night	久 long	侵 encroach	羅 gauze	襪 [muat] stockings	The night is long, invading [her] gauze stockings.
卻 then	下 lower	水 water	精 essence	簾 curtain	[She] lowers the quartz-bead curtain,
玲 [glistening]	瓏	望 gaze	秋 autumn	月 [ŋuat] moon	Glistening as [she] gazes at the autumn moon.

EZRA POUND'S TRANSLATION

The Jewel Stairs' Grievance

The jewelled steps are already quite white with dew,
It is so late that the dew soaks my gauze stockings,
And I let down the crystal curtain
And watch the moon through the clear autumn.

[Pound's] Note.—Jewel stairs, therefore a palace. Grievance, therefore there is something to complain of. Gauze stockings, therefore a court lady, not a servant who complains. Clear autumn, therefore he has no excuse on account of the weather. Also she has come early, for the dew has not merely whitened the stairs, but has soaked her stockings. The poem is especially prized because she utters no direct reproach.

STUDY NOTES AND QUESTIONS

1. Discuss Pound's reading. Did he point to the key elements and implications?

2. Discuss Li Bai's use of light in the poem.

"Question and Answer in the Mountains" by Li Bai

山中問答							Question and Answer in the Mountains[65]
問	余	何	意	棲	碧	山 [ʂəɨn]	You ask me with what intent do
ask	me	what	intent	roost	emerald	mountain	I perch in the green mountains:
笑	而	不	答	心	自	閑 [ɣəɨn]	I smile but do not answer:
smile	and/but	not	reply	mind	of itself	at ease	my mind is fully at ease.
桃	花	流	水	窅	然	去	Peach blossoms, floating on the
peach	flowers	flow	water	distant	-ly	leave	water, leave for far away.[66]
別	有	天	地	非	人	間 [kəɨn]	There is another Heaven and
apart	there is	heaven	earth	is not	people	midst	Earth, not among humankind.

STEPHEN OWEN'S TRANSLATION

Dialogue in the Mountains

You ask me why it is
  I lodge in sapphire hills;
I laugh and do not answer—
  the heart is at peace.
Peach blossoms and flowing water
  go off, fading away afar,
and there is another world
  that is not of mortal men.

STUDY NOTES AND QUESTIONS

1. The obvious first question is whether Li Bai here recounts a dialogue, as the title states, or whether the interlocutor here, like the person in Tao Qian's "Twenty Poems on Drinking Ale" (see chapter 5), is a fiction. Is Li Bai talking to himself?

2. What role is Li Bai adopting here?

65. An alternative title for this poem is "In the Mountains, Answering a Lay Person" 《山中答俗人》.

66. This is an allusion to the Peach Blossom Spring, an idyllic farm community described by Tao Qian in his famous essay, "Peach Blossom Spring." In Tao Qian's story, a fisherman discovers this otherwise hidden land by following peach blossoms floating on a stream.

"Decanting Alone, under the Moon" by Li Bai

月下獨酌四首第一					Decanting Alone, under the Moon, 4 poems, no. 1
花	間	一	壺	酒	Amid the flowers, one pot of ale:
flowers	midst	one	pot	ale	
獨	酌	無	相	親 [tshin]	I pour it alone, without a friend.
alone	pour	without	mutually	close	
舉	杯	邀	明	月	I raise my cup to invite the bright moon.
raise	cup	invite	bright	moon	
對	影	成	三	人 [ɲin]	Facing my shadow, we become three people.
face	shadow	become	three	people	
月	既	不	解	飲	Not only does the moon not understand drinking,
moon	since	not	know	drink	
影	徒	隨	我	身 [ɕin]	My shadow pointlessly follows me.
shadow	in vain	follow	my	body	
暫	伴	月	將	影	For the moment, I'll accompany the moon and my shadow:
moment	befriend	moon	take	moon	
行	樂	須	及	春 [tɕhwin]	Our finding pleasure should last through spring.
carry out	joy	surely	reach	spring	
我	歌	月	徘	徊	I sing, and the moon wavers.
I	sing	moon	go back/forth		
我	舞	影	零	亂 [lwan^h]	I dance, and my shadow grows wild.
I	dance	shadow	in confusion		
醒	時	同	交	歡	While sober, we'll share our pleasure.
sober	time	share	mutual	pleasure	
醉	後	各	分	散 [san^h]	After we're drunk, we'll each go on our way.
drunk	after	each	divide	scatter	
永	結	無	情	遊	Vowing eternally to wander without passions,
always	tie	without	feelings	wander	
相	期	邈	雲	漢 [xan^h]	We agree to meet in the distant Milky Way.
mutually	await	distant	cloud	Milky Way	

ARTHUR WALEY'S TRANSLATION

Drinking Alone by Moonlight

A cup of wine, under the flowering trees;
I drink alone, for no friend is near.
Raising my cup I beckon the bright moon,
For he, with my shadow, will make three men.
The moon, alas, is no drinker of wine;

Listless, my shadow creeps about at my side.
Yet with the moon as friend and the shadow as slave,
I must make merry before the Spring is spent.
To the songs I sing the moon flickers her beams;
In the dance I weave my shadow tangles and breaks.
While we were sober, three shared the fun;
Now we are drunk, each goes his way.
May we long share our odd, inanimate feast,
And meet at last on the Cloudy River of the sky.

Elling Eide's Translation

Drinking Alone in the Moonlight

Beneath the blossoms with a pot of wine,
No friends at hand, so I poured alone;
I raised my cup to invite the moon,
Turned to my shadow, and we became three.
Now the moon had never learned about my drinking,
And my shadow had merely followed my form,
But I quickly made friends with the moon and my shadow;
To find pleasure in life, make the most of the spring.

Whenever I sang, the moon swayed with me;
Whenever I danced, my shadow went wild.
Drinking, we shared our enjoyment together;
Drunk, then each went off on his own.
But forever agreed on dispassionate revels,
We promised to meet in the far Milky Way.

Study Notes and Questions

1. The poem begins with Li Bai drinking alone. Does he escape his solitude through his fanciful imaginings? What is the quality of whimsy here? Is it natural and spontaneous? What is the effect of his listing the faults of his new-found friends, which he immediately forgives and disregards?

2. Li Bai inhabits many personae in his poems. What is the persona here? Do you think that the "implied author" is someone different who is winking at the antics of the persona that he sets out in the poem?

3. What is the high point of the poem? How does Li Bai create the context for it? How does the ending of the poem frame that high point?

Chapter Seven

Du Fu

Du Fu 杜甫 (712–70) is China's greatest poet. His technical range is extraordinary, but what truly sets him apart is how his unfailing poetic inventiveness captures an unprecendented breadth and depth of human experience. Ironically, the scope of the topics in his poetry and the creativity and honesty with which he approached them kept him from being acknowledged as a great writer in his own day. This chapter attempts to introduce his many styles and moods and the sheer originality with which he approached the topics he brought within the scope of poetic composition.

Du Fu's Life

Du Fu was from a well-established aristocratic lineage that claimed descent from the important Jin dynasty general and scholar Du Yu 杜預. His grandfather was Du Shenyan 杜審言 (ca. 646–ca. 708), one of the most important poets of Empress Wu's reign. His father, however, held only minor regional posts. Little is known about Du Fu's early life. He was born in a small town near Luoyang, the eastern capital. After he turned nineteen, he traveled around the southeast (modern Jiangsu and Zhejiang Provinces) for several years before returning to Luoyang to take the *jinshi* examination. He failed. He then spent five years in eastern China (modern Shandong, Hebei Provinces). Turning thirty, he returned to Luoyang, presumably in search of patronage, and remained there for three years. He met Li Bai and the important poet and official Gao Shi 高適 (ca. 705–65) at this time. Finding no advancement, he set off again for the east before deciding to try his luck in Chang'an. At age thirty-six, he took a special examination designed to discover overlooked talent, but Li Linfu 李林甫, the prime minister at the time, was attempting to weed out the "new men" who had come to power via the examination system and to return authority to the major aristocratic lineages. He therefore asserted that the court had not overlooked anyone worthy of attention and failed everyone. Du Fu spent the next few years traveling between Chang'an and Luoyang before finally, at age forty, submitting writings to the throne: he was rewarded with a minor post. The position, however humble, was good enough that Du Fu decided after several years in Chang'an to move his family there from Luoyang. As luck would have it, however, excessive rain in the fall of that year (754) ruined the harvest, driving up prices, so that Du Fu decided that he could not afford to maintain his family in the capital and moved them to the town of Fengxian 奉先 northeast of Chang'an. For the next year he traveled between Fengxian and Chang'an, but then, in late 755, the catastrophic An Lushan Rebellion broke out.

By 755, Emperor Xuanzong had been on the throne for forty-three years. During his later years, he increasingly entrusted rule to his prime ministers, and the relationship between the court and the generals who guarded the borders became increasingly tense. The Song dynasty historian Sima Guang 司馬光 largely blamed this tension on the prime minister, Li Linfu. Control of the northern borders was entrusted to military governors, who had authority over both military and civil rule in their regions.

Because this concentration of power potentially posed a threat to Li Linfu, he specifically appointed non-Chinese generals to these posts to prevent their attaining civil ministerial posts in the capital that might challenge his control. This split between civil and military, the capital and border control, however, led to mutual suspicion. An Lushan, the military governor of three border regions concurrently, effectively had control over northeastern China. Although his relationship with Xuanzong seemed strong, tensions between An and Yang Guozhong 楊國忠, the prime minister after Li Linfu's death, grew ever greater. Either because of his own ambitions or because he felt the need to act preemptively against Yang, An Lushan rebelled in late 755. His army advanced on Luoyang, and in the garrisons in his path most prefects who had responsibility to resist either fled or surrendered. Luoyang fell, and An Lushan turned toward Chang'an. Between the two cities, however, was Tong Pass, a major strategic mountain fortress guarding the entrance to the Chang'an region that would be difficult to capture. Because Yang Guozhong once again did not trust the intentions of Geshu Han 哥舒翰, the non-Chinese general who commanded the imperial troops at the pass, he ordered the army to leave the pass to fight An Lushan in open terrain. Geshu Han had no choice but to obey, and the imperial troops were slaughtered.

When Yang Guozhong and the court heard the news, they, together with Xuanzong's retinue and the emperor's most loyal troops, quietly fled Chang'an in the night. After leaving the city, however, Xuanzong's troops demanded the execution of Yang Guozhong, who had brought the empire to this crisis. They also demanded the execution of Yang Guifei 楊貴妃, Precious Consort Yang, who was a relative of Yang Guozhong and who—according to the legend that grew around these momentous events—had entirely besotted Xuanzong and distracted him from the responsibilities of rule.[1] At this point, his generals also persuaded Xuanzong to flee into the mountainous, easily defended region of Shu 蜀 (Sichuan) and to abdicate to his son, Suzong 肅宗, who would remain in the north to rally the imperial armies and attack An Lushan. Luckily for the new emperor, An Lushan's army itself was in disarray. An Lushan was killed by his own son, An Qingxu 安慶緒, who was then killed by the rebel general Shi Siming 史思明. Shi proved an able leader (hence the rebellion is called the "An Shi Rebellion" in Chinese), but he was killed in turn by his son Shi Chaoyi 史朝義. Despite this internal chaos, the Tang did not completely suppress the rebellion until 763, when Shi Chaoyi committed suicide. As the regional commanders defected to the Tang, however, the Tang court, desperate for their aid and having little choice, granted those regional commanders posts as military governors, which officially ceded to them the combined civil and military authority in the regions they controlled. Thus the Tang central court for the rest of the dynasty was severely weakened. Even though ambitious emperors succeeded in restoring their control over some of this territory, their hold remained tenuous.

Du Fu left Chang'an for Fengxian in the Fifth Month of 756, before Geshu Han led his troops out of the pass. Du Fu led his family from Fengxian, via his maternal uncle's home (the occasion recounted in the "Ballad of Pengya" 彭衙行), to the town of Fuzhou, where he left them in safety as he attempted to join Suzong's court. En route, however, he was captured and taken to Chang'an. By early summer of 757 he had escaped and made his way to Emperor Suzong's encampment where he was appointed a Reminder, a relatively low-ranking court official charged with finding mistakes in official documents in both their wording and content. Unfortunately, Du Fu had the temerity to defend the hapless official Fang Guan 房琯 who, having great faith in the strength of sage virtue, had decided to emulate Zhou dynasty warfare by attacking An Lushan's army with ox-drawn carts. Du Fu spoke up for

1. According to stories, An Lushan, who acted the part of Yang Guifei's "child" to amuse the emperor, in fact had an illicit affair with her.

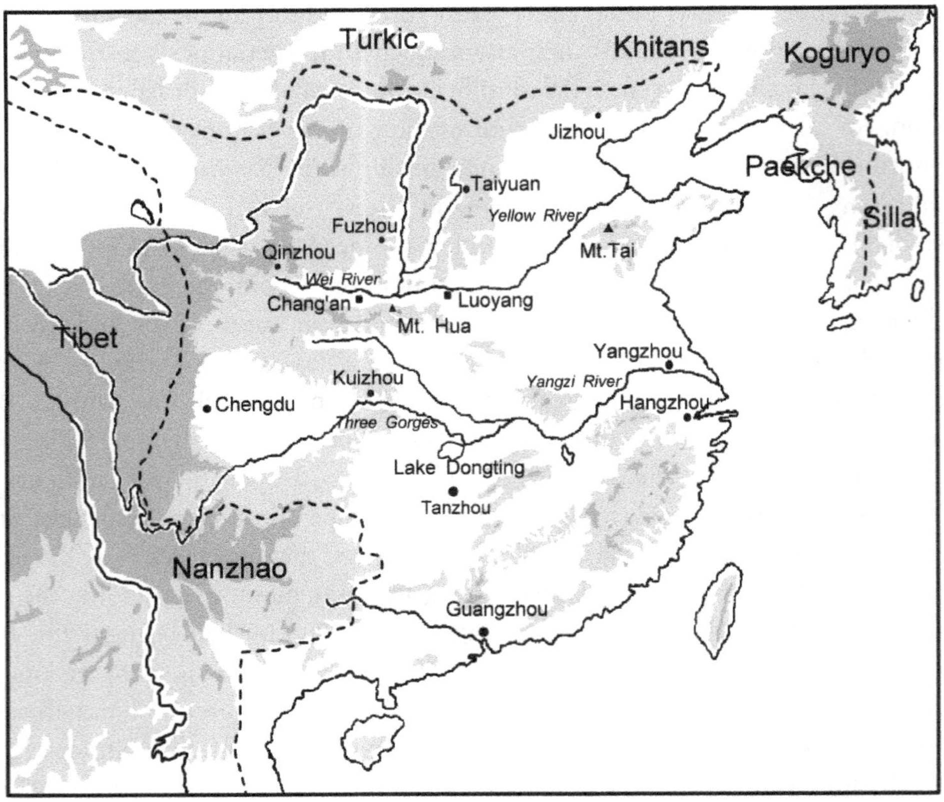

Du Fu's China

his friend after the debacle, was briefly imprisoned, pardoned, and then given permission to visit his family in Fuzhou. In the meantime, imperial troops recaptured Chang'an, so, in early 758, Du Fu led his family from Fuzhou to the capital. However, later in that year as part of a purge of irregularly appointed officials, Du Fu was reassigned to a minor post in the small town of Huazhou 華州 near Chang'an. By the end of the next year, he had resigned his post, given up all hope of an official career, and planned how to provide for his family.

In the Seventh Month of 759 Du Fu and his family left Huazhou for Qinzhou 秦州 (in modern Gansu Province) and then traveled to Chengdu 成都 in Sichuan Province through a pass near Qinzhou. In Chengdu in 760, he had no obvious means of support. Fortunately, an old friend, Yan Wu 嚴武, had been appointed military governor of Chengdu garrison, so Du Fu became a member of his staff and set up a household in his famous thatched cottage or, more humbly named, "grass hut" in the suburbs of the city. Moreover, soon thereafter Gao Shi was appointed governor in Chengdu. The next five years had their moments of crisis but were basically stable. In 765, however, first Gao Shi and then Yan Wu died. By this time the An Lushan Rebellion had been suppressed, and Du Fu resolved to return to the Chinese heartland by heading east on the Yangzi River. By late spring of 766 he had gotten as far as Kuizhou 夔州, next to the Three Gorges 三峽 on the Yangzi. He lingered there for the next year and a half with ever-increasing health problems. In early 768 he and his family were on their way again and traveled slowly down the Yangzi. By 769 they had gotten as far as Lake Dongting 洞庭湖 and visited various friends and acquaintances in nearby cities like Tanzhou 潭州 (Changsha 長沙). Still planning to push on to Luoyang and Chang'an, Du Fu died near Tanzhou in the fall of 770.

Du Fu's Poetry

Scholars usually divide Du Fu's poetry into four periods: his "early" work, the poems during the rebellion before he left for Sichuan (737–59), those he wrote in Chengdu, Sichuan, from 760–65, and the poems of his long, slow journey down the Yangzi in his final years.

Du Fu's "early" poems are not in fact all that early: his earliest extant poems come from his mid-twenties when he already was a mature poet with distinctive stylistic traits. Poems likes "Gazing on the Peak" and "Painting of a Hawk," for example, reveal Du Fu's sweeping imaginative reach and complexity of sensibility. In them he creates multiple perspectives and draws on syntactic ambiguity to undercut the stability of simple viewing positions. "Painting of a Hawk" also wittily shows that Du Fu was strongly aware of the problem of artifice—of making and crafting—that is a constant challenge to the art of writing poetry. His "Ballad of the Army Carts," also from the pre-rebellion period, is a highly ambitious old-style poem, a bravura performance that pulls together all the conventional motifs of the theme into an unflaggingly energetic protest poem. At the same time, it marshals all the techniques that Du Fu used with stunning effect a few years later in the far more focused and specific protest poems in the early years of the An Lushan Rebellion.

Many later Chinese literati especially admire Du Fu's early rebellion-period poetry. The range of ways in which he handles the themes of the war, its hardships, and his own personal dislocation is nothing short of extraordinary. It should be stressed that Du Fu's choosing to write on these topics at all is remarkable and has few compelling precedents. With few models to draw on, Du Fu synthesized the rhetorical and formal techniques he needed to deal effectively with these intensely personal events that also were of great historical moment. For his ability to capture their historical significance, later literati deemed him the "Poet Historian" 詩史. The range of moods and styles in "Moonlit Night," "Lament for Riverbend," and "Spring Vista," all written while Du Fu was captive in Chang'an, suggests Du Fu's confidence both in the power of poetry to speak to all time and in his own ability to craft the forms appropriate to the task. Once he escaped from Chang'an, he developed flexible old-style forms to convey (and shape) the confluence of personal hardship and universal turmoil in such autobiographical poems as "The Ballad of Pengya" and the "Journey North" 北征 and in the protest poems known as the "Three Officers" and "Three Partings."[2]

Scholars may *admire* Du Fu's rebellion-period poetry, but they *love* the poetry he wrote in Chengdu. After long hardship, Du Fu spent a few years of relative ease in Chengdu and produced a poetry that never forgets the problems of the state and society but that does manage to find calmness and often self-mocking humor as well as broader meaning in a wide range of often-trying personal experiences. "My Thatched Roof Was Destroyed by the Autumn Wind: A Song" is a classic example of travail, humor, and a small dash of ironized yet real seriousness.

After Du Fu left Chengdu, his poetic vision and technique grew increasingly intense and difficult. Many later literati who grappled seriously with poetic composition considered this final period Du Fu's greatest, while those who primarily were readers rather than writers considered Du Fu's poems after Chengdu too highly wrought and impenetrably difficult. Du Fu's regulated verse during his final

2. The "Three Officers" are "The Officer at Xin'an《新安吏》, "The Officer at Shihao"《石壕吏》, and "The Officer at Tong Pass"《潼關吏》.The "Three Partings" are the "Parting of the Newlywed"《新婚别》, "Parting of the Homeless"《無家别》,and "Parting of the Old Man"《垂老别》.

years grew especially dark and demanding. He pushed the regulated form to the limits of what it could bear in his effort to forge a vast, coherent vision in which he, insignificant and decrepit, still could play his part. His faith in this possibility gives his late poetry extraordinary power, but it was a faith in a symbolic universe that could be encompassed by language and poetry that died with him. Later readers read and marveled at what had been. Through Du Fu they could catch a glimmer of the grandeur of the world of Emperor Xuanzong's reign that Du Fu created.

"Gazing on the Peak" by Du Fu [old-style verse]

望嶽					Gazing on the Peak[3]
岱 First	宗 Elder	夫 now	如 like	何 what	What is the Primal Elder like?[4]
齊 Qi	魯 Lu	青 green	未 not yet	了 [lɛw'] finish	Through Qi and Lu, its green does not end.[5]
造 create	化 transform	鍾 gather	神 divine	秀 flower	Creation gathered [here] the divine and outstanding.[6]
陰 *yin*	陽 *yang*	割 hack	昏 dark	曉 [xɛw'] dawn	Its sunny and shady sides split dusk and dawn.
盪 wash	胸 chest	生 give birth	曾 layer	雲 clouds	Rinsing [its] chest, it gives rise to layered clouds.
決 split	眥 eye corner	入 enter	歸 return	鳥 [tɛw'] bird	Straining eyes sharply, entering the returning birds.
會 [future]	當 surely	凌 ascend	絕 cut-off	頂 summit	When surely I ascend its utmost summit,
一 one	覽 look	眾 group	山 mountain	小 [siaw'] small	In one gaze, all the mountains will become small.[7]

3. Written around 737, this is one of Du Fu's earliest extant poems. The term "peak" refers to the Five Peaks, the five sacred mountains of Chinese imperial tradition. Mt. Tai is the Eastern Peak.

4. The phrase "primal elder," used to refer to Mt. Tai, appears in the *Bai hu tong* 白虎通, a Han dynasty work.

5. Qi and Lu were states in northeast China during the Warring States period. The *Records of the Grand Historian* notes, "The sunny side of Mt. Tai is Lu, the shady is Qi." 「泰山之陽則魯，其陰則齊 。」

6. The line echoes Sun Cho 孫綽, "*Fu* on Wandering on Mt. Tiantai"《遊天台山賦》:"Tiantai is the most divine and outstanding of mountain peaks." 「天台山者，蓋山嶽之神秀者也 。」

7. Du Fu here draws on the claim in *Mencius* 孟子, "Exhausting the Mind"《盡心》, that "Confucius climbed Mt. Tai and considered the entire realm small."「孔子登泰山而小天下。」

Study Notes and Questions

1. This is a very expansive poem that invokes cosmic processes and a long history of cultural references to Mount Tai. How does Du Fu invoke these contexts in the first four lines?

2. Du Fu in this poem already reveals his taste for difficult diction and imaginative leaps. Note the complex parallelism of lines 5 and 6: "wash chest" parallels "split eye-corner," but in each case we are not sure whose chest and whose eyeballs are involved. It does not quite work for the "chest" to be Du Fu's and then continue with "give rise to layered clouds." Line 6 also presents an interpretive challenge: explain the line using the word-for-word translation. How does an eyeball enter a returning bird? What does this mean? What are we to imagine here?

3. The closure for the poem suits the expansiveness of the first six lines: to whom is Du Fu comparing himself? The ending also is generically appropriate for an account of Mount Tai: what qualities of Mount Tai does the couplet capture?

"Painting of a Hawk" by Du Fu [regulated verse]

畫鷹					Painting of a Hawk
素 white	練 silk	風 wind	霜 frost	起 rise	On white silk, wind and frost rise:
蒼 dark	鷹 hawk	畫 paint	作 create	殊 [dʑuə̌] unique	A dark hawk, an extraordinary painting.
㩳 straight	身 body	思 long	狡 agile	兔 rabbit	Body held high, it longs for a nimble rabbit.[8]
側 sideways	目 eye	似 resemble	愁 sad	胡 [ɣɔ] Hu	Eyes looking aside, it resembles the sad nomad.[9]
絛 ribbon	鏇 axle	光 gleam	堪 willing	擿 pick	The gleam of its tether and ring: it can be picked up.[10]
軒 eaves	楹 post	勢 force	可 can be	呼 [xɔ] call	At the eaves-side post, its stance [is such that] it can be called.
何 what	當 when	擊 strike	凡 ordinary	鳥 bird	When will it strike the ordinary bird,
毛 feather	血 blood	灑 sprinkle	平 level	蕪 [muə̌] brush	Feathers and blood sprinkled on the level bushes?

Stephen Owen's Translation

Painted Hawk

Wind-blown frost rises from plain white silk,
a gray falcon—paintwork's wonder.

Body strains, its thoughts on the cunning hare,
its eyes turn sidelong like a Turk in despair.

You could pinch the rays glinting on tie-ring,
its stance, to be called to the column's rail.

When will it strike the common birds?—
bloody feathers strewing the weed-covered plain.

---

8. In this poem, Du Fu draws phrasing from earlier compositions about hawks. This line echoes Sun Chu 孫楚 (d. 294), "Hawk *Fu*" 《鷹賦》:"It captures the nimble rabbit on the level plain."「擒狡兔於平原。」

9. Sun Chu, "Hawk *Fu*": "With deep-set eyes and moth-eyebrows, his appearance resembles the sad northern nomad."「深目蛾眉，狀如愁胡 。」

10. Fu Xuan 傅玄 (217–78), "Hawk *Fu*": "Decorated with an ornate shackle of rainbow colors, tied to a gold ring with a moving pivot."「飾五彩之華絆，結鏇璣之金鐶。 」

Study Notes and Questions

Earlier poems on painting had played with confusion between art and reality. In this poem Du Fu constantly presents art that is trying to escape from its frame.

1. Which lines refer to the painting, which to Du Fu's imagination, and which to real birds?

2. The poem reflects a common pattern used in regulated verse: how can the second couplet be considered a development of the first line, while the third couplet is a development of the second line? The final couplet then resolves the issues raised in the restatements of the theme presented in the middle couplets.

"Ballad of the Army Carts" by Du Fu [old-style verse]

	兵車行							Ballad of the Army Carts[11]
	車 cart	轔 rumble	轔 rumble		馬 horses	蕭 neigh	蕭 [siaw] neigh	The carts rumble on,[12] The horses neigh.[13]
	行 travel	人 person	弓 bow	箭 arrows	各 each	在 is at	腰 [ʔjiaw] waist	The marchers each with bow and arrows at their waists.
	耶 father	孃 mother	妻 wife	子 child	走 run	相 [d.o.]	送 see off	Father, mother, wife, and children run to see them off.
4	塵 dirt	埃 dust	不 not	見 see	咸 Xian-	陽 yang	橋 [kɦiaw] Bridge	In the dust, one cannot see the Xianyang Bridge.[14]
	牽 pull	衣 clothes	頓 stamp	足 feet	攔 obstruct	道 road	哭 cry	Pulling their clothes, stomping their feet, they block the road, crying.
	哭 cry	聲 sound	直 straight	上 ascend	干 assail	雲 cloud	霄 [siaw] high cloud	The crying sound goes up, piercing the clouds above.
	道 road	旁 side	過 pass-	者 -ers	問 ask	行 travel	人 [rin] person	A passer-by on the roadside asks a marcher.
8	行 travel	人 person	但 only	云 say	點 dot	行 travel	頻 [pɦjin] frequent	The marcher only says, "Campaign conscription is frequent.

11. This poem was written in 751 (Tianbao 10) when Du Fu lived in Chang'an.

12. *Canon of Poetry*, "Carts Rumble"《車轔》(Mao 126): "There is a carriage rumbling."「有車轔轔。」

13. *Canon of Poetry*, "My Chariot Is Strong"《車攻》(Mao 179): "Whinnying, the horses neigh."「蕭蕭馬鳴。」See Karlgren, *The Book of Odes*, pp. 123–24.

14. This is a bridge leading over the Wei River outside of Chang'an.

	或 some	從 from	十 ten +	五 five	北 north	防 guard	河 River	Some from age fourteen have guarded the river in the North.[15]
	便 then	至 arrive	四 four ×	十 ten	西 west	營 encamp	田 [tɦian] field	They reach forty, manning settlements in the West.[16]
	去 leave	時 time	里 village	正 head	與 give	裹 wrap	頭 head	When they left, the village head tied their headbands for them.
12	歸 return	來 come	頭 head	白 white	還 still	戍 guard	邊 [pjian] border	Returning, their heads are white, and still they guard the border.
	邊 border	庭 office	流 flow	血 blood	成 become	海 sea	水 [ʂyjɨ] water	At border posts, flowing blood became an ocean of water.
	武 Martial	皇 Emperor	開 open	邊 border	意 intent	未 not yet	已 [jɨ] finish	Our Martial Emperor's desire to open the borderlands is not fulfilled.[17]
	君 You	不 not	聞 hear					Have you not heard!
	漢 Han	家 clan	山 mountain	東 east	二 2 ×	百 100	州 prefecture	The two hundred prefectures east of the mountains of the Han clan:[18]
16	千 1000	村 village	萬 10,000	落 village	生 grow	荊 brier	杞 [kʰɨ] thorn	A thousand villages, ten thousand hamlets are overgrown with brier.
	縱 even if	有 there is	健 sturdy	婦 wife	把 grasp	鋤 hoe	犁 [liaj] plow	Even if there remains a strong wife who grips hoe and plow.
	禾 grain	生 grow	隴 mound	畝 field	無 has no	東 east	西 [siaj] west	The furrows of growing grain are without any order.
	况 still more	復 again	秦 Qin	兵 troops	耐 bear	苦 hard	戰 battle	Moreover, the Qin troops endure hard fighting,[19]
20	被 endure	驅 drive	不 not	異 differ	犬 dog	與 and	雞 [kjiaj] chicken	Inflicted with being driven along, no different from dogs or chickens.
	長 elder	者 one	雖 though	有 have	問 [ʋùn] ask			Although you, Sir, inquire,

15. In 727 (Kaiyuan 15), Tibetan armies attacked the Tang at the Yellow River in the northern section of what is now Gansu Province. After that, the Tang maintained a standing army in the region.

16. These frontier settlements were farming communities of conscript soldiers. During peaceful times, they produced food to supply the army; during campaigns, they were mobilized to fight.

17. Du Fu refers to Han Wudi, the "Martial Emperor" who brought the Han to the peak of its power. As is often the case, a Han name stands in for a Tang name, here, the reigning emperor himself.

18. That is, the half of Tang China east of the passes between Luoyang and Chang'an and north of the Huai River.

19. Qin is an early name for the region "within the passes" around Chang'an.

22	役	夫	敢	伸	恨 [xɦən]			How can a conscript express his resentment?
	conscript	man	dare	extend	resentment			
	且	如	今	年	冬			Consider this year's winter:
	now	like	present	year	winter			
	未	休	關	西	卒 [tsyt]			Not having rested the troops West of the Passes,[20]
	not yet	rest	Pass	West	troops			
	縣	官	急	索	租			The district officials urgently demand the land-tax.
	district	official	hasten	search	land-tax			
26	租	稅	從	何	出 [tʂʰyt]			Where are the taxes going to come from?"
	land-tax	tax	from	where	come out			
	信	知	生	男	惡			I now truly understand that bearing a male is bad,
	truly	know	born	male	bad			
	反	是	生	女	好 [xǎw]			And, contrarily, bearing a female is good.
	oppose	this	born	female	good			
	生	女	猶	得	嫁	比	鄰	Bearing a female, she still gets to marry into the neighboring household.
	born	female	still	get	marry	next	neighbor	
30	生	男	埋	沒	隨	百	草 [tsʰǎw]	Bearing a male, he is buried amidst the wild grasses.
	born	male	bury	sink	follow	100	grasses	
	君	不	見		青	海	頭 [tɦəw]	Do you not see! By Lake Kokonor,[21]
	You	not	see		blue	sea	head	
	古	來	白	骨	無	人	收 [ʂiw]	From of old, the white bones have had no one to collect them.
	ancient	come	white	bones	have not	people	collect	
	新	鬼	煩	冤	舊	鬼	哭	The new ghosts are greatly grieved, the old ghosts weep:
	new	ghosts	vexed	grieved	old	ghosts	weep	
34	天	陰	雨	濕	聲	啾	啾 [tsiw]	The sky is overcast, rain drizzles, their sound whispers.
	sky	cloudy	rain	wet	sound	twitter	twitter	

Study Notes and Questions

1. Compare this poem to Li Bai's "Fighting South of the Wall" (see chapter 6). What stylistic, visual and emotional elements do they share? What is the role of the speaker in Li Bai's poem? What is the poet's role in "Ballad of the Army Carts"? What effect do these roles have on the tone of the two poems?

2. Ending a poem in a manner appropriate to the themes and emotions it sets out is always a challenge, and the poets developed new techniques like objective closure to handle this task. Compare the last four lines of "Ballad of the Army Carts" with the final couplet of "Fighting South of the Wall." Explain the very different effects.

---

20. "West of the Passes" is another name for Qin, the region around Chang'an.

21. This is a lake in Mongolia at the border of the Tang frontier.

"Lament for Riverbend" by Du Fu [old-style verse]

哀江頭							Lament for Riverbend
少	陵	野	老	吞	聲	哭 [kʰəwk]	The old rustic of Shaoling cries with muffled sobs.[22]
Shao	ling	rustic	old	swallow	sound	cry	
春	日	潛	行	曲	江	曲 [kʰywk]	On a spring day he stealthily goes to the bend in Bending River.[23]
spring	day	submerge	travel	Bend	river	bend	
江	頭	宮	殿	鎖	千	門	The thousand gates of the palaces at the riverbank are all locked
river	head	palace buildings		lock	1000	gates	
細	柳	新	蒲	為	誰	綠 [lywk]	The fine willow fronds and new rushes: for whom are they green?
fine	willow	new	reeds	for	who	green	
憶	昔	霓	旌	下	南	苑	I recall of old: the rainbow banners descended to South Garden:[24]
recall	old	rainbow	banner	down	south	garden	
苑	中	萬	物	生	顏	色 [ʂəə̆k]	In the garden all things acquired a fine appearance.
garden	in	10,000	things	grow	face	appearance	
昭	陽	殿	裏	第	一	人	The first lady of the Gleaming Radiance Palace[25]
Gleaming Radiance Palace			in	number	1	person	
同	輦	隨	君	侍	君	側 [tʂəə̆k]	Rode in the chariot following her lord, and served at his side.
share	chariot	follow	lord	serve	lord	side	
輦	前	才	人	帶	弓	箭	The palace maidens in front of the chariot carried bows and arrows:
chariot	before	talent	people	carry	bow	arrow	
白	馬	嚼	齧	黃	金	勒 [ləə̆k]	The white horse gnashed at his golden bit.
white	horse	chomp	chew	yellow	gold	bit	
翻	身	向	天	仰	射	雲	Turning her body facing Heaven, a maid looked up, shot the clouds:
turn	body	toward	sky	look up	shoot	cloud	
一	笑	正	墜	雙	飛	翼 [jiăk]	A smile just as she felled a pair of flying wings.
one	arrow	truly	fall	pair	fly	wings	
明	眸	皓	齒	今	何	在	Those bright eyes and gleaming teeth, where are they now?
bright	pupils	gleaming	teeth	now	where	are	

22. Du Fu's clan was from Shaoling, on the outskirts of Chang'an.

23. Riverbend was a park on the banks of the Wei River in Chang'an where the course of the river took a bend. Xuanzong and Precious Consort Yang frequently visited the park.

24. Lotus Garden (South Garden) was on the south side of the Riverbend District. The "rainbow banners" alludes to a procession of immortals and thus refers to an imperial excursion.

25. The Palace of Gleaming Radiance was a Han dynasty imperial residence. The "first lady" of that Han palace was Zhao Feiyan, but here the term refers to Precious Consort Yang.

血	污	遊	魂	歸	不	得 [təə̆k]	Blood has spattered the wandering
blood	defile	wander	soul	return	not	get	soul: it cannot return.[26]
清	渭	東	流	劍	閣	深	The pure Wei flows east; the road
pure	Wei	east	flow	Sword	Pavilion	deep	to Sword Pavilion is long:[27]
去	住	彼	此	無	消	息 [sik]	She who went, he who remains: they
go	reside	that	this	lack	news		have no news of one another.[28]
人	生	有	情	淚	沾	臆 [ʔiă̆k]	In life, there are [moments of great]
human	life	has	emotion	tears	drench	chest	emotion: tears drench my chest:
江	水	江	花	豈	終	極 [kɦiə̆k]	How can the river waters and river
river	water	river	flowers	how	end	end	flowers ever end?
黃	昏	胡	騎	塵	滿	城	At yellow dusk, dust from the
yellow	dusk	Tartar	cavalry	dust	fills	city wall	Tartar horsemen fills the city:[29]
欲	往	城	南	望	城	北 [puə̆k]	I want to go south of the city and
want	go	city	south	gaze	city	north	gaze north of the city.

Stephen Owen's Translation

Lament by the River

An old man, a countryman from Shaoling,
sobs swallowing back the sound,
he walks hidden on a day in spring
by a bend of the Bending River.

By the river the palace galleries
locked in by a thousand gates,
thin willow branches and fresh reeds—
for whom do they show their green?

I think back when rainbow banners
came down to this Southern Park,
and the thousands of things within the park
all took on a bright complexion.

That woman, who was first of all
in the Zhao-yang Galleries,

26. During Xuanzong's flight from Chang'an, the troops that accompanied him insisted that he execute the inept, corrupt, and meddlesome prime minister Yang Guozhong as well as his relative, Precious Consort Yang. She was strangled.

27. Sword Pavilion was the name of a strategic pass in Sichuan: Xuanzong was fleeing to Sichuan.

28. See Owen's translation for another interpretation.

29. The Hu are more precisely Turkish, but the name applies generally to northern and northwestern barbarians.

went with her lord in the same palanquin
    and attended by his side.

The handmaidens who rode in front
    all bore arrows and bows
on white horses that chomped and foamed
    on bits of yellow gold.

They bent back and, facing sky,
    shot arrows into clouds;
a single shaft brought plummeting
    a pair of wings in flight.

Those bright eyes and sparkling teeth—
    where are they today?
Blood has stained her roaming soul,
    she cannot make it home.

From here where the clear Wei flows on east,
    to the depths of Sword-Tower Pass;
between those who went and those who stayed,
    there is no exchange of news.

If any man has feelings,
    tears will soak his breast,
the river waters and river flowers
    will never come to an end.

Turkish horsemen in gathering dusk,
    dust is filling the city,
I am on my way to south of the city
    but turn and gaze to the north.

Study Notes and Questions

"Lament for Riverbend" is the beginning of the creation of the romantic myth of Precious Consort Yang, Yang Guifei. "Riverbend" was a scenic park on the banks of the Wei River in the suburbs of Chang'an. Before the rebellion, Du Fu had written several social poems to commemorate outings there.

1. This is an old-style narrative poem. "Old-style" poetry often seeks immediacy and emotional honesty. Note the beginning: why does Du Fu not switch the first and second lines? What is the effect of Du Fu's introducing himself in the third person?

2. Notice the narrative flow of the poem. What is the connection between the second and third couplets? What device does Du Fu use to get from one time frame to the next? Explain.

3. What is the effect of introducing Yang Guifei as "The first lady of the Gleaming Radiance Palace"? Is there a quality of "if not her, then someone else would have been number one, with the same results"? Tone is vitally important here. Does Du Fu seem to be criticizing Xuanzong?

4. What is the point of focusing on the vignette of the shooting of the bird? Who shoots? The image of women carrying bows and arrows is an aspect of *diandao*, a world turned topsy-turvy. Yet Du Fu presents it as a dazzling, utterly captivating spectacle.

5. The "bright eyes and gleaming teeth" are a synecdoche for Yang Guifei. Why does Du Fu use them? Do they make the scene more vivid? Or do they seem oddly disembodied? Are the images related to the events of the previous couplet?

6. At what point does Du Fu return to the narrative present of the poem from his reverie on the past?

7. Does Owen's generalized translation of "those who went and those who stayed" work better than the more specific "She who went, he who remains"? In the one case, Du Fu continues to develop the story of Guifei and Xuanzong. In the other, he has shifted to his concluding responses. Which is better? Explain.

8. What is the relationship between lines 17 and 18? In the context of the events described in the poem, what does line 18 mean? What is the function of this very abstracted, generalized language?

9. The final line always has been considered cryptic. What do you think Du Fu's gesture might mean?

"A Spring Vista" by Du Fu [regulated verse]

春望					A Spring Vista
國 country	破 broken	山 mountain	河 rivers	在 remain	The capital is broken: mountains and rivers remain.
城 wall	春 spring	草 grass	木 tree	深 [ɕim] deep	The city wall in spring: the grasses and trees grow thickly.
感 moved	時 time	花 flower	濺 drench	淚 tear	Moved by the times, flowers drenched with tears.
恨 resent	別 parting	鳥 bird	驚 startle	心 [sim] heart	Resenting the parting, birds startle the heart.
烽 beacon	火 fire	連 connect	三 three	月 month	Beacon fires burn for three months.[30]
家 family	書 writing	抵 exchange	萬 10,000	金 [kim] gold	For a letter from my family, I'd pay ten thousand cash.
白 white	頭 head	搔 scratch	更 again	短 short	My white hair, as I scratch it, grows ever shorter,[31]
渾 complete	欲 want	不 not	勝 sustain	簪 [tʂim] hat clasp	So soon it won't sustain the clasp.[32]

GARY SNYDER'S TRANSLATION

Spring View

The nation is ruined,   but mountains and rivers remain.
This spring the city   is deep in weeds and brush.
Touched by the times   even flowers weep tears.
Fearing leaving   the birds tangled hearts.
Watch-tower fires   have been burning for three months
To get a note from home   would cost ten thousand gold.
Scratching my   white hair thinner
Seething hopes   all in a trembling hairpin.

30. Or, "Beacon fires have burned from Third Month to Third Month."

31. One scratches one's head when unsettled or concerned.

32. That is, the hat-pin for his official's hat.

Stephen Owen's Translation

The View in Spring

A kingdom smashed, its hills and rivers still here,
spring in the city, plants and trees grow deep.

Moved by the moment, flowers splash with tears,
alarmed at parting, birds startle the heart.

War's beacon fires have gone on three months,
letters from home are worth thousands in gold.

Fingers run through white hair until it thins,
cap-pins will almost no longer hold.

Study Notes and Questions

This is perhaps Du Fu's most famous poem, but it is not clear what it means exactly. It seems to invite a sentimental reading that overlooks the complexities that make the poem so famous.

1. Explain the meaning of the first line. Is nature in fact independent of (and indifferent to) human events? Or does nature stand as an emblem of constancy that supports the imperial order in the human realm?

2. In line 2, what is a 城春, which literally reads, "city wall spring"? What does it signify that the grasses are growing well? Is nature replacing the human here, or offering a promise of revival? Does this rework the nature of the relationship between the human and the natural worlds in the first line?

3. In the second couplet, whose heart and whose tears is Du Fu referring to? The line does not say explicitly. What is the point of the ambiguity in terms of the relationship between the human and the natural?

4. How does the third couplet reconfigure the relationships of the human and the natural: once you start seeing them, they leap out at you. For example, the "month" in line 5 also simply means "moon." Similarly, the "gold" in line 6 is taken to mean "money," but it also remains the metal.

5. Finally, how does the conclusion of the poem reshape once again the theme of the human and the natural, and how is it appropriate for a *spring* poem?

"Moonlit Night" by Du Fu [regulated verse]

月夜					Moonlit Night
今	夜	鄜	州	月	Tonight, the moon in Fuzhou:[33]
now	night	Fu-	-zhou	moon	
閨	中	只	獨	看 [k^{h}an]	From the bedroom [you] watch it alone.
bedroom	in	only	alone	look	
遙	憐	小	兒	女	I think fondly of my children far away:
afar	cherish	little	boy	girl	
未	解	憶	長	安 [ʔan]	They don't yet understand [your] recollections of Chang'an.
not yet	understand	recall	Chang-	-an	
香	霧	雲	鬟	濕	The fragrant mist of [your] cloud-ringlets has become damp.
incense	fog	cloud	ringlet	damp	
清	輝	玉	臂	寒 [ɣan]	The pure gleam of [your] jade arms is cold.
is pure	gleam	jade	arm	cold	
何	時	倚	虛	幌	When, leaning on the empty gauze screen,
what	time	rest	empty	screen	
雙	照	淚	痕	乾 [kan]	Will it shine [our] pairs of tear-tracks dry?
pair	shine	tear	trace	dry	

David Hinton's Translation

Moonlit Night

Tonight at Fu-chou, this moon she watches
Alone in our room. And my little, far-off
Children, too young to understand what keeps me
Away, or even remember Ch'ang-an. By now,

Her hair will be mist-scented, her jade-white
Arms chilled in its clear light. When
Will it find us together again, drapes drawn
Open, light traced where it dries our tears?

---

33. In 756 Du Fu took his family to Fuzhou to escape the An Lushan Rebellion. After Suzong (Xuanzong's son) had accepted the throne on his father's abdication, Du Fu, hearing the news, attempted to reach Suzong's new government. He was captured by troops loyal to An Lushan and brought back to Chang'an. This poem was written during Du Fu's forced stay in Chang'an. (See the account in "Du Fu's Life" at the beginning of this chapter.)

Study Notes and Questions

This poem is based on two traditional themes: moon-gazing and the lonely wife. Chinese moon-gazing poems, like the English nursery rhyme ("I see the moon, and the moon sees me"), build upon the idea that the two people (the poet and the desired person) are linked by both looking at the moon at the same time. Even though separated, they still can share the same moon, the same experience. The "lonely woman" theme became a courtly convention during the Southern Dynasties: mannered, elegant, and impersonal. Here Du Fu restores an immediacy and honesty to the topic even as he retains courtly embellishments.

1. The first couplet introduces the idea of sharing at both the physical and the ideational level. How does Du Fu know his wife is watching the moon in Fuzhou? What does this implicitly assert about their relationship? What *is* a "Fuzhou moon"? Is that what Du Fu sees as well?

2. Sometimes a writer simply abandons parallelism in a middle couplet. Although "afar cherish" is parallel with "not-yet understand" and, with a stretch, "boy girl" can be taken as parallel to "Chang -an," the "little" preceding "boy girl" is a modifier while "recall" preceding "Chang -an" is a transitive verb. The grammar of the two lines just does not match. In the couplet, how is "afar" parallel to "not yet"?

3. Burton Watson proposes a translation of line 4 that surely is correct: "They do not yet understand *your* recollection of Chang'an. How does this differ from Hinton's reading? What is the difference in terms of a relationship to the first couplet? What is the effect on the focus and mood of the line in Hinton's adding "what keeps me away" to help clarify the implications of the line?

4. The third couplet is courtly: it describes an elegant woman by focusing on her attire and attributes. A "cloud-ringlet" is part of the hairdo of a well-bred woman. The parallelism in the couplet is rather straightforward. How *do* the words match one another? How do the elements in these lines continue the themes of "moon," "night," and "separation"?

5. Remember the question with which "Painting of a Hawk" ends. Du Fu often uses this sort of imaginative projection to conclude a poem. Here, the final line involves courtly wit to bring together the themes of the poem. According to the line, what dries the tears? What is the image Du Fu paints here? What in fact will dry them? Why indulge in this elegant "misprision"?

6. David Hinton's translation raises some questions both about form and content. Hinton's version is "Americanized." While most lines in Chinese poems are end-stopped—that is, the sentence or phrase comes to an end at the end of the line—Hinton continues the syntax of his sentences across line breaks. Point out some examples of this strategy. Notice that while Hinton breaks the poem into two stanzas, he begins a sentence at the end of the fourth line and continues it into the sixth. What is the effect of this syntactic linking of lines on the cadences in the poem?

7. Consider the shift in stylistic register shaped by word choice in Hinton's translation. Hinton quietly elides the courtly element in replacing Du Fu's wife's "cloud-ringlets" with "hair." Are those ringlets a distraction from the quality of the poet's longing for his wife? Explain.

8. Rewrite the last sentence of Hinton's translation in plain English.

"Grieving for Chentao" by Du Fu [old-style verse]

悲陳陶							Grieving for Chentao[34]
孟	冬	十	郡	良	家	子 [tsɨ̆]	In the first month of winter, the sons of noble
first	winter	ten	district	fine	clan	son	households from the ten districts:[35]
血	作	陳	陶	澤	中	水 [śiɪ̆]	Their blood became water in
blood	make	Chen-	-tao	Marsh	middle	water	the Chentao Marsh.
野	曠	天	清	無	戰	聲	The wilds are broad, the sky clear,
wilds	broad	sky	pure	without	battle	sound	no sound of battle:
四	萬	義	軍	同	日	死 [siɪ̆]	Forty thousand righteous troops
4	10,000	righteous	army	same	day	die	died on the same day.
群	胡	歸	來	雪	洗	箭	The horde of barbarians return
flock	Tartar	return	come	snow	wash	arrow	and wash their arrows with snow,
仍	唱	夷	歌	飲	都	市 [dźɨ̆]	And sing barbarian songs as they
and	sing	barbarian song		drink	capital	market	drink in the capital markets.
都	人	迴	面	向	北	啼	The capital's populace turn their
capital	people	turn	face	facing	north	weep	heads and weep facing north:
日	夜	更	望	官	軍	至 [tśiɪi]	Day and night they ever more look
day	night	more	look for	official	army	arrive	for the imperial army to arrive.

Study Notes and Questions

1. Note the absence of a verb in the first line. If the first line sets out the topic for a sentence that spans the entire first couplet, what one word in the Chinese (and in what position in the line) is the grammatical topic? What is the effect of this linking of the two lines as one single sentence stating the fact of the slaughter?

---

34. Sima Guang 司馬光 (1019–86) in his *Comprehensive Mirror to Aid Governance* (*Zizhi tongjian* 資治通鑑), a history of China up to the founding of the Song dynasty, offers an account of the battle: "On the *xichou* day (11/16/756), the [Central and Northern] Armies met the rebel general An Shouzhong at Xianyang's Chentao Slope. [Fang] Guan imitated the ancient method: he used 2000 ox-drawn war chariots and accompanied by horses. The rebels, being upwind, created a din with drums and shouts, and the oxen all were startled. The rebels released fire to burn them, and men and beast were thrown into great chaos. Those in the imperial army who died or were wounded were more than 40,000 men. The survivors were only a few thousand." 「辛丑，二軍遇賊將安守忠於咸陽之陳濤斜。琯效古法，用車戰，以牛車二千乘，馬步夾之；賊順風鼓譟，牛皆震駭。賊縱火焚之，人畜大亂，官軍死傷者四萬餘人，存者數千而已。」(*Zizhi tongjian* juan 219). Chentao, east of Chang'an, is a boggy area, and thus it is also called Chentao Marsh.

35. *History of the Han*, "Biography of Zhao Chongguo"《漢書・趙充國傳》: "The sons of noble houses from the six districts were selected to serve in waiting in the Yulin Army. They became officials through talent and strength; many of the famous generals came from this group."「六郡良家子，選給羽林期門。以材力為官，名將多出焉。」

2. Consider the time frames—the narrative past and narrative present—in the various lines. Is the first line past, present, or unclear?

3. In line 3, why is there no "sound of battle"? What is the effect of this landscape image? What is the effect of following this quiet, ominous image with line 4? Line 4 is a simple statement of fact, but what is the tone?

4. In the third couplet Du Fu presents a complex set of contrasts with the first half of the poem: refined sons < > barbarian hordes, outland < > market, blood turned to mud < > blood washed off, silence < > song, past < > present, presence < > absence. Discuss the impact of this accumulation of contrasts.

5. Does the poem offer an effective ending? Think of its relation to the use of time in the poem. Think also of the versions of the relation of the martial to social order presented in the poem.

"The Officer at Stone Moat" [old-style verse]

石壕吏					The Officer at Stone Moat
暮 sunset	投 put	石 Stone	壕 Moat	村 [ts'uən] village	At sunset I sought lodging at Stone Moat Village.[36]
有 there is	吏 officer	夜 night	捉 hasten	人 [ńiın] people	There was an officer that night hastening the people.
老 old	翁 old man	踰 jump	牆 wall	走 run	An old man jumped over a wall and ran away:
老 old	婦 wife	出 go out	門 gate	看 [k'ɑn] look	His old wife went out of their gate to look.
吏 officer	呼 shout	一 one	何 how	怒 [nuò] angry	The officer yelled oh how fiercely!
婦 wife	啼 weep	一 one	何 how	苦 [k'uò] bitter	The wife wept oh how bitterly!
聽 listen	婦 wife	前 front	致 deliver	詞 words	I listened when the wife came forward to speak:
三 three	男 son	鄴 Ye	城 city	戍 [śiuò] guard	"My three sons were stationed at Ye.[37]
一 one	男 sone	附 attach	書 letter	至 [tś'iıi] arrive	One son wrote a letter that has arrived.
二 two	男 son	新 new	戰 battle	死 [siıĭ] die	Two sons recently have been killed in battle.
存 survive	者 -er	且 for now	偷 steal	生 life	The remaining son for the moment still survives.[38]
死 die	者 -er	長 always	已 end	矣 [jĭ] -ed	Those who died are gone forever.
室 room	中 middle	更 again	無 without	人 [ńiın] people	In my house, there is no one else—
惟 only	有 there is	乳 suckle	下 below	孫 [suən] grandson	Just a grandson who is still nursing.
有 there is	孫 grandson	母 mother	未 not yet	去 go	Because there is the grandson, his mother has not yet left.
出 go out	入 enter	無 without	完 whole	裙 [giuən] skirt	In her coming and going, she has not a complete dress.

36. The village was between Tong Pass and Luoyang in the Henan region.

37. Guo Ziyi and a large army of military governors laid siege to An Lushan's son, An Qingxu, at the city of Ye. An managed to break through and decisively defeat the combined armies, which then regrouped at the city of Heyang and issued a call for more conscript soldiers.

38. Literally, "he steals a life" that he does not merit.

	老 old	嫗 old woman	力 power	雖 although	衰 [ṣiuɪi] decline	Although, as an old woman, my strength has declined,
	請 request	從 follow	吏 officer	夜 night	歸 [kiuəi] return	Let me follow you to return tonight.
	急 urgent	應 respond	河 He-	陽 -yang	役 duty	You need to urgently respond to the call for conscripts at Heyang:[39]
20	猶 still	得 obtain	備 ready	晨 dawn	炊 [ts'iuɪ] cooking	I still can prepare the morning meals."
	夜 night	久 long	語 speech	聲 sound	絕 [dziuæt] end	The night was long; all sound of speech stopped:
	如 as if	聞 hear	泣 sob	幽 secluded	咽 [ʔiɛt] stifled	It seemed as if I heard stifled weeping.
	天 sky	明 bright	登 climb	前 front	途 road	When the sky grew light, I climbed the road ahead:
24	獨 only	與 with	老 old	翁 old man	別 [biat] part	I took leave of only the old man.

Irving Y. Lo's Translation

Recruiting Officer of Shih-hao

At dusk I sought lodging at Shih-hao village,
When a recruiting officer came to seize men at night.
An old man scaled the wall and fled,
His old wife came out to answer the door.

How furious was the officer's shout!
How pitiable was the woman's cry!
I listened as she stepped forward to speak:
"All my three sons have left for garrison duty at Yeh;
From one of them a letter just arrived,
Saying my two sons had newly died in battle.
Survivors can manage to live on,
But the dead are gone forever.
Now there's no other man in the house,
Only a grandchild at his mother's breast.
The child's mother has not gone away;
She has only a tattered skirt for wear.
An old woman, I am feeble and weak,
But I will gladly leave with you tonight

39. See footnote 37.

To answer the urgent call at Ho-yang—
I can still cook morning gruel for your men."

The night drew on, but talking stopped;
It seemed I heard only half-concealed sobs.
As I got back on the road at daybreak,
Only the old man was there to see me off.

Study Notes and Questions

This old-style protest ballad is part of a set of poems called the "Three Officers and Three Partings." All were written at about the same time in 759 when Du Fu had just returned from Luoyang to his post at Huazhou (on the Yellow River just inside the passes in Guanzhong). The language and technique point back to the narrative poems of the late Han from the anonymous Luofu story to Wang Can's "Seven Laments."

1. Du Fu establishes a *first-person* narrator in the first line. Explain.

2. Note the rhyme scheme of the first quatrain (four lines). Even in Middle Chinese, the rhyme is very loose. This slant rhyme probably created an "old" effect for Du Fu and his contemporaries because the early poetry recorded in the *Literary Anthology* that was their model had ceased to rhyme by the Tang. Notice also that the general rhyme scheme of the poem—*aaba*—takes the quatrain as its unit of organization. Do the shifts in rhyme match the shifts in meaning in the poem? Illustrate your answer with specific examples.

3. Note the use of repetitive, quasi-formulaic language in lines 9–12. The enumerations echo *yuefu* usage.

4. Consider Irving Lo's translation of lines 11 and 12. Should this couplet be taken as a specific comment or as a general observation? The two meanings are irreconcilable. Explain your preference.

5. Note how Du Fu makes the transition from the scene he records to his departure the next morning. Explain the details of the couplet that marks the transition.

6. The final couplet is a form of "objective closure" where the poet lets the presentation of an image stand in for his personal response. Chinese poets often preferred objective closure because it was more resonant than a statement of emotion. What responses does the final image of the old man "stand in for" here?

"Ballad of Pengya" by Du Fu [old-style verse]

	彭衙行					Ballad of Pengya
	憶 recall	昔 former	避 flee	賊 thief	初 beginning	I recall formerly, at the beginning of our flight from the rebels:[40]
	北 north	走 run	經 go through danger	險	艱 [kɛːn] difficulty	Rushing northward, we passed through great difficulties.
	夜 night	深 deep	彭 Peng-	衙 -ya	道 road	Night was deep on the road to Pengya;
4	月 moon	照 shine	白 white	水 river	山 [ʂɛːn] mountain	The moon shone on White Water Mountain.
	盡 finish	室 room	久 long	徒 on foot	步 walk	My entire family was long on foot:
	逢 encounter	人 people	多 most	厚 thick	顏 [ŋɛːn] face	When we met people, they mostly looked at us unmoved.
	參 [uneven array]	差	谷 valley	鳥 bird	吟 chant	High and low, the valley birds sang out;
8	不 not	見 see	遊 wander	子 son	還 [ɣwɛːn] return	We do not see wanderers returning.
	癡 foolish	女 girl	饑 hungry	咬 bite	我 me	My foolish girl in hunger bit me:
	啼 cry	畏 fear	虎 tiger	狼 wolf	聞 [mun] hear	I feared the tigers and wolves would hear her cries.
	懷 chest	中 middle	掩 cover	其 her	口 mouth	Holding her to my chest, I covered her mouth,
12	反 turn	側 side	聲 sound	愈 more	嗔 [dɛn] roar	But, turning her head, she wailed even more loudly.
	小 small	兒 son	強 force	解 understand	事 matter	My young son made an effort to understand the situation:
	故 thus	索 seek	苦 bitter	李 plum	餐 [ts^{h}an] eat	So he went to seek bitter plums to eat.
	一 one	旬 10 days	半 half	雷 lightning	雨 rain	In a ten-day period, half was thunderstorm:
16	泥 mud	濘 mire	相 mutual	攀 climb	牽 [k^{h}ɛn] drag	In the mud and mire we pulled one another along.

40. In the Sixth Month of Tianbao 15 (756), Du Fu and his family fled northward from White Water County and passed through Pengya en route to Fuzhou. This poem was probably written in the autumn of the next year (757) as Du Fu was returning from Suzong's court at Fengxiang to his family in Fuzhou.

既 since	無 have no	禦 guard	雨 rain	備 prepare	Not only had we no preparations for rain,
徑 path	滑 slippery	衣 clothes	又 also	寒 [ɣan] cold	The path was slippery and our clothes cold.
有 there is	時 time	經 go through	契 [hardship]	闊	At times we went through great hardship:[41]
竟 end	日 day	數 several	里 *li*	間 [kɛːn] between	In an entire day, we went only several *li*.
野 wilds	果 fruit	充 fill	糇 provision	糧 grain	Wild fruit served as provisions;
卑 low	枝 branch	成 become	屋 roof	椽 [drwian] beam	Low-hanging branches became our roof.
早 early	行 travel	石 stone	上 on	水 water	Early, we traveled on water pouring over rocks;
暮 dusk	宿 lodge	天 heaven	邊 next	煙 [ʔɛn] mist	At dusk we lodged in the mists at the sky's edge.
小 small	留 remain	同 Tong	家 clan	窪 deep pool	We remained briefly at Tongjia Tarn.[42]
欲 want	出 go out	蘆 Lu	子 Mr.	關 [kwɛːn] pass	We hoped to go out through Lu Zi Pass.[43]
故 former	人 people	有 there is	孫 Sun	宰 Zai	Among my old friends is Sun Zai[44]
高 high	義 righteous	薄 near	曾 layered	雲 [wun] cloud	His towering virtue nears the layered clouds.
延 invite	客 guest	已 already	曛 dusky	黑 black	When he greeted his guests it was already dusk:
張 set out	燈 lamp	啟 open	重 double	門 [mən] gate	He set out lanterns and opened gate after gate.
煖 warm	湯 water	濯 wash	我 our	足 feet	He heated water to wash our feet.
剪 cut	紙 paper	招 summon	我 our	魂 [ɣwən] souls	He cut out paper to summon our souls.[45]

41. The phrase "hardship" 契闊 comes from "Strike the Drum"《擊鼓》, Mao 31 in the *Canon of Poetry*「死生契闊。與子成說。執子之手。與子偕老。」

42. Tongjia Tarn is between Pengya and Fuzhou. Sun Zai lived there.

43. Leaving through this pass suggests that Du Fu planned to go to the temporary court of the newly enthroned Emperor Suzong.

44. It is possible that 宰 refers not to Mr. Sun's personal name but to his role as village head.

45. He cut paper into a banner to call back Du Fu's soul: the belief was that fright or grief scattered one's soul, and it needed to be brought back to the body through a summons.

	從 follow	此 this	出 go out	妻 wife	孥 children	After this, he led out his wife and children.
	相 mutual	視 see	涕 tears	闌 [in streams]	干 [kan]	Seeing one another, tears streamed down.
	眾 crowd	雛 kids	爛 [utterly done]	熳	睡 sleep	My flock of children fell into a deep sleep
36	喚 call	起 rise	霑 soak	盤 platter	飧 [swən] food	But were called to rise when presented platters of food to eat.
	誓 vow	將 [future]	與 with	夫 venerable	子 sir	I vow to be to you
	永 always	結 connect	為 become	弟 younger	昆 [kwən] elder	Always as if younger and elder brothers.
	遂 then	空 empty	所 [where]	坐 sit	堂 hall	Then he emptied the hall where we sat;
40	安 at ease	居 reside	奉 offer up	我 our	歡 [xwan] delight	As I rested at ease, he offered us delight.
	誰 who	肯 willing	艱 hardship	難 trouble	際 border	Who is willing at a time of hardship
	豁 spacious	達 reach	露 expose	心 heart	肝 [kan] liver	With utter openness to reveal his inmost thoughts?
	別 part	來 come	歲 year	月 month	周 cycle	Since parting, a full year has passed,
44	胡 Hu	羯 Jie	仍 still	構 make	患 [ɣwɛːn^{h}] calamity	But the barbarians still create disaster.
	何 what	當 at	有 there is	翅 flight-feathers	翎	When will I come to have wings
	飛 fly	去 leave	墮 descend	爾 you	前 [dzɛn] before	And fly off to land before you?

Study Notes and Questions

A "ballad" is a narrative old-style form. This poem is a splendid expression of Du Fu's gratitude to his friend Sun Zai in a time of great trouble. "Ballad of Pengya" centers on the domestic realm in a way unprecedented in Tang poetry and matched only by Tao Qian (365–427). Yet Du Fu writes of these private materials with complete mastery and naturalness.

1. Note how Du Fu frames the poem. The "Ballad of Pengya" is a "recollection" poem. Who is the speaker? What is the effect of explicitly marking the actions of the poem as "past"?

2. Even as line 8 describes a particular personal situation, it also recalls the generic language of *yuefu* folk poetry and the anonymous lament of separation. What is the effect of this sort of doubled vision?

3. What is the point of the vignette of Du Fu's baby daughter in lines 9–14? That is, what does it mean beyond a simple recounting of events? The incident, its sentiments, and language do not seem "poetic," so, what is it doing in the poem? How does it fit into Du Fu's larger purposes in writing the poem?

4. What is the tone of lines 13 and 14 that describe Du Fu's son's efforts to help?

5. Note the linguistic variety of lines 15–26. The effects are unfortunately hard to see in the English translation. Lines 15 and 16 are roughly parallel in general categories, but their syntax is very different. (Line 15 is a nominal sentence with a nested clause structure, while in 16, two verbs replace the two nouns.) In line 17 the caesura is very weak because the last three characters (a verb-object compound modifying a noun) serve as the object of the verb "have-no." Line 18, in contrast, is a pair of complete short sentences with a correspondingly strong caesura. Lines 19 and 20 form one complete sentence, although all the verbs are in line 19. Then lines 21–22, 23–24, and 25–26 are all strictly parallel couplets. The inevitable question, however, is "So what?" What impact does this crafting have on the narrative of hardship that Du Fu sets out here?

6. The series of parallel couplets in lines 21–26 marks a turn in the story Du Fu tells, for they bring the narrative as far as Mr. Sun's house, although Du Fu does not quite say this. What does he do instead?

7. Why does Du Fu write "When he greeted his guests . . . " rather than "When he greeted us . . . "? Why the third-person perspective?

8. Why do you think Mr. Sun first tended to Du Fu and his family and *then* brought out his own wife and children to greet them?

9. The ending, with its simple depiction of a domestic scene, is very effective. It needs to be strongly stressed that other poets during this time period simply did not write about this sort of situation. How does this private memory become the stuff of public poetry? If "poetry speaks of one's resolve," what are the larger commitments that the poem addresses?

"A Guest Arrives" by Du Fu [regulated verse]

客至							A Guest Arrives[46]
舍	南	舍	北	皆	春	水	South of my cottage, north of
lodging	south	lodging	north	all	spring	water	my cottage, all is spring water.
但	見	群	鷗	日	日	來 [ləj]	I see only the flock of gulls that
only	see	flock	gulls	day	day	come	comes each day.[47]
花	徑	不	曾	緣	客	掃	The flower-strewn path has never
flower	path	not	ever	because	guest	sweep	been swept in hope of a guest.
蓬	門	今	始	為	君	開 [k^{h}əj]	My bramble gate for the first time
bramble	gate	now	begin	for	you	open	I open now for you.
盤	飧	市	遠	無	兼	味	A plate of food, the market being
platter	food	market	far	without	combine	flavor	far, has no mixed flavors.[48]
樽	酒	家	貧	只	舊	醅 [p^{h}əj]	For a jug of ale, my family being
jug	ale	family	poor	only	old	brew	poor, we have only an old brew.
肯	與	鄰	翁	相	對	飲	If you're willing to drink facing
willing	with	neighbor	old man	mutually	face	drink	my old neighbor,
隔	籬	呼	取	盡	餘	杯 [pəj]	I'll shout across the hedge for him
across	hedge	shout	take	finish	remain	cup	to finish off the remaining cups.

Burton Watson's Translation

A Guest Arrives

North of my lodge, south of my lodge, spring rivers all;
day by day I see only flocks of gulls convening.
Flower paths have not been swept for any guest;
my thatch gate for the first time opens to you.
For food—the market's far—no wealth of flavors;
for wine—my house is poor—only old muddy brew.
If you don't mind drinking with the old man next door,
I'll call across the hedge and we can finish off what's left.

---

46. Du Fu's original note for the poem: "I am delighted that Magistrate Cui has visited." 「喜崔明府相過 。」

47. The poem alludes to a story from the late Han dynasty Daoist miscellany, *Lie Zi* 列子. See chapter 6, note 33.

48. This seems to be a fairly conventional way to describe humble fare.

Study Notes and Questions

This seven-character regulated verse poem is a wonderful exercise in studied informality. Its whimsical mood and light tone often are considered representative of Du Fu's frame of mind during his stay in Chengdu. It was late in 759 that he and his family arrived in Sichuan. The next spring, with the help of friends and relatives, he moved into the "Grass Hall" (Caotang 草堂) in the western suburbs of Chengdu. Later readers strongly associated Du Fu with his Grass Hall, and a replica of it in modern Chengdu is a popular tourist site. Although still uncertain about support, he spent a relatively quiet and uneventful year there before further disturbances made life uneasy.

1. The opening line of this poem was endlessly reworked by later poets. Perhaps its major attraction was the simple, repetitious language that in broad brush-strokes evoked a spring scene familiar to readers.

2. The second line suggests that Du Fu is up to something: for Chinese readers, the allusion to the story from *Lie Zi* would be immediately obvious. What is the story? In what part does Du Fu present himself? Such an image in the second line of a regulated verse poem almost inevitably means that Du Fu will be playing with the themes of innocence and spontaneity in the poem.

3. How does the third line reinforce the image of the "natural man" in line 2? According to the line, what sort of person is a "guest"? In what lines does Du Fu imply that in the world of his thatched cottage the binarism of "guest"/"host" seems out of place?

4. Watch boundary crossing in Chinese poems. In how many ways does Du Fu suggest that his guest is not part of the idyllic world in the poem?

5. What do you make of the final line? How would you feel as the guest? Have you ever had this sort of turn of events happen to you? Explain.

"My Thatched Roof Was Destroyed by the Autumn Wind: A Song" by Du Fu

	茅屋為秋風所破歌									My Thatched Roof Was Destroyed by the Autumn Wind: A Song
	八	月	秋	高	風	怒	號 [xɦaw]			In the Eighth Month, in high autumn, the wind roared.[49]
	eighth	month	autumn	high	wind	angry	shout			
	卷	我	屋	上	三	重	茅 [ma:w]			It rolled up the three layers of thatch on my roof.
	roll	my	roof	top	three	layer	thatch			
	茅	飛	渡	江	灑	江	郊 [kja:w]			The thatch flew off, crossing the river, scattered along the bank.
	thatch	fly	cross	river	scatter	river	area			
4	高	者	掛	罥	長	林	梢 [ʂa:w]			Up high, it caught in the branches of tall trees.
	high	one	hang	catch	long	grove	limb			
	下	者	飄	轉	沉	塘	坳 [ʔja:w]			Below, it whirled into pools and puddles and sank.
	low	one	whirl	turn	sink	pool	puddle			
	南	村	群	童	欺	我	老	無	力 [liǝ̆k]	A crowd of boys from the south village cheated me, being old and weak.
	south	village	crowd	boy	cheat	me	old	lack	strength	
	忍	能	對	面	為	盜	賊 [tsɦiǝ̆k]			How could they bear to steal right before my eyes?
	endure	can	oppose	face	do	thief	steal			
8	公	然	抱	茅	入	竹	去			They openly grabbed armfuls of thatch and departed into the bamboo grove.
	public	-ly	enwrap	thatch	enter	bamboo	leave			
	脣	焦	口	燥	呼	不	得 [tǝǝ̆k]			My lips parched and mouth dry, I could not shout.
	lips	parch	mouth	dried	shout	not	obtain			
	歸	來	倚	仗	自	嘆	息 [sik]			Returning, I leaned on my staff and sighed to myself.
	return	come	lean	staff	myself	sigh	exhale			
	俄	頃	風	定	雲	墨	色 [ʂǝǝ̆k]			In a moment, the wind stilled; the clouds turned ink-dark:
	sudden	brief	wind	stilled	clouds	ink	color			
12	秋	天	漠	漠	向	昏	黑 [xǝǝ̆k]			The autumn sky so vast turned autumn black at dusk.
		sky	obscure	obscure	face	dusk	blacken			
	布	衾	多	年	冷	似	鐵 [tʰiat]			My cloth coverlet of many years was cold like iron.
	cloth	coverlet	many	years	cold	like	iron			
	嬌	兒	惡	臥	踏	裏	裂 [liat]			My pettish child slept poorly and ripped up the lining.
	pettish	child	badly	lies	tread	lining	rip			
	床	頭	屋	漏	無	乾	處			At the bedstead the roof dripped: nowhere was dry.
	bed	head	roof	drip	lack	dry	place			

49. "High autumn" refers to the quality of the sky in autumn, which has a particular clarity that makes the vault of the sky seem especially high and open.

雨	腳	如	麻	未	斷	絕 [tsɦyat]			The rainstreaks were like hemp, without break or stop.
rain	feet	like	hemp	not yet	break	cease			
自	經	喪	亂	少	睡	眠			Since going through the turmoil and loss, I have slept little.
since	pass	loss	chaos	little	sleep	sleep			
長	夜	沾	濕	何	由	徹 [trʰiat]			This long night, drenched, how will I get through it?
long	night	drench	wet	what	way	finish			
安	得	廣	廈	千	萬	間 [kja:n]			How can I get a broad villa of ten thousand bays:[50]
how	get	broad	manse	103	104	bays			
大	庇	天	下	寒	士	俱	歡	顏 [ŋja:n]	To greatly shelter the cold gentlemen of the realm, all with happy faces?
great	cover	Heaven	below	cold	gentry	all	happy	face	
風	雨	不	動	安	如	山 [ʂa:n]			Wind and rain would not move it, as secure as a mountain.
wind	rain	not	move	stable	like	mountain			
嗚	呼								Alas, Oh!
Oh!	Ah!								
何	時	眼	前	突	兀	見	此	屋 [ʔəwk]	When will I see this soaring roof before my eyes?
what	time	eyes	before	soaring high		see	this	roof	
吾	廬	獨	破	受	凍	死	亦	足 [tsywk]	If my hut alone is destroyed and I freeze to death, I will be satisfied.
my	hut	alone	break	receive	freeze	die	also	suffice	

Stephen Owen's Translation

My Thatched Roof Is Ruined by the Autumn Wind

In the high autumn skies of September
the wind cried out in rage,
Tearing off in whirls from my rooftop
three plies of thatch.
The thatch flew across the river,
was strewn on the floodplain,
The high stalks tangled in tips
of tall forest trees,
The low ones swirled in gusts across ground
and sank into mud puddles.
The children from the village to the south
made a fool of me, impotent with age,
Without compunction plundered what was mine
before my very eyes,

50. A "bay" (*jian* 間) is the space between the support pillars of a house, so that a "bay" does not correspond directly to "room."

Brazenly took armfuls of thatch,
ran off into the bamboo,
And I screamed lips dry and throat raw,
but no use.
Then I made my way home, leaning on staff,
sighing to myself.
A moment later the wind calmed down,
clouds turned dark as ink,
The autumn sky rolling and overcast,
blacker towards sunset,
And our cotton quilts were years old
and cold as iron,
My poor boy slept poorly,
kicked rips in them.
Above the bed the roof leaked,
no place was dry,
And the raindrops ran down like strings,
without a break.
I have lived through upheavals and ruin
and have seldom slept very well,
But have no idea how I shall pass
this night of soaking.
Oh, to own a mighty mansion
of a hundred thousand rooms,
A great roof for the poorest gentlemen
of all this world,
a place to make them smile,
A building unshaken by wind or rain,
as solid as a mountain,
Oh, when shall I see before my eyes
a towering roof such as this?
Then I'd accept the ruin of my own little hut
and death by freezing.

Study Notes and Questions

1. The great challenge of this poem is to decide on its tone. What does Du Fu, the implied author, think of Du Fu, the hapless narrator of the poem? He certainly sympathizes with the seriousness of his plight, but there is also something sadly comical and slightly ironic in the presentation of the poem. Du Fu adopted this stance of bemusement at the difficulties of the emotionally intense old man, Du Fu.

2. The poem announces itself as a "song," and Tang readers would have expected liberties to be taken with form and content in this old-style genre. The rhyme is quintessentially "old style": *aaaaa bbcbbbb ddedfd ggg hh*. Do the shifts in rhyme match the thematic shifts in the poem?

3. This is another one of Du Fu's poems that was dearly loved by later generations. In particular, writers frequently cited the final lines, 19–25, which come utterly unexpectedly. Here again, however, the tone is complex. This is a brilliant way to conclude a poem about one's roof getting blown off, but what is the difference between these lines being spoken by Du Fu the persona in the poem and Du Fu the actual author of the poem?

"Weary Night" by Du Fu [regulated verse]

倦夜					Weary Night
竹	涼	侵	臥	内	Bamboo coolness invades the bedroom.
bamboo	cool	invade	bedroom	within	
野	月	滿	庭	隅 [ŋuă]	The outland moon fills a corner of the courtyard.
outland	moon	fill	court	corner	
重	露	成	涓	滴	The heavy dew forms water drops that fall.
heavy	dew	form	droplet	drop	
稀	星	乍	有	無 [muə̆]	The sparse stars flicker, now there, now gone.
sparse	star	sudden	there	not there	
暗	飛	螢	自	照	Fireflies gleam in their own light as they fly in the dark.
dark	fly	firefly	of itself	shine	
水	宿	鳥	相	呼 [xɔ]	The birds stopping for the night on the water call out to one another.
water	sojourn	birds	mutually	call	
萬	事	干	戈	裏	Ten thousand affairs all hemmed in with weapons:
10,000	affairs	halberd	spear	inside	
空	悲	清	夜	徂 [dzɔ]	In vain I sorrow that the pure night passes.
in vain	sorrow	pure	night	depart	

Burton Watson's Translation

Restless Night

The cool of bamboo invades my room;
moonlight from the fields fills the corners of the court;
dew gathers till it falls in drops;
a scattering of stars, now there, now gone.
A firefly threading the darkness makes his own light;
birds at rest on the water call to each other;
all these lie within the shadow of the sword—
Powerless I grieve as the clear night passes.

Study Notes and Questions

This poem was written in Chengdu.

1. What oppositions does the first couplet establish? What time of year is it (i.e., when would you notice the coolness coming in to the bedroom)? What seasonal patterns are associated with that time of year? What is a "bamboo coolness," and why is the moon an "outland moon"? What does Du Fu actually see here?

2. What is the relationship of the second couplet to the first? (How does the poet know there is dew? Why are the stars sparse?) How does the parallelism work in the couplet?

3. How is the image of the fifth line related to the images of the first half of the poem? Explain the parallelism of the third couplet. Why are the birds "sojourning"?

4. The most difficult question of all is what the final couplet has to do with the rest of the poem: why is it a brilliant conclusion to the sequence of images of the poem and a fitting end to a poem with the title "Weary Night"?

"Lone Goose" by Du Fu [regulated verse]

孤雁					Lone Goose
孤 lone	雁 goose	不 not	飲 drink	啄 peck	The lone goose neither drinks nor eats.
飛 fly	鳴 cry out	聲 sound	念 recall	群 [giuən] flock	Calling out as it flies, its voice [shows it] longs for its flock.
誰 who	憐 pity	一 one	片 fleck	影 shadow	Who feels sorrow for one fleck of shadow?
相 mutual	失 lose	萬 10,000	重 -fold	雲 [jiuən] clouds	They have lost one another midst ten-thousand layers of clouds.
望 gaze	盡 exhaust	似 seem	猶 still	見 see	Gaze exhausted, as though still seen;
哀 sorrow	多 much	如 resemble	更 again	聞 [miuən] hear	The sorrow increases, as if heard again.
野 outland	鴉 crow	無 without	意 intent	緒 thread	The outland crows are without any thought:
鳴 caw	噪 racket	亦 also	紛 profuse	紛 [p'iuən] profuse	Their cawing is abundantly clamorous.

Study Notes and Questions

This poem was written in the first year of the Dali reign period (766) while Du Fu was living in Kuizhou.

1. Examine Du Fu's use of the regulated verse form here. How does he introduce his topic and themes in the first couplet, develop them in the second, mark a shift in the third, and provide a response in the last?

2. Look in particular at the parallelism of the middle couplets. Explain the parallelism of the second couplet.

3. The third couplet is famous for its ambiguity: does this describe the goose longing for its flock and imagining it hears and almost sees them, or does this describe Du Fu straining to track the bird? What is the effect of this confusion of perspectives?

4. Chinese poetry very much is an art of selection: the poems generally are short, and poets must craft the details carefully. What do the crows in the final couplet signify? Is this another version of objective closure? Discuss the difference between such a use of imagery and the sort of symbolism we are used to in English poetry.

"The Yangzi and Han Rivers" by Du Fu [regulated verse]

江漢					The Yangzi and Han Rivers[51]
江 River	漢 Han	思 longing	歸 return	客 traveler	At the meeting of the Yangzi and the Han, a traveler longing to return.
乾 Qian	坤 Kun	一 one	腐 rotten	儒 [ryə̆] scholar	Between Qian and Kun, one pointless pedant.
片 fleck	雲 cloud	天 sky	共 alike	遠 far	A fleck of cloud, far away in the sky;
永 long	夜 night	月 moon	同 share	孤 [kuə̆] alone	In the long night, alone like the moon.
落 falling	日 sun	心 heart	猶 still	壯 sturdy	As day falls, my heart remains sturdy.
秋 autumn	風 wind	病 sick	欲 about to	蘇 [suə̆] recover	In the autumn wind, from sickness almost recovered.
古 ancient	來 come	存 remain	老 old	馬 horse	From of old, they have preserved old horses.
不 not	必 need	取 take	長 long	途 [tɦuə̆] road	The horse need not take to the long road.

Stephen Owen's Translation

Where Yangzi Meets the Han

Wanderer, homesick, where Yangzi meets Han,
Confucian hack, between Earth and Sky.

Wisp of cloud, the sky shares such distance,
endless night, the moon same as I in solitude.

Setting sun, the mind still has vigor;
autumn wind, sickness almost cured.

From ancient times they have kept old horses;
they need not take to the distant road.

---

51. Du Fu apparently uses Jiang Han 江漢 to refer to two separate regions, one in the Kuizhou 夔州 area and another where the Han 漢 flows into the Yangzi River. Here it is the latter region. Du Fu wrote the poem in 768.

Angus C. Graham's Translation

Yangtse and Han

By Yangtse and Han, a stranger who thinks of home,
One withered pedant between the Ch'ien and K'un.
Under as far a sky as that streak of cloud,
The moon in the endless night no more alone.
In sunset hale of heart still:
In the autumn wind, risen from sickness.
There's always a place kept for an old horse
Though it can take no more to the long road.

Study Notes and Questions

1. This is another of Du Fu's famous, and austere, late regulated verse compositions. Once again, look at his use of the form. What are the themes introduced in the first couplet? How do the images of the second couplet develop those themes? Explain the parallelism, which is rarely simple in Du Fu's late regulated verse.

2. How does the third couplet continue the themes and reframe them in the context of Du Fu's own life? And finally, how does the last couplet build on the third couplet to present Du Fu's stance concerning his own situation as a lone traveler amidst the vast, bleak, yet beautiful, landscape? What meaning has he found or created for himself?

"Traveler's Pavilion" by Du Fu [regulated verse]

客亭					Traveler's Pavilion
秋 autumn	窗 window	猶 still	曙 dawn	色 color	At the autumn window, still dawn's colors;
落 falling	木 tree	更 more	高 high	風 [piung] wind	Trees barren, yet more wind high above.
日 sun	出 come out	寒 cold	山 mountain	外 beyond	The sun comes out beyond the cold mountains;
江 river	流 flow	宿 overnight	霧 mist	中 [ṭiung] middle	The River flows midst the overnight mists.
聖 sage	朝 court	無 without	棄 discarded	物 thing	Our Sage Dynasty is without discarded things:
衰 decline	病 ill	已 already	成 become	翁 [ʔung] old man	Decrepit and ill, I've already become an old man.
多 many	少 few	殘 remnant	生 life	事 affairs	How many matters of this remaining life,
飄 gust	零 fall	任 entrust	轉 turning	蓬 [pung] tumbleweed	Cast to the wind, are entrusted to a rolling tumbleweed?

Study Notes and Questions

Du Fu wrote this poem in 762 while traveling from Jinzhou to Zizhou in Sichuan. His family remained in Chengdu.

1. There is a "High Tang" style of opening a poem: a simple, evocative grandeur of scale that the major High Tang poets (Wang Wei, Meng Haoran, Li Bai, Du Fu) captured. Later poets attempted to duplicate the effect, but rarely with much success. "Traveler's Pavilion," like "The Yangzi and Han Rivers" above, is a famous example of a poem that begins with such an opening couplet. Describe what you see when you envision what the couplet depicts. Explain the logic of the second line. Also notice that the two lines are parallel.

2. The second couplet is much admired for its descriptive power. Consider all the binary oppositions at work in the couplet. Movement/stillness is one: explain how it appears in each line. Also think about boundaries and crossing boundaries: where do these appear in the lines? There is also seen/unseen. Explain how the logic of binarism shapes the implicit meaning of the couplet and the scene it describes.

3. The central issue in this poem is how the third couplet fits into the rest of the poem. Is Du Fu saying what he thinks in the third couplet, or is this a case of "stating the opposite of what one thinks" (*fan yu* 反語)? Explain your position. Are the images of decline and being cut off (rejection) presented in this couplet anticipated in the first four lines? Are those images balanced by other aspects of the scene? Is there balance in this couplet?

4. Du Fu in his poetry often surrenders much in order to retain a little. In a world in which he is cast adrift, even preserving some possibility of effective action and some claim to meaning is a substantial achievement. This poem is one example. In the final couplet, what does he say is possible? What does he give up? How does the final couplet address the concerns of the third couplet? This general approach to finding meaning in events earned Du Fu the epithet "sorrowful yet resolute" (*beizhuang* 悲壯).

From the Series "Autumn Meditations" [regulated verse]

秋興八首 第一							Autumn Meditations, 8 poems, no. 1
玉 jade	露 dew	凋 decline	傷 wound	楓 maple	樹 tree	林 [liɪm] grove	Jade dew withers and wounds the maple groves.
巫 Wu	山 Mountain	巫 Wu	峽 gorge	氣 air	蕭 chill & dreary	森 [ʂiɪm]	In the Wu Mountains and Wu Gorge, the air is chill and drear.
江 river	間 between	波 wave	浪 billow	兼 join both	天 sky	湧 swell	Billows on the river swell to the sky.
塞 pass	上 on	風 wind	雲 clouds	接 connect	地 earth	陰 [ʔiɪm] darken	The winds and clouds above the pass reach their shadows to the ground.
叢 cluster	菊 chrys…-	兩 two	開 open	他 other	日 day	淚 tears	The clustered chrysanthemums twice have opened tears of another day.
孤 lone	舟 boat	一 one	繫 tether	故 old	園 garden	心 [siɪm] heart	A lone boat entirely binds this former garden heart.
寒 cold	衣 clothes	處 place	處 place	催 hasten	刀 knife	尺 ruler	Cold-weather clothes everywhere hasten the scissors and rule:
白 white	帝 emperor	城 city wall	高 high	急 urgent	暮 dusk	砧 [ṭiɪm] fulling	White Emperor City, so high, urges on the sunset fulling.[52]

STEPHEN OWEN'S TRANSLATION

Autumn Stirrings (I)

Jade white dew scars and harms
    forests of maple trees,
on Wu Mountain and in the Wu Gorges,
    the atmosphere bleak and dreary.

Between river's margins the waves
    churn level with sky,

52. Fulling is a process of beating cloth to expand the fibers. This is an autumn activity.

wind-driven clouds over passes
    cast shadows touching earth.

Chrysanthemum clumps twice bring forth
    tears of another day,
and a lonely boat once fastened
    a heart of its homeland.

Everywhere clothes for cold weather
    hasten ruler and blade,
walls of White Emperor Castle high,
    pounding blocks urgent in dusk.

Study Notes and Questions

1. Du Fu's "Autumn Meditations" were written around 766 in Kuizhou. This set of poems is extremely challenging. Its compressed, elliptical language, ambiguous syntax, and enigmatic couplet structure are a culmination of Du Fu's late regulated-verse style.

2. This first poem is the introduction to the series of eight poems and sets out the basic themes. The first two couplets of the poem focus on the autumnal qualities of the vista Du Fu sees. This is not the "high autumn" of Du Fu's "My Thatched Roof Was Destroyed by the Autumn Wind." What are the qualities of autumn that Du Fu stresses in the first two couplets?

3. Explain the parallelism in the second couplet. How difficult is it to identify the categories that link the characters in corresponding positions in each line? Do the lines set out contrasts or similarities within the categories of correspondence?

4. The third couplet is very challenging. Look closely at the parallelism: how are chrysanthemums like a boat? How is "other" like "old"? Think here about questions of presenece and absence.

5. While "tears" and "heart" appear to make a good pairing, "day" and "garden" seem utterly unrelated. However, consider the binary of time/space: what are the binary categories in the parallelism between "tears of another day" and "former garden heart"? Are the tears and the heart part of the present, past, or both? How does considering the parallelism help to define the meaning of the difficult phrases "tears of another day" and "former garden heart"?

6. Coming at the beginning of a sequence of poems, the final couplet does not offer a resolution that synthesizes the oppositions introduced in the first six lines. Instead, the last couplet, presenting a form of objective closure, focuses on the sounds of the fulling blocks and the preparation of winter clothing. This image does not return the reader's attention to Du Fu's immediate circumstances but is a more complex act of imagination that places Du Fu on the edge of a larger community. What is Du Fu's mood here? Why does his attention turn to the fulling blocks in the distance?

秋興八首 第七							Autumn Meditations, 8 poems, no. 7
昆	明	池	水	漢	時	功 [kəwŋ]	The pond waters of Kunming are
Kun-	-ming	pond	water	Han	time	accomplish	an achievement of Han times.[53]
武	帝	旌	旗	在	眼	中 [truwŋ]	The banners and pennants of Emperor
Wu	Emperor	banner	flag	is in	eye	middle	Wu stand before one's eyes.
織	女	機	絲	虛	夜	月	The threads on the loom of the Weaving
weave	woman	loom	thread	empty	night	moon	Maid are empty in the night moon.[54]
石	鯨	鱗	甲	動	秋	風 [puwŋ]	The scales of the stone leviathan
stone	whale	scales	plate	move	autumn	wind	move in the autumn wind.[55]
波	漂	菰	米	沉	雲	黑	Waves toss duckweed, the black of
wave	drench	duckweed		sink	clouds	black	sunken clouds.
露	冷	蓮	房	墜	粉	紅 [ɣəwŋ]	The dew chills the lotus pods, the
dew	cold	lotus	chamber	fall	powder	red	red of scattered pollen.
關	塞	極	天	唯	鳥	道	The mountains and passes extend
pass	fort	extreme	heaven	only is	bird	way	to heaven, a path only for birds.
江	湖	滿	地	一	漁	翁 [ʔəwŋ]	Rivers and lakes fill the land: one
river	lake	fill	land	one	fisher	old man	old fisherman.

STEPHEN OWEN'S TRANSLATION

Autumn Stirrings (VII)

The waters of Kun-ming Pool
  are a deed of the days of Han,
pennons and banners of Emperor Wu
  are right before my eyes.

Loom threads of the Weaving Girl
  lie empty in night's moon,
stone Leviathan's fins and scales
  stir the autumn wind.

---

53. Emperor Wu (the "Martial Emperor") of the Han ordered the building of Kunming Lake to the southwest of Chang'an, the capital, so that he could train his troops for naval warfare. It was modeled on the much larger Lake Kunming in the foothills of the Himalayas in Yunnan Province.

54. The Weaving Maid is a constellation. In Chinese folklore, the Oxherd and the Weaving Maid were lovers set at opposite ends of the Milky Way as punishment for being distracted from their duties. They were allowed to meet only once a year.

55. This line alludes to the Western Han dynasty story collection known as *Miscellaneous Accounts of the Western Capital* 西京雜記: "At Kunming Pond, they carved jade into a leviathan. Whenever there was a thunderstorm, it would always call out. Its tail and fins would all move." 「昆明池刻玉石為鯨魚，每至雷雨，常鳴吼，鰭尾皆動。」

Waves toss a kumi seed
　　sunk in black of cloud,
dew is chill on the lotus pod
　　from which tumbles powdery red.

Fortified passes stretch to the skies,
　　a way only for birds,
lakes and rivers fill the earth,
　　and one old man, fishing.

Angus C. Graham's Translation

Autumn Meditation, number 7

K'un-ming Pool was the Han time's monument,
The banners of the Emperor Wu are here before my eyes.
Vega threads her loom in vain by night under the moon,
And the great stone fish's plated scales veer in the autumn wind.
The waves toss a zizania seed, over sunken clouds as black:
Dew on the calyx chills the lotus, red with dropped pollen.
　Over the pass, all the way to the sky, a road for none but the birds.
On river and lakes, to the ends of the earth, one old fisherman.

Study Notes and Questions

1. In this poem, Du Fu begins with an image from Chang'an. Since he is in Kuizhou, the image is an imagined one. Exactly *how* is it imagined? Are the banners that he evokes in the second line those of Tang Emperor Xuanzong? Or are they those of Emperor Wu of the Han? Is Du Fu leaping time as well as space? What do you think he is trying to do here?

2. The images from Kunming Pool in Chang'an in the second couplet are equally empty and enigmatic. The poem alludes to Ban Gu's 班固 "*Fu* on the Western Capital" 西都賦:

集乎豫章之宇	They gathered at Camphor Lodge,
臨乎昆明之池	And looked down on Kunming Pond.
左牽牛而右織女	To the left is the Oxherd, to the right the Weaving Maid.
似雲漢之無涯	It resembles the boundlessness of the Milky Way.

The early Tang commentary by Li Shan 李善 explains, "At Kunming Pond there are two stone figures, images of the Oxherd and the Weaving Maid." 「昆明池有二石人，牽牛織女象。」 However, the allusion does not clarify Du Fu's usage of the image here. Are we to think of the actual constellation, the Weaving Maid, or the statue? Is the Weaving Maid constellation reflected in the lake? Do her threads empty out the late-night moon, as the syntax suggests? The word "thread" (*si* 絲) is homophonous with "longing" (*si* 思), and the play on words is a standard part of the *yuefu* repertoire. Does Du Fu intend the connection here? Do the stone whale's scales move the autumn wind, or do they move in it?

3. The third couplet is also a mass of images calling on one another without clear order. The syntax is uncertain. Are the wave-drenched duckweed seeds black like sunken clouds? Or do the last three characters constitute a new sentence: "Waves drench the duckweed seeds, and the sunken clouds are black"? If the latter, what is the connection between the two halves of the line? The second half of the couplet offers no help, since it also can be read in two ways:

(a) Dew-chilled lotus pods are red with fallen pollen.
(b) Dew grows cold on the lotus pods; the fallen pollen is red.

We know this is still Kunming Lake. Yet when is it? Now? In Du Fu's remembered past? In Emperor Wu's time? Does it matter?

4. The final couplet seems utterly outside time, and yet it returns us to Du Fu's present world of Kuizhou. Note that it is a parallel couplet. How does line 7 accomplish the transition from Kunming Lake to Kuizhou? What do all the previous images have to do with the final line? Is the final line a positive image? A negative image? Mixed? What is your sense of the line?

秋興八首第八							Autumn Meditations, 8 poems, no. 8
昆	吾	御	宿	自	逶	迤 [ji]	The road from Kunwu to Yusu twists and turns.[56]
Kun-	-wu	Yu-	-su	of itself	thread about		
紫	閣	峰	陰	入	渼	陂 [pi]	The shadow of Purple Chamber Peak enters Meipi Lake.[57]
Purple	Chamber	Peak	shade	enter	Mei-	-pi	
香	稻	啄	殘	鸚	鵡	粒	The fragrant rice: the pecked remains of parrot kernels.
fragrant	rice	peck	remain	parrot		kernel	
碧	梧	棲	老	鳳	凰	枝 [tɕi]	Jade-green pawlonia: roosting-aged pheonix branches.
green	pawlonia	roost	old	pheonix		branch	
佳	人	拾	翠	春	相	問	Fair maidens pick kingfisher feathers, asking one another on spring outings.[58]
fine	person	pick up	kingfisher	spring	mutually	ask	
仙	侶	同	舟	晚	更	移 [ji]	Immortal companions sharing a boat row yet again in the late sun.[59]
immortal	friend	share	boat	late	more	move	
綵	筆	昔	曾	干	氣	象	My rainbow brush once pressed upon nature's primal powers.[60]
colored	brush	in past	once	encroach	*qi*	image	
白	頭	今	望	苦	低	垂 [dʑwi]	With white hair, now I gaze, then in bitter sorrow lower my head.
white	hair	now	gaze	bitter	low	hang	

Angus C. Graham's Translation

Autumn Meditation, number 8

The Kunwu road by Yusu River ran its meandering course,
The shadow of Purple Turret Peak fell into Lake Meipi.
Grains from the fragrant rice-stalks, pecked and dropped by the parrots:
On the green *wutong* tree branches which the perching phoenix aged.
Beautiful girls gathered kingfisher feathers for spring gifts:
Together in the boat, a troop of immortals, we set forth again in the evening....

---

56. Kunwu and Yusu are both regions mentioned in the preface to Yang Xiong's "Hunt *fu*" 《羽獵賦序》. By the Tang, Yusu was the name of a river. Both were in the region near Chang'an on the way to Meipi Lake.

57. Purple Chamber Peak is one of the peaks in the Zhongnan Mountain Range to the south of Chang'an.

58. This may be an allusion to Cao Zhi's "*Fu* of the Luo River Goddess" 《洛神賦》: "Some gathered up bright pearls; some collected kingfisher feathers."「或採明珠，或拾翠羽。」Perhaps the maidens and Du Fu are exchanging greetings.

59. This alludes to a story in the *History of the Latter Han* 後漢書: people watching Li Ying 李膺 and Guo Tai 郭泰 cross a stream in a boat took them to be immortals.

60. The "rainbow brush" refers to a story in Zhong Rong's 鍾嶸 (468–518) *Shi pin* 詩品 in which the poet Jiang Yan 江淹 (444–505) dreamed that an earlier poet Guo Pu 郭璞 (276–324) came to him and demanded the return of a rainbow brush. After giving up the brush in the dream, Jiang Yan's talent vanished.

This brush of many colours once forced the elements.
Chanting, peering into the distance, in anguish my white head droops.[61]

Study Notes and Questions

This poem continues the water theme of poem number 7 even though it moves to a different site.

1. We are back in Chang'an in the first line, but then Du Fu leads us out of town to Meipi Lake. Since this couplet describes geography, it is largely out of time. The statements are true in past, present, and future. Thus we do not know if Du Fu is imagining the present or again recalling better times.

2. The second couplet offers little help in framing the poem. The syntax of the two lines is strange, but both Graham and Owen do their best to naturalize it. We know that the lines somehow describe the scene at Meipi, but why these lines are significant is unclear. Certainly there is the sense of diminishment, that Du Fu points to meager traces of better times. Yet the traces *do* remain, so the better times did exist. If remnant glory is all the glory one can get, so be it.

3. Why does Du Fu mention spring? Who were these maidens? Who were the immortals? Is Du Fu writing from memory, imparting alluring colors to some excursion long ago? Or are these marks of absence, experiences he thinks are possible on the lake that he never quite had? Are the immortals leaving without him?

4. Is the final couplet an ultimate refusal of consolation, a refusal to transform the images? He had done it before, but nothing is left now. Yet he claims he had indeed once grasped that "rainbow brush." Is this remnant glory? Even though he asserts a final failure, it is at the end of a spectacular series of poems: should we believe him, or is this a pose? Is such a pose a fitting end to the poetic sequence?

---

61. Some texts of the poem have "chant" 吟 instead of "now" 今.

"Observing Mistress Gongsun's Disciple Dancing the Sword Dance, A Ballad," with Preface, by Du Fu [old-style verse]

大曆二年十月十九日，夔州別駕元持宅，見臨潁李十二娘舞劍器，壯其蔚跂，問其所師，曰「余，公孫大娘弟子也。」開元三載，余尚童稚，記於郾城觀公孫氏舞劍器渾脫，瀏灕頓，獨出冠時。自高頭宜春梨園二伎坊內人洎外供奉舞女曉是舞者，聖文神武皇帝初，公孫一人而已。玉貌錦衣，〔…〕況余白首。今茲弟子亦匪盛顏。既辨其由來，知波瀾莫二。撫事慷慨，聊為劍器行。昔者吳人張旭善草書，書帖數，嘗於鄴縣見公孫大娘舞西河劍器，自此草書長進，豪蕩感激，即公孫可知矣。

On the nineteenth day of the Tenth Month of the Second Year of Dali, at the house of Yuan Chi, Aide to the prefect of Kuizhou, I saw Ms. Li 12 of Linying dance the Sword Dance.[62] Finding her bold manner grand, I asked with whom she had studied. She said, "I was a student of Mistress Gongsun." In the 3rd year of Kaiyuan, I was still a boy; I remember watching Gongsun dance the Sword and the Huntuo with a lively shifting pace.[63] She was the best of her time. From the masters of the two schools of Yichun to the outside entertainers, among those who knew this dance, at the beginning of Ming Huang's reign, there was Gongsun alone.[64] With a jade face and embroidered clothes [. . . .] yet more since I have white hair.[65] Now this disciple also has lost the glow of youth. Having learned how she came here, I know that our vicissitudes have been the same. Having been deeply moved by touching upon old matters, I decided to compose the "Ballad of the Sword Dance." Formerly Zhang Xu of Wu was good at draft-style calligraphy.[66] Although he often wrote, once he saw Mistress Gongsun dance the Western River Sword Dance at Yan. From that time, his calligraphy advanced greatly, bold, wild, excited: Gongsun['s manner] can be known from this.

觀公孫大娘弟子舞劍器行

Observing Mistress Gongsun's Disciple Dancing the Sword Dance, A Ballad

昔	有	佳	人	公	孫	氏	Of old there was the Fair One, Miss Gongsun.
formerly	there was	fine	person	Gong	-sun	clan	
一	舞	劍	器	動	四	方 [faŋ]	She danced the Sword Dance and moved the Four Directions.[67]
one	dance	Sword	tool	move	four	region	

62. The date corresponds to November 15, 767. Kuizhou is a city amid the Three Gorges on the Yangzi River. "Li 12" refers to her being ranked the twelfth-oldest member of her generation in her clan.

63. Kaiyuan 3, at the beginning of Xuanzong's long reign, was 715. Both the Sword Dance and the Huntuo were Central Asian dances. The culture of cosmopolitan Chang'an enthusiastically adopted the new musical styles from cultures along the Silk Road.

64. The Yichun and the Pear Garden were the two academies that trained the imperial musicians and dancers. Ming Huang, "Bright Emperor," was the name used to refer to Xuanzong ("Mysteriously Dark Ancestor") during his lifetime, and it remained the usual name throughout the remainder of the Tang.

65. This sentence seems to be missing some text.

66. Zhang Xu was one of the great Tang dynasty painters and especially famous for his draft-style calligraphy (*caoshu* 草書).

67. I.e., the whole world.

觀	者	如	山	色	沮	喪	Those who watched [crowded] like mountains; their appearance was dazed.
observe	-ers	like	mountain form		block	mourn	
天	地	為	之	久	低	昂 [ŋaŋ]	Heaven and earth always raised and dropped for her:
sky	earth	for	her	long	lower	raise	
㸌	如	羿	射	九	日	落	Flashing like Yi shooting the nine suns, falling,[68]
flash	like	Yi	shoot	nine	suns	fall	
矯	如	群	帝	驂	龍	翔 [sɦiaŋ]	Soaring like the assembled Ancestors, rising on chariots with teams of dragons,[69]
fly	like	crowd	thearch	3-team	dragons	soar	
來	如	雷	霆	收	震	怒	Coming like a thunder-clap accumulating aroused anger,
come	like	thunder	-clap	collect	quake	anger	
罷	如	江	海	凝	清	光 [kuaŋ]	Finishing like a great river with a stilled pure gleam.
end	like	river	sea	congeal	pure	gleam	
絳	脣	珠	袖	兩	寂	寞	Her carmine lips and pearl-sewn sleeves both have been silenced.
red	lips	pearl	sleeve	both	silent	silent	
晚	有	弟	子	傳	芬	芳 [faŋ]	Late [in life], there was a disciple who transmitted her fragrant charm.
late	there is	disciple		convey	fragrance		
臨	潁	美	人	在	白	帝	The beauty from Linying is at the city of the White Emperor.[70]
Lin	-ying	beauty	person	is at	white	emperor	
妙	舞	此	曲	神	揚	揚 [jiaŋ]	Wonderfully dancing this tune, her spirit ascends upward.
subtle	dance	this	tune	spirit	lift up	lift up	
與	余	問	答	既	有	以	Since she could answer my questions,
with	me	ask	answer	since	there is	means	
感	時	撫	事	增	惋	傷 [ʂiaŋ]	Moved by the times, recollecting events, I am increasingly heart-struck.
moved	times	touch	events	add	regret	hurt	
先	帝	侍	女	八	千	人	Among the eight thousand handmaidens of our Former Emperor,
former	emperor	serve	woman	8 ×	1000	people	
公	孫	劍	器	初	第	一 [ʔjit]	From the beginning Gongsun's Sword dance was the best.
Gong	-sun	sword	tool	at first	number	one	
五	十	年	間	似	反	掌	Fifty years have passed like the turn of a hand:
5 ×	10	years	between	seem	turn	palm	

68. During Yao's reign, ten suns appeared in the sky and threatened to scorch the earth. Yao ordered the great archer Yi to shoot down nine of the suns.

69. Ancestors are both heavenly rulers and the spirits of earthly emperors who have attained god-like status and serve as intermediaries between men and heavenly powers.

70. Linying is a county in present-day Henan. Kuizhou was referred to as the City of the White Emperor.

風	塵	澒	洞	昏	王	室 [ʂit]	Wind and dust, so vast, have darkened the imperial household.
wind	dust	boundless		darken	king	abode	
梨	園	弟	子	散	如	煙	The disciples of the Pear Garden have scattered like mist.
Pear	Garden	disciples		scatter	like	mist	
女	樂	餘	姿	映	寒	日 [rit]	The lingering manner of the imperial musician glows in the cold sunlight.
woman	music	remnant	manner	shine	cold	sun	
金	粟	堆	南	木	已	拱	The trees south of Gold-grain Mound already a hand-span around.[71]
Gold	grain	Mound	south	trees	already	encircle	
瞿	塘	石	城	草	蕭	瑟 [ʂət]	The grasses by stone ramparts at Jutang are sere and forlorn.[72]
Ju	-tang	stone	rampart	grass	forlornly dreary		
玳	筵	急	管	曲	復	終	On the tortoise-shell mat, the strident flutes of the tune again come to an end.
tortoise	mat	urgent	pipes	tune	again	end	
樂	極	哀	來	月	東	出 [tʂʰyt]	When joy reached it height, sorrow came; the sun rose in the east.
joy	extreme	sorrow	come	moon	east	come out	
老	夫	不	知	其	所	往	This old man does not know where he is heading:
old	man	not	know	his	where	goes	
足	繭	荒	山	轉	愁	疾 [tsɦit]	With calloused feet, midst the wild mountains, he becomes grief-stricken.
feet	callous	wild	mountain turn		grief	sick	

Study Notes and Questions

This poem is one of the early examples of a growing interest in capturing the aesthetic effects of music in poetry.

1. The poem also is part of Du Fu's mythologizing the glory of Xuanzong's reign. The former court musician from Xuanzong's Pear Garden adrift in the South becomes a popular figure in later Tang poetry. Du Fu here suggests an important reason: he and later writers saw reflections of their own plight in the musician's fate. What aspects of life and art do they share?

2. The poem itself is a fairly straightforward old-style verse composition with one change of rhyme. Its structure is much like a *fu*, with a mix of narrative and elaborate descriptive sections. Look at the shifting syntax of the lines. Some are extremely prosy: find a few examples. What is the effect of presenting a "poetic" topic through such prosy language?

---

71. Gold-grain Mountain was the site of Xuanzong's tomb.

72. Jutang is one of the Three Gorges on the Yangzi just east of Kuizhou. Here it presumably refers to the entire Three Gorges region.

"South of the River, Meeting Li Guinian" [regulated verse]

江南逢李龜年							South of the River, Meeting Li Guinian[73]
岐	王	宅	裏	尋	常	見	In the home of the Prince
Qi	Prince	house	in	seek	often	see	of Qi we constantly met;[74]
崔	九	堂	前	幾	度	聞 [ʋjyn]	How many times did I hear you
Cui	Nine	hall	before	how many times		hear	before the hall of Cui Nine?[75]
正	是	江	南	好	風	景	It's just now, in the fine scenery of
just	is this	river	south	good	wind	scene	the South,
落	花	時	節	又	逢	君 [kyn]	In the season of falling flowers
falling	flowers	time	season	again	meet	you	I again meet you.

STUDY NOTES AND QUESTIONS

Explain the fittingness of the place and season for the meeting.

73. This poem was written in 770 in Tanzhou (modern Changsha). Li Guinian was a famous singer from the imperial court. During the An Lushan Rebellion he fled south and sought patronage from the local elites of the South.

74. The Prince of Qi was Li Fan, Emperor Ruizong's fourth son.

75. Cui Nine was Cui Di, the younger brother of Cui Shi, the Director of the Secretariat, and a close friend of Emperor Xuanzong. The "Nine" indicates that he was the ninth oldest male child of his clan in his generation.

Chapter Eight

Middle and Late Tang Poetry

The An Lushan Rebellion should not have occurred. The prefects who commanded the defenses for the cities that stood in the way of An Lushan's army were sons of good families who were well versed in the Confucian cultural tradition of their ancestors: they should not have abandoned their cities. But they did. Eunuchs should not have gained control of the palace armies. Regional warlords should not have been able to openly defy Tang imperial authority. After the rebellion was quelled, emperors should have been strong and resourceful rather than susceptible to falling under the influence of the eunuchs, dabbling in Daoist alchemical potions, and dying young.

The civil elite in the wake of the rebellion had to confront the failure of the cultural traditions that had hitherto defined their place in the world. Du Fu tried with desperate genius to sustain his grand vision of an imperial system that participated in the order of the cosmos. Later writers had to confront the possibility that the cosmos in fact cared very little about the human realm. They came to suspect that the correspondences between the human and the natural order upon which earlier poetry relied were but products of deluded human imagining.

In the Mid- and Late Tang, the civil elite thus needed both to renegotiate its relationship with the phenomenal realm and to rediscover the basis for its moral authority. The wide range of poetry during the hundred years after the end of the An Lushan Rebellion reflects this process of rethinking the human in many conflicting and complex ways. Bai Juyi's early poetry of social protest, for example, asserts clear moral positions based on fundamental Confucian values that need no additional support from correspondences drawn from the natural realm. These poems make no attempt to read the landscape as Du Fu's poems do. Han Yu's early poetry shows a similar pattern, although he was less polemically dogmatic. Han Yu, however, also developed a poetry of ironic encounter with the landscape in which he self-consciously imposed a structure of fantastic images and conceits upon the world. Meng Jiao and Li He took a different, though related route: they explored the distortions of subjectivity that stood between humans and their perception of the world. They set out grotesque, traumatized, and ghost-ridden visions of the landscape to foreground the problem of the unreliability of the subject. (It should be noted that these themes of the self shaping the perceived order of the world had been a staple of Buddhist philosophy for centuries before the failures of the An Lushan Rebellion forced literati to confront the possibility that their world too might arise out of dreams of desire and fear.) Other poets like Jia Dao, Yao He 姚合 (fl. 840), Xu Hun 許渾 (fl. 850), and Du Mu explored subjective ordering in a more muted way: they wrote landscape poetry where the crafting of couplets exposed the aesthetic manipulation of the world. They created small vignettes of encounter where the shaping of the moment within the couplet was the central focus. This small, well-crafted landscape verse came to be known as the "Late Tang Style" in the later literary tradition. By the end of this period, Li Shangyin had developed a poetry in which subjectivity turns opaque: the poems, awash in desire, anticipation, and sorrow, never quite allow the reader to see beyond the poet to a world of stable references that would help situate the desires presented in the text within the context of the time, place, and external circumstances under which it was written.

The Tang dynasty did not end for another forty years after the death of Wen Tingyun. There were other poets of note during this last period, but they did not escape the increasingly narrow range of possibilities for what poetry could accomplish. The recasting of poetry to restore its imaginative scope needed to await the broad cultural transformations of the Northern Song dynasty (960–1127).

The Historical Context

Most of the famous Mid- and Late Tang poets were officials or at least sought office in the Tang central bureaucracy. Many also served in the administrations of regional military governors. The political organization of the empire in the ninth century not only shaped the social networks within which these authors wrote but also had a profound impact on their sense of identity as officials, as members of a morally responsible elite, and as inheritors of the Chinese civil (*wen* 文) and literary (*wenzhang* 文章) traditions.

In the wake of the An Lushan Rebellion, the Tang state had the good fortune to have a succession of competent emperors served by a retinue of able advisors. Suzong, having persuaded his father Xuanzong to abdicate, went on to retake the capitals and bring the rebellion to an end. However, he could not undo the damage the rebellion had inflicted on the political structure of the empire. Most crucial was the loss of control over the northeastern provinces: regional commanders—some of whom had served with An Lushan—still had large armies loyal to them rather than to the throne. The commanders refused to pay taxes and refused to accept officials appointed to their regions by the central court. Since the now-independent regions of Hebei and Henan in particular had been important sources of revenue and grain, the southern regions the Tang still controlled became increasingly important, as did the canal system that connected the South to the capitals.

Emperor Daizong 代宗 came to the throne through the intervention of a eunuch who killed Emperor Suzong's widowed empress to remove Daizong's main rival. The empress had been plotting to replace Daizong with one of her own children. However, Daizong, being no fool, had the eunuch assassinated the year he became emperor. He could not deal with external threats to his power quite so easily, and he had to develop measures to preserve the weakened authority of the central court rather than attempt to expand it. That challenge fell to his son Emperor Dezong 德宗. Dezong first sought to stabilize the court's fiscal resources. Many of the land registries upon which the old tax system was based were destroyed in the rebellion, and several important regions were not paying their taxes in any case. So Dezong and his advisors greatly simplified the old, piecemeal tax system by creating a single agricultural tax. The court negotiated quotas with the provinces based on the amount of their cultivated land. The central court acknowledged its decreased control over the provinces by allowing the provincial administrations to determine many of the fine points of how to implement the tax. The policy proved successful: taxes flowed in, and the civilian bureaucracy at least for the moment regained control of the finances of the empire.

Dezong, having access to revenue, next took on the regional military governors. When the military governor of Chengde 成德 (in modern Hebei Province) died, Dezong refused to recognize the claim of the son to succeed the father as governor. The northeastern provinces all recognized this move as an attack, and they broke into open rebellion. To make matters worse, Li Xilie, the governor of Huaixi 淮西 Province, which controlled the crucial canal system, decided to rebel as well and thus cut off the Tang government's access to grain. When the troops of Zhu Ci, a northwestern garrison general, came to Chang'an to help suppress the revolt, they mutinied, and Zhu Ci, whose brother Zhu Tao already had revolted, joined with his troops and forced Dezong to flee the capital. Two generals—Li Huaiguang and Li Sheng—came to Dezong's rescue, but Li Huaiguang, who controlled the province of Hezhong 河中 (in modern Shanxi Province), felt he had been slighted and rebelled as well. Dezong's advisors then strongly urged him to focus on matters closest to hand and deal with Zhu Ci while granting the northeastern governors the authority they sought. Dezong followed this advice, and Li Sheng, proving an able general, defeated both Li Huaiguang and Zhu Ci. Dezong then defeated Li Xilie in Huaixi. The result of Dezong's effort was mixed: the remaining northeastern governors had firmer control over their provinces, but their total land area had diminished.

The people who proved most important in Dezong's time of greatest need were two eunuch commanders and a scholar from the Hanlin Academy, none of whom were part of the regular bureaucracy. The result was that for the rest of his reign, as Dezong concentrated on stabilizing imperial rule in the areas he *did* control, he increasingly turned away from the established institutions—the civil and military bureaucracies—in favor of his own irregular imperial organizations. When he appointed eunuchs to command his palace army, the role of eunuchs became a permanent feature of late Tang rule.

When Dezong died (of natural causes), his first son came to the throne as Emperor Shunzong 順宗 (r. 805). Unfortunately, this son had suffered a stroke the year before his father died and was not really capable of ruling. Wang Shuwen 王叔文 (753–806), a scholar in the increasingly important Hanlin Academy and old acquaintance of Shunzong, appears to have been planning for such a situation with a small group of low-ranking officials. They intended both to amass great power and to institute much-needed reforms by controlling access to the emperor and curtailing the power of the eunuchs and officials who might oppose them. They succeeded for a while, but Shunzong clearly was too incapacitated to continue ruling, and the group failed to secure the military and official support needed to control the inevitable succession. Shunzong abdicated to his oldest son, Wang was executed, and the others in the group—including the writers Liu Yuxi 劉禹錫 (772–842) and Liu Zongyuan 柳宗元 (773–819)—went into exile.

Shunzong's son, Emperor Xianzong 憲宗 (r. 805–20), was young and energetic, and he moved to build upon his grandfather's work of imperial restoration. Xianzong pushed hard to get the resources necessary to wage war against the independent governors. Among other reforms, he began to reassert the central court's ability to directly control taxes rather than rely on regional administrators. Similarly, he increased central control over the regional armies. After some initial setbacks, he managed to defeat or intimidate several important regions and restore imperial authority over them. Xianzong was equally successful in his effort to revitalize the central bureaucracy. He appointed a succession of relatively young but very talented chief ministers. Wu Yuanheng, for example, was charged with the task of organizing preparations for the campaign against the Huaixi military governor, which was especially crucial because Huaixi, in the south, could threaten supply lines to the capital. Other military governors learned of these plans and were so concerned that in 815 they had Wu assassinated. It was to little avail, however: his subordinate, Pei Du 裴度, proved equally competent, and Wu became a martyr whose death helped rally the empire to the cause of defeating Huaixi, which fell in 817. After this important victory, Xianzong appeared to be on the verge of a major dynastic restoration. Unfortunately, he died under mysterious circumstances in 820. In one version of the story, he was murdered by eunuchs who were afraid that he was about to engage in institutional reform that would strip them of access to wealth and power. Another version is that they simply provided him with Daoist elixirs that proved toxic.

Xianzong's son Emperor Muzong 穆宗 (r. 820–24) was just twenty-four when he became emperor. He lacked his father's skill, authority, experience, and committed advisors. In fairly short order he managed to antagonize the northeastern provinces so much that they revolted and recovered much of the independence they had lost under Xianzong. Three years later, in 823, he had a serious accident while playing polo. An invalid, he could barely attend to his duties. The eunuchs were happy to step in, particularly because the regular civil official bureaucracy that should have intervened was distracted by its own internal factional battles. In 821—the second year of Muzong's reign—an official protested that the *jinshi* examination had been rigged to pass the sons of high officials. Yuan Zhen 元稹 (779–831) and other Hanlin academicians supported the protest, so Muzong ordered the candidates retested; most of the previously successful candidates failed. This incident divided the bureaucracy into those who supported the initial results and those who supported the results of the retesting. Muzong lacked the ability to control the high officials who sought to exploit the incident to benefit their associates, and the series of weak emperors who followed him did no better. Thus throughout the remainder of the period covered in this chapter, factionalism between opposing groups that had formed around Niu Sengru 牛僧孺 (779–848) and Li Deyu 李德裕 (787–850) continued to fester and undermine the ability of the regular bureaucracy to stand up to the eunuchs and to the emperors' personal administrative organizations.

When Muzong died of elixir poisoning at age twenty-nine, the palace eunuchs established his fifteen-year-old first son as the new emperor. The son was so disinclined to rise to the responsibilities of rulership that the eunuchs decided he needed to be removed. They had him killed. His younger brother became Emperor Wenzong 文宗 (r. 827–40) at the age of eighteen. Wenzong proved to be a surprisingly good ruler, given the constraints that he faced. He tried to rein in the bureaucratic factions by alternating their access to power at court. During their periods of demotion, the major figures served in the very important positions of governors of the various provinces. That is, they were sent away from court but still maintained their status. Wenzong realized, moreover, that the court factionalism and the power of the eunuchs in the absence of an effective bureaucracy were linked problems, and he sought to fix both at once. Through various maneuvers, he placed men outside the factional disputes into chief ministerial positions and arranged the assassination of the most dangerous of the eunuchs. Then he made a plan to eliminate the rest of the powerful palace eunuchs: he arranged for a report of "sweet dew" (an auspicious omen) to be announced and sent the eunuchs to investigate. They were to be surprised and killed, but unfortunately the troops waiting in ambush were discovered, the plot failed, and the eunuchs regrouped. They then called in the palace army (under eunuch control) and killed all officials who were in any way implicated in the plot, which is referred to as the "Sweet Dew Incident" 甘露之變. After this catastrophe, both the eunuchs and the factions—aware of their vulnerability—grew more cautious in their struggles for power, and Wenzong had no choice but to accept the failure of his aspirations as emperor.

When Wenzong died at age thirty, eunuch factions stepped in to place one of his younger brothers on the throne after killing several other claimants and their supporters. Emperor Wuzong 武宗 (r. 840–46) followed a different strategy from that of his brother: he allowed Li Deyu, the leader of one of the factions, to become a very powerful prime minister. Together they slowly eroded the power of the eunuchs who had made Wuzong emperor by taking away most of their military commands and returning various financial bureaus to regular official (i.e., Li Deyu's) control. Li did not overstep his authority and encroach on Wuzong's final right to decide; instead he used his power merely to send away rather than eliminate the members of Niu Sengru's rival faction. Wuzong, like earlier emperors, took Daoist elixirs that progressively incapacitated him. However, the famous Huichang 會昌 suppression of Buddhism (named for the reign period) that started in 845, the last full year of his life, was less the result of his belief in Daoism and his growing instability than it was an effort to curb the financial drain imposed by the tax privileges that had been granted to the Buddhist monasteries. Li Deyu, waging war on several fronts (against the Uighurs and a provincial military governor), found that the return of thousands of monks and nuns to lay status and the restoration of much of the monasteries' productive farmland to the tax rolls gave him vital resources, so he let the persecution continue. When Wuzong died from elixir poisoning the next year, however, the campaign came to a halt. Nonetheless, the new emperor did not entirely reverse course: he continued to strictly control the ordination of monks and asserted his authority over the major temple complexes.

The eunuchs had killed all of Wuzong's remaining brothers when they put him on the throne. When he died, his children were still young. Therefore, the eunuchs turned to one of Wuzong's uncles to become the next emperor, Emperor Xuānzong 宣宗 (r. 846–59), who ruled for the rest of the period covered in this chapter. Xuānzong had not liked his nephew when Wenzong was in power, so he dismissed Li Deyu and arranged for him to be exiled to far distant Hainan Island on trumped-up charges. Xuānzong, who from the sidelines had witnessed the factionalized bureaucracy during the rule of three nephews, had a strong sense of the need for personal imperial rule. His effort to suppress the factional discord was simplified by the fact that most of the major participants in the feud had died or had become less active. Xuānzong intimidated his officials through his mastery of the details of policy issues. The first years of Xuānzong's reign seem to have gone peacefully enough as he gained control over the court and bureaucracy, but the Tang was under constant financial pressure because of the cost of defense in the north and northeast, and Xuānzong increasingly sought ways to extract revenue from southeast China. By the time of his death in 859, discontent in the south had transformed into popular uprisings. The final slow disintegration of the Tang had begun.

The biographies of the major poets of the Mid- and Late Tang weave themselves through this larger history of eunuch intrigue, bureaucratic factionalism, and the constant efforts of the central court to regain or maintain control of the provinces. Although most of the emperors ruled for relatively short periods, they seem to have had a sense of what needed to be done and managed to command the loyalty of an official elite—including the poets—despite the challenges and dangers presented by life near the throne.

Bai Juyi 白居易 (772–846)

Bai Juyi's grandfather and father had served as local officials in the Yangzi region. He thus was from the lower stratum of the Tang social and political elite. However, he was a talented young man. He passed the *jinshi* examination at twenty-eight years of age but decided to participate in a series of special decree examinations in order to speed his advancement in office. Preparing for these in Chang'an, he witnessed the collapse of Wang Shuwen's regime in 805. The next year he passed a prestigious decree examination and received appointment into the Hanlin Academy and then a series of posts in the capital. In 811, his mother died, and he retired to mourn her.[1] He was summoned back to the capital in 814, but the next year, after the chief minister Wu Yuanheng was assassinated, Bai Juyi wrote a memorial demanding that Wu's killers be caught and executed. Given the complexity of the task of dealing with the provincial governors on the eve of a campaign to defeat one of them, the court decided that Bai had overstepped the authority of his position and demoted him to a post in Jiangzhou 江州 (in modern Jiangxi Province). In 817 he was transferred to another regional post, but in 820 after Xianzong's death Bai was recalled to the capital. In 821 Bai participated in retesting the *jinshi* candidates after the accusations of favoritism that started the factional dispute between Li Deyu and Niu Sengru. He failed most of those who had passed in the first exam. The next year he asked for a post in the provinces to escape the tense situation in the capital and was appointed prefect of Hangzhou. For the next twenty years he moved between important posts in Chang'an, Luoyang, and the provinces (he was in Luoyang during the Sweet Dew Incident) and finally retired at the age of seventy-one as the Minister of Justice and Junior Mentor of the Heir Apparent 太子少傅. He spent his final years in Luoyang organizing his collected writings.

As a poet, Bai Juyi's style shifted dramatically over the years. In 806, the year that he passed the decree examination, he wrote the sentimental "Song of Everlasting Regret" 長恨歌 about Emperor Xuanzong's search for Precious Consort Yang's spirit after her death. This poem became his most famous work. Having attained office at court, he produced the morally outraged, radical poems "New *Yuefu*" 新樂府 and "Chants from Qin" 秦中吟 that drew upon the rhetoric and styles advanced by earlier advocates of the poetry of "Restore the Ancient" (*fugu* 復古) like Chen Zi'ang. These poems stressed the didactic function of writing and eschewed all literary embellishment. Then, after being demoted to a local post in Jiangzhou for demanding the capture of Wu Yuanheng's assassins, he developed a more moderate though still highly accessible style and wrote his other old-style verse masterpiece, the "Ballad of the Pipa" 琵琶行. As he grew older, he perfected a simple, "easy" style that made his poetry very popular but also made him a target of mockery in later dynasties.

Like most of the Mid-Tang poets, Bai Juyi considered the locus of poetic meaning a problem. The emotionally charged narrative of "The Song of Eternal Regret" and the didacticism of the "New *Yuefu*" provide two contradictory although strongly human-centered solutions. His later poetry is more nuanced but preserves the centrality of the human subject in interpreting events. In poems like "Song of the Twilight River" and "Autumn Longings" below, for example, Bai uses similes and other modes of comparison to make the human act of interpreting explicit in reading the landscape.

1. In Chinese ritual practice, a son returned home to mourn his mother's or father's death for a period of three years.

"Gazing at the Moon, I Am Moved" by Bai Juyi

[Complete Title]

自河南經亂關內阻饑兄弟離散各在一處。因望月有感，聊書所懷，寄上浮梁大兄，於潛七兄，烏江十五兄，兼示符離及下邽弟妹

Since the land south of the Yellow River has been in chaos and the region within the Passes blocked and suffering famine, we brothers have all dispersed to different places. Gazing at the bright moon, I am moved and would write out my thoughts to send to Eldest Brother at Fuliang, Seventh Brother at Yuqian, and Fifteenth Brother at Wujiang, as well as my younger siblings at Fuli and Xiafeng.[2]

時	難	年	荒	世	業	空 [kʰəwŋ]	The times are calamitous, the year barren,
times	calamity	year	barren	generation	legacy	empty	our patrimony now empty,
弟	兄	羈	旅	各	西	東 [təwŋ]	We brothers in our official travels
brothers		harness	travel	each	west	east	are all sent east and west.
田	園	寥	落	干	戈	後	The fields and gardens of home
fields	gardens	[neglected]		shield	spear	after	are desolate after warfare.
骨	肉	流	離	道	路	中 [truwŋ]	Flesh and blood have drifted
bone	meat	flow	part	way	road	middle	apart in our travels.
弔	影	分	為	千	里	雁	Lamenting our shadows, we divided
lament	shadow	divide	become	thousand	*li*	goose	to become thousand-*li* geese.
辭	根	散	作	九	秋	蓬 [bəwŋ]	Parting from the stem, we scattered to act
leave	stem	scatter	act as	nine	autumn	tumbleweed	as tumbleweeds of the Ninth Month.[3]
共	看	明	月	應	垂	淚	Together looking at the bright
together	look	bright	moon	ought	hang	tears	moon, we surely all drip tears:
一	夜	鄉	心	五	處	同 [dəwŋ]	For one night, our homeward hearts
one	night	home	heart	five	place	share	in five places are all the same.

Study Notes and Questions

1. This is an early regulated-verse poem, written when Bai Juyi was twenty-eight. Note the combination of intense emotion and formal control. Note also that this is a poem of the social realm, in which the landscape plays no significant role.

2. Look carefully at the parallelism in the middle couplets. Explain, phrase by phrase, how the parallelism works.

---

2. In 799 the troops of a military governor in Jiangnan mutineed after his death. The rebellion was joined by other southern troops and proved difficult to suppress. Because of this, little rice from the region arrived in Chang'an, which was suffering from drought and famine.

3. The Ninth Month is the last month of autumn.

From the "New *Yuefu*," with Preface, by Bai Juyi

序曰：凡九千二百五十二言，斷為五十篇。篇無定句，句無定字。繫於意，不繫於文。首句標其目，卒章顯其志，詩三百之義也。其辭質而徑，欲見之者易諭也；其言直而切，欲聞之者深誡也；其事覈而實，使采之者傳信也；其體順而律，可以播於樂章歌曲也。總而言之，為君、為臣、為民、為物、為事而作，不為文而作也。

In all, there are 9,252 characters divided into 50 pieces. The pieces do not have set line [lengths]; the lines do not have a set [number] of characters. They are bound by intention, not by aesthetic concerns. The first line announces the theme; the final stanza reveals their intent: [this follows] the normative meaning of the *Canon of Poetry*. Their phrasing is plain and direct, easy to understand for those who wish to see. Their words are straight and apt: those who wish to hear are deeply warned. Their events are verified and real, allowing those who select them to transmit them with confidence. Their form is flowing and rhythmic and can be set to music. In sum, these were composed for the sake of the ruler, for the officials, for the populace, for objects and events and were not composed for aesthetic ends.[4]

賣炭翁
苦宮市也

The Old Charcoal Seller
The Hardship of Palace Requisitions

賣	炭	翁 [ʔəwŋ]					The old charcoal seller
sell	charcoal	graybeard					
伐	薪	燒	炭	南	山	中 [triwŋ]	Cuts kindling, makes charcoal in the South Mountains.
cut	kindling	burn	charcoal	south	mountains	middle	
滿	面	塵	灰	煙	火	色 [ʂəə̆k]	His face full of dust and ash, appearing like smoke and fire.
full	face	dust	ash	smoke	fire	appearance	
兩	鬢	蒼	蒼	十	指	黑 [həə̆k]	His temples are hoary and his ten fingers black.
pair	temples	hoary	hoary	ten	fingers	black	
賣	炭	得	錢	何	所	營	Selling charcoal, getting cash, what does he plan?
sell	charcoal	get	cash	what	[d.o.]	plan	
身	上	衣	裳	口	中	食 [ʂɦiə̆k]	Clothes on his body, and food for his mouth.
body	on	clothes	clothes	mouth	middle	eat	
可	憐	身	上	衣	正	單 [tan]	It is so sad that the clothes on his body are now thin.
can be	pity	body	on	clothes	just now	single	
心	憂	炭	賤	願	天	寒 [xɦan]	His heart grieves that charcoal is cheap: he prays for cold skies.
heart	grieve	charcoal	cheap	wish	sky	cold	
夜	來	城	外	一	尺	雪 [syat]	After nightfall, there is a foot of snow outside the city wall.
night	come	city wall	outside	one	*chi*	snow	

4. The preface was written in 809 when Bai Juyi was serving as a Left Reminder (rank 8b), a relatively low-ranking court official charged with finding mistakes in official documents in both their wording and content.

曉 dawn	駕 ride	炭 charcoal	車 cart	輾 turn	冰 ice	轍 [trɦiat] rut	At dawn he mounts his charcoal cart rumbling through icy ruts.
牛 ox	困 in straits	人 person	饑 hungry	日 sun	已 already	高 high	His ox stuggles; he is hungry; the sun already is high.
市 market	南 south	門 gate	外 outside	泥 mud	中 middle	歇 [xiat] exhaust	Outside the market's south gate he rests in the mud.
翩 elegant and stylish	翩	兩 pair	騎 rider	來 come	是 is	誰 [ʂɦyj] who	Who are the pair of stylish horsemen who come:
黃 yellow	衣 clothes	使 envoy	者 [person]	白 white	衫 shirt	兒 [ri] youth	A yellow-clothed envoy and his white-shirted lad.[5]
手 hand	把 grasp	文 text	書 writing	口 mouth	稱 cite	敕 [trʰiə̆k] edict	In his hand he holds a document, his mouth cites an edict.
迴 turn	車 cart	叱 yell at	牛 ox	牽 drag	向 toward	北 [puə̆k] north	He turns the cart, shouting at the ox, pulling it toward the north.[6]
一 one	車 cart	炭 charcoal					One cart of charcoal,
千 thousand	餘 remain	斤 jin					Over five hundred pounds.
宮 palace	使 envoy	驅 gallop	將 take	惜 lament	不 not	得 [təə̆k] obtain	The palace officer appropriated it: there was no point regretting.
半 half	疋 bolt	紅 red	紗 silk	一 one	丈 *zhang*	綾 damask	Half a bolt of red silk, several yards of damask:
繫 tie	向 toward	牛 ox	頭 head	充 fill	炭 charcoal	直 [trɦiə̆k] place	Tied to the ox's head to fulfill the value of the charcoal.

Study Notes and Questions

1. Does this poem meet the guidelines Bai Juyi set for himself in the preface?

2. Although the English translation perhaps makes the difference difficult to see, this poem is not as self-consciously prosy as the more radically "old-style" poetry written by Li Bai and other Tang writers. Compare this, for example, to Han Yu's early poems included in this chapter. However, Bai Juyi uses genuinely vernacular language: the word "to take" 將 in the phrase "The palace official appropriated it" 宮使驅將 is a proto-Mandarin "resultative" construction, a verb phrase combining an action and result.

5. The yellow shirt indicates that this is a palace eunuch.

6. That is, the eunuch is requisitioning the charcoal for the palace.

"Inscribed Again" by Bai Juyi

重題							Inscribed Again[7]
日	高	睡	足	猶	慵	起	The sun is high; I've slept enough,
sun	high	sleep	enough	still	lazy	rise	but I'm too lazy to rise.
小	閣	重	衾	不	怕	寒 [ɣan]	In this small chamber, with my doubled
small	pavilion	double	coverlet	not	fear	cold	coverlets, I don't fear the cold.
遺	爱	寺	鐘	欹	枕	聽	The bell of the Temple of [Buddha's] Bestowed
bestow	love	temple	bell	prop	pillow	listen	Love: I listen propped on my pillow.
香	爐	峰	雪	撥	簾	看 [k^{h}an]	The snow on Incense Burner Peak:
incense	burner	peak	snow	pull	screen	look	I pull up the screen to look at it.
匡	廬	便	是	逃	名	地	Kuang Lu is indeed a place for
Kuang	Lu	just	is	flee	fame	place	fleeing into anonymity.
司	馬	仍	為	送	老	官 [kwan]	An adjutant is still a post at which
Adjutant		still	become	see off	old age	position	one can spend one's old age.
心	泰	身	寧	是	歸	處	Anywhere my mind is peaceful, my
heart	peaceful	body	at ease	this is	return	place	body at ease is a place for return:
故	鄉	何	獨	在	長	安 [ʔan]	Why must my hometown be
old	home	why	alone	is at	Chang-	-an	Chang'an alone?

STUDY NOTES AND QUESTIONS

1. This regulated verse poem develops Bai Juyi's somewhat lazy and easily contented persona. In part, he is putting his demotion to a locale far from the capital in a positive light. Still, his stated resolution to be at peace and discover the joys of Jiangzhou is a distinctive approach.

2. Note that this is a tourist's poem: the scenery serves as an object of aesthetic contemplation but has no significance beyond this. In sharp contrast to Du Fu, Bai Juyi does not "read" the landscape for immanent patterns of which he is a part.

7. This poem was written on the wall of Bai's house in the spring of 817 in Jiangzhou, where he had been exiled and was serving as an adjutant with no actual duties. The various places mentioned in the poem are in the vicinity of Jiangzhou. The Temple of Remaining Love (or perhaps Temple of Leaving Love Behind) is on Incense Burner Peak, which in turn is part of Mt. Lu (a.k.a. Kuang Lu), an important Buddhist site.

"Asking Liu Nineteen" by Bai Juyi

問劉十九					Asking Liu Nineteen[8]
綠 green	螘 ant	新 new	醅 brew	酒 wine	The green ants of newly brewed ale,[9]
紅 red	泥 clay	小 small	火 fire	爐 [luǝ̆] brazier	A small brazier of red clay;
晚 late	來 come	天 sky	欲 will	雪 snow	Since evening, the sky has been about to snow:
能 can	飲 drink	一 one	杯 cup	無 [ʋuǝ̆] not	Can you come drink a cup or not?

Witter Bynner's Translation

A Suggestion to My Friend Liu

There's a gleam of green in an old bottle,
There's a stir of red in the quiet stove,
There's a feeling of snow in the dusk outside—
What about a cup of wine inside?

8. Liu Nineteen was a friend who lived in Jiangzhou while Bai Juyi was in exile there. This poem was written in the winter of 817.

9. The "green ants" are the slightly green clumps of scum and rice that float on the top of unfiltered rice ale as it brews.

"Song of the Twilight River" by Bai Juyi

暮江吟							Song of the Twilight River[10]
一	道	殘	陽	鋪	水	中 [truwŋ]	One path of fading sunlight in the middle of the Pu River:
one	road	remnant	sunlight	Pu	River	middle	
半	江	瑟	瑟	半	江	紅 [ɣəwŋ]	Half the river is dark green, half the river is red.
half	river	dark green		half	river	red	
可	憐	九	月	初	三	夜	Delightful is the third night of the Ninth Month:
can be	loved	nine	month	first	three	night	
露	似	真	珠	月	似	弓 [kuwŋ]	The dew resembles pearls, and the moon resembles a bow.
dew	resemble	real	pearl	moon	resemble	bow	

STUDY NOTES AND QUESTIONS

1. This fine quatrain shows traces of Mid-Tang self-consciousness. Bai Juyi writes to capture the transient beauty of a late autumn sunset. Yet the scene is a moment in human experience, an aesthetic gaze, given its meaning by the active appreciation of the poet rather than hinting at meanings beyond the human that Bai Juyi just happens to come upon. Compare this poem, for example, to Du Mu's "Traveling in the Mountains" (p. 338).

2. Months in China were *lunar* months, where the first day was the new moon. What would the moon look like on the third day of the month? How does it resemble a bow?

3. What is the quality of mood and tone in the poem?

10. Bai Juyi probably wrote the poem in 822 as he was heading to his post in Hangzhou.

"Autumn Longings" by Bai Juyi

秋思					Autumn Longings
夕 dusk	照 gleam	紅 redder	於 than	燒 brushfire	The sunset gleam is redder than brushfire.
晴 clear	空 void	碧 blue	勝 beats	藍 [lam] indigo	The clear-sky void is bluer than indigo.
獸 beast	形 shape	雲 cloud	不 not	一 one	Animal shapes: the clouds are not as one.
弓 bow	勢 force	月 moon	初 first	三 [sam] three	The force of a bow: the moon on the third day of the month.
雁 goose	思 long	來 come	天 sky	北 north	Goose-stirred longings come from the north region of the sky.
砧 pounder	愁 sorrow	滿 fill	水 water	南 [nam] south	The sorrow of the fulling block fills the land south of the Yangzi.
蕭 spare and sere	條	秋 autumn	氣 air	味 mood	The sere mood of the autumn air:
未 not yet	老 old	已 already	深 deep	諳 [ʔam] familiar	Even before I've turned old, I'm deeply used to it.

Study Notes and Questions

1. "Autumn Longings" was a well-established poetic theme by the time Bai wrote this poem, and part of the interest in such a poem is how it develops the theme in a new way. What role do the first four lines play in establishing the poet's situation and introducing "autumn longings?"

2. In line 5, what is a "goose-stirred longing"? (Think back to Yu Xin's "Again Parting with Secretarial Minister Zhou" [chapter 5]; Yu Jianwu's "Responding to Command: Spring Night" [chapter 5]; and Du Fu's "Lone Goose" [chapter 7], for example.) The parallel phrase in line 6 is the "sorrow of the fulling block." Fulling blocks were used to pound wet cloth to thicken it for winter use. Here, preparing clothes points to absent husbands for whom the clothing is being readied.

3. What does Bai Juyi mean by lamenting that he already has gotten used to the sere mood of autumn?

"Aboard a Boat, Reading the Poems of Yuan Nine" by Bai Juyi

舟中讀元九詩							Aboard a Boat, Reading the Poems of Yuan Nine
把 take	君 your	詩 poems	卷 scroll	燈 lamp	前 before	讀 read	I take your scroll of poems and read them before the lamp.
詩 poems	盡 exhaust	燈 lamp	殘 remnant	天 sky	未 not yet	明 [miajŋ] bright	The poems come to an end, the lamp gutters, and still the sky is not light.
眼 eyes	痛 hurt	滅 put out	燈 lamp	猶 still	闇 dark	坐 sit	My eyes hurt, I put out the lamp, and remain sitting in darkness:
逆 head-	風 -wind	吹 blow	浪 waves	打 hit	船 boat	聲 [ɕiajŋ] sound	A headwind blows up waves: the sound as they hit the boat.

ANNA M. SHIELDS'S TRANSLATION

Reading Yuan Ninth's Poems aboard a Boat

By the lamp, I take your scroll of poems in hand to read;
as the poems end, the lamp burns down—the sky not yet light.
My eyes aching, I put out the lamp, yet sit still in darkness—
sounds of waves, blown by a headwind, beating against the boat.

STUDY NOTES AND QUESTIONS

This poem was written to Yuan Zhen while Bai Juyi was en route to his exile in Jiangzhou in 815. Yuan Zhen's answering poem (translated by Anna M. Shields) is:

酬樂天舟泊夜讀微之詩	*Responding to Letian's Poem on Reading My Poems at Night on a Moored Boat*
知君暗泊西江岸	I know that you moored in darkness on the western riverbank,
讀我閑詩欲到明	reading my poems of idleness almost until daybreak.
今夜通州還不睡	This night in Tongzhou I still cannot sleep—
滿山風雨杜鵑聲	through wind and rain in the mountains, the sound of cuckoos.

The beauty of the poem, and its challenge, is in the last line in relation to the first three. Consider Yuan Zhen's answering poem as a form of interpretation. What is the role of the final images in the two poems?

"Ballad of the *Pipa*," with Preface, by Bai Juyi

元和十年，予左遷九江郡司馬。明年秋，送客湓浦口。聞船中夜彈琵琶者，聽其音，錚錚然有京都聲。問其人，本長安倡女。嘗學琵琶於穆、曹二善才，年長色衰，委身為賈人婦。遂命酒，使快彈數曲。曲罷憫然。自敘少小時歡樂事，今漂淪憔悴，轉徙於江湖間。予出官二年，恬然自安，感斯人言，是夕始覺有遷謫意。因為長句，歌以贈之，凡六百一十二言，命曰琵琶行。

In the tenth year of the Yuanhe era (815), I was demoted to the position of adjutant in Jiujiang Prefecture. The next autumn, I was bidding farewell to a guest on the bank of the Pen River. We heard the playing of a *pipa* in a boat that night. As we listened to the music, it had the thrumming sound of the capital. When we asked the player, she originally had been a courtesan in Chang'an. She had studied with the two virtuosos Mu and Cao, but when she grew older and her looks declined, she entrusted herself to become a merchant's wife. I then ordered ale and had her play several tunes. When the tunes had finished, she was pensive: she described the pleasures of her youth, and that now she was adrift and haggard with want. She by turns arrived in the region of rivers and lakes. I had been serving out of the capital for two years, had adjusted, and was content. Moved by this person's words, this evening I began to feel my exile. Because of this, I composed a long poem for her, sang and presented it to her, in all 612 characters, and entitled it "The Ballad of the *Pipa*."

琵琶行							Ballad of the *Pipa*[11]
潯 Xun-	陽 -yang	江 river	頭 head	夜 night	送 see off	客 [kʰaijk] traveler	On the bank of Xunyang River, seeing off a guest at night,[12]
楓 maple	葉 leaf	荻 reed	花 flower	秋 autumn	索 rustle	索 [sak]	The maple leaves and reed plumes in autumn rustled.
主 host	人 person	下 get down	馬 horse	客 traveler	在 is at	船 [ʑwian] boat	The host got off his horse; the guest was on the boat.
舉 lift	酒 ale	欲 about to	飲 drink	無 in no	管 pipe	絃 [ɣɛn] string	Raising their wine cups, about to drink, they were without music.
醉 drunk	不 not	成 complete	歡 joy	慘 dejected	將 about to	別 [biat] separate	Tipsy, they felt no joy; dejected, they were about to part.
別 separate	時 time	茫 vast and vague	茫	江 river	浸 drench	月 [ŋuat] moon	At the time to part, vast and vague, the river drenched the moon.
忽 sudden	聞 hear	水 water	上 on	琵 pi-	琶 -pa	聲 sound	Suddenly, on the water, they heard the sound of a *pipa*.

11. In 814 the independent northern military governors Li Shidao and Wang Chengzong sent assassins to Chang'an, where they killed the hard-line minister Wu Yuanheng. This was part of a campaign to disrupt the reconquest of Huaixi 淮西. Bai was demoted for demanding that the crime be avenged. Jiujiang 九江 is another name for Jiangzhou, in modern Jiangxi Province. Bai was forty-five when he wrote this.

12. Xunyang 潯陽 River leads from Pengli Lake 彭蠡湖 to the Yangzi.

8	主 host	人 person	忘 forget	歸 return	客 traveler	不 not	發 [puat] set off	The host forgot about returning; the traveler did not set out.
	尋 seek	聲 sound	暗 dark	問 ask	彈 play	者 -er	誰 [dʑwi] who	Following the sound, they discreetly asked who the player was.
	琵 pi-	琶 -pa	聲 sound	停 stop	欲 about to	語 speak	遲 [dri] delay	The sound of the *pipa* stopped; about to speak, she paused.
	移 move	船 boat	相 mutually	近 draw near	邀 invite	相 mutually	見 [kɛn^h] see	We moved our boat closer, invited her to meet us.
12	添 add	酒 ale	迴 return	燈 lamp	重 again	開 open	宴 [ʔɛn^h] banquet	We added more ale, relit the lamps, and again set out a banquet.
	千 thousand	呼 call	萬 10,000	喚 shout	始 start to	出 come out	來 come	After a thousand calls, ten thousand shouts, she started to come out.
	猶 still	抱 embrace	琵 pi-	琶 -pa	半 half	遮 block	面 [mjian^h] face	Still her arms held the *pipa*, half covering her face.
	轉 turn	軸 peg	撥 pluck	絃 string	三 three	兩 two	聲 [ɕiajŋ] sound	She turned the pegs, plucked the strings for two or three notes.
16	未 not yet	成 complete	曲 tune	調 tune	先 first	有 there is	情 [dziajŋ] emotion	Not yet starting her tune, the feeling was already there.
	絃 string	絃 string	掩 hide	抑 press	聲 sound	聲 sound	思 [si^h] longing	String after string pressed and pulled, sound upon sound of longing,
	似 resemble	訴 inform	平 level	生 life	不 not	得 attain	意 [ʔi^h] intent	As if to recount a lifetime of aspirations not attained.
	低 lower	眉 eyebrow	信 trust	手 hand	續 continue	續 continue	彈 play	With lowered brows, trusting her hands, on and on she played,
20	說 explain	盡 exhaust	心 heart	中 middle	無 is no	限 limit	事 [dʑi^h] matter	She completely explored the boundless matters of the heart.
	輕 light	攏 press	慢 slow	撚 twist	抹 stroke	復 again	挑 [thɛw] pluck	Lightly pressing, slowly twisting, she strummed and plucked.
	初 at first	為 make	霓 rainbow	裳 skirt	後 after	六 six	么 [ʔɛw] yao	At first she played "Rainbow Skirts," and then "Green Waists."[13]
	大 large	絃 string	嘈 din	嘈 din	如 resemble	急 urgent	雨 [wuă'] rain	The large strings drummed like hard rain.
24	小 small	絃 string	切 light and fine	切	如 resemble	私 private	語 [ŋiă'] speaking	The small strings chirruped like a private conversation.

13. "Rainbow Skirts and Feather Cloaks" was a dance tune that Emperor Xuanzong (r. 713–56) found pleasing. It is strongly associated with the besotted sensuality of the end of Xuanzong's reign.

嘈	嘈	切	切	錯	雜	彈 [dan]	Drumming and chirruping mixed as she played:
din	din	light and fine		interlace	mix	play	
大	珠	小	珠	落	玉	盤 [ban]	Large pearls, small pearls falling onto a jade platter.
big	pearl	small	pearl	fall	jade	platter	
間	關	鶯	語	花	底	滑	The warbler's softly turning voice flowed smoothly under the blossoms.
bird-call		warbler	speaking	flowers	below	glide	
幽	咽	泉	流	冰	下	難 [nan]	The hidden sobs of springs and rills barely moved beneath the ice.
secluded	sob	spring	flow	ice	below	difficult	
冰	泉	冷	澀	絃	疑	絕 [dzwiat]	Icy springs congealed with cold, the string seemed to end.
ice	spring	cold	rough	string	suspect	cut off	
疑	絕	不	通	聲	暫	歇 [xɨat]	Seeming to end, unable to go on, the sound for a while ceased.
suspect	cut off	not	penetrate	sound	sound	cease	
別	有	幽	愁	暗	恨	生 [ʂiajŋ]	There was a new sense of inward grief; a hidden regret took shape.
separate	there is	secluded	sorrow	dark	regret	is born	
此	時	無	聲	勝	有	聲 [ɕiajŋ]	At this time, there being no sound was better than having sound.
this	time	is no	sound	defeat	there is	sound	
銀	瓶	乍	破	水	漿	迸	A silver vase suddenly breaks; liquid pours forth.
silver	vase	suddenly	break	water	broth	disperse	
鐵	騎	突	出	刀	槍	鳴 [miajŋ]	Iron-clad horsemen rush out; knives and spears sing.
iron	rider	spring out	come out	knife	spear	sing out	
曲	終	收	撥	當	心	畫 [ɣwɛːk]	The tune ends; taking the plectrum, she strikes across the middle:
tune	end	gather	plectrum	is at	heart	stroke	
四	絃	一	聲	如	裂	帛 [bɛːk]	Four strings, in one sound, like the ripping of silk.
four	string	one	sound	resemble	rip	silk	
東	舟	西	舫	悄	無	言	The boats to the east and west were silent, without speech.
east	boat	west	catamaran	silent	is not	speak	
唯	見	江	心	秋	月	白 [bɛːk]	We only saw in the center of the river the autumn moon so white.
only	see	river	heart	autumn	moon	white	
沉	吟	放	撥	插	絃	中 [truwŋ]	Deep in thought, she placed the plectrum between the strings.
ponder in doubt		place	plectrum	stick	string	middle	
整	頓	衣	裳	起	斂	容 [juawŋ]	Straightening her clothes, she rose and put on a serious expression.
straighten	shake	clothing		rise	gather	mien	
自	言	本	是	京	城	女 [nrɨə̆^{h}]	She said of herself, "Originally I was a girl from Chang'an.
of itself	say	origin	is	capital	city	girl	

	家	在	蝦	蟆	陵	下	住 [druă^{h}]	My house was at the foot of Toad Mound.[14]
	house	is at	toad		mound	below	reside	
	十	三	學	得	琵	琶	成	At thirteen, I had mastered the *pipa*.
	ten +	three	learn	attain	pi-	-pa	complete	
44	名	屬	教	坊	第	一	部 [bɔʼ]	My name was enrolled in the first rank of the Music School.
	name	attach	instruction	place	[rank]	one	section	
	曲	罷	曾	教	善	才	伏 [buw^{h}]	When my tune ended, I caused even the virtuosos to submit.
	tune	stop	once	compel	fine	talent	submit	
	妝	成	每	被	秋	娘	妒 [tɔ^{h}]	With my makeup complete, I made Qiuniang jealous.[15]
	makeup	complete	each time	incur	Qiu-	niang	jealous	
	五	陵	年	少	爭	纏	頭	The rich youths from the suburbs vied to wrap my hair with silk.
	five	tumulus	year	few	compete	wrap	head	
48	一	曲	紅	綃	不	知	數 [ʂuə̆^{h}]	For one song, they offered countless bolts of fine red silk.
	one	tune	red	fine silk	not	know	number	
	鈿	頭	雲	篦	擊	節	碎	Inlaid combs of silver, I shattered in beating out the rhythm.
	inlaid	head	cloud	comb	beat	rhythm	shatter	
	血	色	羅	裙	翻	酒	污 [ʔɔ^{h}]	My blood-colored filmy skirt was stained with overturned ale.
	blood	color	gauze	skirt	overturn	ale	stain	
	今	年	歡	笑	復	明	年	The joy and laughter of this year will come again next year.
	now	year	joy	laugh	again	next	year	
52	秋	月	春	風	等	閑	度 [dɔ^{h}]	The autumn moon and spring wind passed in idleness.
	autumn	moon	spring	wind	await	idle	cross	
	弟	走	從	軍	阿	姨	死	My younger brother ran off to join the army; my "aunt" died.
	brother	run	follow	army	aunt		die	
	暮	去	朝	來	顏	色	故 [kɔ^{h}]	Dusks departed, dawns came, and my appearance grew old.
	sunset	leave	dawn	arrive	appearance	color	old	
	門	前	冷	落	鞍	馬	稀	My gates became desolate, horses and riders few.
	gate	before	cold	fallen	saddle	horse	few	
56	老	大	嫁	作	商	人	婦 [buwʼ]	Having grown older, I married to become a merchant's wife.
	old	mature	marry into	make	merchant	person	wife	
	商	人	重	利	輕	別	離	Merchants value profit and think little of partings.
	merchant	person	treat heavy	profit	treat light	part	separate	

14. Toad Mound 蝦蟆陵 supposedly was the burial site of Dong Zhongshu 董仲舒, the important Han dynasty Confucian scholar. It originally was called Dismount Horse Mound 下馬陵 (*xiama*, close homophone to "toad," *hama*) because everyone dismounted to show their respect.

15. Qiuniang 秋娘 (Autumn Maid) was Du Qiuniang 杜秋娘, a famous performer who became one of Muzong's consorts. The phrase became a standard way to refer to "famous geishas."

前 former	月 month	浮 Fu-	梁 -liang	買 buy	茶 tea	去 [k^hɨə̆’] leave	Last month he left to buy tea at Fuliang.[16]
去 leave	來 since	江 river	口 mouth	守 maintain	空 empty	船 [ʑwian] boat	Since he left, I have maintained an empty boat by the river.
繞 encircle	船 boat	月 moon	明 bright	江 river	水 water	寒 [ɣan] cold	Surrounding the boat, the moon was bright, the river water cold.
夜 night	深 deep	忽 suddenly	夢 dream	少 few	年 year	事 event	Late at night, suddenly I dreamt of events of my youth.
夢 dream	啼 weep	妝 makeup	淚 tears	紅 red	闌 interweave	干 [kan]	In my dream I cried tears stained with rouge, red streaming down.”
我 I	聞 hear	琵 pi-	琶 -pa	已 already	歎 sigh	息 [sik] breathe	When I first heard the *pipa*, I already sighed with sorrow.
又 again	聞 hear	此 this	語 speak	重 doubled	唧 sighing	唧 [tsik]	Now, hearing these words, my sighs grew yet deeper.
同 share	是 is	天 heaven	涯 shore	淪 drift aimlessly	落	人 person	We both have sunk into oblivion at the edge of the Heavens.
相 mutually	逢 meet	何 what	必 must	曾 once	相 mutually	識 [ɕik] know	Meeting one another, why must we have known one another?
我 I	從 from	去 last	年 year	辭 take leave	帝 emperor	京 [kiajŋ] capital	I have taken leave of the capital since last year,
謫 exile	居 reside	臥 lie down	病 sick	潯 Xun-	陽 -yang	城 [dʑiajŋ] city	Living in exile, abed with sickness in the city of Xunyang.
潯 Xun-	陽 yang	小 small	處 place	無 is no	音 tone	樂 music	Xunyang is an insignificant place without music.
終 end	歲 year	不 not	聞 hear	絲 silk	竹 bamboo	聲 [ɕiajŋ] sound	Through the year one does not hear the sound of pipes or strings.
住 reside	近 come near	湓 Pen	江 river	地 land	低 low	濕 damp	I live near the Pen River: the land is low and damp.
黃 yellow	蘆 reed	苦 bitter	竹 bamboo	繞 encircle	宅 house	生 [ʂiajŋ] is born	Yellow reeds and bitter bamboo surround my house.
其 their	間 midst	旦 dawn	暮 dusk	聞 hear	何 what	物 thing	In the midst of this, from dawn to dusk what do I hear?
杜 cuckoo	鵑	啼 weep	哭 cry	猿 gibbon	哀 lament	鳴 [miajŋ] call out	Cuckoos weep, and gibbons wail.

16. Fuliang 浮梁 was another name for Raozhou 饒州 (Jingdezhen in modern Jiangxi Province), a marketing center for the tea trade in the Tang dynasty.

	春	江	花	朝	秋	月	夜	Mornings of flowers on the spring river, nights of autumn moon,
	spring	river	flower	morning	autumn	moon	night	
76	往	往	取	酒	還	獨	傾 [k^{h}jwiajŋ]	From time to time I would take ale and pour it out alone.
	from time to time		take	ale	and	alone	tip	
	豈	無	山	歌	與	村	笛	How could there not be mountain songs and hamlet piping?
	how	is no	mountain	song	and	village	flute	
	歐	啞	嘲	哳	難	為	聽 [t^{h}ɛjŋ]	Its babble and screech are impossible to listen to.
	babbling		screeching		impossible	enact	listen	
	今	夜	聞	君	琵	琶	語	Tonight, hearing your tale of the *pipa*,
	now	night	hear	you	pi-	-pa	speak	
80	如	聽	仙	樂	耳	暫	明 [miajŋ]	Was like hearing immortals' music: my ears momentarily cleared.
	resemble	listen	ascendant	music	ears	temporary	clear	
	莫	辭	更	坐	彈	一	曲	Don't decline to again sit and play one more tune.
	don't	decline	anew	sit	play	one	tune	
	為	君	翻	作	琵	琶	行 [ɣaijŋ]	For you, I shall compose a "Ballad of the *Pipa*."
	for	you	in turn	compose	pi-	-pa	ballad	
	感	我	此	言	良	久	立 [lip]	Moved by these words of mine, she stood for a long while,
	moved by	my	this	say	truly	long	stand	
84	卻	坐	促	絃	絃	轉	急 [kip]	Then sat, tightened the strings; the strings became more urgent.
	return	sit	tighten	string	string	turn	urgent	
	淒	淒	不	似	向	前	聲	Its desolate sorrow did not resemble the former sound.
	desolate		not	resemble	former	before	sound	
	滿	座	重	聞	皆	掩	泣 [k^{h}ip]	The entire gathering, hearing it again, all wiped away tears.
	full	seat	doubled	hear	all	wipe	tears	
	就	中	泣	下	誰	最	多	In the group, whose falling tears were the most?
	arrive	middle	tear	go down	who	most	many	
88	江	州	司	馬	青	衫	濕 [ɕip]	The adjutant of Jiangzhou's blue clothes were drenched.
	Jiang-	-zhou	adjutant		blue	shirt	moist	

Study Notes and Questions

This is one of the greatest poems in the Chinese tradition, but it is not readily accessible to Western readers. One important context, for example, is the conventional theory of music that is closely related to the canonical view of poetry. The "Record of Music" from the *Record of Rites*, dating from the late Warring States or early Han, presents an initial version of the theory that in turn served as the basis for the "Great Preface" of the *Canon of Poetry*. The "Record of Music" stresses that music is to give inner order to the emotions that inevitably are stirred in people's encounters with objects and events in the world. Music restores harmony by finding proper external expression for the feelings within. Thus, at the very beginning of the "Ballad of the *Pipa*," the narrator explains that the farewell party was close to failing for want of music to allow the host and guests to dispel the sorrow of parting. The party's encounter with the pipa player happened by chance but was extremely welcome, and both their effort to dispel sorrow and their delight in finding music frame the story.

Another underlying context is the idea of the "one who knows the sound" (*zhiyin* 知音), meaning one who has a deep, intuitive knowledge of another person's heart. The source of this important term is an early story about the playing of a zither (*qin* 琴) meeting its ideal listener.

1. This long poem breaks into five parts with a short coda. Part 1 ends on line 14, part 2 on line 38, part 3 on line 52, part 4 on line 62, and part 5 on line 82.

2. Mid-Tang poets took great interest in the challenge of capturing musical performance in poetry. Du Fu's "Observing Mistress Gongsun's Disciple Dancing the Sword Dance" is one early example; Li He also wrote on the theme in such poems as "Song of Li Ping Playing the Harp." In "Ballad of the *Pipa*" lines 19–36 give a virtuoso description of the music. Try to imagine the music associated with each image that Bai Juyi offers. Also try to imagine the playing and what Bai meant by the line, "At this time, there being no sound was better than having sound." Note that when the *pipa* player starts a new song at the end of the poem, Bai states, "Its desolate sorrow did not resemble the former sound" and that the power of the song reduces its audience to tears, but he makes no attempt to describe the music. Why not?

3. The moon first appears in the poem in line 6. Note its reappearance directly following the end of the musical section. What is the effect of this intensely quiet visual image at this point of transition?

4. The narrative of the *pipa* player's life relies on accepted images of the arc of the life of a Chang'an female musician. She is precocious in youth, leads a wild, colorful, heedless life in her prime, but eventually confronts decline and solitude before drifting off. Does the generic nature of her story detract from the impact of that story on her audience or does it add to the emotion?

5. Bai Juyi in the next section explicitly compares his life with that of the *pipa* player. In the preface he states, "I had been serving out of the capital for two years, had adjusted, and was content. Moved by this person's words, this evening I began to feel my exile." Music gives shape to unresolved feelings within: is Bai's reawakened sorrow good or bad, given what he writes in the poem?

6. What claim is Bai Juyi making in saying that he cried the most?

Han Yu 韓愈 (768–824)

Han Yu, like Bai Juyi, was from a family with a record of local service on the periphery of the elite stratum. His father died when he was three, but he was taken care of by his much older brother Han Hui 韓會, who was twenty-eight at the time. Han Hui was caught up in the spectacular collapse of chief minister Yuan Zai's regime during Emperor Daizong's 代宗 reign and in 779 was exiled to a post in Guangdong. Han Yu accompanied his brother to Guangdong, but Han Hui died there two years later, and Han Yu went to live at the estate of his mother's clan in Xuancheng 宣城 (in modern Hubei Province). Han Yu spent the rest of his early years at the estate, but left when he was nineteen to see more of the world and to search for patronage before taking the *jinshi* examination. He passed the examination in 792 at age twenty-five. Since the *jinshi* examination merely made one eligible for office rather than guaranteeing an office, Han Yu, like Bai Juyi, participated in the higher round of decree examinations. Unlike Bai, however, Han Yu failed it three years in a row. Nonetheless, he attracted the attention of Dong Jin, the military governor of Bian-Song Province, to whose staff he received an appointment in 796. He served in Bianzhou 汴州 (modern Kaifeng) until Dong's death in 799, after which he joined the staff of Zhang Jianfeng, the military governor of Xuzhou 徐州 (in modern Jiangsu Province). Having established himself in regional service, Han Yu eventually managed to receive a post in the capital. He was, however, an outspoken official who took his duty to remonstrate seriously and spent the rest of his career moving back and forth between increasingly distant exile and increasingly more important official positions both in the capital and in the provinces. Perhaps his most famous contretemps was his memorial against Xianzong's plan to honor relics of the Buddha's bones, which in its sweeping attack on the history of imperial patronage of Buddhism in Chinese history was deemed to move from honest disagreement to slander. He was sent off to serve as the prefect of Chaozhou 潮州 in Guangdong, where he wrote his equally famous order telling the alligators they needed to leave his prefecture. He was soon transferred to a nearer prefecture (Yuanzhou in modern Jiangxi Province) and then recalled to his former post in the capital. He retired because of illness from the office of Vice Director of the Ministry of Personnel at age fifty-seven and died soon after.

Han Yu was a leading cultural figure during Xianzong's reign. Literary historians usually describe him as the leader of the "Restore the Ancient" (*fugu* 復古) school of prose, but his actual role is broader than that of an arbiter of style. Han Yu, like many other literati of the period, became convinced that the moral failures of the elite during the An Lushan Rebellion and more recent regimes required a renewed commitment to the foundational Confucian values embodied in the early texts. Many layers of accumulated tradition and practice had to be jettisoned. He argued for this paring-away in his policy analyses and memorials, and he drew on it in his own writings in both prose and poetry. In poetry in particular, his discontent with the bland practices of the post-rebellion court led him to champion the highly individualized poetry of Li Bai and Du Fu and, in his own verse, to experiment with a wide range of techniques. His wild old-style poems, like "So Hurried" 忽忽, derived from Li Bai but pushed the style further. He also wrote a series of fabulously imaginative long old-style poems that hearken more to the Han *fu* than to any more recent writing. In both cases, meaning flows out from the active imagination of the author, and the world of phenomena has meaning imposed on it rather than discovered in it. Some of his later poems, like "Autumn Thoughts" 秋懷 and the very late "First Floating on South Creek" 始泛南溪, present a quiet humanism: he is not fighting the landscape but looking to his own internal resources for moving about in it and recreating the human community.

Another important role Han Yu played as a cultural leader was that of patron. He was friends with and supported the poetic efforts of a group of the most distinctive and talented writers of the period, including Meng Jiao, Zhang Ji 張籍 (767–830), Jia Dao, Li He, and others.

"So Hurried" by Han Yu

忽忽

忽	忽	乎	余	未	知	生	之	為	樂	也
hurry	hurry	!	I	not yet	know	life	's	make	merry	is
願	脫	去	而	無	因 [ʔjin]					
desire	shed	leave	but	without	means					
安	得	長	翮	大	翼	如	雲	生	我	身 [ʂin]
how	obtain	long	pinions	big	wings	like	clouds	grow	my	body
乘	風	振	奮	出	六	合	絕	浮	塵 [trɦin]	
ride	wind	stir	shake	go out	six	compass	cut off	float	dust	
死	生	哀	樂	兩	相	棄				
death	life	sorrow	joy	pair	mutual	discard				
是	非	得	失	付	閒	人 [rin]				
right	wrong	obtain	lose	attach	idle	person				

So Hurried[17]

So hurried, I do not yet know what it is to enjoy life.
I desire to cast it all off, leave, but I lack the means.
How can I get long feathers, great wings like clouds to sprout from my body,
Riding the wind, bestir myself to go beyond the Six Directions, leaving behind the floating dust?
Death and life, sorrow and joy: discard both pairs.
Right and wrong, success and failure: leave these to idle people.

Study Notes and Questions

This intense "old-style" poem derives from Li Bai's use of run-on lines with abundant grammatical function words in poems like "Fighting South of the Wall." Li Bai, however, used old *yuefu* titles as the starting point for his performances. Han Yu here frees himself from this constraint, but do the themes that he invokes in the poem remain within the domain of those Li Bai stressed in his "old-style" verse?

---

17. This poem was probably written in 799 when Han Yu was thirty-two. At the time he was serving as an aide to the military governor of Xuzhou, Zhang Jianfeng, after having failed the *jinshi* examination for a second time.

“Goulou Mountain” by Han Yu

岣嶁山							Goulou Mountain[18]
岣	嶁	山	尖	神	禹	碑 [pi]	The tablet to Emperor Yu on the peak of Goulou Mountain:
Gou-	-lou	Mountain	peak	divine	Yu	tablet	
字	青	石	赤	形	摹	奇 [gi]	The glyphs are green, the rock red, the shape striking.
glyphs	green	stone	red	shape	form	strange	
科	斗	拳	身	薤	倒	披 [p^{h}i]	Tadpole’s fisted body, scallion splayed downward,[19]
tadpole		fist	body	scallion	hang	split	
鸞	飄	鳳	泊	拏	虎	螭 [ʈ^{h}i]	A phoenix soars, *feng* bird roosts, tiger and dragon crouch.
phoenix	soar	*feng*	moor	stalk	tiger	dragon	
事	嚴	跡	祕	鬼	莫	窺 [k^{h}jwi]	The matter serious, the trace secret, even ghosts cannot spy on it.
affair	stern	trace	secret	ghost	none	spy	
道	人	獨	上	偶	見	之 [tɕi]	A man of the Way alone ascended and by chance saw it.
Way	person	alone	ascend	by chance	see	it	
我	來	咨	嗟	涕	漣	洏 [ɲi]	I come to sigh, tears streaming unstanched.
I	come	sigh	sigh	tears	torrential		
千	搜	萬	索	何	處	有	After countless searches, where is it?
1,000	seek	10,000	search	what	place	exist	
森	森	綠	樹	猿	猱	悲 [pi]	In the denseness of green trees gibbons and apes wail.
dense	dense	green	trees	gibbon	ape	sorrow	

STUDY NOTES AND QUESTIONS

1. This poem reflects another part of Han Yu’s style. The second couplet in particular has been praised for its dense, virtuosic, imaginative description of the calligraphy of the stele. Search the web for examples of seal-script calligraphy (try “Goulou Mountain”) that might fit the description of the fourth line.

2. Note how the poem ends. Han Yu throughout the poem focuses on human traces, human endeavors, and personal commitments, even if he is happy to invoke ghosts. In the final couplet he presents a vision of nature: how does the “green world” stand in relation to human intentions here?

---

18. Goulou Mountain is part of Mt. Heng, the southern sacred peak. Han Yu visited Mt. Heng on his way to exile in Chaozhou. Little is known with confidence about the tablet commemorating Yu’s accomplishments. If the tablet ever existed, it was lost by the Song dynasty.

19. Early Chinese writing was called “tadpole writing” by the Han dynasty people who could no longer read it. “Upside-down Scallion” is the name for another style of so-called seal script.

From the Series "Autumn Thoughts" by Han Yu

秋懷詩十一首第八					Autumn Thoughts, 11 poems, no. 8[20]
卷 whirl	卷 whirl	落 fall	地 ground	葉 leaf	Whirling, the leaves that fall to the ground,
隨 follow	風 wind	走 run	前 front	軒 [xian] porch	Following the wind, rush by my front veranda.
鳴 sing	聲 sound	若 seems	有 there is	意 intent	Their singing sound seems to have an intent.
顛 topsy	倒 turvy	相 [mutual]	追 chase	奔 [pun] rush	Tumbling over, they scurry chasing one another.
空 empty	堂 hall	黃 yellow	昏 dusk	暮 sunset	In an empty hall, at dusky sunset,
我 I	坐 sit	默 silent	不 not	言 [ŋian] speak	I sit, silent, not speaking.
童 youth	子 child	自 from	外 outside	至 arrive	My boy arrives from outside.[21]
吹 blow	燈 lamp	當 at	我 me	前 [tsɦan] before	Kindling the lamp, he sets it before me.
問 ask	我 me	我 I	不 not	應 reply	He asks me; I do not reply.
饋 bring food	我 me	我 I	不 not	餐 [ts^{h}an] eat	He brings me food; I do not eat.
退 withdraw	坐 sit	西 west	壁 wall	下 below	He withdraws to sit by the west wall.
讀 read	詩 poem	盡 finish	數 several	編 [pjian] piece	Reading poems, he finishes several.
作 make	者 -er	非 is not	今 now	士 man	Their authors are not men of the present.
相 [mutual]	去 leave	時 time	已 already	千 [ts^{h}ian] thousand	Their time is already a thousand years past.
其 his	言 word	有 there is	感 move	觸 strike	Their words move me,
使 cause	我 me	復 again	悽 sad	酸 [suan] acid	Make me once more painfully sad.
顧 turn	謂 address	汝 you	童 youth	子 child	Looking back, I say, "You, child,

20. This series of poems was written in 806 when Han Yu was summoned to Chang'an as an erudite in the State Academy. As always, life at the center of all political intrigue was stressful and frustrating.

21. It is unclear whether this is a servant (or slave) or his own child.

置 put	書 book	且 and	安 quiet	眠 [mjian] sleep	Put aside the book and sleep well.
丈 adult	夫 person	屬 at present	有 there is	念 thought	A grown man right now has much to think,
事 affairs	業 task	無 without	窮 end	年 [nian] year	And duties that have no end."

STEPHEN OWEN'S TRANSLATION

Autumn Thoughts

Blown tumbling, leaves that fall to the ground,
before my porch they run with the wind.

There seems some intent in the sounds they make,
toppling over, chasing swiftly each other.

Then twilight came to my empty hall,
I sat there silent, not speaking.

The boy came in from the outside
and lit the lamp in front of me.

He asked how I was, I did not reply;
he brought me food, I would not eat.

He drew back and sat by the western wall,
read out poems, completing a few.

Their writers were not men of today,
already a thousand years have gone by.

But something touched me in their words,
that made me again feel discouraged.

I looked around, saying "You, boy,
put the books down and go to bed,

There's something on my mind just now,
a task to be done that never ends."

STUDY NOTES AND QUESTIONS

1. It is a challenge to write a poem of autumnal meditations if one is reluctant to mix the realm of human values with the world of nature and phenomenal process. Han Yu here brilliantly acknowledges the power of an autumnal mood but recasts it as a reflection on time slipping away and on withdrawal into melancholy. Central to the poem is the question of speech and of breaking out of isolation. Follow the evolution of images of and references to speech throughout the poem, beginning with the chatter of the whirling leaves, through Han Yu's silence, to the intervention of the boy, to Han Yu's final response.

Consider the complexity of the situation where a young child reads poems of men long dead that, in the end, reach Han Yu and spur him to speech. What is the tone of Han Yu's instruction to the boy? How is it a response to the "autumnal"?

2. What is the effect of the repetitions of the use of the pronoun "I" (*wo* 我) in lines 5–10, where it appears six times? In particular, what is the effect in lines 9–10, where it appears four times?

"Teasing Zhang Ji" by Han Yu

調張籍					Teasing Zhang Ji[22]
李	杜	文	章	在	Li Bai's and Du Fu's writings remain:
Li	Du	writings		remain	
光	焰	萬	丈	長 [trɦiaŋ]	A gleaming blaze ten thousand feet long.
gleam	flame	10^4	fathom	long	
不	知	群	兒	愚	Not knowing, those children are fools:
not	know	gathered	children	foolish	
那	用	故	謗	傷 [ʂiaŋ]	To what end do they slander?
what	use	purpose	slander	harm	
蚍	蜉	撼	大	樹	Ants shaking a large tree,
ant	ant	shake	big	tree	
可	笑	不	自	量 [liaŋ]	Their not taking their own measure is laughable.
can be	laugh	not	-self	measure	
伊	我	生	其	後	And I was born after them.
and	I	born	their	after	
舉	頸	遙	相	望 [ʋaŋ]	Lifting my head, I look afar for them.
lift	neck	afar	[object]	gaze	
夜	夢	多	見	之	In dreams at night I often see them.
night	dream	often	see	them	
晝	思	反	微	茫 [maŋ]	But in daylight these thoughts grow indistinct.
day	long	yet	tiny	vague	
徒	觀	斧	鑿	痕	In vain I observe the traces of the axe and borer.[23]
in vain	observe	axe	borer	trace	

22. Zhang Ji was a younger colleague. He passed the qualifying test to take the *jinshi* exam when Han Yu was the administering official in Bianzhou (Kaifeng). Thus Han Yu became his official patron. Zhang had a successful official career and became a highly regarded poet who specialized particularly in *yuefu* forms. This poem perhaps was written in 816 while Han Yu was serving as a chief secretary in Chang'an.

23. The wording suggests comparison with the legendary Emperor Yu's opening of channels through mountains to control the floods.

不	矚	治	水	航 [xɦaŋ]	I cannot see the sailing that rules the water.[24]
not	see	control	water	sailing	
想	當	施	手	時	I imagine at the time when they set to work:
imagine	at	apply	hand	time	
巨	刃	磨	天	揚 [jiaŋ]	The great blade lifted to brush against the sky.
great	blade	brush	sky	lift	
垠	崖	劃	崩	豁	Riverbanks, hacked, crumble and open.
banks	shores	hack	crumble	open	
乾	坤	擺	雷	硠 [laŋ]	Heaven and Earth heaved with a rumbling thunder.[25]
Qian	Kun	push	thunder	rumble	
惟	此	兩	夫	子	These two Masters
only	these	two	Masters		
家	居	率	荒	涼 [liaŋ]	Lived in homes that were largely desolate.
home	reside	generally	desolate		
帝	欲	長	吟	哦	The Heavenly Emperor wished them to always chant poems:
God	wish	long	chant	mutter	
故	遣	起	且	僵 [kiaŋ]	So he made them rise high and fall low.
thus	send	rise	and	fall over	
翦	翎	送	籠	中	Clipping their wings, he consigned them to cages.
clip	pinions	escort	cage	middle	
使	看	百	鳥	翔 [sɦiaŋ]	He made them watch the other birds soar.
cause	look	hundred	birds	soar	
平	生	千	萬	篇	The tens of thousands of works of their lifetime:
normal	life	1,000	10,000	pieces	
金	薤	垂	琳	琅 [laŋ]	"Gold Hatch" and "Dangled Scallion" suspended like brilliant jade.[26]
Gold	Scallion	hang	brilliant jade		
仙	官	敕	六	丁	The Immortal officials ordered six officers,
immortal	official	order	six	men	
雷	電	下	取	將 [tsiaŋ]	With thunder and lightning, to descend and take away [the poems].
thunder	lightning	descend	take	carry	
流	落	人	間	者	What drifted back to mankind
flow	fall	people	midst	[thing]	
太	山	一	毫	芒 [maŋ]	Is like a single hair compared to Mount Tai.
Tai	Mountain	one	feather	hair	

24. The phrase "rule (control) the water" clearly points to Yu's regulating the rivers. The primary image, however, is of a boat that manages to navigate a difficult river.

25. Qian and Kun are the hexagrams for Heaven and Earth. Du Fu frequently used the pair to suggest the involvement of cosmic forces in the landscape.

26. These are both types of early Chinese writing (unintelligible to all but the specialists from Han dynasty onward).

我 I	願 desire	生 grow	兩 two	翅 wing	I desire to sprout two wings,
捕 capture	逐 chase	出 go out	八 eight	荒 [xuaŋ] wilds	Give pursuit, leaving behind the Eight Wilds.[27]
精 truly	誠 indeed	忽 suddenly	交 communicate	通	Being utterly sincere, I suddenly would communicate with them.
32 百 hundred	怪 strange	入 enter	我 my	腸 [trɦiaŋ] innards	A hundred marvels would enter my innards.
刺 stab	手 hand	拔 pull	鯨 whale	牙 tooth	With bare hands(?), I would pull out the whale's tooth.[28]
舉 lift	瓢 gourd	酌 pour	天 heaven	漿 [tsiaŋ] liquor	Lifting a gourd, I would pour out Heavenly nectar.
騰 leap	身 body	跨 straddle	汗 Vast Emptiness	漫	With vaulting body, I would straddle the Vast Emptiness.[29]
36 不 not	著 attach	織 Weaving	女 Girl	襄 [siaŋ] carriage	I would not be restricted to the Weaving Girl's carriage.[30]
顧 look back	語 inform	地 ground	上 on	友 friend	Looking back, I speak with my friend on the ground:
經 manage	營 plan	無 don't	太 too	忙 [maŋ] busy	In your planning, don't be too busy.
乞 beg	君 you	飛 flying	霞 mist	珮 pendant	I shall give to you a pendant of the flying mists.
40 與 with	我 me	高 high	頡 flutter	頏 [xɦaŋ] flit	With me you can dart on high.

Study Notes and Questions

1. Zhang Ji admonished Han Yu not to write frivolous pieces, but is "Teasing Zhang Ji" frivolous or serious? The tone of the poem is hard to pin down. Does it vary from section to section? Explain.

2. Focusing on its tone, compare this poem to Du Fu's song lamenting the destruction of his roof (pp. 249–50).

---

27. That is, the farthest borders of the eight directions (N, NE, E, SE, S, SW, W, NW).

28. The meaning of the phrase "stab the hand" is unclear.

29. The phrase "Vast Emptiness" (*hanman* 汗漫) comes from the "Responses of the Way"《道應》chapter in the Western Han syncretic philosophical text, *Huainan Zi* 淮南子.

30. The allusion here is to "Great East"《大東》(Mao 203) in the *Canon of Poetry*, which describes the Weaving Girl being moved seven times from star to star in her constellation during each day. Shimizu Shigeru suggests that Han Yu here means that he will be freed from the constraints of time. See Shimizu Shigeru 清水茂, *Kan Yu* 韓愈 (Tokyo: Iwanami shoten, 1958), p. 32.

3. When Li Bai and Du Fu died, they appeared—in the context of their own days—to have failed as poets. This poem, however, reflects the change in Mid-Tang values. Why does Han Yu consider the two poets so great, and what has Han Yu learned from them?

4. Does the poem, in its style, imagery, and organization, resemble Li Bai's or Du Fu's poems? Explain.

"Written on the Wall of the Temple of King Zhao of Chu" by Han Yu

題楚昭王廟							Written on the Wall of the Temple of King Zhao of Chu[31]
邱	墳	滿	目	衣	冠	盡	Burial mounds fill the eye: their clothes and
hill	tumulus	fill	eye	clothes	cap	end	ceremonial caps have vanished.
城	闕	連	雲	草	樹	荒 [xuaŋ]	The city walls and chambers stretch to
city wall	tower	connect	cloud	grass	tree	overgrown	the clouds; the grasses and trees grow wild.
猶	有	國	人	懷	舊	德	Still there are people of this
still	are	kingdom	people	cherish	old	virtue	country who cherish virtue of old:
一	間	茅	屋	祭	昭	王 [yaŋ]	In a thatched house of one room,
one	bay	thatch	roof	sacrifice	Zhao	King	they sacrifice to King Zhao.

STEPHEN OWEN'S TRANSLATION

On the Temple of King Chao of Ch'u

Tombs and mounds fill my eyes, the robes and caps are gone,
Walls and towers stretch to the sky, trees and grass grow over them.
Yet still there are men of his state who feel his former virtue,
And in this single-roomed thatched hut, they pray to King Chao.

STUDY NOTES AND QUESTIONS

1. What role does nature play in this poem? What images belong to "nature," and what belong to the human realm? Does nature affirm, complement, and provide a model for human values, or does it threaten human society and human values?

2. Han Yu, coming upon the small, rustic temple, sees "virtue of old" as persisting in the folkways of the people who maintain the temple, but just barely, and certainly beyond the awareness of those in the

31. In 819, after submitting a vehement Confucian protest against the emperor's honoring bones said to be the Buddha's, Han Yu was banished to Chaozhou in modern Guangdong Province. En route, he stopped in Yicheng (in modern Hubei Province), the former capital of King Zhao of Chu, and visited the temple there. King Zhao moved the capital from Ying in 504 BC to escape the threat of attacks by the kingdom of Wu.

center of power. Han Yu's poem cannot be reduced to allegory, but it has implications for a man who has just been banished to the far south. Explain.

3. The final couplet offers a revelation that is complex in the way that Du Fu's final images often are. Du Fu's images give away much in order to save a little, to preserve his deepest human commitments. He presents himself as very small in a large, desolate world, yet he insists that he will remain and persevere. What does Han Yu give away? What does he preserve?

From the Series "First Floating on South Creek" by Han Yu

南溪始泛三首第二 — First Floating on South Creek, 3 poems, no. 2[32]

南	溪	亦	清	駛	South Creek is pure and rapid,
south	creek	also	pure	rapid	
而	無	楫	與	舟 [tʂiw]	And is without boats and oars.
and	without	oar	and	boat	
山	農	驚	見	之	The mountain farmers are startled to see it.
mountain	farmer	startle	see	it	
隨	我	觀	不	休 [xiw]	Following me, they watch without ceasing.
follow	me	observe	not	stop	
不	惟	兒	童	輩	Not only the youngsters,
not	only	child	youth	cohort	
或	有	杖	白	頭 [tɦəw]	There are also some white-haired ones [leaning on] staffs.
some	are	staff	white	hair	
饋	我	籠	中	瓜	They feast me with melons from the basket.
feast	me	cage	in	melon	
勸	我	此	淹	留 [liw]	They urge me to tarry here.
urge	me	here	tarry	remain	
我	云	以	病	歸	I say that I return because of sickness.
I	say	using	sick	return	
此	已	頗	自	由 [jiw]	Being here already allows me to do rather as I will.
here	already	rather	do from oneself		
幸	有	用	餘	俸	Luckily I have the unused part of my salary.
lucky	there is	use	left over	salary	
置	居	在	西	疇 [trɦiw]	I'll set up a residence in the west field.
set up	reside	in	west	fields	
囷	倉	米	穀	滿	The granary will be full of rice and grain.
granary	storehouse	rice	grain	full	

32. In 824 Han Yu retired to a villa south of Chang'an.

	未 not yet	有 have	旦 dawn	夕 dusk	憂 [ʔiw] grief	I do not yet have worries from dawn to dusk.
	上 above	去 leave	無 without	得 special	得 intent	In the past, leaving, I had no special intent.
16	下 below	來 come	亦 also	悠 afar	悠 [jiw] afar	In the future, as I come, I also am at ease.
	但 only	恐 fear	煩 bother	里 village	閭 hamlet	I only fear I may bother the village:
	時 occasion	有 there is	緩 loose	急 taut	投 [tɦəw] rely	At times I may need help in emergencies.
	願 request	為 become	同 share	社 shrine	人 person	I hope to become a person to share in the altar sacrifices:
20	雞 chicken	豚 pig	燕 feast	春 spring	秋 [ts^{h}iw] autumn	With chickens and pigs feast the springs and autumns.

STEPHEN OWEN'S TRANSLATION

Floating on South Creek for the First Time: second of three poems

South Creek is also clear and rushing,
But there are no boats or oars on it.
Mountain farmers are startled to see this one,
And following me, they won't stop staring.
Not just a group of young boys—
Sometimes there are white-haired men leaning on staffs.
They offer me melons in a basket,
And urge me to linger here.
I say that I've come home on account of sickness,
And feel particularly on my own here.
I hope I'll have a chance to use my remaining salary
To set up a dwelling here on the western fields.
Rice and grains shall fill the granaries,
And I'll have no worries from dawn to dusk.
I never got any satisfaction from rising to a high position,
Coming down from it, I'm also perfectly at ease.
I only fear that I'll be a nuisance to the village,
At times troubling them when there is urgent business.
But I would like to be one who shares their cult,
And with pigs and chickens, feast the springs and autumns.

Study Notes and Questions

With its vision of an aging scholar-official escaping the burdens of irony and self-consciousness and finding his place in a simple rural community, this poem deeply influenced later Song dynasty writers.

Note, however, that the poem transcends rather than eschews self-consciousness about differences in status and culture. The first six lines do not augur well as the villagers gawk at the strange procession of a high official—and a boat—reaching their hamlet. How does Han Yu then go about writing himself into the community?

Meng Jiao 孟郊 (751–814)

Meng Jiao was from Jiangnan, southeast China. His father held one minor post, but there appears to have been no family tradition of service. Meng Jiao was born late in the Tianbao reign period of Xuanzong, that is, before the An Lushan Rebellion. He was twelve when the rebellion ended, but since he lived in the south, it had little direct impact on him. We have little information on Meng Jiao's life before he turned thirty, but this period saw the break-up of the northeastern section of the empire (and parts of the southern section as well) into independent domains with only nominal allegiance to the throne. Meng Jiao surely witnessed the parts of this collapse that affected his region. His biographies state that when young he lived in reclusion near Mount Song (in modern Henan Province), and that he went to Luoyang, presumably looking for patronage, when he was thirty. In approximately 786 he went to Chang'an to take the *jinshi* examination but failed and then went to Suzhou where he associated with the poets there, such as Wei Yingwu 韋應物 (737–92) and the monk-poet Jiaoran 皎然 (ca. 730–ca. 799). In 791 he went to Chang'an to try the *jinshi* examination again, and again he failed. The next year he tried again and, although he failed, he met Han Yu and Li Guan 李觀 (766–94), both of whom passed. He finally passed in his fourth attempt in 795. However, he did not receive a post and instead returned to Jiangnan. He joined Zhang Ji in visiting Bianzhou, where he met Han Yu again. He left Bianzhou before its military governor died and returned to Suzhou and its environs. He returned to Luoyang in 800 in search of a post and received the office of sheriff of Liyang 溧陽 (in modern Jiangsu Province). It was not much but allowed him to take care of his mother there. When his assignment ended, he waited for his replacement to arrive, sent his mother to an estate in Yixing 義興, and then went to Chang'an—where he joined Han Yu, Zhang Ji and others—until he received a post in Luoyang. Once in Luoyang, he stayed there until he died in 814.

Meng Jiao was of a different generation from Han Yu and Zhang Ji (both born in 768), and his career was far less successful than theirs, yet he is strongly associated with them as a poet. He composed linked verse together with them, and the three shared a taste for the strange and grotesque.[33] Like them—and very different from the southeastern poets like Wei Yingwu—he sought ways to foreground the role of the poet's subjectivity in the shaping of experience. Meng Jiao in later dynasties primarily was thought of as "cold" (*han* 寒), since his poems tend to present a poor and bleak world.

33. A "linked verse" poem is a poem written jointly by two or more authors. The participants in linked verse composition took turns writing segments of the poem—often just a line or a couplet at a time—but the conventions were very fluid, and there are examples of poets contributing much longer segments. As Stephen Owen explains, such poetry stresses wit and encourages hyperbole. See Owen's discussion of Han Yu and Meng Jiao's linked verse in *The Poetry of Meng Chiao and Han Yü* (New Haven: Yale University Press, 1975), pp. 116–36.

"Ancient Grievance" by Meng Jiao

古怨					Ancient Grievance
試 try	妾 my	與 with	君 you	淚 [lwi^{h}] tears	You and I, let us try with our tears—[34]
兩 two	處 place	滴 drip	池 pond	水 [ɕwi'] water	In two places, drop them into pond water.
看 look	取 pick	芙 lotus	蓉 	花 flower	Watch, in picking lotus flowers,
今 this	年 year	為 for	誰 who	死 [si'] die	This year, for whose [tears] will they die?

STUDY NOTES AND QUESTIONS

1. The poem's title marks it as "ancient" and signals that the author will be adopting an "ancient" persona. Who is the speaker here? Can we tell if the woman is high-born?

2. The poem drops us into the middle of a frustrated love affair. Can we tell anything about it? Do we need to know? What is the "grievance," and why does Meng Jiao call it "ancient"? Why write a short fragment of a poem like this: with what is Meng Jiao experimenting?

34. The speaker is a wife, as indicated by *qie* 妾, the humble first-person status pronoun meaning a "secondary wife" or concubine.

"Late Vista at a Luoyang Bridge" by Meng Jiao

洛橋晚望							Late Vista at a Luoyang Bridge
天 heaven	津 ford	橋 bridge	下 below	冰 ice	初 first	結 [kjiat] congeal	When the ice first begins to freeze beneath Heaven Ford Bridge,
洛 Lo-	陽 -yang	陌 road	上 on	人 people	行 about to	絕 [tsfiyat] cease	And on the roads of Luoyang, people are almost gone,
榆 elm	柳 willow	蕭 barren	疏 stripped	樓 tower	閣 chamber	閒 idle	The elms and willows stand barren, the buildings are quiet.
月 moon	明 bright	直 directly	見 see	嵩 Song	山 Mount	雪 [syat] snow	The moon is bright: I can see the snow on Mount Song.[35]

STUDY NOTES AND QUESTIONS

1. This is a poem about a special moment. Try to picture the visual image of that moment. How does each element that Meng Jiao describes contribute to that moment?

2. What is the mood of the final line? How do the first three lines shape it?

35. Meng Jiao may be drawing on a couplet from Xie Lingyun's poem, "Year's End"《歲暮》:"The bright moon shines on the accumulated snow; the north wind is strong and mournful."「明月照積雪，朔風勁且哀。」

From the "Cold Creek" Series by Meng Jiao

	寒溪八首 第三					Cold Creek, 8 poems, no. 3[36]
	曉 dawn	飲 drink	一 one	杯 cup	酒 wine	At dawn I drank a cup of ale.
	踏 tread	雪 snow	過 pass	清 pure	溪 [kʰjiaj] creek	Treading snow, I visited the pure creek.
	波 waves	瀾 billows	凍 freeze	為 become	刀 knives	The waves, frozen, had become knives.
4	剸 rend	割 hack	鳧 ducks	與 and	鷖 [ʔjiaj] gulls	They hacked and rent the ducks and gulls.
	宿 roost	羽 feathers	皆 all	翦 cut	棄 discard	Last night's feathers were all cut and abandoned.
	血 blood	聲 sound	沉 sink	沙 sand	泥 [niaj] mud	The blood-drenched sound sank into the mud and sand.
	獨 alone	立 stand	欲 want	何 what	語 say	Standing alone, what could I say?
8	默 silent	念 think	心 heart	酸 grieved	嘶 [siaj] cry	Silently thinking, my heart cried in sorrow.
	凍 frozen	血 blood	莫 do not	作 make	春 spring	Frozen blood, don't become spring!
	作 make	春 spring	生 grow	不 not	齊 [tsɦiaj] even	If you became spring, growth would be unbalanced.
	凍 frozen	血 blood	莫 do not	作 make	花 flower	Frozen blood, don't become flowers!
12	作 make	花 flower	發 emit	孀 widow	啼 [tɦiaj] tears	If you became flowers, you would draw out widows' tears.
	幽 hidden	幽 hidden	棘 bramble	針 needle	村 village	In deep seclusion, a village of brambles:
	凍 frozen	死 dead	難 hard	耕 plow	犂 [liaj] plowshare	Frozen to death, they cannot plow.

36. This series was probably written in 806 when Meng Jiao lived in Luoyang.

STEPHEN OWEN'S TRANSLATION

Cold Creek, III

At dawn I drank a single cup of wine,
Treading the snow I visited the clear creek.
The waves had frozen into knives
That hacked and carved the ducks and widgeons.
Feathers that spent the night, all cut off and lost,
The sound of blood sinking into mud and sand.
Alone I stand—what shall I say?
Silently I brood, my heart cries out bitterly.
Frozen blood will never make springtime,
If it made springtime, inequality would be born.
Frozen blood will make no flowers,
If it made flowers, it would bring the widow's weeping.
Hidden away, village of thorns and brambles,
Frozen to death, there can be no plowing.

STUDY NOTES AND QUESTIONS

1. This poem centers on the reading of nature, which appears vicious and cruel. The story begins calmly enough in the first couplet when the speaker decides to visit the creek. The third line, while odd in asserting that the waves had become knives, still can be naturalized through the image of jagged ice forms. However, the speaker persists with this reading and in the fourth line asserts that the knives have fulfilled their purpose in the slaughter of the birds. The fifth line suggests that the external referent, the element in the scene that inspires the speaker's reading, are the few feathers left on the ice, which are taken as all that remains from the attack. Why, however, did he not hear the cry of the birds? Line 6 proposes that the sounds were swallowed up by the earth.

2. The image of the sound and the blood absorbed by the earth leads to the final section. Why does the speaker address the frozen blood? What is the relation of the speaker's address to the blood and the final couplet? Has the temporal frame shifted? In moving from the creek to the village, the speaker offers one last version of the relation of the human community to nature. What is his central focus here, and how does it relate to the rest of the poem?

Jia Dao 賈島 (779–854)

Not much is known of Jia Dao's life. His ancestors were from Fanyang 范陽 in the northeast, but there was no record of family service in civil administration. In his youth he was poor and joined the Buddhist *sangha*. However, in 811 when Jia Dao was thirty-two, he met Han Yu, Meng Jiao, Zhang Ji, and other poets in Chang'an. They greatly appreciated his abilities and persuaded him to take the *jinshi* examination and seek office. Over the next twenty years he consistently failed the examination. Some sources state that he did finally pass as he approached fifty, but the modern Japanese scholar Arai Ken suggests that he received his first post as registrar in Changjiang 長江 County (in modern Sichuan Province) as a form of exile when he was fifty-nine without ever attaining *jinshi* status. On completion of his three-year posting, he then was transferred to Puzhou 普州 (also in Sichuan), and it appears that he died in office there.[37]

Jia Dao became famous for the intensely self-conscious artistry of his regulated verse poems. In a well-known—though surely apocryphal—anecdote, Jia Dao, having just arrived in Chang'an, was deep in thought trying to decide which of two words was better: "Birds rest in the trees next to the pool; a monk *pushes* the gate beneath the moon" 鳥宿池邊樹，僧推月下門 or "a monk *knocks at* the gate beneath the moon" 僧敲月下門. He was riding a mule acting out "push" and "knock" when, unawares, he ran into Han Yu's horse. Since Han Yu was a high official, this breach was a crime. Han Yu's retainers held Jia Dao, and he explained his poetic predicament. Han Yu thought a while and said, "'Knock' is better." Thus began their friendship.

Jia Dao primarily focused on small-scale landscape poems in which the inner couplets reveal the pressure of crafting, often at the expense of the coherence of the poem as a whole. These characteristics—small-scale landscape regulated verse and careful crafting—came to define the "Late Tang style" 晚唐體 for later writers and were associated with Jia Dao, Du Mu, Yao He, and Xu Hun.

37. See Arai Ken's 荒井健 annotated translation of Jia Dao's funerary inscription in Ogawa Tamaki 小川環樹, ed., *Tōdai no shijin—sono denki* 唐代の詩人—その傳記 (Tokyo: Taishūkan shoten, 1975), pp. 425–35.

"Clear Skies after Snow: Afternoon Vista" by Jia Dao

雪晴晚望					Clear Skies after Snow: Afternoon Vista
倚 lean	杖 staff	望 gaze	晴 clear sky	雪 snow	Leaning on my staff, I gaze at the clear-sky snow:
溪 ravine	雲 clouds	幾 how many	萬 10,000	重 [trɦywŋ] double	The ravine clouds, how many thousand layers?
樵 gather wood	人 person	歸 return	白 white	屋 roof	Woodgatherers return to the white roofs.
寒 cold	日 sun	下 go down	危 perilous	峰 [fjyawŋ] peak	The cold sun sets on towering peaks.
野 outland	火 fire	燒 burn	岡 hill	草 grass	Outland fires burn the knoll grasses;
斷 broken	煙 smoke	生 born	石 rock	松 [sɦywŋ] pine	Puffs of smoke appear amid rock-rooted pines.
卻 retreat	回 turn	山 mountain	寺 temple	路 road	Now I turn back on the road to the mountain temple:
聞 hear	打 beat	暮 sunset	天 sky	鐘 [tʂywŋ] bell	I hear the striking of the vespers bell.

PAUL ROUZER'S TRANSLATION

An evening view, after snow clears

I lean on a staff, view fair-weather snow:
Clouds above the stream in endless folds.
Wood-cutters return to spare lodgings
As the chill sun sets on steep mountains.
A field fire consumes the ridge-top grass,
And sparse mist gives birth to stone-side pines.
I retreat down the path to a mountain temple
And hear them strike the bells of dusk.

STUDY NOTES AND QUESTIONS

1. Compare the first line of this poem to Meng Jiao's "Late Vista at a Luoyang Bridge." The settings are similar: are the moods and authors' stances similar too?

2. Discuss the parallelism of the middle couplets. Within the structure of the second couplet, for example, how is a woodgatherer like the sun?

3. Explain the generic features of the final couplet. Have we seen other poems that end in a similar manner? How do the specific details of this final couplet provide an appropriate conclusion to the poem?

"Staying the Night at a Mountain Temple" by Jia Dao

宿山寺					Staying the Night at a Mountain Temple
衆 crowd	岫 mountains	聳 looming	寒 cold	色 appearance	The crowded mountains loom in the cold.
精 refined	廬 hut	向 faces	此 this	分 [piuən] divide	The purified retreat can be discerned from here.
流 flow	星 stars	透 penetrate	疏 sparse	木 trees	The flowing stars penetrate the thinned trees;
走 run	月 moon	逆 go against	行 travel	雲 [jiuən] clouds	The running moon goes against the moving clouds.
絕 cut-off	頂 top	人 people	來 come	少 few	At the very top, few people come.
高 tall	松 pine	鶴 crane	不 not	群 [giuən] flock	Among the tall pines, the crane does not seek a flock.
一 one	僧 monk	年 years	八 eight	十 ten	One monk, of eighty years,
世 world	事 affairs	未 not	曾 once	聞 [miuən] hear	Has never heard of the affairs of the world.

PAUL ROUZER'S TRANSLATION

I spend the night at a mountain temple

Peak upon peak thrust into cold air;
The monks' pure lodge can be seen from here.
Shooting stars show through the sparse trees;
A rushing moon turns back on scudding clouds.
Few men come here to the steepest crag,
Nor will cranes nest within these tall pines.
A single monk here, of eighty years,
Has never heard of the world's affairs.

STUDY NOTES AND QUESTIONS

Jia Dao earned his reputation as a master stylist of regulated verse. He focused not on recording grand themes and major events but on crafting accounts of everday experience.

1. The second couplet of this poem is especially well-known. Explain the images. How are the stars flowing? Why are the trees in the forest "thinned"? How is the moon running and how does it go against

the clouds? Try to imagine this description of the moon meeting wind-blown clouds. In the end, is his account here a description of the world (the stars and clouds) or of the human perception of the world?

2. People argue that Jia Dao's focus on the crafting of the inner couplets of regulated verse damaged the aesthetic coherence of the poem as a whole. Is this true here?

"Seeing Off Tang Gui to Return to His Estate on the Fu River" by Jia Dao

送唐瓌歸敷水莊					Seeing Off Tang Gui to Return to His Estate on the Fu River[38]
毛 hair	女 woman	峰 peak	當 is at	戶 door	Hairy Woman Peak stands at the door:[39]
日 sun	高 high	頭 head	未 not yet	梳 [ṣio] comb	The sun is high, yet her hair is uncombed.
地 land	侵 encroach	山 mountain	影 shadow	掃 sweep	The land is overborne by the sweeping mountain shadow.
葉 leaf	帶 carry	露 dew	痕 trace	書 [śio] write	The leaves carry the writing of dew tracks.
松 pine	徑 path	僧 monk	尋 seek	廟 temple	Along the pine path a monk seeks a temple.[40]
沙 sand	泉 spring	鶴 crane	見 see	魚 [ŋio] fish	At the sandy spring a crane watches fish.
一 one	川 river	風 wind	景 scene	好 good	The scenery of the entire river is fine.
恨 regret	不 not	有 exist	吾 my	廬 [lio] hut	I regret that it does not have my hut.

PAUL ROUZER'S TRANSLATION

I see off Tang Huan on his return to his Fu River estate

Hairy Girl Peak will face your door,
So when the sun climbs high, you'll leave hair uncombed.
Earth is impinged by sweep of mountain shadow;
Leaves bear the calligraphy of frosty tracks.

---

38. The Fu River 敷水 is in Huazhou 華州, where the Yellow River turns north.

39. Hairy Woman Peak 毛女峰 is one of the four peaks of the Taihua Mountains 太華山 in Tongzhou 同州 (next to Huazhou).

40. Some texts have "medical herbs" (*yao* 藥) rather than "temple" (*miao* 廟).

On a pine path a monk seeks herbs;
At a sandy brook a crane espies fish.
All along your stream the scenery's fine —
I regret not having my own hut there.

Study Notes and Questions

1. Explain the whimsical first couplet. How does "Hairy Woman Peak stand at the door"? What physical aspect of the scene allows Jia Dao to assert that the "hair is uncombed"?

2. Consider the difference in scale in the second couplet. How are the two images of the mountain's shadows and the dew tracks parallel?

3. The third couplet is also slightly off balance. How is a monk seeking a temple like a heron watching fish? Note that the variant, "medical herbs" creates a much easier couplet.

4. The end is very low-key. What is the relevance of Jia Dao's allusion to Tao Qian's "I also love my hut" from "Reading the *Canon of Mountains and Seas*" poem no. 1?

Li He 李賀 (790–816)

Li He seems to have been from a distant offshoot of the Tang imperial lineage. His father, Li Jinsu 李晉肅, had served in minor local offices and apparently had met Du Fu. Li He was raised on a small estate outside of Luoyang. He presented his poetry to Han Yu at age seventeen, and according to the anecdotal literature that developed around the figures of this period, Han Yu was greatly impressed. In another story, Han Yu and a friend heard of the genius of Li He when he was still a child; they paid him a visit, demanded a poem from him, and were suitably startled by the brilliance of the extemporaneous verse. In any case, in 810 Han Yu was serving as the magistrate of Henan County, which contained the city of Luoyang. After Li He passed the initial exam in Luoyang, Han Yu recommended him to take the *jinshi* examination in Chang'an. However, the testing officials in Chang'an refused to allow Li He to take the *jinshi* examination because his father's name had the homophonous character *jin* 晉 in it, and sons should not use words that sound like words in their fathers' names. This rather absurd argument (Han Yu protested it) appears to have been a mere pretext for barring Li He from the exam, but the actual reason remains unclear. The next year, however, Li He did receive a minor post in the capital, apparently through his lineage status. He served his three years at the post but then, pleading illness, returned home. He stayed with a friend in the small town of Luzhou 潞州 (in modern Shanxi Province) in 815 while making one last effort to find a position, but then returned home and died.

Li He today is primarily known for his strange, spirit-ridden poetry. Like Meng Jiao, he explored ways of writing that present overwrought subjectivity in which the obsessive concerns of the author overwhelm the poem. In his own day, however, Li He was admired for the great technical brilliance of his verse.

"The Grave of Little Su" by Li He

蘇小小墓					The Grave of Little Su[41]
幽	蘭	露			The dew on secluded orchids
hidden	orchid	dew			
如	啼	眼 [ŋja:n´]			Resembles weeping eyes.
resemble	weep	eyes			
無	物	結	同	心	There is nothing "to bind our hearts as one."
without	thing	tie	share	heart	
煙	花	不	堪	剪 [tsian´]	The misty flowers: I cannot bear to cut them.
mist	flower	not	bear	cut	
草	如	茵			The grass resembles a mat.
grass	resemble	mat			
松	如	蓋 [kaj`]			The pine resembles a canopy.
pine	resemble	carriage-canopy			

41. Little Su was a famous courtesan during the Southern Qi dynasty (479–502).

	風 wind	為 become	裳 skirt	The wind becomes a skirt.
8	水 water	為 become	珮 [pɦuaj`] belt-pendant	The water becomes pendants.
	油 oil	壁 wall	車 cart	An oil-cloth carriage
	夕 dusk	相 [object]	待 [tɦaj`] await	At dusk awaits him.
	冷 cold	翠 turquoise	燭 candle	A cold blue-glinting candle
12	勞 labor	光 gleam	彩 [ts^{h}aj`] color	Labors to become bright.
	西 west	陵 mound	下 below	At the foot of West Mound
	風 wind	吹 blow	雨 rain	The wind blows rain.

Angus C. Graham's Translation

The Grave of Little Su

I ride a coach with lacquered sides,
My love rides a dark piebald horse.
Where shall we bind our hearts as one?
On West Mound, beneath the pines and cypresses.
(Ballad ascribed to the singing girl Little Su, ca. AD 500)

Dew on the secret orchid
Like crying eyes.
No thing to bind the heart to.
Misted flowers I cannot bear to cut.
Grass like a cushion,
The pine like a parasol:
The wind is a skirt,
The waters are tinkling pendants.
A coach with lacquered sides
Waits for someone in the evening.
Cold blue candle-flames
Strain to shine bright.
Beneath West Mound
The wind puffs the rain.

STUDY NOTES AND QUESTIONS

1. As Graham's note shows, Li He incorporated all the elements of the Southern Qi *yuefu* song, "Song of Little Su," into his poem. A more precise translation of the *yuefu* poem is:

妾乘油壁車	I ride an oil-cloth carriage
郎騎青驄馬	You mount a blue-white horse
何處結同心	Where shall we bind our hearts as one?
西陵松柏下	Under the pine and cypress of West Mound.

2. This poem is as strange as, though less intense than, Meng Jiao's "Cold Creek." How are the grass like a mat and the pine like a canopy? How can the wind become a skirt and the water a belt-pendant? Imagine the scene being depicted and then the sensibility interpreting the scene.

3. Li He's poem seems to be a reenactment of the meeting in the "Song of Little Su." Is the blue-glinting candle the narrator's or is it Little Su's? Descriptions in which one cannot decide between a real presence and a ghostly account are called "fantastic" in Western discussions of literature. Does the term fit here?

"Bring in the Ale" by Li He

將進酒								Bring in the Ale
琉	璃	鍾 [tʂywŋ]						A glass goblet,
glass		goblet						
琥	珀	濃 [nrywŋ]						Amber dark.
amber		dark						
小	槽	酒	滴	真	珠	紅 [xɦəwŋ]		From the small cask,
small	cask	ale	drip	true	pearl	red		ale drips pearls of red.
烹	龍	炮	鳳	玉	脂	泣		Boiled dragon, roast phoenix,
boil	dragon	roast	phoenix	jade	fat	cry		its jade fat weeps.
羅	屏	繡	幕	圍	香	風 [fjywŋ]		Sheer screens, embroidered curtains
gauze	screen	embroider	curtain	surround	incense	wind		close in the fragrant wind.
吹	龍	笛						Blow the dragon reed-pipes!
blow	dragon	reeds						
擊	鼉	鼓 [kuə̆´]						Strike the lizard-skin drums!
strike	lizard	drum						
皓	齒	歌						Glistening teeth sing.
white	teeth	sing						
細	腰	舞 [ʋuə̆´]						Narrow waists dance.
narrow	waist	dance						
況	是	青	春	日	將	暮 [muə̆´]		Especially since this day of
especial	this is	green	spring	day	about to	sunset		green spring nears sunset.
桃	花	亂	落	如	紅	雨 [yă´]		Peach flowers fall chaotically
peach	flower	chaotic	fall	like	red	rain		like pink rain.
勸	君	終	日	酩	酊	醉		I urge you to be completely
urge	you	end	day	blot	-to	drunk		drunk the whole day:
酒	不	到	劉	伶	墳	上	土 [tʰuə̆´]	Ale does not reach the dirt on
ale	not	reach	Liu	Ling	grave	on	dirt	Liu Ling's grave.[42]

Study Notes and Questions

1. Compare this poem with Li Bai's version (chapter 6). How are they the same? How do they differ? Does Li He substitute images while using the same basic tropes?

---

42. Liu Ling 劉伶, one of the Seven Worthies of the Bamboo Grove, wrote "In Praise of Wine's Virtue" 酒德頌 and was famous for drinking.

2. Consider the teeth as synecdoche: they appear earlier in such poems as Du Fu's "Lament for Riverbend." What is the effect of the synecdoche?

"Song of the Bronze Immortal Bidding Farewell to the Han," with Preface, by Li He

魏明帝青龍元年八月，詔宮官牽車西取漢孝武捧露盤仙人欲立置前殿。宮官既拆盤，仙人臨載，乃潸然淚下，唐諸王孫李長吉遂作《金銅仙人辭漢歌》。

In the Eighth Month of the first year of the Green Dragon reign period, Emperor Ming of the Wei ordered his palace officials to bring from the west the bronze immortal dew-platter holders, which he wanted set in front of his palace.[43] When the officials had removed the platters and the immortals were about to be carried off, they copiously wept tears. The royal descendant of the Tang, Li Changji accordingly writes the *Song of the Bronze Immortal Bidding Farewell to the Han.*[44]

金銅仙人辭漢歌並序							Song of the Bronze Immortal Bidding Farewell to the Han
茂 Mao	陵 Tumulus	劉 Liu	郎 Master	秋 autumn	風 wind	客 [kʰja:jk] traveler	Young Master Liu of Maoling, a traveler in the autumn wind.[45]
夜 night	聞 hear	馬 horse	嘶 neigh	曉 dawn	無 without	跡 [tsiajk] trace	At night one heard a horse neigh, at dawn, there are no tracks.
畫 painted	欄 railing	桂 cassia	樹 tree	懸 hang	秋 autumn	香 perfume	The cassia trees by the painted railings cast their autumn incense.
三 three	十 ten	六 six	宮 palace	土 dirt	花 flower	碧 [piajk] green	In the thirty-six palaces the mosses are emerald green.[46]
魏 Wei	官 officials	牽 drag	車 cart	指 point	千 1000	里 [li'] *li*	Wei officials drag the cart, point a thousand *li* ahead:
東 east	關 pass	酸 acid	風 wind	射 shoot	眸 pupil	子 [tsz'] 	The acid wind of the East Pass shoots into my eyes.[47]

43. See Graham's account of the Bronze Immortals in *Poems of the Late T'ang* (p. 107). Emperor Ming of the Wei ruled from 227 to 240. The first year of the Green Dragon reign period was 233. A certain amount of confusion has arisen because of textual variants. One text says "Ninth Year," but the reign period lasted only five years. Moreover, the statues in fact were moved in the first year of the Jingchu reign period (238).

44. Li He was a descendant of the Tang dynasty Prince of Zheng and thus could properly refer to himself as part of the imperial lineage. He uses the name Changji because that is the area outside Luoyang where he lived.

45. Emperor Wu of the Han dynasty was buried at Maoling. A "ling" is a tumulus, a large mound built to house the imperial tomb. "Young Master Liu" refers to Emperor Wu, whose name was Liu Che 劉徹. "Autumn wind" refers to the "Song of the Autumn Wind," which he was said to have written.

46. Ban Gu's "*Fu* on the Western Capital" refers to the thirty-six buildings of Emperor Wu's palace.

47. This is the pass on the road leading from Chang'an to Luoyang.

空 in vain	將 take	漢 Han	月 moon	出 go out	宮 palace	門 gate	In vain they bring the Han moon out of the palace gates.
憶 recall	君 you	清 pure	淚 tears	如 resemble	鉛 lead	水 [ʂyj′] water	Thinking of you, [I shed] pure tears like molten lead.
衰 decline	蘭 orchid	送 see off	客 traveler	咸 Xian-	陽 -yang	道 [tɦǎw′] road	Decayed orchids see off the traveler on the road from Xianyang.[48]
天 heaven	若 if	有 have	情 feelings	天 heaven	亦 also	老 [lǎw′] grow old	If Heaven had feelings, Heaven too would grow old.
攜 hold	盤 platter	獨 alone	出 go out	月 moon	荒 desolate	涼 	Holding the platter, I go out alone: the moon is desolate.
渭 Wei	城 wall	已 already	遠 far	波 waves	聲 sound	小 [siǎw′] small	The Walls of the Wei already are far, the sound of waves faint.

Angus C. Graham's translation

A Bronze Immortal Takes Leave of Han

Boy Liu in Leafy Mound, visitor of the autumn wind . . .
In the night I heard his horse whinny, at sunrise saw no track.
On the cassia tree by the painted rail the scent of autumn hangs:
In his thirty-six palaces the dust blooms emerald.

Wei's servants haul the cart, point ahead a thousand miles:
A sour wind shoots from the east pass at my pupils.
The moon of Han in vain with me I come forth at the palace gate:
At your memory the transparent tears are like molten lead.

Withering orchids escort me along the Hsien-yang road:
If heaven too had passions even heaven would grow old.
With the pan in my hands I come forth alone under the desolate moon:
The city on the Jwei far back now, quiet the waves.

Study Notes and Questions

In this brilliant historical envisioning, Li He creates the persona of a bronze immortal and imagines the perspective of a statue. He surely was drawing upon Li Bai's recreation of poignant scenes from the past, as in the "Song of the Roosting Crows," but his use of the statue goes well beyond Li Bai.

1. The first line is dense with implications. Why introduce Emperor Wu of the Han by referring to Maoling, his burial tumulus? Why then call Emperor Wu "young Master Liu"? How does this shape the persona of the statue?

---

48. Xianyang was the capital of the Qin dynasty, to the west of the Han (and Tang) capital of Chang'an.

2. What does the second line mean? Why are there no traces? Can a statue hear things humans cannot?

3. Why is it a "Han moon" that the Wei officials attempt to bring out of the palace in line 15?

4. The line "If Heaven had feeling, Heaven too would grow old" is very famous, but what does it mean? Does the statue, in the end, take the perspective of Heaven?

5. What is the effect of the objective closure in the final couplet? Does it illustrate the view enunciated in the couplet before it?

"Song of Li Ping Playing the Harp" by Li He

李憑箜篌引							Song of Li Ping Playing the Harp[49]
吳 Wu	絲 silk	蜀 Shu	桐 pawlonia	張 extend	高 high	秋 [ts^{h}iw] autumn	Wu silk and Shu paulownia draw the autumn yet higher.[50]
空 empty	白 white	凝 congeal	雲 clouds	頹 collapse	不 not	流 [liw] flow	In the empty whiteness, frozen clouds break but do not flow.
湘 Xiang	娥 E	啼 weep	竹 bamboo	素 White	女 Maid	愁 [tʂɦəw] sad	The Xiang Wives weep on bamboo; the White Maid is sad.[51]
李 Li	憑 Ping	中 center	國 state	彈 plays	箜 harp	篌 [xɦəw]	Li Ping in the capital plays the harp:
崑 Kun	山 Mountain	玉 jade	碎 shatter	鳳 phoenix	凰	叫 [kjiawˋ] shout	The jade of the Kun Mountains shattering, a phoenix screeching,
芙 lotus	蓉	泣 weep	露 dew	香 fragrant	蘭 orchid	笑 [siawˋ] laugh	Lotus weeping dew, fragrant orchids laughing.
十 ten	二 two	門 gates	前 before	融 melt	冷 cold	光 [kuaŋ] radiance	Before the twelve gates, it fuses with the moon's cold radiance.[52]
二 two	十 ten	三 three	絲 thread	動 move	紫 Purple	皇 [xɦuaŋ] Emperor	Twenty-three strings move the Purple Emperor.[53]

49. Li Ping was a famous contemporary performer who was part of the imperial troupe.

50. Silk is for the strings, and paulownia wood was considered best for the body of stringed instruments.

51. The Xiang Wives are the two wives of the mythical emperor Shun. After he died, their tears stained the bamboo to create a mottled-leaf variety. They then became goddesses who remained in the Xiang region of Chu. The White Maid was a goddess who played the *qin*, or zither, very well. After Fu Xi invented the fifty-stringed zither, he gave it to the White Maid to play. Her performance moved him so strongly that he cut the zither in two to diminish its power.

52. Chang'an had twelve gates in its city wall.

53. The Purple Emperor was a Daoist god, but the term here refers to the reigning Tang emperor.

女	媧	煉	石	補	天	處 [tsʰiɔ̆´]	Where Nü Wa smelted rock
Nü	Wa	smelt	rock	repair	Heaven	place	to repair the Heavens,[54]
石	破	天	驚	逗	秋	雨 [yă´]	The rock broke, the Heavens startled,
rock	break	Heaven	startle	detain	autumn	rain	and drew on the autumn rain.
夢	入	神	山	教	神	嫗 [ʔyă´]	In dream he entered the spirit mountain,
dream	enter	spirit	mountain	instruct	spirit	old lady	instructed the ancient goddess:
老	魚	跳	波	瘦	蛟	舞 [ʋuɔ̆´]	Aged fish jumped the waves;
old	fish	jump	waves	thin	dragon	dance	haggard dragons danced.
吳	質	不	眠	倚	桂	樹 [ʂɦyɔ̆`]	Wu Zhi did not sleep,
Wu	Zhi	not	sleep	lean	cassia	tree	leaning against the cassia tree:[55]
露	腳	斜	飛	濕	寒	兔 [tʰuɔ̆`]	The dew mist flies aslant,
dew	feet	slant	fly	dampen	cold	rabbit	wetting the cold rabbit.[56]

STUDY NOTES AND QUESTIONS

Later readers called Li He the "Ghostly Talent" 鬼才. He earned the name for having written poems like this, as well as for those that directly invoke the ghostly-like: "The Grave of Little Su" and "The Song of the Bronze Immortals."

1. What does it mean to "draw the autumn higher" in the first line? Can you use the images from the next three lines to help explain this idea?

2. Compare the section describing the music in lines 5–6 and 9–12 to Bai Juyi's approach in the "Ballad of the *Pipa*." How are they the same? How do they differ, and what is the effect of those differences?

3. Once again Li He uses objective closure: how does the final couplet work as the end of a poem on playing a harp?

---

54. Nü Wa, sister of Fu Xi, prepared a special rock to repair a hole in Heaven.

55. Li He refers to Wu Gang 吳剛, a Daoist adept who was banished to the moon for violating Daoist practices. He was condemned to constantly attempt to chop down a two-thousand-foot cassia tree that grew on the moon and that repaired itself after each swing of the axe.

56. The "cold rabbit" refers to the moon.

"Song of the Changping Arrowhead" by Li He

長平箭頭歌							Song of the Changping Arrowhead[57]
漆	灰	骨	末	丹	水	砂 [ʂaː]	Black lacquer ash, white bone
lacquer	ash	bone	tip	cinnabar	water	sand	tip, red cinnabar grain:
淒	淒	古	血	生	銅	花 [xwaː]	The oozing of ancient blood
oozing		old	blood	sprout	bronze	flower	sprouted bronze flowers.
白	翎	金	簳	雨	中	盡	The white feathers and metal-tipped
white	feather	metal	shaft	rain	in	exhaust	shaft have vanished in the rain.
直	餘	三	脊	殘	狼	牙 [ŋjaː]	There only remains the three-spined
only	remain	three	spine	remnant	wolf	tooth	remnant of a wolf's tooth.
我	尋	平	原	乘	兩	馬 [maːˊ]	I searched the level plain,
I	search	level	plain	ride	pair	horse	mounting a pair of horses.
驛	東	石	田	蒿	塢	下 [xɦjaːˋ]	At the foot of a weedy hill in the
station	east	rock	field	weeds	hill	below	rocky fields east of the station,
風	長	日	短	星	蕭	蕭	The wind is constant, the daylight
wind	long	sun	short	stars	sparse and dim		short, the stars few and dim.
黑	旗	雲	濕	懸	空	夜 [jiaˋ]	The black banner clouds are damp
black	banner	cloud	wet	hang	empty	night	and hang in the empty night.
左	魂	右	魄	啼	肌	瘦 [ʂəwˋ]	To the left and right, souls wail
left	souls	right	spirits	weep	flesh	thin	their flesh thin.
酪	瓶	倒	盡	將	羊	炙 [tʂiajk]	Pouring out a bottle of curd,
curd	bottle	up-end	finish	take	goat	roast	I carry roast goat.
蟲	棲	雁	病	蘆	筍	紅	The insects rest quietly; the goose
insect	roost	goose	sick	reed	sprout	red	ails; the reed shoots are red.
迴	風	送	客	吹	陰	火 [xuaˊ]	A whirlwind seeing off the
whirl	wind	see off	traveler	blow	*yin*	fire	traveler blows ghostfires.[58]
訪	古	汍	瀾	收	斷	鏃 [tsəwk]	Visiting the ancient, with tears streaming
visit	ancient	drenched tears		pick up	broken	arrowhead	I pick up a broken arrowhead.
折	鋒	赤	璺	曾	刲	肉 [riwk]	In its snapped tip, a crimson crack:
snap	tip	red	crack	once	split	muscle	it once had pierced flesh.

57. During the Warring States period, the Qin general Bai Qi 白起 accepted the surrender of four hundred thousand troops from the state of Zhao at Changping. He then buried them all alive. Li He passed by the site in 814 en route to visiting a friend, Zhang Che, in Luzhou.

58. These foxfires were thought to be the transformation of ancient blood.

	南	陌	東	城	馬	上	兒	The youth on horse-back on
	south	road	east	wall	horse	on	youth	the south road east of the city
16	勸	我	將	金	換	簝	竹 [triwk]	Urges me to take gold to buy
	urge	me	take	gold	exchange	basket	bamboo	a bamboo altar basket.[59]

Stephen Owen's Translation

Song of an Arrowhead from the Battlefield of Chang-ping

Char of lacquer, powder of bone,
pebble of cinnabar:
in the chill gloom in ancient blood
blooms flowers in the bronze.
The white feathers and gilt shaft
have gone in the rains,
and all that remains is this
three-spined, broken wolf's fang.

I went searching over that level plain,
driving my two-horse team,
through the stony fields east of the station
by the foot of a weed-grown slope;
Daylight shortened, the wind was steady,
stars hung in its moaning,
black banners of cloud were draped soaking
in empty night sky.

To my right and left their wraiths
cried out, starving, lean:
I poured a jug of cream in libation,
took a lamb to roast.
Insects settled, the geese flew sick,
the sprouts of reeds turned red,
and spiraling gusts sent the traveler on his way,
blowing their shadowy fires.

Seeker of the past, tears streaming,
I reaped this snapped barb,
whose broken point and red-brown cracks
once cut through flesh.

59. This last phrase is uncertain. It either refers to a basket in which meats for sacrifice are placed, or it means a type of bamboo good for making the shaft of an arrow.

On a southern lane in the capital's eastern ward
  a boy on horseback
tried to get me to trade the metal
  for an offering basket.

STUDY NOTES AND QUESTIONS

1. Li He describes this poem as a "song." This designation often allows a poet to take stylistic liberties with the old-style form. Comparing the poem with Cao Cao's and Li Bai's poems, are there song-like features in this poem?

2. Li He achieves a "fantastic" quality in his poems where one cannot decide if the elements in the landscape are real or phantasms of Li He's imagination. How do the first two couplets set the framework for such fantastic images?

3. In line 8, what are "black banner clouds"? What resonances does "banner" invoke?

4. In the next couplet (lines 9–10), are we to take the ghosts as real? The many Tang stories involving ghosts suggest that people at the time believed in the existence of ghosts, but they also knew that people had vivid, often overly active imaginations. Meng Jiao probably wanted the reader to take the images in "Cold Creek" as distorted by an overwrought sensibility, but what about here? What is the difference between the implied author suggesting that the narrator is imagining the ghosts and their being presented as real within the framework of the poem?

5. The rhymes in lines 9–12 seem wrong, and some editors suspect that the text is corrupt. There is not much to be done but simply to acknowledge the problem.

6. The ending of the poem is something of a puzzle. What do you see as the significance of the callow youth of the city telling the narrator to exchange the arrow tip for the altar basket?

Li Shangyin 李商隱 (ca. 812–58)

The conventional story of Li Shangyin's life stresses the centrality of factional politics, but the account is hard to assess: it is unclear whether Li Shangyin rose to a high enough position to have suffered from the partisan strife. Like many other Tang poets, he was born into a family with a history of local service, which meant that his clan presumably derived most of its financial stability from land holdings but maintained status and tax privileges by sending sons to seek office. When Li Shangyin was a child, he accompanied his father as he served on the staff of various regional officials, but his father died when Li Shangyin was ten, so he and his mother returned to the familiy's estate in Zhengzhou 鄭州 (in modern Henan Province). After the period of mourning, he appears to have moved to Luoyang. At eighteen, he met the important official Linghu Chu 令狐楚 in Luoyang, impressed him, and joined his staff. At twenty-one he attempted the *jinshi* exam but failed and followed Linghu Chu to Taiyuan, where Linghu served as governor. Li soon returned to Zhengzhou, presumably to continue to prepare for the *jinshi* examination. He continued to fail until finally succeeding in 837, apparently with the help of Linghu Chu's son, Linghu Tao. Having passed the examination, Li Shangyin went to rejoin Linghu Chu's staff, but Linghu died in the winter of 837. The next year he received a summons to join the staff of Wang Maoyuan in Jingyuan 涇原 in the northwest (in modern Gansu Province). Wang was sufficiently impressed by the young man that he offered him his daughter in marriage. Li participated in a decree examination to try to advance his career but failed. After that, he had what would appear to be a more or less typical mid-level official's career of postings in the capital, in the provinces, and on the staff of regional governors mixed with periods spent at home. Even so, traditional accounts of his life attribute the difficulties he encountered to the enmity he earned by switching his allegiance from Linghu Chu and Linghu Tao—who were in Niu Sengru's faction—to Wang Maoyuan, who was loyal to Li Deyu. However, even as late as 851, Linghu Tao seems to have helped Li Shangyin attain a post. In any case, the factional dispute has gained importance less as a way to explain Li Shangyin's biography than as a way to interpret his poetry.

During his lifetime and into the Song dynasty, Li Shangyin was primarily admired as a prose stylist in formal, elegant parallel forms. His poetry shares many traits with his prose. It is densely allusive, tightly structured, and difficult for the non-specialist. Some of Li Shangyin's poetry—and especially his so-called "Untitled" poems—have an additional layer of difficulty. They seem to refer to events and to understandings shared by Li Shangyin and his immediate audience but lost to later readers. The poems themselves refuse to be more specific. Critics have taken these poems as referring either to patrons who misunderstood Li (Linghu Tao and the Niu faction) or to lovers with whom he had been forbidden contact. My own reading is that the poems are one more form of late Tang experimentation in how to represent the ways subjectivity interferes with and deeply informs our engagement with the world. Reading Li's most radical poems, one has the sense that we are trapped in a world of loss and longing, unable to see beyond the sorrow.

"Brocade Zither" by Li Shangyin

錦瑟							Brocade Zither
錦	瑟	無	端	五	十	絃 [xɦjian]	A brocade zither, fifty strings to no end.[60]
brocade	zither	with no	end-point	five	ten	strings	
一	絃	一	柱	思	華	年 [nian]	For each string, each peg, thinking about flourishing years.
one	string	one	peg	long for	florid	year	
莊	生	曉	夢	迷	蝴	蝶	Master Zhuang in a dawn dream strayed as a butterfly.[61]
Zhuang	Master	dawn	dream	confuse	butterfly		
望	帝	春	心	託	杜	鵑 [kjyan]	Wang Di's spring heart is entrusted to the cuckoo.[62]
Wang	Emperor	spring	heart	entrust	cuckoo		
滄	海	月	明	珠	有	淚	On the dark sea the moon is bright; for pearls we have tears.[63]
dark	sea	moon	bright	pearls	have	tears	
藍	田	日	暖	玉	生	煙 [ʔjian]	On Indigo Field the sun is warm: the jade gives off haze.[64]
Indigo	Field	sun	warm	jade	grow	mist	
此	情	可	待	成	追	憶	Can this feeling have waited to become a recalled memory?
this	feeling	can be	await	become	chase	recall	
只	是	當	時	已	惘	然 [rian]	It's just that, at the time, it was already indistinct.
just	is	that	time	already	at a loss		

---

60. The "brocade" describes the elaborate decoration on the body of the zither. A *se* 瑟 is a large type of zither like the Japanese *koto*. Even the *se*, however has only twenty-three or twenty-five strings. "Fifty strings" alludes to the story of the Pale Girl 素女. When the mythic emperor Fu Xi was performing a ceremony to Heaven and Earth, the Pale Girl played ritual music on a fifty-stringed *se*. Her playing was so sad that Fu Xi ordered her to stop. Because she refused, he broke the instrument in half to create the twenty-five–stringed zither.

61. The final passage of "Discourse on Equalizing Things"《齊物論》in *Zhuang Zi* describes how Zhuang Zi once dreamed that he was a butterfly unaware that he was in fact Zhuang Zi. On waking, he was not sure whether he was Zhuang Zi who had dreamt that he was a butterfly or a butterfly who now dreamed that he was Zhuang Zi.

62. Wang Di was the king of Shu during the Warring States period. There are various versions of the account of Wang Di's departure from Shu, his regret, and his transformation into a cuckoo. In one version, he assigned Bie Ling 鱉靈, an able minister, to do water conservancy away from the capital. While Bie was away, Wang Di debauched his wife. Ashamed of his action, Wang Di yielded the throne to Bie and left Shu. Later he regretted his exile, and, when he died, his soul was transformed into a cuckoo.

63. Li Shan 李善 (early Tang) explains in his commentary to Zuo Si's "*Fu* on the Capital of Wu"《吳都賦》in the *Zhaoming wenxuan* 昭明文選 that when the moon is full, pearls are completely round, and as the moon wanes, pearls grow smaller. Also, it was believed (or at least there was a story) that merpeople cried tears of pearl.

64. Indigo Field Mountain in Shaanxi Province was famous for its jade. Various stories have accrued around this line. For example, the *Lu yi zhuan* 錄異傳 preserves a tale about Fuchai, a famous king of Wu. He refused to allow his daughter, Purple Jade, to marry the man she loved. After she died of vexation, Fuchai saw some purple jade giving off a strange gleam; his wife ran out to pick up the jade, but it burst into flames and disappeared. Many commentaries also cite Sikong Tu's 司空圖 (837–908) comment that Dai Shulun 戴叔倫 (732–89) wrote, "A poet's scene is like Indigo Field when the sun is warm and fine jade gives off mist: it can be seen from afar, but it cannot be set directly before the eyes."「詩家之景，如藍田日暖，良玉生煙，可望而不可置於眉睫之前也。」

Angus C. Graham's Translation

The Patterned Lute

Mere chance that the patterned lute has fifty strings.
String and fret, one by one, recall the blossoming years.
Chuang-tzû dreams at sunrise that a butterfly lost its way,
Wang-ti bequeathed his spring passion to the nightjar.
The moon is full on the vast sea, a tear on the pearl.
On Blue Mountain the sun warms, a smoke issues from the jade.
    Did it wait, this mood, to mature with hindsight?
In a trance from the beginning, then as now.

Study Notes and Questions

"Brocade Zither" is one of Li Shangyin's most famous poems, and like his "Untitled" poems, readers have no good idea what it means. One important Qing dynasty interpretation is that the poem commemorates the death of Li Shangyin's wife. Since this is the first poem in Li Shangyin's collection as it was transmitted, the modern scholar Qian Zhongshu suggests that the poem is about poetry itself. The poem effectively may be an "Untitled" poem, since its title may have been simply taken from the first two words of the first line. Line by line, the poem presents mysteries.

1. In line 1, why does the zither have fifty strings "to no end," i.e., pointlessly?

2. Does the second line indicate that the author is fifty years old? Unfortunately, Li Shangyin may not have lived that long.

3. Are the inner couplets describing the music? If so, what types of sound are they describing?

4. Try to paraphrase the final couplet. Does comparing the two translations help?

"Untitled" ("Seeing one another is hard") by Li Shangyin

無題							Untitled
相	見	時	難	別	亦	難 [nan]	Seeing one another is hard;
mutually	see	time	hard	separate	also	hard	separation is also hard.
東	風	無	力	百	花	殘 [tsɦan]	The east wind is without force,
east	wind	without	strength	hundred	flowers	remnant	the hundred flowers tattered.[65]
春	蠶	到	死	絲	方	盡	The spring silkworm's silk stops
spring	silkworm	arrive	death	silk	just now	exhaust	only with its death.
蠟	炬	成	灰	淚	始	乾 [kan]	The tears of the wax torch begin to
wax	torch	become	ash	tears	first	dry	dry only when it has become ash.
曉	鏡	但	愁	雲	鬢	改	At the dawn mirror, she only grieves at
dawn	mirror	only	sorrow	cloud	locks	change	the change in her cloud-like forelocks.
夜	吟	應	覺	月	光	寒 [xɦan]	Chanting at night, she surely is aware
night	chant	surely	aware	moon	gleam	cold	that the moon's gleam is cold.
蓬	山	此	去	無	多	路	Mount Penglai is not far from here:[66]
Peng	Mountain	this	leave	without	many	roads	
青	鳥	殷	勤	為	探	看 [k^{h}an]	Bluebird, try your best to spy her out for me.
blue	bird	very diligent		for sake	seek	look	

ANGUS C. GRAHAM'S TRANSLATION

Untitled (vi)

For ever hard to meet, and as hard to part.
Each flower spoils in the failing East wind.
Spring's silkworms wind till death their heart's threads:
The wick of the candle turns to ash before its tears dry.
Morning mirror's only care, a change at her cloudy temples:
Saying over a poem in the night, does she sense the chill in the moonbeams?
  Not far, from here to Fairy Hill.
Bluebird, be quick now, spy me out the road.

65. The east wind is the spring wind.

66. Mt. Penglai is one of the mythical Islands of the Immortals in the eastern ocean.

Study Notes and Questions

Li Shangyin's "Untitled" poems have been subject to endless speculation. Some commentaries have proposed that the poems refer to clandestine love either within the imperial palace or with a woman beyond the reach of propriety. Others have offered political readings, where Li Shangyin is pleading for a renewal of trust within the factional disputes of the day. I prefer to consider them as "tone poems," the orchestration of elements to create a particular subjectivity within the poem.

1. What information can be gleaned from the poem? What is the basic problematic informing the poem? What time of year is it? What is the status of the person described in the poem? What is the attitude of the persona speaking in the poem?

2. Although the fragments are disjointed, is it possible to construct a narrative for the poem?

3. Is there a unity of mood in the poem? Explain.

"Untitled" ("'I'll come' is an empty phrase") by Li Shangyin

無題							Untitled
來	是	空	言	去	絕	蹤 [tsywŋ]	"I'll come" is an empty phrase,
come	is	empty	word	leave	cut off	trace	going leaves no trace.
月	斜	樓	上	五	更	鐘 [tʂywŋ]	The moon slants on the tower
moon	slant	tower	on	fifth	watch	bell	at the bell of the fifth watch.[67]
夢	為	遠	別	啼	難	喚	In a distant parting in a dream,
dream	become	distant	separate	cry	hard	call out	I weep, unable to call out.
書	被	催	成	墨	未	濃 [nrywŋ]	Writing compelled to be finished
writing	[passive]	urgent	complete	ink	not yet	dark	in haste, the ink not yet dark.[68]
蠟	照	半	籠	金	翡	翠	The shining of the wax [candle] half
wax	shine	half	cage	gold	kingfisher		encloses the gold kingfisher.[69]
麝	熏	微	度	繡	芙	蓉 [jywŋ]	The scent of muskdeer faintly drifts
muskdeer	scent	faint	cross	embroider	lotus		over the embroidered lotus.[70]

67. The night is divided into five watch periods. The fifth watch begins at 4:00 AM. A bell would be rung at the beginning of each watch.

68. The Chinese used an ink stick made of compressed charcoal, which they then ground on a stone slab with water. The longer one ground, the darker the ink.

69. The kingfisher is used to describe an iridescent turquoise color. The image here is probably of an embroidered kingfisher in which both turquoise and gold thread were used.

70. The scent gland of the muskdeer was used in the making of incense.

劉	郎	已	恨	蓬	山	遠	Master Liu already regretted that Mount Penglai was far:[71]
Liu	Master	already	regret	Peng	Mountain	far	
更	隔	蓬	山	一	萬	重 [trɦywŋ]	Now, separated from Mount Penglai ten thousand-fold.
again	apart	Peng	Mountain	one	10,000	-fold	

PAUL ROUZER'S TRANSLATION

Untitled

"I'll come" an empty promise;
you left without a trace.
Now the moon sets over the house
and bell of dawn rings out.
I dreamt we were parted by great distance,
and my sobbing could not call you;
Then I hurried to finish a letter for you,
not waiting for ink to darken.
The light of the candle half-enclosed
a screen of turquoise and gold;
Incense fragrance faintly crossed
a robe with embroidered lotus.
Young Liu had always hated
that Penglai was so far
Now he finds that Penglai conceals
a myriad hills beyond.

STUDY NOTES AND QUESTIONS

1. As in the first "Untitled" poem, Li Shangyin here offers fragments of a narrative of separation and longing. What holds these fragments together? Who is the narrator? Where is the narrator?

2. Is there unity of time in the poem, or does it weave together the present moment and past recollection?

3. Are the middle couplets parallel? Explain. How are the lines different if one thinks of them as halves of parallel couplets?

---

71. Penglai was one of the Three Islands of the Immortals of Daoist legend.

"Listening to a Song" by Li Shangyin

聞歌							Listening to a Song
斂	笑	凝	眸	意	欲	歌 [ka]	Gathering her smiles, eyes becoming fixed, she is about to sing.
gather	smile	congeal	pupil	intent	about to	sing	
高	雲	不	動	碧	嵯	峨 [ŋa]	High clouds stop moving, becoming towering emerald mountains.[72]
high	clouds	not	move	emerald	towering		
銅	臺	罷	望	歸	何	處	At Bronze Sparrow Terrace, they have stopped gazing; where have they gone?[73]
bronze	terrace	quit	gaze	return	what	place	
玉	輦	忘	還	事	幾	多 [ta]	The jade chariot has forgotten to return: how many matters have arisen?[74]
jade	chariot	forget	return	matters	how	many	
青	冢	路	邊	南	雁	盡	By the road to Green Mound the south-flying geese are all gone.[75]
green	grave	road	side	south	geese	finish	
細	腰	宮	裏	北	人	過 [kua]	Northerners now visit the slim waists in the palace.[76]
slim	waist	palace	in	North	people	pass by	
此	聲	腸	斷	非	今	日	This sound that rends one's innards is not of today [alone]:
this	sound	innards	break	is not	now	day	
香	灺	燈	殘	奈	爾	何 [xɦa]	As the fragrant [tallow] is consumed, the lamp grows dim, what can you hope for?
incense	burn up	lamp	remnant	avail	you	what?	

72. The clouds' stopping, frequently mentioned in poems on singing, comes from a story in the "Tang Inquired"《湯問》chapter of a late Han dynasty Daoist miscellany, *Lie Zi*. Xue Tan, a student of the singing master Qin Qing, believed that he had learned all that Qin could teach him and asked permission to leave. Qin assented, but at the farewell banquet when Qin sang, "the sound shook the forest and the echoes stopped the clouds." Xue apologized and never again dared to speak of leaving.

73. Cao Cao, on his deathbed, requested that his concubines be gathered into the Bronze Sparrow Terrace, a palatial residence. They were to sing and offer sacrifices to his spirit and were to gaze at his tumulus for a long time and remember him.

74. Two stories are perhaps relevant here. King Mu of Zhou rode throughout his kingdom on a chariot adorned with jade and gold. During his meeting with the Daoist goddess, Queen Mother of the West, he sang a song with her. When the song finished, she rode off into the clouds. Also, the last emperor of the Sui, Sui Yangdi, allowed himself to be distracted by his concubines. After he journeyed to Yangzhou, he did not want to return to the North, which was already in rebellion. He died in the South.

75. Green Mound is the gravesite of Wang Zhaojun, the concubine of Han Yuandi who was given to the Xiongnu to marry their king. She died and was buried in the far north.

76. "Slim waists" alludes to King Ling of Chu: he liked thin waists and thus many women in the country starved themselves to please him. "Northerners" alludes to the Qin conquest of Chu.

STUDY NOTES AND QUESTIONS

1. This is yet another song about a musical performance, but Li Shangyin treats the topic quite differently from Du Fu, Bai Juyi, or Li He. At what points in the poem does he refer to the playing and his reaction to it?

2. What is the function of the parallel inner couplets? Explain in detail how the parallelism works. What do the couplets contribute to the account of the performance?

"Chang E" by Li Shangyin

嫦娥							Chang E[77]
雲 cloud	母 mother	屏 screen	風 wind	燭 candle	影 shadow	深 [ʂim] deep	Behind the mica windscreen, the candle's shadows grow deep.
長 long	河 river	漸 gradual	落 fall	曉 dawn	星 stars	沉 [trɦim] sink	As the long River [of Stars] gradually falls, the dawn stars sink.[78]
嫦 Chang	娥 E	應 ought	悔 regret	偷 steal	靈 divine	藥 herb	Chang E surely regrets having stolen the divine herb:
碧 green	海 sea	青 blue	天 sky	夜 night	夜 night	心 [sim] heart	The green sea, the blue sky, her heart night after night.

ANGUS C. GRAHAM'S TRANSLATION

Ch'ang O

The lamp glows deep in the mica screen.
The long river slowly descends, the morning star drowns.
Is Ch'ang O sorry that she stole the magic herb,
Between the blue sky and the emerald sea, thinking night after night?

STUDY NOTES AND QUESTIONS

1. How do the two couplets of the poem hold together? What does the first couplet have to do with Chang E, and what does Chang E have to do with the scene set out in the first couplet?

2. What is the mood in the poem? Does the poem have a man's voice or woman's, or can't one tell? Does the question of authorial voice matter? Compare the voice here with that in "Night Rain, Sent North" below.

---

77. According to a story in the "Surveying Obscurities"《覽冥》chapter of *Huainan Zi*, Chang E was the wife of Yi 羿. Yi requested an elixir of eternal life from the Queen Mother of the West, but before he could use it, Chang E stole it, drank it, and fled to the moon. In later accounts, she became the moon's presiding spirit.

78. The image here is of the Milky Way slowly rotating as the night progresses.

"Night Rain, Sent North" by Li Shangyin

夜雨寄北							Night Rain, Sent North
君	問	歸	期	未	有	期 [kɦi]	You ask the date set for my return:
you	ask	return	date	not yet	there is	date	no date has yet been set.
巴	山	夜	雨	漲	秋	池 [trɦi]	In the Ba Mountains the night rain
Ba Mountain		night	rain	swell	autumn	pool	swells the autumn pools.[79]
何	當	共	剪	西	窗	燭	When shall we together trim the
what	at	together	trim	west	window	candle	candle at the west window,[80]
卻	話	巴	山	夜	雨	時 [ʂɦi]	And talk about the time of night
but then	talk	Ba Mountain		night	rain	time	rain in the Ba Mountains?

ANGUS C. GRAHAM'S TRANSLATION

Night Rains: To My Wife Up North

You ask how long before I come. Still no date is set.
The night rains on Mount Pa swell the autumn pool.
When shall we, side by side, trim a candle at the West window,
And talk back to the time of the night rains on Mount Pa?

KENNETH REXROTH'S TRANSLATION

When Will I Be Home

When will I be home? I don't know.
In the mountains, in the rainy night,
The Autumn lake is flooded.
Someday we will be back together again.
We will sit in the candlelight by the West window.
And I will tell you how I remembered you
Tonight on the stormy mountain.

STUDY NOTES AND QUESTIONS

1. Note the use of repetition in the poem. The repetition within the first line is later echoed by repeated phrases in the second and fourth lines. What is the effect of these repetitions on the cadence of the poem?

---

79. The Ba Mountains are a mountain range in Sichuan. Li Shangyin presumably sent this poem to his wife in Chang'an in 848, although some scholars argue that the timing does not actually work.

80. The wick of a Chinese candle is made of reed rather than string. It needs to be broken off on occasion.

2. Some scholars suggest that Li Shangyin here consciously echoes the ending of Du Fu's "Moonlit Night" in this poem. Would such an allusion add to or subtract from the poem?

"The Sui Palace" by Li Shangyin

隋宮							The Sui Palace
紫 Purple	泉 Spring	宮 palace	殿 palace	鎖 lock	煙 mist	霞 [xɦa:] cloud	The palaces at Purple Spring are locked in mist.[81]
欲 wish	取 take	蕪 weedy	城 city	作 make	帝 imperial	家 [kja:] household	He wished to make a weed-grown city the imperial dwelling.[82]
玉 jade	璽 seal	不 not	緣 fated	歸 return	日 sun	角 angle	Had the jade seal not been fated to turn to the one with a high forehead,[83]
錦 brocade	帆 sail	應 ought	是 is	到 reach	天 sky	涯 [ŋja:j] border	The brocade sails surely would have reached the edge of the sky.[84]
於 until	今 now	腐 rotten	草 grass	無 with no	螢 firefly	火 fire	Even now the rotting grass is without the firefly's glow.[85]
終 end	古 ancient	垂 hanging	楊 willow	有 there are	暮 sunset	鴉 [ʔja:] crows	For all time there will be sunset crows in the weeping willows.[86]
地 ground	下 below	若 if	逢 meet	陳 Chen	後 last	主 ruler	If, below the ground, he meets the last ruler of the Chen dynasty,[87]
豈 how	宜 proper	重 again	問 ask	後 rear	庭 court	花 [xwa:] flower	How would it be right to ask again about "Flowers in the Rear Courtyard?"[88]

81. "Purple Spring" is a site north of Chang'an, which was the capital of the Sui as well as the Tang dynasty.

82. The Southern Dynasties poet Bao Zhao wrote the "*Fu* on the Weed-grown City"《蕪城賦》to describe the desolation of the city of Guangling 廣陵 (modern Yangzhou) after it had been burnt down in a rebellion. Emperor Yang of the Sui dynasty established Yangzhou as a secondary capital.

83. The Jade Seal is the emperor's official seal used in authenticating his documents. It is a metonym for the emperor's legitimacy of rule. A high forehead with the bones bulging pronouncedly foretells that one will become emperor. The founder of the Tang dynasty was said to have such a physiognomy.

84. The grand ships on which Emperor Yang made his visits to the South as he rebuilt the canal system had sumptuous brocade sails. The "edge of the sky" may echo the account of Emperor Wu of the Han's attempt to reach the Islands of the Immortals far off in the eastern ocean.

85. Emperor Yang once ordered his palace officials to capture thousands of fireflies—which were thought to be produced by rotting grass—so that he could release them on a nighttime excursion to the mountains.

86. Emperor Yang ordered that willows be planted on the banks of the canals that he had rebuilt.

87. The dead go to the Yellow Springs under the ground.

Stephen Owen's Translation

The Sui Palace

The halls of the palace at Lavender Springs
shut in mists and rose clouds,
but he wished to occupy City of Weeds
to serve as the Emperor's home.

Had the jade scepter not, by consequence,
gone to him with the sun-knobs,
I am sure that those brocade sails
would have made it to the horizon.

Even today the rotting plants
are bare of fireflies,
yet for all time the hanging willows
will have their twilight crows.

If under the Earth he happens to meet
the last ruler of the Chen,
it would not be right again to ask
for "In the Rear Court Flowers."

Study Notes and Questions

1. This is a poem in the subgenre of "cherishing the old" (*huai gu* 懷古). How does Li Shangyin see the past inhering in the present scene? How does the exploration of what remains reinterpret the past events? Consider in particular the assessment offered in the second couplet.

2. It remains useful to stress that the poem is regulated verse. Although the second couplet is a single sentence that begins with a counterfactual proposition, it still does so through parallel lines. How does it work? Also explain the implications of the pairings of the third couplet.

88. Yan Shigu 顏師古 (581–645) in the *Sui yilu* 隋遺錄 records how Emperor Yang of the Sui dynasty, while he was still heir apparent, dreamed of the dead last ruler of the Chen. The deceased ruler brought in several palace ladies, one more beautiful than the rest. Emperor Yang requested that they dance to the tune "Flowers in the Rear Courtyard." When they had finished, the Chen ruler asked Emperor Yang if he enjoyed his sailing excursions and argued that each simply pursued that which pleased him and thus, after the Sui conquest of the South, he should not have condemned the Chen ruler for his devotion to his decadent aesthetic ways. For later Tang dynasty literati, Emperor Yang in the end also brought his own empire to ruin through his profligate rule.

Du Mu 杜牧 (803–53)

Accounts of Du Mu tend to present two very different images of the same person, with little effort to reconcile them.[89] The first is based on the historical record and Du Mu's writings in his main collection. The second is a romantic myth based on the poetry that accumulated in his "Separate Collection" 別集.

Du Mu was from an illustrious clan. His grandfather, Du You, had a long career as chief minister under a succession of emperors and wrote the *Tong dian* 通典, a classic study of governmental institutions throughout the imperial period. Du Mu and his cousin Du Cong both continued their family tradition during the difficult years of the late Tang. Du Mu passed the *jinshi* examination at age twenty-six, then passed a decree examination and received a capital posting. Shortly thereafter, however, he left to serve for eight years on the staffs of a series of military governors. He returned to court, but because he had to leave again to take care of his younger brother, who had gone blind, he again sought staff positions. Returning once more to the capital at age thirty-seven, Du Mu remained for three years in various offices before being appointed as prefect to three Jiangnan prefectures in succession. He spent one more period in the capital before being reassigned yet again as a prefect in the southeast. When he finally returned to the capital three years later, he fell ill and died. It would seem that one reason he was constantly sent out to serve as prefect is that he was good at it: in one well-known memorial, Du Mu analyzed the problem of piracy on the Yangzi River and proposed solutions that were supported by Li Deyu but apparently never were implemented. It is worth mentioning that Du Mu wrote a commentary on the *Sun Zi*, a classic of military strategy, and had participated in discussions about the complex military campaigns during Li Deyu's period as the dominant minister under Wuzong.

Du Fu is primarily thought of as a poet of the "Late Tang" style. His best-known poems are indeed calm, crafted regulated verse that reflected on the encountered landscape. His collection also has several famous poems drawing on themes from the pleasure quarters.

89. Zhou Xifu 周錫韍 in his popular anthology of Du Mu's poems, *Du Mu shi xuan* 杜牧詩選 (Hong Kong: Joint Publishing, 1980), does in fact confront the question of the "real" Du Mu and argues that the romantic myth should be set aside as an exaggeration of a commonly shared sensuous aspect of elite life during the Tang.

"Mooring on the Qinhuai River" by Du Mu

泊秦淮							Mooring on the Qinhuai River[90]
煙 mist	籠 cage	寒 cold	水 water	月 moon	籠 cage	沙 [ʂa] sand	Mist veils the cold water; the moon veils the sand.
夜 night	泊 moor	秦 Qin	淮 Huai	近 near	酒 wine	家 [kja:] house	At night mooring on the Qinhuai, we are near a tavern.
商 merchant	女 girl	不 not	知 know	亡 lost	國 kingdom	恨 regret	A singing girl does not know the regret of a doomed country:[91]
隔 across	江 river	猶 still	唱 sing	後 Rear	庭 Court	花 [xwa:] Flowers	Across the river, she still sings "Flowers in the Rear Courtyard."[92]

STUDY NOTES AND QUESTIONS

This poem remains true to its occasional nature: Du Mu captures his sense of what it is like to stop for the night in the "southern" ambience of the Qin-Huai region.

1. Drawing on your own experience, when and why would mist form above a small river? What would it mean for the moon to "veil" (literally, "encage") the sand? How bright is the moon? How sharp a change is there between the sand on the bank and the earth behind and above it?

2. Why *would* a singing girl know "the regret of a doomed country?" Why does this question occur to Du Mu? If the song is a pretty southern tune, why should she not sing it? That is, does Du Mu know too much for his own good here? Does his historical sensibility alienate him from the scene, in which he is, after all, just a stranger passing through? Presumably the scene is quite lovely: across the river, a young girl is singing, but what exactly does her singing reveal?

---

90. The Qinhuai River is a tributary of the Yangzi River, which flows into the Yangzi near present-day Nanjing.

91. The phrase "doomed country" refers in part to the "Great Preface" to the *Canon of Poetry*. The preface argues that one can discern the status of a country by its poetry: "The sound of a doomed country is sad and resentful." See chapter 3 for a translation of the "Great Preface."

92. This song was written by the last emperor of the Chen dynasty, last of the Southern Dynasties. The song is considered emblematic of the frivolous, eroticized, aestheticized Southern court before its much-deserved conquest by the vigorous, martial Sui dynasty.

"Relieving My Thoughts" by Du Mu

遣懷							Relieving My Thoughts
落	拓	江	南	載	酒	行 [xɦja:jŋ]	A knock-about south of the river, I carried ale as I went.
down and out		River	south	carry	wine	travel	
楚	腰	纖	細	掌	中	輕 [kʰjiajŋ]	The waists of Chu are fine and delicate, light in the palm.[93]
Chu	waist	fine	narrow	palm	middle	light	
十	年	一	覺	揚	州	夢	Once wakened from a ten-year Yangzhou dream,[94]
ten	years	one	waken	Yang-	-zhou	dream	
贏	得	青	樓	薄	倖	名 [mjiajŋ]	What I have gained is the name of a dandy in the brothels.
gain	obtain	blue	tower	slight	favor	name	

Angus C. Graham's Translation

Easing My Heart

By river and lakes at odds with life I journeyed, wine my freight:
Slim waists of Ch'u broke my heart, light bodies danced into my palm.
Ten years late I wake at last out of my Yang-chou dream
With nothing but the name of a drifter in the blue houses.*

*'Blue houses': brothels.

Study Notes and Questions

This is an extremely well-known poem that has stuck Du Mu with the reputation of the wastrel lamented here. The poem, however, is not part of his "official" collection. He perhaps excluded it, or it perhaps became attached to his name after his death.

93. One text has "break [my] heart" 斷腸 for "fine and delicate."

94. Yangzhou is a major city in the South (Jiangnan).

"Traveling in the Mountains" by Du Mu

山行							Traveling in the Mountains
遠 far	上 ascend	寒 cold	山 mountain	石 rock	徑 path	斜 [sɦia] slant	Climbing far into the cold hills, the rocky path slants.
白 white	雲 cloud	生 born	處 place	有 there is	人 people	家 [kja:] house	Where white clouds are born there are men's houses.
停 stop	車 cart	坐 sitting-ly	愛 cherish	楓 maple	林 forest	晚 late	Stopping my carriage, I cherish the afternoon in the maple forest:[95]
霜 frost	葉 leaves	紅 red	於 than	二 second	月 month	花 [xwa:] flower	The frosty leaves are redder than flowers in the Second Month.

ANGUS C. GRAHAM'S TRANSLATION

Travelling in the Mountains

Far up the cold mountains the stony path slopes:
Where the white clouds are born there are homes of men.
Stop the carriage, sit and enjoy the evening in the maple wood:
The frosty leaves are redder than the second month's flowers.

STUDY NOTES AND QUESTIONS

The Study Notes and Questions for Bai Juyi's landscape quatrains (p. 280) suggest that comparison with this poem might be useful. Du Mu here exploits the quatrain form where the first two lines set up a situation, the third line raises a question, and the fourth line offers an answer.

1. Here, the first two lines offer a rather sere landscape, high up in cold mountains with clouds drifting in and out and only a few human dwellings. The third line, given this context, raises the question: why tarry in such scenery?

2. The answer in the fourth line seems to present some sort of revelation to be wondered at, a revelation that, in contrast to Bai Juyi's quatrains, seems to reach beyond mere human subjectivity to suggest a significant pattern in the world upon which Du Mu has stumbled. What is that pattern?

---

95. *Zuo* 坐, the word that I awkwardly render as "sitting-ly," is a function word meaning "without doing anything" [an action spontaneously occurs] that derives from the full verbal meaning of the word, "to sit." Note that Graham translates the character as the verb "sit."

From the Series "Presented at Farewell" by Du Mu

贈別二首第二							Presented at Farewell, 2 poems, no. 2
多	情	卻	似	總	無	情 [tsɦiajŋ]	Much emotion resembles a complete lack of emotion.
much	feeling	yet	resemble	entirely	without	feeling	
惟	覺	樽	前	笑	不	成 [ʂɦiajŋ]	We are only aware that in front of the wine cup, no smiles form.
only	aware	goblet	before	smile	not	form	
蠟	燭	有	心	還	惜	別	The wax candle has a heart and laments parting:
wax	candle	has	heart	also	lament	farewell	
替	人	垂	淚	到	天	明 [miajŋ]	For people it drips tears until the sky brightens.[96]
for	people	hang	tears	reach	sky	bright	

ANGUS C. GRAHAM'S TRANSLATION

Farewell Poem (second of two to a girl of Yangzhou)

Passion too deep seems like none.
While we drink, nothing shows but the smile which will not come.
The wax candles feel, suffer at partings:
Their tears drip for us till the sky brightens.

STUDY NOTES AND QUESTIONS

1. The first line is admired for its construction. What do the grammatical function words "yet" (*que* 卻) and "entirely" (*zong* 總), called "empty words" in Chinese, contribute to the cadence and emotional quality of this line? Can you draw on personal experiences to explain this line's meaning and effect?

2. Explain the wit in the final couplet. Also explain how this couplet uses the generic expectations of the quatrain as discussed in the Study Notes and Questions to "Traveling in the Mountains" above.

---

96. The wick of a candle is called its "heart," and candle drippings are called "tears."

"Written on the Wall of the Water Pavilion of Kaiyuan Temple" by Du Mu

[Complete Title]

題宣州開元寺水閣閣下宛溪夾溪居人

Written on the wall of the Water Pavilion of Kaiyuan Temple in Xuanzhou for residents on both sides of Wan Creek below the pavilion[97]

六	朝	文	物	草	連	空 [khəwŋ]	The remains of the Six Dynasties
six	dynasty	culture	object	grass	reach	void	culture: grasses stretch to the void.
天	澹	雲	閑	今	古	同 [tɦəwŋ]	The sky is placid, the clouds idle,
sky	calm	clouds	idle	now	ancient	same	long ago and now the same.
鳥	去	鳥	來	山	色	裏	Birds go, birds come midst the
bird	go	bird	come	mountain	color	in	colors of the mountains.
人	歌	人	哭	水	聲	中 [triwŋ]	People sing, people cry within the
people	sing	people	cry	water	sound	middle	sound of the waters.[98]
深	秋	簾	幕	千	家	雨	The curtains of deep autumn:
deep	autumn	curtain	curtain	thousand	house	rain	rain on a thousand houses.
落	日	樓	臺	一	笛	風 [fuwŋ]	The setting sun on the towers and
fall	sun	tower	terrace	one	pipe	wind	terraces: wind of a single reed pipe.
惆	悵	無	因	見	范	蠡	Dejected, I have no way to see
deeply sad		without	means	see	Fan	Li	Fan Li:[99]
參	差	煙	樹	五	湖	東 [təwŋ]	Uneven misty trees east of the
uneven array		mist	tree	five	lake	east	Five Lakes.

97. Xuanzhou is a city south of Yangzhou. Du Mu took his brother there to try to help him recover from his eye ailment.

98. This is perhaps an allusion to the "Tan gong, part 2"《檀弓下》in the *Record of Rites*. After the Duke of Jin congratulated Master Wen for establishing a new dwelling, the structure was praised, "[People] will sing here. [People] will cry here. The clans of the state will gather here."

99. Fan Li was minister to Goujian, the King of Yue, and aided him in exacting revenge on the state of Wu. After his plan was realized, he sought the life of a recluse and sailed into the Five Lakes.

PAUL ROUZER'S TRANSLATION

I wrote this on the Water Pavilion of Kaiyuan Temple in Xuanzhou; below the Pavilion, residences line either side of Wan Stream.

All those cultured relics of the Six Dynasties:
  now grass stretches to the sky.
The sky grows pale, the clouds drift idle:
  Then and Now the same.
Birds will come and birds will go
  within the colors of the hills;
And men will sing and men will cry
  amid the sound of water.
Curtains and blinds in the depth of autumn:
  rain falls on a thousand homes;
Mansion and terrace in the setting sun:
  the wind carries a single flute.
I grow melancholy as I know
  there's no way to meet Fan Li;
And the misty trees rise unevenly
  to the east of the Five Lakes.

STUDY NOTES AND QUESTIONS

1. This is an extremely well crafted Late Tang poem. Think of it first as an example of regulated verse: what are the themes of the first couplet? Are they developed in the middle couplets, or are the earlier norms of aesthetic unity represented by the phrase "initiate-receive-turn-synthesize" 起承轉合 no longer relevant?[100]

2. The parallelism of the second couplet is not complex: explain the "colors" and "sounds" in the two lines.

3. The third line is especially well crafted. What is "rain on a thousand houses" (literally, a "thousand house rain")? What is the "wind of a single reed pipe"? Explain what they mean when arranged as parallel phrases.

4. Explain the image used in the objective closure at the end of the poem.

---

100. The phrase is in fact a retrospective formulation for the normative structure of a poem proposed in the Yuan dynasty (1271–1368), but it is a good general guide to the organization of Early and High Tang regulated verse in particular.

Wen Tingyun 溫庭筠 (ca. 812–66)

Trying to dissociate fact from myth in the biography of Wen Tingyun is even more difficult than for Du Mu. We know little for sure, but many wonderful stories of Wen's bad behavior accumulated and found their way into the dynastic histories.[101] In any case, he was born around 812. The dynastic histories state that his clan was from Taiyuan in the north and that he was related to the important early Tang official Wen Yanbo 溫彥博 (574–636). The ancestry may be spurious, but he was from a minor lineage of high enough status that he could attempt to pass the *jinshi* examination and qualify for office. He also seems to have been from the Jiangnan region that figures so prominently in his poetry. He took the *jinshi* examination numerous times with no success, and this is blamed on his ability to anger patrons and his reputation as a wastrel. His failure, like that of Li Shangyin, also is ascribed to factional politics. Wen Tingyun appealed to Li Deyu when he dominated the court under Wuzong to no avail and appears to have been a drinking companion of Linghu Tao's son. There are stories of him writing an examination *fu* for a candidate and having this transgression discovered. Perhaps also like Li Shangyin, he was awarded a minor post away in Fangcheng 方城 (in modern Hubei Province) without having passed the examination. While at that post, he impressed the provincial military governor, who gave him a position on his staff. Wen spent more time in the South, getting into various scrapes, and appears to have returned to Chang'an briefly for a capital position but soon lost that post and was sent once more to the South, probably where he died.

Wen Tingyun's poetry shapes the broad contours of his reconstructed biography. Wen was the first major Chinese author to write in the emerging *ci* 詞, or song lyric, form discussed in chapter 9. In poetry, the connection with performance had weakened throughout the Tang, even if quatrains in particular seem still to have been sung. However, the pleasure quarters and banquets continued to demand songs. As new musical forms appeared, singers adapted their repertoire to the new music. As had been the case in the late Han dynasty, literati gradually became interested in writing lyrics for musicians to sing. In *ci*, however, writers preserved the tune title to which their lyrics were written. Wen Tingyun's *ci* survived in a later anthology, and they reflect the ambience of the pleasure quarters in which they ostensibly were written. His *ci* have secured his reputation as a wastrel. However, his *yuefu* and other song forms in *shi* poetry show similar moods, images, and formal techniques. Aside from the song forms, his poems tend to be in the Late Tang style of small, highly crafted landscape scenes.

101. For this summary I rely on Paul Rouzer's judicious account in *Writing Another's Dream: The Poetry of Wen Tingyun* (Stanford: Stanford University Press, 1993), pp. 11–15.

"Traveling Early in the Shang Mountains" by Wen Tingyun

商山早行					Traveling Early in the Shang Mountains[102]
晨 dawn	起 rise	動 move	征 journey	鐸 bell	At dawn rising, I shake my long-traveling [carriage] bells.
客 traveler	行 travel	悲 lament	故 old	鄉 [xiaŋ] region	A traveler goes on, lamenting his old home.
雞 chicken	聲 sound	茅 thatch	店 inn	月 moon	A rooster's call: the moon over the thatched inn;
人 human	跡 trace	板 plank	橋 bridge	霜 [ʂaːŋ] frost	Human tracks in the frost on the plank bridge.
槲 oak	葉 leaves	落 fall	山 mountain	路 road	Oak leaves fall on the mountain road.[103]
枳 bramble	花 flower	明 bright	驛 station	牆 [tsɦiaŋ] wall	Bramble flowers are bright by the post-station wall.[104]
因 rely	思 long for	杜 Du-	陵 -ling	夢 dream	Relying [on these], I long for my dream of Duling:[105]
鳧 duck	雁 geese	滿 fill	回 turn	塘 [tɦaŋ] pool	Ducks and geese filled the curving pond.

PAUL ROUZER'S TRANSLATION

Setting Out Early from Mount Shang

At dawn I rise, stirring my carriage bells.
This traveler goes on, grieving for his home.
Cry of the cock, moon on the thatched inn;
Tracks of someone, frost on the plank bridge.
Oak leaves fall on the mountain road;
Orange blossoms brighten the post-station wall.
And so I long for my Duling dream;
Ducks and geese fill the curving pool.

---

102. Rouzer notes: "Mount Shang is in modern Shaanxi, east of Shang district near the Hubei border."

103. *Hu* 槲 is a type of oak whose dead leaves fall in the early spring.

104. *Zhi* 枳 is a type of bramble with white spring flowers.

105. Duling is in the suburbs of Chang'an and was a popular place for excursions for those who lived in the capital.

STUDY NOTES AND QUESTIONS

This well-crafted poem is in the Late Tang landscape mode. The second couplet is very famous and is the center of interest in the poem.

1. To focus on the crafting of the second couplet, consider first the rooster. Where is Wen Tingyun when he hears it? Why does the rooster crow? Chinese poets explored the use of modifiers to impart particular qualities to the scenes they sought to convey. Du Fu described the "outland moon" in "Weary Night"; Li He wrote of the "Han moon" in the "Song of the Bronze Immortals"; here Wen Tingyun presents a "thatched inn moon." Readers easily take this as a moon over a thatched inn, but the effect is in fact somewhat different, in that this moon somehow has "thatched inn" as an attribute and differs from Du Fu's or Li He's moons, which have their own distinctive qualities imparted by the nouns that modify them. Next, the line is an enjambment of two noun phrases: "rooster sound" and "thatched inn moon," and there is no verb. How do the aural and visual images complement and "interanimate" (i.e., give life and energy to) one another here?

2. The second line of the couplet, although less manifestly crafted, is equally effective as a matching image parallel to the first line. Here too there is no verb, just the transient footprints in the soon-to-melt frost on the plank bridge. Just as today there are signs that warn, "[Ice on] bridge freezes before [ice on] the road surface," here, too, frost still forms on the bridge in the mountains in springtime. How do the moon and the frost relate to one another in the couplet? What does the solitary set of footprints signify for Wen as he sets out?

3. Note that Rouzer treats "bright" in line 6 as a causative usage, "to brighten." Can you picture to yourself how the blossoms might brighten the wall? What effect does this causative reading have on the meaning of the line?

4. In poems about traveling at dawn, poets often refer to dreams interrupted by the need to rouse early. How do the leaves and flowers of the third couplet lead Wen to recall his earlier dream of Chang'an?

"Training for Naval Battle on Kunming Lake" by Wen Tingyun

	昆明治水戰詞							Training for Naval Battle on Kunming Lake[106]
	汪 deep and extensive	汪	積 pile up	水 water	光 gleam	連 connect	空 [khəwŋ] void	Deep and vast are the collected waters: their gleam reaches the void.
	重 doubled	疊 layered	細 fine	紋 pattern	交 cross	激 extend	紅 [xɦəwŋ] red	Circle on circle, the fine ripples link in glowing red.
	赤 crimson	帝 emperor	龍 dragon	孫 grandson	鮮 bright	甲 armor	怒 angers	The Crimson Emperor, dragon's child, in bright armor, grows angry:[107]
4	臨 overlook	流 flow	一 one	眄 glare	生 grow	陰 dark	風 [fuwŋ] wind	Overlooking the current, with his one glare, a dark wind rises.
	鼉 lizard	鼓 drum	三 three	聲 sounds	報 report	天 Heaven	子 [tsẓ̌] son	Lizard-skin drums with three sounds reply to the Son of Heaven;
	雕 falcon	旗 banner	獸 beast	艦 war-boat	淩 ride	波 waves	起 [kʰɪ̌] rise	With falcon banners, the beast-headed warships rise riding the waves.
	雷 thunder	吼 bellow	濤 billows	驚 startle	白 white	若 resemble	山 mountain	Thunder roars, billows startle, white like mountains.
8	石 stone	鯨 whale	眼 eye	裂 split	蟠 curling	蛟 dragon	死 [sẓ̌] die	The stone leviathan's eye splits, the coiling dragon dies.[108]
	滇 Dian	池 pool	海 ocean	浦 shore	俱 both	喧 clamor	豗 [xuaj] clamor	By the bank of Dian Pool, all is dinning clamor:[109]
	青 blue	翰 feather	畫 paint	鷁 heron	相 mutual	次 in order	來 [laj] come	Blue Pinion and Painted Heron come in ordered ranks.[110]
	箭 arrow	羽 feather	槍 spear	纓 chord	三 three	百 hundred	萬 10,000	Arrow feathers and spear cords, in all, three million:

106. Emperor Wu of the Han constructed a model of Kunming Lake near the capital to allow his navy to practice for his campaign against the tribes of Yunnan, who lived on the banks of the real Lake Kunming.

107. The first Han emperor was "revealed to be" the son of the celestial Crimson Emperor; his mother conceived after an encounter with a dragon-spirit.

108. The *Miscellaneous Accounts of the Western Capital* describes a stone whale at the border of the lake that roared and moved its tail whenever there was a thunderstorm. See footnote 55 in chapter 7.

109. Dian Pool was another name for Kunming Lake.

110. These are types of decorations on the warships. The heron was believed to ward off evil spirits

12	蹋	翻	西	海	生	塵	埃 [ʔaj]	They trample the Western Sea
	step	overturn	west	ocean	grow	dust	dirt	and stirring the dust.[111]
	茂	陵	仙	去	菱	花	老 [lǎw]	The Maoling immortal has left,
	Mao	Ling	immortal	leave	caltrop	flower	grow old	as caltrop flowers grow old;
	唼	唼	游	魚	近	煙	島 [tǎw]	Blowing bubbles, the wandering fish
	glub	glub	wander	fish	near	mist	island	draw near the misty islands.
	渺	莽	殘	陽	釣	艇	歸	In the distance, in remnant sunlight
	vast	misty	remnant	sunlight	fish	skiff	return	a fishing skiff returns home;
16	綠	頭	江	鴨	眠	沙	草 [ts^hǎw]	And green-headed river ducks
	green	head	river	duck	sleep	sand	grass	sleep in the grass on sand.

Paul Rouzer's Translation

Song: Naval Battle on Kunming Lake

The deep waters stretch far and wide,
their glitter reaches to the sky.
Delicate patterns, piled up—
joined ripples turn red.
The Crimson Emperor, dragon-scion,
fish-scale armored, rages:
One glance by current's edge and he
glares once: a hidden wind is born.
Lizard-skin drums thrice resound
in reply to Heaven's Son;
With pheasant banners, the beast-
galleons rise as they cross the waves.
Thunder roars as frothy waves startle,
a white the size of hills.
Stone leviathan's eye is split,
coiling sea serpents die.
By the shores of Dian Pool,
all is roar and clash.
As Black Feather and Painted Albatross
come out in their formations.
Arrow-feathers and spear-thongs—
three million in number.
Troops trample the Western Sea
and cause the dust to rise.

---

111. The Western Sea is actually the vast expanse of steppe and desert on the northwest border of China.

Now the Maoling immortal has left,
    as caltrop flowers age;
Blowing bubbles, the playful fish
    approach the misty isles.
Far away, in lingering sunlight
    a fishing skiff goes home;
And green-headed river ducks
    sleep in the sandy grass.

STUDY NOTES AND QUESTIONS

This is another example of a reimagining of an historical event: the practicing of naval warfare. For Wen Tingyun, however, the scene he invokes has lost all present meaning.

1. What is the time frame of the first couplet? When do we first see Emperor Wu, and how is he introduced? Dragons in China are associated with water, where they were thought to have lived.

2. The last reference to Emperor Wu in the poem is as the "Maoling immortal." Maoling is where Emperor Wu was buried. There also were stories that he was destined to reach the Three Isles of the Immortals. What is the effect of conflating the two references?

3. How does the history of the lake inform its present state, described in the final couplet?

Yu Xuanji 魚玄機 (ca. 844–ca. 868)

What we know of the woman writer Yu Xuanji, like her friend Wen Tingyun, is largely shaped by the stories that accumulated around her. She appears to have been from Chang'an, to have been taken as a concubine by an official at age sixteen, and to have separated from him three years later. In the traditional account, she then entered the demimonde as a courtesan but was also a Daoist nun for a period. She reportedly was executed for having killed her maid.

Yu Xuanji is primarily famous as a woman writer whose poems reveal a strong voice struggling against the constraints imposed on women in the late Tang. Her extant collection contains just forty-nine poems.

"Presented to a Neighboring Woman" by Yu Xuanji

贈鄰女					Presented to a Neighboring Woman[112]
羞 ashamed	日 sun	遮 block	羅 gauze	袖 sleeve	Ashamed of daylight, [you] block it with [your] gauze sleeve.[113]
愁 sorrow	春 spring	懶 torpid	起 rise	妝 [tʂaːŋ] make-up	Sorrowing at springtime, [you] are too weary to rise and attend to [your] appearance.
易 easy	求 seek	無 without	價 price	寶 treasure	It is easy to seek a priceless treasure.
難 hard	得 obtain	有 there-is	心 heart	郎 [laŋ] gentleman	It is impossible to find a gentleman with a heart.
枕 pillow	上 on	潛 submerge	垂 hang	淚 tear	On [your] pillow, [you] secretly weep tears.
花 flower	間 among	暗 dark	斷 break	腸 [trɦiaŋ] innards	Among flowers, [you] rend [your] innards unseen.
自 of-itself	能 able	窺 peek	宋 Song	玉， Yu	Since [you] can espy a Song Yu,[114]
何 what?	必 must	恨 resent	王 Wang	昌 [tʂʰiaŋ] Chang	Why need [you] resent Wang Chang?[115]

112. This poem has the alternative title of "Sent to Supernumery Gentleman Li Yi" 寄李儀員外.

113. One text has 障 ("obstruct") for 遮.

114. In the "*Fu* on the Lechery of Master Dengtu" 《登徒子好色賦》,in the *Zhaomin wenxuan*, that was attributed to Song Yu, Song Yu describes how the beautiful daughter in the household to the east looked at him through a hole in the wall for three years, yet he was never tempted by her.

115. Various Tang poems use Wang Chang as an example of a feckless lover.

STUDY NOTES AND QUESTIONS

1. The two titles for this poem present a problem for the reader: we interpret the poem very differently if the poem is being sent to a neighboring woman or to Li Yi, who was Yu Xuanji's former husband.

2. Consider the pronouns absent in the Chinese text but necessarily added in the translation: if the poem is sent to Li Yi, "I" would replace "you" in each line. What happens to the tone and voice in the poem with this change? How would you interpret Yu Xuanji's attitude toward the woman? How would you interpret her attitude toward Li Yi?

"Seeing Where the Names of the *Jinshi* Examinees Are Posted" by Yu Xuanji

[Complete Title]
遊崇真觀南樓覩新及第題名處

On an excursion to the South Tower of Chongzhen Temple, seeing where the names of the newly successful jinshi examinees are posted[116]

雲	峰	滿	目	放	春	晴 [tsɦiajŋ]	Cloudy peaks fill the eye, releasing spring clear skies.
cloud	peak	fill	eye	release	spring	clearing	
歷	歷	銀	鉤	指	下	生 [ʂaːjŋ]	So distinct, the silver hooked [characters] appeared beneath [the scribe's] fingers.
distinct		silver	hook	finger	below	be born	
自	恨	羅	衣	掩	詩	句	I resent that my gauze clothes hide my lines of poetry.
of-itself	resent	gauze	clothes	hide	poem	line	
舉	頭	空	羨	榜	中	名 [mjiajŋ]	Raising my head, I envy in vain the names on the board.
raise	head	empty	envy	board	middle	name	

KENNETH REXROTH'S AND LING CHUNG'S TRANSLATION

On a Visit to Ch'ung-chên Taoist Temple I See in the South Hall the List of the Successful Candidates in the Imperial Examinations

Cloud capped peaks fill the eyes
In the Spring sunshine.
Their names are written in beautiful characters
And posted in order of merit.
How I hate this silk dress
That conceals a poet.
I lift my head and read their names
In powerless envy.

---

116. Chongzhen Temple was a Daoist temple in Chang'an. After the *jinshi* examinations, the names of the successful candidate were posted publicly there.

"Selling Wilted Peonies" by Yu Xuanji

賣殘牡丹							Selling Wilted Peonies
臨 overlook	風 wind	興 arise	歎 sigh	落 fallen	花 flower	頻 [pjin] often	Overlooking the wind, I am frequently moved to sigh over the falling flowers:
芳 fragrant	意 intent	潛 sunken	消 disperse	又 again	一 one	春 [tʂʰyn] spring	Their fragrant aura disperses unseen: yet another spring.
應 ought	爲 for sake of	價 price	高 high	人 person	不 not	問 ask	It surely must be because their price is high that no one inquires.
卻 yet	緣 base on	香 fragrance	甚 extreme	蝶 butterfly	難 hard to	親 [tsʰin] grow close	Yet because their fragrance is so intense, the butterflies cannot draw near.
紅 pink	英 blossom	隻 only	稱 be fitting	生 be born	宮 palace	裏 inside	It is fitting that these pink petals should grow only in a palace:
翠 blue-green	葉 leave	那 how	堪 endure	染 stain	路 road	塵 [trɦin] dust	How can their lustrous green leaves bear to be stained by the dust of the road?
及 reach	至 arrive	移 move	根 root	上 Shang-	林 lin	苑 garden	Only when its roots have been transplanted to the Shanglin Garden,[117]
王 prince	孫 grandson	方 just now	恨 regret	買 buy	無 without	因 [ʔjin] rely on	Will my princely gent then regret that there is no way to buy them.

Stephen Owen's Translation

Selling Tattered Peonies

Facing the wind, my sighs are stirred
at the flurry of falling flowers,
unnoticed, their sweetness melts away,
one more spring goes by.

I'm sure it's because the price is high
that no one wants them,
and due to their overpowering scent
butterflies won't draw nigh.

Blooms of red that are fit to grow
in the palace compound alone—
how can those azure leaves endure
to be stained by dust of the road?
A day will come when their roots are moved

117. Shanglin was the great Han dynasty imperial garden.

to the park of the Emperor,
and then my prince will have bitter regret
that he has no way to buy.

Study Notes and Questions

1. This is a "chanting about objects" (*yong wu* 詠物) poem, and like many poems in this genre, it is allegorical, that is, an extended metaphorical comparison between an object and some aspect of human, usually personal experience. What is the comparison? Explain how the specific details set out in the first four lines work as parts of the comparison.

2. What is the poet's tone here? What difference does it make that we know the author is a woman? What difference does what we "know" from her biography as later readers make when we read the poem?

"Inscribed at Mist-hidden Pavilion" by Yu Xuanji

題隱霧亭							Inscribed at Mist-hidden Pavilion
春	花	秋	月	入	詩	篇 [p^{h}jian]	Spring flowers and the autumn moon enter my poems;
spring	flower	autumn	moon	enter	poem	piece	
白	日	清	宵	是	散	仙 [sian]	In the bright sun or on clear evenings, these are for an unbound transcendent.
white	sun	clear	night	this	dispersed	transcendent	
空	捲	珠	簾	不	曾	下	Completely rolling up the bead curtain, I have never lowered it.
empty	roll up	bead	curtain	not	once	lower	
長	移	一	榻	對	山	眠 [mjian]	I have moved a single bench to sleep facing the mountains.
long	move	one	bench	facing	mountain	sleep	

Study Notes and Questions

1. Poems written for display at a location attempt to convey the author's distinctive sense of the particular qualities of the place. Readers coming to the location would admire both the ways in which the author captured the ambience and the author's sensibility revealed in the poem. From the poem, how would you describe the qualities of the Mist-hidden Pavilion?

2. What is the significance of the gesture of moving the bench by the window, whose curtain is never to be lowered?

3. What difference does it make whether the author of the poem is a man or a woman?

Chapter Nine

The Growth of a New Poetic Form: The Song Lyric

The poetic genres of the Chinese tradition all began as song forms. The poems of the *Canon of Poetry* were part of the ritual repertoire of the Zhou court and were accompanied by both music and dance. The *Lyrics of Chu*, beginning with the meters of the "Nine Songs," also were performances to music that eventually were written as texts. We have seen as well how the pentasyllabic *shi* meter began as a popular musical verse form that grew in popularity and was adopted by elite culture at the end of the Han dynasty. Similarly, we learned in chapter 4 that one stream of influences in the development of the quatrain was a tradition of southern folk songs.

Once writers began to compose in these genres outside of the contexts of musical performance, the initial intimate connection with song gradually disappeared. Still, the successive waves of song forms that were brought into the elite poetic repertoire show that these performance settings, ranging from elaborate formal court rituals to convivial banquets among friends, and from rural religious festivals to courtesans' songs heard at taverns during lonely travel, continued to provide inspiration to poets. The rise of the *ci* 詞 or "song lyric" during the Tang dynasty seems to have had roots in all of these varieties of musical performance: the music performed by Tang Emperor Xuanzong's "Pear Garden" musicians, the southern folk tunes sung at local festivals, the milieu of the entertainment quarters both in Chang'an and in the southern cities that grew increasingly important during the Mid-Tang period. As literati began to experiment with the possibilities of *ci* as a new poetic genre, however, they seem to have respected an important distinction in the manner of its composition: they composed the lyrics of the songs to fit the requirements of the music (*yi sheng* 倚聲). Thus, one name for *ci* is simply "the lyrics for a tune" (*quzi ci* 曲子詞). These requirements included the length of the lines, the pattern of tones within a line, the number of lines in a strophe, and the rhyme scheme for the stanza. This commitment to writing to the music gave *ci* a very different arc of development from *shi* poetry. Of equal significance, scholars have long argued that the appearance of *ci*, with its separate topics and formal characteristics, influenced the development of the *shi* tradition in the Song dynasty (discussed in the next chapter) by providing writers with an alternative genre in which to compose. Poets composed *shi* when their topic and occasion were best written in the *shi* form, but they wrote *ci* when the aesthetic impulse or the occasion called for *ci*. This chapter introduces the typical forms and themes of *ci* as it developed as a genre, while the next explores the works of the later writers who drew on these early innovations.

The Early Development of *Ci* during the Tang Dynasty

The early history of *ci* as a genre remains uncertain, but at the beginning of the twentieth century, song lyrics from the Tang dynasty written to identifiable *ci* tune titles were discovered among texts hidden for centuries in a library in a cave that was part of a Buddhist temple complex outside the city of Dunhuang in far northwestern China. The fact that these songs appeared in Dunhuang, which served as a gateway to the Silk Road (the trading route between China, Central Asia, India, and the Middle East), suggests that *ci* as a genre was well established in the heartland of China by the time the authors of these manuscripts wrote down the lyrics. Some lyrics survive by great serendipity: they appear to have served as writing practice for scribes, who used the back sides of paper—which was still expensive—to write out popular tunes that came to mind at the moment. We know that the earliest lyric in the cache of papers was transcribed around AD 802 because that was the date recorded in a document on the front side of the sheet of paper.

The song lyrics preserved in the Dunhuang texts reveal a broad range of topics, from religious themes to the hardship of conscript duty, from the sorrows of lonely wives to the plight of a merchant's life of constant travel. Consider, for example, the following lyric to the tune (*cidiao* 詞調 or *cipai* 詞牌) "Willow Branch":[1]

"To the Tune 'Willow Branch'"

		【楊柳枝】						To the Tune "Willow Branch"
春	去	春	來	春	復	春，	[tʂʰyn]	Spring departs, spring comes, spring after spring.
spring	depart	spring	come	spring	again	spring		
寒	暑	來	頻。	[pjin]				Cold and warmth come again and again.
cold	hot	come	often					
月	生	月	盡	月	還	新。	[sin]	The moon waxes, the moon wanes, the moon returns anew,
moon	is born	moon	end	moon	return	new		
又	被	老	催	人。	[rin]			Again old age presses us.
again	endure	old-age	urge	person				
只	是	庭	前	千	歲	月，		It's just that the thousand-year-old moon before the courtyard
just	it is	courtyard	before	1,000	year	moon		
長	在	長	存。	[tsɦun]				Is always here, always remains:
long	exist	long	remain					
不	見	堂	上	百	年	人，	[rin]	Do you not see the man of a hundred years in the hall?
not	see	hall	on	100	year	person		
盡	總	化	微	塵。	[trɦin]			In the end [he] transforms into dust.
end	always	transform	minute	dust				

1. This textbook follows the convention of using thick brackets (【…】) to indicate the tune title for a lyric, as in "To the Tune 'Willow Branch'" 【楊柳枝】 below.

This *ci* begins with the themes of mutability and the fragility of life but does not then shift—as conventional treatments of these topics in the *shi* genre might lead one to expect—to a *carpe diem* response, to lines urging the audience to eat, drink, and make merry while the possibility is still at hand.

The generic features of this early *ci* are typical of a so-called "dual stanza" (*shuang diao* 雙調) form. First, although some song tunes require lines that appear identical to a seven-syllable quatrain (i.e., 7-7-7-7), the lines here are uneven, as they are in most *ci*. Hence yet another name for *ci* is "long and short lines" (*changduan ju* 長短句). Later manuals (*ci pu* 詞譜) that reconstructed the prosodic rules for *ci* specify the pattern for "Willow Branch" as:

◎●○○●●△，●○△。◎○◎●●○△，●○△。
◆◎●◎○○●●，●○△。◎○◎●●○△，●○△。

○ = Level tone, ● = Oblique tone, ◎ = either tone category;
△ = Level tone rhyme, ◆ = "change phrase" required

Comparing the Dunhuang song above with this generalized pattern shows another characteristic of the form: the actual prosody here does not match the "expected" form. The second line of each stanza has four rather than three characters, while the fourth has five rather than three. Within the lines, the tonal patterns do not quite work, either. Since *ci*, especially in its early development, was a performance genre, the writer of the lyrics had leeway to interpret flexibly the matching of words to tune, and the tune itself also may have had various versions in circulation. Still, the rhymes remain consistent, and the "change phrase" (*huan tou* 換頭) at the beginning of the second stanza in this lyric, "it's just that . . . " (*zhi shi* 只是), serves its appropriate function of responding to the first stanza while anticipating a shift in perspective in the second stanza.

The song "To the Tune 'Willow Branch' " and the other song lyrics discovered in Dunhuang show that many key generic features of the genre already were mature before elite writers began to take an interest in the *ci* during the ninth century. Not only do many of the later titles appear among these early texts, but lyrics were being composed in the "extended form" (*man ci* 慢詞) as well as in the "short lyric" (*xiao ling* 小令) forms of the "single stanza" (*dan diao* 單調) and the "dual stanza.") Interestingly, the early elite compositions in *ci* form are on a much narrower range of the themes than those found in the Dunhuang texts. In large measure, this seems to be because elite interest in *ci* grew from two sources—the musical performance milieu of the capital and the folk song traditions of the South—and they wrote on themes appropriate to those two contexts. The elite *ci* of the period also often have the appearance of seven-character quatrains rather than texts with varying line lengths: Bai Juyi and Liu Yuxi, for example, wrote an extended series of lyrics to the tune of "Willow Branch," but, in contrast to the Dunhuang example, theirs took the form of quatrains.

"Southern" Ci by Bai Juyi and Liu Yuxi

In addition to the "Willow Branch" lyrics, two groups of the earliest *ci* written by literati reflect the world of southern folk tunes. Bai Juyi wrote a set of lyrics to the tune "Recalling the South," and Li Yuxi wrote answering poems. Liu Yuxi, however, is more famous for writing a longer series of nine *ci* to the "Bamboo

Branch" tune that he justified by citing the example of Qu Yuan. Traditional culture accepted the account that Qu Yuan wrote new lyrics for the "Nine Songs" because he delighted in the music and intentions of the rustic versions of the songs he had heard but lamented the poor quality of the wording and therefore was inspired to provide new lyrics. Liu Yuxi could not actually understand the lyrics of the "Willow Branch" songs he heard, since they were in a local Sichuan dialect, but he found the performance moving and provided appropriate lyrics.

"To the Tune 'Recalling the Southland'" by Bai Juyi

【憶江南】							To the Tune "Recalling the Southland"
江 river	南 south	好， fine					The Southland is fine.
風 wind	景 scene	舊 former	曾 once	諳。[ʔam] acquainted			I once became accustomed to the scenery.
日 sun	出 come out	江 river	花 flower	紅 red	勝 defeat	火， fire	When the sun comes out, the river flowers are redder than fire.
春 spring	來 come	江 river	水 water	綠 green	如 resemble	藍，[lam] indigo	When spring comes, the river water is as green as indigo.
能 can	不 not	憶 recall	江 river	南。[nam] south			Can I help but recall the Southland?

ANNA M. SHIELDS'S TRANSLATION

Yi Jiangnan

The Southland is fine,
Its scenery as fresh in my mind as ever:
When the sun rose, river flowers were redder than fire;
When spring came, river waters were like indigo.
How can we not remember the Southland?

Study Notes and Questions

1. The tune title "Recalling the Southland" is considered the same as "Dreaming of the Southland" 【夢江南】. The tune is a single stanza with the conventionally assigned prosody:

○◎●，◎●●○△。◎●◎○○●●，◎○◎●●○△。◎●●○△

How well do Bai's lyrics match the prescribed pattern?

2. Note how the theme of the poem matches the tune title. This sort of correspondence appears relatively frequently in early *ci* but then disappears in later poems.

3. Reread Bai's quatrains in chapter 8 and compare his use of simile here and in the quatrains. Are they the same?

4. Note that Shields translates the descriptions in the lyric in past tense. What difference does this make for the meaning of the poem? Which tense do you prefer? Explain.

"To the Tune 'Bamboo Branch'" by Liu Yuxi

【竹枝詞】								To the Tune "Bamboo Branch"
山	桃	紅	花	滿	上	頭，	[tɦəw]	The red flowers of the mountain peach fill [the branches] above
mountain	peach	red	flower	fill	upper	part		
蜀	江	春	水	拍	山	流。	[liw]	The spring waters of the Shu rivers flow dashing against the mountains
Shu	river	spring	water	strike	mountain	flow		
花	紅	易	衰	似	郎	意，		The red of the flowers easily fades, like your intent.
flower	red	easy	decline	resemble	your	intent		
水	流	無	限	似	儂	愁。	[tʂ̩ɦəw]	The flow of the waters is without limit, like my sorrow.
water	flow	without	limit	resemble	my	sorrow		

Study Notes and Questions

1. Although the title of the series of poems uses the term "lyrics," the poems are perhaps best considered a transitional form in which Liu composed a quatrain, but at the time of performance the singer would add additional words, usually "harmonizing sounds" (*he sheng* 和聲) or "filler words" (*chen zi* 襯字) as needed to truly fit the tune.

2. The lyrics here express very conventional sentiments associated with the folk tunes of the South. Reread the series of "Midnight's Songs" in chapter 5. Even though Liu Yuxi composed the poem in the upper reaches of the Yangzi River in Sichuan, well away from the lower Yangzi River basin typically associated with "the South," he still uses the conventionalized "Southern" first-person pronoun *nong* 儂.

Wen Tingyun 溫庭筠 (ca. 812–66) and the Entertainment Quarters

Wen Tingyun was the first major writer to leave an important legacy of poetry within the *ci* genre. As discussed in chapter 8, we know little about his life, and the little we do know probably has been embellished by later writers to explain his interest in and mastery of *ci*. The lyrics that he wrote appear to be from the demimonde of the entertainment quarters and reflect an understanding of music unusual for a member of the scholar-official stratum. Most of Wen's extant lyrics come from the Five Dynasties anthology *Among the Flowers* (*Huajianji* 花間集), compiled in the Later Shu court of Meng Chang in Sichuan in 940.

Many of his lyrics are slightly voyeuristic descriptions of women. They appear to focus less on the rather stereotypical figure of the woman herself than on combining the prosodic demands of the *ci* genre with technical aspects of representation in which the objects in the woman's apartment and the scenes that she views convey the emotion and ambience of the lyric.

"To the Tune 'The Water Clock'" by Wen Tingyun

【更漏子】		To the Tune "The Water Clock"
玉 爐 香，	jade / brazier / incense	Fragrance in the jade incense brazier,
紅 蠟 淚，[lyẁ]	red / wax / tears	Red candle tears:
偏 照 畫 堂 秋 思。[sz̨̀]	one-side / shine / painting / hall / autumn / longing	It insistently shines on autumn longings in the painted hall.
眉 翠 薄，	eyebrow / kingfisher / thin	The iridescent green of her brows is pale;
鬢 雲 殘，[tsɦan]	temples / cloud / remnant	The cloud-ringlets at her temples are unkempt.
夜 長 衾 枕 寒。[xɦan]	night / long / coverlet / pillow / cold	The night is long, the coverlet and pillow cold.
梧 桐 樹，	paulownia / tree	The paulownia tree,
三 更 雨，[yǎ́]	third / watch / rain	And the midnight rain,
不 道 離 情 正 苦。[khuǒ́]	not / say / parting / feeling / just now / bitter	Do not say that the feelings of separation just now are hard.
一 葉 葉，	one / leaf / leaf	Leaf after leaf,

一	聲	聲，[ʂiajŋ]			Sound after sound:
one	sound	sound			
空	階	滴	到	明。[miajŋ]	On the empty steps, it drips until dawn.
empty	steps	drip	arrive	bright	

Study Notes and Questions

1. Wen Tinyun presents an observer's account of the forlorn woman that focuses on physical details. However, he points to a hidden, interior sensibility when he tells us directly that she is lonely through the phrase "autumn longings." Why is autumn significant? How do autumn longings differ from spring longings?

2. The other emotive word in line 3 is *pian* 偏, translated as "insistently" but with the sense of "now, at an inappropriate time, it insists on . . . " Why is the "now" of the poem a bad time for the candle to shine?

3. How else does Wen Tingyun depict the mood of the woman? What do each of the objects and events in the lyric (brazier, candle, brows, ringlets, etc.) contribute?

4. The second stanza of the lyric mainly focuses on the paulownia and the rain. What do you recall about paulownia from Li He's "Song of Li Ping Playing the Harp" in chapter 8? What is the effect of the pair of short lines with repetitions ("Leaf after leaf, Sound after sound") in the final strophe in conveying the quality of the scene and mood?

5. Even though the lyric is a seemingly objective description of the scene, there is still an authorial presence and voice in the poem. What, for example, does the statement "[The tree and rain] do not say that the feelings of separation just now are hard" tell you about implied author?

6. The standardization of prosodic pattern for this version of "The Water Clock" is

   ●○○，○●▲。◎●◎○○▲。○◎●，●○△，◎○◎●△。
   ●○○，○●▲。◎●◎○○▲。○◎●，●○△，◎○◎●△。
   (▲ represents a required oblique [*ze* 仄] tone rhyme.)

How well does Wen Tingyun's lyric match this? Note that the last three lines of each stanza are part of a single prosodic unit extending beyond the couplet. Western discussions of this unit call it a *strophe*. Because the prosodic structure of the line is more complex in song lyrics than in *shi* poetry, the textbook in chapters 9 and 10 provides punctuation to mark the minor breaks (、), the major breaks (，), and the ends of lines (。) that are required by the tune titles.

"To the Tune 'Pusa man'" by Wen Tingyun

【菩薩蠻】							To the Tune "Pusa man"[2]
小	山	重	疊	金	明	滅，[mjiat]	On small mountains, layer on layer, gold glints.
small	mountain	repeat	layer	gold	bright	extinguish	
鬢	雲	欲	度	香	腮	雪。[syat]	Her cloud ringlets are about to cross the fragrant snow of her cheeks
temple	cloud	about	cross	fragrant	cheek	snow	
懶	起	畫	蛾	眉，[mi]			She is too listless to rise to paint her moth eyebrows
lazy	rise	paint	moth	eyebrow			
弄	妝	梳	洗	遲。[trɦi]			She delays in applying makeup, combing, and washing.
do	makeup	comb	wash	tardy			
照	花	前	後	鏡，[kiajŋ]			Illumining the flower in mirrors front and behind,
shine	flower	before	behind	mirror			
花	面	交	相	映。[ʔiajŋ]			The flowers and her face brighten one another.
flower	face	mutually		brighten			
新	帖	繡	羅	襦，[ryə̆]			Newly embroidered on her gauze jacket:
new	add	embroider	gauze	jacket			
雙	雙	金	鷓	鴣。[kuə̆]			Pair upon pair of golden partridges.
pair	pair	gold	partridge				

ANNA M. SHIELDS'S TRANSLATION

Hills in many layers, golden glow flickering,
Clouds of hair poised to fall across the snow of her fragrant cheeks.
Languidly rising to paint her moth-brows,
to her makeup and toilette she finally stirs.

Reflected flowers in mirrors front and back;
flowery faces shine upon each other.
Newly stitched on her embroidered gauze gown:
pair on pair of golden partridges.

2. "Pusa man" literally means "Bodhisattva barbarian." By one account, the name derives from the appearance of a troupe of foreign women performers sent to the Tang court: the imperial music school then gave this title to a tune derived from the troupe's repertoire.

Study Notes and Questions

1. This is a much more opaque poem than Wen's "To the tune 'The Water Clock.'" What do we know of the woman's mood? Is she happy or sad? Perhaps the lassitude is because she had a wonderful night but her lover had to leave early. Or perhaps it is because she is all alone with no reason to rise early and prepare herself. Can we know? Is there a narrative here? Is the context clear?

2. What are the "hills in many layers"? Many generations of scholars have debated whether the phrase refers to a painted screen or to her hair or perhaps to something else. Similarly, what exactly is the scene described as "reflected flowers in mirrors front and back"? Critics remain unsure. What is the effect of this presentation of a woman rising from bed, about whom we know nothing? Why focus on the pairs of partridges newly embroidered into her sheer gown?

3. According to traditional lore, the call of the partridge evokes the long to return home because it sounds like the words, "You cannot get to travel, Brother!" (*xing bude ye, gege* 行不得也哥哥). Is this association relevant here?

4. The standardized prosody for "Pusa man" is:

◎○◎●○○▲，◎○◎●○○▲。◎●●○△，◎○◎●△。
◆◎○○●▲，◎●○○▲。◎●●○△，◎○◎●△。

How well does Wen Tingyun's lyric match this standard version?

Literati Appropriation of *Ci* in the Five Dynasties

In 875 Huang Chao 黄巢, a wealthy salt smuggler who organized a private militia, joined forces with Wang Xianzhi 王仙芝 to lead a broad popular rebellion against Tang rule. After the rebels' initial success, imperial forces rallied, reclaimed control of the areas around the capitals, and forced Huang Chao and his army to move south, pillaging as they went. By 879 he had reached Guangzhou, which he sacked. However, his men, hating the far south (an estimated 30 percent of his troops died there), urged him to return north. In 880 he crossed the Yangzi, and by the winter of that year he had captured Luoyang. He then drove Emperor Zhaozong 昭宗 and his retinue out of Chang'an to seek refuge in Shu (Sichuan), as Emperor Xuanzong had done a hundred and twenty years earlier. The imperial forces eventually rallied once again and began a counter-offensive. At a crucial moment, Zhu Wen, one of Huang Chao's generals, surrendered to Tang forces, was appointed a military governor, and joined the offensive against Huang Chao. In the summer of 883, with the aid of a Shatuo Turk general, they drove Huang Chao out of Chang'an (which they then pillaged in turn). After a year-long campaign, impe rial forces with their allies finally suppressed the rebellion and received Huang Chao's head in the summer of 884.

Although the emperor returned to court in Chang'an, the Tang empire never really recovered. Zhu Wen, the general who abandoned Huang Chao, was among a growing list of military governors in regions near the capitals who were effectively beyond the control of the emperor but who continued to support the Tang because they could not yet defeat the collective might of the other warlords with whom they were competing. The next twenty years provide a depressing list of maneuvers and counter-maneuvers, plots and counter-plots, and incessant warfare involving the imperial clan, the civil bureaucracy, the eunuchs (who controlled the palace armies as well as access to the emperor), and the military governors.

In 903 the balance of power shifted significantly. A warlord, Li Maozhen, allied with the eunuchs to counter Zhu's growing power. When Zhu began to prepare to march on Chang'an, the eunuchs fled with the emperor to Fengxiang 鳳翔 (in modern Shaanxi), to the west of the capital, where Li gave them his support. After an extended siege, however, Li negotiated with Zhu to slaughter the eunuchs and give Zhu control of Zhaozong. Zhu took the emperor to Luoyang but soon thereafter decided it was best to eliminate Zhaozong, who proved a threat even as a captive. Zhu had his son assassinate Zhaozong (and then commit suicide to take the blame) and installed a twelve-year-old puppet emperor, later known as Aidi 哀帝, the "Sorrowful Emperor." Many scholars consider the death of Zhaozong in 903 to be the end of the Tang, but others consider 907—the year Aidi was forced to abdicate to Zhu Wen—to be the last year of the dynasty.

In 907 Zhu founded the Later Liang dynasty, and the era of the "Five Dynasties and Ten States" began. The Five Dynasties refers to the five successive northern states:

Later Liang 後梁 (907–923)
Later Tang 後唐 (923–936)
Later Jin 後晉 (936–947)
Later Han 後漢 (947–951)
Later Zhou 後周 (951–960)

The "Ten States," founded by regional warlords, were:

Wu 吳 (907–937)
Wu-Yue 吳越 (907–978)
Min 閩 (909–945)
Chu 楚 (907–951)
Southern Han 南漢 (917–971)
Former Shu 前蜀 (907–925)
Later Shu 後蜀 (934–965)
Jingnan 荊南 (924–963)
Southern Tang 南唐 (937–975)
Northern Han 北漢 (951–979)

For the history of *ci* as a genre, three of the "Ten States" are particularly important. The first part of the story of the literati appropriation of *ci* focuses on the Former Shu and Later Shu states in modern Sichuan. The second part will turn to the Southern Tang.

The Former Shu

Wang Jian 王建 (847–918), the founder of the Former Shu state, had a background similar to the other military men who carved out kingdoms after the collapse of the Tang. He was a native of Henan, and his father reputedly was a baker. After a period of smuggling salt and petty brigandage, Wang and his followers joined the army of one of the independent regional military governors who first submitted to Huang Chao and then, switching sides, died fighting for the Tang. His successor, however, abandoned the Tang and preferred simply to build his own power base and pillage the local countryside. Wang decided to flee to Chengdu to join Emperor Xizong 僖宗 (r. 873–88). The imperial retinue was riven with power struggles, but Wang, having attained appointment to the palace guard, managed to navigate the currents well enough to end up as a prefect in Sichuan. From that position, he gradually gained control over Sichuan during the final decades of the ninth century. In 892, the Tang emperor Zhaozong acknowledged Wang's de facto control of the region and appointed him its military governor. In 903 Wang received further appointment as the King of Shu. When later that year Zhu Wen had Zhaozong assassinated and placed Emperor Aidi 哀帝 (r. 904–7) on the throne, Wang Jian did not acknowledge the succession and instead announced the formation of a new imperial government in exile committed to restoring the Tang imperial line. However, when Aidi abdicated in 907, Wang Jian, accepting the end of Tang imperial rule, proclaimed himself the emperor of Shu.

Wang Jian was not a native of Sichuan, and the men he appointed to his early imperial staff were men who had served with him through his long years of fighting. His chief minister Wei Zhuang (see below) also was not from the region. Thus the culture of this court milieu was largely northern and military. After founding the dynasty, Wang continued to consolidate his position, but he was unfortunate in his appointment of an heir apparent. As he neared death, he reportedly was aware of the inadequacies of the crown prince and planned to replace him, but the prince whom he preferred died suddenly and suspiciously. In 925, seven years after Wang Jian died and the crown prince took the throne, the Shatuo Turkish ruler of the northern state of the Later Tang (which had defeated and replaced Zhu Wen's Later Liang) conquered Shu.

The Later Shu

The Later Tang control of Sichuan did not last long. The founding emperor of the Later Tang, Zhuangzong, died in a mutiny in 926 and an adoptive brother seized the throne as Mingzong. At this point, the military governor of western Sichuan, Meng Zhixiang 孟知祥 (874–934), a native of Henan who had been one of Zhuangzong's officers during his rise to power, joined Dong Zhang, the military governor of eastern Sichuan, in rebelling. When Mingzong sought reconciliation, Dong, whose family had been killed by Later Tang forces, refused. After Meng defeated Dong and gained control over all of Sichuan in 932, Mingzong acknowledged the situation by appointing Meng the military governor of both halves of Sichuan. When Mingzong died in 933, Meng Zhixiang concluded that the Later Tang polity was unstable (indeed, Mingzong's successor ruled for just six months), renounced his allegiance, and in 934 declared himself Emperor of Shu. However, he himself suffered a stroke and died later that year.

Although his son Meng Chang 孟昶 (919–65, r. 934–65) was only fifteen when he came to the throne, he managed to retain his position and ruled for thirty-two years. He initially proved an effective ruler, but after 951 he apparently handed over most of the responsibilities of government to an old friend. Still, the Shu state resisted the armies of the Later Zhou in 955 before the new Song state overwhelmed it ten years later. In 965 after his armies suffered major defeats, Meng Chang accepted the inevitable and surrendered to the Song.

Among the Flowers

The *ci* anthology *Among the Flowers* (*Huajianji* 花間集), compiled in 940 in the court of the Later Shu dynasty just six years after its founding, represents a major turning point in the development of *ci* as an elite poetic form. The anthology contained 500 lyrics by eighteen poets. Among those writers, five, including Wen Tingyun, were from the Tang, although at least three of the five primarily were active at the very end of the dynasty and later. The poet and official selected to write the preface to the anthology was Ouyang Jiong 歐陽炯 (896–971), a Shu native, who later rose to serve as grand councilor. Although the other writers in the anthology were not quite so successful, many held court positions and clearly were part of the elite stratum in Sichuan during the Five Dynasties period.[3] *Among the Flowers* reflects the ways in which elite society—with its complex mix of military and civil, and Sichuan and largely northern backgrounds—appropriated *ci* as a genre. Perhaps the most notable feature, aside from the technical facility of the writers, is the narrowness of the topics explored through the lyrics. As the title suggests, the poets wrote exclusively about elegant women and the travails of love. Ouyang Jiong, following the precedent of the *New Songs of the Jade Terrace* (see chapter 5 under Xiao Gang), pointed to the usefulness of the anthology in social gatherings and in providing replacements for less elegant popular lyrics.[4] In *Among the Flowers*, the other major transitional Tang figure after Wen Tingyun is Wei Zhuang.

---

3. For a list of authors in the collection, see Anna M. Shields, *Crafting a Collection: the Cultural Contexts and Poetic Practice of the* Huajianji *(Collection from Among the Flowers)* (Cambridge: Harvard University Asia Center, 2006), p. 113. Five of the twelve who Shields lists as having been affiliated with either the Former or Later Shu states were in fact from other regions in China, so that the court elites of the two dynasties seem not to have been regional in character.

4. For a translation and discussion of Ouyang's preface, see Shields, *Crafting a Collection*, pp. 150–58.

And among the writers who were Ouyang Jiong's contemporaries, Gu Xiong has a large number of poems in the collection and will serve to suggest the styles of *ci* at the time.

Wei Zhuang 韋莊 (d. 910)

Wei Zhuang, from Duling near the Tang capital of Chang'an, passed the *jinshi* exam in 894 during the final years of the Tang dynasty. He proved a capable administrator and political advisor and was commissioned to convey the letter of appointment that conferred imperial legitimacy upon Wang Jian as deputy military governor. Wei Zhuang stayed in Sichuan and was serving on Wang's staff when Tang Emperor Zhuangzong was assassinated in 903. As noted above, after Aidi's abdication in 907, Wang Jian initially called for a restoration of the empire, but when that produced no popular support, he concluded that the situation was hopeless and, with Wei Zhuang's support, declared himself the emperor of Shu. Wei Zhuang was instrumental in creating an effective bureaucracy for the new state based on the Tang model and in 908 was appointed Wang Jian's chancellor.

Wei Zhuang thus had a career very different from that of Wen Tingyun, and Wei Zhuang's interest in *ci* as a poetic form contributed to its legitimacy (or marked its growing acceptance) as a literati pursuit. His surviving lyrics, while still focusing on women, romance, and longing, were in a much more direct style than Wen's compositions and used simplified, hypotactic syntax, in contrast to Wen's preference for parataxis.[5] Moreover, while Wen Tingyun tended to view women from a distanced, third-person perspective, Wei Zhuang frequently used a first-person, often male, voice.

"To the Tune 'Pusa man'" by Wei Zhuang

【菩薩蠻】							To the Tune "Pusa man"
如	今	卻	憶	江	南	樂，[lak]	Even now I yet recall the joys of the Southland.
resemble	now	but	recall	river	south	joy	
當	時	年	少	春	衫	薄。[pɦak]	At that time, my years were few, and my springtime shirt was thin.
just at	time	year	few	spring	shirt	thin	
騎	馬	倚	斜	橋，[kɦiaw]			Riding a horse, as I inclined against the sloping bridge,
ride	horse	lean	slant	bridge			
滿	樓	紅	袖	招。[tʂiaw]			A full tower of red sleeves beckoned.
full	tower	red	sleeve	summon			

5. The last line of Wei Zhuang's "Pusa man" provides a good example of hypotactic (subordinating) syntax in which the syntactic relations of all the phrases are well-defined: "White-haired, [I] vow never to return home" 「白頭誓不歸」. It uses a standard sentence construction (i.e., subject-verb-object) and clear "modifier-modified" noun and verb phrases. The last two lines of Wen Tingyun's "Pusa man," in contrast, use paratactic syntax in which one element follows another, but the syntactic relation between them is unclear. Line 8—"Pair upon pair of golden partridges" 「雙雙金鷓鴣」—follows line 7—"Newly embroidered on her gauze jacket" 新帖繡羅襦—but the syntactic relation between the two lines is left open.

翠	屏	金	屈	曲，[khywk]	The gold of the kingfisher screen [glints] as it bends:
halcyon	screen	gold	bend	curve	
醉	入	花	叢	宿。[siwk]	Drunk, I entered the cluster of flowers to spend the night.
drunk	enter	flower	cluster	spend night	
此	度	見	花	枝，[tşi]	This time, seeing a branch of flowers,
this	pass	see	flower	branch	
白	頭	誓	不	歸。[kyj]	White-haired, I vow never to return home.
white	head	vow	not	return home	

ANNA M. SHIELDS'S TRANSLATION[6]

Today I yet recall the delights of Jiangnan—
back then I was a young man, in spring clothes so light.
Riding my horse, I'd lean from the bridge to see
towers filled with red sleeves beckoning.

The gilded kingfisher screen around me,
drunk, I'd enter the "flowery groves" to sleep.
Now when I see the flowering branches,
this white-haired old man vows he'll never go home!

STUDY NOTES AND QUESTIONS

1. This lyric uses many markers of time ("just now," "at that time," "this time") to frame the recollection of former joy that is the poem's theme. How do these terms contribute to creating a narrator very different from the silent narrator in Wen Tingyun's poems?

2. Compare this lyric with Bai Juyi's "Recalling the Southland": how does the addition of a second stanza in the "Pusa man" lyric change the treatment of the topic in Wei Zhuang's poem? What is the relation of the first to the second stanza here?

3. What marks the voice of Wei Zhuang's poem as male? (Note that Shields adds "man" to the second line, but it is not explicit in the Chinese text.) What difference would it make if Wei Zhuang wrote these lyrics to sing himself or to be sung by female entertainers?

6. Shields has an extensive discussion of this lyric in *Crafting a Collection*.

“To the Tune ‘Nü guanzi’ (‘Daoist Nun’)” by Wei Zhuang

【女冠子】						To the Tune “Nü guanzi”[7]
昨	夜	夜	半，[puan`]			Last night at midnight,
last	night	night	half			
枕	上	分	明	夢	見，[kjian`]	On my pillow, very clearly in dream you appeared.
pillow	above	divide	clear	dream	see/appear	
語	多	時。[ʂɦi]				When we had spoken a lot,
speak	many	time				
依	舊	桃	花	面，[mjian`]		As before, on [your] peach flower face,
rely	before	peach	flower	face		
頻	低	柳	葉	眉。[mi]		[You] often lowered your willow-leaf brows.
frequent	lower	willow	leaf	eyebrow		
半	羞	還	半	喜，		Half-embarrassed and half-delighted,
half	shamed	and	half	delight		
欲	去	又	依	依。[ʔi]		[You] were about to leave but still lingered.
about to leave		again	linger			
覺	來	知	是	夢，		Awakening, I know this was a dream:
awake	come	know	this/is	dream		
不	勝	悲。[pi]				I cannot bear the sorrow.[8]
not	successful	sorrow				

Study Notes and Questions

1. The situation seems simple enough, but is the dreamer the man or the woman? Explain. What difference does it make for the poem? For the presentation of the poem?

2. The standardized tune pattern for “Nü guanzi” is:

◎○◎▲，◎●◎○◎▲。●○○△。◎●○○●，○○●●△。
◆◎○○●●，◎●●○△。◎●○○●，●○△。

How well does this poem match the later standard? Does Wei Zhuang use the transition (*huantou*) between the stanzas to make a shift, or is the second stanza a continuation of the first?

---

7. Kang-I Sun Chang translates and discusses this lyric in *The Evolution of Chinese* Tz’u *Poetry from Late T’ang to Northern Song* (Princeton: Princeton University Press, 1980), pp. 42–44.

8. The *busheng* 不勝 + Verb construction in the *first tone* means “cannot Verb to completion.”

GU XIONG 顧敻

Very little is known about Gu Xiong. We cannot be sure where he was from. He served as prefect under the Former Shu and received appointment as a "defender-in-chief" (*tai wei* 太尉) from the Later Shu court. His fifty-five surviving lyrics are all from *Among the Flowers*.

"To the Tune 'Speaking of Innermost Feelings'" by Gu Xiong

【訴衷情】		To the Tune "Speaking of Innermost Feelings"
永 夜 拋 人 何 處 去，	long night abandon person what place go	In the long night, where has the one who abandoned me gone:
絕 來 音。[ʔim]	break come sound	Word has stopped coming.
香 閣 掩，[ʔiam´]	fragrant chamber close	[My] fragrant chamber is closed.
眉 斂，[liam´]	brow gather	[My] brows are furrowed,
月 將 沉。[trɦim]	moon about to sink	The moon is about to set.
爭 忍 不 相 尋。[sɦim]	how bear not [d.o.] follow	How can I bear to not follow you?
怨 孤 衾，[khim]	resent lone coverlet	I resent the lonely coverlet.
換 我 心，[sim]	exchange my heart	Changing my heart
為 你 心。[sim]	become your heart	To become your heart,
始 知 相 憶 深。[ʂim]	begin know [d.o.] recall deep	[You] would begin to understand the depth of my recollections.

STUDY NOTES AND QUESTIONS

1. This sort of single-stanza lyric is relatively rare in *Among the Flowers*, but this lyric is well-known even today. Note how compact the lyrics are in presenting the situation of the narrator, and how the lyrics set the time, place, and narrative frame.

2. Also note the use of conventionalized "colloquial" terms: *zheng* 爭 for "how" and *ni* 你 for "you" (this is the standard second-person pronoun in modern Mandarin but was rarely used in Five Dynasties writings).

3. The rhyme scheme for the prosodic pattern for this tune, with six rhyme words for the short lines in the second half of the stanza, differs significantly from those of *shi* poetry:

◎●◎○○●●，●○△。○●▲，○▲，
●○△。◎●●○△，●○△。●●△，●○△，●○○●△。

How does Gu Xiong take advantage of the short phrases and rhyme after rhyme in crafting the mood and theme of the lyric?

The Southern Tang Court

In 937 the last emperor of the Wu dynasty in the south, outmaneuvered by his advisor Xu Zhigao's 徐知誥 (889–943) effort to steadily consolidate power, abdicated and ordered Xu to assume the throne. Xu Zhigao complied but did not continue the Wu dynasty. Two years earlier, in 935, the Later Tang dynasty—whose founder proclaimed his new state to be the successor to the Tang—collapsed, and perhaps because of this Xu decided to claim the succession from the Tang for himself. He asserted his descent from the Tang imperial Li clan, changed his name to Li Bian 李昪, and named his state the Tang. It became known as the Southern Tang.[9]

Xu Zhigao in fact was the adopted son of Xu Wen 徐溫 (862–927), a key advisor of Yang Xingmi 楊行密 (852–905), the founder of the Wu state. While Yang had the sort of humble origins and military background common among founders of states during the Five Dynasties, Xu Wen stressed the transition to a civil government and restarted an examination system. It was in part through his control of personnel that he attained significant control over the Wu government, control that he passed to Xu Zhigao rather than to his natural children. Although little is known about the early life of Xu Zhigao, Xu Wen clearly was correct in judging his potential: as Li Bian, founder of the Southern Tang, he prepared the state so well that when he died six years later in 943, his son Li Jing 李璟 (916–61) had the resources and organization to aggressively expand the Southern Tang territory. However, reunifying large tracts of southern China left Li Jing without the resources to resist the resurgent northern state of the Later Zhou, to which he was compelled to acknowledge fealty in 958. In 960 Zhao Kuangyin 趙匡胤 (927–76), a Later Zhou general, deposed the seven-year-old Later Zhou ruler to found the Song as Emperor Taizu (r. 960–76), and Li Jing accordingly reaffirmed his loyalty as ruler of a vassal state to the Song.

The Song founder had great plans and soon launched a campaign against the surviving southern regimes. He took advantage of opportunities as they arose so that his conquest of the Southern Tang was delayed until 975, when the "Later Ruler" Li Yu 李煜 (937–78) had already succeeded his father. The story of the conquest of the Southern Tang is worth stressing because literary histories routinely present Li Yu as an effete, feckless ruler whose focus on literature rather than rule brought the end of his state. As Hugh Clark describes the final years:

> Li Yu, as ruler of the Southern Tang, had been a loyal and subservient tributary, regularly sending envoys to Kaifeng to affirm his subordinate status. But following the successful conclusion of the campaign against the Southern Han, the Song began deliberately to reduce

9. Later historians added "Southern" to distinguish the dynasty from the earlier Tang. See Hugh R. Clark, "The Southern Kingdoms between the T'ang and the Sung, 907–979" in *Cambridge History of China*, vol. 12, part 1, pp. 166–67.

> Li Yu's status. Late in 971 he was directed to change his title from "Ruler of Tang" to "Ruler of Jiangnan," a demotion that attempted to end the connection between Li Yu and the imperial heritage of the Tang dynasty. The following year, Song Taizu decided to increase the pressure by detaining Li Yu's brother, who had come to Kaifeng on a tributary mission. Li Yu was greatly alarmed by this and restructured his bureaucracy to make it appear less imperial. All this was in vain, however, for Taizu had determined that Li Yu would either yield his kingdom voluntarily or have it taken by force. Through 973 and 974 the two played a delicate minuet. Li Yu was fully aware that resistance to Taizu's appeal would lead to only one outcome, yet he continued to avoid a showdown. In late 975, Taizu's patience ran out and the invasion began. Even Wu-Yue forces participated, launching an assault from the east at the same time that Song forces crossed the Yangzi River and entered Jiangnan from the north. Although Southern Tang resources and power had been reduced by the loss of the Huai-nan prefectures nearly two decades before, the kingdom was still wealthy and its armies strong. The campaign was accordingly slow and difficult. But in late 975, Li Yu accepted the inevitable and surrendered.

The literary myth of Li Yu, based on his interest in and talent for composing *ci*, does not tally very well with the historical record of a wily ruler, who resisted the Song for as long as possible and who was not so vain as to subject his state to further predations of conquest after it became clear he could not hope to win or even reach a military stalemate.

Still, the court of Li Yu was indeed highly cultivated. His grandfather Li Bian had made an effort to recruit talented men for the civil service, and the court drew on a large pool of well-educated men from the heartland of south China. The interest of Li Yu and of the Southern Tang court in composing *ci* therefore clearly marks the genre's growing acceptance in elite culture.

Feng Yansi 馮延巳 (903–60)

Later histories portrayed Feng Yansi as a scheming, reckless man with appallingly poor judgment. Feng was one of the so-called "five demons" (*wu gui* 五鬼), a group of venal, vicious, and incompetent advisors surrounding Li Jing. He kept better officials at a distance from the emperor and encouraged the vacillating Li Jing to adopt bellicose policies that ultimately led to the dynasty's collapse. We cannot entirely rely on this account because history, in the end, is written by the winners, and they paint the failings of those whom they conquered in bright, clear colors. From the perspective of later Song dynasty officials, Li Jing squandered his resources in his efforts to unify southern China, and Feng Yansi, as one of his most important ministers, thus bore much responsibility for this folly.

Feng Yansi's song lyrics reveal clear differences from those of the court of the Later Shu in *Among the Flowers*. Because few song lyrics survive, it is hard to say definitively whether these differences reflect stylistic developments between 940 and 960, or different regional styles, or Feng Yansi's own personal sensibility, or a mix of all these components. In any case, Feng's *ci*, while still drawing on the narrow themes of spring longing, autumnal regret, and abandoned palace women, are often written in a first-person voice closer to the style of Wei Zhuang than to that of Wen Tingyun. The language is plain and hypotactic, but the poet uses questions and modal phrases (expressions of desirability, possibility, or probability like "must," "don't," and "ought") to reflect the persona's direct engagement in the scene portrayed in the lyrics. The lyrics often give the reader a short arc of narrative development to frame the mood of the song.

"To the Tune 'Magpie Treading the Branch'" by Feng Yansi

【鵲踏枝】								To the Tune "Magpie Treading the Branch"[10]
六	曲	闌	杆	偎	碧	樹，	[žhüê`]	The six bends of the railing hug the emerald trees.
six	bend	railing		near	emerald	tree		
楊	柳	風	輕，					Among the willows, the wind is light,
willow		wind	light					
展	盡	黃	金	縷。	[lüê´]			Spreading all the golden floss.
spread	complete	yellow	gold	thread				
誰	把	鈿	箏	移	玉	柱，	[drhüê`]	Who moved the jade pegs of the inlaid zither?
who	grab	inlaid	zither	move	jade	peg		
穿	簾	海	燕	驚	飛	去。	[k'iê`]	Going through the curtain, the ocean swallow, startled, flies away.
pierce	curtain	ocean	swallow	startle	fly	leave		
滿	眼	遊	絲	兼	落	絮，	[siê`]	Filling the view, drifting silk and falling catkins,
fill	eye	wander	silk	combine	fall	floss		

10. The rhymes here follow Daniel Bryant's modification of Pulleyblank's Late Middle Chinese in *Lyric Poets of the Southern T'ang: Feng Yen-ssu (903–960) and Li Yu (937–978)* (Vancouver: University of British Columbia Press, 1982), p. 16.

紅	杏	開	時，				At the time when the pink apricot opens:
red	apricot	open	season				
一	霎	清	明	雨。[ṷê′]			A brief shower of Qingming rain.
one	instant	Qing-	ming	rain			
濃	睡	覺	來	鶯	亂	語，[ŋiê′]	Wakened from deep sleep by the chaotic voice of orioles,
deep	sleep	awake	come	languid	not	speak	
驚	殘	好	夢	無	尋	處。[tš'iê`]	Startled from the remains of a fine dream, there is nowhere to seek it [again].
startle	remnant	good	dream	without	seek	place	

STUDY NOTES AND QUESTIONS

1. This lyric marks a clear shift from the focus of the works in *Among the Flowers*, but it is not a radical change. Is the scene of the poem still in a palace? Do you think the speaker is a man or a woman?

2. Does the second stanza present a unified scene? What is the mood? How does it relate to the scene?

"To the Tune 'Picking Mulberries'" by Feng Yansi

【采桑子】

To the Tune "Picking Mulberries"

花	前	失	卻	遊	春	侶，	Before the flowers, I have lost my companion in spring excursions.
flower	before	lose	withdraw	travel	spring	companion	
獨	自	尋	芳，[faŋ]				Alone I seek out the fragrant verdure.
alone	by myself	seek	fragrant grasses				
滿	目	悲	涼，[liaŋ]				Filling my view, a sad chill,
fill	eye	sad	cool				
縱	有	笙	歌	亦	斷	腸。[drhiaŋ]	If there were pipes and song, it would still break my heart.
even if	there is	panpipe	song	also	break	innards	

林	間	戲	蝶	簾	間	燕，	The sporting butterflies of the grove and the swallows among the curtains,
grove	within	play	butterfly	curtain	within	swallow	
各	自	雙	雙，[šwaŋ]				All are in pairs.
each	by itself	pair	pair				
忍	更	思	量，[liaŋ]				Can I bear to reflect again:
bear	again	long	reckon				
綠	樹	青	苔	半	夕	陽。[yiaŋ]	Green trees, green moss, halfway through dusk.
green	tree	green	moss	half	dusk	radiance	

STUDY NOTES AND QUESTIONS

1. Like the first lyric, this is a meditation on a spring scene. What in the lyrics creates the sense of the author's presence in the scene?

2. The generalized prosody for "Cai sangzi" is:

◎○◎●○○●，◎●○△。◎●○△，◎●○○●●△。
◆◎○◎●○○●，◎●○△。◎●○△，◎●○○●●△。

Does Feng Yansi follow this prosody?

LI YU 李煜 (937–78)

History dealt Li Yu a poor hand as a ruler. As the sixth of Li Jing's eight sons, he was not trained for rule, nor had he cultivated his own group of counsellors (and generals) to help him when he came to the throne. Moreover, from the very beginning of his rule, he had to acknowledge his status as a vassal to the Song state. The large sums of tribute that had to be sent northward left Li Yu with limited resources to prepare for the Song's inevitable campaign against the Southern Tang. He had to improvise, and, given the situation, he managed well.

Perhaps the greatest question surrounding Li Yu's song lyrics is whether they were part of his improvisational efforts to define his role as ruler and his relationship to the Song. Ever since the Song dynasty, readers have taken a handful of Li Yu's approximately thirty extant song lyrics as his response to his captivity in the north. Only one lyric, however, provides sufficient internal evidence to justify taking it as autobiographical reflection. And while Song readers scorned its presentation of the captive Li Yu as more concerned about his palace women than about his state, it served the clear function of declaring that the former ruler's commitments were now personal rather than imperial and that he was not a threat to Song rule. We lack any real evidence to assess the other *ci* of Li Yu's that traditional readers treated as autobiographical. However, those traditional readings underscore the significant development marked by Li Yu's approach to *ci*. He very effectively broadened the content of the song lyric and brought a strong, personal voice to his compositions. Even more than Feng Yansi, he used questions and modal phrases to convey his commitment to the scene depicted in the poem.

In the traditional account of Li Yu's death after he and his court were held as captives in Kaifeng, the very power of his lyrics written in captivity brought about his end. Although some consider the utter despair of the last line of "Billows Scour the Sand" below to have been Li Yu's final composition, the more popular story is that after the Song emperor read "Fair Lady Yu," he decided he could not afford to let such an affecting poet live and had Li Yu poisoned.

"To the Tune 'Billows scour the sand'" by Li Yu

【浪淘沙】							To the Tune "Billows Scour the Sand"
簾 curtain	外 outside	雨 rain	潺 ripple-	潺，[džhan] ripple			Beyond the curtains, the rain rills.
春 spring	意 intent	將 about	闌。[lan] exhaust				The sense of spring is about to end.
羅 gauze	衾 coverlet	不 not	暖 warm	五 five	更 watch	寒。[xhan] cold	The sheer coverlet is not warm in the chill of the fifth watch.
夢 dream	裏 in	不 not	知 know	身 body	是 it is	客， traveler	In my dream I don't know that I am a traveler:
一 one	餉 moment	貪 covet	歡。[xuan] joy				For a moment I am avid for joy.

獨	自	莫	憑	闌。[lan]			Alone, do not lean on the railing!
alone	self	don't	lean	rail			
無	限	關	山，[šan]				[There are] passes and mountains without end,
without	limit	pass	mountain				
別	時	容	易	見	時	難。[nan]	Times of parting are easy; times of seeing one another hard.
part	time	easy		see	time	hard	
流	水	落	花	歸	去	也，	The flowing waters and falling flowers have left,
flow	water	fall	flower	return	leave	[is fact]	
天	上	人	間。[kyan]				In heaven and in the human realm.
heaven	on	people	among				

STUDY NOTES AND QUESTIONS

1. In the first line, do you *see* the rain? Is this an enclosed interior scene, or one open to the outside? Does that make a difference? For example, is the persona in the lyric looking upon a spring scene that is now slipping away, or is the second line more of an internal reverie?

2. In the third line, what time of day is it? (If one looked out through the window what could one see?)

3. Is there an implied narrative? Is the person just now waking from a dream?

4. Is the time of the second stanza the same as the first? What is the relation between the second stanza and the first?

5. Is the very famous ending couplet of this lyric seen or imagined? What difference does it make? (Consider all the images of sight cut off in the poem: is there a cumulative effect?)

6. Compare Li Yu's prosody to the general form:

◎●●○△，◎●○△。◎○◎●●○△。◎●◎○○●●，◎●○△。
◆◎●●○△，◎●○△。◎○◎●●○△。◎●◎○○●●，◎●○△。

"To the Tune 'Fair Lady Yu'" by Li Yu

		【虞美人】					To the Tune "Fair Lady Yu"
春	花	秋	月	何	時	了，[liau′]	Spring flowers and autumn moons, when will they end?
spring	flower	autumn	moon	what	time	end	
往	事	知	多	少。[šiau′]			Of former affairs, how much do we know?
gone	affair	know	much	little			
小	樓	昨	夜	遇	東	風，[fuŋ]	In the small tower last night [I] encountered the spring wind.
small	tower	last-	night	meet	east	wind	

故 國 不 堪 回 首 月 明 中。[trioŋ]
old state not bear turn head moon bright middle
In the bright moonlight [I] cannot bear to turn my head toward my old state.

雕 欄 玉 砌 應 猶 在，[dzhai`]
carved rail jade steps ought still be there
The carved railings and jade steps ought to still be there;

只 是 朱 顏 改。[kai´]
only it is crimson face change
It's just that my ruddy face has changed.

問 君 能 有 幾 多 愁，[džhêu]
ask you able exist how many sorrow
I ask you how much sorrow can there be:

恰 似 一 江 春 水 向 東 流。[liu]
exactly like one river spring water toward east flow
It is exactly like a river of spring-time water flowing to the east.

STUDY NOTES AND QUESTIONS

1. What is the effect of beginning the lyric with a question followed by yet another question? Are these rhetorical questions?

2. From the first two lines, what time of year would you assume it to be?

3. What is the effect of making the third line a comment about an event that happened the previous evening? What tense should the fourth line be read in? What difference does it make to the mood and meaning of the poem?

4. Explain the transition between the first and second stanzas.

5. This is a very coherently crafted lyric. To what in the first stanza does the second line of the second stanza correspond?

6. What is the effect of adding the interlocutor in the seventh line? And how is the final line an answer to the question in the seventh line? How does the last line build upon the images presented earlier in the poem? And what is the effect of the claim that it is "exactly like" the river flowing to the east? (Think, for example, about Bai Juyi's use of simile.)

7. The prosody of "Yu mei ren" is taken to be:

◎○◎●○○▲，◎●○○▲。◎○◎●●○△，◎●◎○◎●●○△。
◆◎○◎●○○▲，◎●○○▲。◎○◎●●○△，◎●◎○◎●●○△。

How well does Li Yu follow this generalized schema?

Poetic Innovations during the Northern Song

Zhao Kuangyin, the general who founded the Song dynasty in 960 by deposing the infant emperor of the Northern Zhou, was determined to avoid letting his own heir meet this fate. Once he had pacified the realm, he began a policy of recruiting men of talent to civil office and weakening the hold of his generals and the military governors who had controlled large domains during the Five Dynasties. Although the period between the fall of the Tang and the founding of the Song was only a little more than fifty years, the social, political, and cultural organization of the realm had shifted profoundly. The Great Clans that had served as the basis of the Tang social, political, and economic order had largely collapsed, and the early Song emperors needed a new mechanism to recruit men to serve in the bureaucracy that administered the empire. They greatly expanded the role of the examination system and in the process created a new stratum of scholar-officials, men from educated families of local prominence but without the political and economic status of the Tang Great Clans.

The new capital of Kaifeng was but one among many important cities. The southern cities that had grown to prominence as economic and cultural centers during the Five Dynasties retained their stature, and when Song dynasty officials took up posts in one of these metropolitan centers, they encountered a stimulating cultural milieu distinct from that of the capital. The growth of cities was aided by a booming economy in the South. Beginning in the late Tang and continuing through the Five Dynasties period, the Chinese population significantly shifted to the south as peasants fled the turmoil of the north and opened up new, rich farmland in the Yangzi River basin. The Northern Song government produced huge quantities of coins, and a monetized economy—including crops for the market rather than just subsistence—developed around the urban areas to support their needs.

Finally, printing began to spread. While printing appears to have begun to develop in the Tang to assist in Buddhist devotional practices (the printing of images and scripture), in the early Song, the imperial government used the technology to help distribute the Confucian canon—on which the examinations were based—to local schools throughout the empire. Commercial printing took root as the economy expanded, and major centers of textual production developed in Sichuan and Fujian. This wider dissemination of texts helped nurture literacy, learning, and the literati culture of the Northern Song.

Although the first fifty years of the dynasty witnessed all of these interrelated transformations, there appear to have been few new literary developments. The *shi* poetry of the first two generations of the Song was largely backward-looking. Similarly, the few lyrics from the early Northern Song that survive seem largely to draw on Tang and Five Dynasties tune titles, themes, and techniques. In fact, however, very few texts remain from the first fifty years; and it is therefore impossible to come to definite conclusions about the literature of the period. The first fifteen authors in the *Complete Song Dynasty Lyrics* (*Quan Song ci* 全宋詞) are:

He Xian 和峴 (933–88): 3 lyrics in 3 tune titles
Wang Yucheng 王禹偁 (954–1001): 1 lyric in 1 tune title
Su Yijian 蘇易簡 (958–96): 1 lyric
Kou Zhun 寇準 (961–1023): 6 lyrics in 6 tunes
Qian Weiyan 錢惟演 (962–1034): 2 lyrics in 2 tunes
Chen Yaozuo 陳堯佐 (963–1044): 1 lyric

Pan Lang 潘閬 (*jinshi* status awarded 995, d. 1009): 11 lyrics in 2 tunes
Ding Wei 丁謂 (966–1037): 2 lyrics in 1 tune
Lin Bu 林逋 (967–1028): 4 lyrics in 4 tunes
Yang Yi 楊億 (974–1020): 1 lyric
Chen Ya 陳亞 (*jinshi* 1002): 4 lyrics in 1 tune
Xia Song 夏竦 (984–1050): 2 lyrics in 2 tunes
Nie Guanqing 聶冠卿 (988–1041): 1 lyric
Li Zunxu 李遵勖 (988–1038): 2 lyrics in 2 tunes
Fan Zhongyan 范仲淹 (989–1052): 5 lyrics in 5 tunes

In other words, there are only forty-six extant lyrics for the writers active in the first fifty years of the dynasty, a period almost as long as the entire Five Dynasties era. Scholars have speculated about why so few *ci* survive from the period. One major argument is that, despite the acceptance of *ci* in the Later Shu and Southern Tang courts, the early Northern Song court and elite society continued to consider song lyrics as simply too plebian to save and pass down. Based on later writings, we can be sure that *ci* continued to be written and performed in major southern cities like Yangzhou, Hangzhou, and Suzhou and that the literati elite continued to enjoy them. They also probably tried their hand at writing in the genre, but their compositions did not survive.

Thus from the perspective of literary history, the story of the growth of song lyrics as a genre begins again in the early years of the eleventh century with the four elite writers whose lyrics do survive: Zhang Xian 張先 (980–1078), Liu Yong 柳永 (987–1053), Yan Shu 晏殊 (991–1055), and Ouyang Xiu 歐陽修 (1007–72). Of these four writers, Yan Shu and Ouyang Xiu largely drew upon earlier *ci* styles, while the lyrics by Zhang Xian and Liu Yong reveal new features that mark a significant development in the Song dynasty elite appropriation of *ci* as a genre. Because Ouyang Xiu's works are similar in style to those of Yan Shu, while Zhang Xian is a transitional figure between Yan Shu and Liu Yong, this section offers two representative lyrics by Yan Shu and Zhang Xian before turning to Liu Yong, who is considered the most important innovator in *ci* of the early Song.

The song lyrics of Su Shi 蘇軾 (1037–1101), that end this section, mark a significant step beyond Zhang Xian and Liu Yong and reflect the literati culture's adoption of the *ci* genre for its own compositional concerns. Su Shi wrote lyrics that greatly expanded the range of topics explored in *ci* and moved the genre out of the entertainment quarters and into the mainstream of elite life.

Yan Shu 晏殊 *(991–1055)*

Yan Shu came from a local elite family in Jiangxi (i.e., the South) and came to the Song court in 1005 at the age of fourteen to take the recruitment examination for young prodigies. He passed, was awarded a status equivalent to having passed the *jinshi* examination, and was appointed to a nominal office in the Palace Library. From that auspicious beginning, he went on to an extremely successful career and eventually rose to the position of chief councilor. One of his very important talents was recognizing and cultivating promising young men: many of the important officials of the next generation received his early support. For example, he presided over the *jinshi* examination through which both Zhang Xian and Ouyang Xiu qualified for government service.

The very fact that a substantial collection of 136 lyrics by Yan Shu survives indicates that he played a role in reasserting the legitimacy of the form within elite culture. His elegant *ci* clearly reflect the models of Wei Zhuang and Li Yu, with many delicate spring and autumn scenes tinged with melancholy.

"To the Tune 'Plaint of Inner Feelings'" by Yan Shu

		【訴衷情】					To the Tune "Plaint of Inner Feelings"
芙	蓉	金	菊	鬬	馨	香，[xiaŋ]	Hibiscus and gold chrysanthemums compete in floating fragrance;
hibiscus	gold	chrys...	compete	dispersed	fragrance		
天	氣	欲	重	陽。[jiaŋ]			The weather nears Double Yang.
sky	air	about to	Double	Yang			
遠	村	秋	色	如	畫，		In the distant village, the autumn colors are like a painting:
distant	village	autumn	color	resemble	painting		
紅	樹	間	疏	黃。[xɦuaŋ]			Red trees interspersed with sparse yellow.
red	tree	come between	sparse	yellow			
流	水	澹，					The flowing waters are placid,
flow	water	placid					
碧	天	長，[trɦiaŋ]					The azure sky is broad,
azure	sky	long					
路	茫	茫。[maŋ]					The road is distant and dim.
road	boundless & distant						
憑	高	目	斷，				From on high, I strain my eyes:
rely on	high	eye	snap				
鴻	雁	來	時，				When swans and geese arrive,
swan	goose	come	time				
無	限	思	量。[liaŋ]				Limitless longing.
without	limit	longing	reckon				

STUDY NOTES AND QUESTIONS

1. Why is the speaker in the poem moved by the arrival of the geese? Do you think the lyric is a form of second-person address, directed to the distant person to whom the speaker cannot send a letter?

2. Explain whether, in your judgment, the speaker in the lyric is male or female. What difference does it make?

3. How does this *ci* differ from those by Li Yu? What is the social status of the speaker in this lyric? Does Yan Shu give the speaker a personalized voice and presence in the lyric that makes you think that the speaker is Yan Shu himself? What about the intensity of the emotion? How is the tone related to the formal features of the poem?

4. Suppose that this is an occasional verse: Yan Shu wrote it for a banquet on an autumn evening in a pavilion next to a river, and he is in fact describing elements of the scenery. Suppose he wrote the lyrics to be sung by a female musician for his guests' entertainment. How would this scenario change your reading of the poem? How would the fact of performance make this lyric different from the many "autumn modal" poems we already have seen from the earlier tradition?

Zhang Xian 張先 *(980–1078)*

Zhang Xian, a transitional figure important in winning elite acceptance for *ci* as a genre, was from the southern prefecture of Huzhou 湖州 (in modern Zhejiang Province). He passed the *jinshi* examination in 1030 at the age of fifty and then served in a variety of substantive regional posts, including prefect, before retiring to Huzhou to live a very convivial, gregarious life as a gentleman recluse. When Su Shi (see below) became vice-prefect of Hangzhou in 1072, he became friends with the ninety-two-year-old Zhang and seemingly was inspired to take *ci* seriously as a literary form by Zhang's example.

Zhang Xian continued the trend, visible in Yan Shu's lyrics, of moving *ci* out of the palace and out of the entertainment quarters. He used song lyrics to write about quotidian life. Even more than Yan Shu's example above, Zhang's lyrics eschew the ornateness and intensity of emotions found in the early *ci* lyrics. However, he also began to apply the discipline of composing striking lines (*jing ju* 警句) to the crafting of song lyrics. As part of the regularization of *ci* as a genre, Zhang added many headnotes to his *ci* that explain the occasion for which he wrote the lyrics. Because three of his most popular lyrics had striking lines that used the character "shadow" (*ying* 影), he frequently was referred to as Zhang "Three Shadows" (Zhang Sanying 張三影). One of those lyrics is presented below.

"To the Tune 'Heavenly Immortal'" by Zhang Xian

時為嘉禾小倅，以病眠，不赴府會。

At the time, I was a junior prefectural aide in Jiahe. Because I was sick and resting, I did not attend the prefectural gathering.

		【天仙子】					To the Tune "Heavenly Immortal"
水	調	數	聲	持	酒	聽，[thiajŋ]	Several notes of "Water Tune": I hold ale as I listen;
water	tune	several	sound	carry	ale	listen	
午	醉	醒	來	愁	未	醒。[siajŋ]	I have sobered from noon drinking but not yet sobered from grief.
noon	drunk	sober	come	grieve	not yet	sober	
送	春	春	去	幾	時	回。	Sending off spring, spring departs: when will it return?
see off	spring	spring	depart	how many time		return	
臨	晚	鏡，					Overlooking a late [afternoon] mirror,
overlook	afternoon	mirror					
傷	流	景，[kiajŋ´]					Pained by the flowing scene,
hurt	flow	scene					
往	事	後	期	空	記	省。[siajŋ´]	I reflect in vain on past matters and future commitments.
depart	affair	later	period	empty	recall	reflect	
沙	上	並	禽	池	上	瞑，	The paired ducks of the sandbank are growing dark on the pond;
sand	on	pair	bird	pond	on	dark	

雲	破	月	來	花	弄	影。[ʔiajŋ´]	The clouds break, the moon arrives, the flowers play with their shadows.
cloud	break	moon	come	flower	dandle	shadow	
重	重	簾	幕	密	遮	燈,	Layer upon layer of blinds and curtains densely shield the lamp.
double	double	blinds	curtain	dense	block	lamp	
風	不	定,[tɦiajŋ`]					The wind is unsettled;
wind	not	settle					
人	初	靜,[tsɦiajŋ`]					As people first grow quiet:
person	first	quiet					
明	日	落	紅	應	滿	徑。[kjiajŋ`]	Tomorrow the fallen red [petals] surely will fill the path.
bright	sun	descend	red	ought	fill	path	

STUDY NOTES AND QUESTIONS

1. How is this lyric a response to its occasion? What is the function of the first stanza? Explain the particular details. How does the closure here draw on techniques used in *shi* poetry to bring an occasional poem to an end?

2. The shift of tone and topic in the first line of a second stanza usually is important in the overall construction of a lyric. What is the function of the ducks? Where are the ducks: does the speaker of the lyric see or imagine them?

3. If the speaker of the lyric is looking out a window in the first two lines of the second stanza, how do you explain the third line? Recall the occasion of the *ci*: do you think that the speaker closed the blinds and curtains where he continues to rest, or do the lamps refer to the bright lights of the prefectural gathering that he has missed?

4. Following the third line, to whom does the line "As people first grow quiet" refer? Zhang Xian? People outside his window? The people at the gathering? Explain your interpretation.

5. The second line of the second stanza is the most famous line from this poem. Wang Guowei, the important early modern critic of *ci*, in particular praised the use of "play" (*nong* 弄) to capture the quality of the scene. How does this attribution of intention to the branches of flowers animate the scene? (Note that all three verbs in the line are active.) Do the flowers relieve the speaker's loneliness, add to it, or have nothing to do with it?

Liu Yong 柳永 *(987?–1053?)*

Liu Yong was the great innovator in the early Song dynasty *ci* tradition. And as was the case for both Wen Tingyun and Li Yu, later scholars shaped their accounts of Liu Yong's life to match the stereotypes suggested by his lyrics. According to the resulting story, he led a dissolute life in the entertainment quarters of the capital and other major cities in the South. He reputedly was so effective as a writer of *ci* in the style of the brothels that whenever a new tune became popular, singing girls sought him out to write new lyrics for them to sing. In one account, the emperor used his prerogative specifically to fail Liu Yong in the final stage of the *jinshi* examination because Liu Yong's morals were too lax. In the usual story, even after Liu did manage to attain the status of *jinshi* and serve in local office, his reputation and behavior kept him from having a significant career. However, the story continues, the lyrics he wrote late in life, chastened by his failures, reflect the sorrows and frustrations of his wandering course as a low-level official, in contrast to the more sexually charged *ci* of his youth.

How much of this is true is hard to say. Scraps of later information (still of uncertain reliability) let us piece together a different account more typical for less prominent members of the newly emerging Song elite: in this version, Liu Yong came from a well-established Southern clan. His father served the Southern Tang and then attained the *jinshi* in the new Song dynasty in 985 and held a variety of provincial and capital posts. Liu Yong passed the *jinshi* in 1034: he could not have done so without sponsors who were willing to take responsibility for his moral conduct. His subsequent career was not brilliant, but few men ever ascended to the higher reaches of the Song bureaucracy. His own son passed the *jinshi* exam in 1046, so he clearly had the resources and commitments required to give his son the education needed to pass the exam.

Despite the uncertainties surrounding Liu Yong's life, his lyrics present a clear set of innovations that surely derived from his mastery of the contemporary modes of writing *ci* in the urban entertainment districts of his day. The number of tune titles he used and their formal features mark a major change from the practice of Yan Shu, Zhang Xian, and Ouyang Xiu:[11]

Author	Number of *Ci*	Number of Tunes	Number of Long *Ci* (80+ characters)
Yan Shu	136	36	3 (1 title)
Zhang Xian	165	96	18 (16 titles)
Ouyang Xiu	240	69	12 (10 titles)
Liu Yong	212	126	122 (87 titles)

Liu Yong used far more tune titles than other contemporary elite writers. Importantly, those tunes were largely in the long *man* 慢 form, with more than eighty characters in a song. The greater room provided by this format allowed Liu Yong to explore the themes of his *ci* in more detail and from more perspectives within a single song. The contemporary tunes with which Liu Yong worked also provided more complex syntactic patterns as well as an additional musical option of "padding words" (*chen zi* 襯字), words added to meet the musical requirements of the tune. The result of such padding was that there was significant variability in the different lyrics that Liu Yong wrote to the same tune title. (Later elite writers who

11. This chart comes from Murakami Tetsumi 村上哲見, *Sō shi kenyū: Tō Godai hoku Sō hen* 宋詞研究：唐五代北宋篇 (Tokyo: Sōbunsha, 1976), p. 218.

learned from books rather than from the performances in the entertainment quarters complained that Liu Yong did not know the tunes and could not provide a reliable model.)

Another formal aspect of the *man* style that Liu Yong introduced to the elite repertoire was the use of "governing words" (*ling zi* 領字), phrases from one to three characters long, to provide a frame for sections of the composition that can range from one to four lines in length. In "Eight Sounds from Ganzhou," translated below, for example, Liu Yong writes:

> **歎**年來蹤跡，何事苦淹留？

Here, "I sigh that" (*tàn* 歎) governs two lines. Also in "Eight Sounds" he writes:

> **漸**風霜淒慘，關河冷落，殘照當樓。

Here, "gradually" (*jian* 漸) governs three lines. Typical examples of governing words cited by the late Southern Song *ci* author and theorist Zhang Yan 張炎 (1248–ca. 1320) in his *Sources of Ci* (*Ciyuan* 詞源) are:

正	"It is just that . . . "
但	"It is only that . . . "
甚	"Very. . . "
莫是	"Is it not . . . ?"
還有	"There also is . . . "
那堪	"How can I bear . . . ?"
最無端	"Most pointless . . . "

These phrases help give the longer *man* lyrics an internal framework to structure the text. Authors and scholars of *ci* later in the tradition sought to develop rules for how governing words were best used in writing lyrics.

In sum, Liu Yong's innovative adoption of the longer *man* form with its greater syntactic and thematic possibilities significantly shaped the future development of *ci* as a genre.

"To the Tune 'Qu yu guan'" by Liu Yong

【曲玉管】

To the Tune "Qu yu guan"

隴 首 雲 飛，
mountain head cloud fly
Over the mountains the clouds fly,

江 邊 日 晚，
river beside sun late
By the river the sun turns to dusk,

煙 波 滿 目 憑 闌 久。[kiw´]
mist wave fill eye lean railing long
Misty waves fill the eye, as I lean long
on the railing.

立 望 關 河，
stand look for pass river
I stand looking at the passes and
river:

蕭 索 千 里 清 秋，[tshiw]
desolate thousand *li* pure autumn
Desolate, a thousand *li* of limpid autumn,

忍 凝 眸。[məw]
endure congeal pupil
Can I bear to fix my gaze?

杳 杳 神 京，
far far numinous capital
Far far away is the divine capital,

盈 盈 仙 子，
alluring immortal person
Alluring is the immortal one,

別 來 錦 字 終 難 偶。[ŋəw´]
part come embroider word to end hard encounter
Since parting, [her] embroidered words
have been impossible to meet.

斷 雁 無 憑，
broken goose with no rely
That isolated goose is unreliable:

冉 冉 飛 下 汀 洲。[tʂiw]
slowly slowly fly descent sandbar islet
Slowly it flies down to the river islets.

思 悠 悠。[jiw]
longing remote remote
Longing thoughts grow distant.

暗 想 當 初，
hidden imagine just at beginning
I inwardly envision the beginning:

有 多 少、幽 歡 佳 會，
there is many few secluded joy fine meet
There were so many private joys and
fine encounters

豈 知 聚 散 難 期，
how know gather scatter hard set time
How could we know meeting and
parting would be hard to arrange,

翻 成 雨 恨 雲 愁。[tʂɦəw]
reverse become rain regret cloud sorrow
Turning into the regrets and sorrows
of rain and clouds.

阻 追 游。[jiw]
block pursue excursion
We cannot pursue [our former]
excursions.

每	登	山	臨	水，		Whenever I climb a mountain or look over a river,
each	climb	mountain	look over	river		
惹	起	平	生	心	事，	It stirs those affairs of my former life,
stir	raise	level	life	heart	affairs	
一	場	消	黯，			A scene of mute sorrow,
one	field	dissolve	darken			
永	日	無	言，			Throughout the long day without speaking—
long	day	with no	speak			
卻	下	層	樓。[ləw]			I then descend the layered pavilion.
then	descend	layer	pavilion			

STUDY NOTES AND QUESTIONS

1. Think about the organization of the lyric and what the tune's longer length allows. How does the first stanza lead into the second and the second into the third? What techniques of repetition does Liu Yong use to link the stanzas? What new material and tone does he use to set apart each of the stanzas?

2. What is the effect of the long strophes that span three, four, or five lines?

3. What is the effect of the objective opening of the first stanza? At what point does Liu Yong begin to set out the specific significance of those images for the persona in the poem? How does he develop that significance? What effect does this slow unfolding of the persona's engagement in the scene have on the persona's voice in the poem?

4. The binomes that begin the second stanza mark a shift in the register of the language. Recall, for example, the beginning of the second of the "Nineteen Old Poems" in chapter 2, which includes the line, "Elegant is the woman in the tower" (盈盈樓上女). What is the effect on the mood of the lyric?

5. The phrase "inwardly envision" (*an xiang* 暗想) is a "governing phrase": how many sentences do you think it "governs?" How does it shape their reading?

6. Consider how the text enriches the resonances of the phrase "rain regrets and cloud sorrows." (This is technically a "doubled phrase" (*huwen* 互文) meaning "the regrets and sorrows of clouds and rain.") We have seen how "clouds and rain" refer to sexual union, but here the phrase links the theme of "gathering and parting" from the line above it with the image of clouds from the first line of the lyric and reanimates an old phrase with more complex metaphorical features. How do you read "the regrets and sorrows of clouds and rain" here?

7. The lyric's conclusion draws on a well-established way of ending a "climbing on high" poem but remains compelling. What standard ending does he borrow from, and how does he build upon it?

"To the Tune 'Settling the Waves'" by Liu Yong

【定風波】		To the Tune "Settling the Waves"
自 春 來、慘 綠 愁 紅，	from spring arrive sad green sorrow red	Since the arrival of spring, I am saddened by green and feel sorrow at red;
芳 心 是 事 可 可。[kʰa´]	fragrant heart this affair can can	Concerning the fragrant heart, all matters are indifferent.
日 上 花 梢，	sun ascend flower branch	As the sun climbs to the flowering branches,
鶯 穿 柳 帶，	oriole pierce willow belt	And orioles pierce the willow streamers,
猶 壓 香 衾 臥。[ŋua`]	still press incense blanket lie down	Still pressed by a fragrant coverlet, I lie down.
暖 酥 消，	warm cream melt	Warm [cosmetic] oil melts,
膩 雲 嚲，	luster cloud droop	My lustrous clouds [of hair] droop:
終 日 厭 厭 倦 梳 裹。[kua´]	end day frail frail tired comb wrap	To day's end, frail, I am too weary to comb and dress my hair.
無 那。[na´]	with no avail	Nothing to be done!
恨 薄 情 一 去，	resent slight feelings once depart	I resent that since that man of slight feelings left,
音 書 無 個。[ka`]	sound letter with no individual	Not a single letter.
早 知 恁 麼，	early know like this	If I had early known it would be like this,
悔 當 初、不 把 雕 鞍 鎖。[sua´]	regret just at beginning not take carved saddle lock	I regret that at the beginning, I did not lock up his carved saddle.
向 雞 窗、只 與 蠻 箋 象 管，	toward rooster window only give Man paper ivory tube	In the study, only give him Man paper and an ivory-handled brush,[12]
拘 束 教 吟 課。[kʰua`]	limit bind instruct chant lesson	Restricting him to chanting his texts.

12. The term "rooster window," used to refer to a study, comes from a story in a compilation of accounts of mysterious events in which a man obtained a rooster that learned to talk. He kept it in a cage outside his study and conversed with it throughout the day, and its wise insights led him to grow very adroit in speech.

鎮	相	隨，						All day we would accompany one another,
entire	mutual	follow						
莫	抛	躲，[tua´]						Not setting the other aside:
don't	discard	hide						
針	線	閒	拈	伴	伊	坐，		Idly plying needle and thread, I would sit by his side,
needle	thread	idle	handle	next to	him	sit		
和	我，[ŋa´]							With me,
with	me							
免	使	年	少，	光	陰	虛	過。[kua`]	We would not allow the days of our youth to pass in vain.
avoid	cause	years	young	gleam	shade	empty	pass	

STUDY NOTES AND QUESTIONS

1. This lyric obviously is in the voice of a woman, in contrast to the male voice in "Qu yu guan." Think of the ways in which Liu Yong defines a gendered identity here: consider, for example, the differences between male and female agency (she regrets not having locked up her lover's saddle and confined him to his study). Consider inside/outside distinctions, the focus on the body, the role of the landscape, and as many other factors as you can find.

2. Continuing the question of gendered voice, when in the lyric does it become apparent that the person *is* female? Explain.

3. Based on the second stanza, is the woman of the same social stratum as her lover? Explain. If the lyric were performed in the entertainment quarters, would there be a distance between the persona in the lyric and the performer singing the song?

4. In an anecdote in which Yan Shu dismisses Liu Yong for writing hopelessly vulgar lyrics very different from his own, more refined *ci*, Yan quotes the line "Idly plying needle and thread, I would sit by his side." This line seems a male projection of a female vision of domestic harmony and a quiet private life rather than the sort of erotically charged line one might have expected. Why do you think the later creator of the anecdote might have chosen this line and this lyric?

"To the Tune 'Eight Sounds of Ganzhou'" by Liu Yong

【八聲甘州】		To the Tune "Eight Sounds of Ganzhou"
對 瀟 瀟、暮 雨 灑 江 天，	facing drizzle drizzle sunset rain sprinkle river sky	Facing the patter: sunset rain scattered in the river and sky,
一 番 洗 清 秋。[ts^{h}iw]	one turn clean pure autumn	A moment clearing the limpid autumn.
漸 風 霜 淒 慘，	gradual wind frost chill wretched	Gradually, the wind and frost grow chill and forlorn,
關 河 冷 落，	passes river cold fallen	The passes and river grow bleak,
殘 照 當 樓。[ləw]	remnant shine just at tower	As remnant sunshine falls on the tower.
是 處 紅 衰 翠 減，	this place red decline emerald decrease	In this place, the red [blossoms] shrivel and the jade-green [leaves] diminish.
苒 苒 物 華 休。[ts^{h}iw]	slowly slowly things florid cease	Slowly the flourishing stops.[13]
惟 有 長 江 水，	only there is long river water	There is only the water of the Yangzi,
無 語 東 流。[liw]	with no speech east flow	Without speaking, flowing to the east.
不 忍 登 高 臨 遠，	not bear climb high look over far	I unwillingly climb on high and overlook the distant view,
望 故 鄉 渺 邈，	look for old village vague remote	Looking for my old village in the dim vastness:
歸 思 難 收。[ʂiw]	return longing hard to draw in	Longing to return is impossible to restrain.
歎 年 來 蹤 跡，	sigh year arrive footprint trace	I sigh for [my vagrant] footsteps during these years:
何 事 苦 淹 留。[liw]	what affair bitter tarry remain	For what matters do I tarry so?
想 佳 人、妝 樓 顒 望，	imagine fair person make-up tower grand gaze	I imagine my fair one in her boudoir tower raising her head to look:

13. Commentaries take *ran ran* 苒苒 as equivalent to *ran ran* 冉冉 ("gradually"), but it also could refer to the flourishing of nature during the year.

誤	幾	回	天	際	識	歸	舟。[tʂiw]	How many times has she mistakenly recognized my returning boat?
err	how many	cycle	sky	border	recognize	return	boat	
爭	知	我、	倚	闌	干	處，		How can she know that I, where I lean on the balustrade,
how	know	I	lean	balustrade		place		
正	恁	凝	愁。[tʂɦəw]					Just now am enmeshed in sorrow like this?
just now	like this	congeal	sorrow					

KANG-I SUN CHANG'S TRANSLATION

I face the scene of a downpouring evening rain,
splashing on the river and sky,—
The clear autumn is washed clean.
Gradually the frosty wind brings a chilly current of air,
The mountain pass and the rivers become desolate,
And the fading sunlight falls on the tower.
Here the red blossoms wither, the green leaves decay—
One by one the beautiful scenes in nature fade away.
Only the water of the Yangzi River
Flows east, without a word.

I cannot bear to view the distance from a high point—
Gazing upon my homeland faraway
Would arouse all my homesick thoughts.
I sigh over my straying steps these years,
Why do I suffer these endless wanderings?
I imagine my fair lady now looking earnestly out from her chamber—
How many times did she take the boat on the horizon for mine?
How would she know that I, leaning here against my balustrade,
Am bursting with grief?

STUDY NOTES AND QUESTIONS

1. This is perhaps Liu Yong's most famous lyric. Compared to the work of Yan Shu and Zhang Xian, what does it add to the *ci* tradition? Are the themes new? What does the spaciousness of the extended *man* form contribute to the development of the themes?

2. Consider how the lyric begins: is the brief autumn rain that clears the air a positive image? Is there a shift in mood between these first two lines and the rest of the stanza? The solemn autumnal mood of the stanza is complex: how do the lines of the stanza modulate the mood? Are there, for example, still flowers and leaves in the scene? Are the distant vista and the sunset light on the tower beautiful even if the persona reads into it signs of the inevitable decline of the year?

3. Why does the persona in the poem lament that the river flows "without a word"? Would you expect it to speak? What would its "speaking" be? How does this absence contribute to the poem and lead into the next stanza?

4. Do the gendered roles in the second stanza repeat those already seen in Liu Yong's two lyrics above? Explain.

5. Liu Yong employs many governing words (*ling zi*) in this lyric:

對瀟瀟	**Facing** the patter...
漸風霜淒慘	**Gradually**, the wind and frost grow chill and forlorn
望故鄉渺邈	**Looking** for my old village in the dim vastness
歎年來蹤跡	I **sigh** for [my vagrant] footsteps during these years
想佳人妝樓顒望	I **imagine** my fair one in her boudoir tower raising her head to look

Explain why each of these is a *ling zi* and what line(s) the word "governs."

6. How does the ending of this lyric draw on earlier techniques of "poetic closure" from both the evolving *ci* tradition and the more established *shi* form? What elements does it draw from each? More crucially, does this use of convention add to or detract from the power of the closing question?

Su Shi 蘇軾 *(1037–1101)*

Su Shi is one of the greatest cultural figures in Chinese history. He was the preeminent writer of prose and *shi* poetry in his generation and one of the central writers of the entire literary tradition. He was an important calligrapher, innovative painter, and high-ranking official. However, he was less than adroit as a politician, and his sharp wit led to a trial for insulting the emperor (a case brought by partisans of a faction he opposed) and to two periods of exile.

From a local elite clan in Sichuan that had little record of service, Su Shi, along with his brother Su Zhe 蘇轍 (1039–1112) and his father Su Xun 蘇洵 (1009–66), made a strong impression on elite society in Kaifeng 開封, the Northern Song capital. The two brothers, attended by their father, came from their home in Meishan 眉山 to pass the controversial *jinshi* examination of 1057, the year when Ouyang Xiu changed the required prose style of the examination from the strongly archaized "Imperial Academy" style to a plainer "old-style" form. Before they could benefit from their success, Su Shi's mother died, and they returned to Meishan to observe mourning. After the mourning period ended, Su Shi in 1061 passed a prestigious imperial decree examination to speed his progress through the bureaucratic system. After he served in his first post, however, his father died and he returned yet again to Meishan to mourn.

By 1069, when Su Shi returned to Kaifeng for a posting, Wang Anshi 王安石 (1021–86) had become the chief minister and was beginning a series of major reforms. Wang designed his "New Policies" (*xinfa* 新法) in part to bring in more funds to support the Northern Song's incessant warfare on its northern frontier and in part to help bring economic stability to China's large agrarian population. Conservatives at court strongly opposed Wang's interventions into the market economy but were driven out one by one. Su Shi stayed as long as he could but also eventually decided to seek an appointment outside of Kaifeng. In 1071 he became the vice-prefect of the important southern city of Hangzhou and subsequently shifted to posts of prefect in Mizhou and Xuzhou, two smaller southern prefectures. During these years in office, the disagreements at court had evolved into increasingly intense partisan struggle. Although Wang Anshi retired in 1076, Wang's partisans accused Su Shi of *lèse majesté* in 1079 in order to intimidate the conservative opposition and used his *shi* poems as evidence. Su was convicted of a minor offense and exiled in 1080 to the small town of Huangzhou in Hubei on the Yangzi River, where he remained until 1084.

After Emperor Shenzong 神宗 (1048–85, r. 1067–85) died in 1085 and his empress became regent for the young Emperor Zhezong 哲宗 (1077–1100, r. 1085–1100), the conservative opposition pushed Wang's clique from power and recalled Su Shi to the capital. Su, however, found himself at odds with the new conservative chief ministers: they wanted to completely undo Wang's "New Policies" reforms, but Su Shi found some of the policies to be useful in helping farmers. He spent the next seven years rotating among regional posts away from the political tensions of the capital, but in the end, he could not escape the factional strife. When Zhezong came to rule for himself in 1094, he restored his father's "New Policies" ministers, who exiled the conservatives, proscribed their writings, and forbade their descendants from even entering the capital. Su Shi first was exiled farther south to Huizhou (in modern Guangdong) and then, when it appeared that he was not suffering enough, the "New Policies" regime exiled him to Hainan Island in the far southeast. Although Su Shi was recalled in 1100 on the death of Zhezong and the ascension of Emperor Huizong 徽宗 (1082–1135, r. 1100–1126), he died one year later.

The details of Su Shi's life and career are important in understanding the development of his approach to *ci*. Although he was a prolific writer of *shi* poetry and prose from early in his life, he showed no significant interest in song lyrics until he received his posting to Hangzhou as vice-prefect in 1071. The Song dynasty, far more than the Tang, had many competing metropolitan cultural centers. Hangzhou was one of the most important cities in the increasingly important Jiangnan region and had a thriving entertainment quarters that probably surpassed those of the capital. In this new milieu, Su Shi met the aging *ci* writer Zhang Xian and was inspired to try his hand at the new musical form. Su's lyrics during his stay in Hangzhou were primarily verse celebrating social occasions and mostly in the short lyric (*xiao ling*) form. However, following a pattern seen in the lives of other poets encountered throughout this textbook, when Su Shi left Hangzhou to become the prefect of Mizhou and then Xuzhou, he began to experiment with a much more personal use for the genre. Following Zhang Xian's example in adding subtitles to explain the context for composition, he wrote lyrics to his brother and to commemorate the tenth anniversary of his wife's death, and these represented a major expansion of the range of *ci* as a form. When the "New Policies" partisans subsequently tried Su for slandering the throne, using his *shi* poetry as evidence and banishing him to Huangzhou, *ci* came to play a yet more significant role in Su Shi's writings. Because *shi* poetry always was susceptible to political readings, Su wrote far less of it in Huangzhou and instead turned his attention to *ci* as a verse form he could more freely share with friends, family, and colleagues. In Huangzhou Su Shi adapted the *ci* form for yet broader and deeper expressive purposes and developed an influential style—especially in the longer *man* format—with a quality of "heroic abandon" (*haofang* 豪放).[14] After his release from exile and return to higher levels of government service, he continued to write *ci*, but his focus largely shifted back to *shi*, and his most innovative period came to a close.

Some important *ci* writers like Xin Qiji later emulated Su Shi's style of "heroic abandon." Others, however, criticized his lack of musicality and his use of song lyrics to explore themes usually considered more appropriate to the *shi* form. They considered Su Shi's *ci* to have lost the "basic character" (*ben se* 本色) of the song lyric.

14. See, for example, Ronald Egan, *The Problem of Beauty* (Cambridge: Harvard University Asia Center, 2006), p. 284; and Kang-i Sun Chang, *The Evolution of Chinese* Tz'u *Poetry From Late T'ang to Northern Sung* (Princeton: Princeton University Press, 1980), p. 201ff.

"To the Tune 'River Goddess'" by Su Shi

乙卯正月二十日夜記夢

On the twentieth day of the First Month of 1075 at night I record a dream

		【江神子】					To the tune "River Goddess"[15]
十	年	生	死	兩	茫	茫。[maŋ]	Through ten years, life and death both have become indistinct.
ten	year	alive	die	two	indistinct		
不	思	量，[liaŋ]					I do not give thought:
not	think	reckon					
自	難	忘。[ʋaŋ]					[She] was impossible to forget.
of itself	hard	forget					
千	里	孤	墳，				A thousand *li* from the lone tomb,
thousand	*li*	lone	tumulus				
無	處	話	淒	涼。[liaŋ]			There is no place to talk of [my] desolation.
with no	place	talk	dreary	chill			
縱	使	相	逢	應	不	識，	Even if we were to meet again, [she] surely would not recognize me:
even	cause	mutual	meet	ought	not	recognize	
塵	滿	面，					Dust fills my face;
dust	fill	face					
鬢	如	霜。[ʂa:ŋ]					My temples are like frost.
temples	resemble	frost					
夜	來	幽	夢	忽	還	鄉。[xiaŋ]	Tonight in secluded dream I suddenly returned home.
night	come	secluded	dream	sudden	return	hometown	
小	軒	窗，[tʂʰwa:wŋ]					By the small veranda window
small	veranda	window					
正	梳	妝。[tʂa:ŋ]					[She] just now brushes [her] hair and applies make-up:
just now	comb	make-up					
相	顧	無	言，				We look at one another without speech;
mutual	look back	with no	speak				
惟	有	淚	千	行。[xɦaŋ]			There are only a thousand tracks of tears.
only	there is	tears	thousand	line			
料	得	年	年	斷	腸	處，	I sense that year after year, at the place that breaks my heart:
reckon	get	year	year	rend	innards	place	

15. Su Shi wrote this *ci* in Mizhou in 1075, when he was serving as prefect. The lyric commemorates his first wife, Wang Fu 王弗, who died in the capital in the Fifth Month of 1065 and was buried in Meishan, their hometown. They were married in 1054, when he was seventeen and she was sixteen. The tune is also called "River Town" 【江城子】.

明 bright	月 moon	夜， night	On a night of a bright moon,
短 short	松 fir	岡。[kaŋ] hill	A hill of short firs.

Ronald C. Egan's Translation

Ten years, the dead and living lie distantly apart.
I do not try to remember,
It is hard to forget.
The lone grave a thousand miles away,
No place to express the heart's chill.
Even if we met, she would not know me,
Face covered with dust,
Hair like frost.

Last night my lonely dream took me home.
By a small window
She was combing and making up.
We gazed at each other, speechless,
Only a thousand rows of tears.
I picture that place of heartbreak year after year,
On moonlit nights,
Low pines beside a mound.

Study Notes and Questions

1. *Shi* poems commemorating the death of one's wife had been part of the Chinese poetic tradition for centuries, but Su Shi here uses *ci* to explore this theme. Still, his very personal response to a particular occasion retains some connection to the more traditional topics, language, and imagery of the song lyric. What elements does the poem share with earlier *ci*? Explain. How does Su Shi use them?

2. The short preface mentions the dream that inspires the poem. Does the first stanza also mention that dream?

3. How would you paraphrase the second and third lines that are parts of one sentence? How do they take up the proposition in the first line? Does the first stanza develop an "argument" that creates a context for the second stanza? What is the relationship of the first to the second stanza?

4. Consider how Su Shi uses the prosody of the *ci* tune. For example, the last three lines of each stanza are a single unit that has a long hypotactically phrased line followed by two three-character lines. Does Su Shi repeat the same syntax in the two stanzas? What is the relationship of the long line to the two short lines in each stanza? What is your rhythm when reading these lines?

5. How would you paraphrase the last three lines of the second stanza?

"To the Tune 'Water Tune Prelude'"

丙辰中秋，歡飲達旦，大醉，作此篇，兼懷子由。

On the night of the Mid-Autumn Festival in 1076, I reveled and drank 'til dawn. Very drunk, I wrote this piece and fondly recalled [my brother] Ziyou.[16]

【水調歌頭】						To the Tune "Water Tune Prelude"
明	月	幾	時	有。		How long has there been a bright moon?[17]
bright	moon	how many	time	exist		
把	酒	問	青	天。[tʰian]		Grasping ale, I ask the blue heavens.
grasp	ale	ask	blue	sky/heaven		
不	知	天	上	宮	闕，	I wonder, in the palaces in the heavens,
not	know	heaven	on	palace	pavilion	
今	夕	是	何	年。[nian]		What year is this night?
now	night	this is	what	night		
我	欲	乘	風	歸	去，	I want to ride the winds to return,
I	want	ride	wind	return	leave	
又	恐	瓊	樓	玉	宇，	But also fear that in the jade towers and nephrite canopies,
also	fear	jade	tower	nephrite	canopy	
高	處	不	勝	寒。[xɦan]		In these high places I could not bear the cold.[18]
high	place	not	defeat	cold		
起	舞	弄	清	影，		I rise to dance and play with my pure shadow;[19]
rise	dance	play with	pure	shadow		
何	似	在	人	間。[kjaːn]		How does this seem like being within the human realm?
how	resemble	be at	people	amidst		
轉	朱	閣，				It circles around the crimson pavilion,
revolve	crimson	pavilion				

16. Su Shi wrote this *ci* in 1076 while serving as prefect of Mizhou 密州 (in modern Shandong). Su Zhe, his younger brother, was serving in Qizhou 齊州 (also in Shandong, but still not a short distance away) at the time.

17. Li Bai's influence looms very large in this *ci*. Here Su Shi echoes Li Bai's poem "Grasping Ale, Asking the Moon" 《把酒問月》, whose first couplet begins: "How long has there been a moon in the blue sky? / I now stop my goblet to ask it." 「青天有月來幾時，我今停杯一問之。」

18. Lines 5–7 expand upon and revise line 3 in Li Bai's "Grasping Ale, Asking the Moon": "One cannot get to climb to the bright moon." 「人攀明月不可得。」

19. Su Shi here echoes Li Bai's "Decanting Alone, under the Moon": "I sing, and the moon wavers. / I dance, and my shadow grows wild." 「我歌月徘徊，我舞影零亂。」 (See chapter 6.)

低	綺	戶，					And descends to the ornate window,
lower	fine silk	door					
照	無	眠。[mjian]					To shine on the sleepless.
shine	with no	sleep					
不	應	有	恨，				[The moon] ought not feel resentment:
not	ought	there is	resentment				
何	事	長	向	別	時	圓。[yan]	Why is it that it always is round at times of parting?
what	matter	long	facing	parting	time	round	
人	有	悲	歡	離	合，		Among people there are sorrow and joy, separation and reunion;
person	there is	sorrow	joy	part	join		
月	有	陰	晴	圓	缺，		For the moon, there are clouds and clearing, waxing and waning.
moon	there is	cloudy	clear	round	lacking		
此	事	古	難	全。[tsfiyan]			These matters, from of old are impossible to make whole.
this	matter	old	hard	complete			
但	願	人	長	久，			I only hope that for us it will always be that
only	want	person	long	long time			
千	里	共	嬋	娟。[?jyan]			Across a thousand *li* we can share [its] allure.[20]
thousand	*li*	together	alluring				

Study Notes and Questions

1. Compare Su Shi's use of the *ci* form here with Li Bai's old-style songs. What does the existence of specific prosodic requirements contribute to Su Shi's verse?

2. Su Shi starts out assuming the role of Li Bai toasting the moon, but then turns to worry that, as a mere mortal, he cannot endure the transcendent world. He then returns to the Li Bai role in his dance. What is the effect of this pause for worried reflection in the poem? How does it shape the persona in the poem? What effect does it have on the implied author?

3. In the zigzags of thought and emotion, is Su Shi trying to capture the qualities of being drunk? Or is the emotion more complex? Explain.

4. How do the movements in the first stanza complicate its final line?

5. How does the tone shift at the beginning of the second stanza?

6. Why does Su Shi suggest the possibility that the moon bears him some resentment?

7. What do the abstractions of the middle section of the second stanza contribute to the verse? Although the treatment of the theme seems to leave the usual world of *ci* sentimentality and intimate

20. Compare this line with the last couplet of Xu Hun's "Cherishing a Comrade in the Southland" 《懷江南同志》: "It surely is that the moon on Lake Dongting, / Across ten thousand *li* we share its allure." 「惟應洞庭月，萬里共嬋娟。」

emotion far behind, can these abstractions be a stand-in for the implied author's emotions? In particular, how does Su Shi develop the theme of "fondly recalling his brother" in the song lyric?

8. What thoughts, feelings, and attitudes does the final couplet capture that make this an appropriate way to serve as a response to the rest of the song and to bring the song to a close? (Do poems missing someone, for example, often end in projections into the future?)

"To the Tune 'A Melody of Yang Pass'" by Su Shi

中秋作

Composed on the Mid-Autumn Festival

		【陽關曲】					To the Tune "A Melody of Yang Pass"[21]
暮 dusk	雲 cloud	收 gather	盡 exhaust	溢 swell	清 clear	寒，[xɦan] cold	The dusk clouds have all receded; a welling of limpid coolness;
銀 silver	漢 Han	無 with no	聲 sound	轉 revolve	玉 jade	盤。[pɦuan] platter	The Silver River, without sound, turns on the Jade Platter.[22]
此 this	生 life	此 this	夜 night	不 not	長 long	好， good	In this life, this night is not forever fine:
明 bright	月 moon	明 bright	年 year	何 what	處 place	看。[kʰan] look	The bright moon next year: from where shall we look at it?

STUDY NOTES AND QUESTIONS

1. "A Melody of Yang Pass" is one of the *ci* tunes that look like seven-character quatrains. What is the difference between writing this poem as a quatrain and writing it as a *ci*?

2. Can you think of a way to translate the last line to preserve the repetition of the word *ming* 明, which appears in "bright moon" 明月 and "next year" 明年? What does one lose when one loses the repetition?

21. Su Shi wrote this verse in 1077 while he served as prefect of Xuzhou. His brother was visiting him at the time. A later note explained that he wrote this poem (*shi* 詩) and sang it to the tune "A Melody of Yang Pass." The fifteenth day of the Eighth Month that year was September 6.

22. The "Silver Han" is the Milky Way, envisioned as a river. The Jade Platter is the moon.

"To the Tune 'The Allure of Niannu'" by Su Shi

赤壁懷古

Cherishing the Past at Red Cliff[23]

【念奴嬌】	To the Tune "The Allure of Niannu"[24]
大 江 東 去， big river east depart	The great river departs eastward:
浪 淘 盡， waves wash exhaust	Its waves have washed away,
千 古 風 流 人 物。[ʋjyt] 1000 ancient wind flow person object	Dashing men of a thousand ages.
故 壘 西 邊， old rampart west side	The west side of the old ramparts,
人 道 是、三 國 周 郎 赤 壁。[pjiajk] person say this is three state Zhou master red wall	People say, is The Red Cliff of Master Zhou of the Three Kingdoms.[25]
亂 石 穿 空， chaotic rock pierce void	Chaotic rocks pierce the void;[26]
驚 濤 拍 岸， startle billow rip bank	Startled billows strike the bank,[27]
捲 起 千 堆 雪。[syat] roll rise 1000 pile snow	Swirling upward a thousand piles of snow.
江 山 如 畫， river mountain resemble painting	The river and mountains are like a painting:

23. Su Shi wrote this lyric in 1082 in Huangzhou, a small town in modern Hubei to which he was exiled in 1080 after a trial for slandering the emperor and his high officials. The "Red Cliff" in Huangzhou is not the actual Red Cliff of the famous battle (see footnote 25), and Su Shi in line 5 seems to indicate that he was aware that the local lore was wrong.

24. Niannu reportedly was a famous singer during the Tianbao reign period of Emperor Xuanzong of the Tang.

25. The Battle of Red Cliff in 208 was a key defeat that ended Cao Cao's effort to conquer the south and reunify China as the Later Han dynasty was disintegrating. Cao Cao had built a fleet for crossing the Yangzi and invading the South, which was controlled by Sun Quan and Liu Biao. Huang Gai, one of Sun Quan's generals, sent Cao Cao a note offering to surrender his fleet, but instead, Huang filled his ships with straw and oil and set them ablaze as they neared Cao Cao's fleet, which lay at anchor. Most of Cao Cao's ships, which were chained together, were burnt, and much of Cao Cao's army was destroyed. "Master Zhou" is Zhou Yu 周瑜 (d. 210), one of Sun Quan's generals, who led the land battles against the remaining Wei troops after the rout of Cao Cao's fleet.

26. There are some variant lines in the sources for this composition. Zou Tongqing 鄒同慶 and Wang Zongtang 王宗堂 prefer "pierce the void" to "collapse the clouds" 崩雲. See Su Shi, *Su Shi's* Ci *Chronologically Arranged and Annotated* 蘇軾詞編年校注, edited by Zou Yongqing and Wang Zongtang (Beijing: Zhonghua, 2002), vol. 2, p. 399.

27. Zou and Wang also accept "strike" 拍 rather than "shatter" 裂.

一 時 多 少 豪 傑。[kɦiat]	one time many few brave grand	At one time, how many grand heroes!
遙 想 公 瑾 當 年，	far imagine Gong- jin at that year	Afar I imagine Gongjin in that year:[28]
小 喬 初 嫁 了，	little Qiao begin marry finish	He had just taken Little Qiao as wife.
雄 姿 英 發。[fjyat]	manly manner splendid come forth	His manly manner stood out clearly,
羽 扇 綸 巾，	feather fan green headcloth	With feather fan and green silk headcloth.
談 笑 間、強 虜 灰 飛 煙 滅。[myiat]	chat laugh amid strong captive ash fly smoke extinguish	Midst chatting and laughter, the strong caitiffs flew as ashes and vanished in smoke.[29]
故 國 神 游，	old country spirit wander	Wandering in spirit to my old state,
多 情 應 笑 我，	many feelings ought laugh me	Filled with emotion: [they] surely would laugh at me,
早 生 華 髮。[fjyat]	early bear florid hair	Early growing grey hair.
人 間 如 夢，	people amid resemble dream	The human realm is like a dream:
一 樽 還 酹 江 月。[ŋyat]	one goblet return libation river moon	A beaker of ale I still pour as libation to the river moon.

Benjamin Ridgway's Translation

"The Charms of Niannu"

"Cherishing the Past" at the Red Cliff

The great river departs for the east,
And in its waves are extinguished,
Romantic men of a thousand years ago.
The old fort on the western bank,
People say was the Red Cliff of Zhou Yu in the Three Kingdoms.
Jagged rocks thrust into the sky,
Startled waves slap the shore,
Rolling up a thousand piles of snow.

---

28. Gongjin was the courtesy name of Zhou Yu. He and his brother married sisters from the Qiao clan: Zhou Yu married the younger of the two sisters.

29. Zou and Wang prefer "strong caitiff" 強虜 to "mast and scull" 檣艣. See Zou and Wang, *Su Shi's* Ci, vol. 2, p. 399.

The river and mountains are like a painting,
At one time how many heroes there were!
Far off I imagine Gongjin in those years,
Little Qiao just married to him,
His brave bearing shining forth,
With feather fan and green silken headband,
Amidst chatter and laughter, the mighty caitiff became ashes in the wind.
My spirit wanders to this ancient kingdom,
So sentimental, one should laugh at me,
With grey hair grown early.
The human world is like a dream,
So let me pour this libation to the river moon.

Study Notes and Questions

1. This song lyric, Su Shi's most famous, defined the "unbridled" (*haofang* 豪放) style of *ci*. Comparing it with earlier lyrics, how would you define the main features of the unbridled style?

2. Paraphrase the first six lines. What is Su Shi's argument about why he cannot say for certain if this is the correct Red Cliff?

3. In the rest of the first stanza Su Shi describes an intensely active scene. Is it past or present? Is it in fact like a painting? In this poem of reimagining, what relation does Su Shi create between imagination and the actual scene?

4. How does Su Shi make the transition from the first stanza to the second?

5. The first six lines of the second stanza are pure imagination, but is it a coherent imagination? Do the various images that Su Shi introduces create a coherent vignette? Explain.

6. Explain the transition from the first six lines of the second stanza to the final five lines. Commentators have long debated what Su Shi meant by "old state." Is it his home region of Sichuan, or is it the Sichuan of 200 AD that was one of the Three Kingdoms? In each case, who does he think would laugh at him, and why would it matter?

7. How does all that has happened in the lyric shape Su Shi's concluding thought that the "human realm is like a dream"?

8. If "the human realm is like a dream," why does the persona in the poem pour the libation? (What is a libation?) And why pour one to the moon in the river? What does the poem say about the interplay of memory, imagination, the landscape, and the intentions of the viewing subject?

9. What does the *ci* form contribute to the thematic development?

Chapter Ten

The Song Lyric in the Twelfth and Thirteenth Centuries

Introduction

The period of formal innovation in the *ci* genre had largely ended by the beginning of Emperor Huizong's 徽宗 reign in 1100. Writers had adopted the extended *man* form, and some continued Zhang Xian's and Su Shi's practice of adding headnotes to their *ci* and treating the genre as one more form of occasional composition. By 1100, composing song lyrics had become part of elite cultural life, and most of the important writers of *shi* poetry in the late Northern Song and throughout the Southern Song also were accomplished composers of *ci*.

For the period after 1100, histories of *ci* focus primarily on those authors who sought to preserve the distinctiveness of the song lyric as a specifically musical genre. Five of the six authors featured in this chapter had a specialist's mastery of music, and most wrote their own tunes. Even among these authors, however, *ci* came to play a broader role as a versatile occasional genre applicable to a wide range of events in elite life. This breadth of occasion and content is especially true of the sixth writer—Xin Qiji—who is mostly known as a patriotic poet but who in fact experimented in many ways with expanding the range of the form.

The time period covered in this chapter extends from Huizong's ascension to the throne in 1100 through the fall of the Northern Song in 1126 to the end of the Southern Song in 1280. In contrast to the significance of the An Lushan Rebellion for Du Fu and the Mid- and Late Tang poets, however, the particular details behind the fall of the north to the Jurchens and indeed behind most of the political and social history of the successor Southern Song dynasty are largely incidental to the writings of the six authors we shall examine. Li Qingzhao and Xin Qiji were deeply affected by the loss of the north on a *personal* level, but the Song dynasty's failure was not a cultural catastrophe that demanded the sort of reflection and questioning occasioned by the crisis after the collapse of Xuanzong's reign in the Tang. In a similar manner, Jiang Kui, Wu Wenying, and Zhang Yan all were affected by the social and political developments of their day, but these larger trends had little direct impact on their *ci* compositions.

Thus this chapter looks less at the intersection of historical circumstances and the development of *ci* as a genre and focuses instead on the actual practice of *ci* composition by the major Song dynasty writers in the form.

Zhou Bangyan 周邦彥 (1056–1121)

Later writers in the *ci* tradition considered Zhou Bangyan the great synthesizer of the genre. Like Liu Yong, he was deeply versed in musical technique and was a master of the long *man* form, but he brought a more refined command of language and phrasing to his lyrics.

Zhou was from an elite clan from Qiantang, the region around Hangzhou, a center of *ci* composition. His uncle Zhou Bin 周邠 (*jinshi* 1063) was a friend of Su Shi's. Zhou Bangyan had a rather successful official career. During the period when Wang Anshi's reform regime stressed the route of entering government service via the Imperial University (Taixue 太學), Zhou became an "outer hall" student there and attracted the emperor's attention by writing an obscurely learned, monumental *fu* on the imperial capital.[1] He received a minor initial appointment but worked his way up to county magistrate, prefect, and finally director of the palace library. Perhaps because of Zhou's reputation as a writer of *ci*, Zhang Yan 張炎 (1248–1320), the late Southern Song writer and critic of *ci*, reported that Zhou was also briefly appointed to the Imperial Music Bureau (Dashengfu 大晟府) when Emperor Huizong created it in 1103 in order to correct the musical tunings and provide court music. While this post became part of Zhou's biography in late imperial times, modern scholars suggest it was a creative reading on Zhang Yan's part. Such loosely substantiated details may have gained credence because, although Zhou Bangyan compiled a literary collection that survived until the early Southern Song, it then disappeared. His only surviving writings are his song lyrics, and stories inevitably accumulated around them, connecting them to putative events and relationships in his life.

Zhou Bangyan was a careful stylist who worked lines from earlier poetry into his lyrics and tended to be reticent rather than explicit in writing emotionally charged scenes. The topical range of his extant lyrics return to the world of Zhang Xian and Liu Yong rather than Su Shi: the joys of the pleasure quarters and the sorrows of travel. He was sufficiently musically accomplished as to write his own tunes, which became popular during his lifetime, and later writers of *ci* treated him as a model throughout late imperial times.

1. There were two thousand students in the "outer hall," three hundred in the "inner hall," and one hundred in the "upper hall."

"To the Tune 'Chant of the Auspicious Dragon'" by Zhou Bangyan

【瑞龍吟】						To the Tune "Chant of the Auspicious Dragon"[2]
章	臺	路。[luǝ̆`]				On the road from Zhang Terrace.[3]
Zhang	Terrace	road				
還	見	褪	粉	梅	梢，	One still sees the fading powder on plum branch-tips,
still	see	fade	powder	plum	branch-tip	
試	花	桃	樹。[ʂɦyǝ̆`]			And first-flowering peach trees.
try	flower	peach	tree			
愔	愔	坊	陌	人	家，	Secluded in the houses of the byways,
secluded		lane	path	people	house	
定	巢	燕	子，			Swallows building their nests
settle	nest	swallow				
歸	來	舊	處。[tʂɦyǝ̆`]			Return to their old places.
return	come	former	place			
黯	凝	佇。[trɦyă`]				Dejected I stand still.
dejected	congeal	stand				
因	念	箇	人	癡	小，	Because I recall how one, a simple child,
rely on	recall	a	person	foolish	small	
乍	窺	門	戶。[xɦuǝ̆`]			Suddenly peeked out from the gate.
sudden	peek	gate	door			
侵	晨	淺	約	宮	黃，	Braving the dawn, with a faintly traced yellow palace moon,[4]
encroach	dawn	shallow	restrict	palace	yellow	
障	風	映	袖，			Blocking the wind, brightened by sleeves,
block	wind	shine	sleeve			
盈	盈	笑	語。[ŋyă`]			Amply alluring, laughter and talk.
abundant		laugh	talk			
前	度	劉	郎	重	到，	Master Liu from last time has arrived again,[5]
former	time	Liu	Master	again	arrive	
訪	鄰	尋	里，			Visiting neighborhoods, inquiring in the wards,
visit	neighbor	search	ward			

2. Zhou Bangyan created this tune.

3. Zhang Terrace was a palace in Xianyang (the Qin capital later replaced by Chang'an) built by a King of Qin during the Warring States period. The "Zhang Terrace road" ornamentally refers to the streets of the capital.

4. This refers to a semicircle of yellow that Song women drew on their foreheads.

5. The line alludes to Liu Yuxi's famous quatrain on the peaches of Xuandu Temple. He wrote an initial quatrain on the peaches before being sent into exile and wrote a second quatrain on returning: "Who knows where has the Daoist master who planted the peaches has gone? / Master Liu from the last time now has come again."「種桃道士知何處，前度劉郎今又來」

Chinese	Gloss	Translation
同 時 歌 舞，	same time sing dance	Of the singers and dancers of that time,
惟 有 舊 家 秋 娘，	only there is old house Qiu- niang	There is only Qiuniang of the old house,
聲 價 如 故。[kuə̆ˋ]	sound price resemble old	Whose reputation is as of old.
吟 箋 賦 筆，	chant paper compose brush	With chanting's paper and composing brush,
猶 記 燕 臺 句。[kyə̆ˋ]	still recall Swallow Terrace line	I still remember the lines on Swallow Terrace.[6]
知 誰 伴、	know who side	Do I know by whose side she is
名 園 露 飲，	famous garden exposed drink	drinking relaxed in a famous garden,[7]
東 城 閒 步。[pɦuə̆ˋ]	east wall leisure pace	Or walking at leisure by the eastern wall?[8]
事 與 孤 鴻 去。[kɦyə̆ˋ]	event with lone swan depart	The matter has departed with a lone swan.
探 春 盡 是，	search spring entirely this is	Searching for spring entirely is this:
傷 離 意 緒。[syə̆ˋ]	wound separate intent thread	Feelings of the pangs of separation.
官 柳 低 金 縷。[lyə̆ˊ]	official willow low gold thread	Low on the office willows: golden threads.
歸 騎 晚、	return ride late	Riding, I return late,
纖 纖 池 塘 飛 雨。[yə̆ˊ]	delicate pond pool fly rain	delicately flying rain on the ponds and pools.
斷 腸 院 落，	break innards court- yard	This heart-rending courtyard:
一 簾 風 絮。[syə̆ˋ]	one curtain wind catkin	A curtain with wind-blown catkins.

6. Liu Zhi (Willow Branch), a young woman of Luoyang, was moved by Li Shangyin's set of four poems on Swallow Terrace and sought to arrange a tryst. It never happened, and she was taken by another. Li then wrote a poem "Presented to Willow Branch."

7. "Exposed drinking" is drinking with one's cap and headband off, that is, a very informal occasion.

8. "Eastern wall" probably echoes Du Mu's poem on the singer Zhang Haohao, occasioned by his meeting her by the eastern wall of Luoyang after four years. By then, she already had been a part of an official's household for two years.

Study Notes and Questions

1. Is the moment at the beginning of the poem the same as the moment at the end? How does the progression of the poem work? Explain the set of emotions Zhou captures in the poem through these scenes and reflections.

2. Notice some of the *ci* cadences in the poem:

Lines 2–3: 還見(褪粉梅梢，試花桃樹)。
Still see: fading powder plum branch-tips
attempt flower peach trees

Lines 8–9: 因念(箇人癡小，乍窺門戶)。
Because I recall: how one, a simple child
suddenly peeked out from the gate

Lines 16–17: 惟有(舊家秋娘，聲價如故)。
There was only: Qiuniang of the former house
reputation was like of old.

How does Zhou Bangyan exploit the line structure of the song lyric in the rhythm of his narrative?

3. Many of the lines are in fact noun phrases rather than full sentences. Can you identify some of them? What is the effect of these phrases (which often contain verb constructions as adjectives)?

4. How does Zhou use the stanza structure? What are the breaks between the three stanzas?

5. What do the allusions to Liu Yuxi, Li Shangyin, and Du Mu (all Mid- or Late Tang poets) contribute to the *ci*?

"To the Tune 'Western River'" by Zhou Bangyan

金陵懷古

Cherishing the Old at Jinling[9]

【西河】		To the Tune "Western River"
佳 麗 地，[tɦi`]	fine ordered place	Fine, lovely place,[10]
南 朝 盛 事 誰 記。[ki`]	south court flourish event who recall	Who recalls the flourishing events of the Southern Dynasty?
山 圍 故 國 繞 清 江，	mountain encircle old state surround limpid river	Mountains enclose the ancient and surround the limpid river:
髻 鬟 對 起，	coiled hair bun face rise	Coiffure rising, facing one another;
怒 濤 寂 寞 打 孤 城，	angry billow silent solitude strike lone rampart	Angry billows in solitude strike the lone rampart,
風 檣 遙 度 天 際。[tsiaj`]	wind mast far cross sky edge	And wind-[borne] masts afar cross to the sky's edge.
斷 崖 樹，	broken cliff tree	A tree on a sheered cliff
猶 倒 倚，	still inverted lean	Still leans upended,
莫 愁 艇 子 曾 繫。[xɦjiaj`]	Mo- chou skiff once tie	Where Mochou's skiff once was tethered.[11]
空 餘 舊 跡 鬱 蒼 蒼，	empty remain old traces dense dark dark	In vain there remain old traces obscure and dark;
霧 沉 半 壘。[lyj´]	mist sink half fortress	Mists sink half the battlements.
夜 深 月 過 女 墻 來，	night deep moon cross parapets come	When night is deep, the moon crosses the parapets,

9. Jinling (or Jiankang, modern Nanjing) was the capital of the southern states during the Southern Dynasties. It was razed at the end of that period but was rebuilt and remained an important city during the Tang and Song.

10. The phrasing echoes such lines as Xie Tiao's "Tune of Entering the Court" 《入朝曲》: "South of the River is a fine, lovely place; / Jinling is the realm of emperors."「江南佳麗地，金陵帝王州。」

11. Mochou ("Don't grieve") was a famous Tang dynasty singer who, according to one source, was from Stone Ramparts 石城 in Hubei (here mistaken for the Stone Ramparts in Jinling).

賞 心 東 望 淮 水。[syjˊ]
appreciate heart east gaze Huai water
With an appreciating mind I gaze east at the Huai River's waters.

酒 旗 戲 鼓 甚 處 市。
ale banner play drum what place market
An alehouse banner, the playing of drums: what town's market?

想 依 稀、王 謝 鄰 里。[liˊ]
imagine faint appearance Wang Xie neighbor ward
In imagination it seems like the precincts of the Wangs and Xies.

燕 子 不 知 何 世，
swallow not know what generation
The swallows don't know what is the age:

入 尋 常 巷 陌 人 家 相 對，
toward ordinary lane path people house mutual face
Entering the houses of the common lanes facing one another,

如 說 興 亡 斜 陽 裏。[liˊ]
resemble speak rise fall slant sunlight in
They seem to speak of rise and fall in the slanting sunlight.

STUDY NOTES AND QUESTIONS

1. Line 3 of the lyric reworks Liu Yuxi's 劉禹錫 quatrain, "Stone Rampart" 石頭城. Stone Rampart was a part of Jinling.

山圍故國周遭在，	Mountains enclose the ancient state, circling all around.
潮打空城寂寞回。	The tide strikes the ramparts and in silence returns.
淮水東邊舊時月，	The moon of old times on the eastern side of the Huai waters,
夜深還過女牆來。	When night is deep, comes crossing over the parapets.

2. The lyric, like Su Shi's "The Charms of Niannu," is a "cherishing of the past" poem. Su's *ci* established the "unbridled" mode of *ci* composition, while Zhou Bangyan keeps his themes, language, and treatment within the mainstream. What about Jinling does Zhou cherish?

3. Recalling Su Shi's use of the imagination in his lyric, how do the roles Zhou assigns to memory and imagination differ in his lyric?

4. The conclusion of the lyric incorporates another of Liu Yuxi's most famous quatrains, "Black-clothes Lane" 烏衣巷:

朱雀橋邊野草花，	Flowers of wild grasses by Crimson Sparrow Bridge:
烏衣巷口夕陽斜。	The dusk sunlight slants at the mouth of Dark-clothes Lane.
舊時王謝堂前燕，	The swallows before the halls of the Wangs and Xies in old times
飛入尋常百姓家。	Have flown into the houses of the ordinary populace.

Black-clothes Lane was named after Black-clothes Camp, established in Jinling during the Three Dynasties period. The Wangs and Xies were the most powerful clans of the Southern Dynasties.

5. Zhou Bangyan builds his composition around two well-known quatrains by Liu Yuxi discussed in study notes 1 and 4 above. How does this affect the tone of the lyric? What do the allusions contribute to the range of meaning in the *ci*? Is the effect similar to that in *shi* poems on "cherishing the past"?

"To the Tune 'Fair Lady Yu'" by Zhou Bangyan

【虞美人】							To the Tune "Fair Lady Yu"
疏	籬	曲	徑	田	家	小 ◦ [siaw′]	A thin hedge and a winding path:
sparse	hedge	bend	path	field	house	small	the farm household is small.
雲	樹	開	清	曉 ◦ [xjiaw′]			Cloud-[draped] trees open in
cloud	tree	open	limpid	dawn			the limpid dawn.
天	寒	山	色	有	無	中 ◦ [triwŋ]	The sky is cold; the forms of the
sky	cold	mountain	aspect	exist	not-exist	middle	mountains half there, half not.
野	外	一	聲	鐘	起、		Beyond the outlands, one sound of a
outland	outside	one	sound	bell	rise		bell rises
送	孤	篷 ◦ [pɦəŋ]					to send off the lone sail.
send off	lone	sail					
添	衣	策	馬	尋	亭	堠 ◦ [xɦəw`]	Putting on more clothes, I whip my
add	clothes	whip	horse	seek	pavilion	outpost	horse to search for the outpost.
愁	抱	惟	宜	酒 ◦ [tsiw′]			For a burden of sorrow, only ale is fitting.
sorrow	wrap	only	fitting	ale			
菰	蒲	睡	鴨	占	陂	塘 ◦ [tɦaŋ]	Among the reeds and grasses, the sleeping
wild-rice	reeds	sleep	duck	occupy	bank	pool	ducks occupy the pool.
縱	被	行	人	驚	散、		Although startled and scattered by this traveler,
even if	by	travel	person	startle	scatter		
又	成	雙 ◦ [ʂwa:wŋ]					they again form pairs.
again	form	pair					

STUDY NOTES AND QUESTIONS

1. How does the pattern of images in the first stanza relate to those in the second?

2. How does the persona in the *ci* fit into the landscape? How do the ducks fit into the landscape? How are they alike, how different?

3. What is the mood and meaning of the final image of the ducks scattering (how did the person in the poem feel as they took flight) and returning?

Li Qingzhao 李清照 (1084–ca.1147)

Zhou Bangyan and, a generation later, Li Qingzhao were the two most important writers of song lyrics during Emperor Huizong's long reign that ended in the Jurchen conquest of north China. Li Qingzhao also was a woman; indeed, she is considered one of the best women writers of premodern China.

Li Qingzhou was from a prominent literati family. Her father, Li Gefei 李格非 (*jinshi* 1076), was an associate of Su Shi and his circle and rose to the important court position of vice-director of the Bureau of Rites. She married Zhao Mingcheng 趙明誠 (1080–1129), the son of Zhao Tingzhi 趙挺之 (1040–1107), who served as Huizong's chief minister early in his reign. Li and Zhao spent the idyllic first years of their marriage collecting books and antiquities and cataloguing them. When the Jurchens invaded, they fled south with their large collection. Unfortunately, Zhao died of sickness en route to taking up a post as prefect of Huzhou, a region on the new border with the Jurchen Jin dynasty. Li kept the collection together as best she could as she struggled to find a secure residence in the south, but as a single woman, she lacked much protection, and most of her possessions were taken by officials or thieves or were lost in transport. During these difficult early years of the Southern Song, she sought the protection and security of a second marriage, but her hasty judgment proved bad, and she attained a divorce after only a few months. Although some later writers reported that Li Qingzhao spent the last decades of her life adrift, Ronald Egan concludes from the sparse surviving evidence that in fact she returned to Lin'an (i.e., Hangzhou), the new "temporary capital" of the Southern Song, spent her final years as a member of elite capital society, and continued to write.

By the time Li Qingzhao began to compose *ci*, it had gained provisional acceptance in elite culture and had largely matured as a form. Zhou Bangyan was writing new tunes, and Su Shi's effort to redirect the focus and tenor of *ci* to bring it closer to *shi* poetry continued to receive some attention, but in general there seemed to be a consensus about the themes, styles, and range of language appropriate to the genre. Li Qingzhao worked within that consensus even though her status as a woman added a distinct quality of voice to her compositions. While she was careful to shape a persona as a woman of her own social stratum, she also had some freedom to explore aspects of women's experience, and this set her works apart from the verse of her contemporary male writers. Like Zhou Bangyan, she was a stylist who delighted in using lines from earlier poetry in her lyrics, and she was strongly committed to the fundamentally musical character of *ci*. In a famous polemical essay on *ci* as a genre, she excoriated those (male) writers who had disregarded or poorly mastered the musical aspect of *ci* or who had failed in their phrasing, or who simply fell short in the overall conception of their compositions. Discussing Yan Shu, Ouyang Xiu, and Su Shi, she noted:

> Their learning plumbed the extremes of heaven and humankind. When they composed little song lyrics, it was like drawing a small gourd of water out from a great ocean. Still, what they wrote reads like nothing more than *shi* poetry that has not been properly polished, and their lines frequently violate the prosodic rules. 學際天人，作為小歌詞，直如酌蠡水于大海，然皆句讀不葺之詩爾，又往往不協音律者。[12]

---

12. Li Qingzhao, "Discussion of *Ci*"《詞論》in *Li Qingzhao ji jianzhu* 李清照集箋注, annotated by Xu Peijun 徐培均 (Shanghai: Shanghai guji, 2002), *juan* 3, pp. 266–67. The translation is from Ronald Egan, *The Burden of Female Talent: The Poet Li Qingzhao and Her History in China* (Cambridge: Harvard University Asia Center, 2013), pp. 77–78.

Following her critique of earlier generations of writers, she made the important—and often repeated—assertion that "we can see therefore that this form of writing is a field unto itself, and those who understand it are few" 乃知別是一家，知之者少。[13]

Only a handful of Li Qingzhao's writings other than her *ci* survive. Her essay "Discussion of *Ci*" was preserved. Later scholars also transcribed the long autobiographical postface she wrote for her husband's *Records of Metal and Stone*, a study of the ancient artifacts they had collected. The letter she wrote to thank an official for helping her extricate herself from her second marriage survives and helps us understand that marriage. Among Li Qingzhao's song lyrics, Ronald Egan concludes that only twenty-three are very securely attributable to her; another seven appear in Southern Song sources, while the remaining forty-five became attached to her corpus of writings as her fame grew in the Ming and Qing dynasties.[14] The song lyrics presented below are from the first two groups that are most likely authentic.

"To the Tune 'Note on Note (extended)'" by Li Qingzhao

【聲聲慢】		To the Tune "Note on Note (extended)"
尋 尋 覓 覓，	search search seek seek	Searching and searching, seeking and seeking,
冷 冷 清 清，	cold cold limpid limpid	Cold, so cold, limpid, so limpid,
凄 凄 慘 慘 戚 戚。[tshiajk]	dreary dreary wretched sorrow sorrow	Dreary, so dreary, so wretched, so sorrowful.
乍 暖 還 寒 時 候，	sudden warm and cold season time	In the season of sudden warming and then cold again,
最 難 將 息。[sik]	most hard take rest	It is most difficult to take care.
三 杯 兩 盞 淡 酒，	three cup two cup weak ale	Three beakers and two cups of weak ale:
怎 敵 他、晚 來 風 急。[kip]	how match it late come wind urgent	How can they fend off the whipping of the wind since evening?
雁 過 也，	goose cross "it is"	The geese have passed:
正 傷 心，	just wound heart	It indeed breaks the heart,
卻 是 舊 時 相 識。[ṣiə̆k]	but this is old time mutual know	But we knew each other in former times.

13. The translation is from Ronald Egan, *The Burden of Female Talent*, p. 78.

14. See the discussion in Egan, *The Burden of Female Talent*, pp. 91–104.

Chinese	Gloss	Translation
滿 地 黃 花 堆 積，[tsiajk]	fill ground yellow flower pile gather	Filling the grounds, chrysanthemum flowers gather in piles:
憔 悴 損，	haggard injure	Haggard and frail,
如 今 有 誰 堪 摘。[tra:jk]	like now there is who willing pick	Now who is there who would pick them?
守 著 窗 兒，	guard -ing window	Staying by the window,
獨 自 怎 生 得 黑。[xəə̆k]	alone myself how get black	By myself, how can [I wait for the sky to] get black?
梧 桐 更 兼 細 雨，	paulownia again join fine rain	The paulownia and the drizzling rain,
到 黃 昏、點 點 滴 滴。[tiajk]	reach yellow dusk dot dot drip drip	Reaching dusk: drop, drop, drip and drip.
這 次 第，	this circumstance	This moment,
怎 一 個、愁 字 了 得。[təə̆k]	how one [measure] sorrow character complete get	How can a single word "Sorrow" get it all?

Stephen Owen's Translation

to "Note after Note"

Searching and searching, seeking and seeking,
so chill, so clear,
dreary,
and dismal,
and forlorn.
That time of year
when it's suddenly warm,
then cold again,
now it's hardest of all to take care.
Two or three cups of weak wine—
how can they resist the biting wind
that comes with evening?
The wild geese pass by—
that's what hurts the most—
and yet they're old acquaintances.

In piles chrysanthemums fill the ground,
looking all wasted, damaged—
who could pick them, as they are now?

I stay by the window,
how can I wait alone until blackness comes?
The beech tree,
  on top of that
    the fine rain,
on until dusk,
the dripping drop after drop.
In a situation like this
how can that one word "sorrow" grasp it?

Study Notes and Questions

1. The tour-de-force opening of this song lyric is one of the most famous in the *ci* tradition. If this is a form of word-painting, do the words paint a scene? An emotion? A mood? Explain the effect of these three lines of repetitions that are all part of one sentence.

2. What is the season? Fall or spring? How do you know?

3. What is the gender of the persona in the *ci*? Explain your choice.

4. What is the significance of the speaker recognizing the geese that pass overhead without stopping in the last line of the first stanza?

5. Note that the romanization (developed for the Tang) does not work precisely here to capture the rhyme: 息 *sik* rhymes with 急 *kip*. At this point the *–k* and *–p* entering-tone words were beginning to fuse into a glottal stop *-ʔ* that then disappears in the northern dialects. Li Qingzhao was from Shandong, in the northeast.

6. Is there a temporal break or a change of scene between the stanzas?

7. Critics have admired the structural echoing of the repetition in the "Drop, drop, drip and drip" 點點滴滴. What is the effect of this echoing?

8. How does Li Qingzhao take advantage of the long *man* form here? Think in particular about the function of the question with which she ends the lyric as a way of pulling together the composition as a whole.

"To the Tune 'Like a Dream'" by Li Qingzhao (first lyric)

【如夢令】						To the Tune "Like a Dream"
昨	夜	雨	疏	風	驟，[tʂɦəw`]	Last night the rain was sparse but the wind buffeted;
yester	night	rain	sparse	wind	gallop	
濃	睡	不	消	殘	酒。[tsiw´]	Deep sleep did not disperse the lingering ale:
strong	sleep	not	melt	remnant	ale	
試	問	捲	簾	人，		I tried asking [the maid] rolling the curtains,
try	ask	roll	curtain	person		
卻	道	海	棠	依	舊。[kɦiw`]	But [she] said the crabapples were as before.
but	say	sea	plum	rely	former	
知	否，[fuw´]					"Do you know or not,
know	"is it not"					
知	否，[fuw´]					Do you know or not:
know	"is it not"					
應	是	綠	肥	紅	瘦。[ʂəw`]	Surely it is, the green grows plump but the pink grows thin."
ought	is	green	plump	pink	thin	

RONALD C. EGAN'S TRANSLATION

To the tune "As If in a Dream"

Last night the rain was intermittent, the wind blustery.
Deep sleep did not dispel the lingering wine.
I tried asking the maid who raised the blinds,
She said the crab apple blossoms were as before.
"Don't you know?
Don't you know?
The greens must be plump and the reds withered."

"To the Tune 'Like a Dream'" by Li Qingzhao (second lyric)

【如夢令】						To the Tune "Like a Dream"
常	記	溪	亭	日	暮，[muǒ`]	I always recall the pavilion by the creek at sunset:
always	recall	creek	pavilion	day	sunset	
沉	醉	不	知	歸	路。[luǒ`]	Deeply drunk, I did not know the route back.
sink	drunk	not	know	return	road	
興	盡	晚	回	舟，		The mood ending, late in the day I turned the boat,
inspire	exhaust	late	turn	boat		

誤	入	藕	花	深	處。[tʂhiə̆`]	And mistakenly entered a place thick with lotus flowers.
err	enter	lotus	flower	deep	place	
爭	渡，[tɦuə̆`]					Striving to cross,[15]
strive	cross					
爭	渡，[tɦuə̆`]					Striving to cross,
strive	cross					
驚	起	一	灘	鷗	鷺。[luə̆`]	I startle to flight a whole shoal of gulls and egrets.
startle	rise	one	shoal	gull	egret	

Stephen Owen's translation

Like a Dream

I will always recall that day at dusk,
  the pavilion by the creek,
and I was so drunk I couldn't tell
  the way home. My mood left me,
it was late when I turned back in my boat
and I strayed deep among lotuses—
how to get through?
how to get through?
and I startled to flight a whole shoal
  of egrets and gulls.

Study Notes and Questions

These lyrics, written to the same tune, show that a tune, even a short form as restrictive as this—with its many required rhymes and duplicated lines—can be used to express many different moods and treat many different topics.

First Lyric

1. Ronald Egan points out that Li Qingzhao here takes elements from a poem, "Too Tired to Rise" 懶起, by the Late Tang writer Han Wo 韓偓 (ca. 842–923):

昨夜三更雨，	Last night, rain at midnight;
今朝一陣寒。	This morning, a gust of cold
海棠花在否，	Do the crabapple flowers remain or not?
側臥卷簾看。	Lying on my side, I roll the curtains to look. (ll. 9–12)

15. Some scholars take 爭渡 ("striving to cross") as 怎渡 ("How do I cross?"). But there are earlier precedents for the phrase in which writers used 爭 in its literal rather than colloquial sense.

This first lyric basically reworks Han Wo's poem in a very condensed manner.[16] What situation and mood is Li Qingzhao trying to capture here? Is it a reenvisioning of the ending of Han Wo's poem? What does she add, and to what effect?

2. Is the persona in the first lyric male or female? Remember that the translation takes the attendant to be female, but the gender is not given in the *ci* itself.

3. What is the meaning of the assertion in the last line? What is the urgency suggested by the duplicated phrases?

Second Lyric

1. In the "Wu songs" from the Southern Dynasties, the person in the small boat among the lotus flowers is usually a woman. But what about here? What is the gender of the persona in this lyric? Are there any other gender cues? Are there aspects of the character and situation of the persona that go against the "female" norms?

2. One modern commentary, perhaps concerned that it would have been improper for Li Qingzhao to have been out in a boat by herself, takes the lyric as literally autobiographical and assumes that Li was with a party of young women in this episode. Assess this reading.

3. Li Qingzhao's second song lyric is much like Zhou Bangyan's tune to "Yumeiren" in that it has the self-contained quality of a quatrain vignette capturing an intense, free-standing moment of experience. Why will the persona "always recall" the experience? What do the various parts of the boat trip contribute to make the final image so compelling?

4. Compare the role of the duplicated phrases here to the phrases in the same position in the first lyric. What is the difference in effect if the phrase is translated as "How to get through" rather than "Striving to cross"? Which do you prefer, and why?

5. What is the quality of the "one" in the last line?

6. Think of the use of time in this lyric. By the time you get to the last line, have you forgotten that this is the record of a past event? At what point does the narrative frame slip?

16. See his discussion in *The Burden of Female Talent*, pp. 327–28.

"To the Tune 'Always Encountering Joy'" by Li Qingzhao

元宵 First Night[17]

【永遇樂】							To the Tune "Always Encountering Joy"
落	日	鎔	金，				The setting sun is molten gold,
fall	sun	melt	gold				
暮	雲	合	璧，				The dusk clouds are joined jade disks:
sunset	cloud	join	jade disk				
人	在	何	處。[tʂhiə̆`]				Where is [that] person?
person	is at	what	place				
染	柳	煙	濃。				Dyeing the willows, the mist is thick.
dye	willow	mist	thick				
吹	梅	笛	怨，				Playing "Plum [Blossoms]," a flute is aggrieved:
blow	plum	flute	aggrieved				
春	意	知	幾	許。[xiə̆`]			Spring thoughts, how many are there?
spring	thought	know	how many				
元	宵	佳	節，				First Night is a fine season:
prime	night	fine	season				
融	和	天	氣，				Balmy air,
fuse	warm	sky	air				
次	第	豈	無	風	雨。[yă´]		Soon now how can there not be wind and rain?
next	rank	how can	without	wind	rain		
來	相	召、	香	車	寶	馬，	[They] come to call on me, the fragrant carriages and precious horses,
come	mutual	summon	fragrant	carriage	precious	horse	
謝	它	酒	朋	詩	侶。[liə̆´]		[But I] bid farewell to other drinking friends and poetry companions.
decline	other	ale	friend	poem	companion		
中	州	盛	日，				In the Central Provinces in their flourishing days,
middle	state	flourish	day				
閨	門	多	暇，				In my chambers I had much leisure:
boudoir	door	many	leisure				
記	得	偏	重	三	五。[ŋuə̆`´]		I recall how I especially valued the Fifteenth.
recall	get	one-side	heavy	three	five		
鋪	翠	冠	兒，				[We] adorned hats with kingfisher feathers,
spread	kingfisher	hat					

17. This is the Lantern Festival, held on the night of the first full moon of the year, the fifteenth day of the First Month.

撚	金	雪	柳，				And twisted-gold sprays of meadowsweet,
twiddle	gold	snow	willow				
簇	帶	爭	濟	楚。[tʂhuə̆ʹ]			Worn in clusters, vying in elegant allure.
cluster	wear	compete	elegant allure				
如	今	憔	悴，				Now, haggard,
resemble	now	haggard					
風	鬟	霜	鬢，				With wind-blown ringlets and frosted temples,
wind	ringlet	frost	temple hair				
怕	見	夜	間	出	去。[khiə̆ˋ]		I fear to go out at night.
fear	[result]	night	midst	go out	leave		
不	如	向、	簾	兒	底	下，	It is better to be by the curtains, lowered,
not	resemble	face	curtains		low	go down	
聽	人	笑	語。[ŋyăʹ]				And listen to people talking and laughing.
listen	people	laugh	talk				

STUDY NOTES AND QUESTIONS

1. Most commentators believe Li Qingzhao wrote this lyric after the fall of the north. What in the *ci* suggests this?

2. The addition of the note "First Night" suggests that this lyric is a reflection on personal experience, just as one reads Su Shi's lyrics as a response to a specific place and time. How does this assumption about the person in the poem change your reading of it?

3. One modern commentary takes the "person" in the third line to be Li Qingzhao, who is now in a strange city (Lin'an) after her flight from the north. What difference does this reading make, in contrast to assuming that the "person" is the generic missing and longed-for "other person" common in song lyrics?

4. What is the mood of the poem? The weather is balmy, the scene lively: what is the quality of sadness in the lyric? What elements in the poem contribute to that sense of sadness?

5. How does Li Qingzhao employ the break between the two stanzas? What are the continuities, and what are the changes in the first few lines of the second stanza?

6. Why does the persona make the gesture of closing herself away? Does the gesture speak to the question of why Li Qingzhao wrote the lyric?

Xin Qiji 辛棄疾 (1140–1207)

Xin Qiji is famous as the great patriotic lyricist of the Southern Song dynasty. However, there was more to his *ci* than patriotic fervor. Xin Qiji was born in Shandong in the north, over a decade after the Jurchen conquest. His father died while Xin Qiji was young, and he was raised by his grandfather, who had served as a county magistrate in the Jin. Xin Qiji seemed well positioned to achieve prominence in the new dynasty: he had distinguished himself as a student of the important official Liu Zhan 劉瞻 (fl. 1155) and obtained the *jinshi* degree in 1160. Nonetheless, at the time of the Prince of Hailing's (Wanyan Liang 完顏亮) disastrous campaign against the Southern Song, Xin Qiji decided to leave the Jin and repatriate himself to the Southern Song.

The usual account, which seems the stuff of legend, is that during Wanyan Liang's failed campaign, a local leader named Geng Jing decided to rebel, and Xin Qiji somehow led two thousand men to join Geng's uprising. Geng sent Xin and some other men south to submit to the Southern Song and was rewarded with the position of "Heaven Pacifying Military Governor." Shortly afterwards, however, Geng was betrayed and killed, and Xin Qiji and his followers returned to Geng's camp, captured and killed the traitor, and then returned south once more.

After submitting to the Southern Song, Xin Qiji had a good if not brilliant career. At the beginning, at age twenty-four, he received the initial minor position of notary of the administrative assistant in Jiangyin 江陰 (in modern Jiangsu) but was promoted to vice prefect of Jiankang 建康 (modern Nanjing), and then to a succession of high-level regional postings. His persistent advocacy of a military campaign to retake the north eventually got him stripped of office, and he retreated to Shangrao 上饒 (in modern Jiangxi), where he set up his new residence. Xin Qiji in retirement became friends with many of the important cultural figures of his day, including Chen Liang 陳亮 (1143–95) and Zhu Xi 朱熹 (1130–1200). After ten years in retirement in Shangrao he was recalled and had the sort of career typical of officials committed to the revanchist cause during the era: short periods of service followed by longer periods in retirement. Xin Qiji lived to see the realization of his long-held hopes—embodied in Han Tuozhou's reckless 1206 campaign against the Jin—collapse in humiliating defeat. He died the next year.

Xin Qiji in his patriotic *ci* availed himself of Su Shi's style of "heroic abandon" (*haofang* 豪放) to express his determination, vexation, and remorse through song lyrics. While such lyrics are part of his large corpus of 626 *ci* (the largest in the Song), it may be better to consider Xin Qiji as a great amateur at the form who, following Su Shi's lead, used song lyrics as he saw fit, without worrying about the generic proprieties that so concerned Li Qingzhao. While Su Shi was accused of using the materials and techniques of *shi* poetry to write *ci* (*yi shi wei ci* 以詩為詞), critics accused Xin Qiji of using prose to write *ci* (*yi wen wei ci* 以文為詞). Xi Qiji delighted in allusive references and inserted snippets from Zhuang Zi and many other texts into his lyrics. Especially during his long years in enforced retirement, he used *ci* to explore many different themes well beyond the range of conventional *ci* practice. Later readers, however, quietly ignored the idiosyncratic aspects of Xin Qiji's lyrics to focus instead on the vehemently patriotic *ci* that his looser approach to the genre made possible.

"To the Tune 'Feeling for Fish'" by Xin Qiji

淳熙已亥，自湖北漕移湖南，同官王正之置酒小山亭，為賦。

In 1179 I was transferred from serving as supply commissioner in Hubei to Hunan. My office colleague Wang Zhengzhi set out ale in a small pavilion, and I composed for him.

【摸魚兒】		To the Tune "Feeling for Fish"
更 能 消、幾 番 風 雨，	anew / can / endure / how many times / wind / rain	Can I again endure how much more wind and rain:
匆 匆 春 又 歸 去。[khy`]	hurriedly / spring / again / return / leave	In a flurry, spring again retreats.
惜 春 長 怕 花 開 早，	cherish / spring / long / fear / flower / open / early	Cherishing spring, I always fear that the flowers will bloom early:
何 況 落 紅 無 數。[ʂu`]	how / more so / fall / pink / with no / number	How much more when the fallen pink [petals] are countless!
春 且 住。[tʂy`]	spring / moment / remain	Spring, stay for a moment.
見 說 道，	see / speak / say	I have heard it said,
天 涯 芳 草 無 歸 路。[lu`]	heaven / edge / fragrant / grass / with no / return / road	From the fragrant flora at heaven's edge, there is no road of return.
怨 春 不 語。[y`]	resent / spring / not / speak	I resent that spring does not speak.
算 只 有 殷 勤，	reckon / only / there is / diligent	I figure there only is the diligent
畫 檐 蛛 網，	painted / eaves / spider / web	Spider's web under the ornate eaves
盡 日 惹 飛 絮。[sy`]	exhaust / day / provoke / fly / floss	All day provoking the flying catkins.
長 門 事，	Long / Gate / affair	In the affair of the Long Gate Palace,
準 擬 佳 期 又 誤。[u`]	expect / plan / fine / date / again / err	She had anticipated a fine meeting but was mistaken.
蛾 眉 曾 有 人 妒。[tu`]	moth / eyebrow / once / there is / person / jealous	Moth eyebrows once made people jealous.

千 金 縱 買 相 如 賦，	thousand gold / even if / buy / Xiang- / ru / *fu*	For a thousand gold [coins], even if she bought Xiangru's *fu*,[18]
脈 脈 此 情 誰 訴。[su`]	silent yearning / this / feeling / who / inform	Silently yearning, whom can I tell of this feeling?
君 莫 舞。[ʋu`]	you / don't / dance	Don't dance!
君 不 見，	you / not / see	Don't you see,
玉 環 飛 燕 皆 塵 土。[thu`]	Yu- / huan / Fei- / yan / all / dust / dirt	[Yang] Yuhuan and [Zhao] Feiyan both are but dust.[19]
閒 愁 最 苦。[khu`]	idle / sorrow / most / bitter	This idle sorrow is the most bitter.
休 去 倚 危 欄，	don't / depart / lean / looming / railing	Don't go and lean on the looming railing:
斜 陽 正 在，	slant / sunlight / just now / is at	The slanting gleam is just now
煙 柳 斷 腸 處。[tʂhy`]	mist / willow / break / innards / place	On the heart-breaking place among the misty willows.

STUDY NOTES AND QUESTIONS

1. This song lyric in later times was much admired for its fervor and has acquired a framing allegorical interpretation. In this reading, in the first stanza, wind and rain in late spring refers to the weakening situation of the dynasty. "Heaven's edge" and "no road of return" point to Xin's demotion, while the spider points to the small-minded men at court who slandered him. The second stanza is taken as criticism of the emperor for neglecting his talent and being swayed by slander. How can you determine whether this reading is legitimate or whether the lyric is more closely focused on the occasion of parting from a friend?

2. From the preface, this would seem to be a parting poem: what themes associated with leave-taking does it invoke? Paraphrase the basic argument of the first stanza. Paraphrase the second. What is the relationship between the first and second stanza? What are the shifts?

---

18. These lines refer to Sima Xiangru's "*Fu* on Long Gate Palace"《長門賦》. Its preface explains that Empress Chen lost the favor of Emperor Wu of the Han and, having heard of Xiangru's abilities, offered him one hundred catties of gold to write a *fu* to make the emperor aware of her worthiness. The preface concludes with Empress Chen restored to the emperor's favor.

19. Yang Yuhuan ("Jade Bracelet") was Precious Consort Yang (Yang Guifei), the great love of Emperor Xuanzong of the Tang. Zhao Feiyan ("Flying Swallow"), a famous dancer who reputedly was so light that she could be held on one's hand, became empress to Emperor Cheng of the Han. The pairing of "plump Yang and thin Zhao" became a standard reference to the range of types of beautiful women.

3. Note how many lines of the second stanza are used to develop the theme of Sima Xiangru, Empress Chen, and the Long Gate Palace. How, in the end, does Xin Qiji use the theme? Do you prefer an allegorical reading here? Why or why not?

4. What is the point of the final gesture of concern over the sorrow of "climbing on high," a theme we have seen frequently in this textbook?

"To the Tune 'Congratulating the Bridegroom'" by Xin Qiji

別茂嘉十二弟，鶗鴂、杜鵑實兩種，見離騷補注

Taking leave of my cousin Maojia, No. 12. The shrike and the cuckoo are in fact two species: see the "Encountering Sorrow, with Supplemented Annotation."[20]

【賀新郎】	To the Tune "Congratulating the Bridegroom"
綠 樹 聽 鶗 鴂。[kjyat] green tree listen shrike	Among green trees I listen for the shrike.
更 那 堪、鷓 鴣 聲 住， yet that endure partridge sound reside	Yet more hard to endure: the sound of the partridge is subdued;
杜 鵑 聲 切。[ts^{h}iat] cuckoo sound cut	The sound of the cuckoo is sharp.[21]
啼 到 春 歸 無 尋 處， cry arrive spring return is no search place	They cry until spring retreats— there is no place to search—
苦 恨 芳 菲 都 歇。[xiat] bitter resent fragrant flora all end	Bitterly resenting that verdure all has faded.[22]
算 未 抵、人 間 離 別。[pɦiat] reckon not yet arrive people among part separate	I reckon it does not compare to parting in the human realm.
馬 上 琵 琶 關 塞 黑， horse on lute pass barrier black	On horseback, with a lute, as the frontier pass darkens;[23]

20. Xin Qiji here refers to Hong Xingzu's 洪興祖 (1090–1155) annotation of "Encountering Sorrow." This important edition was newly published at the time.

21. The call of the partridge is associated with longing for home, and the cuckoo's call sounded like 不如歸去 ("best to go home").

22. Xin here refers to "Encountering Sorrow" and its commentary. "Encountering Sorrow" states, "I fear that the shrike will call out early, / Causing all the flora to not be fragrant." 「恐鶗鴂之先鳴兮，使夫百草為之不芳。」. The early Tang commentary explains "It always calls out at the beginning of summer; If it calls out, the many fragrant plants all fade away." 「常以立夏鳴,鳴則眾芳皆歇。」

23. This line alludes to the story of Wang Zhaojun, the palace woman given as a bride to a Xiongnu chieftain at the end of the Western Han dynasty. Such marriages of "princesses" to create kinship alliances were part of Han dynasty diplomacy with

更	長	門、	翠	輦	辭	金	闕。[khyat]	And at Long Gate, the halcyon carriage takes leave of the gold pavilion.[24]
also	Long	Gate	halcyon	carriage	leave	gold	pavilion	
看	燕	燕，						See "Young Swallow":
see	swallow	swallow						
送	歸	妾。[tshiap]						[She] "sent off the returning consort."[25]
see off	return	concubine						
將	軍	百	戰	身	名	裂。[liat]		The general after a hundred battles— his reputation is rent to tatters.
general	army	100	battles	body	name	shred		
向	河	梁、	回	頭	萬	里，		Facing the bridge over the river, He turns his head to the ten thousand *li* distance:
facing	river	bridge	turn	head	10,000	*li*		
故	人	長	絕。[tsɦyat]					Forever cut off from his old friend.[26]
old	person	long	cut off					
易	水	蕭	蕭	西	風	冷，		The Yi River is forlorn, the west wind cold;
Yi	water	forlorn		west	wind	cold		
滿	座	衣	冠	似	雪。[syat]			The clothes and hats of all attending were like snow.
full	seat	clothes	hat	resemble	snow			
正	壯	士、	悲	歌	未	徹。[trɦiat]		An upright stalwart officer: His sad song was not finished.[27]
upright	stalwart	officer	sad	song	not yet	finish		

the Xiong. The traditional account of Wang Zhaojun explains that Han emperor ordered the plainest woman in his harem be selected as the bride. Because Wang Zhaojun refused to bribe the painter, he falsified her portrait, and she was chosen as the next Han "princess." When the emperor met her at the farewell audience, he deeply regretted that such a beauty was to be sent off to live among the Xiongnu, but it was too late. He had the painter executed. Living among the Xiongnu, Wang Zhaojun became a master of the *pipa*, a lute that is associated with the frontier. Over the centuries, much lore and many poems accumulated around Wang Zhaojun and the sorrows of her leaving the Han to live among the Xiongnu.

24. This line alludes to Empress Chen, who lost the affection of Emperor Wu of the Han and was sent to live in the Long Gate Palace.

25. Here the allusion is to the poem "Young Swallow"《燕燕》(Mao 28), which the Mao commentary explains as "Jiang of [Duke] Zhuang of Wei sent off the returning concubine"「衛莊姜送歸妾」, referring to the story of how the wife of Duke Zhuang of Wei could not conceive a child and had a consort bear a child in her place. That son died soon after taking the throne, and the consort was sent back to her parents in Chen. (Note that the rhyme word is a –p entering tone rather than –t: this reflects the significant phonological shifts, marked by the fusing of entering-tone finals, during the Jin and Southern Song.)

26. The opening vignette alludes to the farewell between the Han general Li Ling and Su Wu when Su was returning to China. Both had been captured by the Xiongnu, but Emperor Wu of the Han had had Li Ling's clan exterminated because Li failed to commit suicide when captured, and Li therefore had no reason to return and became reconciled to life as a captive in the North. In contrast, Su, an envoy, had resisted Xiongnu efforts to accept life among them. The wording of the lyrics borrows from Li Ling's biography in the *Han History* 漢書 and from a poem and letter he supposedly wrote on parting from Su Wu.

啼	鳥	還	知	如	許	恨，		If the singing birds also knew regret like this,
cry	bird	if	know	resemble this		regret		
料	不	啼	清	淚	長	啼	血。[xyat]	I expect they would not cry pure tears but always cry blood.
reckon	not	cry	pure	tears	always	cry	blood	
誰	共	我，						Who, together with me,
who	with	me						
醉	明	月。[ŋyat]						Will get drunk under the bright moon?
drunk	bright	moon						

STUDY NOTES AND QUESTIONS

1. This song lyric is a farewell poem, but it takes the sorrow of parting as its theme and develops it consistently throughout the two stanzas through allusion to famous farewells. What is the effect of the allusions in the song? In particular, what is the effect of the scholarly comment in the preface about the shrike and the cuckoo being different birds?

2. Note how the song begins with birds and then returns to them at the end. Explain the argument of the lyrics as the poem shifts away from the birds and then comes back.

3. How does the treatment of a farewell differ from *shi* conventions in this song? Are there aspects of this song that use the *ci* form especially effectively?

4. Are there particular lines that mark this *ci* as an "unbridled song" that you can compare with the *ci* of Su Shi?

5. Given the themes and development of the *ci*, do you find the final two lines an effective ending?

---

27. The farewell on the Yi River refers to Jing Ke taking his leave as he departs to attempt to assassinate the future first emperor of the Qin dynasty. His biography in the *Records of the Grand Historian* records a song he sang when setting out on his mission: "The wind is forlorn, hey, and the Yi River cold. / A stalwart officer, once departed, hey, will not return again."「風蕭蕭兮易水寒，壯士一去兮不復還。」Those attending the farewell banquet all wore white clothing as a sign of mourning.

Jiang Kui 姜夔 (ca. 1155–1221)

Premodern writers and critics, as well as most modern scholars, consider Jiang Kui's song lyrics to be the culmination of *ci* as a genre in the Southern Song. Jiang Kui had a deep knowledge of music: the scores he recorded for some of the tunes that he composed are the only surviving examples of musical notation from the Song dynasty. He also was a proficient and admired poet in the *shi* genre. Although he followed the more conservative approach in his choice of subject matter seen in the styles of Zhou Bangyan and Li Qingzhao, he still expanded the topics for *ci* composition. Moreover, his use of allusion and flexible handling of syntactic function words reflected the impact of Xin Qiji. His mastery of structure and language produced richly textured compositions more like the art songs of the European traditions than like the lyrics for popular entertainment with which the *ci* tradition began.

Jiang Kui perhaps was born in Shangrao 上饒 in Raozhou (modern Jiangxi), where his clan had been long settled. (Later in life, however, he identified himself as a person from nearby Poyang 鄱陽.) His father had attained the *jinshi* in 1160, and Jiang Kui accompanied him when he took up a post as the local magistrate in Hanyang. When his father died in Hanyang, Jiang Kui then relied on his older sister who had already married into a local family.

Jiang Kui at various times attempted the prefectural qualifying examination that would have allowed him to go to the capital to compete in the *jinshi* examination, but by this time in the Southern Song, competition in the preliminary examination had grown intense, and he never passed. In his forties, he submitted fourteen ceremonial songs to the court and was awarded the privilege of taking the *jinshi* examination without having passed the preliminary test, but he then failed the *jinshi* exam. Thus he remained a commoner throughout his life. He spent his adulthood traveling from patron to patron, meeting and writing with the most important cultural figures of his day, including Xin Qiji and Zhu Xi. Xiao Dezao was an initial patron who helped establish his early reputation as a writer of *shi* poetry, and Fan Chengda, the most successful of his friends politically, was his most prominent and important later patron.

Among his eighty-four extant *ci*, the most famous are "Yangzhou (extended)," an early composition written on the damage suffered by Yangzhou in the war with the Jurchen, and "Hidden Fragrance" and "Sparse Shadows," two innovative *ci* on plums written at the request of Fan Chengda 范成大 (1126–93). These latter two songs are among his many "chanting about objects" (*yong wu* 詠物) *ci*, which proved very influential for the next generation of writers.

"To the tune 'Yangzhou (extended)'" by Jiang Kui

淳熙丙申至日，予過維揚。夜雪初霽，薺麥彌望。入其城則四顧蕭條，寒水自碧，暮色漸起，戍角悲吟。予懷愴然，感慨今昔，因自度此曲。千巖老人以為有《黍離》之悲也。

On the winter solstice of 1176 I visited Yangzhou. The previous night's snow had just begun to clear, and shepherd's purse and wheat filled the view. As I entered the city, the scene was forlorn in all directions; cold water glinted green, and a twilit scene arose, with the mournful chant of the bugle. My breast filled with sorrow, and moved by past and present, I wrote this tune. The Old Man of Qian'yan thought this had the sadness of "Millet."[28]

【揚州慢】		To the tune "Yangzhou (extended)"
淮 左 名 都，	Huai left famed metropolis	Famous city east of the Huai River,
竹 西 佳 處，	bamboo west fine place	The lovely locale west of the bamboo:[29]
解 鞍 少 駐 初 程。[trɦiajŋ]	untie saddle few stop begin journey	Unbinding my saddle, I halt a while at the beginning of my travel.
過 春 風 十 里，	pass spring wind ten *li*	Passing by ten *li* of spring wind,[30]
盡 薺 麥 青 青。[tshiajŋ]	exhaust shepherd's purse wheat green green	Everywhere shepherd's purse and wheat so green.
自 胡 馬、窺 江 去 後，	from Tartar horse peek river leave after	Since the Tartar horses watching the river left,[31]
廢 池 喬 木，	abandoned pond large tree	The abandoned pools and grand trees
猶 厭 言 兵。[piajŋ]	still detest speak weapon	Still detest speaking of weapons.
漸 黃 昏、清 角 吹 寒，	gradual yellow dusk clear horn blow cold	In the gradually growing dusk, A clear horn blows chill,
都 在 空 城。[ʂɦiajŋ]	all is at empty rampart	All within the empty ramparts.

28. "The Old Man of Qian'yan" was Xiao Dezao 蕭德藻 (*jinshi* 1151). "Millet"《黍離》is a poem in the *Canon of Poetry* (Mao 65) expressing sorrow on seeing the ruins of the old Zhou capital.

29. The language is a conventional allusion concerning Yangzhou from the famous final couplet of Du Mu's poem, "Written on the Chan-Wisdom Temple in Yangzhou" 《題揚州禪智寺》:"Who knows that on the road west of the bamboo, / With singing and music is Yangzhou?"「誰知竹西路，歌吹是揚州。」

30. This line echoes Du Mu's "Presented at Farewell"《贈別二首》:"Spring wind along ten *li* of the streets of Yangzhou, / [Those] rolling up the bead curtains cannot at all compare [to you]."「春風十里揚州路，卷上珠簾總不如。」

31. Yangzhou suffered significant damage during Wanyan Liang's disastrous 1161 invasion of the south.

杜	郎	俊	賞，				Master Du was surpassing in appraisal,[32]
Du	Master	excel	appraise				
算	而	今、	重	到	須	驚。[kiajŋ]	But I reckon now, if he came again, he surely would be startled:
reckon	and	now	again	arrive	must	startle	
縱	豆	蔻	詞	工，			Even though the phrasing of "cardamom" was skillful,[33]
even if	cardamom		phrase	skilled			
青	樓	夢	好，				And his dream of blue pavilions fine,[34]
blue	pavilion	dream	good				
難	賦	深	情。[tsɦiajŋ]				It would be hard to set out [these] deep feelings.
hard	set out	deep	feeling				
二	十	四	橋	仍	在，		The Bridge of Twenty-four still is here;[35]
two	ten	four	bridge	still	is at		
波	心	蕩、	冷	月	無	聲。[ʂiajŋ]	The center of the waves stirs: the cold moon is without sound.
wave	heart	agitate	cold	moon	is without sound		
念	橋	邊	紅	藥，			I think on the red peonies by the bridge:
think on	bridge	beside	red	peony			
年	年	知	為	誰	生。[ʂaːjŋ]		Year after year, I wonder for whom they grow?
year	year	know	for	who	live		

32. "Master Du" here is Du Mu, whose poems about Yangzhou Jiang Kui cites through the *ci*.

33. "Cardamom" refers to the first couplet of Du Mu's quatrain "Presented at Parting, 2 poems, no. 1"《贈別二首》. Jiang Kui already has alluded to the second couplet of the poem in line 4: "Delicate and charming, older than twelve, / A cardamom bud on a branch tip at the beginning of the Second Month."「娉娉裊裊十三餘，豆蔻梢頭二月初。」

34. The "blue pavilion dream" refers to the final couplet of one of Du Mu's most famous Yangzhou poems, the quatrain "Relieving My Thoughts"《遣懷》:"Once wakened from a ten-year Yangzhou dream, / What I have gained is the name of a dandy in the blue pavilions [i.e., brothels]."「十年一覺揚州夢，贏得青樓薄倖名。」This poem is fully discussed in chapter 8.

35. The Bridge of Twenty-four was a bridge in Yangzhou. Du Mu mentions it in the quatrain "Sent to Administrative Assistant Han Cho of Yangzhou"《寄揚州韓綽判官》:"At Bridge of Twenty-four on a bright-moon night, / The jade girl: where are you teaching her to play the flute?"「二十四橋明月夜，玉人何處教吹簫。」By one account, the bridge gained its name from twenty-four female performers who played the flute upon it; another version explains that in the Tang dynasty there were twenty-four bridges, but they did not survive into the Song. In the Song, red peonies grew next to the Bridge of Twenty-four.

SHUEN-FU LIN'S TRANSLATION[36]

Yangchow mahn

During the Ch'un-hsi reign period (1174–1189), I passed through Yangchow at the winter solstice of 1176. The night snow began to clear up and the shepherd's purse (*capsella bursa pastoris*) and wheat extended as far as the eye could see. Entering the city walls, I saw ruin and desolation on all sides. Cold water lay jade green. Sunset colors slowly set in and the guard's horn sadly moaned. My spirit was desolate; I sighed over past and present. As a result, I composed this lyric song. The Old Man of a Thousand Cliffs (i.e. Hsiao Te-tsao) felt that it has the sadness of the "Shu-li."

In this most famed city of the south of the Huai,
At Bamboo-west Pavilion, a beautiful place,
I unstrap the saddle for a brief halt at the first stage.
Through ten miles in the spring wind,
There is nothing but green shepherd's purse and wheat.
Since Tartar horses left from spying on the Yangtse,
Abandoned ponds and lofty trees
Still detest talk of warfare.
Gradually it becomes twilight,
A clear horn blows out of the cold,
In the empty city.

Du Mu, the eminent connoisseur,
Were he to return today, could not fail to be astonished.
Though his poem on the cardamom was skillful
And his dream at blue mansion was lovely,
He would find it hard to express these deep feelings.
His Twenty-Four Bridges still exist,
Waves stir at midstream—the cold moon makes no sound.
I pity the peonies beside the bridge,
For whom do they grow year after year?

STUDY NOTES AND QUESTIONS

1. Jiang Kui here strongly shapes his "past" Yangzhou through the poetry of the Late Tang poet Du Mu. Describe this version of Yangzhou. What are its most important features? Is Jiang Kui thinking of the historical past, or is he creating a myth of Yangzhou? What is the difference?

2. What do you think the preface contributes to the composition as a whole?

---

36. See Shuen-fu Lin's discussion of this poem in *The Transformation of the Chinese Lyrical Tradition: Chiang K'uei and Southern Sung* Tz'u *Poetry* (Princeton: Princeton University Press, 1978), pp. 73–82.

3. Explain the syntax of the first strophe. Are there other strophes that comprise single sentences? What is the effect of this extended syntactic structuring?

4. Consider Jiang Kui's use of function words in the *ci*. For example, what is the effect of the pairing of *zi* 自 ("from") and *you* 猶 ("still") in lines 6 and 8? Find other examples.

5. Jiang Kui also uses governing words (*ling zi*) like *suan* 算 ("to reckon") and *nian* 念 ("to think on"). Identify one more. Explain why these are *ling zi* and how they function.

6. How does the landscape "still detest[s] speaking of weapons." What does Jiang Kui's assertion here mean?

7. Consider the larger organization of the lyric: what, for example, is the relation between the two stanzas? What does the specific ordering of images throughout the *ci* contribute to it?

"To the tune 'Seeking Spring' (extended)" by Jiang Kui

予自孩幼從先人宦於古沔，女須因嫁焉。中去復來幾二十年，豈惟姊弟之愛，沔之父老兒女子亦莫不予愛也。丙午冬，千巖老人約予過苕霅，歲晚乘濤載雪而下，顧念依依，殆不能去。作此曲別鄭次皋、辛克清、姚剛中諸君。

As a child I accompanied my father to Mian; my older sister was married there.[37] Having left Mian, I returned there almost twenty years later: how could it be only the love of a brother for an older sister? All of the elders and youngsters of Mian cherished me. In the winter of 1186 the Old Man of Qian'yan agreed to meet me at Tiao and Zha Creeks.[38] The year was late, and I would proceed riding the billows and covered with snow. Thinking [about my sister and friends], I tarried and almost could not leave. I wrote this song to bid farewell to Zheng Zigao, Xin Keqing, and Yao Gangzhong.

【探春慢】						To the tune "Seeking Spring" (extended)
衰	草	愁	煙，			Amid withered grasses and mournful mists,
wither	grass	mourn	mist			
亂	鴉	送	日，			Chaotic ravens see off the sun:
chaotic	crow	see off	sun			
風	沙	回	旋	平	野。[jia']	Wind-blown sand whirls across the level plain.
wind	sand	turn	whirl	level	wilds	
拂	雪	金	鞭，			Brushing the snow with a metal whip,
brush	snow	metal	whip			
欺	寒	茸	帽，			Cheating the cold in a soft hat:
cheat	cold	soft	hat			

37. Mian is another name for Hanyang 漢陽 in modern Hubei Province.

38. The Old Man of Qian'yan is Xiao Dezao. Tiao Creek and Zha Creek were in Huzhou (in modern Zhejiang). Xiao once served as magistrate of Wucheng 烏程 in Huzhou (where Zha Creek is). He moved his residence there, and when he returned after finishing his term in Hunan, he invited Jiang Kui to accompany him.

還 記 章 臺 走 馬。[maː´]	still recall Zhang Terrace run horse	I still recall racing horses along Zhang Terrace Road.[39]
誰 念 漂 零 久，	who think drifting long	Who is concerned that, long drifting about,
漫 贏 得 幽 懷 難 寫。[sia´]	in vain gain get secluded breast hard depict	I in vain have earned solitary thoughts hard to express?
故 人 清 沔 相 逢，	old person clear Mian mutual encounter	Old friends meet one another by the clear Mian;
小 窗 閑 共 情 話。[xɦwaːj`]	small window idle together feeling talk	At ease before a small window talking of [deep] feelings.
長 恨 離 多 會 少，	long regret separate many meet few	I always regret that partings are many and meetings few;
重 訪 問 竹 西，	again visit inquire bamboo west	[About to] again visit "west of the bamboo,"
珠 淚 盈 把。[paː´]	pearl tear fill grasp	Pearls of tears fill my hands.
雁 磧 波 平，	goose sandbar wave level	At the sandbank of geese, waves are calm;
漁 汀 人 散，	fisher isle person scatter	On the fishermen's isles people have scattered:
老 去 不 堪 游 冶。[jia´]	old depart not willing travel amuse	Grown old, I unwillingly go on excursions.
無 奈 苕 溪 月，	without avail Tiao Creek moon	Pointlessly, the moon of Tiao Creek
又 照 我 扁 舟 東 下。[xɦjaː`]	again shine my sliver boat east descend	Again shines on my sliver of a boat as it descends eastward.
甚 日 歸 來，	what day return come	What day will I return,
梅 花 零 亂 春 夜。[jia´]	plum flower scatter chaotic spring night	With plum flowers in profusion on a spring night?

39. Zhang Terrace Road actually was in Chang'an, but Jiang uses it to refer to a grand boulevard.

Study Notes and Questions

1. This is a parting poem, but what is Jiang Kui's view of this occasion? Regret? Anticipation? Explore the series of stances toward farewell that he sets out in the *ci*.

2. The first two strophes form single sentences. What are the connections between these two strophic units? What is the role of imagery in connecting the two strophes?

3. In "Yangzhou" Jiang Kui writes, "It would be hard to set out these deep feelings," and in "Seeking Spring," he laments, "I in vain have earned solitary thoughts hard to express." What is the role of these laments in the two *ci*?

4. What is the relationship between the first and second stanza in this lyric?

5. Consider the arguments of the second stanza within the conventions of parting poems in the *shi* tradition that you have seen in this book. What elements does Jiang Kui take from the earlier tradition?

"To the Tune 'Hidden Fragrance'" by Jiang Kui

辛亥之冬，予載雪詣石湖。止既月，授簡索句，且徵新聲，作此兩曲。石湖把玩不已，使工妓隸習之，音節諧婉，乃名之曰《暗香》《疏影》。

In the winter of 1191, when it was covered with snow, I visited Stone Lake. I stopped there for a month. [Fan Chengda] gave me paper, sought some verses, and requested a new tune.[40] I composed this pair of songs. [Fan] Stone Lake held them in appreciation without end and had skilled female singers practice them. Their sound was harmonious and graceful. I thereupon named them "Hidden Fragrance" and "Sparse Shadows."[41]

【暗香】	To the Tune "Hidden Fragrance"
舊 時 月 色， former time moon appearance	In former times, this sight of the moon—
算 幾 番 照 我， reckon how many time shine me	I reckon—how many times has it shone on me,
梅 邊 吹 笛。[tɦiajk] plum beside blow flute	By the plum trees, playing the flute?
喚 起 玉 人， call rise jade person	I called to the jade one,
不 管 清 寒 與 攀 摘。[traːk] not regard pure cold with climb pluck	Not heeding the pure coolness, to climb and pluck [flowers] with me.

40. The major official, poet, and patron Fan Chengda lived in retirement at Stone Lake near Suzhou.

41. The titles come from a famous couplet in the poem "Plum Flowers"《梅花》by the early Northern Song recluse poet Lin Bu 林逋 (967–1028): "Sparse shadows across the water, pure and shallow; / A hidden fragrance drifts by the moon at dusk."「疏影橫斜水清淺，暗香浮動月黃昏。」His poems on plums were taken to reflect his pure and independent personality.

何 遜 而 今 漸 老，	He Xun and now gradual old	He Xun now is gradually aging,[42]
都 忘 卻、 春 風 詞 筆。[pit]	all forget withdraw spring wind phrase brush	And entirely forgets the lyric brush [inspired by] the spring wind.[43]
但 怪 得、 竹 外 疏 花，	only think odd get bamboo outside sparse flower	I only think it odd that the sparse flowers beyond the bamboo—
香 冷 入 瑤 席。[sɦiajk]	fragrance cold enter jade mat	Their fragrance, cold, enters the jade [banquet] mat.[44]
江 國，	river country	The river countryside
正 寂 寂。[tsɦiajk]	just now silent silent	Just now is silent.
歎 寄 與 路 遙，	sigh send with road distant	I sigh and send them [to her] when the road is distant,
夜 雪 初 積。[tsiajk]	night snow begin accumulate	And the night snow begins to pile high.
翠 尊 易 泣，	azure beaker easy weep	Before the azure beaker, it is easy to weep:
紅 萼 無 言 耿 相 憶。[ʔiǎk]	red calyx without speak troubled mutual remember	The red flower-stems are without speech; troubled, I remember [her].
長 記 曾 攜 手 處，	long recall once hold hand place	I always recall where we once held hands:
千 樹 壓、 西 湖 寒 碧。[piajk]	thousand tree oppress West Lake cold emerald green	A thousand trees weighed upon the cold emerald of West Lake.
又 片 片 吹 盡 也，	again flake flake blow exhaust [it is]	Again, petal after petal, all blown away:
幾 時 見 得。[təǎk]	how many time see get	How many times will I get to see them?

42. Commentaries cite the annotation to a poem by Du Fu concerning the Southern Dynasties poet He Xun's love of the plum blossoms of Yangzhou, but there may have been other sources, now lost, for Jiang Kui's allusion.

43. The rhyme here suggests that the *–t* and *–k* final entering tone endings are fusing to a glottal stop, -ʔ. It remains useful to remember that Pulleyblank's reconstructions are just an approximation.

44. Although standard syntax would suggest the line reads, "The fragrant coldness enters the jade seat," Jiang Kui here seems to be taking liberties with wording.

Stephen Owen's Translation

to "Fragrance from Somewhere Unseen"

The moon's hue of days gone by—
I wonder how often it shone on me
playing my flute beside the plums?
It called awake that woman, white marble,
and heedless of cold
  together we snapped off sprays.
But now this poet grows old,
and the pen that once wrote songs
  of the breeze in spring
  is utterly forgotten;
I'm just intrigued by those sparse blooms
  over beyond the bamboo,
how their chill scent
  seeps into party mats.

These river lands now
lie somber and still,
And I sigh
  to send them to someone traveling far,
as tonight their snow begins to heap high.
With kingfisher cups
  and easily brought to tears,
restive, I recall
  pink petals that never speak.
I always think back where we once held hands:
where the freight of a thousand trees weighed
  on West Lake's cold sapphire.
Now petal by petal once more
  they all blow away,
never again to be seen.

"To the Tune 'Sparse Shadows'" by Jiang Kui

【疏影】		To the Tune "Sparse Shadows"
苔 枝 綴 玉，	lichen / branch / patch / jade	On lichen-covered branches adorned with jade,[45]
有 翠 禽 小 小，	there is / jade green bird / small / small	There are jade green birds, so small,
枝 上 同 宿。[siwk]	branch / on / share / spend night	Roosting together on the branches.
客 裏 相 逢，	traveler / in / mutual / encounter	In my travels we meet,
籬 角 黃 昏，	hedge / corner / yellow / dusk	By the corner of the hedge at dusk:
無 言 自 倚 修 竹。[triwk]	without / speak / of itself / lean / long / bamboo	Without speaking, she leans on the long bamboo.
昭 君 不 慣 胡 沙 遠，	Zhao- / jun / not / accustom / Tartar / sand / far	[Wang] Zhaojun, never accustomed to the distance of the Tartar sands,[46]
但 暗 憶、江 南 江 北。[puə̆k]	only / dark / recall / river / south / river / north	Only inwardly remembers south of the river, north of the river.
想 佩 環、月 夜 歸 來，	imagine / pendant / disk / moon / night / return / come	I imagine [her wearing] a pendant disk on a moonlit night returning,[47]
化 作 此 花 幽 獨。[tɦəwk]	change / make / this / flower / secluded / alone	Changed into this flower, secluded, alone.
猶 記 深 宮 舊 事，	still / recall / deep / palace / former / event	I still recall an affair of old, deep in the palace:
那 人 正 睡 裏，	that / person / just now / sleep / in	That one just then was in sleep,
飛 近 蛾 綠。[lywk]	fly / near / moth / green	[It] alighted upon her moth[-brow's] green.[48]

---

45. Fan Chengda's *Plum Catalogue* 梅譜 lists "lichen-plum" as a particular type of plum tree with lichen-covered branches.

46. Wang Zhaojun was the Han dynasty palace woman married to a Xiongnu prince. See pages 420-21.

47. Jiang Kui adapts a line of a famous Du Fu poem on Wang Zhaojun titled "Chanting My Thoughts at Ancient Sites", 5 poems, no. 3《詠懷古跡五首》:"[Her] pendant disk in vain returns as a soul on moonlit nights."「環佩空歸月夜魂。」

48. The green could refer to a type of powder applied to the eyebrows, or it could simply mean a greenish hue to the black of the eyebrows. Jiang Kui here alludes to the story of a plum blossom that alighted on the forehead of a Southern Dynasties princess and would not come off for several days. The women in the palace thought this so remarkable that they painted plum blossoms on their foreheads in emulation.

莫	似	春	風，				Don't resemble the spring wind,
don't	resemble	spring	wind				
不	管	盈	盈，				Not heeding [her] allure:
not	heed	alluring					
早	與	安	排	金	屋。[ʔəwk]		Be early in arranging a golden room for [her].[49]
early	with	place	arrange	gold	roof		
還	教	一	片	隨	波	去，	And if [you] let a single petal, following the waves, depart,
still	allow	one	flake	follow	wave	depart	
又	卻	怨、	玉	龍	哀	曲。[khywk]	[You] should resent the mournful tune of the jade-dragon [flute].[50]
again	withdraw	resent	jade	dragon	mourn	tune	
等	恁	時、	重	覓	幽	香，	If [you] wait until that time to again seek the secluded fragrance,
wait	this	time	again	seek	secluded	fragrance	
已	入	小	窗	橫	幅。[fjywk]		It already has entered the horizontal scroll by the small window.[51]
already	enter	small	window	across	strip		

Grace Fong's Translation[52]

Mossy branches adorned with jade—
They are tiny green birds roosting together on a branch.
Meeting her on a journey
At twilight by the corner of a fence,
Where wordless she leans next to tall bamboos.
Zhaojun unaccustomed to tartar sands far away
Only longed in secret for her native Southland.
I imagine the one with jade pendants returning on a moonlit night,
Transformed into this flower, hidden and solitary.

I still recall in the old tale of the secluded palace;
That beauty was asleep then

---

49. A story about Emperor Wu of the Han relates how, when he was still small, he told his aunt that if he could wed Ajiao (a young playmate) he would build a golden hall for her. His father had him honor his words, and she later became Empress Chen.

50. Lin Bu, clearly an important model for Jiang Kui, wrote a *ci* on plum blossoms titled "Dawn Horn in the Frosty Sky" 《霜天曉角》. One strophe mentions a "jade dragon" flute: "From somewhere, three trills of a jade dragon; / The sound shakes / the moon at the branch tips." 「甚處玉龍三弄，聲搖動，枝頭月。」

51. Horizontal scrolls (*heng fu* 橫幅) seem to have been placed by windows in the Southern Song, as seen in Lu You's 陸游 line from the poem "Events, Drinking at Night" 《夜飲即事》: "At the small window, the horizontal scroll depicts the Southland." 「小窗橫幅畫江南。」

52. Grace Fong has a very useful discussion of this poem in *Wu Wenying and the Art of Southern Song* Ci *Poetry* (Princeton: Princeton University Press, 1987), pp. 42–43. Shuen-fu Lin also translates the lyric and has a detailed and thoughtful analysis in *The Transformation of the Chinese Lyrical Tradition* (pp. 171–77).

When one alighted beside her dark moth-eyebrows.
Don't be like the spring wind,
Heedless of beauty in full bloom,
But early arrange for it a gold chamber.
If you let one petal flow away with the waves,
You will be resenting the sad tune for the Jade Dragon flute;
If one waits till then to seek again the subtle scent,
It will have entered the horizontal scroll by the small window.

Study Notes and Questions for "Hidden Fragrance" and "Sparse Shadows"

1. The preface tells us that Jiang Kui wrote the two lyrics at the same time, but are they tightly linked?

2. What is the role of memory in defining the meaning of plum blossoms in these poems?

3. How does the past shape the meaning of present experience as Jiang relates it in the poems?

4. Aside from the reference to He Xun, Jiang Kui does not use allusions in "Hidden Fragrance." In contrast, "Sparse Shadows" uses allusions at key points. Identify and explain the functions of these allusions in "Sparse Shadows."

5. Follow the allusions in "Sparse Shadows" that begin with Wang Zhaojun and end with a transformation into plum blossoms. Imagine that the plum blossoms are the transformed jade that had been worn by Wang Zhaojun. What qualities do such plum blossoms possess?

6. How does the first stanza of "Hidden Fragrance" set up the second stanza, and how does the second stanza develop the first stanza? What about in "Sparse Shadows"? What does this illustrate in terms of how Jiang Kui uses the *ci* form in these compositions?

7. How does Jiang Kui take advantage of the long *ci* strophe that continues over two or three lines? What impact does this strophic structure have on the cadences of the poems?

8. How does the final strophe of "Sparse Shadows" bring together the thematic and imagistic elements in the two poems?

Wu Wenying 吳文英 (ca. 1200–ca. 1260, or 1215–76)

The years separating Jiang Kui and Wu Wenying marked a significant shift in Southern Song culture. The cessation of warfare in Emperor Gaozong's 高宗 (r. 1127–62) reign was followed by a long era of relative peace, punctuated by the fiasco of Han Tuozhou's 韓侂胄 (1152–1207) northern campaign in 1206 (which ended with the Southern Song emperor sending Han's head to the Jin ruler, along with significant reparations). Competition in the examination system grew yet more intense in this period, so that for many men, simply participating in the examination at the provincial level—whether one passed or not—served as adequate proof of elite status within their local communities. Even among those who passed the *jinshi* examination, service in one or two posts sufficed to protect their clans' tax privileges and to establish their role as elite families in their local communities. Some men from these local elites, restless and in search of entertainment and good company as well as a reputation outside of the overcrowded examination system, traveled from patron to patron with the hope of establishing themselves as writers. In part, their travels seem to have been supported by their clans, who were happy to have sons making a name for themselves in the larger world.

This group of wanderers formed the broad milieu of the "Rivers and Lakes" writers. "Rivers and Lakes" refers to a social world outside of officialdom, focused more on major cultural centers like Suzhou, Yangzhou, and Jinling than on the capital itself. This world intersected with the official stratum, since officials at both the local and national level served as important patrons for the Rivers and Lakes writers.

Wu Wenying was part of this Rivers and Lakes milieu. Very little is known about his life. Even the dates of his birth and death are uncertain: traditional sources argue that he was born around 1200 and died around 1260, but more recent scholarship places his birth and death fifteen years later. He seems to have had two brothers, Weng Fenglong 翁逢龍 and Weng Yuanlong 翁元龍, and he, like them, was born in Siming 四明 (modern Ningbo 寧波). The different surname suggests that Wu Wenying was adopted into a Wu clan or that his mother remarried. Weng Fenglong appears to have obtained the *jinshi* degree and had a reasonably successful mid-level official career, and some of his and Weng Yuanlong's poetry still survives. Judging from the prefaces to Wu Wenying's *ci*, he remained in the very prosperous and cultured regions surrounding Suzhou, Ningbo, and Hangzhou throughout his life and relied on patrons who offered him staff positions that were outside the regular bureaucratic appointment process.[53]

Wu Wenying's *ci* in part reflect the practices of the Rivers and Lakes community. About half of his 340 extant lyrics are verses written to meet the requirements of a social occasion. That is, *ci* had become sufficiently part of the elite literary world that it was used—like *shi* poetry—as entertainment and as an opportunity for refined competition and display at social gatherings. Wu Wenying's contemporary fame as a *ci* writer reflects both his mastery of the form and his development of a distinctive style that set him apart. Like Jiang Kui, he had a firm grasp of musical technique, and like many other Southern Song writers of *ci*, he was adroit at the use of allusion. In addition, however, he wrote in a very dense style, using few function words and displaying a strong preference for nominal, paratactic constructions. His language is vivid, but verbs appear more as striking adjectives than as full verbs. His *ci* present a flow of images that are elliptical and challenging. Like Li Shangyin's *shi* poetry, they invite allegorical reading.

---

53. For a detailed reconstruction of Wu Wenying's life, see Grace S. Fong, *Wu Wenying and the Art of Southern Song* Ci *Poetry* (Princeton: Princeton University Press, 1987), pp. 3–31.

At the end of the Song dynasty, the critic and writer Zhang Yan compared Jiang Kui's "clarity and spaciousness" (*qingkong* 清空) to Wu Wenying's "density" (*zhishi* 質實). Critics in the Qing dynasty revival of *ci* largely continued this contrastive evaluation, even though some preferred Wu Wenying while others preferred Jiang Kui.

"To the Tune 'Eight Sounds of Ganzhou'" by Wu Wenying

零巖陪庾幕諸公游

At Lingyan, accompanying the worthies of the Stabilization Fund Office on an excursion[54]

【八聲甘州】	To the Tune "Eight Sounds of Ganzhou"
渺 空 煙 四 遠， vague void mist four distant	A hazy void, mist everywhere in the distance:
是 何 年、青 天 墜 長 星。[siajŋ] this what year blue sky fall long star	What year was this, when the meteor fell from the blue sky?[55]
幻 蒼 崖 雲 樹， illusion dark cliff cloud tree	An illusion of dark cliffs and cloudy trees,
名 娃 金 屋， name beauty gold roof	A famous beauty's golden room:[56]
殘 霸 宮 城。[ʂɦiajŋ] ruin warlord palace rampart	The ruined warlord's palace ramparts.
箭 徑 酸 風 射 眼， arrow path sour wind shoot eye	Along Arrow Path a biting wind assails the eyes.[57]
膩 水 染 花 腥。[siajŋ] grease water infuse flower odor	Ointment in the water infuses the flowers rankly.[58]

54. Lingyan was a mountain to the west of Suzhou. The Stabilization Fund Supervisorate operated on the *lu* (circuits) level of jurisdiction. It supervised grain storage and transport, relief granaries, state-monopolized industries and trade, and agricultural development activities (Hucker, p. 493).

55. Local folklore asserted that the mountain fell from the sky.

56. This refers to the palace Fuchai 夫差 (r. 495–473 BC), the King of Wu, built for Xishi 西施. After Fuchai defeated Goujian 勾踐, the King of Yue, Goujian trained Xishi, a young woman of extraordinary beauty, in all the alluring arts and had her presented to Fuchai so that he would be distracted from his responsibilities and allow his kingdom to fall to ruin. Famously, the plan worked. *Wa* 娃 is a conventionally "regional" term dating back to the Han dynasty for how the people of Wu referred to young women.

57. The King of Wu built this very straight canal to allow palace women to go by boat to hills where he had fragrant grasses planted. The women were sent to gather the grasses. The phrase "sour wind assails the eyes" comes from Li He's "Song of the Bronze Immortal Bidding Farewell to the Han." This poem is fully discussed in chapter 8.

58. The palace women of the King of Wu's court reportedly washed off their makeup in "Fragrant Creek," also called "Makeup Pool," which still retained a fragrance.

時 靸 雙 鴛 響，	time tread pair duck echo	At times, the echoes of treading pairs of mandarin duck [slippers]:[59]
廊 葉 秋 聲。[ʂiajŋ]	corridor leaf autumn sound	The autumn sound of leaves on the corridor.
宮 裏 吳 王 沈 醉，	palace in Wu king sunk drunk	In the palace, the King of Wu is dead drunk,
倩 五 湖 倦 客，	rely Five Lakes weary traveler	Relying on the weary traveler of the Five Lakes
獨 釣 醒 醒。[siajŋ]	alone fish sober sober	Who fishes alone, awake and sober.[60]
問 蒼 天 無 語，	ask dark sky without speech	I ask the azure heavens, but it is silent;[61]
華 髮 奈 山 青。[tshiajŋ]	florid hair endure mountain green	Greying hair enduring the green of the mountains!
水 涵 空、闌 干 高 處，	water contain void balcony-rail high place	The waters hold the void: where the balcony is high,[62]
送 亂 鴉、斜 日 落 漁 汀。[thiajŋ]	see off chaos crow slant sun fall fisher isle	I see off the chaotic crows, as the slanting sun falls on the fishing isles.
連 呼 酒，	successive call ale	Calling repeatedly for ale,
上 琴 臺 去，	ascend zither terrace leave	We ascend Zither Terrace:
秋 與 雲 平。[pɦiajŋ]	autumn with cloud level	Autumn is level with the clouds.

59. Fuchai was said to have had Xi Shi and her attendants walk in slippers along a corridor in which the boards resounded when walked upon. (A temple in Kyoto has such a "nightingale corridor.")

60. This strophe returns to Fuchai, Xi Shi, and Fan Li. According to legend, after Goujian's stratagem of distracting Fuchai succeeded, Xi Shi disappeared into the vast lake country with Fan Li, who patiently had waited for Fuchai's downfall. The strophe seems to also allude to Li Shangyin's famous couplet about Precious Consort Yang titled "Dragon Pool"《龍池》, "At midnight, as they return from the banquet, the palace clepsydra is late; / The Prince of Xue was dead drunk, the Prince of Shou was sober."「夜半宴歸宮漏永，薛王沉醉壽王醒。」 The Prince of Xue was the grandson of Tang Emperor Ruizong 睿宗 (that is, Emperor Xuanzong's nephew), one of the feckless members of the imperial court, while the Prince of Shou was Xuanzong's eighteenth son, from whom Xuanzong took Precious Consort Yang.

61. Some texts have "waves" (*po* 波) for "heavens" (*tian* 天).

62. "Hold the Void" is also the name of a pavilion (涵空閣) in the Lingyan (Ethereal Cliff) Monastery.

ZHANG CHEN'S TRANSLATION[63]

To "Eight Notes of Ganzhou"

The Ethereal Cliff. Visited in the company of the gentlemen in the Stabilization Fund Commission.

The vast void in mist, far in all directions—
  when was it, that the sapphire skies dropped a long shooting star?
An illusion cast of dark-green cliffs and trees in clouds,
  the golden bower of the famous belle,
  the palace walls of an eclipsed overlord.
Over the Arrow Path, stinging winds shoot into the eyes,
  oily waters infuse the flowers so pungent.
At times, she steps in mandarin duck slippers, echoing—
  Leaves in the corridor—the sound of autumn.

In the palace, the King of Wu is sunk in drunkenness;
  O step in, weary wanderer of the Five Lakes,
  who alone casts a fishing line, somber sober.
I ask the dark green waves, they do not speak,
  my hoary hair—how can it bear the mountains green?
The waters enfold the void, from on high by the balustrade,
  my eyes follow the disorderly crows in the slanting sunlight that descend on the fishermen's sandbar.
Again and again I call for ale—
  let us go up to the Zither Platform,
  where autumn is level with the clouds.

STUDY NOTES AND QUESTIONS

1. What is the occasion for the lyric? Does it use the conventions of "climbing on high" that we have seen in the *shi* tradition? Explain.

2. What is the tone and stance of the first line? What is its connection to the next two lines in the strophe? What does the reference to the meteor accomplish in shaping the poem?

3. Explain the transition from the first strophe to the second.

4. Is "illusion" (*huan* 幻) a "governing word"? Explain its effect.

5. Does the story of Fuchai and Xi Shi inhabit the landscape in the first stanza? Are there correspondences in what Wu Wenying sees, or is the evocation an act of willed imagination? Explain.

---

63. For a detailed analysis of this poem, see Chia-ying Yeh Chao, "Wu Wen-ying's *Tz'u*: A Modern View," *Harvard Journal of Asiatic Studies*, vol. 29 (1969), pp. 53–92.

6. The third strophe introduces some interpretive difficulties. What is the point of Wu Wenying's allusion to Li He's poem about the bronze dew-catcher of Emperor Wu of the Han? The word 醒 (*xing*) refers to rank odors: Wu Wenying claims that the ancient makeup makes the flowers along the creek rank. What sort of odor do you imagine? What is the tone here?

7. The first strophe of the second stanza continues the story of Fuchai, Xi Shi, and Fan Li. However, Wu Wenying introduces difficulty with the word *qing* 倩, "to entrust [somebody to do something]." In the context of the lyric and the narrative arc of the story of Xi Shi, who is entrusting whom to do what?

8. Explain the transition between the first strophe of the second stanza and the rest of the stanza.

9. Assess the textual variant: "I ask the azure heavens" or "I ask the azure waters" (or "dark green waves" in Zhang Chen's translation). Which works better in the context of the lyric? Explain. What is the persona in the poem asking the heavens or the waters? How does that question lead into the final line of the strophe?

10. Explain the role of the final two strophes in structuring the poem. Do they draw on *shi* conventions?

11. Later critics have greatly praised the final line. Explain it: how can "the autumn [be] level with the clouds"? What do you see in your mind's eye? What is the mood? How does it relate to the rest of the *ci*?

"To the Tune 'The Wind Entering the Pines'" by Wu Wenying

【風入松】							To the Tune "The Wind Entering the Pines"
聽	風	聽	雨	過	清	明，[miajŋ]	Listening to the wind, listening to the rain, passing the Qingming festival,
listen	wind	listen	rain	pass	Qing-	-ming	
愁	草	瘞	花	銘。[mjiajŋ]			Too sad to draft an "Inscription on Burying Flowers."[64]
sorrow	draft	bury	flower	inscription			
樓	前	綠	暗	分	攜	路，	Before the tower, the green grows dark on the road of parting hands:
tower	before	green	darken	split	hold	road	
一	絲	柳、	一	寸	柔	情。[tsɦiajŋ]	One thread of willow, one inch of tender feelings.
one	thread	willow	one	inch	supple	feeling	
料	峭	春	寒	中	酒，		In the chill of spring cold, I am in my cups:
[chilly]		spring	cold	hit mark ale			
交	加	曉	夢	啼	鶯。[ʔja:jŋ]		Mingling with a dawn dream, the cry of an oriole.[65]
[snuggle]		dawn	dream	cry out	oriole		
西	園	日	日	掃	林	亭，	In the western garden, day after day, sweeping the grove pavilion,
west	garden	day	day	sweep	grove	pavilion	
依	舊	賞	新	晴。[tsɦiajŋ]			As of old, I appreciate the new clear skies.
rely	former	praise	new	clear sky			
黃	蜂	頻	撲	鞦	韆	索，	The yellow wasps often strike the cord of the swings:
yellow	wasp	often	strike	swings		cord	
有	當	時、	纖	手	香	凝。[ŋjiǎŋ]	There is a fragrant congealing from her delicate hand at that time.
there is	just at	time	slender	hand	fragrant	congeal	
惆	悵	雙	鴛	不	到，		I grieve that the pair of mandarin duck [slippers] do not arrive:
grieve		pair	duck	not	arrive		
幽	階	一	夜	苔	生。[ʂa:jŋ]		On secluded steps overnight moss has grown.
secluded	steps	one	night	moss	grow		

64. Yu Xin wrote an "Inscription on Burying Flowers." The surviving text attributed to him is probably a forgery rather than the original version.

65. Most commentaries take 交加 *jiaojia* as simply "mingle with," but Han Wo and Wei Zhuang both use the phrase 交加夢 for a "dream of snuggling together."

Grace S. Fong's Translation

Listening to wind, to rain, I pass Grave-sweeping Day,
Too weary to write an epitaph for buried flowers.
Before the pavilion, green shade obscures our path of parting—
One sprig of willow, one inch of tender feeling.
Chilly in the spring cold I got drunk . . .
The chirping orioles mingle in my daybreak dream.

Day after day I sweep the wooded arbor in the West Garden,
Relishing the new clear weather as in the past.
Again and again yellow bees strike the swing's ropes
Where fragrance from her delicate hands still clings.
Grieved that her mandarin-duck shoes do not come,
Overnight, moss has grown on the secluded steps.

Study Notes and Questions

1. This is a much simpler poem than "Eight Sounds of Ganzhou." While there are minor echoes of other lines, this poem does not have the density of allusion of "Eight Sounds." How does allusion change the reading experience? How does it change the nature of meaning?

2. The structure of this lyric is also relatively simple. Explain the progression from line to line in the first stanza. How is the second stanza connected to the first? Are there any shifts in tone, timeframe, or theme?

3. In the final strophe of the lyric, explain the role of imagination in shaping the reading of the encountered scene. Explain the role of the phrase "overnight" in the "objective closure" of the final line.

4. Modern critics take this poem to be an autobiographical lyric about a lost love. How does this framing change the reading of the poem?

Zhang Yan 張炎 (1248–ca. 1320)

Zhang Yan is the last major writer of *ci* in the Song dynasty. He was a descendant of the early Southern Song general Zhang Jun 張俊 and the great-grandson of Zhang Zi 張鎡 (d. 1207), who was a friend and patron of Jiang Kui. His father, Zhang Shu 張樞 (fl. 1208), was well known as a writer of song lyrics. That is, he came from a well-established elite lineage with a tradition of literary accomplishment. However, the textual evidence needed to construct his biography is very sparse.

He seems to have remained in Hangzhou during his early years and was there to witness the surrender of the city to the Mongols in 1276. In 1279, the year the Mongols finally defeated the last of the Southern Song armies in the far south, he participated in a famous meeting of writers who composed a collection of patriotic song lyrics. Nonetheless, in 1290 he joined a steady stream of southern literati who acquiesced to Mongol pressure to travel to the new Yuan dynasty capital of Dadu ("Great Metropolis," modern Beijing) to seek a role in the new hybrid bureaucracy. However, Zhang Yan did not attain a post (he may have made no more than a *pro forma* effort to find one) and returned to the South by the end of 1291. For the rest of his life, he traveled between Hangzhou and major nearby cities like Suzhou, Shaoxing, Yixing, and Mingzhou. He may have lived off of patronage, but his clan holdings, despite the Mongol conquest, may have produced enough income to support his peripatetic lifestyle.

Like Jiang Kui and Wu Wenying, Zhang Yan was a stylist who brought musical expertise to the writing of song lyrics. He also was an influential critic of the *ci* tradition and wrote the *Origin of Lyrics* (*Ciyuan* 詞源), an important discussion of the art of *ci* composition. The first part of the *Origin of Lyrics* explores musical issues, while the latter part focuses on the history of the genre, formal and technical issues, and an assessment of previous writers.

As a writer, Zhang Yan largely follows the precedents of Jiang Kui and Wu Wenying in using the *ci* genre for a broad range of social and aesthetic purposes. Like the other mainstream Southern Song writers, he weaves allusion into the text of his lyrics and writes a significant number of lyrics in the mode of "chanting about objects." However, he argues that Jiang Kui's "clarity and spaciousness" is superior to Wu Wenying's fragmented, dense style, and Zhang's own intensely crafted yet fluid lyrics reflect that preference.

"To the tune 'Gaoyang Terrace'" by Zhang Yan

西湖春感

On West Lake, spring stirrings

【高陽臺】		To the Tune "Gaoyang Terrace"[66]
接 葉 巢 鶯，	connect leaf nest oriole	Among interlacing leaves, nesting orioles;[67]
平 波 捲 絮，	level wave curl floss	On level waves, curling catkins:
斷 橋 斜 日 歸 船。[ʂɦan]	break bridge slant sun return boat	At Duan Bridge, in slanting sunlight, a returning boat.[68]
能 幾 番 游，	able how many times wander	How often can I wander,
看 花 又 是 明 年。[nian]	look flower again is next year	Looking at flowers: can it be again next year?
東 風 且 伴 薔 薇 住，	east wind moment accompany roses reside	East wind, for the moment, stay to accompany the roses:
到 薔 薇、春 已 堪 憐。[lian]	arrive rose spring already bear to cherish	Reaching the rose, spring now is worth cherishing.
更 悽 然，	yet more desolate -like	Yet more desolate:
萬 綠 西 泠，	10,000 green west ling	Amid the ten thousand [forms of] green at West Ling Bridge,[69]
一 抹 荒 煙。[ʔjian]	one smear wild mist	Just one swath of outland mist.
當 年 燕 子 知 何 處，	at that year swallow know what place	The swallows of that year, do I know where [they have gone]?[70]

66. Although many commentaries assume that Zhang Yan wrote this lyric after the surrender of Hangzhou in 1276, Huang She 黃畬, following Zhang Huiyan 張惠言, dates it to 1275, the year before the surrender. See Huang She, *Shanzhong baiyun ci jian* 山中白雲詞箋 (Hangzhou: Zhejiang guji, 1994), p. 5.

67. This line alludes to a line from Du Fu's "Accompanying Zheng Guangwen on an Excursion to General He's Mountain Grove," 10 poems, no. 2《陪鄭廣文遊何將軍山林》十首第二, "On lowly branches, below, ripening fruit, / Among interlacing leaves, hidden, nesting orioles."「卑枝低結子，接葉暗巢鶯。」

68. Duan Bridge is literally "Broken Bridge," but one account explains that its original name was "Duan Clan Bridge" 段氏橋. The Duan surname is homophonous with "break" (*duan* 斷); the bridge was not broken.

69. West Ling Bridge refers to an area by West Lake near "Lone Mountain" Island.

但 苔 深 韋 曲，	only moss deep Wei bend	There is just the moss grown thick in the Wei Precinct[71]
草 暗 斜 川。[tʂhyan]	grass darken Xie river	And the grasses turned dark at Xie River.[72]
見 說 新 愁，	see speak new sorrow	I have heard talk that the new sorrow
如 今 也 到 鷗 邊。[pjian]	seem now also arrive gull side	Now has reached the seagulls.
無 心 再 續 笙 歌 夢，	is no heart again continue *sheng* song dream	I have no heart to renew the dream of pipes and song:
掩 重 門、淺 醉 閒 眠。[mjian]	close double gate shallow drunk idle sleep	Closing my doubled gates, barely tipsy, I shall idly sleep.
莫 開 簾，	don't open curtain	Don't open the window curtains:
怕 見 飛 花，	fear see fly flower	I fear seeing the flying petals;
怕 聽 啼 鵑。[kjyan]	fear listen cry cuckoo	I fear hearing the crying cuckoo.

STUDY NOTES AND QUESTIONS

1. The date of this lyric's composition is uncertain. Explain the differences in its reading if it was written before Hangzhou's surrender to the Mongols or after. What lines are most affected?

2. In the first line of this lyric, is recognizing the allusion to Du Fu's poem important? Explain.

3. While the first strophe contains many verbs, they all serve as modifiers in what proves to be a nominal sentence. What is the effect of this phrasing?

4. Discuss the tone and voice in the first stanza. Who is the audience here?

5. What is the role of time in the shift from the first stanza to the second?

6. Explore the shifts in mood in the second stanza. What is the effect of the imperative "Don't" at the beginning of the final strophe?

7. Why does the persona in the lyric fear the cuckoo?

---

70. This is a stock allusion to Liu Yuxi's famous couplet from "Black Cloth Lane"《烏衣巷》: "The swallows that in former times were before the halls of the Wangs and Xies, / Have flown into the houses of the common folk."「舊時王謝堂前燕，飛入尋常百姓家。」

71. Wei Precinct was an area in Chang'an where the powerful aristocratic Wei clan lived.

72. Xie River, in Jiangxi, had a long literary history (starting with Tao Qian) as a region of elite retreat from the political order.

"To the Tune 'Ganzhou'" by Zhang Yan

辛卯歲，沈堯道同余北歸，各處杭、越。逾歲，堯道來問寂寞，語笑數日，又復別去。賦此曲，並寄趙學舟。

In the year 1291 Shen Yaodao and I returned from the north, and he lived in Hangzhou and I in Yuezhou. After a year, Yaodao came to inquire of my solitude, and we talked and laughed for several days and then separated again. I write this tune and also send it to Zhao Xuezhou.

		【甘州】						To The tune "Ganzhou"
記	玉	關、	踏	雪	事	清	遊，[jiw]	As I recall Jade Gate Pass, treading on snow was a pure excursion,[73]
recall	jade	pass	tread	snow	event	pure	excursion	
寒	氣	脆	貂	裘。[kɦiw]				The cold air made our sable coats brittle.
cold	air	brittle	sable	coat				
傍	枯	林	古	道，				On the ancient road bordering withered groves,
beside	wither	grove	old	road				
長	河	飲	馬，					At the great river watering our horses,[74]
long	river	water	horse					
此	意	悠	悠。[jiw]					This mood was distant and remote.
this	intent	distant and remote						
短	夢	依	然	江	表，			A short dream: as before, south of the River:
short	dream	as before		river	exterior			
老	淚	灑	西	州。[tʂiw]				Old tears scatter at Xizhou [Gate].[75]
old	tear	scatter	West	Prefecture				
一	字	無	題	處，				For even one character, there is no place to inscribe:
one	glyph	is no	inscribe	place				
落	葉	都	愁。[tʂɦiəw]					The fallen leaves all grieve.
fall	leaf	all	sorrow					
載	取	白	雲	歸	去，			You have mounted a white cloud to return;[76]
ride	-ing	white	cloud	return	leave			

73. Jade Gate Pass was in fact a frontier outpost far to the west in Gansu. Zhang Yan uses the name here to refer to the northern frontier long imagined but never seen by Southern Song writers.

74. This line draws on the *yuefu* poem, "Watering My horse by the Great Wall" (see chapter 3).

75. Xizhou was a city near the Eastern Jin capital. Xie An 謝安 (320–85), savior of the Jin dynasty, returned to the capital from Xizhou in his final illness and died soon after. Yang Tan 羊曇, whom Xie An had treated with great respect, vowed to never travel along the road to Xizhou but inadvertently broke that vow when drunk, arrived at Xizhou, wept copiously, and left.

76. Daoist adepts rode on clouds.

問	誰	留	楚	佩，				I ask who left the Chu pendant
ask	who	leave	Chu	pendant				
弄	影	中	洲。[tʂiw]					That plays with sunbeams on the isle?[77]
play	reflection	middle	isle					
折	蘆	花	贈	遠，				Breaking a reed flower, sending it as a present into the distance:
break	reed	flower	present	distant				
零	落	一	身	秋。[tshiw]				Decayed and desolate, [this] body [now] autumn.
desolate	decay	one	body	autumn				
向	尋	常、	野	橋	流	水，		As I face the flowing waters by common rustic bridge,
face	seek	regular	rustic	bridge	flow	water		
待	招	來、	不	是	舊	沙	鷗。[ʔəw]	Awaiting my call, [these] are not the sand gulls of old.
await	summon	come	not	is	former	sand	seagull	
空	懷	感，						In vain I cherish feelings:
vainly	cherish	moved to feel						
有	斜	陽	處，					[Here] is a scene of slanting sunlight,
there is	slant	sunlight	place					
卻	怕	登	樓。[ləw]					Yet I fear to climb the tower.
but	fear	climb	tower					

Study Notes and Questions

1. What is the tone of the first two strophes of the first stanza? What are Zhang Yan's key memories of the north that he presents here?

2. Explain the sadness of the final two strophes of the first stanza. How does it relate to the scene in the first half of the stanza?

3. What is the effect of the allusive "Chu" language at the beginning of the second stanza? How does it relate to the physical scene? How does it connect with the first stanza? How does it relate to the poem's occasion?

4. Discuss the mood of the middle of the second stanza. Are the reeds part of the physical scene or imagined? Is the rustic bridge part of the scene or imagined? What about the gulls? Explain your reading.

5. Explain the relation between the final strophe and the middle strophes. Who is the persona addressing at the end?

---

77. This strophe draws on the language of the *Lyrics of Chu*. The "Lady of the Xiang"《湘君》, one of the *Nine Songs*, for example, has couplets like

> 君不行兮夷猶， The Lady does not travel, she hesitates:
> 蹇誰留兮中洲。 Now, who detains [her] in the isles?

and

> 損吾玦兮江中， I relinquish my "separate" pendant in the river;
> 遺吾佩兮澧浦。 And leave my belt pendant on the bank of the Li River.

"To the Tune 'Qingping le'" by Zhang Yan

【清平樂】							To the Tune "Qingping le"
候 season	蛩 cricket	淒 dreary	斷，[tuan`] break				The plaint of the seasonal crickets breaks off;
人 person	語 speak	西 west	風 wind	岸。[ŋan`] shore			People talk on a shore of west wind.
月 moon	落 fall	沙 sand	平 level	江 river	似 like	練， bleached silk	The moon sets, the sand is level, the river is like white silk;[78]
望 gaze	盡 exhaust	蘆 reed	花 flower	無 is no	雁。[ŋja:n`] goose		As far as the eye can see, reed flowers but no geese.
暗 dark	教 cause	愁 sorrow	損 harm	蘭 Lan-	成，[ʂɦiajŋ] cheng		In secret making Lancheng, who wastes away in sorrow,[79]
可 can be	憐 pity	夜 night	夜 night	關 relate	情。[tsɦiajŋ] feelings		Pitiably, night after night, bound by feelings.
只 only	有 there is	一 one	枝 branch	梧 paulownia	葉， leaf		Here is only one paulownia leaf:
不 not	知 know	多 many	少 few	秋 autumn	聲。[ʂiajŋ] sound		How limitless is its sound of autumn!

Study Notes and Questions

1. Although Southern Song writers of *ci* primarily are famous for their longer lyrics, they also continued to write much-admired shorter compositions. How does the conciseness of the form shape this lyric? What sorts of details disappear?

2. What is the effect of the shorter two-line strophes?

3. How does this *ci* differ from a *shi* poem on autumn? Is the persona similar? Is the implied audience similar?

4. Look again at the early *ci* compositions like Li Yu's "Billows Scour the Sand" and Yan Shu's "Plaint of Inner Feelings" and compare them with this. What has changed? What remains the same?

---

78. Zhang Yan draws on an image of the gleaming whiteness of a river at night that Xie Tiao captured in the line, "The clear river pure as white silk" (澄江淨如練). Li Bai, Yang Wanli, and others admiringly quoted it in their poetry.

79. Lancheng was the childhood name of the poet Yu Xin 庾信, who is discussed in chapter 5.

Conclusion

Zhang Yan was the last major writer of *ci* in the Song dynasty. Indeed, he was the last major writer of *ci* for the next three hundred years. While it seems that *ci* swiftly disappeared as either a popular performance genre or an object of elite literary interest, what is worth stressing at the end of this major period is the arc of the song lyric's development: the form had many sources in popular culture, and then the initial experiments among elite writers were followed by increasing acceptance and by explorations of the representational possibilities of the form. In many cases, writers brought to *ci* techniques that they had learned in writing *shi*, just as early writers in the *shi* tradition used the techniques of the *fu* genre.

In this textbook I have sought to stress the ever-growing power of poetry to capture, reflect, and shape human experience, a power that comes in large measure from the resources of language—allusion, resonance within a tradition, the careful distortions of syntax and reference—and from the power of poetic form and more complex orderings of voice, mood, argument, and imagery made possible by poetic form. The final two chapters on the song lyric present this story of generic development and growing possibilities for shaping experience that I hope offers some insight into the larger processes of poetic development that remain alive today. I hope this textbook will encourage you to explore not just Chinese poetry but the larger world of poetry with an awareness of form and language, to listen attentively and patiently, and to discover how the poetry speaks to you.

Appendix I

List of Poems, Sources, and Translators

Chapter 1: The Classical Chinese Language

Lewis Carroll, "Jabberwocky." In *Through the Looking Glass, and What Alice Found There* (1871).

Li Bai 李白, "Climbing Phoenix Terrace in Jinling"《登金陵鳳凰臺》. In *Li Bai quanji jiaozhu huishi jiping* 李白全集校注彙釋集評, edited by Zhan Ying 詹鍈 (Tianjin: Baihua Wenyi, 1996), vol. 6, *juan* 19, p. 3011.

Du Fu 杜甫, "The Fair One"《佳人》. In *Du Shaoling ji xiangzhu* 杜少陵集詳註, compiled and edited by Qiu Zhao'ao 仇兆鰲 (Beijing: Zhonghua, 1979), vol. 2, *juan* 7, p. 553.

Wang Wei 王維, "The Villa in the Zhongnan Mountains"《終南別業》. In *Wang Wei ji jiaozhu* 王維集校注, compiled by Chen Tiemin 陳鐵民 (Beijing: Zhonghua, 1997), vol. 1, *juan* 2, p. 191.

Du Fu 杜甫, "Thinking of Li Bai at the Sky's Edge"《天末懷李白》. In *Du Shaoling ji xiangzhu*, vol. 2, *juan* 7, p. 591.

Yuan Jie 元結, "Instructing a Former Campaigner"《喻舊部曲》. In *Quan Tang shi* 全唐詩 (Beijing: Zhonghua, 1960), vol. 8, *juan* 241, p. 2708.

Li Bai 李白, "Resentment"《怨情》. In *Li Bai quanji jiaozhu huishi jiping*, vol. 7, *juan* 24, p. 3693.

Wang Wei 王維, "Visiting Incense Accumulation Temple"《過香積寺》. In *Wang Wei ji jiaozhu*, vol. 2, *juan* 7, p. 594.

Wang Wei 王維, "At Wang River Living at Ease, Presented to Pei Di"《輞川閑居贈裴秀才迪》. In *Wang Wei ji jiaozhu*, vol. 2, *juan* 5, p. 429.

Jia Dao 賈島, "Enjoying the Moon"《玩月》. In *Jia Dao ji jiaozhu* 賈島集校注, edited by Qi Wenbang 齊文榜 (Beijing: Renmin wenxue, 2001), p. 17.

Li He 李賀, "Ballad of the Fierce Tiger"《猛虎行》. In *Sanji pingzhu Li Changji geshi* 三家評注李長吉歌詩 (Shanghai: Shanghai guji, 1998), p. 138.

Wang Wei 王維, "Seeing Off Yuan Two to Serve as Envoy to Anxi"《送元二使安西》. In *Wang Wei ji jiaozhu*, vol. 2, *juan* 4, p. 408.

Li Bai 李白, "At the Tower of Xie Tiao in Xuanzhou, a Farewell Feast with Editor Shu Yun"《宣州謝脁樓餞別校叔雲》. In *Li Bai quanji jiaozhu huishi jiping*, vol. 5, *juan* 16, p. 2567.

Chapter 2: The Formal and Rhetorical Features of Chinese Poetry

William Wordsworth, "Ode: Intimations of Immortality from Recollections of Early Childhood." In *Complete Poetical Works of William Wordsworth* (Cambridge: Houghton Mifflin, 1904), p. 353.

Wang Wei 王維, "Song of a Pair of Yellow Swans: A Farewell" 《雙黃鵠歌送別》. In *Wang Wei ji jiaozhu*, vol 1, *juan* 2, p. 141.

Wen Tingyun 溫庭筠, "To the Tune 'Geng lou zi'" 【更漏子】. In *Huajian ji* 花間集, edited by Ouyang Jiong 歐陽炯, annotated by Xiao Jizong 蕭繼宗 (Taipei: Student Book Store, 1977), p. 25.

Alexander Pope, "An Essay on Criticism." In *The Poems of Alexander Pope*, edited by John Butt (New Haven: Yale University Press, 1963), p. 160.

Du Shenyan 杜審言, "Matching the Rhymes of Assistant Lu of Jinling's 'Early Spring Excursion'" 《和晉陵路丞早春遊望》. In *Quan Tang shi*, vol. 3, *juan* 62, p. 734.

Lu Ji 陸機, "Imitation of 'In the Northwest There Is a Tall Tower'" 《擬西北有高樓》. In *Lu Ji ji* 陸機集, edited by Jin Taosheng 金濤聲 (Beijing: Zhonghua, 1982), p. 60.

D. C. Berry, "On Reading Poems to a Senior Class at South High." In Laurence Perrine and Thomas R. Arp, *Sound and Sense: An Introduction to Poetry*, 8th edition (Fort Worth: Harcourt Brace, 1992), p. 268.

Thomas Hardy, "Channel Firing." In *The Complete Poetical Works of Thomas Hardy*, edited by Samuel Hynes (Oxford: Oxford University Press, 1984), vol. 2, p. 9.

Anonymous, "Barred Gate" 《衡門》. In *Canon of Poetry* (Mao 138). In *Shijing tonggu* 詩經通詁, edited by Luo Jiangsheng 雒江生 (Xi'an: Sanqin, 1998), p. 343.

Percy Bysshe Shelley, "Ode to the West Wind." In *The Poems of Shelley, Volume 3: 1819–1820*, edited by Jack Donavan et al. (Harlow: Longman Press, 1989), pp. 211–12.

Emily Dickinson, "I'm Nobody." In *The Complete Poems of Emily Dickinson*, edited by Thomas H. Johnson (Boston: Little, Brown, and Company, 1960), p. 133.

Anonymous, "Big Rat" 《碩鼠》. In *Canon of Poetry* (Mao 113). In *Shijing tonggu*, p. 279.

Anonymous, "Picking Kudzu" 《采葛》. In *Canon of Poetry* (Mao 72). In *Shijing tonggu*, p. 193.

Robert Browning, "Childe Roland to the Dark Tower Came." In *Robert Browning: The Poems*, edited by John Pettigrew (Harmondsworth: Penguin Books, 1981), vol. 1, p. 585.

Don Marquis, "The Coming of Archy." In *archy and mehitabel* (New York: Doubleday, 1927), n.p.

Interlude: On the Translation of Poetry

Vladimir Nabokov, "On Translating '*Eugene Onegin*,'" *The New Yorker*, January 8, 1955, p. 34.

Translations of Du Fu 杜甫, "Spring Vista" 《春望》:

David Hawkes, "Spring Scene," in *A Little Primer of Tu Fu* (Hong Kong: Renditions, 1987), p. 48.

David Hinton, "Spring Landscape," in *Classical Chinese Poetry: An Anthology* (New York: Farrar, Straus, and Giroux, 2008), p. 198.

Gary Snyder, "Spring View," in *The Gary Snyder Reader* (Berkeley: Counterpoint, 1999), p. 542.

Chapter 3: Origins of the Poetic Tradition

Attributed to Bu Zixia 卜子夏 or Wei Hong 衛宏, "Great Preface" to the Mao version of the *Canon of Poetry* 毛詩大序. In *Wenxuan* 文選, compiled by Xiao Tong 蕭統 (Taipei: Wenyi, 1974), *juan* 45, pp. 648–49. This edition is a facsimile reprint of the Hu Kejia 胡克家 (1796–1820) recarving of the Song dynasty printed edition of the *Wenxuan* with Li Shan's 李善 commentary.

Anonymous, "The Peach Is Fresh-Blooming"《桃夭》. In *Canon of Poetry* (Mao 6), in *Shijing tonggu*, pp. 13–15. Translated as "Young Peach" by Joseph R. Allen, courtesy of the author.

Anonymous, "In the Field There Is a Dead Deer"《野有死麇》. In *Canon of Poetry* (Mao 23), in *Shijing tonggu*, pp. 48–51. Translated by Ezra Pound, *Shih-Ching: The Classic Anthology Defined by Confucius* (Cambridge: Harvard University Press, 1982), pp. 10–11. Translated by Joseph R. Allen, courtesy of the author.

Anonymous, "My Lord Is on Campaign"《君子于役》. In *Canon of Poetry* (Mao 66), in *Shijing tonggu*, pp. 180–81. Translated by Ezra Pound, *Shih-Ching: The Classic Anthology Defined by Confucius*, p. 34. Translated as "My Man Is on Corvee Duty" by Joseph R. Allen, courtesy of the author.

Anonymous, "The Cock Crows"《雞鳴》. In *Canon of Poetry* (Mao 96), in *Shijing tonggu*, pp. 239–41. Translated by Joseph R. Allen, courtesy of the author.

Anonymous, "Yellow Bird"《黃鳥》. In *Canon of Poetry* (Mao 131), in *Shijing tonggu*, pp. 325–28.

Anonymous, "The Birth of the People [of Zhou]"《生民》. In *Canon of Poetry* (Mao 245), in *Shijing tonggu*, pp. 727–34.

Anonymous, "Fruitful Year"《豐年》. In *Canon of Poetry* (Mao 279), in *Shijing tonggu*, pp. 852–53.

Attributed to Qu Yuan 屈原, *Encountering Sorrow* 離騷. In Wang Yi 王逸, ed., *Chu ci buzhu* 楚辭補注, supplemental annotation by Hong Xingzu 洪興祖 (Beijing: Zhonghua, 1983), *juan* 1, pp. 1–13.

Attributed to Qu Yuan 屈原, "Lord amidst the Clouds"《雲中君》. In *Chu ci buzhu*, *juan* 2, pp. 57–59. Translated as "The Lord within the Clouds" by David Hawkes, *The Songs of the South: An Ancient Chinese Anthology of Poems by Qu Yuan and Other Poets* (Harmondsworth: Penguin, 1985), pp. 103–4.

Attributed to Qu Yuan 屈原, "Those Who Died for the State"《國殤》. In *Chu ci buzhu*, *juan* 2, pp. 82–83. Translated as "Hymn to the Fallen" by David Hawkes, *The Songs of the South*, pp. 116–17.

Attributed to Qu Yuan 屈原, "Lament for Ying"《哀郢》. In *Chu ci buzhu*, *juan* 4, pp. 132–36.

Attributed to Song Yu 宋玉, *Nine Transformations*, first section《九辯》. In *Chu ci buzhu*, *juan* 8, pp. 182–83.

Anonymous, "The Fisherman"《漁父》. In *Chu ci buzhu*, *juan* 7, pp. 179–81.

CHAPTER 4: POETRY IN THE HAN, WEI, AND JIN DYNASTIES

Anonymous, "There Is One I Long For"《有所思》. In Guo Maoqian 郭茂倩, *Yuefu shiji* 樂府詩集 (Taipei: Liren shuju, 1981), vol. 1, *juan* 16, p. 230. Translated as "The One I Love" by Stephen Owen, *An Anthology of Chinese Literature: Beginnings to 1911* (New York: W. W. Norton & Company, 1996), p. 227.

Anonymous, "Oh, Above!"《上邪》. In Guo Maoqian, *Yuefu shiji*, vol. 1, *juan* 16, p. 231. Translated as "Heaven Above" by Stephen Owen, *An Anthology of Chinese Literature*, p. 227.

Anonymous, "A Ballad: Watering My Horse by the Great Wall"《飲馬長城窟行》. In Guo Maoqian, *Yuefu shiji*, vol. 1, *juan* 38, p. 556. Translated as "Watering My Horse by the Great Wall" by Stephen Owen, *An Anthology of Chinese Literature*, p. 258.

Anonymous, "Nineteen Old Poems, no. 1"《古詩十九首》第一. In Xiao Tong, *Wenxuan*, *juan* 29, p. 417. Translated by Burton Watson, *Chinese Lyricism:* Shih *Poetry from the Second to the Twelfth Century* (New York: Columbia University Press, 1971), p. 20.

Anonymous, "Nineteen Old Poems, no. 2"《古詩十九首》第二. In Xiao Tong, *Wenxuan*, *juan* 29, p. 417. Translated by Arthur Waley, *Translations from the Chinese* (New York: Knopf, 1941), p. 38.

Anonymous, "Nineteen Old Poems, no. 5"《古詩十九首》第五. In Xiao Tong, *Wenxuan*, *juan* 29, p. 418. Translated by Burton Watson, *Chinese Lyricism*, p. 25.

Anonymous, "Nineteen Old Poems, no. 15"《古詩十九首》第十五. In Xiao Tong, *Wenxuan*, *juan* 29, p. 420. Translated by Burton Watson, *Chinese Lyricism*, p. 29.

Anonymous, "Nineteen Old Poems, no. 19"《古詩十九首》第十九. In Xiao Tong, *Wenxuan*, *juan* 29, p. 420. Translated by Arthur Waley, *Translations from the Chinese*, p. 48.

Cao Cao 曹操, "Ballad of Bramble Village"《蒿里行》. In *Cao Cao ji* 曹操集 (Hong Kong: Zhonghua, 1973), p. 4. Translated as "Wormwood Village Song" by Meow Hui Goh, courtesy of the author.

Cao Cao 曹操, "Short Ballad"《短歌行》. In *Cao Cao ji*, p. 5. Translated as "Short Song" by Stephen Owen, *An Anthology of Chinese Literature*, pp. 280–81.

Cao Zhi 曹植, "Miscellaneous Poem"《雜詩》. In *Cao Zhi ji jiaozhu* 曹植集校注, edited by Zhao Youwen 趙幼文 (Beijing: Renmin wenxue, 1998), *juan* 2, p. 251. Translated by Meow Hui Goh, courtesy of the author.

Cao Zhi 曹植, "Seeing Off Mr. Ying, 2 poems, no. 1"《送應氏二首》第一. In *Cao Zhi ji jiaozhu*, *juan* 1, p. 3. Translated as "The Ruins of Lo-yang" by Arthur Waley, *Translations from the Chinese*, p. 64.

Wang Can 王粲, "Seven Laments, 2 poems, no. 1"《七哀詩》. In *Wang Can ji zhu* 王粲集注, edited by Wu Yun and Tang Shaozhong (Xinyang: Zhongzhou shuhua she, 1984), p. 15. Translated by Wendy Swartz, courtesy of the author.

Ruan Ji 阮籍, "Chanting My Thoughts, no. 1"《詠懷》第一. In *Ruan Ji ji jiaozhu* 阮籍集校注, edited by Chen Bojun 陳伯君 (Beijing: Zhonghua, 1987), *juan* 2, p. 210. Translated as "Songs of My Cares, 1" by Stephen Owen, *An Anthology of Chinese Literature*, pp. 256–57.

Xiang Xiu 向秀, "Thinking of Former Times"《思舊賦》. In Xiao Tong, *Wenxuan*, *juan* 16, pp. 234–35.

Pan Yue 潘岳, "Mourning the Departed, 3 poems, no. 1"《悼亡詩》三首 第一 . In *Pan Huangmen ji jiaozhu* 潘黃門集校注, edited by Wang Zengwen 王增文 (Zhangzhou: Zhongzhou guji, 2002), p. 284. Translated as "Lamenting the Dead" by Burton Watson, *Chinese Lyricism*, pp. 96–97.

Zuo Si 左思, "Chanting of History, 8 poems, no. 6"《詠史詩》八首第六. In Xiao Tong, *Wenxuan*, *juan* 21, p. 304.

Lu Ji 陸機, "Imitating 'How Radiant Is the Bright Moon'"《擬明月何皎皎》. In *Lu Ji ji*, *juan* 6, p. 58. Translated as "Imitating 'How the Bright Moon Is Gleaming'" by Meow Hui Goh, courtesy of the author.

Lu Ji 陸機, "Again on the Road to Luoyang, 2 poems, no. 2"《又赴洛道中作詩》二首第二. In *Lu Ji ji*, *juan* 5, p. 41.

Guo Pu 郭璞, "Poems on Wandering Immortals, 14 poems, no. 1" 《遊仙詩》十四首第一. In Xiao Tong, *Wenxuan*, *juan* 21, p. 313.

Cao Pi 曹丕, "A Discourse on Literature"《典論 · 論文》. In Xiao Tong, *Wenxuan*, *juan* 52, pp. 733–34. Translated by Stephen Owen, *An Anthology of Chinese Literature*, pp. 360–61.

Chapter 5: Northern and Southern Dynasties Poetry

Tao Qian 陶潛, "Reading the *Canon of Mountains and Seas*, 13 poems, no. 1" 《讀山海經詩》十三首第一. In *Tao Yuanming ji jiao jian* 陶淵明集校箋, edited by Gong Bin 龔斌 (Shanghai: Shanghai guji, 1996), *juan* 4, pp. 334–35. Translated by Stephen Owen, *An Anthology of Chinese Literature*, pp. 318–19.

Tao Qian 陶潛, "Returning to the Fields to Live, 5 poems, no. 1" 《歸園田居》五首第一. *Tao Yuanming ji jiao jian*, *juan* 2, pp. 73–77. Translated as "Returning to the Farm to Dwell" by James Robert Hightower, *The Poetry of T'ao Ch'ien* (Oxford: Oxford University Press, 1970), p. 50.

Tao Qian 陶潛, "Twenty Poems on Drinking Ale, no. 5" 《飲酒》二十首第五. In *Tao Yuanming ji jiao jian*, *juan* 3, pp. 219–22. Translated by Wendy Swartz, courtesy of the author.

Xie Lingyun 謝靈運, "Returning from the Purification Hall at Stonewall, Written on the Lake" 《石壁精舍還湖中作》. In Xiao Tong, *Wen xuan*, *juan* 22, pp. 321–22. Translated by Burton Watson, *Chinese Lyricism*, pp. 80–81. Translated as "Written on the Lake, Returning from the Chapel at Stone Cliff" by Stephen Owen, *An Anthology of Chinese Literature*, pp. 320–21.

Xie Lingyun 謝靈運, "Climbing the Tower by the Pond" 《登池上樓詩》. In Xiao Tong, *Wen xuan*, *juan* 22, p. 320. Translated as "Climbing an Upper Story by the Pool" by Stephen Owen, *An Anthology of Chinese Literature*, p. 321.

Bao Zhao 鮑照, "Imitating 'Traveling the Road Is Hard,'" no. 6《擬行路難》第六. In *Bao Canjun shi zhu* 鮑參軍詩注, edited by Ye Jusheng 葉菊生 (Hong Kong: Zhonghua, 1972), *juan* 2, p. 57. Translated as "Hard Traveling VI" by Paul Rouzer, courtesy of the author.

Xie Tiao 謝朓. "Jade Staircase's Grievance"《玉階怨》. In *Xie Xuancheng ji jiaozhu* 謝宣城集校注, edited by Cao Rongnan 曹融南 (Shanghai: Shanghai guji, 1991), *juan* 2, pp. 188–89. Translated as "Grievance on the Jade Stairs" by Xiaofei Tian, courtesy of the author.

Anonymous, "Midnight's Song"《子夜歌》("Ever since I parted from him" 自從別郎來). In Guo Maoqian, *Yuefu shiji*, vol. 1, *juan* 44, p. 642.

Anonymous, "Midnight's Song"《子夜歌》("When young, one should act in season" 年少當及時). In Guo Maoqian, *Yuefu shiji*, vol. 1, *juan* 44, p. 642.

Anonymous, "Midnight's Song"《子夜歌》("I throw on my skirt, not yet tying its belt" 攬裙未結帶). In Guo Maoqian, *Yuefu shiji*, vol. 1, *juan* 44, p. 643.

Anonymous, "Midnight's Song"《子夜歌》("I recall our pleasure so clearly" 我念歡的的). In Guo Maoqian, *Yuefu shiji*, vol. 1, *juan* 44, p. 643.

He Xun 何遜, "At Parting"《相送》. In *He Xun ji jiaozhu* 何遜集校注, edited by Li Boqi 李伯齊, revised edition (Beijing: Zhonghua, 2010), *juan* 2, p. 174. Translated by Burton Watson, *Chinese Lyricism*, p. 89.

Xiao Gang 蕭綱, "Chanting about Late Evening in the Bedroom"《詠晚閨》. In Xu Ling 徐陵, *Yutai xinyong jianzhu* 玉臺新詠箋注, annotated by Wu Zhaoyi 吳兆宜, collated by Mu Kehong 穆克宏 (Beijing: Zhonghua, 1985), vol. 2, *juan* 7, p. 298. Translated as "Another Three Couplets on 'Spring Boudoir Feelings'" by Xiaofei Tian, courtesy of the author.

Xiao Gang 蕭綱, "At Night, Gazing at a Lone Flying Goose" 《夜望單飛雁》. In Ouyang Xun 歐陽詢, *Yiwen leiju* 藝文類聚 (Beijing: Zhongwen, 1980), vol. 2, *juan* 91, p. 1579. Translated as "Gazing at a Lone Wild Goose Flying at Night" by Xiaofei Tian, courtesy of the author.

Yu Jianwu 庾肩吾, "Responding to Command: Spring Night"《應令春宵》. In Xu Ling, *Yutai xinyong jianzhu*, vol. 2, *juan* 8, p. 339. Translated as "Spring Night Respectfully Presented as a Companion Piece Written at the Prince of Xiangdong's Command" by Xiaofei Tian, courtesy of the author.

Yu Xin 庾信, "Dusty Mirror"《塵鏡》. In *Yu Zishan ji zhu* 庾子山集注, edited by Ni Fan 倪璠 (Beijing: Zhonghua, 1980), vol. 1, *juan* 4, p. 378. Translated by Xiaofei Tian, courtesy of the author.

Yu Xin 庾信, "Again Parting from Secretarial Minister Zhou"《重別周尚書》. In *Yu Zishan ji zhu*, vol. 1, *juan* 4, p. 370.

Wang Xizhi 王羲之, "Preface to the *Orchid Pavilion Collection*" 《蘭亭集序》. In *Jin Wang Youjun ji* 晉王右軍集 (Taipei: Student Bookstore, 1987), *juan* 2, pp. 335–36. This is a facsimile of a Guangxu reign period (1875–1908) reprint of a Ming edition compiled by Zhang Pu 張溥. Translated as "Preface to *Collected Poems from the Orchid Pavilion*" by Richard Strassberg, from Victor Mair, ed., *Columbia Anthology of Traditional Chinese Literature* (New York: Columbia University Press, 1994), pp. 565–67.

Chapter 6: Early and High Tang Poetry before Du Fu

Wang Bo 王勃, "The Pavilion of the Prince of Teng"《滕王閣》. In *Wang Zi'an ji zhu* 王子安集注, annotated by Jiang Qingyi 蔣清翊 (Shanghai: Shanghai guji, 1995), *juan* 3, pp. 76–77.

Song Zhiwen 宋之問, "Written on the Wall of the North Post Station of the Dayu Range"《題大庾嶺北驛》. In *Shen Quanqi Song Zhiwen ji jiaozhu* 沈佺期宋之問集校注, annotated by Tao Min 陶敏 and Yi Shujiong 易淑瓊 (Beijing: Zhonghua, 2001), vol. 2, *juan* 2, pp. 427–28.

Shangguan Wan'er 上官婉兒 "An Excursion to Prince Changning's Pond of Floating Cups, 25 poems," no. 9《遊長寧公流杯池二十五首》第九 . In *Da Tang cainü Shangguan Wan'er shi ji* 大唐才女上官婉兒詩集, annotated by Wang Lusheng 王盧生 (Zhengzhou: Zhongzhou guji, 2011), p. 56.

Chen Zi'ang 陳子昂, "Song of Climbing Youzhou Terrace"《登幽州臺歌》. In *Chen Zi'ang shi zhu* 陳子昂詩注, edited by Peng Qingsheng 彭慶生 (Chengdu: Sichuan renmin, 1981), pp. 208–9. Translated as "The Ancients" by Robert Payne, *The White Pony* (George Allen and Unwin, 1949), p. 149.

Wang Zhihuan 王之渙, "Climbing Stork Tower"《登鸛鵲樓》, In *Quan Tang shi*, vol. 8, *juan* 253, p. 2849. Translated as "Climbing the Stork Pavilion" by Richard Bodman, from Victor Mair, ed., *Columbia Anthology of Traditional Chinese Literature*, pp. 193–94. Translated by Stephen Owen, *An Anthology of Chinese Literature*, p. 408.

Meng Haoran 孟浩然, "On Pengli Lake, Gazing at Mount Lu"《彭蠡湖中望廬山》. In *Meng Haoran shiji jianzhu* 孟浩然詩集箋注, annotated by Tong Peiji 佟培基 (Shanghai: Shanghai guji, 2000), *juan* 1, pp. 49–52.

Meng Haoran 孟浩然, "Staying the Night on the Jiande River"《宿建德江》. In *Meng Haoran shiji jianzhu*, *juan* 3, p. 360. Translated as "Spending the Night on the Chien-te River" by Stephen Owen, *The Great Age of Chinese Poetry: The High Tang* (New Haven: Yale University Press, 1981), p. 86.

Wang Wei 王維, "Deer Stockade"《鹿柴》. In *Wang Wei jiao zhu*, vol. 2, *juan* 5, pp. 416–17. Translated as "Deer-Park Hermitage" by Witter Bynner, *The Jade Mountain* (Knopf, 1929), reprinted 1972 by Vintage (Random House), p. 189. Translated as "Deer Enclosure" by Richard Bodman and Victor Mair, from Victor Mair, ed., *Columbia Anthology of Traditional Chinese Literature*, p. 198.

Wang Wei 王維, "Bamboo Village Hostel"《竹里館》. In *Wang Wei jiao zhu*, vol. 2, *juan* 5, p. 424. Translated as "Bamboo Mile Lodge" by Burton Watson, *Chinese Lyricism*, p. 173. Translated as "In a Retreat among Bamboos" by Witter Bynner, *The Jade Mountain*, p. 189.

Wang Wei 王維, "Arriving at the Border as an Envoy"《使至塞上》. In *Wang Wei jiao zhu*, vol. 1, *juan* 2, pp. 133–36. Translated as "Arriving at the Frontier on a Mission" by Stephen Owen, *The Great Age of Chinese Poetry: The High Tang*, p. 33.

Wang Wei 王維, "At Farewell"《送別》. In *Wang Wei jiao zhu*, vol. 2, *juan* 7, pp. 565–66. Translated as "On Going Away" by Robert Payne, *The White Pony*, p. 153.

Wang Wei 王維, "Written on Returning to Mt. Song"《歸嵩山作》. In *Wang Wei jiao zhu*, vol. 1, *juan* 2, pp. 108–9. Translated as "Returning to Mount Sung" by Stephen Owen, *The Great Age of Chinese Poetry: The High Tang*, p. 41.

Wang Wei 王維, "After Long Rains, Written at Wang River Villa"《積雨輞川莊作》. In *Wang Wei jiao zhu*, vol. 2, *juan* 5, pp. 444–47. Translated as "Written at My Estate at Wang Stream, after Long Rains" by Paul Rouzer, courtesy of the author.

Cui Hao 崔顥, "Yellow Crane Tower"《黃鶴樓》. In *Quan Tang shi*, vol. 4, *juan* 130, p. 1329. Translated by Stephen Owen, *The Great Age of Chinese Poetry: The High Tang*, p. 62.

Li Bai 李白, "Song of the Roosting Crows"《烏棲曲》. In *Li Bai quanji jiaozhu huishi jiping*, vol. 1, *juan* 3, pp. 342–48. Translated by Stephen Owen, *The Great Age of Chinese Poetry: The High Tang*, p. 121.

Li Bai 李白, "Fighting South of the Wall"《戰城南》. In *Li Bai quanji jiaozhu huishi jiping*, vol. 1, *juan* 3, pp. 349–57.

Li Bai 李白, "Bring in the Ale"《將進酒》. In *Li Bai quanji jiaozhu huishi jiping*, vol. 1, *juan* 3, pp. 357–67. Translated as "Bring the Wine" by Burton Watson, *Chinese Lyricism*, pp. 144–45.

Li Bai 李白, "Ancient Airs, 59 poems, no. 1"《古風五十九首》第一. In *Li Bai quanji jiaozhu huishi jiping* vol. 1, *juan* 2, pp. 19–29. Translated as "Poems in an Old Style, No. 1" by Victor Mair, in Victor Mair, ed., *Columbia Anthology of Traditional Chinese Literature*, pp. 205–6. (Mair's translation initially appeared in Victor Mair, *Four Introspective Poets: A Concordance to Selected Poems by Roan Jyi, Chern Tzyy-arng, Jang Jeouling, and Lii Bor* [Tucson: Arizona State University Press, 1987], p. 92.)

Li Bai 李白, "Jade Staircase's Grievance"《玉階怨》. In *Li Bai quanji jiaozhu huishi jiping*, vol. 2, *juan* 5, pp. 727–31. Translated as "The Jewel Stairs' Grievance" by Ezra Pound, *Cathay* (London: Elkin Matthews, 1915), p. 13.

Li Bai 李白, "Question and Answer in the Mountains"《山中問答》.Given as "In the Mountains, Answering a Lay Person"《山中答俗人》in *Li Bai quanji jiaozhu huishi jiping*, vol. 5, *juan* 16, pp. 2623–26. Translated as "Dialogue in the Mountains" by Stephen Owen, *An Anthology of Chinese Literature*, p. 403.

Li Bai 李白, "Decanting Alone, under the Moon, 4 poems, no. 1"《月下獨酌四首》第一. In *Li Bai quanji jiaozhu huishi jiping*, vol. 6, *juan* 21, pp. 3267–72. Translated as "Drinking Alone by Moonlight [1]" by Arthur Waley, *Translations from the Chinese*, p. 118. Translated as "Drinking Alone in the Moonlight" by Elling Eide, from Victor Mair, ed., *Columbia Anthology of Traditional Chinese Literature*, p. 203.

CHAPTER 7: DU FU

Du Fu 杜甫, "Gazing on the Peak"《望嶽》. In *Du Shaoling ji xiangzhu*, vol. 1, *juan* 1, pp. 3–5.

Du Fu 杜甫, "Painting of a Hawk"《畫鷹》. In *Du Shaoling ji xiangzhu*, vol. 1, *juan* 1, pp. 19–20. Translated as "Painted Hawk" by Stephen Owen, *An Anthology of Chinese Literature*, p. 428.

Du Fu 杜甫, "Ballad of the Army Carts"《兵車行》. In *Du Shaoling ji xiangzhu*, vol. 1, *juan* 2, pp. 113–18.

Du Fu 杜甫, "Lament for Riverbend" 《哀江頭》. In *Du Shaoling ji xiangzhu*, vol. 1, *juan* 4, pp. 329–33. Translated as "Lament by the River" by Stephen Owen, *An Anthology of Chinese Literature*, pp. 422–23.

Du Fu 杜甫, "A Spring Vista" 《春望》. In *Du Shaoling ji xiangzhu*, vol. 1, *juan* 4, p. 320–21. Translated as "Spring View" by Gary Snyder, *The Gary Snyder Reader* (Berkeley: Counterpoint, 1999), p. 542. Translated as "The View in Spring" by Stephen Owen, *An Anthology of Chinese Literature*, p. 420.

Du Fu 杜甫, "Moonlit Night" 《月夜》. In *Du Shaoling ji xiangzhu*, vol. 1, *juan* 4, pp. 309–10. Translated by David Hinton, *Selected Poems of Tu Fu* (New York: New Directions, 1988), p. 25.

Du Fu 杜甫, "Grieving for Chentao" 《悲陳陶》. In *Du Shaoling ji xiangzhu*, vol. 1, *juan* 4, pp. 314–15.

Du Fu 杜甫, "The Officer at Stone Moat" 《石壕吏》. In *Du Shaoling ji xiangzhu*, vol. 2, *juan* 7, pp. 528–30. Translated as "Recruiting Officer of Shih-hao" by Irving Y. Lo from Victor Mair, ed., *Columbia Anthology of Traditional Chinese Literature*, p. 214.

Du Fu 杜甫, "Ballad of Pengya" 《彭衙行》. In *Du Shaoling ji xiangzhu*, vol. 1, *juan* 5, p. 413–17.

Du Fu 杜甫, "A Guest Arrives" 《客至》. In *Du Shaoling ji xiangzhu*, vol. 2, *juan* 9, p. 793. Translated by Burton Watson, *Chinese Lyricism*, p. 166.

Du Fu 杜甫, "My Thatched Roof Was Destroyed by the Autumn Wind: A Song" 《茅屋為秋風所破歌》. In *Du Shaoling ji xiangzhu*, vol. 2, *juan* 10, pp. 831–33. Translated by Stephen Owen, *The Great Age of Chinese Poetry: The High T'ang*, pp. 207–8.

Du Fu 杜甫, "Weary Night" 《倦夜》. In *Du Shaoling ji xiangzhu*, vol. 3, *juan* 14, p. 1176–77. Translated as "Restless Night" by Burton Watson, *Chinese Lyricism*, p. 167.

Du Fu 杜甫, "Lone Goose" 《孤雁》. In *Du Shaoling ji xiangzhu*, vol. 4, *juan* 17, pp. 1530–31.

Du Fu 杜甫, "The Yangzi and Han Rivers" 《江漢》. In *Du Shaoling ji xiangzhu*, vol. 5, *juan* 23, p. 2029–30. Translated as "Where Yangzi Meets the Han" by Stephen Owen, *An Anthology of Chinese Literature*, p. 439. Translated as "Yangtse and Han" by Angus C. Graham, *Poems of the Late T'ang* (New York: NYRB Classics, 2008), p. 48.

Du Fu 杜甫, "Traveler's Pavilion" 《客亭》. In *Du Shaoling ji xiangzhu*, vol. 2, *juan* 11, pp. 932–33.

Du Fu 杜甫, "Autumn Meditations, 8 poems, no. 1" 《秋興八首》第 一. In *Du Shaoling ji xiangzhu*, vol. 4, *juan* 17, pp. 1484–85. Translated as "Autumn Stirrings (I)" by Stephen Owen, *An Anthology of Chinese Literature*, p. 434.

Du Fu 杜甫, "Autumn Meditations, 8 poems, no. 1" 《秋興八首》第七. In *Du Shaoling ji xiangzhu*, vol. 4, *juan* 17, pp. 1494–96. Translated as "Autumn Stirrings (VII)" by Stephen Owen, *An Anthology of Chinese Literature*, p. 438. Translated as "Autumn Meditation, number 7" by Angus C. Graham, *Poems of the Late T'ang* (NYRB Classics), pp. 54–55.

Du Fu 杜甫, "Autumn Meditations, 8 poems, no. 1" 《秋興八首》第八. In *Du Shaoling ji xiangzhu*, vol. 4, *juan* 17, pp. 1497–99. Translated as "Autumn Meditation, number 8" by Angus C. Graham, *Poems of the Late T'ang* (NYRB Classics), p. 55.

Du Fu 杜甫, "Observing Mistress Gongsun's Disciple Dancing the Sword Dance, a Ballad" with preface 《觀公孫大娘弟子舞劍行》并序. In *Du Shaoling ji xiangzhu*, vol. 4, *juan* 20, pp. 1815–18.

Du Fu 杜甫, "South of the River, Meeting Li Guinian" 《江南逢李龜年》. In *Du Shaoling ji xiangzhu*, vol. 5, *juan* 23, pp. 2060–61.

Chapter 8: Middle and Late Tang Poetry

Bai Juyi 白居易, "Gazing at the Moon, I Am Moved" 《自河南經亂關中阻饑兄弟離散各在一處。因望月有感，聊書所懷，寄上浮梁大兄，於潛七兄，烏江十五兄，兼示符離及下邽弟妹》. In *Bai Juyi ji jianjiao* 白居易箋校, annotated by Zhu Jincheng 朱金城 (Shanghai: Shanghai guji, 1988), vol 2, *juan* 13, pp. 781–83.

Bai Juyi 白居易, "Preface to the *New Yuefu*" 《新樂府序》. In *Bai Juyi ji jianjiao*, vol. 1, *juan* 3, pp. 136–39.

Bai Juyi 白居易, "The Old Charcoal Seller" 《賣炭翁》. In *Bai Juyi ji jianjiao*, vol. 1, *juan* 4, pp. 227–29.

Bai Juyi 白居易, "Inscribed Again, 4 poems, no. 3" 《重題》四首第三. In *Bai Juyi ji jianjiao*, vol. 2, *juan* 16, p. 1030.

Bai Juyi 白居易, "Asking Liu Nineteen" 《問劉十九》. In *Bai Juyi ji jianjiao*, vol. 2, *juan* 17, pp. 1075–76. Translated as "A Suggestion to My Friend Liu" by Witter Bynner, *The Jade Mountain* (New York: Alfred A. Knopf, 1929), p. 118.

Bai Juyi 白居易, "Song of the Twilight River" 《暮江吟》. In *Bai Juyi ji jianjiao*, vol. 3, *juan* 19, pp. 1300–1301.

Bai Juyi 白居易, "Autumn Longings" 《秋思》. In *Bai Juyi ji jianjiao*, vol. 3, *juan* 26, p. 1859.

Bai Juyi 白居易, "Aboard a Boat, Reading the Poems of Yuan Nine" 《舟中讀元九詩》. In *Bai Juyi ji jianjiao*, vol. 2, *juan* 15, pp. 947–48. Translated as "Reading Yuan Ninth's Poems aboard a Boat" by Anna M. Shields, courtesy of the author.

Yuan Zhen 元稹, "Responding to Letian's Poem on Reading My Poems at Night on a Moored Boat" 《酬樂天舟泊夜讀微之詩》. In *Yuan Zhen ji biannian jianzhu* 元稹集編年箋注, annotated by Yang Jun 楊軍 (Xi'an: San Qin, 2002), p. 656. Translated by Anna M. Shields, courtesy of the author.

Bai Juyi 白居易, "Ballad of the Pipa, with Preface" 《琵琶行》並序. In *Bai Juyi ji jianjiao*, vol. 2, *juan* 12, pp. 685–98.

Han Yu 韓愈, "So Hurried" 《忽忽》. In *Han Yu quanji jiaozhu* 韓愈全集校注, edited by Qu Shouyuan 屈守元 and Chang Sichun 常思春 (Chengdu: Sichuan University Press, 1996), vol. 1, p. 73.

Han Yu 韓愈, "Goulou Mountain" 《岣嶁山》. In *Han Yu quanji jiaozhu*, vol. 1, pp. 217–20.

Han Yu 韓愈, "Autumn Thoughts, 11 poems, no. 8"《秋懷詩十一首》第八 . In *Han Yu quanji jiaozhu*, vol. 1, p. 366. Translated by Stephen Owen, *An Anthology of Chinese Literature*, pp. 484–85.

Han Yu 韓愈, "Teasing Zhang Ji"《調張籍》. In *Han Yu quanji jiaozhu*, vol. 2, pp. 703–9.

Han Yu 韓愈, "Written on the Wall of the Temple of King Zhao of Chu"《題楚昭王廟》. In *Han Yu quanji jiaozhu*, vol. 2, pp. 767–68. Translated as "On the Temple of King Chao of Ch'u" by Stephen Owen, *The Poetry of Meng Chiao and Han Yü* (New Haven: Yale University Press, 1975), p. 283.

Han Yu 韓愈, "First Floating on South Creek, 3 poems, no. 2"《南溪始泛三首》第二. In *Han Yu quanji jiaozhu*, vol. 2, p. 906. Translated as "Floating on South Creek for the First Time: second of three poems" by Stephen Owen, *The Poetry of Meng Chiao and Han Yü*, p. 286.

Meng Jiao 孟郊, "Ancient Grievance"《古怨》. In *Meng Jiao shiji jiaozhu* 孟郊詩集校注, annotated by Hua Chenzhi 華忱之 and Yu Xuecai 喻學才 (Beijing: Renmin wenxue, 1995), *juan* 1, p. 20.

Meng Jiao 孟郊, "Late Vista at a Luoyang Bridge"《洛橋晚望》. In *Meng Jiao shiji jiaozhu, juan* 5, p. 219.

Meng Jiao 孟郊, "Cold Creek, 8 poems, no. 3"《寒溪八首》第三. In *Meng Jiao shiji jiaozhu, juan* 5, p. 233. Translated by Stephen Owen, *The Poetry of Meng Chiao and Han Yü*, p. 144.

Jia Dao 賈島, "Clear Skies after Snow: Afternoon Vista"《雪晴晚望》. In *Jia Dao ji jiaozhu* 賈島集校注, annotated by Qi Wenbang 齊文榜 (Beijing: Renmin wenxue, 2001), *juan* 6, pp. 327–28. Translated as "An evening view, after snow clears" by Paul Rouzer, courtesy of the author.

Jia Dao 賈島, "Staying the Night at a Mountain Temple"《宿山寺》. In *Jia Dao ji jiaozhu, juan* 8, pp. 387–89. Translated as "I spend the night at a mountain temple" by Paul Rouzer, courtesy of the author.

Jia Dao 賈島, "Seeing Off Tang Huan to Return to His Estate on the Fu River"《送唐環歸敷水莊》. In *Jia Dao ji jiaozhu, juan* 4, pp. 179–81. Translated as "I see off Tang Huan on his return to his Fu River estate" by Paul Rouzer, courtesy of the author.

Li He 李賀, "The Grave of Little Su"《蘇小小墓》. In *Li Changji geshi Wang Qi hui jie* in *Sanji pingzhu Li Changji geshi, juan* 1, p. 46. Translated by Angus C. Graham, *Poems of the Late T'ang*, p. 113.

Li He 李賀, "Bring in the Ale"《將進酒》. In *Li Changji geshi Wang Qi hui jie* in *Sanji pingzhu Li Changji geshi, juan* 4, pp. 164–65.

Li He 李賀, "Song of the Bronze Immortal Bidding Farewell to the Han"《金銅仙人辭漢歌》並序. In *Li Changji geshi Wang Qi hui jie* in *Sanji pingzhu Li Changji geshi, juan* 2, pp. 66–67. Translated as "A Bronze Immortal Takes Leave of Han" by Angus C. Graham, *Poems of the Late T'ang*, p. 106.

Li He 李賀, "Song of Li Ping Playing the Harp"《李憑箜篌引》. In *Li Changji geshi Wang Qi hui jie* in *Sanji pingzhu Li Changji geshi, juan* 1, p. 35.

Li He 李賀, "Song of the Changping Arrowhead"《長平箭頭歌》. In *Li Changji geshi Wang Qi hui jie* in *Sanji pingzhu Li Changji geshi, juan* 4, pp. 158–59. Translated as "Song of an Arrowhead from the Battlefield of Chang-ping" by Stephen Owen, *An Anthology of Chinese Literature*, pp. 489–90.

Li Shangyin 李商隱, "Brocade Zither"《錦瑟》. In *Li Shangyin shige jijie* 李商隱詩歌集解, annotated by Liu Xuekai 劉學鍇 and Yu Shucheng 余恕誠 (Beijing: Zhonghua, 1988), vol. 3, pp. 1420–38. Translated as "The Patterned Lute" by Angus C. Graham, *Poems of the Late T'ang*, p. 171.

Li Shangyin 李商隱, "Untitled"《無題》("Seeing one another is hard" 相見時難別亦難). In *Li Shangyin shige jijie*, vol. 4, pp. 1461–67. Translated as "Untitled Poems (vi)" by Angus C. Graham, *Poems of the Late T'ang*, p. 150.

Li Shangyin 李商隱, "Untitled"《無題》("'I'll come' is an empty phrase" 來是空言去絕蹤). In *Li Shangyin shige jijie*, vol. 4, pp. 1467–69. Translated as "Untitled" by Paul Rouzer, courtesy of the author.

Li Shangyin 李商隱, "Listening to a Song"《聞歌》. In *Li Shangyin shige jijie*, vol. 5, pp. 1859–63.

Li Shangyin 李商隱, "Chang E"《嫦娥》. In *Li Shangyin shige jijie*, vol. 4, pp. 1694–97. Translated as "Ch'ang O" by Angus C. Graham, *Poems of the Late T'ang*, p. 155.

Li Shangyin 李商隱, "Night Rain, Sent North"《夜雨寄北》. In *Li Shangyin shige jijie*, vol. 3, pp. 1420–38. Translated as "Night Rains: To My Wife Up North" by Angus C. Graham, *Poems of the Late T'ang*, p. 159. Translated as "When Will I Be Home" by Kenneth Rexroth, *One Hundred More Poems from the Chinese: Love and the Turning Year* (New Directions, 1970), p. 77.

Li Shangyin 李商隱, "The Sui Palace"《隋宮》. In *Li Shangyin shige jijie*, vol. 3, pp. 1395–1400. Translated by Stephen Owen, *An Anthology of Chinese Literature*, p. 516.

Du Mu 杜牧, "Mooring on the Qinhuai River"《泊秦淮》In *Fanchuan shiji zhu* 樊川詩集注, edited by Feng Jiwu 馮集梧 (Shanghai: Shanghai guji, 1978), *juan* 4, pp. 273–74.

Du Mu 杜牧, "Relieving My Thoughts"《遣懷》In *Fanchuan shiji zhu*, *waiji* 外集, p. 369. Translated as "Easing My Heart" by Angus C. Graham, *Poems of the Late T'ang*, p. 123.

Du Mu 杜牧, "Traveling in the Mountains"《山行》. In *Fanchuan shiji zhu*, *waiji*, p. 370. Translated as "Travelling in the Mountains" by Angus C. Graham, *Poems of the Late T'ang*, p. 133.

Du Mu 杜牧, "Presented at Farewell, second of two"《贈別二首》第二. In *Fanchuan shiji zhu*, *juan* 4, pp. 311–12. Translated as "Farewell Poem (second of two to a girl of Yang-chou)" by Angus C. Graham, *Poems of the Late T'ang*, p. 134.

Du Mu 杜牧, "Written on the Wall of the Water Pavilion at Kaiyuan Temple"《題宣州開元寺水閣閣下宛溪夾溪居人》. In *Fanchuan shiji zhu*, *juan* 3, pp. 202–3. Translated as "I wrote this on the Water Pavilion of Kaiyuan Temple in Xuanzhou; below the Pavilion, residences line either side of Wan Stream" by Paul Rouzer, courtesy of the author.

Wen Tingyun 溫庭筠, "Traveling Early in the Shang Mountains"《商山早行》. In *Wen Feiqing shiji jianzhu* 溫飛卿詩集箋注, edited by Zeng Yi 曾益 et al. (Shanghai: Shanghai guji, 1980), *juan* 7, pp. 155–56. Translated as "Setting Out Early from Mount Shang" by Paul Rouzer, *Writing Another's Dream: The Poetry of Wen Tingyun* (Stanford: Stanford University Press, 1993), p. 18.

Wen Tingyun 溫庭筠, "Song: Naval Battle on Kunming Lake"《昆明治水戰詞》. In *Wen Feiqing shiji jianzhu*, *juan* 2, pp. 32–33. Translated by Paul Rouzer, *Writing Another's Dream*, pp. 134–35.

Yu Xuanji 魚玄機, "Presented to a Neighboring Woman"《贈鄰女》. In *Yu Xuanji shi biannian yizhu* 魚玄機詩編年譯注, edited by Peng Zhixian 彭志憲 and Zhang Yi 張燚 (Ürümqi: Xinjiang University Press, 1994), pp. 108–9.

Yu Xuanji 魚玄機, "On an excursion to the South Tower of Chongzhen Temple, seeing where the names of the newly successful jinshi examinees are posted"《遊崇真觀南樓覩新及第題名處》. In *Yu Xuanji shi biannian yizhu*, pp. 80–82. Translated as "On a Visit to Ch'ung Chên Taoist Temple I See in the South Hall the List of Successful Candidates in the Imperial Examinations" by Kenneth Rexroth and Ling Chung, *The Orchid Boat: Women Poets of China* (New York: New Directions Publishing Corp., 1973), p. 19.

Yu Xuanji 魚玄機, "Selling Wilted Peonies"《賣殘牡丹》. In *Yu Xuanji shi biannian yizhu*, pp. 80–82. Translated as "Selling Tattered Peonies" by Stephen Owen, *An Anthology of Chinese Literature*, p. 509.

Yu Xuanji 魚玄機, "Inscribed at Mist-hidden Pavilion"《題隱霧亭》. In *Yu Xuanji shi biannian yizhu*, pp. 78–80.

Chapter 9: The Song Lyric as a New Form

Anonymous, "To the Tune 'Willow Branch'" 【楊柳枝】. In Zeng Zhaomin 曾昭岷 et al., eds., *Quan Tang Wudai ci* 全唐五代詞 (Beijing: Zhonghua, 1999), vol. 2, p. 893.

Bai Juyi 白居易, "To the Tune 'Recalling the Southland'" 【憶江南】. In *Bai Juyi ji jianjiao*, vol. 4, *juan* 34, pp. 2353–54. Translated as "Yi Jiangnan (1st of 3)" by Anna M. Shields, *Crafting a Collection* (Cambridge: Harvard University Asia Center, 2006), p. 44.

Liu Yuxi 劉禹錫, "To the Tune 'Bamboo Branch'" 【竹枝詞】. In *Liu Yuxi ji* 劉禹錫集, edited by Bian Xiaoxuan 卞孝萱 (Beijing: Zhonghua, 1990), vol. 2, *juan* 27, p. 359.

Wen Tingyun 溫庭筠, "To the Tune 'The Water-clock'" 【更漏子】. In *Huajian ji*, pp. 32–34.

Wen Tingyun 溫庭筠, "To the Tune 'Pusa man'" 【菩薩蠻】. In *Huajian ji*, pp. 4–7. Translated as "Pusa man (1st of 14)" by Anna M. Shields, *Crafting a Collection*, p. 178.

Wei Zhuang 韋莊, "To the Tune 'Pusa man'" 【菩薩蠻】. In *Huajian ji*, pp. 102–4. Translated as "Pusa man (1st of 14)" by Anna M. Shields, *Crafting a Collection*, p. 196.

Wei Zhuang 韋莊, "To the Tune 'Nü guanzi'" 【女冠子】. In *Huajian ji*, pp. 143–45.

Gu Xiong 顧敻, "To the Tune 'Speaking of Innermost Feelings'" 【訴衷情】. In *Huajian ji*, pp. 367–69.

Feng Yansi 馮延巳, "To the Tune 'Magpie treading the Branch'" 【鵲踏枝】. In *Quan Tang Wudai ci*, vol. 1, pp. 658–59.

Feng Yansi 馮延巳, "To the Tune 'Picking Mulberries'" 【采桑子】. In *Quan Tang Wudai ci*, vol. 1, p. 664.

Li Yu 李煜, "To the Tune 'Billows Scour the Sand'" 【浪淘沙】. In Li Jing 李璟 and Li Yu, *Nan Tang erzhu ci jiaoding* 南唐二主詞校訂, edited by Wang Zhongwen 王仲聞 (Hong Kong: Daguang, 1972), pp. 49–50.

Li Yu 李煜, "To the Tune 'Fair Lady Yu'" 【虞美人】. In *Nan Tang erzhu ci jiaoding*, pp. 9–11.

Yan Shu 晏殊, "To the Tune 'Plaint of Inner Feelings'" 【訴衷情】. In Liu Naichang 劉乃昌 and Zhu Decai 朱德才, eds., *Song ci xuan* 宋詞選 (Beijing: Renmin wenxue, 2003), p. 78.

Zhang Xian 張先, "To the Tune 'Heavenly Immortal': At the time, I was a junior prefectural aide in Jiahe. Because I was sick and resting, I did not attend the prefectural gathering." 【天仙子】「時為嘉禾小倅，以病眠，不赴府會」. In *Zhang Xian ji biannian jiaozhu* 張先集編年校注, edited by Wu Xionghe 吳熊和 and Shen Songjin 沈松勤 (Hangzhou: Zhejiang guji, 1996), pp. 7–9.

Liu Yong 柳永, "To the Tune 'Qu yu guan'" 【曲玉管】. In *Liu Yong ji* 柳永集, annotated by Sun Guanggui 孫光貴 and Xu Jing 徐靜 (Changsha: Yuelu, 2003), pp. 147–48.

Liu Yong 柳永, "To the Tune 'Settling the Waves'" 【定風波】. In *Liu Yong ji*, pp. 111–12.

Liu Yong 柳永, "To the Tune 'Eight Sounds of Ganzhou'" 【八聲甘州】. In *Liu Yong ji*, pp. 105–6. Translated as "*Pa-sheng kan-chou*" by Kang-i Sun Chang, *The Evolution of Chinese* Tz'u *Poetry* (Princeton, 1980), pp. 127–28.

Su Shi 蘇軾, "To the Tune 'River Goddess': On the twentieth day of the first month of 1075 at night I record a dream" 【江神子】「乙卯正月二十日夜記夢」. In *Su ci huiping* 蘇詞彙評, edited by Huang Lixin 黃立新 and Zhu Lan 朱蘭 (Chengdu: Sichuan wenyi, 2000), p. 159. Translated as "To the tune, "River Town" Recording a Dream on the Night of the 20th Day of the 1st Month of Yimao [1075]" by Ronald C. Egan, *Word, Image and Deed in the Life of Su Shi* (Cambridge: Harvard University Council of East Asian Studies, 1994), p. 316.

Su Shi 蘇軾, "To the tune 'Water Tune Prelude': On the night of the Mid-Autumn Festival in 1076, I reveled and drank 'til dawn. Very drunk, I wrote this piece and fondly recalled [my brother] Ziyou." 【水調歌頭】「丙辰中秋，歡飲達旦，大醉，作此篇，兼懷子由」. In *Su ci huiping*, pp. 27–34.

Su Shi 蘇軾, "To the Tune 'A Melody of Yang Pass': Composed on the Mid-Autumn Festival" 【陽關曲】「中秋作」. In *Su ci huiping*, pp. 218–21.

Su Shi 蘇軾, "To the Tune 'The Allure of Niannu': Cherishing the Past at Red Cliff" 【念奴嬌】「赤壁懷古」. In *Su ci huiping*, pp. 41–53. Translated as "The Charms of Niannu": *"Cherishing the Past" at the Red Cliff* by Benjamin Ridgway, courtesy of the author.

CHAPTER 10: THE SONG LYRIC IN THE TWELFTH AND THIRTEENTH CENTURIES

Zhou Bangyan 周邦彥, "To the tune 'Chant of the Auspicious Dragon'" 【瑞龍吟】. In *Qingzhen ji jiaozhu* 清真集校注, edited by Sun Hong 孫虹 (Beijing: Zhonghua, 2002), *juan* 1, pp. 1–7.

Zhou Bangyan 周邦彥, "To the tune 'Western River': Cherishing the Old at Jinling" 【西河】「金陵懷古」. In *Qingzhen ji jiaozhu*, pp. 287–91.

Zhou Bangyan 周邦彥, "To the tune 'Fair Lady Yu'" 【虞美人】. In *Qingzhen ji jiaozhu*, pp. 363–64.

Li Qingzhao 李清照, "To the tune 'Note on Note (extended)'" 【聲聲慢】. In *Li Qingzhao ji jianzhu* 李清照集箋注, annotated by Xu Peijun 徐培均 (Shanghai: Shanghai guji, 2002), *juan* 1, pp. 161–73. Translated as "to 'Note After Note'" by Stephen Owen, *An Anthology of Chinese Literature*, p. 581.

Li Qingzhao 李清照, "To the tune 'Like a Dream'" 【如夢令】("Last night the rain was sparse but the wind buffeted" 昨夜雨疏風驟). In *Li Qingzhao ji jianzhu*, pp. 14–17. Translated as "To the tune 'As If in a Dream'" by Ronald C. Egan, *Burden of Female Talent: The Poet Li Qingzhao and Her History in China* (Cambridge: Harvard University Asia Center, 2013), *juan* 1, p. 232.

Li Qingzhao 李清照, "To the tune 'Like a Dream'" 【如夢令】("I always recall the pavilion by the creek at sunset" 常記溪亭日暮). In *Li Qingzhao ji jianzhu*, *juan* 1, pp. 40–42. Translated by Stephen Owen, *An Anthology of Chinese Literature*, p. 580.

Li Qingzhao 李清照, "To the Tune 'Always Encountering Joy': First Night" 【永遇樂】「元宵」. In *Li Qingzhao ji jianzhu*, *juan* 1, pp. 150–57.

Xin Qiji 辛棄疾, "To the Tune 'Feeling for Fish': In 1179 I was transferred from serving as supply commissioner in Hubei to Hunan. My office colleague Wang Zhengzhi set out ale in a small pavilion, and I composed for him." 【摸魚兒】「淳熙已亥，自湖北漕移湖南，同官王正之置酒小山亭，為賦」. In *Jiaxuan ci biannian jianzhu* 稼軒詞編年箋注, annotated by Deng Guangming 鄧廣銘 (Shanghai: Shanghai guji, 1993), *juan* 1, pp. 66–68.

Xin Qiji 辛棄疾, "To the Tune 'Congratulating the Bridegroom': Taking leave of my cousin Maojia, No. 12. The shrike and the cuckoo are in fact two species: see the 'Encountering Sorrows, with Supplemented Annotation.'" 【賀新郎】「別茂嘉十二弟，鵜鴂、杜鵑實兩種，見離騷補注」. In *Jiaxuan ci biannian jianzhu*, *juan* 4, pp. 526–29.

Jiang Kui 姜夔, "To the Tune 'Yangzhou' (extended)" 【揚州慢】. In *Jiang Baishi ci biannian jianzhu* 姜白石詞編年箋注, annotated by Xia Chengdao 夏承燾 (Shanghai: Shanghai guji, 1998), *juan* 1, pp. 1–3. Translated as "Yangchow mahn" by Shuen-fu Lin, *The Transformation of the Chinese Lyric Tradition* (Princeton: Princeton University Press, 1978), pp. 72–73.

Jiang Kui 姜夔, "To the Tune 'Seeking Spring' (extended)" 【探春慢】. In *Jiang Baishi ci biannian jianzhu*, *juan* 1, pp. 17–18.

Jiang Kui 姜夔, "To the tune 'Hidden Fragrance'" 【暗香】. In *Jiang Baishi ci biannian jianzhu*, *juan* 3, p. 48. Translated as "To 'Fragrance from Somewhere Unseen'" by Stephen Owen, *An Anthology of Chinese Literature*, pp. 586–87.

Jiang Kui 姜夔, "To the Tune 'Sparse Shadows'" 【疏影】. In *Jiang Baishi ci biannian jianzhu*, *juan* 3, pp. 48–51. Translated by Grace S. Fong, *Wu Wenying and the Art of Southern Song* Ci *Poetry* (Princeton: Princeton University Press, 1987), pp. 41–42.

Wu Wenying 吳文英, "To the Tune 'Eight Sounds of Ganzhou': At Lingyan, accompanying the worthies of the Stabilization Fund Office on an excursion" 【八聲甘州】「零巖陪庾幕諸公游」. In *Mengchuang ci huijiao jianshi jiping* 夢窗詞彙校箋釋集評, annotated by Wu Bei 吳蓓 (Hangzhou: Zhejiang guji, 2007), pp. 677–82. Translated as "To Eight Notes of Ganzhou: The Ethereal Cliff. Visited in the company of the gentlemen in the Stabilization Fund Commission," by Zhang Chen, courtesy of the author.

Wu Wenying 吳文英, "To the Tune 'The Wind Entering the Pines'" 【風入松】. In *Mengchuang ci huijiao jianshi jiping*, pp. 455–60. Translated by Grace S. Fong, *Wu Wenying and the Art of Southern Song* Ci *Poetry*, pp. 107–8.

Zhang Yan 張炎, "To the Tune 'Gaoyang Terrace': On West Lake, spring stirrings" 【高陽臺】「西湖春感」. In *Shanzhong baiyun ci* 山中白雲詞, edited by Wu Zeyu 吳則虞 (Beijing: Zhonghua, 1983), *juan* 1, p. 2.

Zhang Yan 張炎, "To the Tune 'Ganzhou'" 【甘州】. In *Shanzhong baiyun ci*, *juan* 1, p. 9.

Zhang Yan 張炎, "To the Tune 'Qingping le'" 【清平樂】. In *Shanzhong baiyun ci*, *juan* 4, pp. 83–84.

Appendix II

List of Variant Characters

Chapter 3: Origins of the Poetic Tradition

Page 73: Qu Yuan, *Encountering Sorrow*
Line 5: Some texts do not have 于, "on."
Line 22: Some texts do not have 乎, "on."
Line 76: Some texts have 時, "[present] time," for 世, "[present] generation."

Page 81: Anonymous, "Those Who Died for the State"
Line 18: Some texts have 子魂魄, "Your souls," for 魂魄毅, "[Their] souls are strong."

Chapter 4: Poetry in the Han, Wei, and Jin Dynasties

Page 95: Anonymous, "There Is One I Long For"
Line 15: Some texts do not include this line.

Page 112: Cao Cao, "Short Ballad"
Lines 11–12: Some texts do not have these two lines.

Page 117: Cao Zhi, "Seeing Off Mr. Ying," 2 poems, no. 1
Line 15: Some texts have 平常居, "where [I] used to dwell," for 平生親, "one with whom [I] have been close all my life."

Page 119: Wang Can, "Seven Laments," 2 poems, no. 1
Line 4: Some texts have 委, "to entrust," for 遠, "to [make] distant."

Page 130: Pan Yue, "Mourning the Departed," 3 poems, no. 1
Line 16: Some texts have 周, "thoroughly," for 回, "to turn."

Page 133: Zuo Si, "Chanting of History," 8 poems, no. 6
Line 2: Some texts have 振, "to agitate," for 震, "to stir" (lit., "earthquake").

Chapter 5: Northern and Southern Dynasties Poetry

Page 153: Tao Qian, "Twenty Poems on Drinking Ale, no. 5"
Line 6: Some texts have 見, "to see," for 望, "to look for."
Line 9: Some texts have 還, "to return," for 中, "midst."

Chapter 6: Early and High Tang Poetry before Du Fu

Pages 180–81: Wang Bo, "The Pavilion of the Prince of Teng"
Line 4: Some texts have 朱, "vermilion," for 珠, "pearl [bead]."
Line 6: Some texts have 度幾, "pass how many," for 幾度, "how many pass."

Pages 190–91: Meng Haoran, "On Pengli Lake, Gazing at Mount Lu"
Line 5: Some texts have 遙島, "distant island," for 匡阜, "Kuang Mountain."
Line 11: Some texts have 尚, "Shang," for 向, "Xiang."

Page 202: Cui Hao, "Yellow Crane Tower"
Line 1: Some texts have 黃鶴, "yellow crane," for 白雲, "white cloud."
Line 6: Some texts have 芳, "fragrant," for 春, "spring."

Page 210: Li Bai, "Bring in the Ale"
Line 17: Some texts have 側, "incline," for 傾, "incline."
Line 19: Some texts have 復, "again," for 用, "use"; others have 願, "vow," for 用.

Chapter 7: Du Fu

Page 227: Du Fu, "Ballad of the Army Carts"
Line 13: Some texts have 亭, "post," for 庭, "office."

Page 230: Du Fu, "Lament for Riverbend"
Line 18: Some texts have 草, "grasses," for 水, "water."

Page 240: Du Fu, "The Officer at Stone Moat"
Line 4: Some texts have 看門, "attend to the gate," for 門看, "[go to the] gate to look."

Chapter 8: Middle and Late Tang Poetry

Page 275: Bai Juyi, "Gazing at the Moon, I Am Moved"
Line 1: Some texts have 饑, "starve," for 荒, "barren."

Page 276: Bai Juyi, "Preface to the New *Yuefu*"
Line 3: Some texts have 肆, "unbridled," for 律, "regulated."

Page 278: Bai Juyi, "Inscribed Again"
Line 8: Some texts have 可, "can be," for 何, "why?"

Page 283–88: Bai Juyi, "Ballad of the *Pipa*"
Preface, Line 1: Some texts have 舟, "boat," for 船, "boat."
Preface, Line 3: Some texts have 憫默, "pensively silent," for 憫然, "pensive."

Line 14: Some texts have 把, "to hold," for 抱, "to enwrap."
Line 22: Some texts have 綠腰, "green waist," for 六么, taken as homophonous for 綠腰.
Line 28: Some texts have 水, "water," for 冰, "ice."
Line 69: Some texts have 地僻, "region is remote," for 小處, "insignificant place."
Line 74: Some texts have 血, "blood," for 哭, "weep."
Line 87: Some texts have 座中, "within the seated [group]," for 就中, "in [their] midst."

Page 310: Jia Dao, "Seeing Off Tang Gui to Return to His Estate on the Fu River"
Title: Some texts have 環, "Huan," for 瓌, "Gui."
Line 5: Some texts have 藥, "medicinal herbs," for 廟, "temple."

Page 318–19: Li He, "Song of Li Ping Playing the Harp"
Line 3: Some texts have 江, "river," for 湘, "Xiang [River]."
Line 11: Some texts have 坤, "Kun," for 神, "spirit."

Page 329: Li Shangyin, "Listening to a Song"
Line 8: Some texts have 光, "radiance," for 殘, "remnant."

Page 336: Du Mu, "Relieving My Thoughts"
Line 1: Some texts have 魄 as a variant way of writing 拓.
Line 2: Some texts have 腸斷, "innards rend," for 纖細, "fine and delicate."
Line 4: Some texts have 占, "seize," for 贏, "gain."

Page 344: Wen Tingyun, "Training for Naval Battle on Kunming Lake"
Line 2: Some texts have 晴漾, "bright ripples," for 交瀲, "crisscrossing ripples."
Line 4: Some texts have 時, "time," for 眄, "glare."
Line 10: Some texts have 青幟白旌, "blue flags and white banners," for 青翰畫鷁, "Blue Feather and Painted Fish Hawk."

Chapter 9: The Song Lyric as a New Form

Page 352: Anonymous, "To the Tune 'Willow Branch'"
Line 7: Some texts have 人, "people," for 上, "on."
Line 8: Some texts have 為陳, "become set-out [traces]" for 微塵, "minute dust."

Page 373: Li Yu, "To the Tune 'Fair Lady Yu'"
Line 5: Some texts have 依然, "as before," for 應猶, "ought still…."
Line 7: Some texts have 都, "in total," for 能, "able to."

Chapter 10: The Song Lyric in the Twelfth and Thirteenth Centuries

Page 405: Zhou Bangyan, "To the Tune 'Western River'"
Line 10: Some texts have 遺, "leave behind," for 餘, "remain."

Page 420: Xin Qiji, "To the Tune 'Congratulating the Bridegroom' "

Line 11: Some texts have 烈, "blazing," for 裂, "shredded."

Line 16: Some texts have 澈 as a variant form for 徹, "thoroughly complete."

Page 445: Zhang Yan, "To the Tune 'Ganzhou' "

Preface, Line 1: Some texts have 庚寅, the stem-and-branch year designation for 1290, for 辛卯, the designation for 1291.

Suggested Readings

General Histories, Anthologies, and Essay Collections

Kang-i Sun Chang and Stephen Owen, eds., *The Cambridge History of Chinese Literature*, Volume 1: To 1375 (Cambridge: Cambridge University Press, 2010).

Paul W. Kroll, ed., *Reading Medieval Chinese Poetry: Text, Context, and Culture* (Leiden: Brill, 2015).

Shuen-fu Lin and Stephen Owen, eds., *The Vitality of the Lyric Voice: Shih Poetry from the Late Han to the T'ang* (Princeton: Princeton University Press, 1986).

Victor Mair, ed., *The Columbia Anthology of Traditional Chinese Literature* (New York: Columbia University Press, 1994).

_____, *The Columbia History of Chinese Literature* (New York: Columbia University Press, 2001).

Stephen Owen, *An Anthology of Chinese Literature: Beginnings to 1911* (New York: W. W. Norton and Company, 1996).

_____, *Readings in Chinese Literary Thought* (Cambridge: Harvard University Press, 1992).

Pauline Yu, *The Reading of Imagery in the Chinese Poetic Tradition* (Princeton: Princeton University Press, 1987).

Chapter 1: The Classical Chinese Language

William H. Baxter and Laurent Sagart, *Old Chinese: A New Reconstruction* (Oxford: Oxford University Press, 2014).

William G. Boltz, *The Origin and Early Development of the Chinese Writing System* (New Haven: American Oriental Society, 1994).

Michael A. Fuller, *An Introduction to Literary Chinese* (Cambridge: Harvard University Asia Center, 2004).

Paul W. Kroll, *A Student's Dictionary of Classical and Medieval Chinese* (Leiden: Brill, 2015).

Jerry Norman, *Chinese* (Cambridge: Cambridge University Press, 1988).

Edwin Pulleyblank, *Outline of Classical Chinese Grammar* (Seattle: University of Washington Press, 1999).

Chapter 2: The Formal and Rhetorical Features of Chinese Poetry

Thomas R. Arp and Greg Johnson, *Perrine's Sound & Sense: An Introduction to Poetry*, 13th ed. (Boston: Wadsworth, 2011).

Zong-qi Cai, ed., *How to Read Chinese Poetry: A Guided Anthology* (New York: Columbia University Press, 2008).

John Hollander, *Rhyme's Reason: A Guide to English Verse*, 3rd ed. (New Haven: Yale University Press, 2001).

X. J. Kennedy and Dana Gioia, *An Introduction to Poetry*, 13th ed. (London: Longman, 2009).

James J. Y. Liu, *The Art of Chinese Poetry* (Chicago: University of Chicago Press, 1966).

Charles Olsen, *The Collected Poems of Charles Olson* (Berkeley: University of California Press, 1987).

CHAPTER 3: ORIGINS OF THE POETIC TRADITION

David Hawkes, *The Songs of the South: An Anthology of Ancient Chinese Poems by Qu Yuan and Other Poets* (Harmondsworth: Penguin Press, 1985).

Bernard Karlgren, *The Book of Odes* (Stockholm: Museum of Far Eastern Antiquities, 1950).

Steven Van Zoeren, *Poetry and Personality: Reading, Exegesis, and Hermeneutics in Traditional China* (Stanford: Stanford University Press, 1991).

Arthur Waley, *The Book of Songs: The Ancient Chinese Classic of Poetry*, edited by Joseph R. Allen (New York: Grove Press, 1996).

_____, *The Nine Songs: A Study of Shamanism in Ancient China*, 2nd ed. (San Francisco: City Lights Books, 1973).

Ching-hsien Wang, *The Bell and the Drum: Shih Ching as Formulaic Poetry in an Oral Tradition* (Berkeley: University of California Press, 1974).

_____, *From Ritual to Allegory: Seven Essays in Early Chinese Poetry* (Hong Kong: Chinese University of Hong Kong Press, 1988).

CHAPTER 4: POETRY OF THE HAN, WEI, AND JIN DYNASTIES

Hans H. Frankel, "The Development of Han and Wei *Yüeh-fu* as a High Literary Genre," in Shuen-fu Lin and Stephen Owen, eds., *The Vitality of the Lyric Voice: Shih Poetry from the Late Han to the T'ang* (Princeton: Princeton University Press, 1986), pp. 255–86.

David R. Knechtges, "From the Eastern Han through the Western Jin (AD 25–317)," in *The Cambridge History of Chinese Literature*, Volume I: To 1375, edited by Stephen Owen and Kang-i Sun Chang (Cambridge: Cambridge University Press, 2010), pp. 116–98.

Shuen-fu Lin and Stephen Owen, eds., *The Vitality of the Lyric Voice: Shih Poetry from the Late Han to the T'ang* (Princeton: Princeton University Press, 1986).

Ronald C. Miao, *Early Medieval Chinese Poetry: The Life and Works of Wang Ts'an (A.D. 177–217)*, Münchener Ostasiatische Studien, vol. 30 (Wiesbaden: Fritz Steiner, 1982).

Stephen Owen, *The Making of Early Chinese Classical Poetry* (Cambridge: Harvard University Asia Center, 2006).

Chapter 5: Northern and Southern Dynasties Poetry

Robert Ashmore, *The Transport of Reading: Text and Understanding in the World of Tao Qian (365–427)* (Cambridge: Harvard University Asia Center, 2010).

Kang-i Sun Chang, *Six Dynasties Poetry* (Princeton: Princeton University Press, 1986).

J. D. Frodsham, *The Murmuring Stream: The Life and Works of Hsieh Ling-yün* (Kuala Lumpur: University of Malaya Press, 1967).

James Robert Hightower, *The Poetry of T'ao Ch'ien* (Oxford: Clarendon Press, 1970).

Shuen-fu Lin and Stephen Owen, eds., *The Vitality of the Lyric Voice: Shih Poetry from the Late Han to the T'ang* (Princeton: Princeton University Press, 1986).

Richard B. Mather, trans., *The Age of Eternal Brilliance: Three Lyric Poets of the Yung-ming Era (483–493)* (Leiden: Brill, 2003).

Stephen Owen, *The Making of Early Chinese Classical Poetry* (Cambridge: Harvard University Asia Center, 2006).

Stephen Owen and Wendy Swartz, trans., *The Poetry of Ruan Ji and Xi Kang*, Library of Chinese Humanities (Boston and Berlin: Walter de Gruyter, Inc., 2017).

Paul Rouzer, *Articulated Ladies: Gender and the Male Community in Early Chinese Texts* (Cambridge: Harvard University Asia Center, 2001).

Wendy Swartz, *Reading Tao Yuanming: Shifting Paradigms of Historical Reception (427–1900)* (Cambridge: Harvard University Asia Center, 2008).

Tian, Xiaofei, *Beacon Fire and Shooting Star: The Literary Culture of the Liang (502–557)* (Cambridge: Harvard University Asia Center, 2007).

______, *Tao Yuanming and Manuscript Culture: The Record of a Dusty Table* (Seattle: University of Washington Press, 2005).

Xu Ling, ed., *New Songs from a Jade Terrace: An Anthology of Early Chinese Love Poetry*, translated by Anne Birrell (Harmondsworth: Penguin, 1986).

Chapter 6: Early and High Tang Poetry before Du Fu

Paul W. Kroll, *Meng Hao-jan* (Boston: Twayne, 1981).

Stephen Owen, *The Great Age of Chinese Poetry: The High Tang* (New Haven: Yale University Press, 1980).

_____, *The Poetry of the Early Tang*, reprint (Basel: Quirin Press, 2012).

Paula M. Varsano, *Tracking the Banished Immortal: The Poetry of Li Bo and Its Critical Reception* (Honolulu: University of Hawai'i Press, 2003).

Arthur Waley, *The Poetry and Career of Li Po, 701–762* (London and Boston: George Allen and Unwin, 1979).

Ding Xian Warner, *A Wild Deer amid Soaring Phoenixes: The Opposition Poetics of Wang Ji* (Honolulu: University of Hawai'i Press, 2003).

Pauline Yu, *The Poetry of Wang Wei* (Bloomington: University of Indiana Press, 1980).

CHAPTER 7: DU FU

Eva Shan Chou, *Reconsidering Tu Fu: Literary Greatness and Cultural Context* (Cambridge: Cambridge University Press, 1995).

David Hawkes, *A Little Primer of Tu Fu* (Oxford: Clarendon Press, 1967).

David R. McCraw, *Du Fu's Lament for the South* (Honolulu: University of Hawai'i Press, 1992).

Stephen Owen, *The Great Age of Chinese Poetry: The High Tang* (New Haven: Yale University Press, 1980).

_____, trans., *The Poetry of Du Fu*, Library of Chinese Humanities (Boston and Berlin: Walter de Gruyter, Inc., 2015).

CHAPTER 8: MIDDLE AND LATE TANG POETRY

J. D. Frodsham, *Goddesses, Ghosts, and Demons: The Collected Poems of Li He (790–816)* (London: Anvil Press Poetry, 1983).

Charles Hartman, *Han Yu and the T'ang Search for Unity* (Princeton: Princeton University Press, 1985).

Jeanne Larsen, *Brocade River: Selected Works of the Tang Dynasty Courtesan Xue Tao* (Princeton: Princeton University Press, 1987).

James J. Y. Liu, *The Poetry of Li Shangyin* (Chicago: University of Chicago Press, 1969).

Stephen Owen, *The End of the Chinese "Middle Ages": Essays in Mid-Tang Literary Culture* (Stanford: Stanford University Press, 1996).

_____, *The Late Tang: Chinese Poetry of the Mid-Ninth Century (827–860)* (Cambridge: Harvard University Asia Center, 2006).

_____, *The Poetry of Meng Chiao and Han Yu* (New Haven: Yale University Press, 1975).

Paul Rouzer, *Writing Another's Dream: The Poetry of Wen Tingyun* (Stanford: Stanford University Press, 1993).

Graham Sanders, *Words Well Put: Visions of Poetic Competence in the Chinese Tradition* (Cambridge: Harvard University Asia Center, 2006).

Edward H. Schafer, *Mirages on the Sea of Time: The Taoist Poetry of Ts'ao T'ang* (Berkeley: University of California Press, 1985).

Anna M. Shields, *One Who Knows Me: Friendship and Literary Culture in Mid-Tang China* (Cambridge: Harvard University Asia Center, 2015).

Chapters 9 and 10: The Song Lyric

Daniel Bryant, *Lyric Poets of the Southern Tang: Feng Yansi (903–960) and Li Yu (937–978)* (Vancouver: University of British Columbia Press, 1982).

Kang-i Sun Chang, *The Evolution of Chinese Tz'u Poetry: From Late T'ang to Northern Sung* (Princeton: Princeton University Press, 1980).

Ronald Egan, *The Burden of Female Talent: The Poet Li Qingzhao and Her History in China* (Cambridge: Harvard University Asia Center, 2013).

_____, *The Literary Works of Ou-yang Hsiu (1007–72)*, reprint (Cambridge: Cambridge University Press, 2009).

_____, *Word, Image, and Deed in the Life of Su Shi* (Cambridge: Harvard University Asia Center, 2006).

Grace S. Fong, *Wu Wenying and the Art of Southern Song* Ci *Poetry* (Princeton: Princeton University Press, 1987).

Xinda Lian, *The Wild and Arrogant: Expression of Self in Xin Qiji's Song Lyrics* (New York: Peter Lang, 1999).

Shuen-fu Lin, *The Transformation of the Chinese Lyrical Tradition* (Princeton: Princeton University Press, 1978).

Anna M. Shields, *Crafting a Collection: The Cultural Contexts and Poetic Practice of the* Huajian ji (Cambridge: Harvard University Asia Center, 2006).

Robin D. S. Yates, *Washing Silk: The Life and Selected Poetry of Wei Zhuang (834?–910)* (Cambridge: Harvard Council on East Asian Studies, 1988).

Pauline Yu, ed., *Voices of the Song Lyric in China* (Berkeley: University of California Press, 1994).

Permissions

ALLEN, JOSEPH R. The following unpublished translations are reprinted with the kind permission of the translator: Anonymous, "In the wilds is a dead doe" (Mao 23); Anonymous, "Young Peach" (Mao 6); Anonymous, "My Man is on Corvee Duty" (Mao 66); Anonymous, "The Cock Crows" (Mao 96).

BODMAN, RICHARD. The translation of Wang Zhihuan, "Climbing the Stork Pavilion" from Victor Mair, ed., *Columbia Anthology of Traditional Chinese Literature* (New York: Columbia University Press, 1994), pp. 193–94, is reprinted by permission of the publisher. Copyright © 1994 Columbia University Press.

BODMAN, RICHARD, AND VICTOR MAIR. The translation of Wang Wei, "Deer Enclosure" from Victor Mair, ed., *Columbia Anthology of Traditional Chinese Literature* (New York: Columbia University Press, 1994), p. 198, is reprinted by permission of the publisher. Copyright © 1994 Columbia University Press.

BYNNER, WITTER. The following translations from *The Jade Mountain* translated by Witter Bynner (New York: Alfred A. Knopf, 1929) are reprinted by permission of Alfred A. Knopf, an imprint of the Knopf Doubleday Publishing Group, a division of Penguin Random House LLC: Bai Juyi, "A Suggestion to My Friend Liu," p. 118; Wang Wei, "Deer Park-Hermitage," p. 189; Wang Wei, "In a Retreat among Bamboos," p. 189. Translation copyright © 1929, renewed 1957 by Alfred A. Knopf, a division of Penguin Random House LLC. All rights reserved.

CHANG, KANG-I SUN. The translation of Liu Yong, "*Pa-sheng kan-chou*" from *The Evolution of Chinese* Tz'u *Poetry* (Princeton: Princeton University Press, 1980), pp. 127–28, is reprinted by permission of the translator. Copyright © 1980 Kang-i Chang Sun.

EIDE, ELLING. The translation of Li Bai, "Drinking Alone in the Moonlight" from Victor Mair, ed., *Columbia Anthology of Traditional Chinese Literature* (New York: Columbia University Press, 1994), p. 203, is reprinted by permission of the Elling O. Eide Foundation. Copyright © 1994 Elling Eide.

FONG, GRACE. The following translations from Grace Fong, *Wu Wenying and the Art of Southern Song* Ci *Poetry* (Princeton: Princeton University Press, 1987) are reprinted with the permission of the press: Jiang Kui, "To the tune 'Sparse Shadows,'" pp. 41–42; Wu Wenying, "To the Tune 'The Wind entering the Pines,'" pp. 107–8. Copyright © 1987 Princeton University Press.

GOH, MEOW HUI. The following unpublished translations are reprinted with the kind permission of the translator: Cao Cao, "Wormwood Village Song"; Cao Zhi, "Miscellaneous Poem"; Lu Ji, "Imitating 'How the Bright Moon Is Gleaming.'"

GRAHAM, ANGUS C. The following translations from *Poems of the Late T'ang* (New York: NYRB Classics, 2008) are reprinted with the permission of the press: Du Fu, "Yangtse and Han," p. 48; Du Fu, "Autumn Meditation, number 7," p. 55; Du Fu, "Autumn Meditation, number 8," pp.

55; Du Mu, "Easing My Heart," p. 123; Du Mu, "Travelling in the Mountains," p. 133; Du Mu, "Farewell Poem (second of two to a girl of Yang-chou)," p. 134; Li He, "A Bronze Immortal Takes Leave of Han," p. 106; Li He, "The Grave of Little Su," p. 113; Li Shangyin, "The Patterned Lute," p. 171; Li Shangyin, "Ch'ang O," p. 155; Li Shangyin, "Night Rains: To My Wife up North," p. 159; Li Shangyin, "Untitled Poems (vi)," p. 150.

HAWKES, DAVID. The following translations from *Songs of the South: An Ancient Chinese Anthology of Poems by Qu Yuan and Other Poets* translated by David Hawkes (Harmondsworth: Penguin Classics, 1985) are reprinted with the permission of the press: Attributed to Qu Yuan, "The Lord within the Clouds," pp. 103–4; Attributed to Qu Yuan, "Hymn to the Fallen," pp. 116–17. Copyright © 1985 David Hawkes.

HIGHTOWER, JAMES ROBERT. The translation of Tao Qian, "Returning to the Farm to Dwell, First of Five poems" from James Robert Hightower, trans., *The Poetry of T'ao Ch'ien* (Oxford: Oxford University Press, 1970), p. 50, is reprinted by permission of Oxford University Press. Copyright © 1970 Oxford University Press.

HINTON, DAVID. The translation of Du Fu, "Moonlit Night" is from David Hinton, *The Selected Poems of Tu Fu* (New York: New Directions, 1988), p. 25. Copyright ©1988 by David Hinton. Reprinted by permission of New Directions Publishing Corp.

LIN, SHUEN-FU. The translation of Jiang Kui, "Yangchow mahn" from Shuen-fu Lin, *The Transformation of the Chinese Lyric Tradition* (Princeton: Princeton University Press, 1978), pp. 72–73, is reprinted with the permission of the translator. Copyright © 1978 Shuen-fu Lin.

LO, IRVING. The translation of Du Fu, "Recruiting Officer of Shih-hao," from Victor Mair, ed., *Columbia Anthology of Traditional Chinese Literature*, p. 214, is reprinted with the permission of the press. Copyright © 1994 Columbia University Press.

MAIR, VICTOR. The translation of Li Bai, "Poems in an Old Style, No. 1," from Victor Mair, ed., *Columbia Anthology of Traditional Chinese Literature*, pp. 205–6, was first published in Victor Mair, *Four Introspective Poets: A Concordance to Selected Poems by Roan Jyi, Chern Tzyy-arng, Jang Jeouling, and Lii Bor* (Tucson: Arizona State University Press, 1987), p. 92. Copyright © 1987 Arizona State University Press. Reprinted with the permission of the Arizona State University Press.

OWEN, STEPHEN. The following translations from Stephen Owen, ed., *An Anthology of Chinese Literature: Beginnings to 1911*, translated by Stephen Owen (New York: W. W. Norton & Company, Inc., 1996) are used by permission of W. W. Norton & Company, Inc.: Anonymous, "Heaven Above," p. 227; Anonymous, "Watering My Horse by the Great Wall," p. 258; Anonymous, "The One I Love," pp. 227; Cao Cao, "Short Song," pp. 280–81; Cao Pi, "A Discourse on Literature," p. 360–61; Du Fu, "The View in Spring," p. 420; Du Fu, "Painted Hawk," p. 428; Du Fu, "Autumn Stirrings (eight poems) I," p. 434; Du Fu, "Autumn Stirrings (eight poems) VII," p. 438; Du Fu, "Where Yangzi Meets the Han," p. 439; Du Fu, "Lament by the River," pp. 422–23; Han Yu, "Autumn Thoughts, Eighth of Eleven," pp. 484–85; Jiang Kui, "to 'Fragrance from Somewhere Unseen,'" pp. 586–87; Li Bai, "Dialogue in the Mountains," p. 403; Li He, "Song of an Arrowhead from the Battlefield of Chang-ping," pp. 489–90; Li Qingzhao, "To the tune 'Like a Dream,'" p. 580; Li Qingzhao, "to 'Note After Note,'" p. 581;

Li Shangyin, "The Sui Palace," p. 516; Ruan Ji, "Song of My Cares, I," pp. 256–57; Tao Qian, "Reading the *Classic of Mountains and Seas*, 13 poems, No. 1," pp. 318–19; Wang Zhihuan, "Climbing Stork Tower," p. 408; Xie Lingyun, "Climbing an Upper Story by the Pool," p. 321; Xie Lingyun, "Written on the Lake, Returning from the Chapel at Stone Cliff," pp. 320–21; Yu Xuanji, "Selling Tattered Peonies," p. 509. Copyright © 1996 by Stephen Owen and The Council for Cultural Planning and Development of the Executive Yuan of the Republic of China.

The following translations from Stephen Owen, *The Great Age of Chinese Poetry: The High Tang* (New Haven: Yale University Press, 1981) are used with the permission of the press: Cui Hao, "Yellow Crane Tower," p. 62; Li Bai, "Song of the Roosting Crows," p. 121; Meng Haoran, "Spending the Night on the Chien-te River," p. 86; Wang Wei, "Arriving at the Border as an Envoy," p. 33; Wang Wei, "Returning to Mount Sung," p. 41. Copyright © 1981 Yale University Press.

The following translations from Stephen Owen, *The Poetry of Meng Chiao and Han Yü* (New Haven: Yale University Press, 1975) are used with the permission of the press: Meng Jiao, "Cold Creek, third of eight poems," p. 144; Han Yu, "On the Temple of King Chao of Ch'u," p. 283; Han Yu, "Floating on South Creek for the First Time: Three Poems II," p. 286. Copyright © 1975 Yale University Press.

PAYNE, ROBERT. The following translations from *The White Pony* (London: George Allen and Unwin Ltd., 1949) are reprinted with the permission of the press: Chen Zi'ang, "The Ancients," p. 149; Wang Wei, "On Going Away," p. 153. Copyright © 1949 George Allen and Unwin.

POUND, EZRA. The translation of Li Bai, "The Jewel Stairs' Grievance" is from Ezra Pound, *Cathay* (London: Elkin Matthews, 1915), p. 13. Copyright ©1915 by Ezra Pound. Reprinted by permission of New Directions Publishing Corp.

The following translations from Ezra Pound, *Shih-Ching: The Classic Anthology Defined by Confucius* (Cambridge: Harvard University Press, 1954) are reprinted by permission of the President and Fellows of Harvard College: Anonymous, "My Lord Is on Campaign" (Mao 66), p. 34; Anonymous, "In the Field There Is a Dead Deer" (Mao 23), pp. 10–11. Copyright © 1954, 1982 by the President and Fellows of Harvard College.

REXROTH, KENNETH. The translation of Li Shangyin, "When Will I Be Home" is from Kenneth Rexroth, *One Hundred More Poems from the Chinese: Love and the Turning Year* (New York: New Directions Publishing Corp., 1970), p. 77, and is reprinted by permission of New Directions Publishing Corp. Copyright ©1970 by Kenneth Rexroth.

REXROTH, KENNETH, AND LING CHUNG. The translation of Yu Xuanji, "On a Visit to Ch'ung-chên Taoist Temple I See in the South Hall the List of the Successful Candidates in the Imperial Examinations" is from Kenneth Rexroth and Ling Chung, *The Orchid Boat: Women Poets of China* (New York: New Directions Publishing Corp., 1982), p. 19, and is reprinted by permission of New Directions Publishing Corp. Copyright ©1973 by Kenneth Rexroth and Ling Chung.

Ridgway, Benjamin. The unpublished translation of Su Shi, "The Charms of Niannu: 'Cherishing the Past' at the Red Cliff," is reprinted with the kind permission of the translator.

Rouzer, Paul. The following unpublished translations are reprinted with the kind permission of the translator: Bao Zhao, "Hard Traveling VI"; Du Mu, "I wrote this on the Water Pavilion of Kaiyuan Temple in Xuanzhou; below the Pavilion, residences line either side of Wan Stream"; Jia Dao, "An evening view, after snow clears"; Jia Dao, "I spend the night at a mountain temple"; Jia Dao, "I see off Tang Huan on his return to his Fu River estate"; Li Shangyin, "Untitled"; Wang Wei, "Written at My Estate at Wang Stream, after Long Rains."

The following translations from Paul Rouzer, *Writing Another's Dream: The Poetry of Wen Tingyun* (Stanford: Stanford University Press, 1993) are used with the permission of Stanford University Press: Wen Tingyun, "Song: Naval Battle on Kunming Lake," pp. 134–35; Wen Tingyun, "Setting Out Early from Mount Shang," p. 18. Copyright © 1993 by the Board of Trustees of the Leland Stanford Jr. University. All rights reserved.

Shields, Anna M. The following unpublished translations are reprinted with the kind permission of the translator: Bai Juyi, "Reading Yuan Ninth's Poems aboard a Boat"; Yuan Zhen, "Responding to Letian's Poem on Reading My Poems at Night on a Moored Boat."

The following translations from Anna M. Shields, *Crafting a Collection* (Cambridge: Harvard University Asia Center, 2006) are reprinted with the permission of the press: Bai Juyi, "Yi Jiangnan (1st of 3)," p. 44; Wei Zhuang, "To the tune 'Pusa man,'" p. 196. Copyright © 2006 President and Fellows of Harvard University.

Snyder, Gary. The translation of Du Fu, "A Spring Vista" from Gary Snyder, *The Gary Snyder Reader* (Counterpoint, 1999), p. 542, is reprinted by permission of Counterpoint. Copyright © 1999 Gary Snyder.

Strassberg, Richard. The translation of Wang Xizhi, "Preface to *Collected Poems from the Orchid Pavilion*," is from Victor Mair, ed., *Columbia Anthology of Traditional Chinese Literature*, p. 565–67, and is reprinted with the permission of the press. Copyright © 1994 Columbia University Press.

Swartz, Wendy. The following unpublished translations are reprinted with the kind permission of the translator: Tao Qian, "Twenty Poems on Drinking Ale, No. 5"; Wang Can, "Seven Laments."

Tian, Xiaofei. The following unpublished translations are reprinted with the kind permission of the translator: Xiao Gang, "Another Three Couplets on "Spring Boudoir Feelings"; Xiao Gang, "Gazing at a Lone Wild Goose Flying at Night"; Xie Tiao, "Grievance on the Jade Stairs"; Yu Jianwu, "Spring Night Respectfully Presented as a Companion Piece Written at the Prince of Xiangdong's Command"; Yu Xin, "Dusty Mirror."

Waley, Arthur. The following translations from *Translations from the Chinese* (New York: Alfred A. Knopf, 1941) are now in the public domain: Anonymous, "Nineteen Old Poems, no. 2," p. 38; Anonymous, "Nineteen Old Poems, no. 19," p. 48; Cao Zhi, "The Ruins of Lo-yang," p. 64; Li Bai, "Drinking Alone by Moonlight [1]", p. 118.

WATSON, BURTON. The following translations from *Chinese Lyricism:* Shih *Poetry from the Second to the Twelfth Century* (New York: Columbia University Press, 1971) are reprinted with the permission of the press: Anonymous, "Nineteen Old Poems, no. 1," p. 20; Anonymous, "Nineteen Old Poems, no. 5," p. 25; Anonymous, "Nineteen Old Poems, no. 15," p. 29; Du Fu, "A Guest Arrives," p. 166; Du Fu, "Weary Night," p. 167; He Xun, "At Parting," p. 89; Li Bai, "Bring the Wine," pp. 144–45; Pan Yue, "Lamenting the Dead, First of Three," pp. 96–97; Wang Wei, "Bamboo Mile Lodge," p. 173; Xie Lingyun, "Returning from the Purification Hall at Stonewall, Written on the Lake," pp. 80–81. Copyright © 1971 Columbia University Press.

ZHANG, CHEN. The unpublished translation of Wu Wenying, "To 'Eight Notes of Ganzhou.' The Ethereal Cliff. Visited in the company of the gentlemen in the Stabilization Fund Commission," is reprinted with the kind permission of the translator.

Harvard East Asian Monographs
(most recent titles)

358. Michael Wert, *Meiji Restoration Losers: Memory and Tokugawa Supporters in Modern Japan*
359. Garret P. S. Olberding, ed., *Facing the Monarch: Modes of Advice in the Early Chinese Court*
360. Xiaojue Wang, *Modernity with a Cold War Face: Reimagining the Nation in Chinese Literature Across the 1949 Divide*
361. David Spafford, *A Sense of Place: The Political Landscape in Late Medieval Japan*
362. Jongryn Mo and Barry Weingast, *Korean Political and Economic Development: Crisis, Security, and Economic Rebalancing*
363. Melek Ortabasi, *The Undiscovered Country: Text, Translation, and Modernity in the Work of Yanagita Kunio*
364. Hiraku Shimoda, *Lost and Found: Recovering Regional Identity in Imperial Japan*
365. Trent E. Maxey, *The "Greatest Problem": Religion and State Formation in Meiji Japan*
366. Gina Cogan, *The Princess Nun: Bunchi, Buddhist Reform, and Gender in Early Edo Japan*
367. Eric C. Han, *Rise of a Japanese Chinatown: Yokohama, 1894–1972*
368. Natasha Heller, *Illusory Abiding: The Cultural Construction of the Chan Monk Zhongfeng Mingben*
369. Paize Keulemans, *Sound Rising from the Paper: Nineteenth-Century Martial Arts Fiction and the Chinese Acoustic Imagination*
370. Simon James Bytheway, *Investing Japan: Foreign Capital, Monetary Standards, and Economic Development, 1859–2011*
371. Sukhee Lee, *Negotiated Power: The State, Elites, and Local Governance in Twelfth-Fourteenth China*
372. Foong Ping, *The Efficacious Landscape: On the Authorities of Painting at the Northern Song Court*
373. Catherine L. Phipps, *Empires on the Waterfront: Japan's Ports and Power, 1858–1899*
374. Sunyoung Park, *The Proletarian Wave: Literature and Leftist Culture in Colonial Korea, 1910–1945*
375. Barry Eichengreen, Wonhyuk Lim, Yung Chul Park, and Dwight H. Perkins, *The Korean Economy: From a Miraculous Past to a Sustainable Future*
376. Heather Blair, *Real and Imagined: The Peak of Gold in Heian Japan*
377. Emer O'Dwyer, *Significant Soil: Settler Colonialism and Japan's Urban Empire in Manchuria*
378. Martina Deuchler, *Under the Ancestors' Eyes: Kinship, Status, and Locality in Premodern Korea*
379. Joseph R. Dennis, *Writing, Publishing, and Reading Local Gazetteers in Imperial China, 1100–1700*
380. Catherine Vance Yeh, *The Chinese Political Novel: Migration of a World Genre*
381. Noell Wilson, *Defensive Positions: The Politics of Maritime Security in Tokugawa Japan*
382. Miri Nakamura, *Monstrous Bodies: The Rise of the Uncanny in Modern Japan*
383. Nara Dillon, *Radical Inequalities: China's Revolutionary Welfare State in Comparative Perspective*
384. Ma Zhao, *Runaway Wives, Urban Crimes, and Survival Tactics in Wartime Beijing, 1937-1949*
385. Mingwei Song, *Young China: National Rejuvenation and the* Bildungsroman, *1900-1959*
386. Christopher Bondy, *Voice, Silence, and Self: Negotiations of Buraku Identity in Contemporary Japan*
387. Seth Jacobowitz, *Writing Technology in Meiji Japan: A Media History of Modern Japanese Literature and Visual Culture*
388. Hilde De Weerdt, *Information, Territory, and Networks: The Crisis and Maintenance of Empire in Song China*
389. Elizabeth Kindall, *Geo-Narratives of a Filial Son: The Paintings and Travel Diaries of Huang Xiangjian (1609–1673)*
390. Matthew Fraleigh, *Plucking Chrysanthemums: Narushima Ryūhoku and Sinitic Literary Traditions in Modern Japan*
391. Hu Ying, *Burying Autumn: Poetry, Friendship, and Loss*
392. Mark E. Byington, *The Ancient State of Puyŏ in Northeast Asia: Archaeology and Historical Memory*
393. Timothy J. Van Compernolle, *Struggling Upward: Worldly Success and the Japanese Novel*
394. Heekyoung Cho, *Translation's Forgotten History: Russian Literature, Japanese Mediation, and the Formation of Modern Korean Literature*
395. Terry Kawashima, *Itineraries of Power: Texts and Traversals in Heian and Medieval Japan*
396. Anna Andreeva, *Assembling Shinto: Buddhist Approaches to Kami Worship in Medieval Japan*
397. Felix Boecking, *No Great Wall: Trade, Tariffs, and Nationalism in Republican China, 1927–1945*
398. Chien-Hsin Tsai, *A Passage to China: Literature, Loyalism, and Colonial Taiwan*
399. W. Puck Brecher, *Honored and Dishonored Guests: Westerners in Wartime Japan*
400. Miya Elise Mizuta Lippit, *Aesthetic Life: Beauty and Art in Modern Japan*
401. Brian Steininger, *Chinese Literary Form in Heian Japan: Poetics and Practice*

402. Lisa Yoshikawa, *Making History Matter: Kuroita Katsumi and the Construction of Imperial Japan*
403. Michael P. Cronin, *Osaka Modern: The City in the Japanese Imaginary*
404. Soyoung Suh, *Naming the Local: Medicine, Language, and Identity in Korea since the 15th Century*
405. Yoon Sun Yang, *From Domestic Women to Sensitive Young Men: Translating the Individual in Early Colonial Korea*
406. Michal Daliot-Bul and Nissim Otmazgin, *The Anime Boom in the United States: Lessons for Global Creative Industries*
407. Nathan Hopson, *Ennobling the Savage Northeast: Tōhoku as Japanese Postwar Thought, 1945–2011*
408. Michael Fuller, *An Introduction to Chinese Poetry: From the Canon of Poetry to the Lyrics of the Song Dynasty*
409. Tie Xiao, *Revolutionary Waves: The Crowd in Modern China*
410. Anne Reinhardt, *Navigating Semi-colonialism: Shipping, Sovereignity, and Nation Building in China, 1860–1937*
411. Jennifer E. Altehenger, *Legal Lessons: Popularizing Laws in the People's Republic of China, 1949–1989*
412. Halle O'Neal, *Word Embodied: The Jeweled Pagoda Mandalas in Japanese Buddhist Art*
413. Maren A. Ehlers, *Give and Take: Poverty and the Status Order in Early Modern Japan*